The Ascendancy of Europe, 1815–1914

M S ANDERSON

The Ascendancy of Europe
1815–1914

THIRD EDITION

Routledge
Taylor & Francis Group

LONDON AND NEW YORK

First published 1972 by Pearson Education Limited

Second edition 1985
Third edition published 2003

Published 2013 by Routledge
2 Park Square, Milton Park, Abingdon, Oxon OX14 4RN
711 Third Avenue, New York, NY 10017, USA

Routledge is an imprint of the Taylor & Francis Group, an informa business

ISBN: 978-0-582-77259-5 (pbk)

British Library Cataloguing in Publication Data
A CIP catalogue record for this book can be obtained from the British Library

Library of Congress Cataloging in Publication Data
A CIP catalog record for this book can be obtained from the Library of Congress

Set in 10/13pt Sabon by Graphicraft Limited, Hong Kong

Contents

Preface to the Second Edition

The twelve years which have elapsed since the first appearance of this book have seen the publication of a great deal of new work, much of it of high quality, on every major aspect of the life of nineteenth-century Europe. I cannot pretend that I have been able to give adequate attention to all this writing, or even to all that published in English; however a considerable amount of new information and ideas, and a number of new examples and illustrations of the arguments put forward, have been incorporated in the revised version. More important, an effort has been made to widen its scope and make its coverage of the subject more complete by adding a substantial chapter on economic and social history, an aspect of nineteenth-century Europe which, I have increasingly felt, was inadequately served in the first edition. I have also done some pruning of the footnotes, which it may be argued were at times somewhat self-indulgent, and have added a bibliography, though inevitably a brief and summary one. I hope these changes may make the book more useful to the students who are the most numerous and important readers of a work of this kind.

M. S. ANDERSON

Preface to the Third Edition

It is very gratifying that three decades after the first publication of this book it should be thought worthy of a new edition, and I am grateful to the publishers for making this revised one possible. I have taken the opportunity to add a good deal of new illustrative material and also to improve or clarify the wording at a small number of points. The Bibliography as well has been considerably altered. I have tried to bring it up to date by including at least the more important work in English which has appeared since the second edition of the book was published in 1985, though the stream of relevant writing, much of it of high quality, is now so great that this in itself is no small undertaking. I have also confined it, more than in earlier editions though by no means entirely, to books and a small number of articles in English. This I have done with some reluctance; but I hope that these changes will not merely prevent it becoming too long and complex but also make it more useful to the students who are the largest and most important group of potential readers.

I have also made one or two changes of some substance as my view of the subject has developed over the years. In the last chapter I have added a brief discussion of the continuing importance in the intellectual and social life of nineteenth-century Europe of traditional forms of religious belief. This is a significant aspect of the period which I now feel sure was given less weight than it should have been in earlier editions. The conclusion I now think stressed rather one-sidedly the conservative and backward-looking aspects of European life. It has now, I hope, been given more balance by reminding the reader how powerful the forces of change had become by about 1880 and how reasonable it was by 1914 for many Europeans to look forward to a future of progress and steady improvement in their lives. Finally, the general effect of the additions to and small changes in the text has been to emphasize the importance of the new united Germany after 1871 and of Russia throughout this entire period. This has tilted the balance of the book to some extent towards them and away from France, the Habsburg empire and even Great Britain. The change has not been very marked; but again I feel it is justified. By

1914 both Germany and Russia, more than ever before, were dominant forces, or potentially so, in many aspects of European life. The tendency for a west European writer to give slightly too much prominence to the affairs of the western states, Great Britain and France, is no doubt natural. But it is right to make some effort to resist the temptation; and this I have tried to do.

M. S. ANDERSON
London, October 2002

Introduction

The generation or more which separates the 1780s from the battle of Waterloo saw the beginnings of modern history in Europe. During the eighteenth century the continent was still, in its everyday life, closer to the twelfth century than to the twentieth. Economic change, though real and important, was by the standards of succeeding generations very slow. Though there was a remarkable growth of population, industrial organization remained for the most part highly traditional. Technology, largely unaffected by scientific discovery, advanced slowly and erratically. As late as 1776 Adam Smith could tacitly assume, in his *Wealth of Nations*, that the economies of the European states were static, or growing only very slowly. Society continued almost everywhere to be, as it had been for centuries, a complex network of groups often enjoying, by law or tradition, important corporate privileges – village communities, guilds, towns, churches, universities. It was still, over much of the continent, divided into traditional 'orders' – church, nobility, burghers, peasantry – whose members enjoyed different legal rights, bore different legal burdens and had different legal personalities.

The governments of continental Europe before the French Revolution, with a few rather unimportant exceptions, were, as they had been for generations, monarchies of a more or less absolute kind. It is true that absolutism was now being challenged and tempered by new forces. 'Enlightened despots', inspired largely by the example and success of Frederick II of Prussia, began to pride themselves on working for (though hardly ever with) their peoples, and as a rule accepted the idea that they and their subjects were bound together by some vague form of quasi-contractual relationship. Moreover the commercial, naval and colonial successes achieved by Britain had now made ideas of limited and parliamentary monarchy more acceptable than ever before, at least in parts of western Europe. The monarchical mystique was thus less pervasive and demanding than in the seventeenth century; the two or three generations before the French Revolution produced no Bossuet or Filmer. None the less no major continental state possessed in the 1780s an effective parliament;

and republicanism was a remote classical tradition, a piece of political anti-quarianism rather than a living idea. Even the armed forces of which rulers made use in the furtherance of their territorial disputes and dynastic claims were highly traditional. The sailing man-of-war armed with smooth-bore cannon using crude black gunpowder had not changed in essentials for well over two centuries: armies were relatively small and often dynastic rather than national in their outlook.

By 1815 this traditional structure had changed almost beyond recognition over much of western Europe and had been seriously shaken in central Europe. This dramatic change was the work in part of the British example. Britain's wealth, her ability to sustain unflinchingly an unprecedentedly expensive and difficult struggle with France which dragged on for more than two decades (1793–1814, with an interval of fourteen months from March 1802 to May 1803) were a spectacular advertisement for industrialization and parliamentary government. But incomparably more important in precipitating change was the challenge and later the overwhelming threat of revolutionary France. The Declaration of the Rights of Man of August 1789, and the spirit which it embodied, made impossible the continuance in France of a society based on inequalities sanctified by law and tradition. They also aroused over much of Europe, at least among the educated minority, intense admiration and genuine sympathy. A vast wave of constructive change in France during the two or three years which followed – the ending of feudalism, the reform of local government, the sweeping away of internal barriers to trade and of obstructive corporate bodies such as the *parlements* and the guilds, the new moderate monarchical constitution of 1791 – seemed to radicals and idealists everywhere to point the way forward to the rest of Europe and to show that the traditional mould of government and society could be broken. The idea that a people, independent of or even against the wishes of its rulers, could and must control its own destiny, the alluring and potentially dangerous belief that no established right had any validity against the popular will, had now been asserted with exciting and terrifying force.

The revolutionaries were not content to preach merely by example. By the spring of 1792 the increasingly messianic tone of the revolution, coupled with the complexities of the struggle for power in Paris, had led to the outbreak of war between France and the powers of the old Europe. In 1793–94 the threat of foreign invasion and civil war established in France, though for little more than a year, the Jacobin dictatorship which was for a century to come to symbolize for most Europeans the cruelty and terror of revolution. From the brief and violent life of this régime was to spring one of the most powerful and durable of all political myths, a grim warning to many and a glowing inspiration to a few for future generations. The drive towards genuine social and economic change, always a minor aspect of the Jacobin régime, was decisively defeated in 1794–95; and this defeat was driven home by the seizure of power by General Bonaparte in 1799. But however conservative the social outlook of the Emperor Napoleon I (as he became in 1804), he represented to the full the expansionist tendencies which had shown themselves in France from 1792 onwards. Under him the sheer military power of the country, based ultimately on its great superiority in population to almost all other European states, appeared to threaten the permanent subordination of most of the continent to French rule. For a decade or more he seemed to have overthrown the balance of power, perhaps for ever. The Habsburg empire, Prussia, to a lesser extent even Russia, all fell before him in the campaigns of 1805–7; and the years 1807–10, when his empire in Europe was at its height, saw his power apparently beyond challenge. His own lack of moderation and statesmanship destroyed that power in 1812–14. But his career had shown with frightening clarity the potentialities of the new forces – the impatience of traditional restraints, the demand for a more fluid type of society and for more rational and effective government – released by the revolution in France.

The Europe of 1815 was thus in some ways and in some parts of the continent (above all east of a line from Hamburg to the head of the Adriatic and south of the Alps and the Pyrenees) still traditional, but one struggling to come to terms with a series of challenging and indeed revolutionary forces. Industrialism, mass conscript armies, reformed and rationalized bureaucracies, most of all the new and dynamic political ideals of popular sovereignty and national self-determination radiating from France, were beginning to transform the old Europe of monarchs, landed nobilities, often unfree peasants, the Europe of tradition, privilege and ancestral pieties. By 1914 that transformation was far advanced. The story of its advance is the theme of this book.

I

The political and economic balance of power

THE CONCERT OF EUROPE, 1815–c. 1850

The peace settlement of 1814–15 attempted, with considerable success, to restore in Europe an effective balance of power and hence pave the way to a long period of international peace. In the west France, which during the previous two decades had destroyed the balance and threatened the continent with the spectre of 'universal monarchy', of dominance by a single state and a single ruler, was now effectively restrained. The kingdom of the Netherlands had been created; Prussia had been strengthened in the Rhineland; an international guarantee of Swiss neutrality had been given; the kingdom of Piedmont-Sardinia had been enlarged by the annexation of Genoa. Most fundamental of all, French expansionism had been checked, at least for the time being, by the restoration of the Bourbons to the throne. In the east Russia, her frontier in Poland pushed further west than ever before, her military strength displayed with unprecedented effect in 1812–14 and her prestige therefore at its height, now seemed the most obvious threat to the balance. But the strengthening of central Europe by the enlargement of both Prussia and the Habsburg empire, by cooperation between them and by the formation of a German Confederation, appeared to offer a means of checking any further advance of Russian power. If such an advance were to take place it might now at least be deflected into the Balkans, an area about which as yet few European statesmen knew or cared much. 'Placed equally between the great empires of East and West,' wrote Metternich, the Austrian chancellor, to Hardenberg, the chief minister of Prussia, 'Prussia and Austria are completing their systems of defence; united, the two monarchies form an unconquerable barrier against the enterprises of any conquering prince who might perhaps once again occupy the throne of France or that of Russia.'[1] The statesmen of Europe had accomplished the considerable feat of ending more than two decades of unprecedentedly large-scale war by a peace which left no major state, not even defeated France, nursing an irreconcilable grievance.

Yet it was a peace based, understandably, on fear. It had its roots in the capacity to destroy the established political order which the French Revolution had shown and in the threatened outbreak in the near future of another great cycle of international conflict. Even in 1815 the Hundred Days of Napoleon's return to power in France, and the failure of the French people to support Louis XVIII against this new usurpation, seemed striking proofs of the fragility of the essentially conservative international system which was under construction. Friedrich von Gentz, secretary to the Vienna congress, predicted another major war within five years; and even Viscount Castlereagh, the British foreign secretary, hardly expected peace to last for more than a decade. This widespread fear of revolution and war (the latter envisaged as the inevitable result of the former) was by no means confined to rulers and their ministers, and showed itself in various forms. In Alexander I of Russia it can be seen in a proposal in October 1815 that the four powers of the anti-French alliance – Great Britain, Austria, Prussia and Russia – should jointly guarantee one another's frontiers, as well as assuming a right of surveillance over the internal affairs of the other European states and of collective intervention in them to suppress revolution. Representatives of the four powers, he proposed, should meet periodically to organize this policy of intervention and suppression. Such a far-reaching innovation in international affairs was quite unacceptable to Castlereagh. He, in sharp contrast, was willing to guarantee only the existing boundaries of France, and to agree to collective intervention of the powers in the smaller states only in case of a revolution there which menaced the general peace of Europe. The result was that the Quadruple Alliance of November 1815 involved the signatories in a formal guarantee only of the French frontiers, though one of its clauses, which provided for their meeting in periodic congresses, meant that some general guarantee system might still emerge in course of time.

It could be argued that the Holy Alliance, signed in September 1815 by the rulers of Russia, Austria and Prussia, involved at least an implied guarantee of the frontiers of these states; but this famous document was in effect a mere declaration of intent, more lacking in precision than any other international agreement of modern times. Moreover the alliance (which was aimed by Alexander at least in part against the Austro-British cooperation which had been a marked feature of the Vienna negotiations) was never liked by Metternich, or its signature regarded by him as more than a necessary sop to the tsar. In fact Alexander's grandiose schemes for the forcible regulation of the affairs of Europe by the great conservative powers had been seriously checked in 1815. The same fate awaited his suggestion in October 1818 of a 'general alliance' which should be open to all states and become the basis of a system of collective guarantee of the status quo by the contracting powers. Castlereagh opposed the idea (the tsar seems to have envisaged the guarantee as extending to existing régimes as well as frontiers). Metternich, though his attitude was more favourable, feared that the proposal might mean that the smaller states became mere Russian satellites; and his reaction to the apparent dangers of the international position showed none of Alexander's idealism and vision. Stripped of the verbiage and pretentious theorizing in which he liked to clothe it, it took the form of mere repression, of efforts to keep revolutionary tendencies within the European states, tendencies whose real strength Metternich grossly exaggerated, under strict surveillance and control. 'You see in me', he boasted in 1817, 'the chief Minister of Police in Europe. I keep an eye on everything. My contacts are such that nothing escapes me.'[2] In July of the same year he proposed unsuccessfully that the conference of ambassadors of the allied powers which had been set up in Paris to supervise the detailed application of the peace settlement with France should collect and collate police reports from the governments concerned. Thus, he argued, revolutionary tendencies throughout the continent could be more effectively combated.

Nevertheless Alexander's idealism, however impractical, struck a chord which reverberated widely in the Europe of the years after the Napoleonic catastrophe. The cosmopolitanism of the later eighteenth century had been based largely on speculation and a priori thinking, and had envisaged the whole of humanity as a unity, in some ultimate sense a single family. It had now been replaced by a narrower current of feeling, one which confined its attention largely to Europe and which was based on the harsh experience of the last quarter-century.[3] In intellectual circles, perhaps even in ruling ones, agreement on the need to make Europe more united and endow it with some form of political organization, however rudimentary, was now for the first time a factor of some practical significance. In Germany the Catholic mystic Baader advocated a federation of the European states based on the Christianity which they all professed. In France Bergasse suggested the more limited expedient of a permanent alliance of sovereigns, while the utopian socialist Saint-Simon sketched the plan of a great European society, democratic and parliamentary, of which the nucleus was to be formed by an alliance between France and Britain. Metternich himself had some sympathy with this type of feeling, arguing that

since no State is any longer isolated ... we must never lose sight of the *society* of States which is an essential condition of the modern world. ... One characteristic of the present world which distinguishes it fundamentally from the ancient is the tendency of nations to draw closer together and to set up a kind of corporate body resting on the same basis as the great human society which grew up at the heart of Christianity.[4]

3

The genuine though limited impulse of these years towards some institutionalized form of European unity found practical expression only in the form of the congresses of heads of state and foreign ministers which met periodically between 1818 and 1822 (at Aix-la-Chapelle in 1818; at Troppau in 1820; at Laibach in 1820–21; and at Verona in 1822, with a last unimportant and unsuccessful effort to hold one in St Petersburg in 1824–25). This 'Congress System', a very tentative approach to international government, soon proved inefficient and short-lived. The congresses never attempted to establish any kind of international institution, or even to set up any kind of permanent secretariat, so that there was no continuity from one meeting to another. Neither the Prince Regent for Britain nor Louis XVIII for France ever appeared at any of them, and Frederick William III of Prussia did so only rarely; so that Alexander I and Francis II of Austria were the only heads of state to attend regularly. Above all, lasting cooperation of the powers was made impossible by the rivalries and disagreements between them. The British government (which in effect meant in this context Castlereagh) was quite unwilling to accept any unlimited right of interference by the great states in the affairs of the smaller ones to prevent or stamp out revolution. Yet this the three conservative eastern powers, Austria, Prussia and Russia, increasingly claimed; and such a right was enshrined in the 'Troppau Protocol' to which they agreed in November 1820.

To Castlereagh the wholesale intervention to which this seemed to open the door was dangerous to the stability of the continent. In his eyes only revolutionary outbreaks which clearly threatened the peace of Europe needed or deserved such treatment. The British government therefore rejected the Troppau Protocol, in the drawing-up of which it had refused to take any share. By the end of 1820 the breach between Britain and the more conservative powers of eastern and central Europe on this issue was wide and the unity of the alliance which defeated Napoleon had been broken. France, though her position was more ambiguous, was also not a reliable supporter of the conservative forces which by 1820 had come to control the congresses. At Aix-la-Chapelle she had been admitted to participation on equal terms in these gatherings. Unlike Britain, she sent representatives to the Troppau and Laibach meetings. But because of the danger of seriously offending liberal opinion within France the French government did not sign the Troppau Protocol; and when in 1823 Louis XVIII sent a French army into Spain to crush the liberal and military revolt which had broken out there three years earlier, he acted independently and made no mention of the mandate for intervention which the conservative powers had previously given him.

Accompanying and underlying these differences of outlook and attitude was a widespread uneasiness inspired by the apparently menacing strength of Russia, and by the highly personal and increasingly erratic policies of Alexander I. In 1820 Metternich, by playing on the tsar's more and more paranoiac fears of revolution, had won his support for an Austrian and highly conservative attitude in international affairs. But this position was slowly altered by the outbreak of revolt in Greece against Turkish rule in the spring of 1821. Alexander was at first willing, under Metternich's influence, to see events there as merely another manifestation of the revolutionary threat to the entire European order. But this attitude was soon eroded by territorial and commercial disputes between Russia and the Ottoman empire, and by the powerful religious sympathies for the Greeks which Orthodox Russia could hardly avoid feeling and which were strengthened by the massacres which punctuated the ferocious war for Greek independence. Before his death at the end of 1825 the tsar had already set in motion the chain of events which culminated in the Russo-Turkish war of April 1828: the British ambassador in St Petersburg reported in November 1825 that Alexander 'was now perfectly habituated to the Idea of War as the only means of compelling Turkey to enter into an arrangement respecting Greece'.[5] Such an attitude meant the likelihood of a break with Austria and the possibility of serious friction with her in the Balkans. Both came to pass under Alexander's successor, his brother Nicholas I.

This growing estrangement dealt a death-blow to any lingering hope of maintaining some system of regular international meetings of the sort which had existed for a few years after 1818. After 1822 the 'Congress System' survived only in the much whittled-down form of conferences of ambassadors to discuss and settle specific international problems. Some of these did very important constructive work. In particular that which sat in London from 1830 onwards settled, after much labour and long delays, the problems created by the Belgian revolution of that year. But a workmanlike *ad hoc* body of this kind, engrossed largely in practical details, was a poor substitute for the gatherings of heads of state, united by religious belief and ties of personal friendship and regulating with Olympian detachment the affairs of Europe, of which some idealists had earlier dreamed.

The way in which the Congress System broke down strengthened a very important assumption which had for the past generation been rooting itself in the mind of Europe. This was the concept of much of the west of the continent (France, from the 1830s the new state of Belgium, above all Great Britain) as standing for liberty, political, personal and intellectual, while its eastern half, and most of all Russia, represented by contrast the forces of autocracy, militarism and oppression.[6] In the 1790s the revolution in France, and even more the final destruction of Polish independence, had been decisive events in the consolidation of this attitude. For a century or more it was to provide a large part of the intellectual and emotional background to the relations of the European states. Much more than any other factor it explains the mingled fear and contempt with which so many west Europeans throughout the century which followed Waterloo regarded the peasant society and military autocracy of Russia.

In the years immediately after 1815 this fear was very understandable. The destruction of Napoleon's *Grande Armée* in 1812, the advance of Russian armies across Poland and Germany in 1813 culminating in their triumphal entry into Paris with the forces of the other allies in April 1814, seemed to mark Russia as a power whose military strength, and therefore whose political potentialities, were of a different order of magnitude from those of the other states of Europe. 'This monster of an empire . . . the most enormous empire, in extent, that ever spread over the face of the earth',[7] now appeared to many observers to threaten the liberties, even the civilization, of Europe.

These fears were grossly exaggerated. The policies of Alexander I helped to ensure that his empire would remain for another century socially, economically and administratively weak by comparison with most of the other great European states. During the first decade of his reign progressive and constructive change in Russia was probably more practicable than at any time until at least the 1860s. Yet from 1811–12 onwards the real interests and needs of the empire – social change, administrative reform and economic development – were consistently sacrificed to the tsar's grandiose and often erratic idealism. By the time of Alexander's death the social and economic gap between Russia and much of western Europe was wider than ever before. Moreover the tsar, in spite of the suspicions of many contemporaries, was little interested in territorial expansion. Even in Poland in 1814–15 he was inspired not by a desire for territory but by a genuine wish to re-establish some form of Polish state. Another aspect of his idealism is seen in his real interest in the creation of moderate constitutional régimes in many parts of Europe (in the Grand Duchy of Finland in 1809, in France and Poland in 1815).

More important than the personal attitude of Alexander and his successors was the fact that Russia's industrial and technological resources were, until well into the second half of the century, grossly and increasingly inferior to those of Britain, and in many ways to those of France or Belgium. In 1850 British consumption of iron, on a per capita basis, was more than fourteen times that of Russia, French consumption four and a half times as great. Of cotton, on the same basis, Britain consumed more than nine times as much as Russia, France almost three times as much.[8] Russia's heavy dependence on foreign technology illustrates her backwardness from a different point of view. The first steam-engine in the country was produced, in 1790, in a factory set up by an Englishman; while the first production of railway locomotives, in 1844, was the work of American entrepreneurs and engineers. Throughout the generation 1836–65 the Russian railways (whose mileage was still tiny in terms of the size and needs of the empire) imported seven-eighths of their rails, three-fifths of their locomotives and two-thirds of their freight cars, while Russian ironmasters showed themselves markedly reluctant to attempt the building of large metal structures such as bridges or to depart in any way from the routine to which they were accustomed.

Nevertheless the deep-rooted and crippling weaknesses of Russia during the decades after 1815 were largely hidden from contemporaries. To them the menacing façade of military power which she presented to the outside world still carried conviction. 'There is evidently nothing in Europe', wrote an influential American pamphleteer in 1822, 'capable of making head against such a power as this. Not all Europe combined in opposition will be able to resist its progress, whenever this vast machinery is seriously brought to bear upon the independence of other nations by an able and ambitious emperor.' He went on to argue that Russian military strength was now so great that a balance of power was forever impossible in Europe, and to speculate that 'we may see at last the two-headed eagle extend his wings and unfurl his charts triumphantly over the Tower of London itself'.[9]

To many observers it appeared that one state above all was equipped to hold its own against the apparently overwhelming power of Russia: Great Britain. Like Russia, though in a very dissimilar way, Britain seemed a power of a different order from those of west and central Europe. Like her she seemed (in both cases with much justification) to be in a sense un-European, with fundamental interests outside Europe and little stake in the welfare of the continent. It was even possible to argue that the real Europe, the Europe of Charlemagne, of Charles V, of Napoleon, had now a choice, in the long run, only between accepting a British or a Russian protectorate.[10]

The bases of Britain's extraordinary international position during the half-century after Waterloo were magnificent in their simplicity and solidity. She was during these decades much the greatest colonial power in the world, much the greatest naval power, and much the greatest industrial power. Her colonial empire, though still undeveloped, made her the one true world power. Her naval strength, in spite of occasional alarms,[11] gave her a degree of physical security matched by no continental state and meant she could safely have only a small and inefficient army. No other state has ever combined a position of such strength with such modest military expenditure. Worldwide colonial possessions and a navy supreme on every sea if it so chose bred in British governments something more clearly approaching a world outlook than had been seen before in any country. Above all Britain's industrial and technological development, as yet unapproached anywhere in Europe except to some extent in Belgium, gave her economic resources quite different in scale from those of her political rivals. She was still far from being a completely industrialized country. The 1851 census showed that agriculture was still Britain's largest single industry (though manufacturing of all kinds now employed considerably more people); and landed property and farms still accounted in that year for about 40 per cent of her total capital. But what mattered was the comparison with other states; and by any standards that comparison was highly favourable to Britain.

Russia and Britain, military power and autocracy on the one hand, industry and individual freedom on the other, thus seemed to some of the most acute observers after 1815 the two poles of attraction between which Europe must, in the long run, choose. In totally dissimilar ways each appeared a power different in magnitude from the other states of the continent. In military and political terms none of these, it seemed, could hope to hold its own against Russia. The Habsburg empire was a multinational agglomeration with all the disadvantages this increasingly involved as the nineteenth century progressed. It was also handicapped by a creaking traditional administrative system and blessed with few easily defensible natural frontiers. All these weaknesses condemned it to a cautious, defensive, conservative and essentially timid stance in international affairs. Metternich himself was well aware of this. In 1822 he complained that 'Today I spend my time shoring up crumbling edifices. I should have been born in 1900 with the twentieth century before me'; and complaints of this kind are frequent in his correspondence. His pessimism was echoed by foreign observers. 'This country', wrote the French ambassador to Vienna in 1817, 'keeps going by its own size, but the government has no energy and none is to be found anywhere ... there is here neither will nor authority, everyone does more or less as he likes, and it is the subordinates who are the masters. ... We look everywhere for the government, and none can tell us where it is.'[12]

Prussia, the other major German or largely German state, seemed even less well equipped to counterbalance the threatening power of Russia. In the making of the 1814-15 settlement she had ranked, at least by courtesy, as a great power; but even after the gains she achieved at Vienna her territory and population scarcely fitted her to play this role. As Metternich put it in 1833 'she shares in the duties of the leading Powers, but her geographical boundaries, combined with a lack of certain essential internal resources, force her back into the second rank'.[13] Nor were these material weaknesses compensated for by the dynamism of her government. There still existed in Prussia a current of radical reformism closely associated with German national sentiment. This can be seen in an early and extreme form in the great soldier Gneisenau's proposals of 1809 for the launching in Germany of a ferocious people's war against Napoleon. It also underlay the military reforms of 1813–14, the introduction of universal military service and the formation of the *Landwehr* by the liberal war minister Boyen; and it received powerful support not merely from soldiers such as Gneisenau and Grolman but also from statesmen such as Wilhelm von Humboldt and Freiherr vom Stein. But side by side with this current ran a stronger one, conservative and legitimist, which had urged caution during the dark days after Jena and which triumphed with the fall of Boyen in 1819. For the next generation Prussia was to pursue a limited and remarkably unobtrusive foreign policy and to be very much overshadowed in European affairs by Austria and Russia.

Even France, a greater power than Austria and a much greater one than Prussia, seemed after 1815 scarcely the equal of Russia and Britain. Her now established status as the centre for all Europe of revolutionary thought and aspiration made her, even under a restored Bourbon dynasty, distrusted and suspected by conservatives everywhere. The constant threat of political instability, seen in the murder in 1820 of a member of the royal family, the Duc de Berri, in Carbonarist conspiracies and in the successful revolution of 1830, emphasized her position as a centre of revolutionary infection. In particular it contrasted unfavourably in the eyes of many observers with the political stability of Britain and Russia.[14] Moreover in the simple terms of military strength the defeats of 1812–14 seemed to mark her as the inferior of the tsarist empire.

Economically the truly European great powers – Austria, Prussia, France – were in 1815 decisively, indeed overwhelmingly, inferior to Britain. Moreover Britain's virtual monopoly of advanced technology, her highly developed financial structure, even her rapidly increasing population, allowed her during the following generation substantially to increase her lead over them. In particular the whole economic and therefore in the long run political balance of Europe was now being powerfully affected by the relative decline of France. In 1850 French production of pig-iron (in the first half of the nineteenth century perhaps the best of all indices of industrial strength) was less than twice what it had been in 1806: in both Britain and Germany its production had grown eight or nine times in the same period. In the two most important technological developments of the age, coke-smelting of iron and railway-building, France lagged far behind Britain. At the end of the Napoleonic Wars a ton of British iron, even after paying transport costs and a heavy import duty, could be sold in France for the mere cost of the charcoal needed to smelt a ton of French iron. The result was a vociferous demand for further protection for the French industry, so that by 1822 the duty on imports of British iron was 120 per cent *ad valorem*.[15] Even as late as 1842, of the 462 French blast-furnaces (the great majority very small and inefficient) only 41 used coke as their fuel. Though railway-building began in France in 1828 she possessed by 1850 only about half the mileage of the German states, and little more than a quarter of that of Britain. Moreover the slow growth of the French railway network, by delaying the complete economic integration of the country, prolonged the life of archaic techniques and out-of-date methods of economic organization. Industrial stagnation was reflected in the fact that between 1801 and 1851 the percentage of Frenchmen living in towns of over 10,000 people grew from 9.5 to only 10.6. In Britain during the same fifty years the growth was from 23.3 to 39.5 per cent. All this did not mean that daily life in France was less agreeable than in Britain. On this observers with experience of both countries agreed. The British agricultural labourer driven into the industrial city by the very unequal ownership of land had many fewer counterparts across the Channel. But the contrast in terms of industrial production is clear. Different factors contributed to the slowness of French industrial growth – lack of coalfields as compared to Britain or Germany, tariff protection against foreign competition and its stimulating if uncomfortable effects, a population which was growing only very slowly. But whatever the exact balance of causes which underlay this decline in France's relative economic strength, the decline was lasting. By the middle of the century her status as a great economic power was menaced not only by the undeniably greater strength of Britain but also by the new threat of German superiority.

That superiority was still far from established. Of the total pig-iron production of the *Zollverein* (the customs union which by then covered most of Germany) in 1850 less than 11 per cent was coke-smelted, a much smaller proportion than in France. The Ruhr, which in 1815, when it became Prussian territory, produced each year only 300–400 tons of iron, remained in the first half of the nineteenth century a metal-working rather than a metal-producing area. It still imported much of its iron from Belgium and Britain. Not until the 1850s did railways link effectively the coal of the Saar basin, the iron ore of Luxembourg and the growing market of the *Zollverein* states in general, thus paving the way for a great expansion of iron production during the second half of the century. Even as late as 1850 French industry used about three times as much steam power as that of Prussia.

Nevertheless German heavy industry, as compared with that of France, probably already enjoyed before the middle of the century one supremely valuable asset. It had more, and more active, entrepreneurs. In the growing Silesian industrial area these were often noble landowners: the obvious example is Count Henckel von Donnersmarck, who in 1837–40 created the Laurahütte complex of blast-furnaces, puddling-ovens and rolling-mills, the first thing of its kind anywhere in Europe east of the Elbe. In west Germany the typical entrepreneur was a member of the middle classes, sometimes of humble origin – Matthias Stinnes, Franz Haniel, most notably Alfred Krupp, who inherited from his father a tiny factory with four employees in which he himself at first worked with his own hands. To these the de Wendel family were perhaps the only real equivalent in the French metal industries. Moreover Prussian industry benefited from two factors little seen in France (or for that matter in Britain) – the assistance of enlightened officials and an increasing application of scientific knowledge to technological problems. Of the first Ludwig von Vincke, first president after 1815 of the new Prussian province of Westphalia, is a good example. The second can be seen in the engagement by the industrialist Friedrich Harkort, to the astonishment of contemporaries, of the first academically trained chemist ever to be employed in the metallurgical industries. The shape of things to come was seen in unmistakably material form when at the Crystal Palace exhibition of 1851 Krupp startled British ironmasters by showing a block of cast steel weighing two tons, an achievement they could not match.

If France, Germany and the Habsburg empire could not face Britain and Russia on equal terms, still less could the other states of Europe. The great-power status which Spain had managed to retain during the eighteenth century was lost for ever when in 1814 her representatives were excluded from any real influence over the work of the Vienna congress. Henceforth, economically and socially backward and politically unstable, afflicted by revolution in 1820, by French intervention in 1823 and by a savage civil war in the 1830s, she was scarcely a respectable second-rate power. Savoy-Sardinia and the Two Sicilies, the most important of the Italian states, were even less able to play significant roles in international affairs. The Ottoman empire from the 1820s onwards was being driven by its ruler, the Sultan Mahmud II, towards some limited modernization. But this remained, even in the military sphere to which the sultan devoted most attention, in many ways superficial. Above all the economic backwardness of the empire, with no modern industry whatever, with its international trade and financial life increasingly in the hands of foreigners, with internal communications so bad as hardly to be paralleled anywhere in Europe save in parts of Spain and southern Italy, was a permanent and fundamental obstacle to the achievement of real strength.

The political events of the generation from the 1820s to the 1850s reflected in many ways British and Russian superiority to the other states of the continent. It was clear that throughout a great area in eastern and south-eastern Europe Russia now occupied a leading position which could be seriously shaken only by defeat in war. In 1826 George Canning, the British foreign secretary, found himself compelled to ally with her in order to prevent her taking uncontrolled and independent action in the Balkans in support of the Greek rebels and of her own claims against the Ottoman empire. Two years later, after Canning's successors had abandoned his policy, she went to war with the Turks and in September 1829 at Adrianople forced them to sign a peace which made the independence of Greece inevitable. In 1830–31 she crushed a serious revolt against her rule in Poland, in spite of the vociferous sympathy for the Poles expressed by liberals throughout western Europe.[16] In 1833 she appeared to some observers, notably to the British foreign secretary, Lord Palmerston, to have reduced the Ottoman empire, by the treaty of Unkiar-Skelessi, very nearly to the position of a satellite. In the same year she endowed the Danubian principalities of Moldavia and Wallachia, which her armies continued to occupy until 1849, with their first approach to a constitution. In 1839–40 it was her temporary cooperation with Britain which allowed Palmerston to play a dominant role in the Near Eastern crisis of these years. The revolutions of 1848, which in the spring of that year seemed to have swept away existing régimes almost everywhere in western and central Europe, left her virtually unscathed; and in 1849 her armies, by dealing the *coup de grâce* to the Hungarian nationalist revolt which had broken out in the previous year, re-established the Habsburgs in the most intractable of all their territories.

Of course there were limits to what Russia could achieve. She was unable, partly because of the revolt in Poland, to take any action against the revolution of 1830 in France; and though Nicholas I always bitterly disliked and distrusted the new régime of Louis-Philippe there he could do little to shake it. Russia's freedom of action in international affairs was already being limited by the financial weakness from which her government was to suffer throughout the nineteenth century; lack of money was one reason for the unwillingness of Nicholas to take an independent line in the Near East in 1839. In 1849 the Turks, supported by Palmerston, were able successfully to resist Russian demands for the extradition of Hungarian and Polish refugees who had taken refuge in the Ottoman empire after the collapse of the revolt in Hungary. But for nearly four decades after 1815 Russia suffered no serious defeat in international affairs.

To the increasingly numerous russophobes in western Europe this success seemed sinister in the extreme. To them it appeared the product not merely of Russia's own inherent strength but also of a cunning and a sustained will to domination which threatened the whole of Europe, and which the fumbling statesmen of the western powers could never meet effectively. To liberals the crushing of Poland, the autocracy of Nicholas I and the intervention of 1849 in Hungary seemed to mark the tsarist empire more clearly than ever as the bulwark of despotism throughout the continent, the 'gendarme of Europe'. This fear and condemnation was not universal. Some observers continued to see in the tsarist régime a potential saviour of Europe from the forces of anarchy which they believed to threaten the continent.[17] One or two even realized that there were important aspects of Russian life which were not authoritarian and which might eventually permit the development of the country along new and different lines.[18] There was also a slowly growing realization that Russia's failure to keep pace with the growth in western Europe of technology and economic life must weaken her international position, that the military strength of a state was no longer a matter of mere ability to put in the field large numbers of illiterate peasant conscripts. It could now be argued that great armies, the basis of Russian power in Europe, would in future influence the movement of history and the development of humanity much less than the new forces of industry and technology. Thus the great English radical, Richard Cobden, in his *Russia* (London, 1836) contended that in the face of modern weapons wild hordes from the east could never conquer Europe and overthrow civilization as the extreme russophobes still feared, and predicted that 'the steam-engine . . . will at no distant day produce moral and physical changes, all over the world, of a magnitude and permanency surpassing the effects of all the wars and conquests which have convulsed mankind since the beginning of time'. But in spite of all this, to the average educated west European during the four decades after Waterloo Russia stood for autocratic power, arbitrary authority and the denial of freedom. To him she seemed a standing menace to the political balance of Europe and the independence of the European states.

During these decades Britain also enjoyed great diplomatic success and international influence. In the early 1820s her naval strength allowed Canning to make a larger contribution than any other European statesman to the achievement of independence by Spanish America. In the 1830s Palmerston, after the revolt of the southern Netherlands against Dutch rule, became the main creator of an indepedent Belgian state. In 1840–41, during the eastern crisis of these years, he achieved a personal triumph which has few equals in the history of European diplomacy. This crisis saw France isolated and humiliated and her protégé Mehemet Ali, viceroy of Egypt, forced to make peace with his overlord the sultan on moderate terms which ensured the continued existence of the Ottoman empire. In part, it is true, these successes were made possible by the fact that the structure of international relations was unusually favourable to Britain. The isolation of France for long periods, the fact that Austria and Prussia had no territorial ambitions and that even Russia (except to some extent in the Near East during the 1820s) showed no desire to increase her territory in Europe, made the task of British governments easier. But external factors of this kind were only one part of the story. The other, and the more permanent, was Britain's own strength and prestige.

In spite of what has been said in the preceding pages it would be highly inaccurate to think of the decades which followed Waterloo as an age of acute and self-conscious competition between states on the economic or even the political plane. By comparison with the period from the 1860s to 1914 they were in general remarkably lacking in feeling of this kind. Alexander I's dream of some kind of formalized international cooperation had faded beyond recall by the early 1820s; but the idea of the 'Concert of Europe' continued to influence statesmen and to blunt the edge of national and state selfishness, though with slowly declining effect, until the middle of the century. The effective cooperation of the great powers in the interests of international peace and stability continued to be an ideal to which something more than lip-service was paid. There was still a widespread feeling that, in particular, significant territorial changes in Europe should be made only with the agreement of these powers. The emergence of an independent Belgium in 1830–39, the product of very long and difficult negotiations, was a triumph for the 'concert' idea. So was the establishment, by the Straits Convention of June 1841, of a set of internationally agreed rules regarding the passage of ships of war through the Bosphorus and Dardanelles which were to last, in essentials, for over eighty years.

The Concert of Europe idea, like every aspiration towards order and stability, was at bottom conservative. Its most consistent supporter, Metternich, whose policy from 1822 until his fall in 1848 has been described as 'a continuous chain of rearguard actions to delay, to cover, and to argue away the breakdown of the Concert of Europe and all it stood for',[19] was influenced above all by forebodings about the future of the Habsburg empire, which an effective concert of the powers would do much to safeguard. In particular his desire for cooperation with Russia in the 1830s and 1840s was based in part on his morbid fear of the forces of revolution in Europe. Also the concert had important practical limitations. It could not prevent Russia from independently imposing peace terms on the Turks in 1829; and there was never any suggestion that it should operate outside Europe. Even the French conquest of Algeria after 1830 lay outside its scope. Nevertheless, vague and restricted though it was, within its limits it was real, perhaps all the more so for being unspecific and therefore flexible.

Moreover the ideal of giving the political unity of Europe some visible institutional form had never been completely abandoned. By the middle of the century it was assuming a new shape, as to the alleged threat to Europe from Russia in the east was added the new one apparently created by the phenomenally growing United States across the Atlantic. The American republic had not played a significant role in the calculations of any statesman during the peace settlement of 1814–15. Between the 1830s and 1850s, however, it was visited and studied by a number of the most important writers on politics of the period – de Tocqueville, List, Fröbel – and their books spread the idea that Europe's leadership of the world was now threatened by the growth of these gigantic extra-European states in east and west and perhaps must inevitably be lost to them as their overwhelming power developed. 'There are only two peoples', wrote the French critic Sainte-Beuve in 1847. 'Russia is still barbarous, but she is great. . . . The other youthful people is America . . . the future of the world is there, between these two great worlds.'[20] Almost simultaneously in Germany the radical Bruno Bauer was speculating gloomily on the imminent emergence of Russia and the United States as the only true world powers.[21] Such forecasts tended to the conclusion that European union (most usually envisaged as some form of federation) was essential if the world centre of civilization and progress were to escape eclipse and even subjection. A series of writers – J. E. Jörg, Fröbel and Constantin Frantz in Germany, the historian Henri Martin in France – put forward in varying forms ideas of this kind around and just after the middle of the century.[22] But the fears which inspired them, though not unreal, were soon shown to be premature. Russia's defeat in the Crimea, and the internal stresses which this exposed and which erupted in populist terrorism during the 1870s and 1880s, did not destroy the view of her as an imminent threat to the independence of Europe; but they greatly weakened it. The backwardness of her society, which had seemed in the first half of the century to make her largely impervious to radical ideas and hence to the weakening effects of revolution, now aroused from the later 1850s onwards pity and even contempt as much as fear. Almost simultaneously the prestige of the United States, and with it that of federalist ideas in general, fell catastrophically as the result of the Civil War of 1861–65. The apparent failure of Russia and America meant that the idea of European union, always confined to a very limited circle of intellectuals and without real influence on statesmen or soldiers, steadily lost ground. Formal political links now seemed unnecessary for the defence or survival of the European states. Europe during the 1850s and 1860s was moving into a new epoch, one dominated not by fears of revolution or of Russian armies but by the problems of nationalism and of a great unified Germany.

THE BALANCE OF POWER REVOLUTIONIZED, c. 1850–1871

'Infallible signs', wrote the French historian Henri Martin in 1847, 'show that in a few years questions of nationality, combined with social questions, will dominate all others on the continent.'[23] He was an accurate prophet. The nationalism which had for almost a century been gathering strength was by the 1870s clearly the most dynamic force in the political life of most of Europe. By then even feelings of monarchical solidarity were obviously unable to hold their own against it. 'There does not now exist', wrote the journalist and economist Walter Bagehot in 1865, 'a human being who could write a letter to every great sovereign in Europe with a certainty that his words would be weighed as those of a wise king, friendly to the person addressed.'[24] Less spectacularly, but with almost equal significance, social and economic changes were influencing the relations between states in ways not hitherto seen. The factors of production could now overstep or bypass political frontiers with unprecedented ease. Large-scale international movement of capital was not new. In the eighteenth century the Dutch republic had lent and invested abroad quite lavishly; and in the first half of the nineteenth Britain had begun to do the same. By the middle of the century, however, one or two countries were beginning to be able to act in this way on a hitherto unknown scale, and such investments now grew with unprecedented speed. By the early 1850s Britain had exported about £200–230 million of capital. By 1875 the total had risen to over £1,000 million. More important to the strictly European picture (since so much British capital went to North and South America, India and Australasia) was France, which under Napoleon III became for a time the greatest of all lenders, the 'banker of the universe'. In 1868 fourteen different states sold in all 2,127 million francs worth of their government bonds in Paris. Emigration on a large scale from some parts of western Europe to America, and on a smaller scale to Australasia and even South Africa, was again not new; but it was now beginning to affect areas hitherto untouched by it, particularly in eastern Europe. Thus in Russian Poland and still more in Galicia, during the second half of the century, the steady growth of a landless peasantry, and of rural overpopulation and

unemployment, began to produce large-scale emigration, either permanently to America or on a seasonal basis to Germany, where spectacular
economic progress was creating an increasing demand for labour. Most of
all the growth of industry, the fact that the 1850s and 1860s saw great
progress in this respect in both France and Germany,[25] was beginning to
alter the situation fundamentally. Britain's lead was still imposing; but
there were signs that it would soon diminish.

These decades were the greatest of the nineteenth century and perhaps
the greatest in all modern European history. During them the world was
bound together with startling speed by a new network of up-to-date communications. They were the supreme age of railway-building not merely
in continental Europe (where 50,000 miles of track were laid in 1850–70
as against only 15,000 before 1850) but in North America and India; and
there seemed hardly any limit to what might be possible with the coming
of this revolutionary new technique of transport. A 'world's highway'
linking western Europe, through the Near and Middle East, with India,
was more than once seriously proposed, and the first serious suggestion of
a trans-Siberian line to link European Russia with the Far East was made
in 1858. The coming of the steamship was, more slowly, revolutionizing
transport by sea and consolidating Britain's position as the greatest of all
maritime powers, since she adopted this new technique earlier and more
wholeheartedly than any of her rivals. The Suez Canal, completed in 1869,
provided, though at high cost in human lives, the most spectacularly successful of all examples of what might be achieved by the building of new
world communication links. (It also saw, in the later years of its construction, the first really large-scale use of mechanical power on any public
work; 10,000 horsepower of mechanical excavators and other machines
were then in use on it.) The telegraph was now allowing a nearer approach
than ever before to the instantaneous transmission of information throughout the world, thus making possible something like a world political system
and a world economy based on world markets and commodity prices.
New gold supplies from the United States and Australia heightened financial
confidence, increased the note circulation of banks and made credit easier
and cheaper to obtain. In every material aspect of life Europe was in rapid
and brilliant development, able as never before to surmount difficulties
and to respond successfully to a challenge.[26] It was the triumphs of these
decades which underlay the optimistic evolutionary materialism increasingly dominant in their intellectual life.[27]

The international influence of a state was still in these years largely a
function of its military power. But that, more than ever before, was now
in turn a function of its economic maturity and financial strength. 'It is
the budget', noted a contemporary, 'which prevents many states, in spite of

conscription, from being ready for war.'[28] This position was very far from new. The difficulty of fighting a successful war without adequate supplies of money is as old as war itself. But by the 1860s the inability of some states – Spain, the Habsburg empire, Russia – to use their military man-power to the full for lack of the economic resources to maintain large armies was a more important factor in the international relations of Europe than ever in the past. In particular the defeat of the Habsburg empire by Prussia in 1866, with all its long-term implications for Europe, was brought about largely by the mere poverty of the Austrian government. Its credit badly shaken by the international financial crisis of 1857, it was simply too poor to afford the reorganization and re-equipment of its army which the Emperor Francis Joseph and his advisers clearly saw was needed.

The increased competitiveness which becomes visible in the international relations of the 1850s and 1860s, and the spectacular changes in the European state system which these years witnessed, were in part the result of the collapse of the Concert of Europe idea. This in turn was largely the result of the defeat of Russia by Britain and France in the Crimean War. No power had wanted that war; and many of the provisions of the treaty of Paris which ended it in March 1856 soon became a dead letter. Yet so far as international relations were concerned it was this struggle far more than the spectacular upheavals of 1848 which ended the Europe of Castlereagh, Metternich and Alexander I. On both sides it brought to the surface antagonisms which had been forming for decades. In Britain in particular its outbreak was accompanied and to some extent caused by a violent outbreak of anti-Russian hysteria. 'The people', wrote an observer in June 1854, 'are wild about this war, and besides the general confidence that we are to obtain very signal success in our naval and military opera-tions, there is a violent desire to force the Emperor (i.e. Nicholas I of Russia) to make a very humiliating peace, and a strong conviction that he will very soon be forced to do so.'[29] Throughout the war it was the British government much more than its French ally which pressed for severe peace terms. In Russia, again, though a public opinion of the kind which now existed in some parts of western Europe was as yet hardly possible, the war could be seen as a proof of the essential hostility to the country and to Orthodoxy of the western states. In particular the humili-ating clause in the peace treaty signed at Paris in March 1856 which neutralized the Black Sea and made it impossible for Russia to maintain a naval squadron there aroused bitter resentment. It was a restriction of a kind which no other European state was to suffer until the much more stringent limitations imposed on German military power in 1919; and to throw it off became at once a major objective of Russian foreign policy.

The growth of Panslav feeling which was so marked in Russia during the next two decades was in part a response to the defeat of 1856.

Above all the war brought a decisive break between Russia and Austria. It destroyed the *entente* between them which, sometimes considerably strained, had none the less endured for over a generation. In December 1855 the Habsburg government at last 'astonished the world with its ingratitude' and presented in St Petersburg the ultimatum, threatening intervention in the war, which forced Russia to make peace. Henceforth relations between the two empires were dominated, on the Russian side, by bitter resentment. Count Nesselrode, the aged chancellor, remained faithful to the end to the conservative, monarchical, anti-Polish and therefore by implication Austrophil policy which he had upheld for so long.[30] But he had never counted for much in the formation of Russian policy and his urgings went unheeded. His successor, Prince Gorchakov, was strongly anti-Austrian. Even during the peace negotiations of 1856 there were clear signs that Russia and France were drawing closer to each other; and this *rapprochement* continued to be an important factor in European diplomacy for several years, until it was disrupted by a new revolt in Russian Poland in 1863. That Russia should thus become openly the friend of Napoleon III, a self-made plebiscitary ruler despised and distrusted by Nicholas I to the day of his death in March 1855, was a genuine diplomatic revolution.

The real importance of the Crimean War, therefore, its status as a genuine dividing-line in the history of the European state system, lies not in its relatively mediocre achievements in the Near East but in the isolation and weakening of Austria which indirectly flowed from it. In November 1850, while she still enjoyed Russian backing, Austria had been able to force Prussia by the humiliating Olmütz Punctation to abandon a short-lived scheme for a union of German princes under her leadership and agree to the restoration of the position of 1815. After 1854–55 another such victory was scarcely to be hoped for. The 'unification' of most of Italy and Germany between 1859 and 1867 took place at the expense above all of the Habsburgs. Something of the sort would have happened in the long run, at least in Germany, even had there been no previous transformation of Russia into an aggrieved revisionist power. German nationalism had asserted itself in 1848; and with the rapid economic development of the country its demands were becoming more and more impossible to deny. It could well be argued, moreover, that the expulsion of Austria from Germany and Italy was in her own long-term interests and those of Europe. 'Hitherto', noted the most acute of all British observers of the German scene in 1866, 'the main cause of her [Austria's] ruin has been the unnatural attempt to exercise a sort of indirect universal dominion from the Eider to Brindisi, but the old imperial purple cannot afford to continue to be sewn on to the new garment of Italian and German progress, and the sooner the rent takes place the better.'[31] But the fact that the Habsburg empire, industrially undeveloped, financially weak, internally divided, was now without the Russian support which had helped to preserve it in 1849, greatly eased the task of the forces which were, within a few years, to turn the whole political balance of Europe upside-down.

These forces owed a good deal of their success to the actions and failures to act of Napoleon III. This strange man united within himself, in unstable and shifting equilibrium, many of the dominant tendencies of the age. He benefited from a width of experience unique among its rulers and statesmen. He had studied at the *Gymnasium* in Augsburg, been a cadet and then an officer in the Swiss army, taken part in the risings of 1831 in Italy, lived in exile in London, and even visited New York. This gave him a range of sympathies, and in some ways at least a grasp of realities, which Alexander II, Francis Joseph and William I of Prussia could not match. He had moreover a sincere sympathy with the national idea and some grasp of its enormous and growing importance. He shared the belief of many of his contemporaries in the advantages of large political units and dreamed of a union of Portugal with Spain and of Denmark and Finland with Sweden. On the other hand he was far from being an out-and-out idealist. He did not push his nationalism or his belief in the superior rationality of large states to the point of desiring the union of Germany or Italy under powerful centralized governments. Such a change would make almost impossible the political influence which in both areas France had usually been able to exercise since the end of the Middle Ages. He was quite willing to see, indeed wished to see, a Prussian-dominated north Germany and a Savoy-Sardinian-dominated north Italy. Both of these would be strong enough to be useful allies; but neither would be strong enough to withstand French hostility. In Germany the power of Prussia would be balanced not merely by that of the Habsburgs but also by that of the small states of the south and west, perhaps banded together in some form of union reminiscent of the *Rheinbund* created by Napoleon I in 1806. In Italy the influence of an enlarged Savoy-Sardinia would be limited by the continued existence of Tuscany, the Papal States and the kingdom of the Two Sicilies, all four if possible united in a federation presided over by the Pope. A scheme of this kind was in fact laid down in his famous Plombières interview with Count Cavour, the Savoy-Sardinian prime minister, in July 1858; and Napoleon envisaged such an Italy as one of the subordinate allies with which he hoped to provide France, which he saw as the natural leader of the Mediterranean states in general.[32]

His policies were not aggressive or expansionist in any important territorial sense. The annexation to France of Savoy and Nice which took
place in 1860 had not been foreseen when his intervention in Italian affairs
began in 1858–59. Though he wished to extend French power towards
the Rhine he thought not in terms of conquest in western Germany but
rather in those of the creation, in 1864, of an independent and neutral
kingdom of the Rhineland under French influence. Nevertheless his most
fundamental objective was the safeguarding of French interests. The uneasy
tension between this element in his policies and that of nationalist and
other idealism was complicated by his personal vacillations, by his taste
for secret diplomacy (which grew from about 1860 onwards), and by the
frequently conflicting advice of his ministers. All these factors explain the
inconsistency of so much of his diplomacy during these crucial years.

It would be a great mistake, however, to think of Napoleon III's foreign
policies exclusively in terms of failure. Certainly his contemporaries, at
least until very late in his reign, did not see him in this light. To Italian
unification he made an essential contribution by his defeat of the Austrian
army in the short war fought in Lombardy in 1859. After the hard-won
victories of Magenta and Solferino, horrified by the slaughter and alarmed
by the hostile attitude which Prussia was taking on the Rhine, he made
peace with the Habsburgs quickly and in the eyes of Italian nationalists
prematurely. The kingdom of Sardinia, to the bitter disappointment of
Cavour, received only Milan by the peace terms and not Venetia, which
had also been promised her at Plombières. Yet the essential break in the
status quo had been achieved. Its one effective defender, the Austrian
army, had after a few weeks' fighting been eliminated from the picture
over most of the peninsula. The way had thus been opened for the overthrow of the flimsy régimes which ruled the different Italian states and
whose Austrian support had now been snatched from them. In Tuscany,
Parma and Modena the rulers were driven out with ease in the spring of
1859. By the end of the year Napoleon had decided to allow the union of
these states with Sardinia in return for the compensation of France with
Savoy and Nice. In the kingdom of the Two Sicilies Garibaldi, taking
advantage of a ferocious and essentially unpolitical peasant revolt in Sicily,
overthrew the last Bourbon ruler in May–September 1860 in the most
spectacular episode of the entire Risorgimento. The annexation to Sardinia
of the princedoms of central Italy and of Naples and Sicily was then
confirmed by plebiscites in the areas concerned.

This whole process was in an important sense artificial. Whatever claims
the Italian nationalists might make it is clear that the movement for national
unity was not one of the mass of the population. It was rather one of the
educated, of the urban middle classes and in some areas of the nobility

(Baron Ricasoli, the outstanding figure in the Risorgimento in Tuscany, is the best example of the last). It depended on organizations such as the National Society founded in 1856; and still more on the drive and initiative of local leaders such as Farini in Modena, Cipriani in Bologna and Ricasoli in Florence. Cavour himself, the most realistic and farsighted figure in the history of nineteenth-century Italy, was very far from being a nationalist. His intellectual affinities were with France and Britain: about Italy in many ways he knew remarkably little. It was only after Garibaldi's astonishing successes in the south had forced his hand that he announced his conversion to the idea of a united Italy, which he had hitherto despised as an impracticable and undesirable Mazzinian dream.

The plebiscites which produced overwhelming majorities in favour of a united Italy under King Victor Emmanuel of Piedmont-Sardinia were largely formalities. (But significant ones: they were among the most important formal concessions yet made anywhere in Europe to the idea of direct expression of the popular will and to the populist attitudes inherent in the mythology of nationalism.) In Tuscany one nationalist told Ricasoli frankly that hardly a peasant would trouble to vote unless he were driven to the polls by nationalist intrigues; and it was widely feared in the summer of 1860 that the indifference or even hostility of the Tuscan countryside to what had been achieved in the last year would be embarrassingly revealed by large-scale abstentions.[33] In the kingdom of Naples, where only 15 per cent of the male population voted, the British minister correctly pointed out that the plebiscite was made a sham by the fact that the only alternative offered to union under Sardinia was the continuation of the present state of near-anarchy; southern Italy, far from producing any genuine nationalist revolution, had simply been conquered by Garibaldi and his army.[34] In Sicily, for years after the unification, *Italia* was widely believed to be the name of the king's wife.[35] Everywhere there was active and pervasive official propaganda in favour of union. Nowhere was the voter given the chance to express a positive preference for the old régime. Yet in spite of all the chicanery, the false claims and nationalist rhetoric, something potentially great had been achieved; and its achievement had been made possible by the international situation. The isolation of Austria and the ambitions and ideals of Napoleon III had given the Italian nationalists, with all their limitations, the freedom of action they had never achieved in 1848.

Different relationships between the powers in the 1850s and 1860s might have stultified completely the movement towards Italian unity and allowed Italy to drag on indefinitely in the weakness and division of 1815. The growth of a great Prussian-dominated German state, on the other hand, incomparably the most important political development of these years, was beyond the ability of any statesman to halt, far less reverse.

The battle of Sadowa in July 1866 was the foundation on which, more than any other, the international relations of late nineteenth-century Europe were built. It provided an unprecedented demonstration of the efficiency of the Prussian war machine and ushered in an age in which military efficiency, expressed in up-to-date armaments, rapid mobilization and movement and competent staff-work, was to count for more than ever before in the power balance between states.[36] It drove the Habsburg empire out of Germany, forced it to make in the following year great concessions to its Hungarian subjects, and in the long run diverted what expansionist energies remained to it towards the south-east, with important and eventually disastrous results. Within the German world it raised the prestige of Prussia to an unprecedented height and placed her beyond all challenge as the only possible leader of a united Germany. By allowing her to annex Hanover, Hesse-Kassel, Nassau and the free city of Frankfurt it also made the process of unification, in the most literal sense, one of Prussian conquest. Within Prussia it consolidated the power of Otto von Bismarck, minister-president since 1862, and of the authoritarian and monarchical outlook which he personified. It thus inflicted on Prussian liberalism and constitutionalism, with which Bismarck and William I had hitherto been locked in bitter conflict over the remodelling of the army,[37] a defeat from which they never recovered. With the formation in 1867 of the North German Confederation, which bound together under Prussian control all the German states north of the Main in a union far closer than that provided by the confederation of 1815, Prussia had established herself for the first time indisputably as a great power. The secret offensive and defensive alliances which Bismarck concluded in the same year with Baden, Württemberg and Bavaria meant that her dominant influence, if not her open control, now extended to the whole of what in 1871 was to become the German empire.

It is easy enough to blame France and to a lesser extent Russia for allowing Prussia, to their own great future detriment, a free hand in 1866–67. With the advantage of hindsight it can easily be argued that German political unity was in the long run a disaster for Europe. The new Germany was too strong for the peace of the continent: but it was also too weak completely to dominate Europe or to overcome by force the antagonisms which it aroused. Yet it is difficult not to feel that this disaster was in some sense inevitable. By the 1860s national feeling and industrial growth were together making more and more unavoidable the creation of some kind of unified and very powerful German state.

There was still far to go before German economic life was completely modernized. In the metal-working industries during the early 1860s, for example, there were still about five times as many men employed in workshops as in factories. The guilds and the restrictions on economic freedom associated with them, which had survived the upheaval of 1848, lingered on for more than another decade. In Austria they were swept away and freedom of enterprise finally established only by an edict of December 1859 (one of the results of the defeat which the Habsburgs had just suffered in Italy); and this example was followed in the next five years by virtually all the German states in which such restrictions still existed. Nothing illustrates better the suddenness of Germany's emergence as a great modern economic power than the fact that even as late as the mid-1860s several millions of her people were still affected to varying extents by traditional limitations of this kind. Nevertheless great economic progress was being made. This sharply increased the desirability, on purely material grounds, of some form of German unity, and made the proliferation of small states and its economic results seem more and more archaic and irritating. The inspiring and terrifying rationality of modern economic life now cut more and more deeply at the roots of traditional Germany. By the 1860s important middle-class groups were demanding with increasing insistence the rationalization on a national scale of many aspects of the economy – a national system of commercial law and patent legislation, the abolition of tolls on the German rivers and the creation of a national system of coinage, weights and measures. 'Legitimacy, Caesarism, Republic, etc.,' complained a writer in April 1866, 'all of that is intertwined with cotton, brandy, coal and iron. A terrible time is coming for thinking men, but the bourgeoisie will wallow in rapture and bliss ... People want to trade, earn, enjoy and get along; they want not a state but a trading company.'[38]

There were still powerful forces, particularly in Prussia, which deeply distrusted national feeling, particularly because of the popular sovereignty which, however vaguely and indirectly, it implied. To a Prussian conservative such as Leopold von Gerlach, and of course to Frederick William IV or William I, the supreme duty was to uphold the institution of monarchy, which was ultimately based, like all enduring institutions, on religion. Their Lutheran piety went so far in some cases as to look back with nostalgia to the Holy Alliance. They resented, for example, the existence of the new kingdom of Italy, based as it was on an impious assault on the established rights of monarchs. But such attitudes, such respect for religion and contempt for economics, could not hope, in the climate of the 1860s, to stem in Germany the movement towards national unity. That movement, like the corresponding one in Italy, was the work of an educated and well-to-do minority. The masses were still, as everywhere in Europe, politically inert. Even in the Landtag election of 1862, at the height of the constitutional crisis over the government's proposals for army reform, hardly more than a third of the Prussian electorate went to the polls. In part this indifference was the result of preoccupation with the more immediate problems of making a living. A handicraft worker threatened by economic liberalism and power-driven machinery was unlikely to have much interest in politics, nationalist or otherwise, beyond a vague tendency to anti-Semitism. Even more, apathy was the result of mere ignorance.

It has been calculated that in Prussia the circulation of newspapers in the 1860s in proportion to population was only about a sixth as great as in England, and that of the 19 million inhabitants of the state there were not more than 1.5 million with a reasonable understanding of public affairs derived from the press. Even among adult males, the only group which mattered politically, only about a fifth could be considered well informed. 'The most significant world events', wrote a German newspaper in 1864,

especially in the towns and villages which lie far from cities, come to the know-ledge of the inhabitants only through oral communication, and even then rather late. It is obvious, however, that under this method of transmitting information we can speak in only very rare cases about a real understanding of the state of affairs, and it is just as obvious that a livelier interest or an enthusiasm for an idea cannot even exist.[39]

In Germany, then, as in Italy, national unity was not the work of the nation at large but of active and self-conscious pressure-groups. Bismarck was no more a true nationalist than Cavour. As a young man, after leaving Prussian government service, he had contemplated joining the British army in India, and the driving intellectual and emotional force in his life, after his religious conversion in the early 1840s, was a conventional Lutheran piety. His allegiance was to Prussia, not to Germany. His essential objective was Prussian dominance of north Germany rather than national unity. But there were two fundamental differences between the two new national states. In Germany, though particularist feeling existed, it was much weaker than in Italy, so that adjustment to the new position after 1866–67 was correspondingly easier. More important, the different parts of Germany were now increasingly bound together by economic links which were much less developed or non-existent in Italy. The very different histories of the two countries after unification can be explained largely in these terms.

The Prussian victory of 1866 over the Habsburg empire, the decisive step towards German unity, had as a postscript that of 1870–71 over France. What effect prompt French intervention on the anti-Prussian side would have had on the course of events in 1866 it is impossible to say. Bismarck in a Reichstag speech of 1874 alleged that 'it would have immediately forced us to cover Berlin and abandon all our successes in Austria'. On the other hand Moltke, the chief of the Prussian general staff, complained to Lord Clarendon, the British foreign secretary, in October 1868, that ignorance of the military weakness of France had prevented Prussia's forcing a settlement of accounts with her two years earlier.[40] In the event Napoleon did not act. He received conflicting advice from his ministers. He was probably influenced by the knowledge that French public opinion, to which he always paid considerable attention, was in favour of peace. His own poor health and his concentration, until it was too late, on Italian affairs at the expense of events in Germany, helped to ensure that he did nothing. But Sadowa left a deep and justified sense of alarm, even of humiliation, in France. Henceforth feeling there, though unwilling to support Napoleon's proposals for army reform and the sacrifices they involved,[41] was deeply suspicious and intensely touchy where Germany was concerned. A crisis of April–May 1867 over an unsuccessful French proposal to buy from the king of Holland the Duchy of Luxemburg with its German population sharpened these feelings. Most of all the prospect that the smaller states of south and west Germany, which were traditional protégés of France, might soon be forced or enticed into union with the rest of the country under Prussian dominance aroused great resentment. 'Between 1866 and 1870 I spoke to numberless Frenchmen,' wrote the British diplomat Sir Robert Morier in January 1871. 'I never heard a different opinion. That the north and south of Germany should unite without the consent of France and without an equivalent to France was simply a thing that could not be. In this respect the most moderate and the most *exalté* thought precisely alike.'[42] The situation between France and Prussia in 1866–70 was therefore tense and unstable. It could be resolved only by war.

Whether and in what sense Bismarck can be said to have planned this war is not important. If the 'logic of history' has any meaning at all then a Franco-Prussian conflict was probable if not inevitable after Sadowa. Quite apart from any question of the rights and wrongs of the candidature of a Hohenzollern prince to the Spanish throne which provided the immediate origin of the war, or of the position in Germany, or even of the balance of power in Europe, there was now on both sides an accumulated fund of resentment which demanded expression. To Frenchmen it seemed that France's rights and prestige must be asserted forcibly against an unscrupulous enemy seeking to destroy them. To most Germans a struggle with France appeared as a continuation of the 'War of Liberation' waged by their grandfathers against Napoleon I in 1813, a war now encrusted with legend and buttressed by a stout structure of nationalist mythology, or even as a continuation of the conflicts of the age of Louis XIV. The result, the Franco-Prussian War of 1870–71, was not merely a military and political but even more a psychological dividing-line in European history. For the first time two great European peoples fought to the point of total collapse, using against each other all the resources provided by developed economies, mass armies and mass hatreds. The result was that the peace terms which ended the war were severe and almost unprecedentedly humiliating to the defeated. France surrendered Alsace and much of Lorraine and paid a war indemnity of five milliard francs. These terms were also, a significant point, deeply influenced by military considerations and military advice. It was Moltke who was responsible for the triumphal entry of the German armies into Paris at the end of the war; and his contention that possession of the great fortress of Metz was the equivalent in any future war of an army of 120,000 men played an important part in Bismarck's decision to retain the city when peace was made.

The upheavals of the 1850s and 1860s did not nullify the special position which Britain and Russia had for the last half-century enjoyed, as powers in Europe but not completely of it. Certainly Britain's military reputation was damaged by the failures of the Crimean War and still more by her obvious inability to play, even had she wished to do so, any effective role in the great struggles of 1866 and 1870–71. She had, admitted Morier in 1870, an army 'which frightens Continentals about as much as an old horse-pistol of the last century'.[43] But her influence in Europe had never been primarily a military one; and these decades saw not merely the continued growth of her industrial, commercial and financial power, but also the consolidation of her empire in India after the Mutiny of 1857 and of her leadership in the forcible opening of China to western trade and influence. Those who in the 1860s wrote her off as a serious factor in the political affairs of Europe were realistic, at least in the short run; but in 1870 her position as the one true world power was still almost as strong as it had been in 1815. Russia enjoyed in some ways a similar fate. Her military prestige was much more severely shaken by the Crimean War; and for the following two decades her expansionist impulses were channelled towards the Far East and later towards central Asia. Her role in Europe, though it could never be unimportant, was for the time being essentially passive. In 1859, 1866 and 1870 she was significant above all for what she did not do. Nevertheless her enormous potentialities, the thought of what this superpower, once her resources were effectively mobilized, might do, continued to worry statesmen and diplomats. All the great states of Europe combined, wrote the American minister in St Petersburg in 1859, 'have not power enough to alter her boundaries or possessions', for 'now this is the Court where all Europe will in reality look, for Russia will be the final arbiter of all'.[44] Palmerston himself was preoccupied in the last weeks of his life, before his death in October 1865, by the thought of what she might achieve once she had acquired the two essentials of good government and railways.

The events of 1859-70 had thus not swept away all the landmarks which had distinguished international relations in the first half of the nineteenth century. But they had made revolutionary changes, above all in the creation of the new Bismarckian Germany. To these the continent now had to adjust.

GERMANY AND EUROPE, 1871-1914

During these forty-three years the most important single fact in the international relations of Europe was the power of Germany. This was seen at every level and in every aspect of international life.

The creation of the German empire had been above all a military achievement, and Prussian-dominated Germany was now the supreme exemplar of a military power. 'Germany', wrote Odo Russell, the British ambassador in Berlin, in March 1873, 'is in reality a great camp ready to break up for any war at a week's notice with a million of men.'[45] In fact the strength of the German standing army was not in the 1870s and 1880s much, and sometimes not at all, superior to that of France.[46] But Germany's military prestige was immense; and as time went on her superiority in arms over her most obvious potential antagonists seemed to increase. By the turn of the century the slow growth of France's population was making it impossible for her to keep pace in military terms with her great rival. Even more important, the difficulties encountered by the Russian army in the Turkish War of 1877-78, and even more its staggering defeat by the Japanese in 1904-5, showed that the country's enormous reserves of manpower, unmatched by adequate organization, transport or equipment, could not by themselves make Russia the military equal of Germany.[47] From 1879 the Habsburg empire and from 1882 Italy (at least on paper) were the allies of Germany; and quite apart from this neither of them had the resources to maintain a truly great army. Britain was still a negligible factor in the European military balance. Germany was thus marked out, at least until serious efforts to modernize the Russian army began in the years just before 1914, as the greatest military power in Europe.

In diplomacy also, until Bismarck's fall from power in 1890, she was the leading European state. The wonderful successes which Prussia under his leadership had achieved in 1862-71 gave him among his contemporaries a reputation for almost superhuman cunning and sagacity which he did not altogether deserve. In Germany his position seemed impregnable.

In international affairs his triumphs were admired and envied so that, as one historian has said with some exaggeration, 'he created . . . a community of nations animated by his maxims in their dealings with one another'. After his fall this position rapidly changed and German diplomacy quickly lost the aura of skill and success with which he had surrounded it; but during the 1870s and 1880s he was clearly the dominant figure in the European state system.

The great success story which the German empire presented to the world had also considerable repercussions on intellectual life. It encouraged an admiration for German education, one which was generally deserved since long before the unification of 1866–71 the German states had achieved a higher level of literacy than any other part of Europe[48] and German higher education was the best in the world. 'In their powers of thought and intelligence, the Germans are so superior to other nations', wrote in the early 1870s an Englishman with long experience of Germany, 'that Englishmen have always something to gain by studying the nature and progress of the German mind.'[49] German predominance also meant that after 1870 the fears of an imminent overshadowing of Europe by Russia and the United States, which had exercised a good many writers in the middle decades of the century, died away. A Europe in whose heart such a great new concentration of strength could develop had as yet little to fear from the outside world.

The great advances of Germany meant a marked decline in the relative economic power of Britain. That power was still, in 1870, very great. In the year of the Franco-Prussian war Britain still produced as much pig-iron as the rest of the world combined. But such a position could not be retained much longer. By the 1870s she was already being compelled to surrender world economic leadership, at least in some respects, to the United States; but given the enormously greater natural and human resources now available in North America this could hardly be regarded as a real defeat. An expert American observer thought that in the 1870s the productivity of labour in most industries was only about 10 per cent lower in Britain than in the United States, and in textiles only 6–8 per cent lower.[50] Much more immediately serious was the fact that for the first time for well over a century Britain's position as the most advanced and productive industrial power in Europe was beginning to be seriously challenged. While during 1870–1913 Germany's share in the world's output of manufactures was increasing that of Britain was falling by more than half, from 32 to 14 per cent. Some of this relative decline was inevitable and indeed on a wide view desirable. Until the 1860s Britain's industrial and technological lead over the rest of the world had been far too great to be permanent; and for one power to hold for ever a position of such superiority would have had unhealthy results both for it and for its competitors. The improvement in Germany's relative position in the 1870s and 1880s was largely the inevitable result of the 'innovation effect' of really large-scale use in her industry of steam-powered machinery; and her less developed economy and possession of a pool of underemployed agricultural labour allowed her in these two decades to make more rapid progress than Britain. But there is little doubt that from the 1890s onwards Britain surrendered to Germany leadership in many branches of industry more quickly and completely than she need have.[51] In 1860 her industrial leadership had still been so great that only three per cent of her imports had been of 'manufactures and miscellaneous goods'; by 1913 the proportion was a quarter. The new position was underlined by the sudden discovery at the outbreak of war that all the magnetos in use in Britain were imported from Germany.

Some of the reasons for this seem in retrospect clear, as indeed they often seemed to observers at the time. British industry, much more than that of Germany, tended to be dominated by the small or at best medium-sized firm. In 1914, of about 63,000 active joint-stock companies in Britain four-fifths were private ones, the great bulk of them small family concerns. In Germany, on the other hand, the leadership of industrial development to an extent unknown elsewhere by a small number of great investment banks encouraged the growth of large enterprises and a stress on 'technological rationality' as against the 'pecuniary rationality' dominant in much British business thinking.[52] In the steel industry, for example, the greater size of her blast-furnaces and processing plants was the most important explanation of Germany's greater efficiency. Even the new British steel-mills being set up in the 1890s were only a quarter to a third of the size of their German competitors, and the average German open hearth was half as large again as the average British one.[53] Perhaps equally important, Britain was no longer the main originator of new methods, techniques and machines. From the 1850s onwards she had rapidly lost to the United States her former leadership in the machine-tool industry. From the 1880s at latest many of the important new machines were American – the Northrop automatic loom, the turret lathe, the linotype machine. The inventions which made possible the modern internal combustion engine originated not in Britain but in France and even more in Germany, from the Lenoir engine of 1860 to the Diesel engine of 1893.

Moreover even when important technological discoveries were made in Britain they were often not exploited there very energetically. In British industry the scrapping and replacement of equipment was often governed by habit and tradition rather than by considerations of technical efficiency or profit maximization. Thus in the steel industry the Gilchrist-Thomas process developed in Britain by 1879 was used more effectively in Germany than in the country of its birth; and the continuous rolling-mill, another British innovation, was adopted in Britain only slowly. A whole series of new techniques – interchangeable parts, the use of jigs, limit gauges, high-speed steel for cutting tools, automatic equipment in general – was adopted more slowly than it could have been. Most of all the inferiority of the electrical and chemical industries to their German competitors was a fundamental weakness. British industry could still achieve impressive increases in output; but they were made in traditional products like cotton textiles and coal. In 1913 chemicals made up 14.4 per cent of German exports by value but only 5.1 per cent of those of Britain. In the same year 48.8 per cent of British exports consisted of coal against only 23.9 per cent in Germany.[54] Even of iron and steel, of which Britain had been the leading world supplier for over a century, Germany became a greater exporter from 1910 onwards. At the outbreak of war in 1914 she was the greatest exporter of machinery in the world and produced 40 per cent of world exports of chemicals and 38 per cent of those of steel. Too much British effort went into producing more of the same things by essentially traditional methods rather than into producing new things by new methods. 'The case against the late Victorians', it has been argued, 'can hardly depend on neglect to nourish and develop their own inheritance. It will have to rest on failure to plant enough seeds which the next generation could similarly bring to fruition.'[55] The result was that from the 1890s onwards the productivity of industrial labour increased considerably more slowly in Britain than in Germany, and much more slowly than in the United States.

Britain had still great sources of economic strength. Her power to generate new ideas was far from extinct; for example the first modern book on factory organization was published in England in 1896. She was still by far the biggest builder and operator of ships in the world: by 1880 she owned half of all the world's steamer tonnage. She was even more dominant in the ownership of world telegraph lines. London was the greatest world financial centre; and Britain exported capital on a greater scale than any other state and thus drew more investment income from abroad than any other. Moreover investment in farms and plantations overseas ensured her a flow of imported food and raw materials at relatively low prices. It is also possible to overestimate the German achievement, remarkable as it was. In 1913 per capita production was still higher in British than in German industry as a whole; and side by side with its great successes in steel, chemicals, electricity, engineering and shipbuilding there were still large sectors of the German economy – retail trade, building, much of agriculture – which were traditional and inefficient (though a contrast of this kind could be found, to varying degrees, in every industrial state). Nevertheless the balance was moving steadily against Britain. Her advantages in shipping, finance and foreign investment were not in every respect an adequate substitute for physical productive power. Moreover all of them depended to a greater or less degree on the existence of a truly international economic system and on the free play of economic forces across political frontiers. Britain was thus more vulnerable than any other great power to the economic nationalism which began to be increasingly influential from the 1880s onwards. By the end of that decade it was clear that there had been in Europe 'a shift from monarchy to oligarchy, from a one-nation to a multi-nation industrial system'.[56]

Why was British industry inferior in dynamism and the innovative impulse to that of Germany? It is generally agreed that the answer does not lie in any shortage in Britain of the physical factors of production or in purely economic constraints. It is true that her population was increasing more slowly than those of Germany and the United States, and that her domestic market and physical resources were smaller (though not a great deal smaller than those of Germany). It is also true that she inevitably incurred 'the penalty of taking the lead' in the form of heavy investment in obsolescent equipment which had often to be written off as the price of innovation. But there is no evidence that these factors were the real explanation of the sluggishness of a good deal of her industry. Moreover the British economy retained in many ways a far more competitive psychology than that of Germany. The formation of cartels which was so marked a feature of German industrial life from the 1880s, and the price-fixing and market-sharing which this involved, were far rarer in Britain. Moreover the British do not seem to have been notably less willing than the inhabitants of other economically advanced countries to save and invest during this period. It has sometimes been argued that from the 1880s onwards British exports of capital to the empire and to semicolonial areas such as Latin America helped to divert exports thither and away from the increasingly difficult and competitive markets of Europe and North America. The availability of these colonial outlets, it is contended, encouraged British industry to take the line of least resistance, to earn there, at least for a time, relatively easy profits, and to lose still further its ability to adapt to new conditions and its impetus towards technological change.[57] The case is difficult either to prove or to disprove conclusively. Certainly British foreign investment was mainly in government bonds and railways (70 per cent in 1913) and very much less in manufacturing (only four per cent in the same year). But equally certainly there is no straightforward correlation between capital exports and the slowing of industrial growth: the heaviest exports of capital came in 1907–14, long after the weaknesses of

British industry had become apparent. Moreover there appears to be no real evidence that heavy capital exports limited industrial investment at home. Again, the fact that government spending on public health and education was increasing can hardly explain Britain's tendency to fall behind Germany, for though expenditure of this kind may have had some slight effect in slowing the rate of economic growth it was Germany rather than Britain which led the way in the development of state paternalism.[58]

Britain's fundamental weaknesses, it is now widely agreed, were social and in a sense intellectual.[59] Weaknesses in the economy were merely the outward signs of deep-seated national attitudes. The stability of British society and the fact that entrepreneurship, however lucrative, still had a low social status compared to the professions, politics or government service, meant that industry recruited fewer men of first-class ability than it otherwise would have done. In its lower and middle ranks wage and salary levels tended to be largely customary. They were decided by social and traditional as much as by economic factors, a state of affairs which made for absence of social tension but not for economic efficiency. In its upper ranks surprisingly often an industrialist, inheriting a family firm built up by previous generations, would lose interest in it and devote himself instead to politics, local government, or even scholarship. Such a scheme of values in some ways greatly benefited British life. It had the great virtue of ensuring that the level of intelligence and integrity in political life was high by comparison with that in any other major country. The fate of Germany, where during this period business expertise and energy in general superior to that in Britain was combined with political stultification, suggests that in the long term the British scale of priorities was not merely more 'civilized' but also more realistic. But it was not a scale which made it easy for the country to hold its own against the increasing pressure of great new industrial powers.

German society was at least as rigidly stratified as that of Britain, in some ways a good deal more so. There was in Britain no social group with the combination of great political power and narrow selfish conservatism which distinguished the *Junker* in Prussia east of the Elbe. There was also no British parallel to the unpleasant adulation of titles and official status which marked German society. The failure of the Second Reich to produce any great liberal and reforming aristocrat of the type not altogether uncommon in Britain is one of the major indictments which can be brought against it. But in Germany the economic effects of class barriers and traditional prejudices were considerably weakened by the great superiority of technical education to anything available in Britain, and by the general acceptance of the idea that high industrial posts should be accessible only to men who had received rigorous training for them.

33

The combination of high culture, intellectual power and width of ideas, which distinguished for example several members of the Siemens family, or Walther Rathenau, outstanding figures in the history of the German electrical industry during this period, was rare among business men everywhere. But it was less rare in Germany than in any other country in the world. The superior efficiency of German industry was in the last analysis the outcome of an intellectual and educational superiority. In particular the lead of Germany over all her competitors in applied science was very marked. It was this which made her so pre-eminent in the chemical and to a lesser extent the electrical industries; but it pervaded every aspect of her industrial life. In 1902 the President of the British Association for the Advancement of Science estimated that German industry employed 4,000 highly trained chemists and British industry only 1,500.[60] By 1914 Germany was the only state in which powerful forces of traditional conservatism, those of the monarchy, the court and the army, existed side by side with a highly dynamic economy and a highly educated population. It was this which made her a potential danger to the rest of Europe.

If even Britain could be overtaken in this way by Germany it was clear that no other European state could as yet compete with the new giant in terms of industrial strength. In the long run the one power which could hope to do so was Russia. By the 1860s there were signs that her potentially vast economic resources might now be developed, on government initiative and under government control, with some of the effectiveness which had hitherto been notably lacking. There was beginning in the 1860s and 1870s to be a new consciousness, the product largely of defeat in the Crimea, of the impossibility of maintaining the country's political influence in Europe, or even securing her against attack, without large-scale economic development. Baron Reutern, finance minister 1862–78, told Alexander II plainly that 'without railways and mechanical industries Russia cannot be considered secure in her boundaries. Her influence in Europe will fall to a level inconsistent with her international power and her historic significance.'[61] And in fact during these years a good deal was done to develop the Russian economy: above all there was railway-building on an unprecedented scale, a scale which by the end of the century had become very impressive. In 1896–1900 over 10,000 miles of track were laid in Russia, in the peak year of 1899 well over 3,000 miles. By the end of the century the railway network, employing 400,000 people, was the country's largest industry. Moreover the generation before 1914 saw, especially in the decade of the 1890s, remarkable growth in every major branch of Russian industry – iron and steel, coal, oil, textiles.[62]

The social and human costs of this growth were heavy. These achievements inflicted much suffering on exploited and impoverished peasants.

They also drew complaints from agrarian interests, which argued that protection, by raising the price of tools and metal goods in general, impeded the modernization of Russian agriculture. Nevertheless the achievements of these years were very real. Control and regimentation by the state, heavy forced contributions by agriculture to the development of industry, a stress on capital goods at the expense of consumer goods and resulting holding down of mass consumption, rigid protectionism, all coloured by fear of economically stronger foreign powers and a perceptible element of xenophobia – Russia in the 1890s exhibited the first clear example of a now familiar picture, that of a backward traditional society having economic growth forced upon it from above.

Nevertheless in spite of these spectacular advances it was still difficult for Russia to compete with Germany as an economic power. Her educational backwardness, though considerable attempts were being made to overcome it, meant that she could not as yet aspire to technological leadership of the kind which Germany had now so clearly achieved. The social and institutional obstacles to economic advance remained more deep-rooted than in any other major state in Europe. Witte, the minister of finance associated with the advances of the 1890s, had been opposed even at the height of his success by the ministry of the interior, which stood for the perpetuation of the traditional Russia of landlords and peasants. Nicholas II himself and the court circle around him remained to the end hostile to industrial capitalism and technological change. The empire in fact faced a fundamental problem which it never solved. Russia had to modernize, and quickly, to hold her own in an increasingly competitive world. Yet modernization must create great problems for her internal stability and perhaps for the very survival of the ruling dynasty.

These difficulties of economic development in part underlie the general failure of Russia's foreign policy during the period between the peace of 1871 and the war of 1914. In 1877–78 the short war with Turkey strained her finances severely: a billion roubles of new paper currency had to be issued in 1877 and Reutern, who had opposed the war from the first, resigned when it ended. Moreover the still incomplete railway system notably failed to supply the Russian armies in the Balkans effectively. These weaknesses do much to explain the Russian government's bowing to British and Austrian demands that the peace settlement imposed by Russia on the Turks at San Stefano in March 1878 should be revised by an international congress. This congress, when it met in Berlin in June, confirmed the specific concessions to Britain and Austria which Russia had already been compelled to make before it opened. The former Turkish provinces of Bosnia and Herzegovina were placed under Austrian occupation. The large autonomous Bulgaria created at San Stefano, stretching to the Aegean and incorporating much territory in Old Serbia, which had been seen by both Britain and Austria as a Russian satellite and a standing threat to the survival of Turkish power in Europe, was diminished territorially and divided between an autonomous province and one still ruled by a Turkish governor. The settlement was not by any means a total defeat for Russia, who made important gains on her Caucasian frontier. But there was widespread Russian resentment of what were felt to be its humiliating terms and of the fading of the dream of leading and protecting the Balkan Slav peoples which had bulked so large in 1876–77. This feeling that the powers of western Europe were hostile or at best indifferent to Russia and her interests was intensified by the prolonged Bulgarian crisis of 1885–87, when the two provinces into which the country had been divided at Berlin were reunited. This was now achieved, by a curious paradox, with British and Austrian support and against Russia's opposition. It therefore amounted to another serious diplomatic setback for her.

By the middle 1890s, with the Near East apparently barred for the time being as a field of expansion, Russia was turning increasingly to east Asia, to Manchuria, Korea and the northern provinces of China. But here there awaited her a much more serious defeat, and one much more clearly the outcome of her economic and technological weakness. The victories of the Japanese in the war of 1904–5 were greatly helped by the still very limited capacity of the Trans-Siberian railway, the immensely long and tenuous line of communications upon which the whole Russian war effort in the Far East had to depend. The fleet which the Japanese navy annihilated in the Straits of Tsushima in May 1905, in the battle which ended the war, was composed mainly of obsolete and in some cases almost defenceless vessels brought with great slowness and difficulty from the Baltic. Its fate seemed to exemplify the continuing material and organizational backwardness of the tsarist empire. Russia had still the immense advantage over Germany and even more over Britain of being virtually unconquerable so long as she could maintain internal cohesion. 'Compared to our Empire', wrote a British cabinet minister in 1901, 'hers is invulnerable. We must be on the defensive in a contest because there is, speaking generally and roughly, no part of her territory where we can hit her. . . . Defeat, diplomatic, naval or military, matters less to her than any important Power.'[63] But these were negative strengths, though important ones. Russia's industries in the years before 1914, though growing rapidly, had still important defects; and until she could raise her armed forces, her administration and perhaps most of all her railway system to a respectable level of efficiency[64] she could hardly hope to win a struggle with a first-class opponent.

The tsarist empire at least possessed the physical resources needed to challenge German leadership of Europe, inefficiently though she deployed them in many ways. No other continental state was in this position. France was increasingly debarred from facing on equal terms her great rival across the Rhine by the stubborn refusal of her population to grow appreciably. The demographic disparity was reflected, in spite of heroic French efforts, in a growing imbalance in the military strength of the two states.[65] In industry the contrast was even more marked. Though after 1896 there was a period of vigorous growth in French production which continued until 1914, France was never in this respect a power able to hold its own with Germany. In 1900, for example, she produced a mere 1.9 million tons of steel against Germany's 7.4 million tons.

The Habsburg empire, tormented by nationality problems and with Hungary, Galicia, Slovenia and other areas still economically and socially among the most backward parts of Europe, now found it increasingly hard to act as a great power. For a century or more its rulers had faced a problem which overrode all others – that of extracting from an agglomeration of territories so disunited and for the most part so poor the means of sustaining the powerful army which its exposed frontiers demanded. This problem was now more insoluble than ever. Italy was in even worse plight. The instability and factiousness of her governments after the end of political dominance by the Right in 1876, the hostility of the Papacy to the new Italian state after 1861, most of all the intractable problem of the backwardness and discontent of the south after unification,[66] meant that she had to face internal difficulties quite comparable to those of Russia or Austria-Hungary during this period. The *guerra di brigantaggio* which raged in the south as a futile separatist reaction against unification until 1867; the great revolt of 1866 in Palermo, which had to be bombarded into submission by the Italian navy; or the peasant risings of 1893 in Sicily and the violent industrial and social unrest of 1898, underline this point. Above all the country was far too poor to do more than make the gestures of a great power. Industrial growth, at least in parts of northern Italy, was substantial during the two decades before the First World War.[67] But in economic terms as well as in military ones she was still in 1914 almost puny compared to Germany, on whom she had indeed come to depend considerably by the 1890s for capital and industrial expertise.

It was scarcely to be expected that Germany, suddenly finding herself in so strong a position in Europe, should not try to use it to her own advantage. The 'War of Liberation' of 1813 and the revolutions of 1848, though each of them had contained an element of aggressive nationalism, had also embodied genuine ideals. Each of them could call upon the spirit of freedom and draw support from the deep wells of romantic sensibility. The Bismarckian Reich of 1871, by contrast, could make little appeal of this kind. It had been created from above, the result of diplomacy and military planning. It stood for strength and efficiency rather than for any ideal. Moreover after the events of 1866–71 it was easier than ever before to think of international influence in terms of measurable material power, in terms which were mechanistic and rationalistic, and to draw from this the conclusion that principles, ideals and the rights of small states and small nationalities now mattered little. This attitude, it must be emphasized, was by no means distinctively German or confined to political conservatives. It underlay the contempt of Marx and Engels for the smaller Slav nationalities:[68] it was well developed in some circles in Russia. It would be difficult, for example, to find a clearer statement of it than that given by the Panslav pamphleteer, General R. A. Fadeev, in 1870. 'In these days', he wrote, 'when Europe is divided into a few enormous masses, when only that State which can put forward half a million of soldiers has a right to separate existence, when even such old countries as Holland and Switzerland are beginning to fear for their future, who cares for such international rubble as the Czechs, Croats and others . . . ?'[69] On this point the tsarist general was one with the founders of 'scientific' socialism: all agreed that the future lay with large political units and that history (increasingly the nineteenth-century substitute for God) was on the side of the big battalions. This attitude, so appropriate to a scientific, materialist and therefore quantitatively minded age, was now very widespread and could be reconciled with political attitudes of otherwise radically differing kinds. But the appeal of expansionist ideas, of ambitions which were to be realized by the use of brute military and economic strength, was by the end of the century greater in Germany than in any other power.

So far as expansion in Europe was concerned, the idea of *Mitteleuropa*, of an economic and perhaps also political union of the German world with Belgium, Holland, Denmark and Switzerland which would create a coherent power structure extending from the Baltic and North Sea far into the Balkans, had begun to take shape in the 1830s. Stimulated by the writings of List, the German prophet of economic nationalism, and still more by the dreams and ambitions of 1848, its importance had reached a peak in the 1850s when a number of Austrian statesmen, notably Baron Bruck, the minister of commerce, gave it active encouragement. After this it had declined rapidly as Austro-Prussian rivalry in Germany came to a head; but this vague and alluring current of ideas was only dormant, not dead. The idea of expansion outside Europe, of a German colonial empire overseas, had less weight of tradition behind it. Nevertheless by the 1870s there were clear signs that it too was developing an appeal for some sections, though as yet limited ones, of German opinion. Until his fall Bismarck was able to keep these expansionist dreams under fairly effective control. He had not a flicker of sympathy for the *Mitteleuropa* attitude, which was impossible to reconcile with the limited, Prussian-dominated Germany which was all he ever wanted to create. Nor had he any personal interest whatever in the acquisition of a colonial empire; his limited move in this direction in 1884–85 was the outcome in the main of domestic political, and perhaps also social, pressures.[70] After his effective disappearance from the political scene in 1890, however, German policy and still more German feeling became increasingly dominated by a disorganized, resentful and in the event rather unsuccessful expansionism.

In particular it was now urged more and more insistently that German power must no longer be confined to Europe. The future belonged to a small number of world powers, of which Germany must become one by building a great fleet and acquiring overseas territory, trading and railway concessions and sources of raw materials. 'Bismarck's problems and achievements lay in European politics, and what we must now carry on is a global policy, a world policy', wrote one of the most influential propagandists of this view in 1903.[71] By the 1890s a whole battery of societies and pressure-groups – the Colonial League, the Pan-German League, the Navy League and others – were urging the necessity and moral justification (the two tended to become synonymous) of a German bid for world power. The real influence of some of these groups can easily be exaggerated. To the landowning and military aristocracy imperial expansion, at least outside Europe, was associated with industrialization and a lessening of the importance of agriculture, and with the growth of the new navy at the expense of the army. Even German finance and industry were more interested in the building up of a kind of informal empire in the Near East and Latin America than in the mere acquisition of territory. It was much more from middle-class and professional groups that the loudest expansionist demands came. From 1909 onwards at least the Pan-German League was on very bad terms with the German government because of its criticisms of what it saw as the unduly slow growth of the German navy.[72] But there is no doubt that the call for an empire reflected a genuine change in the outlook of most politically conscious Germans. Side by side with these naval and colonial ambitions, and with the danger of a collision with Britain which they inevitably involved, went some revival of interest in the possibility of expansion in Europe, of union with the Germans of Austria, Switzerland and the Netherlands and of the formation of a great German-dominated economic union covering the remaining Habsburg territories and much of the Balkans. The most obvious systematic expression of such ideas was the work of the Swedish inventor of 'geopolitics', Rudolf Kjellén, whose *Die Grosmächte der Gegenwart*, published in 1914, called for the creation of a European federation under German leadership to pave the way to the acquisition of a great German colonial empire.

Such schemes and the men who put them forward were usually tinged with anti-Russian feeling: and this was strengthened by the growing discontent of the Baltic Germans under Russian rule from the middle 1880s onwards as attempts to russify them became more blatant and oppressive. By the end of the century Baltic *émigrés* in Germany had become a focus of hostility to Russia: the most important of them, the historian and journalist Theodore Schiemann, had some influence on William II himself. Moreover there was an increasing tendency for ambitions in Africa, the Pacific or the Near East to fuse with those in Europe, so that the same group or the same individual would very often demand the realization of them all more or less indiscriminately.[73] In this way there emerged by the early years of the twentieth century a generalized expansionist drive which often had no clear or specific aims and which was all the more dangerous because it was so amorphous and unfocused.

That the German government should have allowed this state of affairs to develop was in itself a confession of failure. The régime established in 1871, monarchical, Prussian, military and Protestant, never felt able to rely on the active support of large parts of the German people. Distrustful of Catholics and even of non-Prussians, bitterly hostile to the Social Democrats,[74] it represented until its collapse in 1918 sectional interests, some of them numerically quite limited. From the middle 1890s onwards, with his personal power for the time being secured, William II and his advisers attempted increasingly to give the régime popularity, to present it as truly national and weaken the hold in Germany of the 'international' and 'anti-Reich' forces of catholicism and socialism, by showy expansionist gestures and a continual harping on the theme of national interests, honour and rights. 'Only a successful foreign policy can help to reconcile, pacify, rally, unite,' wrote Bülow, the foreign minister, in December 1897. Almost simultaneously Captain von Tirpitz, associated more closely than anyone except the emperor himself with the building of the new fleet, argued that Germany needed a world policy so that new national tasks and the gains to be made from their fulfilment might be used to weaken the hold of socialism on the working classes of the Reich. A military would-be divine-right monarchy was trying to adjust to the age of mass politics; and though its efforts did little to weaken the Catholic Centre party or to slow the growth of the Social Democrats they did a good deal to stimulate aggressive nationalism and to weaken German liberalism still further. The expansionism of Wilhelmine Germany was thus in a very important sense a confession of weakness. It was an implicit admission that the Bismarckian

Reich was really at bottom a mere agglomeration of interests, that it lacked any generally accepted principle of unity and the coherence which a state normally achieves, if at all, only after a long period of organic growth. The best summing-up of this aspect of the situation was made by *The Times* correspondent in Berlin in June 1902. 'Germany', he wrote, 'is a *new*, crude, ambitious, radically *unsound* Power.... The artificial Army system, the pampered commerce and shipping, the Agrarian-industrial cleavage, the unfamiliarity with the perils of civilization – a thousand things, convince me that Germany, with all her phenomenal development, is radically unsound and unhealthy.'[75]

German expansionism was in an important sense highly irrational. Underlying it were not merely hopes and ambitions but also fear – fear that Germany, lacking a great colonial empire and command of the seas, lacking therefore secure supplies of some essential raw materials, might find herself victimized and denied the means of maintaining her great industries by the rivals who did possess these things. Her economic future, it was insistently argued, could not be allowed to depend upon the goodwill of others; only world power could give her the necessary guarantees for the future. The term *Lebensraum* was, probably significantly, coined by the German geographer Friedrich Ratzel in 1901.

Such attitudes were not particularly German. Every great European people was now thinking, more naturally and consistently than ever before, in terms of a world political and economic balance, in those of world strategy and worldwide interests. From the 1870s onwards, for the first time, the world ceased to be divided into great trading areas, to varying extents distinct from one another. For the first time it became effectively a unity so far as commerce and international payments were concerned. The clearest sign of this was perhaps the steady spread of the gold standard. Germany, Holland and the Scandinavian countries had adopted it in the early 1870s; France, Switzerland and Belgium did so in 1878 and the Habsburg empire by laws of 1892 and 1900. Even India, the staunchest supporter of silver, made the gold sovereign legal tender in 1899. The structure of international finance was becoming truly worldwide in its scope, while labour and capital could cross national frontiers more easily than ever before. This meant that increasingly the developed countries could draw on a wide variety of sources for many of their imported foodstuffs and raw materials and that primary producing countries began in many cases to have a wide choice of imported goods. Thus in Britain a good domestic harvest, still of great, sometimes overwhelming, economic importance even as late as the 1870s, had become a much less crucial necessity by the 1880s. The growth of a world economy could also be seen in a tendency for business cycles to affect different countries, particularly if their trade and industry were well developed, in much the same way and at much the same time. Increasingly boom and slump tended to react on them all alike, so that prices, interest rates and probably profits altered in geographically widely separated economies with a hitherto unknown unanimity.

World communications and a world economy inevitably bred world politics and world strategy. By the 1880s each great imperial power had to take account of the effect of its policies in any given area upon its own and its rivals' position in other areas, perhaps thousands of miles away. Thus the building by Russia of the Trans-Caspian railway from Krasnovodsk to Tashkent from 1880 onwards was intended in part to offset the strengthening of the British position in India which had resulted from the opening of the Suez Canal in 1869.[76] Similarly French schemes in the 1890s of cutting a canal through the Kra isthmus and of opening a new trade route into China by the Mekong river were meant to bypass and weaken the great established British trading bases in Singapore and Hong Kong. More significant still, the minor collision between Russian and Afghan forces in March 1885 at Penjdeh, on the northern frontier of Afghanistan, which produced a brief though acute Anglo-Russian crisis, had immediate repercussions in both Europe and the Far East. In the former it produced Russian measures to guard against any effort by Britain to force the Straits and enter the Black Sea: in the latter the temporary occupation by both powers of naval bases in Korea. No previous international confrontation had shown so clearly the extent to which the entire world was now becoming a strategic unity.

Moreover the later nineteenth and early twentieth centuries, as international communications grew and change in so many aspects of life became swift, were a period of unprecedented self-consciousness and uneasiness in the relations between the great states. An unsophisticated semi-educated public opinion created by the new large-circulation newspaper was ready in many states to believe, passionately if intermittently, in the existence of foreign threats and conspiracies. A quite remarkable number of political slogans and catch-phrases which included the words 'danger' or 'peril' came into currency during the period: the 'Yellow Peril', the Chinese and Japanese threat to European civilization which William II thought he detected in the later 1890s, is merely the best known of these.[77]

Nevertheless the wonderful success of Germany made all these fears appear in her case particularly misplaced. Far from suffering from a lack of raw materials or markets, her industry, right down to 1914, was expanding and threatening increasingly to dominate that of her neighbours. In the years immediately before the First World War, for example, German heavy industry was gaining a secure foothold in Normandy and French

Lorraine, and it was not very fanciful to speculate that France, in spite of her great colonial empire, might before very long find herself in some sense the economic satellite of Germany.[78] By 1914 there were more Germans settled in France than Frenchmen in all the French colonies acquired during the previous half-century. A continuation of these trends must end by making Germany the wealthiest as well as the most powerful state in Europe. 'If people in Germany would only sit still,' said an irritated senior diplomat in 1901, 'the time would soon come when we can all have oysters and champagne for dinner.'[79] A few years later in 1911 Hugo Stinnes, one of the captains of west German heavy industry, made the same point in rather different terms. 'Give us three or four more years of peaceful progress', he told Heinrich Class, the leader of the Pan-German League, 'and Germany will be the undisputed economic master of Europe. The French are lagging behind us: they are a nation of *rentiers*. And the English dislike hard work and lack the mettle for new ventures. Apart from them there is no one in Europe to compete with us. Three or four years of peace, then, and I assure you that Germany will secretly come to dominate Europe.' They were quite right. If the Germans had wanted merely to make money and had acted rationally to this end they would never have endangered international peace. Unfortunately they increasingly wished to make history, a much more risky ambition.

Underlying this desire was another feeling which is only too understandable. This was a sense of having been cheated by the past, defrauded of all Germany might have achieved, in imperial terms, during the centuries when she was fragmented and weak and Britain, France and even Russia were united and strong. From her history, with its lost opportunities, sprang a querulous feeling that the world owed her something, that any territorial demands she might put forward in East Africa, Morocco, Samoa or anywhere else, had behind them a kind of historic justice irrespective of the rights and wrongs of the particular case at issue. It is difficult for a historian with any imagination not to feel some sympathy for this attitude. It was in a sense ridiculous that the greatest concentration of physical and intellectual power in Europe should count for less in the non-European world territorially or even culturally, than Holland or Portugal. But the workings of history have produced many ridiculous results; and to arraign them in the name of justice is usually futile. To expect that Germany's ambitions would be considered, because of her history, more valid than those of other states, was unreasonable. The strain of self-pity which is audible in many of the German demands of this period could easily turn into a feeling that Germany was threatened by the plots and conspiracies of her jealous rivals. In particular it helped to ensure acceptance of the belief, very widespread by 1914, that British diplomacy was constructing a worldwide coalition to deprive Germany of the international position which was her due.

The feeling of so many Germans that their country's immense economic progress ought to be reflected in an enhanced international status was, on the other hand, perfectly reasonable. It appeared by the end of the nineteenth century to some observers that the international struggles of the future would be waged increasingly by peaceful, or at least not overtly warlike, means. To an unprecedented extent the great European powers, it seemed, now competed with each other, sometimes bitterly, using as their weapons not armies, navies or even diplomatic services, but loans, railway concessions, commercial treaties and other economic inducements and pressures. Even in Europe itself, to say nothing of the areas of colonial rivalry, there was abundant evidence of this. Thus the growth of German influence in Italy from the early 1880s onwards was based largely on economic strength. A violent press campaign in France against Italy's credit and government securities, and a sharp decline in French investment there after 1888, paved the way for the creation in 1890 of a German syndicate to support the country's finances and develop Italo-German financial relations. The Banca Commerciale Italiana, founded in 1894, was backed by German capital and soon became the most important instrument in the tightening of Germany's commercial and financial hold on the peninsula. In the same way the growth of German influence in the Ottoman empire was accompanied and consolidated by the development of financial links between the two countries. In 1888 the Turkish government raised a loan of 30 million marks from the Deutsche Bank: this was its first important borrowing without the cooperation of the Anglo-French Banque Impériale Ottomane since the foundation of the latter in 1863, and thus clear evidence of the emergence of the new Germany as a financial power in the Near East. Again in 1910 the Young Turk régime, established in power by the revolution of 1908, tried unsuccessfully to raise a loan in London and Paris: the money it desperately needed was provided by a consortium of German and Austrian bankers whose formation for the purpose was urged by Bethmann-Hollweg, the German chancellor. In 1880 only about 5 per cent of the Ottoman public debt had been in German hands; by 1914 about 20 per cent was held in Germany. Still more clearly, the movement of Serbia towards the Franco-Russian side in international affairs after the revolution of 1903 in Belgrade can be seen in the replacement of Vienna by Paris as the source on which the Serbian government relied for its foreign borrowing. The decision to place the loan of 1906, and the armaments order for the Serbian army which was tied to it, in France, was an unmistakable sign of this changed attitude and one which provoked bitter Austrian resentment.

Most important of all loans were used by successive French governments from the end of the 1880s onwards as a means of strengthening
France's relations with Russia. It was money which consolidated the political and military alliance between the two powers which began to emerge
in 1891. Bismarck's prohibition in 1888 of the acceptance on the Berlin
bourse of Russian government bonds as security for loans was intended to
make the tsarist government more amenable to German political pressure.
In itself, therefore, it was a good illustration of the growing use in international affairs of economic forces as a weapon of state policy. It was a
disastrous failure. Though it was revoked in 1894 and minor Russian
loans were raised in Berlin in 1902 and 1905, henceforth Paris became
overwhelmingly the most important source of external finance for the
Russian government. French money was an essential foundation of
Witte's neomercantilist industrial policies. The great loan of 1906, in which
German bankers were once more forbidden by their government to take
part and which was raised mainly in Paris, was a matter almost of life and
death to the tsarist government floundering in the aftermath of defeat by
Japan and still at grips with the revolution which had followed. For some
time to come, therefore, it would clearly be very difficult for Russia to
follow policies likely to be unpopular with French investors.

It is easy to give too much weight to facts of this kind. To speak, as
one well-informed contemporary did, of 'the stupendous modern fact of
the predominance today of economic over political conditions' was a vast
exaggeration. In particular there is little basis for the claim, frequently
made during the 1920s and 1930s, that bankers and investors before
1914 were able to control the policies of governments and dictate the
course of diplomacy. It would be much truer to say that foreign offices
and sometimes service ministries distorted or tried to distort the workings
of the machinery of international investment. Thus the German government on several occasions in the decade before 1914 pressed German
financiers to invest in the Balkans and the Near East when, left to themselves, they would have put their money to safer and more lucrative uses.
In the same way the success of the prolonged Anglo-German negotiations
of 1913–14, which led to the formation of the Turkish Petroleum Company
to exploit the oil resources of Mesopotamia, was made possible by the
willingness of both governments to override the claims and feelings of the
business men concerned.[80] Yet observers during the quarter-century which
followed the fall of Bismarck were not wrong in feeling that the economic
element in international relations had now become so important as
almost to add a new dimension to them. In the twentieth century national
achievement has become more and more typically economic achievement.
Well before 1914 it was clear that international status was now, to an

unprecedented degree, a matter of wealth, of productive power and capacity for economic growth, and that this development would be continued and intensified in the future. The wars of the future will be for markets, wrote a typical observer in 1903:

> they will be wars of necessity, or rather, perhaps, prompted by the hope of material gain. Many of them will be fought with other weapons than cannon and money. Established commerce, a firm hold of trade-routes, preponderance at a trading-post, effective occupation of a produce exchange – in the struggle for markets these will be points of vantage worth more than battalions and a short railway may be of greater value than a fleet of battleships.[81]

Of this materialist, rationalistic, quantitative approach to international affairs German expansionism, in its more realistic aspects, was the most striking and important example.

This atmosphere of intensified international competition, whether political or economic, meant the end of the Concert of Europe as an idea with any effective influence. Already weakened by the events of the 1850s and 1860s – the rift between Austria and Russia after the Crimean War, the increasing isolationism of Britain – it had by the 1880s become little more than a phantom, a concept to which lip-service might still sometimes be paid but to which no leader of any state now owed a serious allegiance. Gladstone, its last important defender, exposed its real weakness when he said, in a speech in November 1879, that 'common action means common objects'.[82] It was impossible to pretend after 1871 that a France and Germany divided by the unhealed sore of Alsace-Lorraine could ever have, at bottom, common objects, at least in Europe. It was difficult to claim, from the 1880s or 1890s onwards, that Russia and the Habsburg empire, increasingly likely to be divided by conflicting ambitions in the Balkans, or Russia and Britain, clearly separated by bitter rivalries in Persia and the Far East, were in a much better position. The dominant characteristic of the diplomacy of the generation which began in the 1870s was the emergence of alliances which divided the major European powers into often competing groups of a closeness and permanence hitherto unknown.

In 1879 Germany signed with the Habsburg empire an alliance which was to remain the pivot of the foreign policies of both governments until they collapsed together in 1918. In 1882 this grouping of powers was joined by Italy; and the treaties which bound together this Triple Alliance continued to be renewed at intervals until 1914. It found itself faced, a decade later, by a combination of tsarist and Orthodox Russia with anti-clerical and republican France, the grouping whose formation Bismarck had wished at almost any cost to prevent. That two states so completely divided not merely in official ideology but also in popular feeling should have come together in this way was a striking fact. It throws into sharp relief the decline of political idealism and prejudice as a factor in international relations since the days of Metternich and Alexander I and its submergence by purely material interests. In Russia even the most conservative and militarist Panslav now tended to see in conservative and militarist Germany a territorial and imperial rival rather than an ideological ally. As early as 1870 General Fadeev could write that 'except as regards a certain community of interests in the Polish question . . . all the more substantial interests of Russia and Prussia are much more antagonistic than those of Russia and France'.[83] In France radical hostility on principle to the Russian alliance and particularly to the French loans with which it was associated was always a factor of some significance. But it was overwhelmed by the belief that a reversal of the verdict of 1871, and from the end of the 1890s perhaps even France's future as an imperial power in Africa and her influence in the Mediterranean, depended on Russian support. Such feelings, aided by the clumsiness of German diplomacy after Bismarck's fall, underlay the conclusion of a Franco-Russian *entente* in general terms in August 1891. This was followed by the signature of a military convention, the real core of the alliance, a year later and its final confirmation by the heads of both states in January 1894.

Neither the Austro-German combination of 1879 nor the Franco-Russian one of 1891–94 was for many years very rigid or inflexible. Bismarck had no intention of allowing his hands to be tightly bound by the combination with the Habsburgs. Both the *Dreikaiserbund* agreement which he signed with Austria and Russia in 1881 and the Reinsurance Treaty which replaced it as a link between Germany and Russia in 1887 contained clauses which contradicted the terms agreed in 1879. In 1897 an Austro-Russian understanding, which for the time being put an end to the rivalry of these states in the Balkans, was also in some of its stipulations not easy to reconcile with the 1879 treaty. The Björkö agreement of 1905, signed by William II and Nicholas II without the knowledge of their foreign ministers and thus at once a dead letter, also contradicted Germany's obligations to her Austrian ally. Nor did the Franco-Russian agreement for a good many years control much more effectively the policies of the two signatories, and particularly those of Russia. In Paris it was regarded above all as an anti-German instrument; while to the government in St Petersburg it was for well over a decade directed rather against Britain. Moreover the imperial ambitions of the two powers were very different. Those of France centred on driving the British from Egypt, which they had occupied, to the intense chagrin of all patriotic Frenchmen, in 1882.[84] Russia by contrast cared little for Egypt, where bad feeling between Britain and France was in many ways useful to her, and was willing to come to terms with Germany in the Near East. For several months, in April–June 1899, the Russian government tried unsuccessfully to secure German agreement to future Russian control of the Straits as compensation for the proposed building of the largely German-financed Baghdad railway. In St Petersburg it was on north China and to a lesser extent the associated territories of Mongolia and Korea that imperial ambitions were now focused; and these areas meant nothing to France.

Nevertheless there was a tendency for both these combinations to become more rigid and exclusive, and therefore more potentially dangerous, as time went on. In 1899 in particular the declared objectives of the Franco-Russian alliance were widened after a visit by Delcassé, the French foreign minister, to St Petersburg. Henceforth the alliance was to maintain the balance of power in Europe, not merely as hitherto to safeguard peace there; and the Franco-Russian military convention was not to come to an end, as had been agreed in 1892, with the break-up of the Triple Alliance. Moreover defeat by Japan and growing dependence on French money both considerably reduced Russia's freedom of action in international affairs after 1905 and made her more vulnerable to pressure from Paris. The Triple Alliance did not change its formal character in the same way. It remained in theory, and so far as Italy was concerned in practice, essentially defensive. But like the Franco-Russian combination it bred, in the years before 1914, increasingly detailed arrangements between its signatories for naval and military cooperation in case of a new war. Thus, for example, in 1913 a convention provided for the cooperation of the Italian and Austrian navies, and of a German squadron, in the Mediterranean if war should break out with France and Russia. And rather as Russia was forced into some degree of dependence on France so Germany, increasingly isolated, was driven to regard the Habsburg empire, in spite of its obvious internal weaknesses, as her one reliable ally in a potentially hostile world. In this way her freedom of international manoeuvre, mainly through her own blunders, was dangerously curtailed.

The decisive check to German hopes of European dominance came with the growing alignment of Britain, from 1904 onwards, with the Franco-Russian camp in international affairs. This quite understandably surprised contemporaries. To Britain, colonial rivalries with Germany had sometimes been irritating; but they had never approached in practical importance and sustained bitterness those which divided her from France in Egypt and from Russia in Persia and the Far East. German claims and gestures aroused resentment in Britain; but there was no tradition of hostility to Germany of the kind which had for decades provided the background to relations with France and even more with Russia. Moreover the alarm aroused by German industrial growth, strong in Britain during much of the 1890s, was now being replaced by a more realistic attitude and a resignation to German competition as a fact of economic life. The Navy Laws of 1898 and 1900 in Germany, with all their implications,[85] were surprisingly slow to arouse British fears; and there was in Britain a vague but significant feeling of racial kinship with the Germans which did not exist where France, still less Russia, were concerned. For all these reasons Britain's first attempts to escape from the isolation and general hostility which seemed by the later 1890s to threaten her throughout the world took the form of advances to Germany. Between 1898 and 1901 Joseph Chamberlain, the headstrong and precipitate colonial secretary, made several efforts to achieve an Anglo-German agreement. They failed and were probably bound to fail.[86] William II and his ministers were now preoccupied by the building of a great German navy, a policy directed, at least in the first place, entirely against Britain. Though they did not wish to antagonize her unnecessarily in the early stages of this process, when the new fleet was felt to be very vulnerable to British attack, a belief that the two powers must ultimately come into conflict was now gaining ground rapidly in Germany. The German government was convinced that the rivalries and hatreds which separated Britain from France and Russia were unappeasable. It therefore believed that it had only to wait for the renewed advances which Britain would soon be forced to make to exact better terms than had hitherto been offered from London, in particular a formal British adherence to the Triple Alliance.

This calculation was not unreasonable in terms of history. It proved tragically wrong as a guide to the future. The insistence of Lord Salisbury, prime minister until 1902, that Britain was not threatened by her isolation was becoming increasingly difficult to sustain. Harassed by France in Egypt and west Africa, her Asiatic position threatened by the advance of Russian power in Persia and north China, faced with an unprecedented exhibition of European hostility during the Boer war of 1899–1902, her world position, if not as yet dangerously threatened, was increasingly uncomfortable. Moreover its maintenance was proving increasingly expensive even in strictly financial terms. In 1893–1904 Britain's naval estimates rose by more than the corresponding expenditures of France, Germany and Russia combined. Her spending on the army also rose more than that of any other great power in the same period; and in proportion to its level in the early 1890s much more than that of either France or Germany. The desire to save money played a considerable part in disposing some members of the cabinet to envisage a German alliance. Once hopes of such an agreement had faded the same factor played an equally important role in the creation of the 1904 *entente* with France.

By the end of 1903 feeling in the British cabinet was moving in favour of such an *entente* and the two powers were tentatively cooperating in Morocco, now much the most important area of Franco-German competition. By April 1904 this *rapprochement* had culminated in a formal agreement. It settled a number of minor though irritating colonial conflicts. More important, it provided for mutual diplomatic support in Egypt, where France at last abandoned her fruitless opposition to the British occupation, and in Morocco, which was now becoming in effect a French protectorate. The forces which favoured an Anglo-French agreement urged still more strongly the conclusion of an Anglo-Russian one. French claims and protests in west Africa or Egypt were hardly more than a nuisance, though sometimes a serious one, to Britain. The Russian advance in central Asia on the other hand, might become an imminent danger to her by threatening her position in India. The growth of the French fleet merely forced Britain to spend more on her own navy; growing Russian military strength in Turkestan meant that the defence of the north-west frontier of India became more than ever the central problem of British imperial strategy, and one which raised great difficulties.[87] An Anglo-Russian agreement therefore seemed likely to save at least as much money as an Anglo-French one in reduced expenditure on the fighting services – a powerful inducement to the Liberal government which had won the election of 1906 with retrenchment in government expenditure as one of the planks in its platform. Fear of Russia was by far the most important single factor in British policy in 1902–4, while the *entente* with France was taking shape; and that *entente* was desired in London because it seemed to open the way to a better understanding with France's ally, as well as for its own sake.

The Russo-Japanese war transformed this situation very much to Britain's advantage, above all by destroying Russia for the time being as a serious naval power. By 1905 the British fleet was, at least for the moment, superior to those of France, Germany and Russia combined and dominant as it had not been since the 1880s. To some observers the war seemed to have made possible once more for Britain a policy of isolation and the avoidance of commitments to other powers. Nevertheless both in London and in St Petersburg readiness for agreement was growing. In Russia the catastrophe of 1904–5 and the revolutionary upheaval which followed led to a greater willingness to make concessions to Britain in Persia, the area of most acute Anglo-Russian conflict and suspicion. In Britain the idea of safeguarding India by an agreement with Russia was as attractive as ever. Most of all on both sides there was now a growing distrust of Germany. The agreement of 1904 had been seen in Paris as strengthening France's hand in any future Franco-German diplomatic conflict; but in London Chamberlain was almost alone among members of the cabinet in seeing that it possessed such potentialities. By 1907 this situation had changed drastically. In March 1905 the German government launched a diplomatic offensive with a very threatening tone against the dominant position which France was now acquiring in Morocco. Britain gave France the diplomatic backing promised in 1904; and the result of the German action was merely to give substance to what had hitherto been a somewhat tenuous Anglo-French understanding.

The international conference which met at Algeciras in January–April 1906 to settle the Moroccan crisis saw Britain give consistent support to France so that, as one French commentator wrote, 'at Algeciras the Entente passed from a static to a dynamic state'.[88] In January 1906, during the Moroccan crisis, there were Anglo-French military conversations about cooperation in a possible war with Germany. By the end of the month the British General Staff had told its French counterpart that in such a struggle it hoped to mobilize over 100,000 men for despatch to France within fifteen days of the beginning of hostilities. British strategy and military preparations were beginning to centre on the idea of action with France in Europe rather than on the traditional preoccupation with the defence of India – a revolutionary change. Though these conversations were unknown to the majority of the British cabinet they had in fact if not in form altered the whole basis of the 1904 agreement. By 1906, moreover, the growth of the German fleet was at last becoming a central issue in Anglo-German relations, while on the Russian side the development of German ambitions in the Near East, typified above all by the Baghdad railway scheme, was arousing deep suspicion. The result was that the Anglo-Russian convention of August 1907, which attempted to settle outstanding Anglo-Russian rivalries in Persia and to regulate the position of the two powers in Afghanistan and Tibet, was so far as Britain was concerned more clearly anti-German in inspiration than the Anglo-French agreement of 1904.

The 1907 agreement was far from completely successful. On each side voices were raised in complaint that too much had been conceded to the other. The government of India, more distrustful of Russian intentions than the ministers in London, opposed its conclusion to the last moment. On the Russian side it was argued, perhaps with more justification, that the Persian settlement[89] was less favourable than the intrinsic strength of the Russian position there justified. Britain's alignment with the Franco-Russian alliance was still, therefore, limited and tentative. She had still no formal military obligations to either France or Russia. In France anti-British feeling was very far from dead. In Russia German influence, backed by feeling in favour of monarchical solidarity against democracy and republicanism, was still powerful in court circles. There were thus still many issues on which the three powers were not prepared to act in concert.

In October 1908 the Habsburg government formally annexed Bosnia and Herzegovina, which had been under Austrian military rule since the Congress of Berlin. This action set off a dangerous explosion of hostility in Serbia, which had Russian backing, and led to the most ominous international crisis for a generation, with a real risk of an Austro-Russian war which might well spread to engulf the whole of Europe. France made it clear in St Petersburg that she was unwilling to give any effective support to Russian ambitions in the Balkans or at the Straits, and there was never any question of Britain doing so. This helped to ensure that in March 1909 a still weak Russia was forced, under heavy German pressure, to abandon her support of the Serbs and submit to the greatest diplomatic humiliation she had suffered since the peace of 1856. France took advantage of the crisis to strike with Germany a favourable bargain over Morocco, by which her political predominance there was recognized in return for a promise not to injure German economic interests. It was possible for the German chancellor, Prince Bülow, later to claim, with a good deal of exaggeration, that in 1908-9 'the group of powers whose influence had been so much overestimated at Algeciras fell to pieces when faced with the tough problems of continental policy'.[90] Moreover in August 1911 Russia made with Germany an agreement over Persia and the Baghdad railway without consulting Britain or France, while in 1912 there were active Anglo-German naval negotiations.[91] None of the Entente powers wanted bad relations with Germany. All were willing to come to terms with her independently on specific issues when it suited them to do so.

Nevertheless the Triple Entente was slowly acquiring effectiveness and gaining coherence. This consolidation was largely the work of Germany herself. After 1907 she was more and more a prey to the fear of 'encirclement' by her enemies. This fear, like Germany's colonial ambitions, was understandable. But like them it led her into ill-judged efforts at self-assertion which in the long run damaged further her international position by intensifying the distrust and ill-feeling which she now increasingly aroused. Nicholas II of Russia, in the immediate aftermath of the Bosnia-Herzegovina crisis, well expressed these feelings in his complaint that 'the form and method of Germany's action – I mean towards us – has simply been brutal and we won't forget it'. In July 1911 the German government set off another Moroccan crisis by the typical gesture of sending a gunboat to the port of Agadir. This was a clumsy attempt not so much to substitute German for French influence in Morocco as to obtain handsome compensation from France elsewhere in Africa as the price of recognizing her *de facto* Moroccan protectorate. It failed. Of the French Congo, which had been hoped for, Germany received only a small part. More serious, the crisis evoked the most forthright public statements of British support for

France hitherto made. On both sides alarm and hostility had been intensified. In Germany there was bitter disappointment at the outcome, widespread criticism of the 'weakness' of the government and of William II
himself, and general agreement that Germany's diplomatic defeat was above
all the result of British hostility. In France, with much less justification,
colonial pressure groups were dissatisfied with the concessions made to
Germany. In Britain, an exchange of letters in November 1912 between
Sir Edward Grey, the foreign secretary, and the French ambassador promised consultation in case of an apparently imminent attack or threat to
the general peace by a third power. The Anglo-French *entente* was now
beginning to resemble, in fact if not in form, an alliance, and one of a
dangerously vague kind.

1914: THE END OF THE OLD EUROPE

The war of 1914 therefore engulfed a Europe politically divided in a more
clear-cut way than ever before. The closeness of the Austro-German combination, based on the dangerous willingness of the German government
to back to the hilt its one remaining genuine ally, had been shown by the
Bosnian crisis of 1908-9. Confronting it was a Triple Entente less united
and less purely European in its outlook but slowly gaining effectiveness
and self-confidence. But it would be misleading and superficial to discuss
the outbreak of war merely in these conventional political terms. The
attitudes of the powers in the crisis of July 1914 might well have been
the same had the alliance systems built up during the past generation or
more never existed. It is at least doubtful whether France, for example,
would have entered the struggle merely because of the terms of her alliance with Russia. Her attitude was determined not by paper obligations
but by her previous history and her interests – by her desire to recover
Alsace-Lorraine and to ward off possible German hegemony in Europe.
Moreover in 1914 she had no third course between submission to German
dominance and armed resistance. A neutrality which left her international
status unimpaired was not open to her. In the same way the worsening
of relations between Germany and Russia after 1908 was not the result
of a Franco-Russian treaty which had already existed for fifteen years,
while Germany was driven to support Austria-Hungary in 1909 and 1914
not by the terms of the alliance of 1879 but by her fear of isolation
and perhaps of Panslav ambitions. Moreover it is misleading to discuss
Britain's entry into the conflict mainly in terms of moral obligations to
France. If these had not squared with her interests they might not have
influenced her actions much more than the military conventions stemming

from the Triple Alliance influenced those of Italy, which remained neutral in 1914.

The details of the purely diplomatic exchanges are interesting above all for what they reveal of the forces which underlay them. In the conventional terms of 'war-guilt', Germany's responsibility for the disaster was much greater than that of any other power.[92] Yet as historical perspective lengthens, a view of the war as in the deepest sense 'caused' by acts or omissions of specific individuals during a few days in the summer of 1914 becomes more and more unsatisfactory. The disparity between the commonplace agents and the overwhelming result is too incongruous for such a view to be easily accepted. It would be hard to show that the statesmen, generals and diplomats of 1914 were either more or less unscrupulous, either cleverer or more stupid, than their predecessors in, say, 1853. Yet the repercussions of what they did were incomparably greater; and some of them at least seem to have felt in the final crisis that they were little more than the puppets of forces which they could not control. The coming of the war was far more than a landmark in diplomatic history. In the domestic politics and even the social history of the European states it was the end, or at least the beginning of the end, of an epoch. It meant 'the passing of the age of monarch and frock-coat and the advent of the age of dictator and coloured shirt'.[93] In the history of political psychology and mythology it marked the final triumph of nationalism and therefore of the populist attitude, the vulgar dynamism, inherent in nationalism. In Europe's relations with the rest of the world it was again a dividing-line, perhaps the most important of all. The self-confidence, the sense of imperial mission, of divinely imposed destiny and obligation, which had achieved so much in the last generation,[94] were mortally wounded by the war.

It was a European war. Its roots were entirely European; and the imperial rivalries of the powers outside Europe provided no more than a background to its outbreak. It is true that in the previous decade German expansionism had taken the form of imperial claims in Morocco, the Congo or the Near East. But the discontent and aggressiveness which underlay these claims were not based on rational calculation of the advantages of world power; by comparison with Britain, and to a lesser extent with France and even Russia, Germany remained parochial in her outlook and in the scope of her policies. Her rather ineffective imperial ambitions were no more than an outgrowth of her position in Europe, of her industrial progress and the history which had made her a late starter in the colonial race. Moreover by 1914 Morocco had ceased to be a serious issue in international affairs and relations between the British and German colonial offices were better than for many years. Nor is it easy to see the war as the result of

Anglo-German industrial and commercial competition. The most politically influential figures in both British and German economic life threw their weight, in the crisis of 1914 as in previous conflicts, whole-heartedly on the side of peace. The shipowner Albert Ballin in Germany, the financier Sir Ernest Cassel in Britain, are only the best-known examples of this attitude; there were many others. Thus, for instance, Sir Robert Hadfield, a leading British ironmaster, suggested in a newspaper interview in 1912 that Britain and Germany should form an *entente*, together with the United States, to exploit the economic resources of China. They should improve relations between them by the setting-up of an Anglo-German board with twenty members; this was to be dominated by business men and in particular to include no diplomats, or army or navy officers. There is a distinctly Cobdenite ring about the proposal, while during the 1914 crisis Lord Rothschild tried unsuccessfully, through its financial editor, to stop *The Times'* advocacy of British intervention on the Franco-Russian side should war break out.[95]

The immediate cause of the war, the Austro-Serb conflict brought to a head by the assassination of the Archduke Francis Ferdinand and his wife in Sarajevo on 28 June, illustrated what had become long before 1914 the most fundamental political difficulty of east and east-central Europe – the impossibility of reconciling existing state frontiers with explosive and demanding nationalism. The revolution of 1903 in Belgrade brought into power there the anti-Austrian Karageorgevich dynasty; no longer was Serbia a virtual satellite of the Habsburgs. The way was thus opened to a rapid growth of Serb territorial ambitions at the expense of the Habsburg empire. The loss of south Slav-populated territory which these ambitions involved would deal that empire, many observers believed, a mortal blow. Once its structure began to crumble, it could be argued, there was no logical end to the process but its dissolution into national states.[96] Bosnia and Herzegovina were therefore annexed in 1908, as the Austrian chancellor admitted, 'to deal a death blow at Serb irredentism'.[97] However, Serb irredentism refused to die; and the result was that in the years which followed the idea of a preventive war against Serbia, to remove once and for all the danger which her claims and ambitions presented to the Habsburg empire, gained ground in Vienna. Conrad von Hötzendorff, the Austrian chief of staff, had pressed in June 1909 for such a war while the international situation was favourable. He repeated these urgings in December 1912, and early in the following year was planning for a conflict with both Serbia and her Russian backer which he hoped would break out in March 1913.

Neither Count Berchtold, the chancellor, nor the Emperor Francis Joseph himself much liked the idea of an aggressive policy in the Balkans. Only after the Sarajevo murders were they fully reconciled to the inevitability of war with Serbia. But even before 1914 there increasingly seemed no alternative if the empire were to survive. Moreover this attitude had come to be shared by controlling elements in Germany, without whose backing the Austrians could do nothing. By July 1914 it was almost as generally agreed in Berlin as in Vienna that the position and even the existence of the Habsburg empire could be defended only by aggression against Serbia. 'Among us,' wrote a high-ranking German soldier early in July 1914, 'the view is predominant that the Austrians should act against Serbia, the sooner the better, and that the Russians, although they are friends of the Serbs, will not interfere.'[98] It was German pressure which persuaded Count Tisza, the prime minister of Hungary, who opposed a conflict which he thought certain to damage the interests of the Hungarian ruling class, to agree to war. With the way thus cleared, Austrian efforts to humiliate and subject her dangerous little neighbour could be embodied in the ultimatum of 23 July, the beginning of the process which culminated ten days later in the outbreak of general European war.

The problem of Austro-Serb relations does more than illustrate the way in which nationalism undermined and disrupted the old Europe. It also brings out two other essential characteristics of the 1914 situation – the dominance of military influences and alleged necessities; and the widespread feeling among peoples as well as statesmen, at least in Germany and the Habsburg empire, that a great international conflict was now inevitable.

Of the first of these points Germany is the most important illustration. There military considerations completely decided, without regard for political ones, the strategy to be followed in case of war. The Schlieffen plan, elaborated in successive versions since 1892 and from 1897 onwards the basis of all German war planning, was based on the assumption of a two-front war against France and Russia, and of an overwhelming offensive in the west involving the violation of Belgium. To this strategy all German military planning was geared. If Germany were to fight she must do so in this way and in no other. The rigidity which this introduced into German policy in the crisis of 1914 was tragic. When William II, with characteristic futility, suggested on 1 August that it might be possible to limit the war by concentrating the German armies against Russia and abandoning the idea of an attack on France he received the inevitable reply: the plans elaborated over many years could not possibly be undone at a moment's notice. The significance of the Schlieffen plan, through the invasion of Belgium which it demanded, in easing the otherwise very difficult task of the Asquith cabinet in bringing Britain into the war has been so often emphasized that it hardly needs repetition here.

Apparent military necessities also made it appear to many Germans in the years immediately before 1914 that a war, if it must come, should be fought as soon as possible. Here the decisive factor was the growth of Russian strength. For several years after the disaster of 1904–5 the Russian army remained weak. This led some German officers, and William II himself, to consider seizing the opportunity of a preventive war against Russia; but at least her power did not seem in Berlin to be immediately menacing. What altered this state of affairs was the marked rise in military expenditure in Russia and even more the growth of the network of strategic railways in her western provinces. Even in 1914 the Russians were badly off so far as railways were concerned. Their front with Germany and Austria was then served by only eighteen tracks, while their enemies had twice as many at their disposal. Moreover their plans for the use of the railways in mobilization (which had in any case been drawn up in 1910 and therefore did not take account of the increased rail capacity made available in the immediate pre-war years) were not efficiently carried out. Nevertheless Russia's capacity to strike a really heavy blow against Germany or Austria-Hungary was undoubtedly increasing. Her vast resources of manpower[99] might now begin to be translated into effective strength in the field. Moreover the French government was doing its best to speed her strategic railway-building and thus make her a more effective weapon against Germany.

All this was bound to create alarm in Berlin. In the crisis of 1914 the leading German military periodical spoke for most of the army leadership when it argued that 'if we do not decide for war, that war in which we shall have to engage at the latest in two or three years will be begun in far less propitious circumstances. At this moment the initiative rests with us: Russia is not ready, moral factors and right are on our side, as well as might. Since we have to accept the conflict some day, let us provoke it at once.'[100] The younger Moltke, the German chief of general staff, had warned both the war minister and the chancellor in December 1912 that though the military situation in the east was still favourable to Germany and Austria-Hungary it would not long remain so as Russia's strength grew. Though even in 1914 he himself seems not to have favoured a preventive war he naturally felt it his duty to see that Germany's position was not permanently weakened vis-à-vis her great eastern neighbour. By 1916 or 1917 the Russian railway network would be complete. Until then Russia would not willingly go to war. But once her preparations were complete she might be impossible to defeat. If war must come, therefore, the sooner the better; and there were observers in 1914, notably Schiemann, who argued that Germany had stolen a march on her enemies by forcing them to fight before they were fully ready to do so. This growing predominance of military considerations in Germany was merely the most important example of a trend which could be seen in varying forms during the last years of peace in many parts of Europe. It is visible in the accelerating military competition between France and Germany.[101] On the personal level it can be seen in the reappointment of Conrad in December 1912 as chief of the Austrian general staff after a temporary demotion, and in the fall from power in St Petersburg early in 1914 of the relatively pacific chief minister, Kokovtsev. Even in Italy the chief of staff, General Pollio, spoke in April 1914 to the German military attaché in Rome of the possibility of a preventive war in response to the continual tightening, as he saw it, of the ring of hostility now surrounding the powers of the Triple Alliance.

In the English-speaking world, where the optimistic, humanitarian, internationalist assumptions of liberalism still had real vitality, the war came generally as a shock. There it seemed to many people a departure from normality explicable only in terms of the deliberate wickedness of a few powerful individuals, above all William II. In continental Europe, notably Germany and Austria-Hungary, the position was different. There long habituation to military influences and modes of thought made it easy to believe that a great international conflict was sooner or later inevitable. In April 1913, for example, von Jagow, the German foreign minister, spoke in confidence to a number of Reichstag deputies of 'the coming world war'. It is clear that by the summer of 1914 there was in Berlin a widespread and fatalistic acceptance of war as unavoidable, and that this had great influence in weakening the will to keep the peace.[102] Bethmann-Hollweg, the chancellor, is reported as saying on 20 July that he saw 'a doom greater than human power hanging over Europe and our own people'. Certainly he was more concerned to throw blame for the catastrophe on Russia, in the futile hope of securing British neutrality, than to preserve peace. At the deepest level such attitudes were nourished throughout Europe by the debased Darwinism which now formed part of the mental furniture of every educated man.[103] In Germany in particular there could be found a social Darwinism more wholehearted and more explicitly brutal than that normally put forward in other parts of the continent, and a resulting rejection of the desirability as well as the possibility of a secure and lasting peace. In every belligerent state, however, the war was not merely accepted but to a greater or less extent welcomed as a positive good. In part this was because it often seemed an escape from, or at least a postponement of, apparently insoluble internal difficulties and conflicts. So intractable and widespread were these in many states that it was possible to compare the position in 1913 with that in the first months of 1848. In Germany the unprecedented success of the Social Democrats in the 1912 Reichstag elections showed that after forty years of effort the imperial régime had failed to win anything more than passive acceptance at best from the majority of industrial workers. The hitherto relatively liberal franchise in Hamburg and Saxony, both strongholds of socialism, had been restricted. Bülow had formed an anti-Social Democrat *Kartell* of parties to fight the 1907 election. Neither expedient had achieved any permanent success in halting the growth of what every conservative regarded as an imminent threat to the existence of the empire. The result was that a *coup d'état* to establish undiluted authoritarianism in the form of a nakedly military monarchy without democratic trappings, an idea which William II had seriously considered in 1897, now seemed more than ever attractive to many members of the Prussian ruling class. In December 1913 such a coup was urged by the Crown Prince William, the heir to the throne. Simultaneously some of the Pan-German leaders were hoping for a remodelling of Germany's political structure along authoritarian lines which would involve the overthrow of Bethmann-Hollweg and permanent exclusion of the Jews from political life. Elsewhere domestic problems were equally serious. In Britain civil war in Ireland seemed imminent and the prime minister, Asquith, though alarmed by the July crisis, hoped that it 'may incidentally have the effect of throwing into the background the lurid pictures of civil war in Ulster'.[104] In the Habsburg empire national antagonisms, seen above all in Hungarian intractability and in the growth of south Slav discontent, were less insistently threatening than in the terrible years 1896–99. But they were as difficult as ever to appease. Francis Ferdinand was bitterly anti-Magyar; and there is evidence that during the emperor's serious illness in the spring of 1914 he had made plans for a military *coup d'état* should Francis Joseph die. In Italy the period of liberal reform presided over by Giovanni Giolitti ended with the Turkish war of 1911–12; and the years immediately before 1914 saw a marked growth of the streak of violence and intolerance which had always been latent in Italian politics. The most notable symptom of this was the victory of Mussolini and his supporters at the Reggio congress of the Italian Socialist Party in 1912. In Russia, though after 1907 the threat of social revolution was no longer imminent, the discontent of the non-Russian national groups was still intense; and the existence of the Duma which Nicholas II had been forced to concede in 1905 was still far from accepted by the more reactionary elements around the tsar. In the eighty years between the accession of Nicholas I in 1825 and the 1905 revolution fewer than two hundred people were executed in the Russian empire for political offences; but in the five years 1906–10, when the existence of the empire seemed sometimes to hang by a thread, the number was almost twenty times as great. In many parts of Europe, moreover, the years just before 1914 saw industrial unrest and strikes, often violent, on an unprecedented scale. It is not surprising, then, that war was sometimes welcomed as an escape into simplicity from the intolerable complexities of peace; and indeed it often did temporarily appease peacetime conflicts, or at least push them into the background. In every belligerent the coming of war meant for the time being a suspension of domestic disputes in face of the external challenge. Even in Russia the gulf dividing the government from the country's intellectuals and liberals was temporarily bridged. But it must be emphasized that the conflict was welcomed for more than these merely rational, or rational-seeming, reasons. To many it seemed not a disaster but a fulfilment, one which was personal rather than national. It brought release from the frustrations, the artificialities, the compromises of peacetime. It confronted the individual with clear, inescapable and, it could be claimed, ennobling duties. 'War, what an exalting thing!' exclaimed a young lieutenant to King Albert of the Belgians on the presentation of the German ultimatum in 1914.[105] This outburst, to which a multitude of parallels can be found in every country involved,[106] represented the mood of Europe, and certainly the mood of the men who were to do the fighting, at least as faithfully as the gloom of liberals, internationalists and believers in the myth of international working-class solidarity. In literature and the arts the avant-garde had already broken through traditional limitations and renounced traditional certainties by 1914.[107] Now an increasing number of people were willing and even anxious to extend this to life in general. The achievements of the old Europe during the nineteenth century had been without parallel in human history. It was now on its deathbed, partly through the mistakes and weaknesses of its leaders and partly through the only half-understood destructive powers with which its own achievements had endowed it. Most fundamentally of all, however, it was doomed by the fact that an appreciable fraction of its own most influential and most idealistic inhabitants did not, in their hearts, want it to continue and were willing and even anxious, in a supreme moment of romantic blindness, to leap forward into a new and more emotionally satisfying future.

NOTES

1. J. B. Duroselle, *L'Idée d'Europe dans l'histoire* (Paris, 1965), p. 195.
2. G. de Berthier de Sauvigny, *Metternich and his Times* (London, Darton, Longman & Todd, 1962), p. 105.
3. M. Bourquin, *Histoire de la Sainte Alliance* (Geneva, 1954), pp. 75–6.

4. Berthier de Sauvigny, *Metternich*, p. 75.

5. Patricia K. Grimsted, *The Foreign Ministers of Alexander I* (University of California Press, 1969), p. 285.

6. For the evolution of this idea in the period 1789–1830 see the discussion of west European (mainly French and German) writing about Russia during these years in D. Groh, *Russland und das Selbstverständnis Europas* (Neuwied, 1961), Pt III, Ch. i, especially pp. 85–6.

7. *Eclectic Review*, n.s., iv (1815), 375.

8. B. Gille, *Histoire économique et sociale de la Russie* (Paris, 1949), p. 152.

9. A. H. Everett, *Europe: or a general survey of the present situation of the principal powers* (London, 1822), pp. 319–20, 323, 360.

10. This was the view of perhaps the most widely read political work of the immediate post-Napoleonic period, the Abbé Dufour de Pradt's *Parallèle de la puissance anglaise et russe relativement à l'Europe* (Paris, 1823), Ch. i, *passim*.

11. See p. 320.

12. Berthier de Sauvigny, *Metternich*, p. 158. Nor was realization of Austrian weakness confined to official circles. See for example the realistic discussion of it in *The State of the Nation at the Commencement of the Year 1822* (London, 1822), pp. 108–10.

13. Berthier de Sauvigny, *Metternich*, p. 175.

14. Neither the unsuccessful Decembrist revolt in Russia in 1825 nor the rather pathetic Cato Street conspiracy of 1820 in London did much to shake this generally accepted picture.

15. H. Rieben and others, *Un Centre de gravité européen* (Lausanne, 1969), pp. 314–15.

16. For the effect of the Polish revolt in intensifying anti-Russian feeling in Britain see J. H. Gleason, *The Genesis of Russophobia in Great Britain* (Harvard University Press, 1950), Ch. v; for its effect on German opinion see Groh, *Russland und das Selbstverständnis Europas*, pp. 159–60.

17. The most important spokesman for this attitude was the Prussian Baron A. von Haxthausen, whose *Studien über die inneren Zustände, das Volksleben und inbesondere die landlichen Einrichtungen Russlands*, the first really penetrating study of Russian agrarian problems in any western language, appeared in 1847–52.

18. The most significant of these was the liberal educationalist, Julius Fröbel, who proclaimed in his *Wien, Deutschland und Europa* (Vienna, 1848) that 'in the Russian people, as in all Slavonic peoples, I see a great democratic future' (Groh, *Russland und das Selbstverständnis Europas*, p. 294).

19. R. A. Kann, 'Metternich: a reappraisal of his impact on international relations', *Journal of Modern History*, xxxii (1960), 337.

20. Duroselle, *L'Idée d'Europe*, p. 231.

21. Groh, *Russland*, p. 270.

22. Groh, *Russland*, pp. 283ff; G. Barraclough, 'Europa, Amerika und Russland in Vorstellung und Denken des 19 Jahrhunderts' *Historische Zeitschrift*, cciii (1966), 300–8.

23. Duroselle, *L'Idée d'Europe*, p. 209.

24. *The Collected Works of Walter Bagehot*, ed. N. St John-Stevas, iv (London, The Economist, 1968), 448.

25. According to perhaps the best contemporary estimate the total steam power available to industry increased over fivefold in France in 1844–64 and over sixfold in Prussia in 1846–61 (M. Block, *L'Europe politique et sociale* (Paris, 1869), p. 106). Modern calculations tell the same story (e.g. T. S. Hamerow, *The Social Foundations of German Unification, 1858–1871* (Princeton University Press, 1969), p. 33).

26. A good example is the rapid conquest of cholera. The disease was probably unknown in Europe until the epidemic of the early 1830s; and though the organism which causes it was isolated by Koch only in 1883 a good empirical knowledge of the means by which it was transmitted, and therefore of how to combat it, existed by the 1860s. The moralistic explanations of the disease generally accepted in the 1830s – e.g. that the victims had weakened their constitutions by excess and thus exposed themselves to infection – were soon discarded in favour of a more open-minded and experimental one (C. E. Rosenberg, 'Cholera in nineteenth-century Europe; a tool for economic and social analysis', *Comparative Studies in Society and History*, viii (1955–56), 452–63).

27. See pp. 367ff.

28. Block, *L'Europe politique et sociale*, p. 78.

29. H. Reeve, ed., *The Greville Memoirs: A journal of the reigns of King George IV, King William IV and Queen Victoria* (London, 1903), vii, 170.

30. See his memorandum of February 1856 in *Lettres et papiers du chancelier Comte de Nesselrode* (Paris, n.d.), xi, 112–16.

31. Mrs Rosslyn Wemyss, ed., *Memoirs and Letters of the Right Hon. Sir Robert Morier* (London, 1911), ii, 67.

32. The best brief analysis of Napoleon's ideas on foreign policy is perhaps still A. Pingaud, 'La politique extérieure du second empire', *Revue Historique*, clvi (1927), 41–68.

33. W. K. Hancock, *Ricasoli and the Risorgimento in Tuscany* (London, Faber & Gwyer, 1926), p. 287.

34. Sir H. G. Elliot, *Some Revolutions and other Diplomatic Experiences* (London, 1922), pp. 101, 112.

35. D. Mack Smith, *A History of Sicily: modern Sicily after 1713* (London, Chatto & Windus, 1968), p. 44.

36. See pp. 328ff.

37. See pp. 105–6.

38. Hamerow, *Social Foundations*, p. 43.

39. *Ibid*, pp. 286–90, 397.

40. Lord Newton, *Lord Lyons: a record of British diplomacy* (London, 1913), i, 202.

41. See p. 325.

42. Wemyss, *Memoirs*, ii, 216–17.

43. *Ibid*, ii, 208.

44. Rosemary K. I. Quested, *The Expansion of Russia in East Asia, 1857–1860* (Kuala Lumpur–Singapore, 1968), p. 193.

45. Newton, *Lord Lyons*, ii, 41.

46. See p. 332.

47. In 1909 General Sukhomlinov, the Russian chief of staff, pointed out that in Russia only three field-guns were available for each infantry battalion, whereas in France and Germany there were four to six. Germany had eighteen howitzers for each of her army corps and the Habsburg empire even more, while Russia had only 174 for 31 army corps (A. M. Zaionchkovskii, *Podgotovka Rossii k mirovoi voine. Plany voiny* (Moscow, 1926), pp. 85–6). In 1914 the Russian army was still only about half as well equipped with artillery as the German one; and for each of its heavy field-guns it possessed only about 1,000 rounds of ammunition (in theory: in practice it was 850 rounds) against the German 3,000 (General Andolenko, *Histoire de l'armée russe* (Paris, 1967), p. 307).

48. During the 1820s the ratio of children in school to the adult population was in Prussia 1 to 8, in England 1 to 16, in France 1 to 30 and in Russia 1 to 700: an estimate of 1845 gave Prussia an illiteracy rate of less than 10 per cent as against 36 per cent in France and 93 per cent in Russia (Hamerow, *Social Foundations*, pp. 279–80).

49. J. Ward, *Experiences of a Diplomatist* (London, 1872), p. 1.

50. E. Young, *Labor in Europe and America* (Washington, 1876), p. 369.

51. Though for a dissenting opinion on this point see D. N. McCloskey, 'Did Victorian Britain fail?' *Economic History Review*, 2nd ser., xxiii (1970–71), 446–59.

52. D. S. Landes, 'The structure of enterprise in the nineteenth century: the cases of Britain and Germany', *Congrès International des Sciences Historiques, Rapports*, v (Stockholm, 1960), 121.

53. See the detailed comparison of the two industries in D. Burn, *The Economic History of Steelmaking* (Cambridge University Press, 1961), p. 191.

54. A. L. Levine, *Industrial Retardation in Britain, 1880–1914* (London, Weidenfeld & Nicolson, 1967), pp. 134–5.

55. W. Ashworth, 'The late Victorian economy', *Economica*, n.s., xxxiii (1966), 32.

56. D. S. Landes, *The Unbound Prometheus: technological change and industrial development in Western Europe from 1750 to the present* (Cambridge University Press, 1969), p. 247.

57. For a good statement of this argument see C. P. Kindelberger, *Economic Growth in France and Britain, 1851–1950* (Harvard University Press, 1964), Ch. xii, especially pp. 272ff.

58. See pp. 191–2, 245.

59. The best general discussion of the points which follow is to be found in Landes, *The Unbound Prometheus*, pp. 336ff.

60. Levine, *Industrial Retardation in Britain*, p. 71. Another estimate was that in the German chemical industry there was one university-trained scientist to every forty other workers, 'a ratio of science to labour probably excelled in no other country in the world' (W. H. Dawson, *The Evolution of Modern Germany* (London, 1908), p. 86). The first chair of applied chemistry in the world had been founded at the university of Giessen as early as 1838.

61. T. H. von Laue, *Sergei Witte and the Industrialization of Russia* (Columbia University Press, 1963), p. 9.

62. See p. 207.

63. G. Monger, *The End of Isolation: British foreign policy, 1900–1907* (London, Nelson, 1963), p. 7.

64. Labour productivity on the railways of Russia in 1913 was little more than a seventh of that on those of the United States: almost twice as many workers in proportion of the total length of track were employed as in France (J. N. Westwood, *A History of Russian Railways* (London, Allen & Unwin, 1964), p. 159).

65. See pp. 332–3.

66. For a good discussion of this backwardness see S. B. Clough and C. Livi, 'Economic Growth in Italy: An analysis of the Uneven Development of North and South', in B. Supple, ed., *The Experience of Economic Growth* (New York, Random House, 1963), pp. 354–66.

67. See pp. 143–4.

68. See p. 247.

69. *Opinion on the Eastern Question* (2nd edn, London, 1876), pp. 81–2. The Russian original, *Mnenie o vostochnom voprose*, was published in 1870.

70. See p. 289.

71. Paul Rohrbach, in his *Deutschland unter den Weltvölkern*, quoted in H. Gollwitzer, *Europabild und Europagedanke* (Munich, 1964), p. 328.

72. R. Chickering, *We Who Feel Most German: a cultural study of the Pan-German League, 1886–1914* (London, Allen & Unwin, 1984), pp. 227ff. See also Mildred S. Wertheimer, *The Pan-German League, 1890–1914* (New York, 1924), especially Chs vii and ix.

73. A good example is General Theodor von Bernhardi, who in perhaps the most extreme of the demands for forcible expansion put forward before 1914, his immensely successful *Germany and the Next War* (English translation, London, 1914; German original, Stuttgart, 1912) demanded simultaneously dominance of Europe, seizure of a great colonial empire, and the achievement of German world power.

74. See p. 119.

75. *The History of the Times* (London, The Times, 1935–52), iii, 366.

76. See p. 279.

77. H. Gollwitzer, *Die gelbe Gefahr* (Göttingen, 1962), pp. 38–42.

78. R. Poidevin, *Les Relations économiques et financières entre la France et l'Allemagne de 1898 à 1914* (Paris, 1969): see especially Pt III, Ch. iii.

79. *Die Grosse Politik der europäischen Mächte* (Berlin, 1922–27), xxix, no. 10750.

80. M. Kent, *Oil and Empire: British Policy and Mesopotamian Oil, 1900–1920* (London, Macmillan, 1976), Chs 4 and 5 *passim*.

81. W Gerrare (i.e. W. Greener), *Greater Russia: the continental empire of the Old World* (London, 1903), pp. 306–7.

82. H. W. V. Temperley and Lillian Penson, *Foundations of British Foreign Policy from Pitt (1792) to Salisbury (1902)* (Cambridge University Press, 1938), p. 392.

83. *Opinion on the Eastern Question*, p. 39.

84. See p. 280.

85. See p. 343.

86. The best account of these negotiations is J. A. S. Grenville, *Lord Salisbury and Foreign Policy* (London, Athlone Press, 1964), Chs vii and xv. See also P. M. Kennedy, 'German world policy and the alliance negotiations with England, 1897–1900', *Journal of Modern History*, xiv, no. 4 (Dec. 1973).

87. On the part played by considerations of Indian defence in bringing about the Anglo-Russian agreement see Beryl J. Williams, 'The strategic background to the Anglo-Russian entente of August 1907', *Historical Journal*, ix (1966), 360–73.

88. A. Tardieu, *La Conférence d'Algésiras* (Paris, 1907), quoted in H. Nicolson, *Sir Arthur Nicolson, Bart., First Lord Carnock: a study in the old diplomacy* (London, Constable, 1930), p. 199.

89. See p. 282.

90. Prince B. von Bülow, *Imperial Germany* (London, 1914), p. 53.

91. See pp. 343–4.

92. The best short statement of the case for German guilt is probably I. Geiss, 'The outbreak of the First World War and German war aims', *Journal of Contemporary History*, i, no. 3 (1966), 75–91. The most detailed indictment is F. Fischer, *War of Illusions: German Policies from 1911 to 1914* (London, Chatto & Windus, 1975: first published 1961).

93. J. Michael Kitch, 'The promise of the new revisionism', *Past and Present*, no. 36 (April 1967), 164.

94. See pp. 296–7.

95. H. Wickham Steed, *Through Thirty Years* (London, Heinemann, 1924), ii, 8–9. For a well-known general statement of the case against attributing the outbreak of the war to the workings of capitalism see Sir J. H. Clapham, *An Economic History of Modern Britain*, iii (Cambridge University Press, 1951), 511–18.

96. Though this attitude may have taken too pessimistic a view of the persisting vitality of the Habsburg empire: cf. p. 237.

97. *Grosse Politik*, xxvi, no. 9386.

98. R. Ropponen, *Die Kraft Russlands* (Helsinki, 1968), p. 263.

99. In 1914, according to an official German estimate, she had 6,300,000 trained men as against 4,900,000 in Germany (Reichsarchiv, *Der Weltkrieg, 1914–1918, Kriegsrüstung und Kriegswirtschaft* (Berlin, 1930), p. 221).

100. *Militarische Rundschau*, July 1914, quoted in *Annual Register*, 1914, p. 305.

101. See p. 335.

102. J. B. Joll, *1914: the unspoken assumptions* (London, Weidenfeld & Nicolson, 1968), p. 6.

103. See pp. 376–7.

104. J. A. Spender and C. Asquith, *Life of Lord Oxford and Asquith* (London, Hutchinson, 1932), ii, 83.

105. J. Lestocquoy, *Histoire du patriotisme en France* (Paris, 1968), p. 196.

106. See for example the quotations in Joll, *1914*, p. 15; and for Italy p. 115 below.

107. See pp. 389–92.

2

The mechanics of government: freedom and authority

In 1815 the governments and societies of continental Europe were in some respects as close to those of the thirteenth century as to those of the twentieth. The growth areas, both economic and intellectual, of the continent were now far removed from the Middle Ages; and large-scale industry, technological change and new currents of feeling and ideas were rapidly carrying them further away. The last two decades of the eighteenth century had seen Britain begin to make the decisive transition to a distinctively modern productive system. Almost simultaneously France had not merely enunciated the creative and disruptive concept of popular sovereignty but attempted, with for a time terrifying success, to put it into practice. In different and less far-reaching ways both the mercantile and middle-class civilization of the Netherlands and to a lesser extent the urban-orientated one of parts of Italy had for long been far from 'medieval'. Yet it is easy for historians, in this as in other contexts, to go too far in stressing the new, the seminal, at the expense of the more typical and therefore the less interesting and the easier to take for granted. 'Typical', admittedly, is a word to which it is difficult to attach any precise meaning in a continent so heterogeneous as Europe had become by 1815. In social structure, in methods of government, in wealth and productive power, the Europe of the Vienna congress was already very disparate indeed.[1] Nevertheless, in so far as the word can legitimately be used, the continent as a whole in 1815 was still typically traditional and backward-looking at least as much as radical and innovating.

Except in one or two areas (France was the only significant one) there was still almost universal acceptance of hereditary monarchy as the normal and indeed the only conceivable constitutional form. The legal nature and powers of this monarchy varied widely between different states. At the one extreme stood Great Britain, where the powers of the ruler had been in decline since the seventeenth century, a decline which had accelerated from the 1780s. By 1815, faced by a powerful and self-confident parliament, by political parties which were slowly acquiring some cohesion, and above all by a now well-established tradition of cabinet independence and unity, the British monarchy was limited and constitutional beyond all possibility of denial. At the other end of the spectrum was Russia. There since the reign of Peter the Great the religious awe which for centuries had buttressed the position of the tsar had been supplemented by a bureaucratic and military structure inspired largely by west European and particularly German models, of which the ruler was in theory the absolute master. There was never during the nineteenth century any clear distinction in Russia between law, in the sense of general rules, and imperial decrees, in the sense of orders implementing the law in particular cases. Moreover it was generally admitted that administrative action by the emperor had the power to override the law. Neither the Council of State set up in 1810 nor the Council of Ministers created two years later had any of the powers of a cabinet: until 1864 the judiciary was simply a branch of the administrative machinery.[2] The rulers of Russia thus enjoyed powers to which no other European monarch could aspire; and of this they showed themselves fully conscious. From the coronation of the Empress Elizabeth in 1742 onwards they regularly placed the crown with their own hands upon their heads during the coronation ceremony in the Cathedral of the Dormition in the Kremlin, the senior archbishop merely handing it to them. This was a formal symbolic assertion, unparalleled in any other European state, of the ruler as absolute, 'owing nothing to anything outside of himself and limited by nothing outside of himself', in other words a kind of deity.[3]

Formal powers and legal rights were far from being the whole of the picture. In Britain the monarchy, stripped of much of its active political role, could still exert appreciable influence on some aspects of government, notably foreign policy and military affairs. More important, it could still influence deeply the tone of the nation's life if the throne were occupied by a ruler capable of appealing to a really profound strain of public feeling, as Queen Victoria did in the last two decades of her reign. In Russia on the other hand the power of the autocracy, whatever the symbols with which it adorned itself, was drastically limited in practice. The sheer size of the empire, the inadequacy of its internal communications and the intractability of the problems it faced, set bounds to what any autocrat could in fact achieve. Observers in the west usually failed to see this, and as a result grossly exaggerated the effective control of the tsars over events. Friedrich von Gentz, secretary of the Congress of Vienna and one of the best-informed men in Europe, told the Hospodar of Moldavia in 1818, for example, that 'None of the obstacles that restrain and thwart the other sovereigns – divided authority, constitutional forms, public opinion, etc. – exists for the Emperor of Russia. What he dreams of at night he can carry out in the morning.'[4] But in fact the Russian monarchy had functioned since the reign of Peter I, and still more since that of Catherine II, as a partnership between the ruler and the privileged landowning class. The tsar gave to the landowner virtually untrammelled control over his peasant serfs and the life of his own estates and locality. In return the landowner accepted an obligation (since 1762 moral rather than legal, but little less effective for that) to serve in the armed forces or the bureaucracy, and did not interfere with the conduct of central government by the tsar and his ministers. Without such a partnership (of which the maintenance of serfdom was an integral part) the ruler, as the conservative ideologist Karamzin pointed out in his *Memoir on Ancient and Modern Russia*, written in 1810–11, would have to bear the whole burden of administering the country and would find it too much for him – a judgement which the course of events after the emancipation edict of 1861 did something to bear out.

The other great monarchies of Europe fell between the British and Russian extremes. In France the monarchical régime restored in 1815 was very different from that of Louis XIV or Louis XV. This difference did not lie, in the last analysis, in the fact that it had been forced to issue in June 1814 a Constitutional Charter which gave France some approach to parliamentary government and accepted some important results of the revolution, notably its land settlement. Nor did the new insecurity of the French monarchy even stem from the fact that it had been restored, after the Hundred Days in 1815, by the power of the anti-Napoleonic allies and the defeat of France. What was of fundamental importance was a change of atmosphere, of psychology. For a vast number of Frenchmen the revolution had shattered, brutally and irrevocably, the myth of monarchy formerly so potent. The years between the effective collapse of the old régime in 1791 and the final catastrophe of Napoleon in 1815 had been too many and too eventful for a legitimist outlook to have survived except in the minds of a minority. Nothing is more difficult than to breathe life into a myth mortally wounded by events, as Charles X was to find. His efforts to revive the ceremonial and atmosphere of the old régime, after his accession to the throne on the death in 1824 of his more moderate elder brother Louis XVIII, were a total failure. They contributed largely to the revolution of 1830 which drove him into exile. In particular his efforts to revive ultra-catholicism as a prop for the throne, by savage legislation against blasphemy and sacrilege and by encouragement of the Jesuits, aroused bitter hostility. It is noticeable that in the fighting of July 1830 in Paris the fury of the insurgents was directed against religious establishments much more than against government ones. But well before

1830 the king's failure was evident. The resurrection at his coronation at Rheims in May 1825 of all the ceremonial of the old régime, and even of the Middle Ages, aroused ridicule as well as alarm among liberals and radicals.

Even more revealing was the plain evidence that popular belief in the quasi-divine character and powers of the ruler had evaporated. In 1774, when Louis XVI was crowned, 2,400 sufferers from scrofula came to Rheims to receive the king's magically healing touch, as their predecessors had done for centuries. In 1825, after his own coronation, Charles was persuaded reluctantly to revive the hallowed practice. But by then only a few fanatical legitimists still regarded it as more than a charade; and a mere 120 or so sufferers appeared in the hope of benefiting from it.[5] This fiasco was the last instance in Europe of a king attempting to act in this way. It can therefore be regarded as one of the great symbolic events in the continent's history. It was the last dying flicker of an idea which goes back far beyond written history, that of the king as a being tinged with divinity and endowed with supernatural powers. Monarchy was an absolute necessity to France after 1815. A moderate constitutional monarchy was the form of government which divided Frenchmen least; and neither a Napoleonic restoration nor a republic would have been tolerated for a moment by the other powers of Europe. But the mystique of monarchy, the 'divinity that doth hedge a king', was dead beyond recall. France, in the eighteenth century the pre-eminent example of a country passionately loyal to its rulers, felt this emotion during the nineteenth century much less vividly than Britain, which since the civil wars of the seventeenth century had seemed to most continental observers outstanding in its disloyalty and factiousness.

In the Habsburg empire and Prussia the monarchy was essential above all as a unifying force. In each case a state which was the result of the haphazard accumulation over generations of territories with no common interest or history was held together by the dynasty, and by the army and bureaucracy which that dynasty had built up around itself. In the Habsburg empire the disasters of the Napoleonic period had shown that the monarchy was the one institution able to act as a rallying point for the peoples of central Europe in face of the hurricane now blowing from France.[6] After 1815 the very backwardness of the empire, the weakness of its central institutions, the rejection of even very moderate proposals for change by the narrow-minded and slow-moving Francis II, consolidated the position of the dynasty. The emperor was not merely the symbol of unity but its active guardian and the only effective guarantee of its continuance. An illustration of this is the *Hausgesetz* of 1839 which gave him for the first time authority over all members of the Habsburg family and their private affairs. In Prussia the forces which threatened to tear the state apart were far less strong than in the Habsburg empire. Prussian rule was widely disliked in the Catholic Rhineland areas which fell under it in 1815. There was even a certain amount of separatist feeling there of which signs were to be visible in 1848. But this was never more than a nuisance; and in particular Prussia had to cope with only one national minority, the Poles, who were in general fairly well treated and thus quiescent during the generation after the Vienna settlement.

Monarchy was therefore a dominant institution in the Europe of the first half of the nineteenth century. Nowhere except in France was there a current of republican feeling able to offer a real threat to the status quo. 'We find everywhere', wrote Metternich in a famous 'Confession of Faith' in December 1820, 'the people praying for the maintenance of peace and tranquillity, faithful to God and their Princes, remaining proof against the efforts and seductions of the factious who call themselves friends of the people and wish to lead them to an agitation which the people themselves do not desire.'[7] This was not the view of an impartial observer; but it was in general a realistic one. Even in 1848 the revolutions in the smaller German states usually began by the revolutionaries declaring their loyalty to the ruling dynasty. The demonstrations of 13 March in Vienna which set off the revolution there, though very hostile to Metternich and one member of the imperial family, the Archduke Louis, were not at all directed against the emperor himself. His flight from the capital two months later produced consternation and strengthened the forces of conservatism in the city, such were the fear and dislike which the possibility of a republic aroused.[8]

This popularity of monarchy had at least two roots. In the first place rule by an individual was of all forms of government the one most comprehensible to the ordinary man, particularly as it was often still possible for the ruler to have some approach to personal contact at least with the people of his capital. Thus it was the custom of the king and queen of Saxony, for example, to dine in public on New Year's Day, and in Dresden there was free admission to the public galleries to see the great court balls given there during the winter season. Secondly, on a more intellectual and less instinctive level, it was widely accepted that only a hereditary monarch could rise above sectional interests and party quarrels and be guided by the permanent interests of the state and its people as a whole. 'Monarchy', wrote the Austrian theorist Lorenz von Stein in 1848, 'represents the autonomous power which alone is able, indeed which is forced by its very nature, to contain within itself the interests of all status groups and classes.'[9] Moreover, the argument often continued, the ruler, unlike a minister or politician, could not resign and thus run away from the results of his own actions. This gave him a uniquely strong sense of responsibility, and to that extent fitted him uniquely to wield supreme power. Such assertions reflected the very widespread continuing attachment all over Europe to the idea of a society which was paternalistic, even patriarchal. They also owed something to provincial and regional patriotisms, to the particularism which still played so great a role in the political life of many states. The indispensability of the monarchy in Prussia and the Habsburg empire as the one force capable of overcoming such forces has already been mentioned. The same factor is seen at its most extreme in the kingdom of the Two Sicilies. This was profoundly divided by the hostility between Sicily and the mainland. It was equally split within Sicily by the vicious centuries-old rivalry between Palermo and Messina which found expression in the terrible civil war begun in the island by the abortive revolution of July 1820 in the former. Such a state, totally devoid of all public spirit and sense of unity, could not exist except as a more or less absolute monarchy.

The monarchies of this period were not liberal or consciously progressive. They disliked changes which might weaken or threaten their own position. They made little overt appeal for popular support, and little effort to create truly representative institutions or to inform themselves systematically about movements of public opinion. Yet they were not reactionary. They made in general no attempt after 1815 to return to the state of things which had existed before 1789. They recognized, however tacitly and reluctantly, that the work of the French Revolution and Napoleon was beyond their power to undo, and that concessions must be made to the ideas and emotions which the last quarter-century had unleashed. The generation which followed Waterloo saw therefore in many parts of Europe a remarkable proliferation of written constitutions and an approach, however hesitant, to representative institutions. There were strict limits to the concessions of this kind which the great conservative monarchies were willing to make. The constitutions were granted by rulers and therefore at least in theory could be revoked by them. The legislative bodies which were set up in France, the Netherlands and some of the German states, were elected in every case by a very small segment of the population and had strictly limited powers. Nevertheless within its own narrow bounds this legitimist constitutionalism was usually genuine. In all the more socially and economically developed parts of the continent the ruler had now to recognize that there were limits to what he could do and boundaries, even if partly self-imposed ones, which he could not overstep.

Because most rulers were still traditional in their outlook and methods they were not as a rule oppressive, at least by the standards of the twentieth century. The Karlsbad decrees of 1819 by which the Austrian and Prussian monarchies attempted to control liberalism in Germany, particularly in the universities, were remarkably moderate in terms of the sophisticated oppressions and censorships of today. More striking is the fact that even the Neapolitan government in the very disturbed and uncertain years 1815–20 did not pronounce a single death sentence for a political offence. By their very nature the régimes of the age of Metternich could not but be respectful of traditional rights of all kinds; and when they were oppressive it was sometimes with fumbling good intentions. Thus the Third Department of the Imperial Chancery, the secret political police organization set up by the Tsar Nicholas I in 1826 which has become a byword for stupid and brutal repression, was staffed by men who were undoubtedly well-meaning. They tried to protect serfs both from their landlords and from local officials, urged improvement of the conditions of industrial workers and the abolition of brutal punishments in the army, and showed some awareness of the urgent need for economic development in Russia.[10]

The traditionalism of the European monarchies was matched by that of the administrative systems which served them. A society over most of the continent as yet little affected by modern industry and its repercussions had only limited need or desire for innovating officials or rational administrative institutions. The first half of the century saw some progress in organization and methods; but it was slow and half-hearted. The evolution of efficient organs of central government went on, but without any sense of urgency, while new institutions often existed for decades side by side with archaic ones. In France, which in this respect led Europe, ministries with more or less clearly defined functions had come into existence well before the revolution. In Russia they began to be created in 1802 and in Prussia in 1808; but in each case the impression of growing modernity which this statement gives is to some extent false. The ministries set up by Alexander I were often poorly organized, with real authority quite frequently not in the hands of their formal head.[11] Those of Prussia continued until 1849 to be governed by the collegiate principle, so widely accepted throughout Europe during the previous century, by which all important decisions were taken by groups or committees rather than by individuals. In the Habsburg administration, though some constructive changes took place (notably the creation of a ministry of finance in 1816) a clear division of the work of government along functional lines was not established until 1848. Until then, moreover, the collegiate principle held sway in Vienna as in Berlin. In Britain, after the creation of a secretaryship of state for war and colonies in 1794, no further post of this kind was set up until 1854, when a new office of secretary of state for the colonies was established. The fact that society was so often still traditional in structure and outlook meant in particular that there was as yet little effective demand for government regulation of economic life. In the few states whose economies had decisively broken with the past, moreover, above all Great Britain and later Belgium, *laissez-faire* attitudes now increasingly influenced thinking on social and economic problems and inhibited official initiatives or interference of any kind.

In the bureaucracies which administered the European states there was sometimes considerable change and improvement, most noticeably in Prussia. In 1809 the Prussian government introduced a system of examinations for candidates for official posts; and this was soon copied by several of the smaller German states. In Württemberg, for example, after 1819 no one could hold a government appointment without having passed the appropriate examination. Also throughout the German world there was now a consistent tendency to make the official secure in his post and even in his retirement. In the Habsburg empire retirement pensions had made their appearance in legislation of 1771 and 1781, though not until after the middle of the nineteenth century did they reach an adequate level. In Prussia a similar system was established in 1825. In Bavaria tenure of most official posts was made permanent during good behaviour as early as 1805, as part of the remarkable round of reforms inspired there by the influence of Napoleonic France; while in Prussia a systematic procedure for the dismissal or disciplining of delinquent officials was built up from the 1820s onwards, and in the Habsburg empire after 1848.

The existence of such safeguards was of the greatest importance; they meant that the official was no longer subject to arbitrary punishment or loss of his post. Moreover in no continental state during this period was it possible for him to be proceeded against in the courts for a civil wrong except with the consent of his superiors in the official hierarchy. This state of affairs, which owed much to the example set by Napoleon I in France, immensely strengthened the position of the official. If he achieved a minimum level of honesty and competence he was now over much of Europe secure, unassailable by political parties or even to a large extent by the law. Also bureaucracies were now more and more organized as fixed hierarchies, with the salary paid to each member dependent entirely upon his official rank. The not very uncommon eighteenth-century practice of paying an official of high social rank more than one of lower status doing the same work was now a thing of the past. Fixed hierarchies, fixed pay scales, fixed entry and disciplinary procedures, pensions, all meant that in some parts of Europe truly modern civil services were now coming into existence. The official could now feel as never before that his position had been given him by the state, not by a patron or even the monarch himself, and that his only loyalty was to the state. This can be seen in the formal establishment in Prussia in 1832 of the principle that he now served the state not the ruler, that he was appointed to the public service in general and not to a specific office, and must therefore be prepared to go wherever the interests of the state demanded.

In some parts of Europe developments of this kind aroused bitter opposition from vested interests. In others they were not attempted at all. In Russia, the most bureaucratic and at least on paper the most centrally controlled of all European states, legislation of 1809 demanded possession of appropriate educational qualifications or the passing of an examination before any official could be promoted above a certain rank in the bureaucracy; but this was deeply disliked by the privileged landowning class and came to nothing. Little in the way of new institutions or methods could be expected from Alexander I in his last years (though M. M. Speransky, the greatest of his ministers, was allowed to carry out significant economic and administrative reforms in Siberia in 1822); and even less from Nicholas I. The Russian empire was therefore left to stagger through much of the nineteenth century in the hands of a bureaucracy which had no standardized recruitment procedures and no common educational tradition or specialized training, which was underpaid, often corrupt and, at least in its lower ranks, bitterly hostile to any suggestion of new methods. Moreover since reform could come only from the tsar, or at least only with his agreement, even liberal reformers continually found themselves compelled to seek his favour and thus strengthen the autocracy which was largely responsible for the evils they wished to abolish. By comparison with the streamlined and scientific Prussian model the Russian administrative machine was until late in the nineteenth century a mere aggregate of officials rather than a true bureaucracy.[12]

In France, again, the great structure of centralized and rationalized administration perfected by Napoleon I, based on the twin foundations of the *conseil d'état* and the prefects, was left virtually untouched by his successors. Not until the coming of the Third Republic in the 1870s was it to undergo serious change.

Above all in Great Britain, economically and socially the pacemaker for Europe, the machinery of administration remained surprisingly backward. There, until after 1832, reform meant above all parliamentary reform. The 1830s and 1840s saw administrative progress, in some ways remarkable, as the state began to grapple, reluctantly and half-comprehendingly, with the unprecedented problems of an industrialized and highly urbanized society. The Factory Acts of 1833 and 1844 (and notably the new inspectorate which alone gave them practical force), the Poor Law Amendment Act of 1834 and the Boards of Guardians which it set up, the creation of county courts in 1846 and the passing in 1848 of the Public Health Act with its immense implications for the future of local government, were all facets of a confused but genuine effort to cope with new social problems. The appointment of a comptroller and auditor-general (though the office assumed its modern form only in 1866) began to make parliamentary control of public finance for the first time really effective. Nevertheless the machinery of administration remained, by French or Prussian standards, small and primitive. In particular it continued to rely heavily on unpaid and amateur administrators, whether in the traditional form of the justices of the peace or in the new one of the poor law guardians. Nowhere else in Europe was so small an area of life regulated, even indirectly, by the state.

Moreover throughout the continent administrative fossils, methods and attitudes normal under the *ancien régime* but increasingly hard to reconcile with an age of industrialism, nationalism and mass armies, lingered on. The payment of officials and even judges by fees rather than by salaries was slow to die. Even in the German states, in administrative efficiency the leaders of Europe, judges in Schleswig-Holstein were paid by fees until 1864. Payment in kind or by perquisites was also far from being completely a thing of the past in the first half of the nineteenth century.

If change were slow it was none the less real. One aspect of this was the continuing movement towards legal codification, very much a legacy from the eighteenth-century Enlightenment, which can be seen in the Civil Code of 1811 in Austria and in the *Polnoe Sobranie Zakonov* (Complete Collection of Laws) published in Russia in 1830. Another was that bureaucracies were beginning systematically to assemble on a hitherto unknown scale information about the resources at their disposal and the people they administered.[13] This development had two roots. First, as states and governments ceased to be the concern merely of rulers, information of this kind became more necessary: the greatest political achievement of the age was the creation and strengthening of nations, and for this knowledge of their resources more precise than in the past was increasingly demanded. Also greater mobility, social as well as geographical, created a new need for the individual to be able to prove his status and identity (which in a static society could normally be done simply by the testimony of his neighbours) by the production of some appropriate document.

But improved administrative structures and more plentiful and reliable official information are in themselves politically neutral; they say nothing about the essential nature of the régimes they serve. These régimes, in spite of the aids to efficiency with which some of them were equipping themselves, present during the generation after 1815 a picture overwhelmingly of conservatism, of political and social timidity. Their leaders often thought of change as inevitable and as impossible to halt once it had begun. This was the attitude of Metternich, and of many of the conservative opponents of the parliamentary reform of 1832 in Britain. In this sense they were believers in progress. But they believed with reluctance; and their belief bred in them a profound pessimism which does much to explain the astonishing ease with which they capitulated to their opponents in the spring of 1848.

The conservative régimes of 1815–48 were by no means free from opposition. Contemporaries were well aware that industrialization often dislocated or destroyed traditional social frameworks and caused real suffering. They were often uneasily aware that rapidly growing cities held potentially dangerous concentrations of impoverished workers against whom the comfortable and the educated might eventually have to defend themselves. 'The barbarians who threaten society', wrote a French newspaper in 1831, 'are not in the Caucasus or on the Steppes of Tartary: they are in the suburbs of our industrial towns.' But this threat was unfocused and long-term. On the political level existing regimes came under attack from two main directions. Firstly and less seriously they were challenged by the secret societies, usually with radical or at least vaguely liberal aims, which proliferated in the last years of the Napoleonic period and during the two decades after 1815. These groups, with roots partly in the masonic movement which had begun to develop in the early eighteenth century and partly in the traditions of the French Revolution, gained for a time widespread support in Italy, above all in Naples. The Carbonari, the most famous and important of them, had probably by 1820 somewhere between 300,000 and 600,000 Italian adherents and dominated the unsuccessful Neapolitan revolution of that year. In France its approximate counterpart, the *Charbonnerie*, had at its peak of activity in the last months of 1821 and the first half of 1822 perhaps 40,000 to 80,000 members. The social and intellectual environment of the period was favourable to organizations of this romantic, emotive, pseudo-religious kind. In the aftermath of a period of unprecedented conflict, with France and Italy in particular full of dismissed Napoleonic officials and unemployed officers with nothing to hope from the new régimes, some development of this kind was perhaps inevitable. In France, for example, the *Charbonnerie* relied for support mainly on the 15,000 or so half-pay officers, social flotsam left behind by the revolutionary and Napoleonic tide.

Nevertheless these secret societies and their attempts at revolution were never a serious threat to the status quo anywhere outside southern Italy, and perhaps not even there. They had no unity. The Carbonari, even within the Italian context, were no more than a series of roughly similar societies and not at all an organized group. These societies existed side by side with a bewildering array of others, some of them like the San Fedists and the Calderari strongly Catholic and conservative in outlook. Moreover they had no clear or unified programme. In Italy most of the Carbonari aimed vaguely at some form of national unity to be achieved by the expulsion of foreign rulers and accompanied by the establishment of some kind of constitutional monarchy; and a large majority of them expected this unity to take a federal form. This was a moderate programme. But side by side with it there existed much more revolutionary ideas, the work of a minority which was radical, egalitarian and anticlerical. In the same way in France the *Charbonnerie* had no unity of outlook: it was merely a miscellaneous collection of opponents of the restored Bourbon régime. Not merely Bonapartists but also Orleanists and Republicans could find a place in it. The spectre of the revolutionary secret society, organized on a European, not a merely national scale, continued to haunt courts and chanceries for a generation; and there was now taking shape a tradition of genuinely radical conspiracy, the work above all of the socialist propagandist Filippo Buonarotti, which was to make a real contribution to European and even world history.[14] But as a serious threat to the status quo the secret society, whether in the hands of the Carbonari or those of its most famous exponents, the Italian nationalist Mazzini or the French socialist Blanqui, was ineffective.

The second and more serious challenge to the conservative monarchies came from the growing pressure in many parts of western Europe for effective parliamentary government. This meant limitation of the power of kings and often also of established churches and landed aristocracies. It also tended to imply the grant of voting rights to at least a substantial proportion of the middle classes. An important stimulus to this current of feeling was provided by the example of Great Britain. Her power and wealth seemed to many continental observers (and to virtually all British ones) to be the result of the excellence of her constitution. She could therefore excite the admiration, on purely material grounds, of many people who were essentially lukewarm in their attitude to liberalism and constitutionalism. She appeared to show that these things could pay, and pay handsomely. On a rather different level she could appeal to more convinced liberals and constitutionalists because of the personal freedom enjoyed by her people and the relatively wide diffusion of political power among them. Even before the great parliamentary reform of 1832 there were about 440,000 men entitled to vote in Great Britain in a total population of 28 million; and after the changes of that year the number increased to about 717,000. In terms of the crude equation of democracy with voting rights and head-counting Britain was the most democratic country in Europe; after 1832 one adult male in five was enfranchised. For more than one reason, then, her influence on the growth of constitutionalism in

Europe was appreciable; the French constitutions of 1814 and 1830, those of the kingdom of the Netherlands in 1815 and of Belgium in 1831, all owed a good deal to British example.

Nevertheless it would be misleading to suggest that pressures for parliamentarism in Europe were exclusively or even mainly a result of British influence. They drew for support still more on the ideas released by the French Revolution, above all on that of popular sovereignty. Moreover Britain had no written constitution which could be easily copied and to which appeal could easily be made. To imitate her institutions it was first necessary to discover what they were and how they functioned – by no means an easy task. It was difficult therefore for the British political structure to be explicitly adopted as a model in the way that the Spanish constitution of 1812 was by the Italian revolutionaries in 1820, or that the Belgian constitution of 1831 was later by liberals all over Europe. Most of all Britain's suitability as a political model was limited by the fact that she was in many ways so un-European. Her society and government lacked, in varying degrees of completeness, three elements fundamental to nearly all continental states – a peasantry, a large centralized bureaucracy and an army recruited by conscription. 'We are', wrote an intelligent observer in the middle of the century, 'in our social life, arrangements, and institutions, much more distinct and widely apart from the Continental people, since the peace and settlement of Europe in 1815, than we ever were at any former period of our History.'[15] The comment had much force; and it meant that a good deal of British experience was simply irrelevant in a truly European context.

The victories won by parliamentarianism in Europe during this period were not negligible. But neither were they anything like complete. The French Constitutional Charter of 1814 set up an elected Chamber of Deputies side by side with a Chamber of Peers nominated by the king; but it was elected by a tiny minority even of that part of the nation which was literate and had some knowledge of public affairs. Only those who paid 300 francs or more in direct taxes (at that time about 90,000 Frenchmen in all, less than one in 300 of the total population) had the right to vote. In the whole island of Corsica there were only about sixty electors. Moreover the principle of monarchy by divine right was expressly reaffirmed in a long preamble to the constitution, while the king had the sole right to summon the two chambers and decide the length of their sessions, and could dissolve the Chamber of Deputies at his pleasure. After the revolution of 1830 which ended the rule of the direct Bourbon line some amendments were made. The much-resented preamble was suppressed and the Chambers were given the right to initiate legislation. More important, the tax qualification for the franchise was lowered by a law of April 1831 from 300 to

200 francs, so that by the time of the 1848 upheaval there were about 240,000 voters in France. Nevertheless this was still not a true parliamentary régime. Corruption and government influence still dominated elections, while in his later years Louis-Philippe, the representative of the younger Orleans branch of the royal family placed on the throne in 1830, became increasingly conservative and hostile to any proposal which tended to limit his power. The continuing narrowness of the franchise, the refusal of the vote to large numbers of educated, politically conscious and therefore potentially dangerous men simply because they were not wealthy, was resented with increasing bitterness. Very soon after 1830 the 'revolution stopped halfway' had begun to be seen as a disappointment, indeed a betrayal, by radicals and even liberals. Their criticism of the Orleans régime was to grow in vehemence for the next eighteen years.

If constitutional progress in France was disappointing, in most of the rest of western Europe it was even more so. The constitution of the kingdom of the Netherlands, drawn up in 1815 with great difficulty, was undermined from the beginning by the Belgian discontents and resentments which disrupted the new state fifteen years later. In Germany effective political change was largely non-existent. The constitution of the German Confederation established in 1815 and guaranteed by the powers at Vienna was rigid and essentially illiberal. The smaller German states were grossly over-represented in the diet which met at Frankfurt, while the ability of any member to veto changes in the structure of the confederation meant that progress either in the direction of liberalism within the German states or of closer union between them was very difficult. Article 13 of the constitution of the Confederation, it is true, provided for the establishment in each member-state of assemblies of estates, a limited gesture towards political progress. In some of its smaller members – Baden, Bavaria, Württemberg, Hesse and Weimar – constitutions rather like that of France, with some guarantees for civil rights and with weak representative bodies chosen on the basis of a very narrow franchise, were established in 1816–20. Again there were limited constitutional experiments in Saxony, Brunswick and Hanover in 1831–33. But neither of these little waves of constitution-mongering was important. Neither affected the only members of the Confederation which really mattered in European terms – Prussia and the Habsburg empire. In both of these what suggestions for constitutional change there were took the form of proposals to revive or strengthen provincial diets of a medieval kind based on the traditional social orders. Thus in the Habsburg territories Metternich helped the Tyrol and Galicia to recover their old provincial constitutions in 1816 and 1817 and promoted the creation of new diets in Carniola in 1818 and Salzburg in 1826, although all of these had very limited powers. About 1817 he even proposed, without result, the creation of a purely advisory central assembly (*Reichsrat*) made up of representatives of the different provincial diets. His hope was that the empire might develop as a federation of historic provinces, each ruled by essentially traditional institutions uncontaminated by the dangerous ideas of liberalism. In Prussia Frederick William III in a rescript of May 1815 promised that the provincial estates should elect delegates to a united assembly in Berlin; but nothing came of this in practice. A generation later his successor, Frederick William IV, allowed the diets of the different Prussian provinces to meet for the first time for several years; and in 1847 he attempted to satisfy growing demands for constitutional change by summoning to Berlin a united diet composed of representatives of these provincial bodies. Gestures of this kind in Vienna and Berlin were far from indicating a desire for a more modern political life. They expressed rather the wish to strengthen the moribund traditional and patrimonial political structures still normal in central Europe.

In one state liberal constitutionalism and parliamentary government did win a clear-cut victory. The Belgian constitution of 1831 became from the moment of its birth a model for liberals all over Europe. As an example of limited constitutional monarchy it was more influential, because clearer and more comprehensible, than that of Britain. Under it political power was still very narrowly diffused. It limited the franchise on the basis of wealth, so that in 1831 only 46,000 Belgians, not much more than 1 per cent of the total population, had the right to vote. But under it both houses of the legislature were elected and judges and clergy were independent of the government; while the declaration of rights which it embodied represented faithfully the tradition of 1789.

The harvest of successful constitutional progress yielded by the decades which followed Waterloo was therefore not a large one. Widespread adoption of parliamentary government, or even widespread lip-service to it, were still things of the future. Nevertheless there were powerful elements in the whole development of Europe during this period, and particularly in its intellectual development, which favoured change in a parliamentary direction.

For the first time the universities had now become, at least in some parts of the continent, centres of political radicalism. It would be possible to study in detail events in Paris in 1789–95 without realizing that the city possessed during these years the largest university in the world. Students as such played no role whatever in the great French Revolution. In 1848, on the other hand, they had great and sometimes disastrous influence on events in Vienna and to a lesser extent in much of Germany and Italy. Moreover by then the foundations had been laid for the most disruptive of all university radicalisms, that of Russia. Wherever in Europe during this period there was serious political commitment in the university world it favoured liberalism and radical political change. Thus in Italy the students of Turin and Pavia were implicated in the attempted revolution of 1821 in Piedmont-Sardinia; and the universities of Turin, Modena and Genoa were closed by the government in 1831 because of their hostile political attitude. Many régimes had therefore now to face a type of criticism and opposition which the rulers by divine right of the seventeenth century and the enlightened despots of the eighteenth had never encountered.

The political challenge offered by this new element in the situation was moreover increased by the creation of new universities in capital cities which went on during the early decades of the nineteenth century – in Berlin in 1808, in Madrid in 1821, in London from 1828 onwards. In Britain and France, each of which had, in very different ways, an active political life, university unrest was unimportant or non-existent. Both of these were politically mature and experienced in a way that made it impossible for much real power to be wielded, even in moments of crisis, by enthusiastic adolescents or theorizing professors. But throughout central Europe political *naïveté* and lack of experience were reflected in a tendency for hopes of change and faith in progress to be largely centred on the universities. 'The German thrones have been undermined by the German universities,' wrote a British observer in 1850. 'A social interest and influence independent of, and adverse to, the German governments, wielded by the universities in one direction, may be considered the great political power in Germany, and that which will ultimately triumph over all the existing institutions.'[16] This was an exaggerated estimate. The institutions which were in the end to dominate Germany, the Prussian monarchy, army and bureaucracy, were much tougher than he supposed. But he was quite right in seeing that in future it would be difficult for German political life to develop with success in any direction clearly opposed by the universities (twelve new ones were founded in 1871–1918). Acceptance of the Bismarckian Reich after 1871, and the Nazi one after 1933 owed a good deal to the support which these régimes received from the official leaders of German intellectual life.

Another sign of underlying political change, and one which again threatened the conservative status quo, was the slow emergence in some parts of the continent of a significant public opinion on political issues. This was the product of developing social communications. In particular it owed much to a growth of newspapers and periodicals and to a gradual increase in the amount of political information available to the ordinary man. In Germany the development of communications and in particular of the press had produced something like a national public opinion by the 1840s; and in Denmark the Press Society, founded in 1835 to protest against the censorship in force there, soon had branches throughout the country and was an important force in the growth of an effective liberal movement. In Italy, again, one historian has spoken of 'a veritable Risorgimento of journalism . . . before the third decade of the Restoration had passed'.[17] The scale of this development should not be exaggerated. There were probably only about 180,000 Italians in all in the 1830s who read journals of any kind. Even in the incomparably better-educated Germany a generation later only a fairly small minority of the population was effectively reached or influenced by the press.[18] But what mattered was the direction in which events were moving as much as the distance they had travelled. By comparison with the eighteenth century or even with the age of Napoleon political information was by the 1840s widely available in many parts of Europe. This was an important sign of the forces of change at work under the conservative political surface which most of the continent still presented; for this reason many governments looked on it with suspicion.

Here, as in so many respects, Britain differed from continental Europe. The absence of any censorship of the press, the limited effectiveness of government efforts to influence newspapers, the publishing from the 1830s onwards of official information in the form of Parliamentary Papers on a scale unequalled elsewhere in Europe, all marked her as distinctive. In no continental state, by contrast, were newspapers and periodicals free during this period. In France a law of October 1814 established a system of preliminary censorship and authorization for newspapers and period- icals; and control of the press was made significantly more severe in the early 1820s. The revolution of 1830 brought little relief; in 1830–34 over 500 press cases were heard in Paris alone (though a considerable majority of these resulted in acquittals) and one newspaper appeared in the courts well over 100 times. The extreme of official censorship and control was reached in Russia under Nicholas I, especially after the revolutions of 1848 and the alarm they aroused. It was claimed in 1850 that there were more officials engaged in censorship in Russia than there were books published there in a year.

In their fear and distrust of the press the rulers and governments of Europe during this period were, it may be argued, justified by events, particularly in France. The newspaper with a really mass circulation was still a thing of the future. In 1814 the *Journal des Débats*, by far the most widely read French paper, had a circulation of only about 23,000 while in 1830 the main Paris papers together printed only about 61,000 copies each day. In England *The Times* at the end of the Napoleonic wars had a circulation of little more than 5,000: heavy taxation (newspapers paid a stamp duty of fourpence each during the period 1815–35) helped to keep sales low. Over eastern and most of central Europe the whole social and intellectual environment – the weakness of the middle class, the unimportance of towns, mass illiteracy – made large circulations impossible even had newspapers been left free to aspire to them. Nevertheless the press was clearly a growing force in western Europe. Indeed in its implications this growth was the most fundamental though also the most informal of all political innovations there during this period. By 1836 total sales of London newspapers were not far short of three times what they had been in 1801, and in the decade 1836–45 the main Paris political dailies doubled their circulation, from 73,000 copies to 148,000.[19] In 1836 the greatest journalist of the age, Emile de Girardin, was able to set up in Paris *La Presse*, a paper sold more cheaply than any before, relying heavily on advertisements for revenue and aiming at the widest possible circulation. This was a real portent. For the first time in European history a newspaper achieved great commercial success by appealing to an audience which was not in any sense a social or intellectual élite. Fundamentally, growing circulations were a result of increasing wealth, rising intellectual standards and a widening of political interest and consciousness to embrace strata of the population hitherto little touched by them. They were also a matter of technical changes which made it possible to print newspapers much more rapidly and cheaply than ever before. Their production was now becoming an industry rather than as hitherto a craft. Until 1811, when the new Koenig press was introduced, the best rate of printing on a handpress was 200 copies per hour. By 1814, using steam power, 500 an hour was possible. By 1847 the most up-to-date press in France could print 16,000 an hour. By the later 1840s, moreover, the coming of wood-pulp paper was helping to reduce costs still further; and already the first of the great news agencies had been set up in Paris by Charles Havas in 1832. Some years later, in 1846 Charles Mitchell began publishing in London his *Newspaper Press Directory*, probably the first of its kind in Europe; and well before the middle of the century it had begun to be argued that a flourishing newspaper press was an essential sign of a free and flourishing society. 'The prevalence or scarcity of newspapers in a country', claimed a British writer in 1850, 'affords a sort of index to its social state. Where journals are numerous the people have power, intelligence and wealth; where journalists are few, the many are in reality mere slaves.'[20]

These developments had indirect repercussions on almost every aspect of life in western Europe. It was now becoming possible to disseminate information and ideas to the general public on a hitherto unheard-of scale. Much of this information was purely practical and utilitarian. The emergence of cheap periodicals with large circulations designed to satisfy an insatiable public appetite for useful knowledge was one of the features

of the 1830s in the more developed parts of western Europe. Thus in France
de Girardin, before setting up *La Presse*, had achieved great success from
1831 onwards with his *Journal des Connaissances Utiles*, which rapidly
amassed 130,000 subscribers. But it was obviously possible to present the
new mass reading public with less utilitarian and more heady fare.

The growth of such powerful engines of information or misinformation
inevitably had large political implications. In the two great western powers,
Britain and France, these differed considerably. In Britain the press was
undeniably important. Statesmen such as Canning, Brougham and Palmerston attached great importance to good relations with editors and
newspapers. But no British government during this period was brought
down by a press campaign: by 1815 newspapers were more and more
reflecting at least as much as creating political opinion in Britain. In France
the position was different. There conservative fears that an irresponsible
trouble-making press, given enough rope, might become a danger to political stability and public order, seemed fully justified. Throughout the
period 1815–48 newspapers which supported the government, any government, were always less popular in France than those which opposed it.
Worse still from the conservative point of view, these opposition papers
were more often than not factious, irresponsible and sometimes dangerously violent. In 1819–20 they accused the government and its head, the
Duc de Decazes, of at least moral responsibility for the murder by a
lunatic of the Duc de Berri, a member of the royal family. In 1825 one of
them began a very exaggerated campaign against clerical influences in the
government; while in 1829 they whipped up a widespread assumption
that the new Polignac ministry must be reactionary, though for months it
did nothing to justify this accusation. For weeks before an attempted
revolt in Lyons in 1834 local newspapers were inciting rebellion; and at
least one in Paris openly called on the other cities of France to follow the
lead of Lyons.[21]

All this criticism and opposition had important practical effects. In
January 1828 Villèle, perhaps the ablest chief minister of the Restoration
period in France, was driven from power largely by press opposition – the
first clear example of this in the history of Europe. The revolution of 1830
began with a protest of journalists (drawn up by the journalist-politician
Thiers in the offices of the liberal *National*) against the suppression of
press freedom by Charles X. The July monarchy was seriously weakened
by irresponsible opposition journalism of the type represented by de
Girardin; and the conservative equation of an uncontrolled press with
instability and revolution seemed to be confirmed by the extraordinary
efflorescence of newspapers in Paris after the fall of Louis-Philippe. In a
few months from the end of February 1848 as many as 450 appeared, a

high proportion for only a few days or even a single issue. By the middle of the century France was not merely the centre of the revolutionary impulse in Europe. She was also the possessor of the most irresponsible, factious and sometimes venal press which the continent could boast. Her experience does not altogether excuse the timidities of Metternich, far less the brutal intolerances of Nicholas I: but it does something to explain, even to justify, them.

In one way in particular governments during the generation after Waterloo revealed their fear of the dissemination of political information. Almost everywhere where quasi-representative institutions existed they showed a strong desire to prevent full reporting, or even any reporting at all, of parliamentary debates. In France under the Restoration newspapers which reported the proceedings of the Chambers laid themselves open to severe penalties. In Hungary Louis Kossuth created a sensation and made his name as a liberal leader merely by circulating in the later 1830s hand-written reports of debates in the House of Tables. Nevertheless in spite of restrictions and censorship it was impossible for governments lacking in self-confidence and the will brutally to repress, to prevent the trickle of political information hitherto available becoming, if not a river, at least in many cases a respectable stream. And the more copious the information available the stronger the case and the heavier the pressure for some broadening of the basis of political power. To some extent also the growth of newspapers had a direct effect of this kind as well as an indirect one. It allowed a few journalists and editors to achieve great influence and opened a narrow chink through which they might enter the citadel of the ruling establishment. The emergence in France of such a figure as Adolphe Thiers in the later 1820s is a case in point; and in 1829 an English commentator thought that 'the example of France will soon be contagious and we shall see men of high hopes and attainments conducting journals and obtaining, at last, through their literary character, seats in the House of Commons'.[22] It was no coincidence that many of the leading figures of the middle decades of the century – Kossuth, to some extent Cavour, perhaps even Louis Napoleon – first achieved prominence as journalists or writers on political questions.

THE REVOLUTIONS OF 1848

Over most of Europe the picture of general political stability which had prevailed since Waterloo was shattered irreparably by the revolutions of 1848. The unheard-of speed with which the revolutionary tide swept across the continent in the spring of that year seemed to bear out all the worst forebodings of pessimistic conservatives. The fragility of legitimate régimes and the weakness of the forces of order appeared only too clearly. By the same token the revolutions seemed to radical idealists everywhere to hold the promise not merely of new constitutions and methods of government but often of a new society, a new world.

The first outbreak, that in Palermo in January 1848, was essentially a separatist movement against rule from Naples, and hence untypical. Far more important was that in Paris at the end of February and the fall of Louis-Philippe which it at once produced. This let loose a tidal wave of upheavals all over Germany and central Europe. Early in March the rulers of all the small west and south German states were forced to make concessions to liberal demands – changes in the composition of their governments, the abolition of surviving feudal rights, alterations in systems of taxation. Above all in the middle of March Metternich, faced by popular hostility in Vienna and demands for his resignation from the Diet of Upper Austria, fled without resistance from the Austrian capital. Serious unrest had begun in Berlin a week earlier; and on 19 March Frederick William IV, after fighting between the citizens and his troops, gave way and withdrew the soldiers to their barracks. In the same extraordinary month the Hungarians proclaimed their autonomy. By the end of the year they had embarked on a war for outright independence which if they were victorious would mean the end of the Habsburg empire. In Italy the success of the revolutionary wave came very early. From the end of January onwards all the independent or quasi-independent states in the peninsula – Naples, Tuscany, Piedmont-Sardinia, the Papal State – were compelled to grant liberal constitutions; and in March there were successful risings against Austrian rule in Milan and Venice. Even on the eastern fringes of Europe similar impulses could be seen in movements in Bucharest against the Russian influence which had dominated the Danubian principalities for two decades, and in the Ionian islands against the British protectorate there.

The revolutionary storm did not burst from a completely clear sky. There had been signs, visible at least to the eye of hindsight, that an upheaval might be imminent. In Germany discontent with the structure of the Confederation, and frustrated nationalism, were by the 1840s more powerful than ever before. Joint conventions of German liberal leaders had met every year since 1839. In 1847 Prince Leiningen, with the support of Prince Albert, the husband of Queen Victoria, had presented to Frederick William IV one of a number of schemes put forward in these years for the reform of the Confederation. At the beginning of 1848 the Prussian minister Radowitz had opened negotiations in Vienna to this end. In Italy Pope Pius IX, elected in June 1846, was far from being a real liberal and even further from being a genuine nationalist. But he was at least prepared to contemplate change in the way his own territories were governed; and this stimulated throughout the peninsula the hopes of enemies of the status quo. The issue by him of a new press law in March 1847 meant that by the beginning of the following year about 100 newspapers and periodicals were being published in Rome. These were later to play an important role in making Pius's position there untenable. The establishment in October 1847 of a small indirectly elected representative Consulta was a gesture in the Papal State towards liberal constitutionalism all the more striking for the completely unexpected quarter from which it came. Moreover the new Pope's opposition in August of that year to the strengthening of the Austrian garrison in Ferrara meant that all over Italy he at once became identified with the national cause. In France criticism of Louis-Philippe and his régime in the press had reached by 1847 a pitch of irresponsible virulence hitherto unequalled, one which astonished many foreign observers.

Most of these portents of change were not new. For all of them except a quasi-liberal Pope precedents could be found in the 1830s and 1840s. Few members of the ruling classes of Europe realized at the beginning of 1848 that they might be on the brink of a precipice. Even in France the great liberal Alexis de Tocqueville was laughed at when at the end of January, in a famous speech in the Chamber of Deputies, he warned of the imminence of savage class struggles for political and even more economic power.[23] The 1848 upheavals overthrew opponents who in the main did not expect or truly understand them: this was a major reason for their rapid and delusive success.

The causes of their outbreak and short-lived victory inevitably varied considerably in different parts of Europe. The original eruption in Palermo in January, the crucial one in Paris at the end of February and that in so remote a capital as Bucharest which broke out in June, all sprang from very different roots. Nevertheless it is possible to make some generalizations which are valid in many at least of this wide variety of contexts. Economic strain undoubtedly played a large part in preparing the way for the outbreaks. Since 1845 much of Europe had suffered a series of bad, sometimes disastrous, harvests. The failure of the potato crop in many areas in 1845 was followed by a generally bad cereal harvest in 1846. The high food prices which resulted pressed heavily not merely on the very poor but also on the ordinary peasant or artisan. Often they pushed him over the frontier, all too easily crossed, which separated a customary and therefore tolerated standard of living from destitution. Expensive food, by absorbing a growing fraction of his already barely adequate purchasing power, inevitably reduced the demand for manufactured goods and meant a serious growth in industrial unemployment. In this way the events of 1845–47 constituted an economic crisis of the typical old régime type.

The social repercussions of these economic strains are clear. They are visible in a growth in the number of beggars and vagabonds (in Bavaria and the Palatinate, for example, the size of this group almost doubled in 1845–47) and in the frequency of food riots (the potato riots of April 1847 in Berlin are a good example). In some cases they helped to generate protracted social struggles in the great European cities, as in the serious disturbances which afflicted the Italian port of Leghorn for about a year from September 1847 onwards.[24] Sometimes suffering intensified hostility to the power-driven machinery which, in the short run, increased misery by reducing employment. In Vienna the demonstrations of the evening of 13 March 1848 and of the following day, which began the revolution in central Europe, were accompanied by much machine-breaking. More constructively, poverty and unemployment underlay the marked growth of emigration to North America from some parts of Europe, notably from western Germany, in 1845–47.

Yet to see the revolutions of 1848 merely or even mainly as the outcome of economic forces, something to be explained in terms of unemployment and prices, would be an untenable oversimplification. The economic situation of 1845–47 certainly provided an important part of the background to the revolutions. It helped to shake still further the prestige and self-confidence of existing régimes in many parts of Europe and to make the ordinary worker, often himself essentially unpolitical, willing to aid in their downfall or at least to see it without regret. But there is no clear correlation, either in time or space, between extreme economic suffering and revolutionary political activity. By the spring of 1848 the worst of the economic crisis was over and food prices were falling. In Germany they were already approaching the level of 1844 and a marked recovery of industrial production and employment was beginning there. Much the same was true in most other parts of Europe. The revolutions thus took place against a background of generally improving economic conditions – a fact which blunted social antagonisms and strengthened the conservative forces almost everywhere.

Moroever the areas which had suffered worst in 1845–47 were not necessarily those in which revolutionary action and ideals were strongest in 1848. Even leaving aside the special case of Ireland, where the potato famine and resulting epidemics produced from 1845 onwards suffering on a scale which virtually obliterated the possibility of revolution, there are many illustrations of this. Thus in the Dutch provinces of the Netherlands a working class largely dependent on the potato suffered greatly from 1845 onwards. In some areas the number of those receiving poor relief grew by 50 per cent in 1844–47. There was the inevitable increase in begging and theft (notably thefts of food). In 1847 the population of the kingdom of Holland fell – the only year since its formation in 1839 when this has happened.[25] Yet all this produced no significant political repercussions. Again in Belgium, which as the most industrialized part of continental Europe was particularly vulnerable to economic fluctuations, 87 per cent of the potato crop was lost in 1845 and the price of bread more than trebled in the following year. In Flanders there was suffering on a scale unseen since the Middle Ages; in Bruges the mortality was so appalling that burials took place only at night for fear lest their number should terrify those who survived. Yet though there was much petty disorder (riots, attacks on bakeries and grain convoys) no effective impulse towards revolution showed itself.[26] Even in France or Germany the areas of maximum suffering did not coincide with those of most intense revolutionary activity. Thus in the French textile centre of Roubaix half the population was living on public charity in the early months of 1848; and in the neighbouring city of Tourcoing the number of workers in employment had fallen by over half in the previous three years.[27] Yet neither saw any serious attempt at revolutionary action.

Moreover it is important to remember that the strains of the years 1845–47 fell most heavily on the handicraft worker, who suffered in general a good deal more than workers in the new factories. The growth of large-scale industry, of factories and power-driven machinery, was therefore largely irrelevant to the events of 1848 over most of Europe. The revolutions were overwhelmingly urban, indeed metropolitan. They were revolutions in Paris rather than in France, Berlin rather than Prussia, Vienna and Prague rather than the Habsburg empire, Naples, Rome, Milan and Venice rather than Italy. Except in backward Hungary none of the movements of this year had real roots in the countryside. Yet modern factory-based industry was still the exception in the capitals, indeed in all the great cities, of continental Europe. The modern industrial town was beginning to show itself. But of the few examples of it yet in existence many were still relatively small (Roubaix, Tourcoing, Mulhouse and Le Creusot in France; Seraing in Belgium; Essen in Germany) and none of them played a role of significance in 1848. Most important of all there was hardly any capital in which factory workers were a large fraction of the population. In Paris, now well established as the centre of the revolutionary impulse in Europe, there were in 1848 about 350,000 industrial workers; but only a very small minority of these were in factories. Moreover the artisan tended, in France as everywhere else, to have more education and more active political consciousness than the factory-hand. It was workers in traditional handicraft trades who formed the backbone of political and social radicalism in the French capital in 1848: tailors and workers in the building trades were particularly prominent.[28] In Vienna,

where socialist ideas were unknown, the most extreme working-class radicals were usually not factory-hands but journeymen embittered by the
growing competition of factory-produced goods. To see the upheaval of
1848 therefore as the work of a proletariat driven to despair by the inhu-
man demands of the new large-scale industry is an error.

If then the rapid spread and brilliant short-lived success of the 1848
revolutions cannot be explained in simple economic terms, in what terms
can they be explained? A single factor in the situation more than all others
combined, holds the answer to this question. It is the weakness, the blindness, above all the lack of self-confidence often carried to the pitch of
absurdity, of the régimes which collapsed, virtually without an attempt to
defend themselves, in the spring of that year. There is no more astonishing
series of events in the history of modern Europe than this collective and
cumulative failure of nerve on the part of monarchies and governments
which were, in a physical sense, fully able to control events and repress the
sometimes almost trivial movements before which they hastened to abase
themselves. They showed a remarkable lack of ability either to negotiate
with the popular movements which now faced them or to crush them
effectively.

Paris is the best known and most important case. There the decision to
proceed with a political demonstration forbidden by the government, the
crucial decision which led to the collapse of the July monarchy, was taken
by no higher or more representative authority than a small group of radicals meeting in the office of an unimportant student newspaper, the *Avant-
Garde*, on 21 February. Only after the king had abdicated, on the 24th,
did the more moderate and better-known radicals begin to play a role;
and even then the direction which events took was to some extent a
matter of pure chance. The seven republican members of the Chamber of
Deputies who were to form a hastily chosen provisional government (as
soon as it was clear that there would not be a regency until Louis-Philippe's
young grandson was old enough to rule) at once hurried off to the Hôtel
de Ville, the traditional centre of revolutionary Paris. There they met
crowds who agreed to accept the seven only if the chief editors of the two
main republican newspapers, the *National* and the *Réforme*, were added
to the new government. The crowds also demanded, as a guarantee that
serious attention would be given to social problems, the admission to
the government of the socialist Louis Blanc, famous as the author of
L'organisation du travail (1840) and the leading exponent of the idea of
national workshops to relieve unemployment, and of a worker, Albert. In
this haphazard way chance, personal factors and mob pressures gave
France, after an unexpected and unplanned revolution, a government completely lacking in unity and without any agreed programme.

The opposition to Louis-Philippe had grievances which were genuine so far as they went – the narrow franchise, corruption and government influence in elections to the Chamber of Deputies, illiberal press laws, a generally uninspiring and unsuccessful foreign policy – but these were too limited to generate the deep and sustained popular hostility which can destroy almost any government. France at the beginning of 1848 was bored and unenthusiastic rather than outraged. That a régime still apparently well entrenched in power should surrender so easily in the face of opposition so lacking in almost everything but the ability to make a noise can be explained only in terms of personalities. Louis-Philippe in February 1848 had about 40,000 soldiers at his command in the capital. But the king was unwilling to save his throne at the cost of possibly large-scale bloodshed; and this was decisive. There were other personal factors involved. In particular Louis-Philippe knew that his régime was disliked by the most vocal sections of the population of the capital, and that the National Guard was unreliable. Nevertheless what happened in Paris during the crisis of 22–24 February can be understood only in terms of an old man, humane, timid and unwilling to struggle for his position, surrendering almost without resistance to forces which he could easily have repressed had he been willing to fight.

The same timidity and lack of self-confidence can be seen in the other great capitals which succumbed to the revolution. In Vienna the imbecile Emperor Ferdinand III was in no position to master or even understand events, while Metternich took a grossly defeatist view of the strength of the revolutionary forces throughout Europe. Thus on 1 March he wrote that the continent was now where it had been in 1791 and 1792 and asked, 'Can 1793 fail to follow?'[29] The analogy was a false one, as events were clearly to show; but the old statesman, the victim of the pessimism which he himself had been propagating for a generation or more, fled without a struggle from the Austrian capital. Nor was this defeatism peculiar to himself; it had infected many of his subordinates. In Venice, notably, the Austrian officials and military commanders were totally defeatist about the position and the possibility of maintaining their hold on the city. In Berlin the erratic and unbalanced Frederick William IV completely lacked the tenacity and ruthlessness needed to cope successfully with the situation. Here also a humane timidity, an unwillingness to shed blood, was for the time being dominant. The result was that the rising of 18 March forced him into surrender to rebellion and a series of unplanned and humiliating concessions – freedom of the press, the calling of the Landtag, a responsible ministry of liberals. 'The Crown itself', said the young Otto von Bismarck, 'has thrown the earth upon its coffin.'[30]

In France, in Austria, in Prussia, the rulers and the régimes had ample physical resources with which to combat the revolution. 'I am strong enough to take Berlin,' said General von Prittwitz, the military commandant of the Prussian capital, 'but that means more fighting. What can we do after the King has commanded us to play the part of the vanquished? I cannot attack without orders.'[31] This remark applied, to varying extents, in all the capitals which succumbed to the revolution. The monarchs and their governments had not been vanquished. But they chose to believe that they had been. Their eclipse was the result above all of a simple loss of nerve; and this was obvious to any clearsighted contemporary. The British diplomat Stratford Canning, for example, travelling to Constantinople by way of the German capitals, summed up his impressions of central Europe by saying that 'the prevalent weakness of almost every constituted authority is of a moral rather than a material character'.[32] An elderly gentleman in Paris, an imbecile in Vienna, an unbalanced romantic in Berlin, a well-meaning apparent liberal in Rome, proved quite unable to ride the storm. The revolutionary tide seemed for a time irresistible; but this was merely because no one was resisting it.

This diagnosis is borne out by the speed with which most of the movements of 1848 collapsed once the forces of resistance recovered their nerve and began to act effectively. In Paris the more radical wing of the revolutionary movement was crushed in the savage 'days of June'. By November 1848 a republican constitution had been established there which, though not in itself conservative, in effect consolidated the victory already won by the moderates. In Berlin Frederick William IV, cured of the fears of March, had regained his position, with the help of the army, by November. In Vienna the conservatives, again with the essential help of the army, had reasserted themselves at the end of October. Mainly as the result of this defeat of the revolution in the two great German capitals the German national representative body, the 'Frankfurt Parliament', which had emerged in the spring of 1848 and been engaged ever since in drawing up a constitution for a united Germany, had lost most of its influence by the end of the year. In Lombardy Austrian power had been reasserted in August, after a war with Piedmont-Sardinia, though Venice did not fall for another year. In Naples the revolution, one of the first to break out, was also one of the first to collapse. It had been crushed as early as May 1848. In Rome the revolutionaries, led by Mazzini and Garibaldi, held out until the beginning of July 1849; while in Hungary the nationalists were finally crushed only in August of that year, and then only because of the intervention of a large Russian army on the side of the Habsburgs. In other words revolution, victorious or apparently so almost everywhere in March 1848, was defeated or weakened almost everywhere six months later, and completely crushed by the end of the summer of 1849.

The essential reason for the rapid defeat of the 1848 upheavals is clear. Since they were in most cases a kind of confidence trick based on the weakness and timidity of the existing régimes in Europe, their fundamental weakness became clear as soon as they had to shoulder real responsibilities and meet real opposition.

This weakness was, at the deepest level, a social one. Except to some extent in Paris the leadership of these movements, and their programmes and objectives, were completely middle class. Written constitutions of a liberal kind, guarantees for freedom of speech and of the press, parliamentary government, representative bodies elected on a widened franchise perhaps even extending to all adult males, the replacement of professional standing armies by citizen militias – these were the typical demands of the middle class revolutionaries. But to the artisan or the peasant, struggling with more immediate problems of low wages, land hunger or unemployment, such ambitions meant much less than to the urban professional man or intellectual. Perhaps the best, and certainly the most frequently quoted, illustration of the middle class character of so much of the revolutionary leadership of 1848 is the Frankfurt Parliament in Germany. Of its rather more than 600 members all save a handful can be classified as professional men or intellectuals. It included 106 professors, 223 lawyers, 118 officials, mostly of high rank, 16 army officers (all from small west German states), and by contrast precisely one peasant (a Pole from Silesia). This highly educated membership did not, perhaps, impede its work so much as is often alleged. The accusation that the Frankfurt professors wasted time in arguing constitutional niceties and debating abstract ideas instead of acting is easily pressed too far. But it did mean that the assembly was not and could not hope to be representative of the German people as a whole. Quite apart from any consideration of equity, its effectiveness was reduced by the fact that there were simply too many important forces in German society (the landed nobility for example) which were not adequately represented in it. In France too the socially limited and politically cautious nature of the leadership thrown up by the revolution can be seen, at least after its early stages. The Constituent Assembly elected at the end of April had among its 880 members about 325 lawyers, 160 landowners and 95 officers or retired officers. Only 34 of its members could be considered in any sense working class; and they showed themselves far from radical in practice.

It would be a mistake to put too much weight on figures of this kind. No nineteenth-century representative body reflected directly in its composition that of the society which it claimed to represent; for that matter none does so today. Nor was it necessarily the case that a revolution led by the middle classes must be moderate or lacking in dynamism. The great outbreak of 1789-94 in France had been the work of a middle class and urban minority unrepresentative of Frenchmen in general. But the social background and above all the attitudes of many of the revolutionaries of 1848 destroyed any slight chance they had of arousing true mass support. In 1789 the collapse of the old régime in France had been brought about in part by a great though unorganized peasant revolt. What remained of feudalism there was abolished *de facto* from below before this victory was enshrined in legislation. Nothing at all comparable happened in 1848. In France the revolution was not the work of the peasant and did little for him. Indeed, he was seriously antagonized when the new republican government, in grave financial difficulties, tried to raise revenue by increasing all direct taxation. To the peasant it seemed that he was being made to pay to keep the workers of Paris in idleness in the ill-fated National Workshops; and 50,000 soldiers (more than were used in the June days in the capital) were needed to suppress the unrest which his resentment produced. In the Habsburg empire the manifesto of 11 April which promised the peasant freedom from all surviving feudal services and dues in fact decreased his interest in the revolution; he now began to wish merely for the re-establishment of law and order. Nor did the Frankfurt Parliament in Germany do enough for the peasant to gain his support. It abolished feudal dues arising from the personal subservience of the peasant to his lord; but it tried to maintain those that could be seen as a normal form of property right. Nowhere did the tiller of the soil, almost everywhere in continental Europe the largest single element in the population, play an active revolutionary role in 1848.

The social limitations of the movements of that year and the extent to which they were 'revolutions of the intellectuals' are seen again in the important role often played in them by students. In Vienna the Academic Legion, a disorganized and badly disciplined body which soon numbered about 5,000, had an important share in the confused events of the spring and summer. The upheaval of 26 May, the most radical of this very turbulent year in the Austrian capital, was set off by an unsuccessful attempt to disband it; and at the German student congress held at Eisenach in September the Viennese representatives found themselves lionized as heroes. In Berlin teachers and students of the university, which temporarily suspended its courses, played a significant role in the March revolution and also formed their own armed corps. In Hesse during the same month the students of the University of Giessen put themselves at the head of the insurgents. In June 1848 Field Marshal Radetzky, the commander of the Habsburg forces in Italy, wrote contemptuously of 'the intelligentsia of our time, the law-giving bands of students with their bought communist allies, the workers'. That young men so inexperienced and often so irresponsible were allowed, even by default, to wield power in this way shows both the weakness of the old régimes which they helped to overthrow and the even greater weakness of those which replaced them.

The lack of mass social backing for these revolutions was both a cause and a result of the fact that, except among the radicals in Paris, they had little social or economic programme. Concentration on constitutional and political issues, characteristic of European liberalism before 1848, meant that in that year the liberals were unable and unwilling to bid for mass support by adopting radical economic and social policies. This is again seen most clearly in Germany. The economic programme of the Frankfurt liberals, in so far as they had one, was based on liberty of the classical individualist kind (freedom of trade, of enterprise, etc.) which the great British economists had now done so much to make the norm in intellectual discussion. But this attitude was quite unacceptable to most German workers, who still thought in traditional guild terms and were still organized on a traditional workshop basis. A congress of representatives of guilds and handicraft industries was held in Frankfurt in July. Far from taking the liberal view it denounced freedom of enterprise and demanded government action to maintain protective guild restrictions. It even went so far as to envisage the creation of a hierarchy of guild councils which might form a kind of federal industrial government side by side with the political one which seemed to be in embryo. There was thus not merely a difference but a head-on collision between the economic ideas of the Frankfurt liberals and those of the ordinary urban worker.

Given their own position, education and interests it is unfair and unrealistic to imagine that the German liberals could have acted otherwise. Nevertheless their attitude to economic life was a serious weakness in their position. In particular it allowed intelligent conservatives to see that it might be possible to outflank and outbid them by a programme of paternalist economic and social change carried out from above, by monarchs and their ministers. The Prussian statesman Radowitz urged Frederick William IV to check the revolution by just such methods; and in February 1849, when royal power had been securely re-established, there was an effort to halt by legislation the movement towards economic freedom and to bolster up the guild system in Prussia. This combination of political reaction with paternalist economic policies (particularly in the form of concessions to the peasants) was also soon to be seen in several of the smaller German states, and even in southern Italy. There 1848 saw the emergence of widespread peasant discontent centred on demands for land redistribution. Such a movement of the countryside could not but embarrass the liberal leadership of the revolution, centred on the city of Naples. For this very reason it was encouraged by royalists anxious to put the liberals between the two fires of monarchical conservatism and agrarian radicalism. The peasant rebels were even equipped with Bourbon flags (though red emblems, a sign of half-assimilated socialist influence, were also prominent among them).[33] Later, in April 1849, Radetzky urged that 'to exalt the poorer classes of the peasantry' should be a major objective of the restored Habsburg régime in Lombardy-Venetia.

Almost everywhere, then, the revolutions suffered from the narrowness of their social base. In particular the dislike felt by the peasant for educated urban revolutionaries who pursued objectives which he did not understand and was not expected to understand showed itself almost everywhere. For a moment one of the greatest of the submerged social resentments of the eighteenth and first half of the nineteenth centuries, that of the country-side for the increasingly dominant and apparently exploiting town, showed itself with unusual clarity.

But the hopes of 1848 were dashed also by many other factors. The revolutions suffered from their own lack of unity; from the poor quality of their leadership and its frequent lack of realism; and from the fact that there was in 1848 no international war of the sort which, by intensifying the popular sense of crisis, might have strengthened the position of polit-ical radicals as had happened in France in 1793. Most of all, perhaps, they were doomed by the general success of the old régimes in retaining the loyalty of their armies.

The divisions of the revolutionaries were of at least three different types. The first, and intellectually the least profound, was that which arose from the survival in Germany and much more in Italy of particularist feelings and traditions in the different states. These raised an important obstacle in the way of the national unity which all German revolutionaries and most Italian ones desired. They therefore helped to ensure that in this respect the revolutions were a failure. In Germany particularist resistance to national unity centred above all on the unwillingness of many Prussians to see their state, which they had learned to think of as the finest expres-sion of the German spirit, merged in a united Germany, at least in the way which the Frankfurt Parliament hoped for. 'The colours black, red and gold [those of the proposed German national state] shall not supplant my cockade, the honoured colours of black and white [those of Prussia],' said Frederick William on 23 March to a group of delegates from south Ger-many who had hoped to persuade him to become ruler of a united nation. Many of his subjects shared this attitude, if they did not express it so flamboyantly. The result was bitter rivalry between the national assembly in Frankfurt and the Prussian Landtag in Berlin. Could two parliaments, one drawing up a constitution for Germany the other creating one for Prussia, coexist? Should a Prussian constitution be drawn up before one for Germany as a whole, with the resulting risk of tying the hands of the legislators in Frankfurt? Many of the latter gave a negative answer to both questions. 'It is highly dangerous that a constitution is being framed in Prussia,' said Robert Blum, one of the most radical of the Frankfurt liberals, on 27 May 1848, 'for once it is completed we are no longer free.' By November another, Rumelin, was arguing that 'a complete victory for the Berlin assembly would be dangerous for the work of this assembly', and that the Prussian Landtag was 'a dangerous rival that by rights should never have convened'.[34]

The rivalry between the two bodies did not confine itself to speeches. It showed itself repeatedly in practice. Thus in June 1848 a provisional government for the new united Germany was formed, with the Habsburg Archduke John as Regent, without even the pretence of consulting Prussia. A proposal in the draft national constitution that the German states should give up the right to separate diplomatic representation in foreign capitals and put their armed forces under the control of the new national government aroused violent opposition in Prussia, not merely from conservatives but from public opinion as a whole. Equally serious, Prussia ostentatiously showed her independence of Frankfurt by signing in August an armistice with Denmark, thus ending for the time being the war between them which had broken out a few weeks earlier over the claims of the Germans of Schleswig and Holstein. Welcomed in Berlin, the agreement seemed in Frankfurt a betrayal of the national cause: the assembly there made the futile gesture of refusing to accept it. The promulgation of a new Prussian constitution in December 1848 was also bitterly opposed from Frankfurt. Though by April 1849, with its power clearly ebbing, the assembly there had been forced to make an unsuccessful offer of the German crown to Frederick William IV, there was still a strong feeling among its members that if he became ruler of Germany the unity of Prussia, and hence her ability to dominate the new national state, ought to be weakened. (For example by providing that her representatives in the new German parliament should be elected by the diets of her different provinces and not by a central Prussian assembly.) The Frankfurt parliamentarians did not want the revolution in Berlin to be crushed. But they wished it to be successful only within manageable limits and if possible only through the help it received from Frankfurt and from the German national and liberal movement.

In Italy particularism had a strength and an edge of real bitterness generally lacking in Germany. Moreover there was no effort in 1848 to create any national Italian representative body. The result was that particularist conflicts crippled the revolutions in the peninsula. Italy was not merely divided by the long history of separatism in the country and by the still powerful traditional loyalties which centred on the different

Italian states and their rulers. She was also plagued by the fact that there were deep divisions between different parts of what were formally political unities. In Sicily there was ferocious separatism and violent rejection of rule from Naples. In the Legations, in the north-east of the Papal State, local patriotism, centring on Bologna rather than Rome, weakened what little unity the Papal State possessed. In the mainland cities of Venetia (Treviso is a good example) there was centuries-old resentment against Venice, their conqueror in the later Middle Ages. Most fundamental of all, the peninsula was already divided by the social and economic gap between north and south which was in the future to become the most intractable of all its problems.

Nevertheless these difficulties sprang, both in Germany and in Italy, from traditions and the emotions these had accumulated around them, from regional and sometimes even personal rivalries (for example between followers of Mazzini and those of the great local revolutionary, Manin, in Venice) as much as from conflicts of ideology. On a deeper level two really profound conflicts of ideas can be seen in 1848: that between moderate advocates of an essentially political revolution and radical supporters of one which would also be social; and that between the irreconcilable presuppositions of liberalism and nationalism.

Revolutionaries who dreamed of an upheaval which would remould society and not be confined to constitution-making could be found in many of the great cities of Europe. But only in Paris were they powerful enough to have any decisive influence on events. There the way in which Louis Blanc and Albert had been forced into the provisional government showed the existence in the city of a significant force of this kind; and until it was crushed in the street-fighting of 22–26 June it generated middle class fear and dislike. The prophecies of de Tocqueville, which had seemed a subject for laughter in January, had now been completely justified. The inevitable result was bitter division between moderate and more extreme revolutionaries. 'The republic of February', complained the moderate republican Garnier-Pagès, 'is no longer a refuge; it is an arena to which each of us comes to cut the throats of the others.'[35] In Vienna the course of events was somewhat similar, though less spectacular and with less far-reaching results. There the uneasy alliance between the workers of the suburbs and the students and middle class liberals of the city was decisively broken by the crushing, on 19–23 August, of disturbances provoked by the efforts of the government to reduce the rate of pay for those employed on public works. A 'social republic' had probably no chance in France in 1848 and certainly none elsewhere in Europe. In a continent which was still so largely agrarian and in which military power lay still in the hands of the conservatives it was no more than a noble and pathetic dream. Yet the forcible suppression of the dream in the 'days of June' was a great event in European history. It completed the disillusionment with middle-class leadership of the politically conscious working class of Paris, the vanguard of European social radicalism, and thus helped to pave the way for the greater violence and more spectacular failure of the Commune in 1871. It added emotional weight to the new political vision which was just beginning to take shape, that of the industrial proletariat as the standard-bearer of a new age, defeated, suppressed, but in the end unconquerable and inevitably triumphant.

The intellectual and above all emotional conflict between liberalism and nationalism and the triumph of the latter, one of the great lessons of modern history, was first clearly exposed in 1848, above all in the German world. Until the failures of that year, it had been possible to believe that the triumph of the national idea, the freeing of the nations from a foreign yoke and all artificial constraints, would by some never-explained alchemy usher in an age of international peace and harmony. The newly freed peoples, in obedience to their own nature, which was at bottom good and virtuous beyond the possibility of corruption, would treat one another as brothers and equals. This was the greatest of the dreams of Mazzini; but it was shared by many other idealists. Garnier-Pagès produced in the first stages of the revolution one of the best statements of this delusion. When the hour of liberty and independence struck, he wrote,

there will be no wars on questions of partition, domination, nationality and influence. No more weak and strong, oppressed and oppressors. Every country, free to enjoy its liberties and to live its own life, will hasten to join the life and liberty of all. . . . No masters will decide on peace and war, no millions will be squandered irresponsibly, and no streams of blood will flow any more. The representatives of peoples, arbiters of common destinies, will freely submit themselves to the general law, which will be equal for all. . . . The reign of peace, order and harmony will be founded. We are marching towards it with mighty steps.[36]

The events of the year of revolutions showed how hollow, even dangerous, such expectations were. In both Vienna and Frankfurt liberals, faced with a challenge to the interests of their national group, abandoned or compromised their political principles in order to repel it. In Vienna the revolutionaries had no intention of breaking up the Habsburg empire into national states. An end to its rule by German bureaucrats was to them a disastrously retrograde step as well as one fatal to their own interests. All of them bitterly resented Czech claims to autonomy and the refusal of the Czech revolutionaries to admit that Bohemia was part of the German world by sending representatives to Frankfurt. Their attitude to Italian national claims was at first more hesitant; but when Sardinia-Piedmont declared war on the Habsburg empire on 23 March these hesitations vanished. The Austrian army in northern Italy was quickly given the support of a volunteer corps formed for the purpose in the Austrian capital. The attitude of the Viennese revolution to the Hungarians also became steadily more hostile as the strength of the demand for Hungarian independence became impossible to ignore. The result of all this was that Vienna saw without regret the crushing of the revolution in Prague in June 1848 by the artillery of Prince Windischgrätz and found pleasure later in the victories of Field Marshal Radetzky and the imperial army in Italy. The movements of 1848 in the Habsburg empire, therefore, far from forming any kind of unity, were bitterly divided. Their intrinsic weaknesses probably doomed them from the start, at least in Vienna and Prague; but the almost total lack of cooperation between them made their fall quicker and more certain than would otherwise have been the case.

In Germany the victory of national over liberal aspirations was even more marked and more important. In the attitude of the Frankfurt Parliament towards the Poles of Posnania or the Danes of Schleswig-Holstein 'healthy national egoism' proved a far stronger force than liberal ideas of self-determination or equality for other national groups. Even the dream of consolidating the revolution by a national war against Russia provoked by the resurrection of an independent Poland, an idea dear to many west and south German radicals, proved quite unable to persuade most of them to surrender any of the Polish territory gained by Prussia since 1772. Indeed on the Polish and Danish issues there was considerably more genuine liberalism in Berlin than in Frankfurt. The large majority of the Frankfurt parliamentarians wished for a Great Germany, a *Grossdeutschland* which would include, as well as Polish and partly Danish territory, the German parts of the Habsburg empire (including Bohemia), Luxemburg and perhaps the German-speaking parts of Switzerland (though not, interestingly enough, Alsace and Lorraine; the strength of France made such a claim appear futile). They had indeed been driven, by the beginning of 1849, to accept a German state which ended at the existing western frontier of the Habsburgs; but only *faute de mieux*, since it was clear that the collapse of the revolution in Vienna and the victories of Radetzky in Italy had now made a Great Germany impossible. All of them, again, wanted a Germany which was militarily strong. Every group at Frankfurt, whatever its attitude on other issues, favoured compulsory military service in the new national state.

There is a strong whiff of hypocrisy about many conventional criticisms of the expansionism which showed itself at Frankfurt. To condemn the self-appointed leaders of a great nation, in an age of increasingly rampant nationalism, for wishing to create a national state, even one pushed to its furthest territorial limits, is unfair. The men of Frankfurt were no more wicked than any other group of nationalists in nineteenth-century Europe. But they were blind to the implications of their ambitions. A Great Germany, for that matter a united Germany of any kind, could not possibly be created without the acquiescence, and probably the active support, of the greatest organized force in German life – the Prussian army. The realization of national ambitions was dependent on the goodwill of the men who controlled that army; and they were not liberals. They had no intention of seeing true liberalism triumph in the new state. The issue of this conflict between liberal and national objectives in Germany was not, therefore, seriously in doubt in 1848. The formal abdication of liberalism which began in 1866 was already foreshadowed. But the violence of the conflict and the rapidity with which it emerged were yet other factors which helped to frustrate the revolutionary hopes which had at first run so high.

The failure of the revolutions to gain mass support, the divisions between revolutionary groups, the clash of revolutionary objectives, were all to some extent inevitable. Radical mass movements could not be conjured into existence in a continent still populated mainly by an ill-educated, distrustful and in many ways bitterly conservative peasantry. Nationalism was the one revolutionary principle to which there was really widespread agreement in 1848. Even in Paris, though there were no territorial demands which France could reasonably put forward on her own account, the emotion expressed itself vicariously in calls for the resurrection of Poland and sympathy for the Italians and Hungarians. Yet nationalism was also the principle by its very nature most certain to create rivalry and disruption. Nevertheless these unavoidable weaknesses were compounded by the indecisiveness and unrealism shown by many of the revolutionaries.

The psychological effects of this lack of grip were considerable. It had been possible before 1848 to believe, essentially in the style of the eighteenth-century Enlightenment, that the complexities and dilemmas of political life were largely artificial, the creation of corrupt and oppressive government or of illiberal constitutions. Under a new, free, truly representative régime these difficulties would hardly need to be solved; they would in some unexplained way simply evaporate as the natural virtue and common sense of the people, 'incorruptible as the sea', were given free play. These dreams, sometimes noble, were doomed to disappointment from the start. One of the great discoveries of 1848 was that revolutionary politics was not necessarily much different from other sorts of politics, that revolutionaries were merely men like other men, selfish, shortsighted and even oppressive, that the people could not be redeemed overnight by deposing a dynasty or rewriting a constitution.

It was in France that pre-revolutionary idealism had been strongest. It was there that disillusionment was most acute. Moreover French radicals were hindered as well as helped by possessing the one true tradition of revolution in Europe, for this tended in practice to breed empty rituals and a kind of revolutionary name-dropping. Too often some action taken in 1789–94 was imitated, or some title used then was revived, without considering whether this traditionalism had anything to do with the real tasks of the moment. This backward-looking aspect of 1848 in Paris is in many ways quite as noticeable as its significance for the future. Thus the left in the Constituent Assembly of 1848 called itself the Mountain, in imitation of its predecessors of 1792: the difference was that in 1792 the Mountain was about to take over the revolution and change the world, while in 1848 those who assumed the name were already a defeated minority. There were even proposals that the assembly should wear an official costume based on the dress of members of the Convention in the 1790s, while the new democratic and radical newspapers which sprang up in such numbers in Paris had very often titles which harked back to 1789 – the *Carmagnole*, the *Journal des Sans-Culottes*, the *Tribunal Révolutionnaire*.[37] This use of revolutionary gestures and terminology as a kind of totem to conjure away danger and conceal real weakness was to be seen again in the Commune of 1871.[38] The revolution in Paris was unique in both its opportunities and its difficulties. It cannot be regarded as typical. But there was widespread agreement after the event that throughout the more advanced parts of Europe the upheavals of that year had failed because of the lack of realism and grip shown by their leaders. Engels's savage onslaught a year or two later in his *Germany: revolution and counter-revolution* on 'the Frankfurt collective tomfoolery' is fairly well known.[39] Walter Bagehot, an equally impressive witness, wrote in 1852 that 'if the revolutions of '48 have clearly brought out any fact, it is the utter failure of newspaper statesmen. Everywhere they have been tried: everywhere they have shown great talents for intrigue, eloquence and agitation – how rarely have they shown even fair aptitude for ordinary administration.[40] Another British observer comfortably concluded that the events of 1848–49 'give proof of the inferior education of the Continental people for practical life, and of the want of judgement and common sense even amongst the most educated men'.[41]

The monarchies and the conservatives were thus able to recover from the collapse of February–March 1848 in large part because of the weakness, on several different levels, of their opponents. They were also, however, able to achieve this because they never lost, and the revolutionaries never gained, the loyalty of the armies which could make or break any régime over most of Europe. In the eighteenth century the army had nowhere been an autonomous or self-conscious political force. Army officers were either non-political professionals or noblemen and courtiers playing at soldiers. Though the latter might sometimes be politically significant, as in the case of the guards regiments in Russia during the four decades after the death of Peter I, armies in general had no politics other than a reflex of unthinking loyalty to the monarch they served. By the early nineteenth century there were signs that this position was changing: the active reforming ambitions of some of the ablest Prussian officers during the decade or more after the battle of Jena are the best indication of this. The confusion of 1848, which often left the army as the only institution still standing firm in a flux of change, almost forced it to play an active and sometimes independent role in events. This was above all the case in the Habsburg empire. There military commanders, Windischgrätz, Radetzky and Jellaćić, with very little control from the emperor, the young Francis Joseph who succeeded the imbecile Ferdinand III in December 1848, saved the imperial régime and the unity of the empire largely on their own initiative. In Prussia also the unquestioning loyalty of the army allowed Frederick William IV to recover much of his power by the end of the year and thus escape paying the price of his own weakness in March. In France it was the army (helped by the Gardes Mobiles) which destroyed in June any remaining chance of social revolution. In Italy it was military power, that of Radetzky's regiments, which brought hopes of national unity to the ground and allowed the dynasties to recover the position they had lost in the spring.

Never had anything like this been seen before. Neither in Paris in 1789 nor in Brussels in 1830 had there been any serious threat of a military counter-revolution. Throughout central and eastern Europe, perhaps even in France, the ultimate guarantee of political stability was now an army of peasant conscripts, poorly educated and unsympathetic to town-bred radicals, officered by landowners or at least by members of well-to-do families. It was no accident that in the second half of the century military uniform was to be more than ever before the garb in which the monarchs of Europe usually appeared in public. It was also, a significant point, the one which many of them preferred to any other. 'As long as the army hold loyal the people can use no physical force', wrote the historian von Sybel of the position in Prussia in 1863. 'Their régime [i.e. that of the king and his supporters] will continue until the army declares for the constitution or until it is defeated in a foreign war.'[42] This had been true not merely of Prussia but of most of Europe ever since 1849 and continued to be true long after 1863. No army ever 'declared for the constitution'. It was the military defeats of 1859 and above all 1866 which made inevitable the internal rearrangement of the Habsburg empire which took place in 1867. It was the military catastrophe of 1870 which doomed the Second Empire in France. It was the brilliant success of the Prussian army until 1918 that ensured the dominance in Germany of social and political conservatism, with all this implied for the continent at large. The hopelessness of any attempt at revolution which was not supported by the army or preceded by its total demoralization was to be demonstrated beyond all reasonable doubt by the fate of the Commune of 1871 in Paris. This outbreak of exasperated patriotism and disorganized idealism was the last serious attempt at a repetition of 1789. Noble and petty, generous and brutal, it was crushed in May 1871 because the provisional government, headed by Thiers, retained the allegiance not merely of virtually the whole of France outside the capital but above all of the army.

The revolutions of 1848 failed, and often conclusively. Nowhere was the defeat pressed home with the ferocity to which the twentieth century has accustomed us. In Vienna, when the city was recaptured by the imperial forces, 1,600 people were arrested; but of these only nine were executed and another nine given long prison sentences. In Hungary 114 people were executed after the surrender and almost 1,800 sentenced to varying terms of imprisonment; but even these were not very high figures for an area where the struggle had been more savage and prolonged than anywhere else in Europe. Nevertheless the defeat of the revolution was everywhere clear. Yet something had been achieved. There was in 1849 no possibility of putting the clock back. For good or ill the age of Metternich and Louis-Philippe had gone for ever. It had been an age in which, over much of Europe, politics had seemed marginal to most aspects of life. In the Habsburg empire, in much of Italy, even in Prussia, political life had centred around the rulers, their ministers and the officials who served them. Parties, programmes, ideologies, had scarcely existed or had appeared of little significance. These societies had been regulated not by political but by administrative or judicial means. For all its follies and futilities, 1848 politicized Europe in a way hardly conceivable a generation earlier. West of the Russian frontier no government, no ruler, was now above or outside politics in the way that Francis II or Frederick William III had been. Now liberal demands or national dreams might be opposed but could not be ignored. Every European government henceforth lived in an environment affected as never before by political discussion and political ideas.

The governments which reasserted themselves after the revolutions were much stronger than their pre-revolutionary predecessors. To some extent this was merely a matter of physical factors. The new railways were making it easier than ever before to move soldiers quickly to crush rebellion before it could offer a serious threat. They also made it possible to transport food rapidly to areas of dearth and thus stave off the famine which alone could produce mass disorder. The new telegraph was allowing a central government to be informed almost instantaneously of events in the most distant parts of its territory, and thus to control these events and still more the day-to-day activity of its own officials. More fundamentally, however, the new régimes of the 1850s embodied attitudes different from those of the age of Metternich, and reflected a changing intellectual climate. Positivism and materialism were now helping to give to the actions of governments a cutting edge of ruthlessness, as well as an energy which they had generally lacked before 1848. In France Louis Napoleon had dreams, and capacities for good and evil, which were quite beyond the scope of Louis-Philippe, as well as an apparatus of political control much more efficient than any possessed by his predecessor. In the Habsburg empire Bach and Kübeck, the dominant ministers of the 1850s, were men of a very different stamp from Metternich. In Prussia, now beginning a period of spectacular economic growth, the medievalist dreams of Frederick William IV had lost all significance before he himself collapsed into insanity in 1858. Tempered by the fires of successfully resisted revolution, fortified by new technical aids and helped by a favourable economic climate, the governments of Europe were entering a new era.

THE AGE OF RECONSTRUCTION, 1849–1871

The more effective authoritarianism of the new régimes is easily illustrated. In Prussia the constitution of January 1850, though it included guarantees of individual freedom, confirmed the king's right to appoint and dismiss ministers and based elections to the Landtag on a three-tier suffrage system which was heavily biased in favour of wealth and the countryside as against the middle and working classes and the cities. Moreover it was accompanied by a series of conservative social and administrative measures – the recalling of provincial diets; the re-establishment of entailed estates; conservative changes in municipal government. The continuing reality of royal and military power was to be demonstrated most clearly of all, however, by the great constitutional crisis which broke out early in 1860 over reform of the army. Prince William, regent for his insane brother Frederick William IV from 1858 and king from January 1861, was purely military in experience and interests. He therefore supported passionately the proposals of his war minister, General Albrecht von Roon, for a three-year period of military service and for the incorporation of the reserve army, the Landsturm, into the regular forces. In spite of repeated victories for the liberal opposition in the elections to the Landtag and the formation of a new Progressive party to assert the principle of parliamentary control over military expenditure, he refused any concession on the issue of three-year service, the question around which the whole dispute soon came to revolve. To give way on this was in his eyes to compromise fatally the whole Prussian tradition (which he thought of in entirely military terms) as well as the position of the monarchy. By September 1862, desperate and contemplating abdication, he turned as a last resort to his ambassador in Paris, Count Otto von Bismarck. For the next four years Bismarck, as minister-president, headed a Prussian government which had no Landtag majority. Slowly, by appealing to the desire for German unity and by the example which he provided of strong-minded and resolute leadership, he improved his position. The elections of July 1866, held on the day of the battle of Sadowa, saw the Progressive party suffer a sharp setback; and in September the new Landtag gave Bismarck, at his own request, a vote of indemnity for the years of unparliamentary government. This was a moral triumph for the king and the government and a surrender by the liberals and parliamentarians whose consequences were to reverberate through the next half-century of German, and even European, history.

Nowhere else was the victory of authoritarianism during these decades so far-reaching in its consequences. Yet in the other great powers which had been affected by the cataclysm of 1848 it seemed at least as visible, particularly during the 1850s. In the Habsburg empire the remarkably liberal Kremsier constitution for the Austrian provinces, drawn up at the beginning of 1849, never came into operation. By the end of 1851 all pretence of constitutional rule there had been swept away; and for the next decade ministers were to be responsible to the emperor alone and the army independent of civil authority. In France the elections of May 1849 showed a marked swing of public feeling towards Catholic and monarchist candidates, and a year later the Constituent Assembly severely restricted the universal suffrage introduced in 1848. Meanwhile the president, Louis Napoleon, was building up with considerable skill a Bonapartist party and fostering his popularity with the army. By these means, and by striking populist attitudes, he was paving the way for the *coup d'état* of 2 December 1851 which overthrew the republic and ushered in a new personal régime, that of the Second Empire. By the end of 1851, therefore, Belgium, Sardinia-Piedmont and the Swiss Confederation were the only states of continental Europe with constitutions which were in any significant sense liberal.

Nevertheless, whatever its defects in the eyes of the constitutionalist, this was an age of real administrative progress in Europe. The running of a great state was now recognized, more clearly than ever before, to require skill, training and plentiful supplies of accurate information. Official statistics were still in many ways primitive. Even population figures were often of only limited value. In Switzerland, for example, registration of births, deaths and marriages was on a purely cantonal, not a national, basis until 1874. In Russia, although the old system of 'revisions', dating from 1719, was abandoned in 1858, there was no attempt at a real census until 1897. Above all no major government except that of Great Britain collected an adequate amount of economic and particularly industrial information.[43] Yet it was increasingly realized that efficent administration in more and more centralized mass societies must be increasingly dominated by quantitative considerations and therefore statistically based. In 1853 the International Statistical Congress held its first meeting, largely on the initiative of the Belgian, Adolphe Quetelet, the greatest statistician of the century. (He had already been responsible for the very efficient Belgian census of 1846.) In France the new attitudes can be seen in a consistent effort to use the census machinery to collect information on the religious life, employment and education of the population; and in 1866 there was even an attempt there at a census of domestic animals. The statesmen of the 1850s and 1860s, sometimes against their will, were being carried by events into an age dominated by size and quantity and by the rationality or pseudo-rationality which these generate.

Moreover the improvement in administrative machinery, in the methods by which officials were selected, trained and controlled, continued. In Britain an Order in Council of May 1855, inspired by the model of the new Indian Civil Service and by the Northcote–Trevelyan *Report on the Organization of the Higher Civil Service* of 1853, opened the way to competitive recruitment. As yet there was competition merely between previously approved candidates; but the further step of open competition (save for the small but important exception of the Diplomatic Service) came in 1870. By then, in spite of the sarcasms of conservatives and doubts of 'the dangerous optimism of competitive choice',[44] a great if belated step towards the modern world had been taken. Moreover the multiplication in every advanced state, again notably in Britain, of new agencies of social provision and control was rapidly increasing the element of professional expertise in the ordering of society. Factory and prison inspectors, medical officers, railway officials in countries such as Belgium, Austria and France where the railways were wholly or partially government-owned, were all examples of this. In Russia in particular the setting-up in 1864 of the *Zemstvo* system[45] led to a rapid multiplication of doctors, medical auxiliaries and teachers employed by these new bodies. This, coupled with the judicial reforms of the same year which created for the first time in Russian history a class of practising lawyers, injected into the life of the country a powerful and fruitful dose of professionalism. Unspectacular and relatively slow-acting, these developments did more to undermine the old Russia of autocracy, of lord and peasant, officer and bureaucrat, than any of the revolutionary visions of the century.

The régimes of the 1850s and 1860s were therefore in many cases progressive, administratively if not politically. Many of the undoubted advances of these decades were not their doing. In particular the marked growth of production and living standards over much of agrarian Europe during these decades owed nothing to them. The introduction of new agricultural techniques, breaking the stagnation in this respect which had generally prevailed during the first half of the century, the warding off of the danger that much of peasant Europe might soon eat potatoes rather than bread, were above all the results of the coming of the railway to the European countryside; and this was a development in which, except in France, governments played little part.[46] But although throughout continental Europe these governments were predominantly authoritarian, stressing their own power and deeply distrusting any kind of popular initiative, they were by no means indifferent to the feelings of those they ruled. However effective railways, telegraphs and new weapons were now making the coercive power of governments, however limited the constitutional rights they conceded to their subjects, their authority was in a very real sense based on the consent of the governed. The 1850s and 1860s were permeated as no period in history had been before by the realization that revolution was possible, perhaps imminent. This meant that governments had to try as never before to win the positive loyalty and support of their subjects, or at least to prevent their discontent reaching a dangerous pitch.

Dynastic loyalties still counted for a good deal in the German world and in central and eastern Europe. In particular they were more than ever the most important prop of the Habsburg empire and gave the autocracy in Russia much of what vitality it still retained. Sheer habit, as always, continued to be a force ensuring that what was continued to be, again especially east of the Rhine or at least the Elbe. But forces of this inarticulate and instinctive kind had already been pushed into the background in the more politically minded parts of western Europe, above all in France, and were losing ground everywhere. The régimes of the two decades after 1848 therefore either themselves contained a more or less explicitly populist element, as that of Napoleon III in France did, or were faced by populist movements which they might despise but could not totally ignore. Thus the Prussian government found itself compelled to take some account of German nationalism and the tsarist one of Panslavism. In no great state except the Habsburg empire and Russia (admittedly very important exceptions) were a written constitution and some form of parliamentarianism rejected by the governments of the 1850s. The idea that the powers of governments must be explicitly limited by constitutional provisions and the rule of law was becoming increasingly universal. Even the very imperfect constitution of 1850 gave Prussia for almost two decades a considerable psychological advantage over the Habsburgs in their struggle for leadership in Germany; for she could claim to be a *Rechtstaat* and the Habsburg territories, after 1851, could not. Governments, however authoritarian and undemocratic in reality, had increasingly to present to the world a façade of popular support. Sometimes this was achieved by influencing and manipulating elections, as in France under Napoleon III. Sometimes it meant playing off the peasant against his more politically conscious and less docile brother in the towns. Thus at the end of 1861 Napoleon III urged the introduction of universal suffrage in Prussia since 'in this system the conservative rural population can vote down the liberals in the cities', a suggestion which Bismarck seems seriously to have considered in the difficult years 1862–66.[47]

Moreover the defeat in Italy in 1859 forced even Francis Joseph and his advisers to recognize that simple bureaucratic absolutism of the type established in 1849 was no longer a going concern. The result was the unsuccessful constitutional experiments of 1860–61, the 'October Diploma' and 'February Patent'; while the much more serious defeat in Germany in 1866 made a drastic change in the political structure, and thus concessions to the Hungarians, unavoidable. The Compromise (*Ausgleich*) of 1867 divided the Habsburg lands into two political entities, one a Hungarian-dominated unitary pseudo-state in the eastern half of the empire, the other a federation of provinces in the west. Except for questions of foreign policy and defence, and the finances required by these, the two parts of the monarchy were effectively independent of each other, each with its own parliament. In essence this was an agreement between the emperor and the Hungarian nationalist leaders, one which Francis Joseph then forced the Germans who controlled the western half of the empire to accept. But it meant that after 1867 the empire had a constitution, and one which, for all its defects, lasted for over half a century. It could also now claim to be a parliamentary state, though in the western half of the new Dual Monarchy parliamentary life was soon to be disrupted by vicious national feuds, and in the eastern half distorted by Hungarian discrimination against the non-Magyar nationalities.

The evolution of Europe since Waterloo had not made authoritarian government impossible: in some important respects it had made it easier. But it had made necessary the evolution of new forms of authoritarianism – more flexible, better informed and better served, more conscious of and responsive to the feelings of the ordinary man. Rouher, the most authoritarian and efficient of the ministers of Napoleon III, summed up one aspect of the position when he said that after the establishment of the Second Empire in 1852 'everybody thought it impossible not to take into account the new political habits which the country had acquired in the preceding fifty years'.[48] Most of the rest of continental Europe had not yet acquired these habits, at least in an engrained form. But the fear that they might take root outside France's borders and that discontent, if ignored, might erupt once more in revolution, was a considerable factor in the attitudes of other European governments. It seemed less and less possible, in the mass age towards which Europe was visibly advancing, for any individual, however great his gifts, to withstand or even deflect a truly popular demand. 'In speculating on the probable course of events in critical and menacing conjunctures,' wrote Bagehot in November 1863, 'we now enquire much more anxiously what are the sentiments and interests of such and such *peoples*, than what are the views and characters of such and such rulers. . . . No influential man in any nation is so influential as the aggregate of men.'[49] The remark was justified. Of the two outstanding statesmen of the generation 1860–90 Gladstone seldom told the British people anything which he did not believe it already wished to hear; and when he did (as over Home Rule in Ireland) it did not listen to him very attentively. The other, Bismarck, borrowed from Napoleon III, in a less explicit form, some of the populism and the continual search for popularity and a good press which distinguished his defeated rival.[50]

The governments of Europe were now being made aware, to an unprecedented degree, of the feelings of at least substantial groups of their subjects, and of the political dangers these might present, by the continued growth of the newspaper press. The scope and speed of this development varied widely between different European states. In Germany the circulation and influence of newspapers was still limited.[51] In central Europe it was even less. In Russia censorship prevented the emergence of any approach to an independent press until the early 1860s, though then the growth was rapid: in a decade or less after the Crimean War the number of Russian-language periodicals grew from 25 to almost 200.[52] The revolutionary upheaval of 1905–7 ushered in another period of rapid growth: by 1913 there were almost 1200 newspapers of various kinds appearing in the Russian empire. In France, on the other hand, the inferiority of imperialist newspapers to opposition ones in circulation and often in quality was always a major worry to the régime of Napoleon III. In August 1861, for example, the government press in Paris had a total circulation of less than 53,000 against the more than 91,000 copies of republican and progressive newspapers sold in the capital; and one result of this position was the payment of subsidies, though not very large ones, by the government to influence or support selected papers – another parallel with the methods of Bismarck.[53] Moreover France was by the 1860s pioneering the really large-circulation newspaper and thus breaking a trail which the rest of the continent was later to follow. The *Petit Journal*, founded in 1863, sold for only five centimes and by the end of 1865 had a circulation of well over a quarter of a million. More ominous from the standpoint of the régime, Henri de Rochefort's scandalous and viciously anti-government weekly *La Lanterne*, launched in May 1868, had reached the unheard-of sale of over half a million by the following summer.

Apart from the growth of education and wealth which made an increasing number of people all over Europe able to read and afford newspapers, a whole series of technical innovations (notably the development of lithography with its implications for the growth of illustrated periodicals) were steadily increasing the appeal of the press. Through it, more completely and continuously than through any form of voting, the ordinary man was able at least to touch the fringes of political life and scent the distant aroma of high policy. Through it also some impression of popular feeling, however incomplete or distorted, could reach the governments of Europe. Through it therefore that feeling might, at least in western Europe, exert some influence on the policies of states. Perhaps the best and most obvious index of the fear which the press aroused on the part of governments is their continuing refusal to grant it complete freedom. In Prussia a law of 1854 deprived those accused of offences against the censorship of the right to trial by jury; while in France the severe restrictions on newspapers introduced in the first days of the Second Empire were not substantially relaxed until 1868. It is also significant that several foreign governments thought it worth while during the 1860s to spend substantial sums in attempts to influence French newspapers in their favour, while Count von Beust, the Austrian foreign minister, made considerable efforts in 1867–71 to secure support of this kind in London and Paris. Even in Russia there was by the 1870s a press which, though it touched directly only a small minority of the population, was capable of commenting forcibly on government policy. By then Mikhail Katkov, the greatest journalist in Russian history, had become in his advocacy of reaction at home and nationalism abroad a man of very real political influence.

Most important of all, the régimes of the 1850s and 1860s were not socially reactionary. In their social policies the note which they sounded was that of a realistic and often progressive conservatism. In Prussia a decree of March 1850 abolished virtually all the servile obligations still owed by peasants to landlords, while all other surviving manorial dues were converted into money rents redeemable at eighteen years' purchase. In the next fifteen years 640,000 peasants in the eastern provinces of the kingdom took advantage of these provisions. The last vestiges of Prussian feudalism as a system of legal obligations were thus swept away; and there is little doubt that the monarchical and aristocratic paternalism of the 1850s achieved considerable popularity with the ordinary subjects of Frederick William IV. Even more important, in Russia the famous edict of March 1861 granted the serfs on private estates immediate personal freedom and embarked upon the appallingly difficult task of trying to establish them as peasant proprietors. It was merely the first, though also the greatest, of a series of similar enactments – for Russian Poland in 1864, for state peasants and those on the lands of the imperial family in 1866 and 1867, for the Cossack areas in 1869 and for Transcaucasia in 1870 – which occupied the following decade. The complexity of this legislation reflected the complexity of the situation in a huge multinational empire with enormous variations between different areas in climate, soil and density of population. The intricacies of the system by which, under the decree of 1861, the serf was to compensate his lord for the labour services and other rights lost by the latter form the most labyrinthine social and administrative story of the nineteenth century. But with all its deep-seated weaknesses (above all the fact that over most of Russia the former serf now had less land to till than he had had under the old agrarian régime) the grant of individual freedom and a minimum of civil rights to 20 million people previously in legal bondage was the greatest single liberating measure attempted in the whole modern history of Europe. It was unique. Russia's problems, in nature and size, were quite unlike those of any other European state. But more than anything else done or attempted during the 1850s and 1860s it marks these decades as a period of constructive social change over much of the continent. Moreover it was followed in Russia by a series of new departures which came close to revolutionizing the national life, above all the reforms in local administration and the judicial system which followed in 1864 and the military reforms of a decade later.[54] No European state during the nineteenth century attempted so much so quickly as Russia in these years. Though this great effort to enter fully the modern world was not sustained and was in many ways a failure this should not blind us to its scope and to the force of its tragic drama.

THE GROWTH OF STATE POWER, 1871–1914

Most Europeans during these four decades believed that they lived in an age of increasing political liberty. They could point to an impressive array of facts to support this belief. The movement towards constitutionalism and legal guarantees of individual freedoms, towards representative government and the placing of increasing political power in the hands of the ordinary man, which had been only partially interrupted in the aftermath of 1848, now seemed irresistible. Almost everywhere in western and central Europe universal male suffrage was achieved or at least approached. Both the new German empire and the new Third Republic in France proclaimed it in 1871. In Britain the parliamentary reform of 1867 marked the most important of all steps towards it; and it had been for most practical purposes achieved there by 1884. In Italy the right to vote, narrowly restricted by the Piedmontese constitution of 1848, was considerably broadened in 1882 so that the electorate rose from 500,000 to 3 million: finally most of the male population was enfranchised in 1912. In the parts of the Habsburg empire ruled from Vienna the franchise was considerably extended in 1896. Eleven years later universal male suffrage was introduced, largely in the desperate hope that this might help to weaken the national antagonisms which threatened to tear the empire apart. In Belgium, the great showpiece of constitutionalism in nineteenth-century continental Europe, where in 1890 there were still only 133,000 voters in a total population of over 6 million, their number was multiplied tenfold at a stroke with the introduction of manhood suffrage in 1892. Of the other minor states Switzerland gave all male citizens the vote in 1874, Spain in 1890, the Netherlands in 1896 and Norway in 1898.

This tendency was far weaker in eastern and south-eastern Europe. Russia had no approach to parliamentary life until the establishment of the Duma in 1906; and this, forced on the régime by the defeat in the Far East and the revolution of 1905, was a weak body elected by a complicated system of mainly indirect voting. In Hungary, right down to the collapse of 1918, hardly a quarter of the male population were voters in fact;[55] while in the Balkans and the Iberian peninsula, though voting rights might be extensive on paper, they were often drastically limited in practice by official pressure and the illiteracy of so much of the electorate.[56] Nevertheless the general picture appeared to be one of increasingly complete diffusion of political power throughout society, of the bringing into the 'political nation' over the greater part of Europe of millions hitherto excluded. Moreover one part of Europe, small but a political model which attracted widespread attention, had already carried democracy to what seemed in one respect the highest attainable pitch: the Swiss constitution of 1874 introduced the device of the referendum, and in 1891 added to it that of the initiative in respect of amendments to the constitution.

Nevertheless this triumph of democracy (at least in the head-counting sense of the term) and of parliamentary government was more apparent than real. In the first place there were often sharp disparities and unfairnesses in the working of the electoral systems which were now proliferating throughout most of Europe. In Germany the 397 one-member Reichstag constituencies set up in 1871 remained completely unchanged down to 1914. The result was increasingly gross over-representation of the eastern agrarian areas of east Prussia, Posnania and Pomerania and under-representation of the towns. In 1912 in the agrarian provinces the number of those eligible to vote in each constituency averaged about 15,000: in one Berlin constituency at the same time there were over 200,000 electors. More strikingly, in the Russian Duma from 1907 onwards each gentry deputy represented 16,000 voters and each peasant one 1.7 million. However these were in a sense merely mechanical difficulties and always in principle avoidable. More fundamental was the fact that the results of parliamentary government, at least in the short run, were disruptive rather than constructive. Constitutionalism and parliamentarianism could not appeal to the ordinary man (or for that matter usually even to the sophisticated and educated man) with the power and directness of nationalism. More and more the national state was becoming the only acceptable political unit.[57] More and more the national dream was acquiring a sacredness with which no other ideology could effectively compete. The impotence of merely political or constitutional principles when confronted by national emotions, first seen clearly in 1848, was now unmistakable. This meant that in areas of mixed nationality a parliament might become little more than an arena in which conflicting national groups struggled with one another, and extension of the suffrage merely a weapon in this struggle. This was seen above all in the western provinces of the Habsburg empire, where after 1897 parliamentary government, always weak, virtually collapsed for several years because of Czech-German antagonism and the resulting Czech obstructionism and growth of pan-German feeling.

There were, however, a number of more generally applicable reasons why the growth of parliaments and the extension of the suffrage failed to transform European political life as liberals and democrats hoped. Effective parliamentary government could normally work only through effective political parties, stable and reasonably responsible; and over much of Europe these hardly existed. In the Austrian provinces of the Habsburg empire the different parliamentary groups usually found it much easier to unite in opposition to the government in power than in its support or in advocacy of constructive alternative policies. In France a plethora of small parties and frequent and unpredictable changes in their relationships helped to make governments under the Third Republic notorious for their instability. They thus prolonged the paradox of the continuance of a highly authoritarian administrative system, largely unchanged since the innovations of Napoleon I, in a society in which the tradition of political liberty had an almost anarchical strength unequalled elsewhere in Europe. In Germany the overwhelming prestige of Bismarck after 1871 and his almost unquestioned political dominance, perhaps coupled with a tendency for able men to prefer careers in industry, banking or the bureaucracy to those available in politics, led to frequent complaints of the low quality of the leadership of all parties. An acute observer as early as 1873 spoke of 'the complaint of all parties that they lack leaders'; and at the end of his life Bismarck himself said that 'the Centrum [the Catholic Centre party founded in 1870] is the only party of which I can say that it has not been incapably led'.[58]

The failure of parliamentary leadership can be seen very clearly in Italy. Even in the 1870s disillusion with the fruits of unification was widespread there. Defeat at the hands of Austria in 1866, and the acquisition of Rome in 1870 only after the overthrow of France by Prussia, had shown up the military weakness of the new state. It was clearly impossible for it to gain Trieste and the Trentino, the central objective of Italian nationalists, by its own efforts. The sense of humiliation which this bred, intensified by official corruption and economic difficulties, is clearly visible in the writings of the greatest of the nationalist authors of the period, Giosuè Carducci. Moreover the sense of lacking real national traditions, inevitable in a state recently formed and in a sense still artificial, contributed to the general feeling of instability. With the evolution from the early 1880s of 'transformism', which meant that every Italian government was a loose coalition of shifting and selfish political groups which made and unmade governments in the pursuit of their own interests, Italian parliamentary life fell increasingly into contempt. The one commanding figure it produced in the generation before 1914, Giovanni Giolitti, was bitterly disliked by many of his fellow-parliamentarians at least in part because he seemed a possible centre of political stability. Such stability would limit the freedom of manoeuvre which the increasing chaos in the Chamber of Deputies gave them.

In yet another respect, moreover, Italy was unlucky. During the later nineteenth and early twentieth centuries coherent political parties in continental Europe were, with few exceptions, either socialist or Catholic in inspiration. Only in terms of these two great ideologies, as a rule, was it as yet possible to organize mass parties with the distinguishing marks of modern groupings of this kind – large memberships, some degree of internal discipline and the formulation of policy, at least in form, by party congresses rather than by small controlling cliques. Yet in Italy a strong Socialist party was slow to develop. More serious, Pope Pius IX in 1874 issued the decree *Non expedit* which forbade good Catholics to play any role in the politics of the ungodly new Italian kingdom. Not until 1905 was this prohibition relaxed by allowing individual bishops to decide whether their flocks might safely take part in political life. Sustained for over a generation, it helped in particular to deprive Italy of the strong and responsible conservative party which would have done more than anything else to raise the tone of her political life.

In Germany too parliamentary government was defeated; and since from 1870 onwards Germany was in most ways the leading state in Europe this defeat was crucial. It was implicit in the foundation of the German empire in 1871. Bismarck, who far more than anyone else determined the structure of that empire, regarded it above all as an instrument for the safeguarding of Prussian greatness. To him it was something forced on Prussia by circumstances, by the need to make a gesture to German national feeling and by the impossibility of leaving the south German states free to fall under the influence of the Habsburgs or of a resuscitated France. His inspiration was neither German unity, as with the nationalists, nor any general political or religious principle, as with the true Prussian conservatives, but rather the unique position and achievements of Prussia. His contempt for German nationalism, shared by most of the German princes, is seen in the complete absence of any elected representatives of the German people from the ceremony in the Hall of Mirrors at Versailles in January 1871 when the empire was proclaimed. From the beginning power over it was to be, and to be seen to be, in the hands of rulers and of the generals and officials who served them, not in those of party leaders or political theorists. Its constitution, based on the North German Confederation of 1867, was that of a federation of monarchs, though one made unreal from the beginning by the predominance of one of their number, the king of Prussia, who was to bear the imperial title. (Some of the new imperial ministries, notably those for war and foreign affairs, were merely extensions of the corresponding Prussian ones.) The upper house of the legislature, the Bundesrat, made up of representatives of the state governments, was so arranged that Prussia, though she had no numerical majority in it, could scarcely be outvoted.

The lower house, the Reichstag, was a concession to national and democratic feeling, popularly elected on the basis of universal manhood suffrage. But its real powers were in many ways very limited. The ministers, who were in any case merely the subordinates not the colleagues of the imperial chancellor, were not members of it. Its control over military affairs was slight, especially after Bismarck succeeded in 1874 in persuading it to vote army expenditure for a seven-year period in advance. Similar votes were given in 1881 and 1887; and the 'septennate' system became an important factor in German politics during the 1880s. Again the control of the

Reichstag over the finances of the imperial government was lessened by the fact that these depended on the contributions made by the different German states, and on the yield of indirect taxation, rather than on direct taxes. But these limitations were merely the outward sign of deeper weaknesses. Any increase in the power of the Reichstag would be opposed implacably by the emperor and by the aristocratic and military influences which dominated the court. To the more extreme of these, ideas of divine right were as valid as they had been to the Prussian conservatives of the 1850s; and they were profoundly contemptuous of middle-class, civilian or parliamentary leadership. The Prussian tradition, of which both William I and William II were proud to regard themselves as the heirs and defenders, was one profoundly hostile to party-political conflict of any kind; its ideal was one of honest and unbiased administration by trained officials controlled only by their official superiors and ultimately by the emperor himself. Moreover since the Reichstag represented the unitary as opposed to the particularistic elements in the structure erected in 1871, any strengthening of it would also arouse the hostility of the smaller German princes.

Perhaps most important of all, the political parties in general showed themselves unable to rise to the opportunities which social and political change in Germany were now opening to them. They offered, in the event, no effective challenge to the forces of autocracy and of military and bureaucratic conservatism which dominated the new empire. Their number, and the bitterness with which they disputed over differing programmes and ideologies, meant that there was little stability in German party politics and that the government, by manoeuvring between the different groups, had to construct a series of constantly changing majorities in the Reichstag in order to pass essential legislation. The National Liberals, the most important party since the great watershed of 1866–67, were beginning to lose some of their strength even before Bismarck broke off his alliance with them in 1879: this break was a death-blow to liberalism as an effective political force in Germany and a turning-point in the country's history. By pushing through the Reichstag in that year a programme of protective tariffs, the chancellor hoped not merely to safeguard German heavy industry, and even more German agriculture, against threatening foreign competition,[59] but also to increase substantially the income from customs duties of the imperial government. The change ushered in a decade during which he relied for support above all on the conservatives, a period during which agriculture became dependent on guaranteed prices and industry dominated by cartels.

The imperial régime had now turned its back on even a diluted form of liberalism and identified itself with agrarian conservatism and with an industrial system which increasingly demanded and expected government support. Moreover the changes of 1879 increased if anything the weakness of the German parties. They destroyed the National Liberals, while the conservatives, themselves divided into two main groups, overwhelmingly Prussian and agrarian, remained too backward-looking and in some cases too hostile to the unification of 1871 to have real mass appeal. Two great parties did indeed show a capacity for rapid growth and real coherence. These were the Centre and the Social Democrats, in spite of the fact that the latter were for over a decade (1878–90) forbidden to organize or carry on propaganda in Germany. But the Centre was the pressure-group of one segment of society, the Catholics, rather than a force aiming at the improvement of the existing political structure; and even the Social Democrats, for all their revolutionary rhetoric, came to have something of the same character with the industrial workers as the objects of their solicitude. Moreover both, even more than the liberal or conservative groups, stood for the propagation of distinctive views of the world (*Weltanschauungen*) rather than for the shouldering of the humdrum tasks and responsibilities of day-to-day government. No party leader during the Bismarckian period became a minister, and only once was such a contingency even seriously discussed (in 1877, when Bismarck broached the possibility to the National Liberal leader, Rudolf Bennigsen). Formal court functions throughout the history of the empire were attended only by the diplomatic corps, high officials and the greater Prussian nobility, with a few nobles from the other states included for the sake of appearances. Party leaders were excluded from them. The Reichstag's lack of real power meant that an industrialist, a landowner or a colonial expansionist tried to achieve his aims through direct contact with ministers, officials, or if possible the emperor himself, rather than through the elected representatives of the German people. Such a system could produce pliant courtiers and skilled lobbyists. It was not likely to produce statesmen. In Britain, even in France, the state, as the organization of power in and over society, was in a real sense the continual creation of the political parties and their activities. In imperial Germany, by contrast, it was something given, imposed in its essentials once for all from above, into the interstices of which the parties and indeed political life in general had to fit themselves as best they could. It would be unfair to accuse the German people of a lack of interest in politics. Though under Bismarck only a little over half of those entitled to vote in Reichstag elections in fact did so, in those of 1907 and 1912 the turnout rose to 84 per cent. But the structure of government ensured that the mere ability to vote in the last analysis counted for little.

The end-product of all this was a Germany which, deeply impressive on the surface, was in many ways strikingly lacking in real unity. Rivalries between the German states meant that strenuous efforts were made to ensure that each was represented in the bureaucracy in proportion to its size; thus appointments to the Supreme Court in Leipzig were made on the basis of state quotas. The continuing dislike in the smaller states of the Prussian predominance consecrated in 1871 meant that all candidates for high official position were carefully scrutinized for signs of particularist sympathies. More serious, great sections of the population were treated as untrustworthy and potentially disloyal. Social Democrats were understandably excluded from government office of any kind, while there was also, and far less justifiably, severe discrimination against Catholics and Jews.[60] During the 1880s Bismarck, showing great adroitness and drawing on his overwhelming reputation and prestige, was able to maintain the status quo and his personal control over it by playing off one institution or group against another – Prussia against the smaller states, the Reichstag against the Budesrat, the parties against each other. Even before the death in 1888 of William I, his invariable though sometimes reluctant supporter, his position had begun to be difficult and he had doubted the permanence of the imperial structure.[61] By 1890, when he was forced to resign by the headstrong and conceited young William II, the old statesman had been driven to envisage a military *coup d'état* which would overthrow the existing constitution and replace it by one giving greater powers to the German rulers and permanently outlawing the Social Democrats.

Under the new emperor the autocratic and military influence hitherto kept at bay by the prestige of the chancellor and his control over William I rose to new heights. Even as early as 1890 William II did not trouble to inform Bismarck's successor, General von Caprivi, of so important a change as the appointment of a new war minister; and in the following year he drafted in person a new Army Bill with the help merely of one of his aides-de-camp and without consultation with any minister. In March 1896 he wrote that 'a Prussian Minister is in the fortunate position of not having to worry whether his Bills succeed or not.... He is *not* appointed to office at the behest of this or that party in the Chamber. On the contrary, my Ministers are chosen quite freely by me through All-Highest confidence; and so long as they enjoy that confidence they do not have to bother about anything else at all.'[62] By the summer of the following year, after serious consideration of a *coup d'état* to halt the threatening growth of the Social Democrats, William had successfully asserted his personal dominance of the government and its policies. His control of appointments was now complete and the ministers no more than his agents, carrying out his instructions without regard to any other consideration. It is significant that throughout his reign the head of his military secretariat normally had audience with him three times a week, and the heads of his naval and civil secretariats twice a week; whereas the chancellor did not as a rule see him more than weekly and most of the ministers only once a year – at the Kiel regatta. Complete personal rule in a society as sophisticated as that of Germany was impossible. The sheer number of decisions to be taken and amount of work involved made it out of the question for a man of William's limited abilities to achieve this ideal.[63] Nevertheless for a number of years he was able, with considerable success, to exploit the potentialities of the position he had inherited. Together with Nicholas II of Russia he made a last stand, however misguided and even ridiculous, on behalf of the moribund idea of divine-right monarchy.

Moreover he was able to do this without effective opposition from the well-to-do middle classes, the very groups which had led the struggle elsewhere in western Europe for parliamentary government and the destruction of autocratic power. This was partly because since 1871, and especially since 1879, the imperial régime had largely favoured middle-class interests. William II himself was keenly conscious of his obligation to help in the expansion of German trade. He combined the functions of divine-right monarch, however incongruously, with those of an imperial commercial traveller. The German middle class was also quiescent because from the 1890s, if not earlier, it was widely feared that reform, once set in motion, might become uncontrollable, and that genuine parliamentary rule might be merely the prelude to that worst of all fates, the victory of socialism. German achievements during the period 1871–1914 were in many ways so great that it is hard not to sympathize with this unwillingness to interfere with what seemed obviously a going concern. Most middle-class Germans accepted the Second Reich for the reason that nearly all their British counterparts supported parliamentary rule – because by and large it seemed to work. Intellectually there was perhaps little to choose between the two attitudes. But Germany paid in the long run a heavy price for this complacency. In 1914 she was in some ways less united and stable than in 1871. Particularism had died down. But the deeper social cleavages revealed in the rise of the Social Democrats had replaced it, the pressures of competing economic interest-groups were sharper, and military influences on the government were stronger than ever.

The stultification of efforts at parliamentary government by the survival of monarchical, military and bureaucratic power was not confined to Germany. In the Habsburg territories the increasingly erosive effect of nationalism made the ruler, the army and the bureaucracy seem even more than in the past the only real unifying forces in the empire. The mere continuance of Francis Joseph for so long on the throne added to his stature in this respect and to his popularity generally. Like Queen Victoria, who benefited in a somewhat similar way from the length of her reign, he was able through the mere passage of time to acquire a symbolic status to which his own abilities scarcely entitled him. The celebration of his eightieth birthday, in 1910, had for central Europe some of the significance that the Diamond Jubilee of 1897 had possessed for Britain and her colonies. Moreover he felt a real personal responsibility to God for the fate of the territories entrusted to his care and, like William II, he thought it the duty of his ministers to accept any post he offered them and to fill it so long as he wished them to. The development of a parliamentary system both in the Hungarian and the Austrian parts of the empire from the 1860s onwards, the extension of the suffrage in the Austrian provinces in 1896 and 1907, made no difference to this attitude; for Hungary was now autonomous and in the provinces governed from Vienna national antagonisms and party weaknesses meant that real authority was left in the hands of the ruler. In particular, like his predecessors, Francis Joseph felt a heavy responsibility for the military strength of his territories and for their foreign policy. When in 1911 Conrad von Hötzendorff criticized the attitude of the foreign minister, Baron Aehrenthal, as too pacific, the emperor replied that 'I make policy; it is my policy. . . . My policy is a policy of peace. . . . My minister of Foreign Affairs carries on my policy in this sense.'[64] Nor were these words an empty boast. To the last days of his life the emperor read assiduously the papers sent him in quantity by the foreign ministry; and in 1913, for example, he showed his independence by ignoring a demand of the Council of Ministers, during the Balkan crisis of that year, for the presentation of an ultimatum to Montenegro.

More important, and to the country concerned more damaging, was the fact that in Russia also the power of the monarch remained essentially unshaken until the twentieth century. The murder of Alexander II in March 1881 ended any possibility of the creation of some limited form of national representative body with advisory functions, an idea with which the tsar had been very cautiously dabbling just before his death. Under his successor, Alexander III, the highly conservative Count D. A. Tolstoy became minister of the interior in 1882, a post which he retained for seven years. His influence, and still more that of the reactionary, intelligent and deeply pessimistic Procurator of the Holy Synod, K. P. Pobedonostsev, inspired a whole conservative programme – Russianization of the national minorities, particularly in the Baltic provinces; restriction of the access of the lower classes to secondary and higher education; strengthening of the position of the landowning class against the peasantry, notably by the creation of the new office of 'land captain' in 1889; weakening of the Zemstvos; intensified anti-Semitism – erected on the foundation of undiluted imperial autocracy. 'The voice of God', Pobedonostsev told the new tsar in 1881, 'orders us to stand boldly by the task of governing, relying on Divine Providence, with faith in the strength and truth of autocratic power, which we have been called to confirm and protect for the good of the people, against all encroachments.'[65] Not until November 1905, in the aftermath of humiliating defeat by Japan and under the impact of revolution, was Nicholas II, who succeeded Alexander III in 1894, compelled to promise the summoning of a form of parliament. This promise was at most half-kept, for the Duma established in the following year was no more than the hollowest pretence of parliamentary government. It had no control over the administration, and could be suspended or dissolved by the ruler at his pleasure. It had no jurisdiction over naval or military expenditure or over that of the ministry of the imperial court. Ministers were still responsible solely to the tsar and did not need its confidence or support. The 'Fundamental Laws' of April 1906 made Russia at most a quasi-constitutional state, for they could be amended only by the tsar and left him with immense personal power. They formally recognized him, for example, as 'supreme director of all the external relations of the Russian state'.

In spite of the revolutionary warning delivered in 1905, therefore, Nicholas and his advisers pinned their faith not on a gradual movement towards constitutionalism and parliamentary government but on the construction of a refurbished and more efficient autocracy. But for the outbreak of war in 1914 their hopes might have been justified, at least in the short or even the medium term. The great wave of disorder which began in 1905 had died down in exhaustion by 1907; and the agrarian policies of P. A. Stolypin, chief minister in 1906-11, produced remarkable progress in many ways in the Russian countryside.[66] It was only the military disasters of 1914-16 and the reaction to them in Russia which showed conclusively the weaknesses of the policies followed a decade earlier.

Throughout central and eastern Europe, therefore, traditional forms of political authority – monarchies, armies, bureaucracies – stood out against the constitutional and parliamentary groundswell which washed round them. In this resistance they were powerfully aided by one of the nineteenth-century developments most neglected by historians – the ability of governments of any political complexion, working through bigger and more effective bureaucracies, to collect taxes more efficiently than ever before. Everywhere they suffered some erosion; and in Russia in 1905-6 they seemed for a moment to totter under the impact of a hurricane. Nevertheless in general they stood firm, and by doing so ensured that a great part of the continent would, at least for the time being, follow neither the British nor the French path to political maturity. Moreover even in western Europe there were increasingly audible doubts whether these paths were the only ones worth following, whether the wind of change was really after all blowing irresistibly in the direction of parliamentary government.

These doubts showed themselves in one way, and perhaps the most intellectually profound one, in the growth of syndicalism.[67] On a more instinctive and emotional level escape could be found from the frustrations of party politics in extreme and visionary nationalism: pan-Germanism in the Habsburg empire was an example of this. Most obviously in Italy a whole series of writers from the 1870s onwards – Carducci, Oriani, Corradini, D'Annunzio – presented nationalism, with its demands for heroism and self-sacrifice, as the obvious means of escape from the suffocating triviality and irrelevance of parliamentary government. Francesco Crispi, the 'strong man' of Italian politics in the 1880s and early 1890s, achieved a great personal following above all because he seemed to personify the heroic aspects of the Risorgimento which the parliamentary régime mocked and degraded. By the end of the century the dangerous idea of a purifying war as the necessary substitute for the revolution which Italy needed, but of which she had been cheated, was being insistently put forward.[68] Just as the foundation for some form of socialist explosion had been laid in Russia by 1914 so had those for some form of Fascism in Italy. In each it was the war and the strains it set up which brought tension to a head and destroyed the old régime

It would be wrong to imply that the Europe of 1914 was uniform, either in its society or in its government and administration. The more developed parts of the continent all possessed, to varying extents, relatively fluid societies based on an ethos of individualism, economies based on technological rationality and the play of market forces, and sophisticated administrations. They also possessed the large educated middle class needed to make such economies and administrations work. Side by side with them, however, there were great areas in which society was still powerfully influenced by ideas of inherited status and group loyalties, and where the social influence of rationality and market forces was still limited. In them government and administration were likely to retain elements of overt class domination and military influence which had been largely discarded in most of western Europe.

Nevertheless by the eve of the First World War the governments and societies of Europe, like the economies which sustained them, seemed to be moving in the direction of greater uniformity. It was possible to believe that everywhere, in spite of hesitations or setbacks, history was advancing towards a form of society which would be unprecedentedly fluid and directed above all towards maximum economic efficiency. In such a society a man's status (which meant increasingly his economic status) would more and more be determined by his own abilities. This society of the future also seemed likely everywhere to be served by administrative machinery in which efficiency and specialized knowledge would be much more important than ever in the past. For the first time truly scientific government, basing policy on accurate information conscientiously collected and impartially weighed, seemed to be possible. Moreover most contemporaries were still able to believe that this gleaming new machinery might remain the servant of the parliamentary democracy which now seemed destined to triumph, not merely in a few favoured states of western Europe and their offshoots overseas, but throughout the world.

NOTES

1. See pp. 5–13.
2. For a useful general conspectus see M. Szeftel, 'The form of government of the Russian Empire prior to the constitutional reforms of 1905–6', in J. S. Curtiss, ed., *Essays in Russian and Soviet History in Honor of Geroid Tanqueray Robinson* (Leiden, 1963).
3. M. Cherniavsky, *Tsar and People: studies in Russian myths* (Yale University Press, 1961), p. 90. The Tsar Paul at his coronation in 1796 carried the assertion of the priestly character of the ruler and his quasi-divinity a stage further by giving himself communion. This was never repeated by his successors; but it is of some interest that as late as the reign of Alexander II there was an attempt in some court circles to bring about Paul's canonization.
4. Quoted in M. Walker, ed., *Metternich's Europe* (London, Macmillan, 1968), p. 80.
5. M. Bloch, *Les Rois thaumaturges* (Paris, 1924), pp. 402–4.
6. See pp. 221–2.
7. The entire document is printed in *Mémoires, documents et écrits divers laissés par le Prince de Metternich* (Paris, 1880–4), iii, 425–45.
8. J. R. Rath, *The Viennese Revolution of 1848* (University of Texas Press, 1957), pp. 198–9.
9. Quoted in E. N. Anderson and P. R. Anderson, *Political Institutions and Social Change in Continental Europe in the Nineteenth Century* (University of California Press, 1967), p. 174.
10. P. S. Squire, *The Third Department. The establishment and practices of the political police in the Russia of Nicholas I* (Cambridge University Press, 1968), pp. 205–7.
11. For illustrations of this point with regard to the Foreign Ministry, see Patricia K. Grimsted, *The Foreign Ministers of Alexander I* (University of California Press, 1969), p. 25.
12. For an excellent survey see M. Raeff, 'The Russian autocracy and its officials', *Harvard Slavic Studies*, iv (1957), 77–91.
13. On the most fundamental aspect of this, the collection of population statistics, see p. 128.
14. See p. 360.

15. S. Laing, *Observations on the Social and Political State of the European People in 1848 and 1849* (London, 1850), p. 15.

16. Laing, *Observations*, p. 220.

17. K. R. Greenfield, *Economics and Liberalism in the Risorgimento: a study of nationalism in Lombardy, 1814–1848* (Baltimore, John Hopkins Press, 1934), p. 171.

18. See p. 25.

19. C. Bellanger and others, eds, *Histoire générale de la presse française* (Paris, 1969), ii, 120.

20. F. Knight-Hunt, *The Fourth Estate* (London, 1850), i, 292.

21. For these examples see Irene Collins, *The Government and the Newspaper Press in France, 1814–1881* (Oxford University Press, 1959), pp. 27–8, 40.

22. *The History of The Times* (London, The Times, 1935–52), i, 228.

23. The crucial passage of this speech is printed in J. P. Mayer, ed., *The Recollections of Alexis de Tocqueville* (London, Harvill, 1948), pp. 12–15.

24. G. Luzzatto, 'Aspects sociaux de la révolution de 1848 en Italie', *Revue Socialiste* (1948), p. 83.

25. M. Bergman, 'The potato blight in the Netherlands and its social consequences', *International Review of Social History*, xii (1967), esp. pp. 394–402.

26. H. Pirenne, *Histoire de Belgique* (Brussels, 1902–32), vii, 128–9.

27. J. Toulemonde, *Naissance d'une métropole: histoire économique de Roubaix et Tourcoing au XIX siècle* (Tourcoing, n.d. [? 1967]), p. 84.

28. G. Duveau, 'L'ouvrier de Quarante-Huit, *Revue Socialiste* (1948), p. 74.

29. *Mémoires*, vi, 568.

30. *Bismarck, the Man and the Statesman: being the reflections and reminiscences of Otto Prince von Bismarck*, trans. A. J. Butler (London, 1898), ii, 335.

31. *Ibid.*, i, 24.

32. E. De Groot, 'Contemporary political opinion and the revolutions of 1848', *History*, n.s., xxxix (1953), 144.

33. C. Scarfoglio, *Il mezzogiorno e l'unità d'Italia* (Florence, 1953), pp. 401ff.

34. F. Meinecke, *Cosmopolitanism and the National State* (Princeton University Press, 1970), pp. 264, 275.

35. F. Ponteil, *1848* (Paris, 1937), p. 185.

36. *Histoire de la révolution de 1848* (Paris, 1866), vii, 177; quoted in J. L. Talmon, *Political Messianism: the romantic phase* (London, 1966), p. 479.

37. G. Duveau, *1848: the making of a revolution* (London, 1967), pp. 51, Introduction xix, 102: Bellanger, *Histoire . . . de la presse française*, ii, 120.

38. Which produced, for example, newspapers called *L'Oeil de Marat*, *La Patrie en Danger*, and *Le Père Duchêne*, all titles saturated in nostalgia for the great days of 1793.

39. For the most recent reprinting of the book see L. Krieger, ed., *The German Revolutions* (University of Chicago Press, 1967), pp. 169, 171, 239.

40. N. St John-Stevas, ed., *The Collected Works of Walter Bagehot*, iv (London, 1968), 75. Bagehot is here thinking mainly of France, and particularly of Thiers and Emile de Girardin.

41. Laing, *Observations*, pp. 315–16; see in particular his criticisms of the Frankfurt Parliament on pp. 428, 430, 450–1.

42. E. N. Anderson, *The Social and Political Conflict in Prussia, 1858–1864* (University of Nebraska Press, 1954), p. 237.

43. See the comments of an American statistician in E. Young, *Labor in Europe and America* (Washington, 1876), pp. 644–5; much of the enormous amount of detailed information in his book is based on British consular reports.

44. Anthony Trollope, *An Autobiography* (Fontana edition: London, 1962), p. 48. For the most famous example of conservative satire on the new ideas see T. L. Peacock, *Gryll Grange* (London, 1860).

45. The Zemstvos (*Zemstva*) were bodies elected, at the district and provincial level, by rural and urban property owners and by the electors chosen by peasant cantons. They had wide powers over public health, communications, famine relief and education, which they generally used constructively.

46. For a good discussion of this see F.M.L. Thompson, 'The Revolution in World Agriculture', in A. Briggs, ed., *The Nineteenth Century: the contradictions of progress* (London, Thames & Hudson, 1970), p. 155.

47. Meinecke, *Cosmopolitanism and the National State*, p. 365, n. 4.

48. T. Zeldin, *The Political System of Napoleon III* (London, Macmillan, 1958), p. 101, The remark was probably made in 1864.

49. St John-Stevas, ed., *Works*, iv, 101.

50. 'Coquetting with the "mob"', wrote the embittered widow of the short-lived Emperor Frederick III in 1890 to her mother, Queen Victoria, 'has always been part of the Prince Bismarck's programme, as it was the Emperor Napoleon III's' (F. E. G. Ponsonby, ed., *Letters of the Empress Frederick* (London, Macmillan, 1928), p. 405.

51. See p. 25.

52. P. L. Alston, *Education and the State in Tsarist Russia* (Stanford University Press, 1969), p. 71; for a convenient short account of the growth of the press in Russia from the reign of Nicholas I onwards see I. A. Fedosov and I. I. Astaf'ev, eds, *Istochnikovedenie Istorii CCCP XIX-nachala XXV* (Moscow, 1970), pp. 244ff.

53. Bellanger, *Histoire . . . de la presse française*, ii, 259; Collins, *The Government and the Newspaper Press in France*, p. 146.

54. See pp. 330–1.

55. In principle the right to vote was possessed by all male citizens from 1874 onwards; but this was hedged about with so many restrictions that the effective franchise was extremely restricted.

56. According to one report only 5 per cent of the Bulgarian electorate, for example, voted during the Stambolov dictatorship (1887–94), though official records purported to show that two-thirds of it had done so (T. Stoianovich, 'The social foundations of Balkan politics', in C. and Barbara Jelavich, eds, *The Balkans in Transition* (University of California Press, 1963), p. 322).

57. See pp. 216–17.

58. F. B. M. Hollyday, *Bismarck's Rival: a political biography of General and Admiral Albrecht von Stosch* (Duke University Press, 1960), p. 121; *Bismarck the*

Man and the Statesman: being the reflections and reminiscences of Otto Prince von Bismarck, trans. A. J. Butler (London, 1898), ii, 335.

59. See p. 245.

60. J. C. G. Röhl, 'Higher civil servants in Germany, 1890–1900', *Journal of Contemporary History*, ii, no. 3 (1967), 109ff.

61. M. Busch, *Bismarck: some secret pages of his history* (London, 1890), p. 445. A good brief account of the difficulties of governing Germany under the 1871 constitution can be found in J. C. G. Röhl, *Germany without Bismarck: the crisis of government in the Second Reich* (London, Batsford, 1967), pp. 20–6.

62. Röhl, *Germany without Bismarck*, p. 150.

63. It is estimated that at the end of the nineteenth century the Civil Secretariat alone was sending to the emperor for consideration 70,000–80,000 documents a year (Röhl, *Germany without Bismarck*, p. 273).

64. F. Engel-Janosi, 'Der Monarch und seine Ratgeber', in F. Engel-Janosi and H. Rumpler, eds, *Probleme der Franzisko-Josephinischen Zeit, 1848–1916* (Munich, 1967), p. 17.

65. *K P Pobedonostsev i ego korrespondenty* (Moscow, 1923), i, 52.

66. See p. 200.

67. See p. 384.

68. J. A. Thayer, *Italy and the Great War: politics and culture, 1870–1915* (University of Wisconsin Press, 1964), Chs i–vii *passim*.

3

Economy and society:
the new and the old

THE GROWTH OF POPULATION

Underlying everything else that happened in nineteenth-century Europe was one brute and basic fact: the number of Europeans was growing with unprecedented speed and steadiness. For the first time, moreover, this growth could be measured with considerable accuracy. Governments, at least in the developed parts of the continent, were now collecting and publishing vital statistics on an increasing scale and taking periodic censuses which became more complete and reliable as the century went on. Civil registration of births, deaths and marriages was introduced in France in 1792 and consolidated a few years later by Napoleon I. There were censuses there at five-year intervals from 1801 onwards, with one or two gaps usually caused by war (there was none in 1816 and that of 1871 was postponed to the following year). In Britain the first census came also in 1801 and was repeated at ten-year intervals throughout the century, though that of 1841 is the first regarded as really reliable. Systematic civil registration of births, deaths and marriages came later there than in France – not until 1836 in England and as late as 1856 in Scotland. However by the later nineteenth century the published British vital statistics had become in many ways very detailed and complete, while from 1887 the French ministry of the interior compiled a *Statistique sanitaire des villes de France* which brought together a great deal of information on population movements, causes of death in different age-groups, etc. In other parts of Europe there were comparable developments. The partial unification of Italy in 1861 was followed almost at once by the taking of a national census, as was the formation of the German empire a decade later. Belgium, relatively advanced in this as in other ways, had already taken a particularly accurate census in 1846.

The main facts of what happened are therefore not in doubt. In 1800 Europe west of the Urals had a total population of about 187 million. A century later it had one of 401 million: and this increase had been achieved in spite of huge emigration to Europe's offshoots overseas, in the Americas,

Australia, New Zealand and parts of Africa. Britain sent during the century about 21 million of her people overseas to settle, and there was also heavy German emigration, especially in its later decades. There was an enormous exodus from Italy, above all from the poverty-stricken south, from the 1890s onwards, and from the 1880s very large-scale emigration of the Polish and Jewish minorities within the Russian empire. In 1846–50, before the steamship and the railway had had much effect, about one in every thousand Europeans emigrated each year: in 1901–5 the rate was 2.5 per thousand and in 1913 4.3. Looked at in the broadest geographical perspective, this combination of population growth and emigration meant an enormous strengthening of Europe's world position and influence, even from a crude numerical point of view. In 1800 a fifth of the world's population lived in Europe or the new quasi-Europes it was creating overseas. By 1914 the proportion was close to a third; and the proportion of the earth's surface inhabited by Europeans had grown even more rapidly. This quantitative change in itself, quite apart from the economic and technological leadership which Europeans were now achieving, was unprecedented in world history.

Within Europe, in the century 1801–1901, the population of Germany rose from 24.8 million to 56.3 million, that of Britain from 15.2 to 38.7, that of Italy from 18.1 to 32.4 and that of European Russia, including the Caucasus, from 35 to 103.4.[1] France lagged notably far behind with a rise merely from 27.3 to 38.9 million; and her showing would have been appreciably worse but for the fact that she, alone among the European states, gained substantially more inhabitants by immigration than she lost by emigration. She was the only European country in which the absolute number of births fell during the nineteenth century. In 1826–30 it averaged 975,000 a year, in 1906–10 only 830,000.

At a rather superficial level this enormous growth of Europe's population is not difficult to account for. High birth-rates are part of the explanation. That for England and Wales reached its peak, at about 35 per thousand of population, in the 1860s, as did that for Russia at the extraordinarily high level of 50 per thousand. For the new German empire the peak came in the 1870s at about 39 per thousand of population, and for Italy in the following decade at almost 38. Families were still by present-day standards very large. In Britain during the second half of the nineteenth-century 43 per cent of marriages produced seven or more children.[2] However the growth of population owed much more to a large and continuing fall in death-rates. In the first half of the century this fall was still relatively modest, and infant mortality rates in particular remained virtually at the eighteenth-century level. In Britain and France one child in five still died before it was a year old, in the German states one in four, and in eastern Europe one in three. Real progress in reducing death-rates at all ages came during the second half of the century, and markedly during the years between about 1890 and 1914. Between 1850 and the First World War mortality in Germany fell from 26 per thousand population per annum to 18, a fairly typical example of what could be achieved. Most of Europe thus found itself in a situation in which, in the later nineteenth century, death-rates were coming down quite fast while birth-rates, though slowly falling, remained relatively high. There was thus a very substantial surplus of births over deaths which for many countries reached its highest point in the first years of the twentieth century. In Germany, for example, it was about 14 per thousand population per annum in 1901–5, and in Italy about 12 per thousand in 1903–13.

The obvious question, though not an easy one to answer, is: what caused this fall in death-rates? There was significant medical progress during the latter decades of the century. The systematic use of antiseptics began at the end of the 1860s, and had the very important result of making childbirth much safer; this was of far greater real benefit to many women than any agitation about political rights could ever be. The bacillus which caused tuberculosis was identified in 1883 and that of cholera in the following year. By 1900 even the existence of different blood groups had been recognized. But the effects of much of this, at least in the short or even the medium term, were limited. There were often long delays between making a discovery and applying it on a large scale to improve public health. Even vaccination of children against smallpox was not made compulsory in France until as late as 1902. It has sometimes been argued that the decline in deaths from the infectious diseases which had for centuries been the great killers – typhus, typhoid, smallpox, diphtheria – was caused by a reduction, for unknown reasons, in the virulence of the disease-causing organisms. Certainly this decline was spectacular. During the 1870s in Britain in every 100,000 people about 64 died each year of typhoid, about 48 of smallpox and about 12 of typhus. By the decade 1901–10 the figures were 18 for typhoid and 2 for smallpox, while typhus had in effect been wiped out. But that these diseases were becoming in themselves less deadly is difficult to prove in any satisfactory way.

The fall in death-rates, and particularly the fall in deaths among young children which was its most striking feature, was almost certainly in the main the result of better elementary hygiene and better nutrition. The former was more than anything else a matter of improving water supplies: it is notable that in many parts of Europe there was for a long time a marked tendency for infant mortality to increase in the summer months, when water supplies were less plentiful and those available more likely to be contaminated in some way. The results, in the form of epidemics of gastro-enteritis and other diseases among especially vulnerable young children can be seen in France as late as 1900 and in nearly all of southern and eastern Europe down to 1914. So far as nutrition was concerned, improved communications from the middle of the century were a powerful force making for more varied diets and most important of all for more reliable supplies of all the basic foods.[3] It has been suggested that in particular more plentiful supplies of milk, at least in some parts of Europe, and by the later years of the nineteenth century better methods of processing and storing it, played an important role in allowing many more young children to survive. Certainly it is suggestive that north-western Europe, where infant mortality fell first and most sharply, was in general an area with extensive mixed farming and relatively abundant supplies of milk.[4] In this respect it contrasted sharply with most of southern and much of eastern Europe, where cattle were fewer and of poorer quality. Certainly also the improvement in infantile mortality was by 1914 very unequally distributed between different countries. At the outbreak of war fewer than one child in ten in Norway and Sweden was dying before it was a year old: in Russia the toll was still about one in four. There were also within each country very marked differences in this as in all other life-chances between different social classes, while some specific disadvantaged groups remained particularly vulnerable. In both Britain and France, for example, the infant death-rate in 1914 was still about twice as high among illegitimate as among legitimate children. But in spite of great regional and class variations the general direction of change is clear. Until the 1880s even in the most advanced parts of Europe most people died of causes which were centuries old – infectious and contagious diseases, malnutrition, the effects of heavy and sustained physical labour. By 1914 the great present-day killers – viral infections, functional disorders and the effects of old age – were increasingly important.

By the later decades of the nineteenth century Europe as a whole was entering a period when the demographic situation was in many ways unprecedentedly favourable to economic advance. The fall in infant mortality was reducing the waste of resources involved when very large numbers of children died before they could enter the working population. At the same time falling death-rates had not yet gone far enough to produce a really large proportion in the population of those too old to work. The economically active population was thus an unusually large fraction of the total; and this in itself favoured a rise in living standards. A growing population meant a growing market and the possibility of growing profits: this helped to encourage investment of all kinds. More specifically, more people meant that more infrastructure in the form of houses, communications, water supplies and so on was needed; and this again was a factor which encouraged economic activity. In Germany, for example, an insistent demand for houses from the 1870s onwards, as population increased and urbanization rapidly advanced, played an essential role in the remarkable general economic growth of the period. In France, by contrast, with an almost stagnant population, there was a corresponding stagnation in house-building from about 1880 onwards which slowed economic advance as a whole.[5] The demographic foundations of Europe during the century 1815–1914, therefore, and especially during its later decades, were in many ways strongly favourable to a growth of production and a general rise in standards of consumption.

THE GROWTH OF INDUSTRY AND THE EMERGENCE OF INDUSTRIAL MAN

Side by side with this growth in the number of Europeans went an even more rapid growth in the economy which sustained them. The result was that by 1914 the vast majority of them, though their standards of physical consumption, health and education were still low by comparison with those of the present day, were decidedly better off than their ancestors a century earlier. For the ordinary peasant or artisan every previous age had been, at least at times, a struggle for mere survival. Now increasingly life could become an aspiration for more. Moreover this growth, once it was fairly under way by the middle of the century, tended to become more rapid with each successive decade. For a generation after 1815 Great Britain and Belgium were the only European states which could claim to be industrialized in a modern sense of the term to any significant extent. It was in them alone that there could be found large factories using power-driven machinery on a considerable scale, together with the substantial engineering and machine-building industries which were now the most reliable indices of a productive system of the new type. Until the cycle of revolution and war which began in 1789 France had not been strikingly inferior to Britain in terms of industrial techniques and productivity; and the Dutch Republic, though now only a secondary industrial power, had remained until the French conquest of 1795 the greatest centre of banking, insurance and international investment in the world. For both the events of 1789–1815 were in varying degrees disastrous. Revolution and war imposed upon both damaging disruptions, losses and discontinuities, destroyed much of their formerly very flourishing overseas trade and denied them the stimulating effect on their economies in general which this trade would have had.

Even in the 1780s Britain, by comparison, had clearly possessed very important economic advantages. A great and increasing foreign trade, plentiful supplies of capital for investment in new processes, good internal communications, plentiful supplies of coal (of which in 1800 she already produced twenty times as much as France), a spirit of enterprise perhaps more widespread than anywhere in continental Europe – all these were already equipping her to lead Europe into an entirely new era of economic growth. By 1815 this leadership was beyond question: the generation which followed widened still further the gap between Britain and her main continental competitors. By the early 1830s she produced ten times as much coal as France, whose population was still about 40 per cent larger, and more than forty times as much as Prussia. She produced more than three times as much iron as France and more than six times as much as Prussia. It was thus from Britain that the new productive techniques and the new methods of industrial organization, taking shape from the 1760s if not earlier and becoming well established in a few parts of the country by the end of the eighteenth century, spread first to Belgium and then to continental Europe as a whole. The 'demonstration effect' of British success, made unmistakable by the flood of cheap British textiles and metalwares which threatened to sweep over Europe with the coming of peace in 1814–15, was an essential part of the entire process. For the other European states the problem thus became to a large extent one of bringing into effective use within their own territories methods and processes which were already known and tested rather than of making for themselves new industrial discoveries. The export of British machines, the emigration to other European countries of British technicians and skilled workers, the registration of patents which diffused knowledge of innovations (British inventors quite often patented their discoveries in Paris as well as in London) all played important roles in this.

The process can be seen in operation first of all in Belgium, whose nearness to Britain, large domestic resources of coal and iron, good internal communications by water and access to large potential markets in France and Germany explain her early industrial growth. A few years after Waterloo John Cockerill, the English entrepreneur who played the most prominent role in the industrialization of Belgium, claimed that he had available in his great metallurgical and machine-building enterprise at Seraing every new technical innovation within ten days of its being introduced in England. Two decades later, in 1839, another observer noted that 'when new machines appear in England, Seraing obtains them to use as models, and supplies them afterwards not only to Belgium but to the entire continent'.[6] By then the Seraing factory had become the greatest integrated metallurgical and machine-building enterprise in the world, with a labour-force of 2,500 men. Certainly Belgium's achievements were striking. In 1830 the country contained 428 steam-engines, of which 74 (21 per cent) were foreign built. By 1844 there were 1,606, of which only 110 (7 per cent) came from abroad; already in the 1830s she was exporting engines worth seven times as much as those she imported.[7] The state-owned Belgian railway network planned in 1834 was completed only a decade later, while the country's coal production almost trebled in 1830–50. Nor was Belgium in any way unique in benefiting from British expertise. During the 1820s there were at least 15,000 British workers active in France; and Germany also drew extensively on the fund of experience which Britain had now accumulated. In 1838–39 Alfred Krupp, bearer of what was to become the greatest name of all in the European metallurgical industries, came to study on the spot British methods of steelmaking; and a Parliamentary Select Committee in 1841 was told that the owners of a factory recently built in Hamburg worked 'with English iron, with English coals, with English models, all their tools English, their director an Englishman, and of the 150 hands who were in their employment, 90 were likewise English'.[8]

By the 1840s and 1850s the pace of advance was quickening. These decades saw a decisive change from what was, for most of Europe, still an essentially eighteenth-century economic and social situation to one in which many aspects of the later nineteenth and even the twentieth centuries are clearly visible. There was a sharp increase in emigration to other parts of the world, and entirely new and important areas of settlement (New Zealand from 1838, Algeria from the early 1840s) began to be accessible to Europeans who wished to attempt a new life in another continent. There was a considerable widening of the markets overseas for European products, which was mainly the result of this emigration but also often the result of force used or threatened by the European states, as with the imposition on China of the 'Treaty Port' system by the treaty of Nanking in 1842 or the great extension of British-held territory in India in the 1840s and 1850s. Railways and steamships were transforming communications, producing unprecedented possibilities of rapid movement and exerting great indirect effects on every aspect of economic life. The gold discoveries of 1849 in California and 1851 in Australia meant a sudden and vast increase in the supply of the metal (the world gold supply grew at least sevenfold in less than a decade) and helped to produce a moderate rise in prices and a measure of profit inflation in the 1850s and 1860s which encouraged business enterprise of all kinds. In less than thirty years, between 1845–47 and 1873–75, the volume of Europe's exports quadrupled; this rate of increase was not to be surpassed until the wonderful decades of the 1950s and 1960s.

All this was ushering in a new era, one marked perhaps most fundamentally by new outlooks and psychologies. Until the middle of the century merchants, bankers, industrialists, entrepreneurs of all kinds in much of continental Europe and indeed in Britain herself had been still very often dominated by attitudes generated in an earlier age. They had tended to think in terms of limited and traditional markets, of slow, expensive and unreliable communications, of the uncertainties and losses which could be produced by the vagaries of the weather. All this meant a somewhat wary and defensive, occasionally outright hostile, attitude to new technology. The expansion and success of the 1850s and 1860s helped to generate greater confidence and therefore greater willingness to invest in new techniques which seemed to hold out the promise of increased profits. Henceforward accelerating technological advance was to be backed and given practical wealth-producing effect by increasingly large amounts of capital. These two factors, technical progress and capital formation, worked together over much of Europe in the later nineteenth century to produce the greatest and most sustained improvement hitherto achieved in any comparable period in the life of the ordinary man.

The acceleration in the flow of new discoveries and new industrial techniques in the second half of the century is unmistakable. A series of new processes (Bessemer, 1855; Martin, 1865; Gilchrist–Thomas, 1878) revolutionized the production of iron and steel. The Solvay process did the same for the production of soda, one of the most essential of all industrial chemicals, so that in 1900 it cost a seventh of what it had in the 1850s. Synthetic dyestuffs, whose development began in the 1860s, became almost at once one of the brightest jewels in Germany's increasingly resplendent industrial crown. Aluminium, first fabricated in minute quantities at great expense in 1854, had become by 1914 a widely used material whose price had fallen spectacularly. In 1860 a kilo of the metal cost 1,250 French francs: half a century later the same quantity could be bought for less than two francs. New alloys and special steels meant that world production of nickel, only 300 tons in 1874, had grown to 20,000 tons at the outbreak of the First World War. The first European pipeline for the transport of petroleum was built by the Nobel interests in Russia in 1877: the first oil-tanker, tiny by present-day standards, followed two years later. An internal combustion engine powered by gas was invented in Belgium in 1860 and became a significant source of power for industry (its original exorbitant fuel consumption of 3,000 litres of gas for every horsepower of usable energy produced had been reduced by 1890 to only 100 litres). By 1914 the presence on Europe's roads of 2 million motor vehicles showed that one of the most far-reaching of all the new industries was well established and growing.

Perhaps most important of all, the growth in the use of electrical power and of a great and increasingly complex electrical industry had begun to revolutionize many aspects of European industrial life. It was now tilting the economic balance perceptibly in favour of countries such as Italy and Switzerland, which had little or no coal resources of their own, and in the process throwing up some of the greatest entrepreneurs of this entire period: Anton and Gerard Philips in the Netherlands, Werner von Siemens and Emil Rathenau in Germany. The improvement by the 1880s of the turbine to a point at which hydroelectricity became a practical proposition, and the development in the following decade of effective means of transmitting electric power over long distances, were the crucial steps in this process. Moreover the increasing complexity of technology meant that the linkages between different industries, the 'multiplier effect' which changes in one might exert on others, became more complex and far-reaching. Thus the rapidly growing importance of electricity stimulated the production of copper and lead; thermally generated electricity meant an increased demand for coal; electric trams (the first way in which the age of electricity was brought home to many ordinary men) meant a growth in the building of coaches and wagons; and trams and the mobility they brought encouraged the growth of cities and hence gave an important impetus to the building trades. (Cement began to be manufactured on an industrial scale from about 1870.) Moreover the completion over much of Europe by the 1870s or 1880s of a good deal of the infrastructure of a modern industrial state in the form of railways, and to a lesser extent roads and port facilities, probably meant that a greater proportion of investment than in the past could find its way directly into productive industry. The result of all these forces was a marked tendency for Europe's industrial production, in spite of inevitable and sometimes sharp fluctuations, to grow at an increasing rate in the two decades or so before 1914. The best calculation available suggests that in 1860–90 the rate of growth may have averaged about 2 per cent each year, while in 1890–1913 it rose to 3.7 per cent (and in 1910–13 to 5.1 per cent).[9]

It is important to stress how uneven and incomplete this process of industrialization was. It would be quite wrong to imagine that traditional small-scale handicraft and workshop methods of production were ever reduced to insignificance, even at the end of the period and in the most highly industrialized countries. In Britain herself true factory methods were until far into the nineteenth century effectively confined to the production of cotton textiles: of the 50,000 or so mechanical looms in 1830 the overwhelming majority were in cotton factories and there were still fewer than 100,000 factory workers in the whole country. Not until the 1850s did factory methods begin to displace traditional ones outside the textile industries, and the most recent study of the subject has concluded that the effect of the steam-engine on industrial growth in Britain was relatively small in the first half of the century.[10] Moreover factory production in its early stages often increased the demand for domestic workers: the new, cheap, mass-produced cotton cloth, for example, had to be made up into dresses and shirts by an army of very badly paid seamstresses working individually or in small groups. In a somewhat similar way the coming of the railways, by the fillip it gave to transport and the distributive trades generally, actually increased substantially the number of horses in use in Britain, and no doubt in all other countries, throughout the second half of the century and therefore the number of men needed to drive and care for them. One recent writer has argued that 'The industrial revolution, far from abridging human labour, created a whole new world of labour-intensive jobs' and that 'mechanisation in one department of production was usually accompanied by an increase of drudgery in others.'[11] Certainly the existence almost everywhere in Europe of large reserves of cheap labour, of workers who could be employed when demand was high and dismissed when it slackened, men towards whom their employers felt only a minimum of obligation and the state virtually none, helped to prolong the use of hand technology. It is very significant that so much of the labour-saving technology of the nineteenth century originated in America, where this labour reserve did not exist. A high proportion of the technological development in European industry, by contrast, was designed to save capital, for example by reducing fuel consumption, rather than to economize in the use of labour.

Everywhere the traditional industries gave ground only slowly to the more rapidly growing ones. Even in Britain there were still more leatherworkers than coal-miners in the middle of the nineteenth century; and it was not until about 1870 that factory workers began to make up more than half the total British work force (though by then they accounted for much more than half of total production). In some types of agriculture also traditional small-scale peasant production for long held its own very well. From the early 1870s cereal producers, and a little later those of meat also, were facing an unprecedented threat in the vast growth of imports from the United States, Canada, Argentina and Australasia; but market gardening, fruit-growing and the supply of eggs and dairy products remained areas in which the small traditional producer was still strong. By the 1870s and 1880s the decline of the old-style self-employed skilled artisan with the essential advantage of direct personal access to the market, the figure who had dominated so much of Europe's industrial life for centuries, was becoming clear. He was now condemned to an increasingly minor role by the relative technological stagnation of the industries in which he was still most prominent – building, clothing, furniture – and by his lack of access to capital and to increasingly complex, distant and rapidly changing markets. In terms of material wealth, as well as of significance in the mechanism of production, he was now being rapidly overhauled by the skilled or even semi-skilled factory worker. In Paris, for example, the real value of the personal estates left by master-artisans rose in the period 1820–1911 from an index figure of 65 to one of 100. For the population in general the rise over the same period was from 18 to 100 and for wage-earners from 10 to 100.[12] But for much of the nineteenth century and over much of Europe it is the persisting vitality of the old rather than the challenge and victory of the new which seems to many present-day historians remarkable.

The triumph of factory production was also for long delayed by the stubborn rearguard action fought by the putting-out system, the working-up in their own homes or in small workshops by individuals or small groups, often scattered over a wide geographical area, of materials supplied to them by an entrepreneur who organized and controlled (sometimes with a good deal of difficulty) the whole productive process. In Germany in the 1840s about two-thirds of all the industrial workers in Prussia and Saxony were still organized in this way; and though the advantages of the factory system inevitably became more obvious as technologies grew more complex and machines more expensive, putting-out retained much of its importance for a very long time. The silk industry of Lyons grew rapidly on this basis from the 1820s onwards; and even in the early twentieth century putting-out still flourished in, for example, the specialized metal trades of Sheffield or in the rapidly growing cotton industry of Piedmont. Until the 1880s or even the 1890s the majority of the European working class was still labouring in ways which had been, in many of their essentials, quite familiar in the eighteenth century.

Until late in the nineteenth century, moreover, the lack of a stable workforce was often a serious check on the advance of modern large-scale factory industry. It was still very common for workers to move frequently from one job to another, and between industry and agriculture or between different branches of industry. In societies where large-scale industrialization was recent or only beginning it was still even in the early twentieth century very common for industrial workers to leave the factories in the summer to work the land in their native villages. This was a serious obstacle in Russia to the growth of a reliable and reasonably skilled labour-force for the country's rapidly developing industries. In the coal-producing areas of the Ukraine in 1893–1902 less than a quarter of the miners actually worked all year in the mines, while in the mines and foundries of Silesia, another area of spectacular growth in heavy industry, there was

a heavy dependence on the labour of migrant Polish workers.[13] From the
1880s onwards the number of factory workers began to increase rapidly
in all industrialized states; and this growth was particularly marked in
those like Germany and Russia which were starting from a lower level
of industrialization than Britain, Belgium or even France. In the German
empire there were about 5 million people employed in factories in 1882
and about 9 million a quarter of a century later. Those employed in industry,
trade and financial services outnumbered those in agriculture for the first
time in 1890. In Russia the number of factory workers doubled, from 1.5
million to 3 million, in 1890–1914. Moreover the newly industrializing
countries were marked by a greater prominence of very large enterprises
than the older industrial states of western Europe. In Hungary, a formerly
very backward area now in rapid transition, 1.5 per cent of the enterprises accounted for not far short of half the industrial work force in the
years before 1914, while in Russia in 1908 over half the industrial workers were in factories employing more than 1,000 people. By the outbreak
of the First World War, therefore, the predominance everywhere on the
continent of modern industry was assured. But it is important to remember how recent many of its successes had been. Until late in the nineteenth
century the large factory, with its expensive machinery, long production
runs and disciplined labour-force was very much the exception. Until then
the economic map of Europe was one showing only islands of modern
industrialization, islands which became distinctly rarer as one moved further east and south from modern industry's Anglo-Belgian roots, islands
still surrounded by a sea of traditionalism.

This was a fundamentally important limit to the scope of industrialization. Its geographical distribution, not merely between states but within
them, was extremely uneven. In some areas, usually relatively small ones,
it came to transform totally the whole texture of life, of material production, of working habits, of social relationships. Outside these areas direct
manifestations of it might be almost imperceptible and traditional methods,
outlooks and values might remain for long unchallenged. The political
units which made up nineteenth-century Europe present a picture therefore not of economic or industrial homogeneity, even of the roughest
kind, but of sharp internal variations and inequalities. Industrialization
meant in practice the establishment of enclaves of large-scale power-driven
industry against a background which was still traditional and usually in
the main agrarian. All the large European states, it has been said, were in
fact 'patchwork quilts of very different economic regions'.[14] In the first
half of the century in England industrial Lancashire contrasted sharply
with the rest of the country; and from the middle of the century or earlier
even sharper contrasts could be seen between the remarkable development

of heavy industry in west-central Scotland and the totally different situation of the Highlands and the Borders. In France again the large-scale industry of Lille, Roubaix or St Etienne was a different world from the traditionalism of much of the south and west of the country. In Germany in 1913 official figures showed Hamburg, for generations at the forefront of the country's commercial growth and an industrial centre in its own right, with a per capita income four times that of the agrarian province of Posen in Polish Prussia. Russia is an outstanding example of the development of very large-scale industry in a few areas against a background of agrarian backwardness, of 'the idiocy of rural life' in Marx's phrase, over much the greater part of the country. In Italy by the early twentieth century the contrasts were perhaps sharpest of all, between the terrible poverty and backwardness of Sicily, Sardinia and much of the south and the relatively sophisticated industrial development which was making a few parts of the north far more akin to Switzerland than to the despairing Mezzogiorno. Such examples could easily be multiplied, and inequalities of this kind have led some historians to query how far the growth of industrial society can be usefully discussed at all in the traditional terms of separate sovereign states.

Nevertheless these states were the framework on which very many aspects of European life depended, the skeleton, so to speak, which for good or evil shaped and controlled the growth of the continent. Without them nineteenth- and twentieth-century Europe is hardly conceivable, and so far as relations between the states were concerned the general effect of industrialization was to increase inequalities and disparities. The fact that it affected different parts of the continent at different times and to widely differing extents meant that the relative economic strength of different states, and hence increasingly their weight in the international balance of power, fluctuated sharply over time. Down to the 1880s Great Britain was in most respects the leader of Europe in industrial organization and techniques, financial institutions and foreign trade. In 1870 she was still producing more than five times as much iron as France and more than four times as much as Germany, both of whom still had appreciably larger populations. At the end of the 1870s British industry had at its disposal two and a half times as much steam power as its French competitors and about half as much again as its now rapidly advancing German ones. In 1913 Britain's per capita Gross National Product was still the highest in Europe. Long before then, however, other countries had begun to overtake and in some respects to surpass her, both in terms of gross production and in per capita ones. Of the greater European states France was not, in most respects, a serious challenge to her. An almost stagnant population; lack of coal deposits on the scale of those of Britain and

Germany; agricultural techniques which changed only very slowly; an inheritance system which tended to keep peasants on the land rather than to drive them to the cities and the factories; perhaps complex interlinked social and historical factors which made large-scale factory industry seem foreign to French traditions and aptitudes – all these meant that France's economic growth during the nineteenth century was slower than that of any other major European state. In 1830 she may have accounted for almost 15 per cent of the total gross product of the continent as a whole: by 1913 her share was probably less than 11 per cent.

Her economic performance has sometimes been excessively written down by historians. The French growth-rate during the half-century 1860–1910 was distinctly better than in the preceding decades and perhaps indeed somewhat above the European average.[15] Even in 1913 her real income per capita was at least equal to that of Germany, though in total volume of production the latter, because of her much larger population, was now far ahead. In many consumer goods industries high quality and relatively high productivity gave France a strong position: and in the years before the cataclysm of 1914 she showed considerable ability to develop new industries such as motor vehicles and the cinema. In some of the last years of peace Charles Pathé, one of the pioneers of the cinema as an industry, sold to the United States more than twice as many films as the entire American industry produced. From the 1850s onwards, moreover, the abundant supplies of investment capital available in France made a very important contribution to economic advance in many parts of Europe. By 1914 there was more than four times as much French money as British invested throughout the continent (including the Ottoman empire and Egypt). Banking systems in many parts of Europe under the Second Empire, heavy industry in west Germany until the 1870s, railway-building in Spain, Italy and the Habsburg empire, later a wide range of enterprises in Russia, all benefited from the flow of capital made available by French investors.[16] But there is no mistaking the general lack in France, except in short periods such as the 1850s and 1896–1914, of the kind of industrial dynamism which some of the other European states were to show during this period.

The stability, sometimes verging on stagnation, of so much French economic life contrasts sharply with the spectacular growth of the new German empire after the unification of 1866–71. There had been clear foreshadowings of this long before the treaty of Frankfurt and the new constitution of 1871. There were some years of very rapid industrial growth in the early 1850s; and it was in that decade that several of the great banks which were later to be the most important controlling influence on German industrial development were founded – the Diskontogesellschaft

(1851), the Darmstadter Bank (1853), the Berliner Handelsgesellschaft (1856). Railway mileage in Germany trebled during the 1850s and 1860s, and by the outbreak of the Franco-Prussian war German industry had at its disposal almost 2.5 million horsepower of steam-engines as against only 1.85 million in France. By the early 1870s Krupp in Essen was already the greatest industrial enterprise in Europe, employing 16,000 men, and there were other outstanding industrial successes like the Borsig concern in Berlin. The speculative boom which followed the end of the war with France set a pace which could not be sustained for more than a few years (the value of the new joint-stock companies set up in Prussia in 1870–74 was greater than that of all those created in the previous half-century) and was followed by a severe slump.

But in spite of inevitable fluctuations the achievement of Wilhelmine Germany was very remarkable. Machine-building, the most telling of all indicators of essential industrial strength in this period, employed 51,000 men in Germany in 1861, 356,000 in 1882 and 1.12 million in 1907.[17] In the great new industries of chemicals and electricity she led the world. A single firm, Badische Anilin und Soda Fabrik, which had employed 7,000 men in 1870, was employing 77,000 only twelve years later: in the years immediately before 1914 it produced more benzol than France, Britain and Belgium combined and about a third of the whole world output of the basic fertilizer sulphate of ammonia.[18] The electric railway, electro-chemistry, electrometallurgy, were all in the main German creations; and though the first public electric power station in Europe was built in England, in 1881, it was the work of a firm, Siemens Brothers, founded by a German. Germany's exports, in money values, doubled in 1872–1900 and then more than doubled again in 1900–13. Moreover their composition was significantly changing. In 1873 38 per cent of them by value had been manufactured goods; forty years later 63 per cent were.[19] In 1871 the German merchant fleet had been a mere 82,000 tons; by 1913 it amounted to 4.38 million tons. From the moment of its foundation Wilhelmine Germany was rapidly overhauling, and in some essential respects surpassing, Great Britain as an economic power. The social and other roots of this splendid German success and relative British decline, which have been briefly discussed in an earlier chapter of this book, are not altogether easy to distinguish and still to some extent the subject of debate;[20] but the extent and nature of the change in the economic balance is not in doubt.

Much of the economic history of nineteenth-century Europe has to be written in terms of the great states – Britain, France and Germany – which have been briefly discussed in the preceding paragraphs and of Russia which will be discussed later and in a rather different context.[21] Some of the smaller states, however, found their position changing, for better or worse, in equally or even more striking ways. Whether they benefited or suffered from economic change depended above all on whether and how fast they could adapt to changing conditions, grasp new opportunities, and find some relatively secure and comfortable niche for themselves in an increasingly complex structure of international trade and comparative national economic advantages. Some, at least in the later decades of this period, were remarkably successful. Switzerland, with few natural resources and a highly educated population, sensibly concentrated on types of production where skill, inventiveness and quality of product rather than large-scale consumption of raw materials were important – machinery, watches and chemicals. By 1914 she had the highest per capita exports of machinery in the world.[22] Over the half-century 1860–1910 the highest growth-rates in Europe were probably those achieved by Sweden and Denmark,[23] and in each case intelligent specialization and the ability to adapt and innovate were crucial. In Sweden the growth of an advanced engineering industry and the exploitation of new markets for forest prod- ucts, paper and wood-pulp, were brilliantly successful. In this half-century her export trade grew almost twice as fast as that of Europe as a whole. Denmark, by developing a very advanced and highly intensive form of agriculture based on the production of eggs, dairy products and bacon for the rapidly growing British market, achieved the unique position of hav- ing a very high rate of economic growth which owed hardly anything to factory or any other kind of industrial production.

Italy, though by no means a small state, could be considered no more than a very minor industrial power during almost the whole of the nineteenth century. Yet in spite of great handicaps – widespread illiteracy, a long history of political division, lack of adequate domestic supplies of coal and iron – she also showed in the last years of this period some real capacity for growth. The difficulties under which she laboured make direct comparisons between her and Switzerland or the Scandinavian states impossible to draw with any fairness; but she displayed, at least in the industrializing areas of the north, in the Milan–Turin–Genoa triangle which was already developing, some of the same adaptability and enterprise. More than any other large European state she benefited from the coming of electrical power, especially from the hydroelectricity which did some- thing to compensate for her lack of coal. In 1897–1913 her industrial production rather more than doubled (starting, of course, from a relatively low base) and in 1903–11 the mechanical power used in Italian industry also doubled, with about half of the total supplied by electricity. More- over the changes were qualitative as well as quantitative. Although the industrial census of 1911 showed that a third of all workers in Italian industry were still in the traditional fields of silk and cotton textiles, the appearance of names such as Fiat, Olivetti and Pirelli showed that in spite of the backwardness of so much of the country and the appalling poverty of the south and the islands some of the new high-technology industries, office machines and motor vehicles, had now established a foothold in a few parts of the more favoured north.

Few of the lesser states of Europe were able, however, to react to the changing economic environment, with all its dangers and opportunities, as successfully as Switzerland or Scandinavia. A country with the will and means to adopt modern industry on a large scale could increase its wealth relatively quickly; but it was equally true that one unable or unwilling to modernize in this way was doomed to see itself decline, sometimes quite rapidly, in terms both of the relative living standards of its people and of its international importance. Until well into the nineteenth century the prevalence of primitive technologies and small-scale handicraft production had tended to prevent the growth of very marked economic inequalities between the states of Europe. Some considerable disparities certainly existed; but until modern industry had developed it was not easy to push them to extremes. As the century went on, however, the gap between states (or rather favoured regions within states) which were adapting and growing, which had factories, investment capital and supplies of skilled labour, and other areas which had none of these things, between winners and losers, grew steadily wider. One effort to give precision to this point has calculated that in 1800 the three richest countries in Europe had an average per capita Gross National Product only some 45 per cent greater than that of the three poorest, but that by 1860 the difference was about 160 per cent and by 1913 about 240 per cent. The gap between rich and poor widened in every decade between 1830 and 1914, though the rate at which it did so appears to have slackened somewhat after the 1860s. Another calculation of the same kind concludes that in 1800–60 the more developed European states more than doubled their per capita incomes, whereas in Scandinavia (only on the threshold of development in 1860), the Mediterranean countries and Austro-Hungary such incomes grew by only 40 per cent and in eastern Europe by a mere 10 per cent.[24]

From the 1860s onwards the balance tilted sharply in favour of northern, mainly Protestant, relatively well-educated Europe. The tremendous achievements of German industry are the main explanation for this; but the even more remarkable progress of Scandinavia also played a part. In the half-century 1860–1910 the Nordic countries (Denmark, Norway, Sweden and Finland) increased their per capita Gross National Product at an average annual rate of 1.6 per cent. For the Mediterranean countries (Spain, Portugal, Italy, Greece and Serbia) in the same period the comparable figure was a mere 0.28 per cent. This progression reflects a growth of international economic inequalities unprecedented in all Europe's previous history (and the disparities between the advanced parts of Europe and the poverty of Asia and even more of Africa were much more striking still). The contrast between the fates of Denmark and Portugal makes the point very well. Denmark in the first years of the nineteenth century accounted for only about 0.4 per cent of Europe's gross product; but by 1913 intelligent adaptation had more than doubled this, to 0.9 per cent. Portugal during the same period saw her contribution drop from about 2 per cent to a mere 0.7 per cent (though how much of this stems from the loss of her empire in Brazil in the 1820s is not clear). From being one of the richer countries of western Europe she had now become the poorest. In 1800 she had been still the fifth or sixth most important trading state in Europe: by 1910 she had sunk to seventeenth place.[25] The unforgiving rationality of modern economic life was now exacting a toll in terms of international inequality such as had never been seen before. These sharp differences in economic performance were now being reflected more clearly and on a larger scale than ever before, moreover, in the migration of workers from one part of the continent to another. Unprecedented numbers were now voting with their feet not merely for promised lands beyond the Atlantic but for European countries other than their own where they hoped to find the work, the wages and the opportunities in general which were lacking at home. The movement of Italian workers into France and of Polish ones into Germany in the later decades of the century were the most obvious examples of this tendency.

Small countries such as Switzerland and the Scandinavian states (and outside Europe Australia, New Zealand and Argentina) were able to do increasingly well for themselves from the 1870s onwards because of the enormous growth of world trade which was another striking result of industrialization and general economic growth. The total value of international trade has been estimated at 10 milliards of French gold francs in 1830, 30 milliards in 1850, 58 milliards in 1870 and perhaps 200 milliards in 1914[26] – a twentyfold increase in three-quarters of a century. This rate of growth, which of course depended very heavily on the development of new techniques of transport, opened important opportunities to small economies which could adapt quickly to the demands of bigger ones. Thus Denmark from the 1870s and New Zealand from the 1880s were flourishing as large-scale suppliers of food to Britain, while Sweden was profiting from the increasing demand of more numerous and more literate Europeans for unheard-of quantities of cheap paper. In this massive growth of world trade an important role was of course played by the United States and, from the 1890s, an increasingly significant one by Japan. But

Europe's role was always the leading one; even in 1913 well over two-fifths of the world's trade was carried out by Europeans. By then the basic pattern of Europe's trade had for long been fixed. On the one hand massive imports from the non-European world of food and raw materials (increasingly in addition to traditional raw materials such as cotton new ones which Europe herself could not produce, such as rubber, or could produce only in inadequate quantities, such as petroleum and copper). On the other hand, counterbalancing and making possible this vast inflow of essential commodities, a great outflow of European manufactured goods of all kinds. This system of international exchanges, the application on an unprecedented scale of the idea of differing comparative productive advantages, was to be seen in its most complete and developed form in the case of Britain. By 1910–1914 she was importing 81 per cent of her wheat, 75 per cent of her butter and 42 per cent of her meat; such a degree of dependence on essential imports by one of the largest markets in the developed world was in itself a powerful force making for a high level of world trade.

This trade growth, and the increasing economic unification of the world which it was bringing about, made an essential contribution to the most obviously and immediately beneficial result of industrial progress – the marked and sustained rise in material living standards to be seen over much of Europe from the middle of the nineteenth century onwards.

Until the 1850s this rise was to many observers hardly perceptible. Until then it was quite plausible to argue that the development of the new-style industry had reduced the standards of the industrial worker without doing very much to lift those of the population in general. Apart from the squalor, the disease, the social disintegration and the apparent political dangers of the new industrial cities or the unprecedentedly rapid growth of older ones, which so impressed and often frightened contemporaries,[27] there were other factors which gave colour to this view. Working hours in the new factories remained everywhere very long, often quite irrationally so, at least until the 1860s: there seems little doubt that, in the words of one writer, 'the first decades of capitalist development involved increased labour effort'.[28] The rigid discipline in many of the new factories and the harshness with which workers were often treated[29] also helped to strengthen the view that much economic change had been for the worse. More important, it was not until the middle of the century that western Europe at least began to shake itself free from the most basic and ingrained of all economic fears, that of really serious food shortage, of crippling rises in the price of the necessities of existence and in the extreme case of simple death through hunger. The crises of the mid-1840s,[30] seen in their most devastating form in the famine which killed half a million people in

Ireland in 1845–47 and led to the emigration of a million others in the following few years, were a grim reminder of how slowly and partially Europe was escaping from these ancestral terrors.

After the watershed of the 1840s, however, the picture changed rapidly and permanently. In France the price of a quintal of wheat fell in 1850, for the first time in the country's history, to the equivalent of less than 100 hours of a labourer's work: 1856 was the last year in which its price exceeded that of 200 hours of such work, and 1891 the last in which it was more than 100 hours.[31] It is significant that the quite serious shortage and rise in food prices from which Europe suffered in 1853–55 (though this was not on the tragic scale of 1845–47) was weathered without serious political unrest; and after that the spectre of famine and increasingly that even of serious shortage steadily receded so far as most of western Europe was concerned. This was partly because of the growing efficiency and productivity of European agriculture and of improved transport with its price-equalizing effects, but still more because from the 1870s onwards the continent could increasingly draw for its food on the resources of vast areas of the rest of the world. A growing market in Europe and improved methods of transport meant that grain from Canada, the United States, Australia and Argentina, meat from Argentina and New Zealand, dairy products from New Zealand, fruit from the Caribbean, could now form a permanent part of the European diet. The growth of international trade of this kind was an important stimulus to economic growth everywhere. If the farmer in the Middle West or the pampas of Argentina, or in New Zealand or Australia, produced food or raw materials for Europe and received manufactured goods in return this normally meant that each of these parts of the world was doing what it was best suited to. Specialization of this kind meant economies of scale and increased productivity, and a more rational and efficient allocation of resources on a world scale.

As food supplies became more secure they began also to absorb a smaller proportion of the purchasing power of the ordinary man. Until the middle of the nineteenth century the position in this respect for the vast majority of Europeans did not vary essentially from what it had been before the French Revolution, when one or two basic foodstuffs, bread above all, absorbed much the greater part of their income, and in periods of high prices absorbed it all. In pre-industrial Europe, it has been said, 'Eating consists of a lifetime of consuming bread, more bread, and still more bread.'[32] In the years after 1815, even in Britain, about two-thirds of an average worker's income went on food and drink. As all the essential foods became cheaper, however, it became possible to spend progressively more on non-essentials, on semi-luxuries and especially on imported food-stuffs: the British per capita consumption of tea, for example, trebled in

1844-76, and in the same years that of sugar increased from about 17 to about 60 pounds per head per year.[33] From the 1860s-1870s onwards technological changes were having a great and increasing effect on the diet of the more developed parts of Europe. Rail transport and refrigeration were making it possible, as nothing else could have, to supply rapidly growing great cities with fresh milk. They were also helping to make a range of fresh fish available as never before in at least some parts of the continent (by 1914 there were over 25,000 fish and chip shops in Britain consuming at least a quarter of all the fish landed in the country).[34] Not all of these changes were for the better nutritionally. Increasingly refined flour meant a considerable loss of nutritional value and the consumption of more and more refined sugar meant a great deal of painful, disfiguring and largely untreated tooth decay (false teeth begin to be common, outside the wealthier classes, only after about 1850). But the contrast with the restricted and often insecure diet of any earlier age was very striking. It was, however, a contrast which was much less marked even at the end of the century in the peasant Europe of the south and east of the continent than in the industrialized societies of the north-west. Until the end of this period the diet of most Russians, for example, remained extremely monotonous. 'The food of the peasants', reported a Moscow doctor in the 1880s, 'is terribly uniform: day in and day out rye bread, potatoes, cabbage; the remaining foods are merely a sort of seasoning for these three.'[35]

The same widening of the effective range of choice was produced by the rapidly increasing quantities of cheap mass-produced manufactured goods. Of these textiles were the first and most striking example; and as early as 1846 the French historian Jules Michelet had clearly grasped their importance and described it in a passage in his book *Le Peuple* which has been frequently quoted. 'Machine production', he wrote

brings within the reach of the poor a world of useful objects, which they never could reach before . . . the great and fundamental revolution has been in cotton prints. . . . Every woman used to wear a blue or black dress that she kept for ten years without washing, for fear it might tear to pieces. But now her husband, a poor worker, covers her with a robe of flowers for the price of a day's labour. All the women of the people who display an iris of a thousand colours on our promenades were formerly in mourning.

From the middle of the century the range of cheap consumer goods began to widen rapidly. From the 1850s-1860s onwards new and mainly American machines, notably the first practicable sewing-machine and the band-saw for cutting-out, paved the way for a really large ready-made clothing industry and for the mass production of cheap boots and shoes. It became unnecessary for the poor to dress, as they had largely done hitherto, in the cast-offs of the more well-to-do. Moreover mass-produced clothing meant that local and regional styles, which in many countries had varied endlessly and strikingly between very small adjacent areas, were by the later decades of the century becoming somewhat despised relics of the past or mere tourist attractions. This growing uniformity in dress within the boundaries of each nation-state may have made a significant contribution to the growth of popular national feeling.[36] By the middle of the century, again, American and Swiss watches and clocks were making what had hitherto been beyond the reach of the ordinary worker into an article of mass consumption, and in the process contributing powerfully to that sharpening of the sense of time and feeling for 'time-thrift' which was one of the most fundamental and lasting legacies of industrialism.[37] More and more, in fact, a worker in steady and reasonably well-paid employment now had access to an increasing range of goods hitherto completely beyond his purse. Books were greatly cheapened by the coming of cheap paper and the complete mechanization of bookbinding in the 1840s. In the early nineteenth century the cost of paper accounted for about two-thirds of the total cost of a moderate-sized edition of a normal book. By its end, vast quantities of paper made from wood-pulp and esparto grass had reduced this proportion to only a tenth.[38] Machine-made carpets were becoming widely available, though even in the 1890s they were beyond the reach of most industrial workers. By 1867 it was possible in Britain to buy a cheap package-tour week in Paris to see the great international exhibition there for thirty shillings (£1.50). By the end of the century very large numbers of workers in the textile towns of Lancashire were taking seaside holidays – the first appearance anywhere in Europe of what was to become a major feature of working-class life.[39] Professional sport was becoming the relaxation of millions (though overwhelmingly male millions). In 1913 in England 120,000 people watched the football Cup Final, while from 1903 onwards more and more Frenchmen could become excited by the greatest of all bicycle races, the Tour de France. By 1914 the cinema had achieved even wider popularity, notably among women: the first custom-built cinema in Britain was erected in Lancashire in 1908.[40] For the first time new synthetic materials – artificial silk (1889), Bakelite (1909), cellophane (1912) – began to play a role in mass standards of living.

The growth of this more varied pattern of consumption was connected, particularly for the middle classes and the more well-to-do working class, with changes in the pattern of retail trade. In the first half of the nineteenth century this remained essentially what it had been for generations. For the majority of Europeans the pedlar, carrying in his pack a small selection of goods, remained the main and often the sole source of the few non-essentials which most people could afford, and even of many essentials. Trade of this kind was a well-established source of employment for the men of particular areas, particularly poor mountainous ones with few resources of their own: the region around Paris, for example, was served largely by pedlars from the Auvergne, and the Po basin and some other parts of Italy by those from the highlands of Piedmont. The fair was still of central importance because of the way in which it brought together buyers and sellers in numbers and on a scale otherwise unparalleled; in some cases it still had international and not merely local or regional importance. Both these venerable institutions showed considerable staying-power in the nineteenth century. In France the fair of Beaucaire remained important until about 1850, and in Germany those of Frankfurt and Leipzig declined only slowly. In Russia the greatest of all, that at Nizhnyi Novgorod, was founded only in 1817 and reached the height of its prosperity as late as the 1880s. Nevertheless this traditional structure was now being steadily replaced by a more modern one based on the shop and the new and important figure of the commercial traveller who carried samples of his wares and acted as a travelling wholesaler. In Prussia, to take one example, there were three times as many retail shopkeepers in 1900 as there had been fifty years earlier.[41] In major cities by the second half of the century another institution of modern life was beginning to be visible – the great store selling, at fixed prices, in a large number of different departments, a very wide range of goods, and attempting through small profit margins and a very large and rapid turnover to reach the widest possible buying public. The first great example of this was the Bon Marché, founded in Paris in 1852 by Antoine Boucicault. In 1863 its turnover was 7 million francs: by 1877, when Boucicault died, it had grown to 77 million and by the 1890s to 150 million. By then the store had forty-seven different departments and did an enormous trade through mail order and the distribution of samples.

Underlying all this was the fact that throughout the period 1850–1914, in spite of inevitable and sometimes sharp fluctuations, the general tendency was for prices to fall. Sometimes, as with new and relatively high-technology goods such as aluminium and most chemicals, the fall was very sharp. This tended to raise real wages. It also subjected many entrepreneurs, faced with falling prices for their products, to considerable financial pressures. These the more successful and enterprising of them usually met by adopting more technically advanced and capital-intensive methods of production. These in their turn tended to make the goods in question still cheaper. In this way there developed, however imperfectly, however distorted by resistance to change, personal greed, tariff barriers and all the inevitable frictions and inefficiencies of any economic system, a beneficent cycle which was all the time tending, however blindly, to raise general standards of living in at least considerable parts of Europe.

Even if much of this growth of mass consumption is dismissed as essentially unimportant, as mere crumbs from the capitalist's table thrown to elements of the working class to divert and appease them (and it would be unfair and superficial to regard it in this way), it was underlain by more fundamental changes in conditions of life for the masses. Hours of work were falling quite sharply in the later decades of the nineteenth century and the early years of the twentieth. In Germany for example the working year in mining and factory industry fell in the period 1850–1913 by about 30 per cent, and that for the employed population in general by about half as much.[42] This reduction in the sheer quantity of labour (or at least in time spent at the workplace) demanded of the ordinary man was probably the most important single element in raising working-class standards of living in the industrially developed parts of Europe. Against this must be set a tendency, at least in some countries, for a greater use of machinery and perhaps a greater intensity and pace of work as factories became increasingly the industrial norm, to increase industrial accidents and the psychological stress of work in industry. In Germany in 1900, 7 industrial workers in every thousand were killed in this way and 37 injured, as against corresponding figures of only 2 and 24 in 1886. But even allowing for this it is difficult to deny that the general direction of change as regards hours of work and working conditions was in the right direction. It can also be argued that there was an underlying long-term tendency throughout the whole century for rates of economic growth and economic conditions in general to become more stable and to fluctuate less sharply. Agriculture, because of its dependence on the weather, was inherently the most variable and unpredictable component in the wealth of all European societies; yet its relative importance was decreasing almost everywhere. The new service industries, notably all sorts of clerical and administrative work, were the most stable element of all; and these were now beginning that inexorable growth which has continued to the present day. It may have been, therefore, that over the long term the forces making for economic stability and security of employment were very slowly tending to increase; but there are both conceptual and practical difficulties in the way of either proving or disproving this contention with any certainty.

This improvement in consumption and conditions of work in working-class life generally, which is visible from the later decades of the nineteenth century, probably owed little to the activities of trade unions. These were certainly growing. In Britain they had about 750,000 members in 1888 and 4 million in 1914: the great dock strike of 1889 is usually taken as marking the beginning of their extension to unskilled workers, though it can be argued that the formation of the National Union of Railwaymen in 1910 was a more important step in the growth of mass union membership. At the outbreak of war in 1914 about 44 per cent of male British manual workers were trade union members. In Germany, where their development had begun later and where official and employer hostility had always been much more marked, trade unions still had 3.3 million members by 1913, the great majority of them in the Free (i.e. at least theoretically Marxist) unions. In France they were at last given a secure legal status in 1884, though they remained for long after that date small, poor and ideologically divided. Yet it is very doubtful whether in any country trade unions did much to increase the share of national wealth and income going to labour in general. What they could and did achieve was to increase the wages of members of powerful unions (which invariably meant skilled men) at the expense of workers who were members of weaker and less tightly organized unions, or of none at all.

Government action, on the other hand, becoming wider in scope and more determined and effective in execution as the century drew to a close, made a real contribution to improving conditions of work, to shortening hours and to banishing child labour from the industrial picture. Here again Britain led the way. The Factory Act of 1833, which limited the hours of work of children (those under nine to be banished from factories, those under thirteen not to work more than 9 hours in any one day), also set up an inspectorate to see that this legislation was enforced. This was a crucial step. Though the number of factory inspectors was at first very small their scope, originally limited entirely to textile factories, grew rapidly. In 1850 it was extended to mines; and the Factory Act of 1867 greatly widened their activities. Perhaps most important of all, their reports provided a fund of detailed and reliable information about working conditions of a kind which no government had ever before possessed and which could form a relatively secure basis for official action. The Unemployed Workmen's Act of 1905, though relatively ineffective in itself, was the first serious suggestion in Britain, and probably in any major European state, of government action to reduce unemployment; and in 1908 the Coal Mines Act, which established an eight-hour day in the mines, was the first government regulation in Britain of the hours of work of adult males. It is one of the paradoxes of history that Britain, where economic liberalism and *laissez-faire* were more of an article of faith than anywhere else in Europe, should have taken the lead in this way in interfering between employer and employed and in tampering with the free working of the labour-market. That this should have been so was a remarkable tribute to the power of the humanitarian impulses which were the main inspiration of government activity of this kind. There developed from the 1830s onwards, and perhaps still more notably from the 1880s, what one historian has called an 'extraordinary heightening of the sense of what the minimal conditions for human existence should be'.[43] This increasing sensitivity to the poverty and suffering of others was buttressed by the growing professionalism of the factory inspectorate and from the 1890s onwards by a fear that a depressed, poverty-stricken and demoralized working class might prove a very serious check on national strength and achievement. Together these forces were strong enough to produce in Britain legislation on factory conditions which was earlier and more far-reaching than that to be found elsewhere in Europe.

France by comparison had no legislation regulating the work of women and children which was even partially effective until 1874. More effective legislation was passed in 1892; but even after this it was possible for some children to be employed when they were only twelve years old. Most significant of all, until 1890 every French worker had to carry the identity paper, the *livret*, introduced under Napoleon I, which constituted a record of his employment and seemed to mark him out as suspect, dangerous, in some sense outside normal society. Germany, which took the lead in the development of a recognizably modern system of social insurance, also lagged behind Britain in effective control of hours of work and working conditions. A law of 1891 forbade night work for women and children and regulated their hours of work; but here again much less was done to extend this sort of protection to men. Nevertheless government action, though it varied widely in scope and effectiveness in different countries, made a real contribution to improving conditions of work; and increasingly by the first years of the twentieth century this was being supplemented by the still more important schemes of state-controlled social insurance which were taking shape in the more advanced states.

The rosy picture drawn in the preceding paragraphs needs modification in some important respects. It has been argued, though this is inherently difficult to prove satisfactorily, that the purchasing power of the masses in fact grew more slowly than it might have done in 1850–1914, since the ruling groups in all the industrializing European countries were able to hold down mass consumption, make society as a whole live less well than it could have done, and thus provide the resources needed for investment. This they could do because almost everywhere the middle-class values of economy, saving and more or less unquestioning acceptance of society as it stood were still dominant.[44] Certainly higher production and productivity, and economic progress generally, did little to produce greater economic equality between different social groups. Serious economic change of any kind meant and could only mean relative and often even absolute loss, even extinction, for some groups in society and gains and expansion for others. In Britain the trail-blazing industrialization of the first half of the nineteenth century was certainly not reflected in any comparable improvement in real wages in general. Largely because population growth was making labour plentiful and cheap, the share of wages in Gross National Product fell considerably; perhaps somewhere between 6 and 14 per cent of national income was diverted during that period away from wages to profits, rents and investment. Even in the 1860s, it can be plausibly argued, a third of the population of Britain was in poverty by the standards of that age. The benefits of industrialization and change were enormous; but for very large parts of society they were slow to show themselves. Eventually they filtered downwards in the form of improved housing, more plentiful and varied food, better education and access to a greatly widened range of goods and services; but over most of Europe this process was hardly clear until the 1870s or 1880s.

Even within the working class there were very wide, indeed unbridgeable, divisions. As modern industry developed there could be seen everywhere to varying extents a distinction between an aristocracy of skilled men and the great body of the unskilled. The former, especially if they could control entry to their trade, could ensure for themselves a high degree of security of employment and stability in the wages they received. The latter, without skills or the ability to influence their conditions of work, were much more at the mercy of market forces and trade fluctuations. Both their employment and the wages they might hope to receive were much less secure than for the privileged skilled men. In Britain in particular, it has been argued, skilled industrial workers formed a distinctive and important group, since Britain, unlike France or Germany, did not have large numbers of well-to-do peasants, minor public officials, schoolmasters and priests who might have challenged the social and political importance which the skilled worker was now assuming.[45] It should not be forgotten that when we speak of a rising standard of living and increasing and more varied consumption, at least in the later nineteenth century, we are often speaking of the skilled minority rather than the unskilled majority so far as the industrial working class is concerned. Thus the average value of the estates left by manual workers in general in Paris in 1820 was 24 francs, while in 1911 it was 200 francs. For skilled workers, however, the rise was from 69 francs to 914; and throughout this period 80-90 per cent of workers normally left no estate at all. The rise in standards is none the less clear: in 1820 45 per cent of the total of these estates consisted of absolute necessities, the meagre possessions without which it was hardly possible to exist, whereas by 1911 this proportion had fallen to a mere 6 per cent. Moreover this rise in standards was clearly the outcome, in the main, of the growth of industry. A study by the same author of five French provincial cities shows that in Lille, the most industrialized of the sample, the increase in private wealth in the period was greatest while in Toulouse, the most traditional of the sample and the one least affected by modern industry, it was least.[46] Even in Britain the gulf between skilled and unskilled was slowly closing from the 1880s onwards. By then cheap food from Europe's overseas settlements, together with the increasing cheapness of many consumer goods and perhaps also the growth of publicly-provided basic education, were slowly eroding the advantages which the skilled had hitherto possessed. Really drastic and rapid levelling, however, in this as in other aspects of society, was hardly visible until after the war of 1914.

As has been pointed out above, it was only in a few areas that the factory worker could at any time be regarded as the dominant or typical worker. Over great parts of the continent he was, even at the end of the century, almost unknown; and even in the most industrialized parts of Europe old-style artisans and handicraft workers, though giving ground, remained a significant element in the industrial picture in 1914. Yet the factory worker had a significance which depended hardly at all on numbers. He represented what was new and potentially disruptive in the structure of European society. The factory was in this period the cutting edge of history. It demanded new attitudes, a new psychology, almost a new sort of man. In the eighteenth century most workers in industry had had considerable control over their hours of work and the way in which they worked. Small units of production, small and cheap machines where machines were used at all, the almost complete absence of any idea of scientific management, all made this possible. The working day and the working week were both very irregular by the standards of what the nineteenth century was to bring; and their irregularities were contained within a year which was still broken up by a considerable number (in Catholic countries many people were beginning to consider a quite excessive number) of traditional holidays, fairs and saints' days. In many industries, notably those dependent on water power as a prime mover, the pace of work, and sometimes the possibility of working at all, were determined by the weather. There were already some foreshadowings of what was to come. As early as the 1770s Josiah Wedgwood had intro-duced in his Etruria factory in Staffordshire the first known clocking-in system for his workers. But to modern eyes the predominant impression is one of little work-discipline, of a lack of close supervision and of essenti-ally traditional attitudes to time, attitudes which had their roots in the immemorial peasant routines of the countryside. One of the most import-ant accomplishments of the nineteenth century was to break down these attitudes, to substitute for them others which stressed systematic work and the keeping of fixed and regular hours, a work-discipline which was strict and exacting, and a general revaluing of time and stress on the importance of making good use of it. These attitudes, once established in the factories, spread from them to working-class society in general.

This process was not a quick or easy one. The early stages of modern industrialization were often marked by difficulty in persuading workers to remain for long in the new factories, or to work regular hours and appear regularly for work. The result was a high turnover of labour and great difficulty in building up a stable and reliable work-force. Moreover a very high proportion of factory workers had a completely rural background and retained close contacts with their native villages. The result was their frequent disappearance in autumn to help bring in the harvest, as continued to happen in Russia until to 1914. A more fundamental difficulty was that many workers still aspired not to maximize their earnings or accumulate money but simply to achieve a purely traditional standard of living and consumption. Their time-horizons tended to be short. They thought in terms of spending money when they had it on immediate gratifications and hardly at all in those of saving. Pay-day was therefore very often followed by heavy drinking and a widespread failure to appear for work. This was a serious difficulty in much of British industry until at least the middle of the nineteenth century; and 'Saint Monday', the tradition of doing no work, or little work, on Mondays while recovering from the weekend's drinking, until then or even later remained an important feature of much British industrial life.[47] As in pre-industrial or only partly industrialized societies, work was still not clearly separated from life in general. The boundary between the two was much less definite than it is today.

These attitudes were irreconcilable with modern industrialism. Power-driven machinery housed in large factory buildings represented a considerable investment which must be efficiently used. Bad time-keeping and absenteeism (which might also reduce the quality of the goods being produced) therefore could not be tolerated. The result was an array of sanctions and inducements designed to produce a more disciplined and reliable work-force. In the early stages of industrialization, at least in Britain, defaulting workers were sometimes beaten, though this was relatively rare. More effective was dismissal or the threat of it, though employers were usually much more reluctant to use this weapon against skilled than against unskilled men. Here again the markedly superior status and greater independence and security of the skilled is clearly visible: it was in the skilled trades in Britain that 'Saint Monday' survived longest. Fines were extensively used, especially for the punishment of relatively minor faults. More positively, payment by results, bonus payments, and even the award of prizes to the best workers, might be used as induce-ments.[48] Clearly the self-interest of employers underlay most of this. But it would be a mistake to think of these efforts entirely in terms of material self-interest. They were also buttressed by a deeply rooted feeling, cer-tainly in Britain and probably in other countries also, that any form of idleness was inherently bad, an encouragement to vice and a waste of the priceless God-given asset of time. The factory system, it could be argued, performed a truly moral function by imposing on the worker a salutary discipline and preventing him from giving way to his baser appetites: it was pointed out that Leeds, a factory town, had higher standards of behaviour than Sheffield, a stronghold of small workshops and independ-ent artisans where the worker was under no such control.[49] Such attitudes were widely propagated in Britain by the schools and largely explain the considerable efforts which were made to see that child workers in factor-ies attended at least Sunday school and if possible received some basic education. It is probably also true that in some cases efforts to organize production more effectively on the basis of stricter work-discipline were inspired by a desire for efficiency for its own sake, a dislike of waste and of obviously faulty organization, an effort, it may not be too fanciful to say, to make factory production an art. The heroic age of British industri-alization saw the appearance in 1832 of the first systematic study of the problems of industrial organization and management, Charles Babbage's *On the Economy of Machinery and Manufactures.*

By the second half of the nineteenth century, first of all in Britain and then in the rest of industrialized Europe, the new outlook was rapidly overcoming the old. Almost everywhere, to varying extents, middle-class values were being adopted by the working class; and this adoption was often at least in part voluntary and spontaneous and not merely the result of compulsion or indoctrination.[50] Rising standards of living were encouraging ideas of steady work and, at least among the better-off part of the working class, even of saving. Railways and newspapers were widen-ing horizons hitherto often very narrow and weakening the more or less unquestioning acceptance of customary standards of living. Most funda-mental of all, the idea of 'time-thrift', of the need to use effectively this priceless and irreplaceable asset, was now being securely implanted in the consciousness of industrialized Europe and was more and more imposed on the other, older, peasant Europe which surrounded it. The Europe of the later nineteenth century was increasingly one of watches and clocks, of timetables, calendars and appointment books. More and more it was a Europe in which people's movements had to be exactly controlled and accurately timed, one in which the working day had a clear beginning and end which had to be adhered to. As time became more and more a pseudo-commodity which was precisely measured out, so it also became something which could be 'lost', an idea foreign to peasant communities where the distinction between time productively used and time wasted was much less sharp. The speed of events was increasing. There was far more, and far more rapid, change in Europe in the generation before 1914 than in that which followed 1815; and this in itself almost certainly helped to sharpen consciousness of time and a feeling for its precise measurement and allocation and effective use. By the outbreak of the First World War European society had already become what one commentator has called a 'civilization of impatience'.[51] It was also a society in which a sharp distinction was now drawn between work and leisure. Such a distinction is inherent in the regularity and discipline of an effective factory system and is probably inevitable in any mature industrial society.[52]

THE DEVELOPMENT OF TRANSPORT
AND ITS IMPLICATIONS

Side by side with the growth of the factory and the increasing size and complexity of its power-driven machinery went the growth of new forms of transport whose effect was in some ways almost as great – the railway and the steamship. Both developed with at times explosive rapidity. The opening of what is generally regarded as the world's first railway using steam-propelled locomotives, the line between Stockton and Darlington, in 1825 did not at first lead to a very rapid transformation of the transport picture even in Britain. In 1840 she had still only 800 kilometres of line; but by 1850 she had 10,500, while Germany already possessed 5,800 and France had built 3,000. Russia by contrast had as yet laid down only a line from St Petersburg to Moscow, a mere 470 kilometres in all: nothing shows more clearly the difficulty with which she adapted to the modern world than the slowness with which this huge country, which stood to gain far more from railways than any other in Europe, exploited the new possibilities which they offered. By 1914 Britain had 38,000 kilometres of line and Germany 63,000. The Russian network had grown spectacularly to 74,000; but this meant that there was still less than a third of a kilometre of railway line for every 100 square kilometres of the Russian empire. By contrast little Belgium, with close on 9,000 kilometres of line in all, had 30 kilometres for every 100 square kilometres of territory – the densest national railway network in the world.[53]

The steamship took somewhat longer to make its full impact. By the 1820s steam tugs were being used to tow sailing-ships out of harbour (hitherto it had been very difficult and often impossible for a sailing-ship to escape from harbour under its own power in the face of unfavourable winds) and in 1819 steam power was used for the first time to assist an Atlantic crossing. However it took several decades for steam-driven vessels to become the dominant element in seaborne trade. Their engines were for long very greedy and inefficient consumers of fuel as well as being not very reliable; and the generation 1820–50 saw the sailing-ship reach its final and most efficient form. Not until the 1870s did the steamship begin to assert its mastery; but when it did the results were striking. By the later 1880s more than half the world's merchant tonnage was steam-propelled. By the end of the century the great advantages of oil fuel, more easily handled than coal and with a higher calorific value, were beginning to be seen. An oil-fired ship crossed the Atlantic for the first time in 1894: more impressive, in 1902 another reached Britain after a voyage from Singapore during which it had burned nothing but oil.[54]

The results of these developments were immense. They transformed the economic life not merely of Europe but of the world; and in the longer term their social implications were at least as important as their economic ones. They generated a series of technological changes – the more powerful and efficient compound steam-engine (developed first for ships and then adopted for railway use); better quality and more durable rails (the demand for these was the most powerful driving force behind the production from the 1850s onwards of cheap steel made possible by the new Bessemer and Gilchrist–Thomas processes); improvements in braking and signalling systems (the important development here was the electric telegraph, used in railway signalling in Britain from the early 1840s); improvements in artificial lighting. In the Habsburg empire up until the 1880s, in Russia until 1914, the railways were the biggest single customer for the products of heavy industry and the main support of the metallurgical industries. Some of their technological spin-offs were very important in their own right. This was notably true of the electric telegraph. Europe had 2,000 miles of telegraph lines in 1849 and 111,000 twenty years later. Railways also rapidly became very large employers in their own right. Rather less than 32,000 people worked on them in France in 1850, when really large-scale construction was only beginning there: by 1914 the corresponding figure was about 360,000.[55] But more important than this was the gigantic increase in the movement of people and goods and the lowering of the cost of transport which the new methods brought. In Britain 60 million tons of goods were carried by rail in 1850 and 410 million in 1900. In Germany the change was more explosive: passenger traffic grew in 1855–1908 by a factor of 29 and goods traffic by one of 42, while the cost of passenger traffic fell by 43 per cent and that of goods traffic by 55 per cent.[56] The cost of transport by sea fell even more sharply in the later decades of the century. In 1869 it cost eleven shillings to transport a quarter of wheat from Chicago to Liverpool: by 1902 the cost was only two shillings and tenpence.

On industry the effects of all this were striking. Railways and later and to a lesser degree steamships made coal, increasingly the basic industrial fuel, more easily available. A very high proportion of the first railways almost everywhere in Europe were built to bring coal either directly to industrial centres or to navigable water on which it could be relatively easily transported to an industrial consumer. Reliable supplies of cheap coal made possible in many cases an increasing geographical concentration of industry in locations favourable to it; and this in turn led to important advantages in price and even in quality derived from large-scale production. In this way in Germany in the mid-century railways helped industry to concentrate in the Ruhr and to some extent in the Berlin area, while other areas with older industries based on water-power, such as the Black Forest, the Harz and the Eifel, began to decline. Later, from the 1880s onwards, the cheap imported coal made possible by steamships played an important role in the belated growth of large-scale industry in Italy. Equally important, railways made supplies of goods of all kinds more certain, speedy and predictable than ever before. This meant that it was less important than in the past for manufacturers or merchants to hold stocks of raw materials or finished goods sufficient to cope with any interruption of supplies; and this in turn released for investment capital which would otherwise have been tied up in this way. Before the coming of the railways, to take an extreme case, pig-iron produced in the Urals took two years to travel to St Petersburg, and much of it still longer to reach its final consumer in western Europe. Transport so painfully slow as this meant an inevitable locking-up of large amounts of capital in goods in transit; railways and steamships freed much of this for other uses.

Improved transport had the even more important effect of widening markets, making them national or international rather than merely regional as so often in the past. It thus eliminated or greatly reduced the sharp price differences, at least for bulky or heavy commodities, which had hitherto existed not merely between countries but between different parts of the same country. In the bad year of 1816, for example, wheat had cost three times as much in Alsace, far from seaborne supplies, as in Poitou on the Atlantic coast of France which did not suffer from this disadvantage.[57] A pood (36 pounds) of Russian iron sold at the Nizhnyi Novgorod fair on the Volga for one rouble in the pre-railway age could sometimes fetch three times as much in the western provinces of the empire because of the cost of transport. Carrying cheap and bulky products overland for a mere twenty-five miles might double their price in some parts of Europe. In plentiful years in Russia much of the harvest was often left in sheaves in the fields, since the grain could be neither sold nor transported to where it could find a buyer. The new capacity to move heavy and bulky goods easily and cheaply over long distances ended a great deal of waste of this kind, made markets more efficient and greatly reduced the sharp and arbitrary local price fluctuations which had been so damaging in the past. This had the result, politically as well as economically and socially important, that after the crisis of 1845–47 famine, and even really severe food shortages, became progressively less likely in the developed parts of Europe. From about 1870 onwards, moreover, railways directly raised standards of living and consumption by making possible the rapid transport of perishable foods such as milk, fruit and vegetables. This helped the growth of specialized production of these commodities, with a consequent gain in efficiency, in some areas within reach of large urban markets. Simultaneously cheap sea transport of bulk cargoes meant that nitrates from Chile and guano from Peru could provide European agriculture with new and very important sources of fertilizers.

The material benefits brought by the new modes of transport were therefore very great. They were not, perhaps, truly revolutionary, at least in the countries of western Europe, which had already fairly well-developed road and canal systems before the railway age dawned. Recent studies suggest that the railways brought a very important acceleration of a process of growth already well under way rather than a quantum jump to an entirely new level of economic activity. In Russia, with her enormous distances, scattered population and huge unexploited resources the potential benefits of railways were much greater; but it can be argued that in western and central Europe their influence was as much on men's minds as on the physical processes of production and distribution. They were not merely a new means of transport but a symbol, the supreme symbol of speed, of progress, of the new world towards which, especially in the optimistic 1850s and 1860s, many Europeans felt themselves to be moving. Railways, more compellingly than factories, or the spread of education, or newspapers, gave men the certainty that they lived in an age of change, an age of almost infinite possibilities. (In the decade before 1914 the still very primitive aircraft and the increasingly popular motor car had in a rather less fundamental way some of the same effects.) Sometimes the glamour of railways and their status as badges of modernity may have led some of the less developed European countries to invest too much of their scarce capital resources in them at the expense of industry. It is arguable that this happened in Spain, for example.[58] But of their value as a symbol and a stimulus there is no doubt.

It is not an accident that so many statesmen who stood for significant political change, normally in a nationalist direction, were strong advocates of railways. Cavour in Italy, Szechenyi and Kossuth in Hungary, later Witte in Russia, are good examples of this; and clearly railway-building sometimes helped in an important way towards the consolidation of new national or pseudo-national states as they came into existence. Italy is a good case in point. She had less than 1,500 kilometres of track at the outbreak of the Austro-Sardinian war in 1859; but by 1864 this had grown sharply to over 4,000 kilometres. The rapid growth was meant, not altogether without success, to stitch together more effectively what was still a deeply divided country. Even in states which were older and better integrated than the new Italian kingdom the coming of railways had profound implications for the growth of national consciousness and a wider social and political vision. The best study of social and economic modernization in any European country has concluded that in France in the 1870s and 1880s the large-scale building of secondary railway-lines in the provinces, and of the new or improved roads which served them, 'resulted in a crash program of national integration of unparalleled scope and effectiveness'. The stimulus offered to hitherto isolated, introverted and tradition-bound regional societies by the new ease of movement could certainly be tremendous and was much more than merely economic in any strict sense. Better communications, according to the same author,

introduced new foods into the diet, new materials in the building of the house, new objects in its interior, new tools in the fields about it, new things to do on holidays, and new kinds of clothes to wear. They offered opportunities for enterprise and hence for social mobility that were not there before; the jobs that went with roads and railways alone were temptations that set many on the move.[59]

In Britain regional differences, even those which distinguished Scotland and Wales from England, were less sharp than those which separated the historic provinces of France, to say nothing of the more deeply divided Spain and Italy. This fact, added to her relatively small geographical area and good pre-railway internal communications, meant that in Britain's case the politically and socially unifying effects of railways were less than in many other parts of Europe. But even here they were visible. The clear emergence of a more nation-wide structure of political feeling and opinion, the reduction of sharp local variations in support for the main political parties which is clearly visible in the 1870s,[60] owed much to the new ease and speed of communication.

Factories using power-driven machinery of increasing size and complexity; a new, more intensive, more systematically enforced labour discipline which stressed the supreme value of time; new methods of transport which made the carriage of both goods and people cheaper, faster and more predictable; wider and more effective markets; increasingly large economic units of all kinds with resulting economies of scale – all this meant the application to economic life more than ever before of rationalizing and innovating intelligence. The Industrial Revolution in its first stages had not owed any great debt to the physical sciences. Most of the new machines and techniques on which it depended had been the product of empiricism, of the enterprise and practical experience of men with little formal education. As it progressed, however, it developed an increasing emphasis on organized and consciously deployed knowledge. As the nineteenth century went on a higher and higher proportion of new inventions and techniques were based upon scientific discoveries and were introduced by men with some scientific training. These increasingly close links between industry and science also worked to some extent in the opposite direction; industrial development could aid the progress of scientific theory, as when the improvement of the steam-engine stimulated advances in thermodynamics. By the end of the century there were signs, in the most advanced industrial powers, that industry had not merely ceased to be indifferent to pure science but was even beginning to take it over. By the 1890s a few great firms in science-based industries – General Electric and Westinghouse in America, the major German chemical companies – were setting up large organizations of their own to carry out fundamental research independent of any immediate practical needs or applications. Slowly but surely the industrialized world was becoming one in which it was assumed that everything could and should be explained and subjected to human control. The pre-industrial or at best early industrial eighteenth century, with its dependence on seasonal rhythms and fluctuations, its slowness and difficulty of movement, its interruptions in the flow of raw materials, its locking-up of capital in often deteriorating stocks, its reliance on irregular supplies of water- and wind-power, was now increasingly remote, not merely in time but in spirit.

AN AGE OF CITIES

Population growth, industrialization, vastly improved transport, more ample and reliable food supplies, all meant rapid growth of towns and especially of large, sometimes enormous, towns. This urban growth made more immediate difference to the lives of more people than anything else which happened during the nineteenth century. The figures are striking. In 1800 there were 21 European cities with populations of over 100,000 and a little over 4.5 million people, less than 3 per cent of the total for the continent, lived in them. In 1900 there were 147 such cities with a population of 40 million, about a tenth of the total. By then the six largest by themselves contained well over 13 million people. When the First World War broke out almost three-quarters of the whole population of the British Isles and over three-fifths of that of Germany, the two most developed great European states, lived in urban rather than rural environments (though here 'urban' is used in the wide sense of settlements with a population of over 2,000).[61] For many individual cities the figures are even more remarkable. Between 1800 and 1914 Stockholm grew from 6,000 to 350,000, Odessa from 6,000 to 480,000, Budapest from 50,000 to 900,000. None of these was primarily an industrial city. But there were industrial cities where growth was equally explosive. Essen had 6,000 inhabitants in 1850 and 300,000 in 1900: Lodz, the greatest producer of textiles in the Russian empire, grew from 31,500 in 1860 to 315,000 in 1897. These were growth-rates which it would have been hard to surpass even in North America.[62] On a smaller scale, to take only one example, Middlesborough, a mere village until the 1830s, grew on the back of the booming local iron industry from 8,000 people in 1851 to 40,000 twenty years later. Simultaneously the discovery of a great deposit of iron ore meant that Barrow-in-Furness, a tiny hamlet of 150 inhabitants in 1846, had a population of 40,000 by 1874. Probably the most striking case of all, so far as the European capitals are concerned, is that of Berlin. In 1800 it was smaller than Moscow or St Petersburg and only a third of the size of Paris. By 1914 it was almost twice the size of either of the Russian capitals and larger than Paris; over this period as a whole it grew twice as fast as the capital of any other major European state.[63] What is really striking about nineteenth-century Europe, therefore, is not so much the growth of towns in general as the phenomenal growth of a relatively small number of great cities; the rise in the urban population was heavily concentrated in them in almost every country. In France in 1801–81 the total population grew by only 40 per cent; but that of Paris went up by 314 per cent and that of the nine other cities which had over 100,000 inhabitants in 1881 by 185 per cent. In Hungary in 1850–90 total population rose by 31 per cent; but Budapest grew by over 214 per cent and the seven next largest cities by 120 per cent.[64]

There were several reasons for this urban growth; they interacted in complex ways and affected different parts of Europe to differing extents and at different times. It had little to do with the existing density of population: Italy, much of which was more densely populated than most of Europe and which had strong urban traditions, saw less growth of this kind than many other parts of the continent. Nor can it be correlated at all closely with systems of land tenure. There was movement to the cities not merely from the great estates of Pomerania and east Prussia but also from the small family holdings of west Germany, and from the highly capitalized commercial farms of England as well as from the peasant ones of France. Sometimes negative factors were predominant; people were driven from the countryside to the cities by unemployment, land hunger and sheer physical want. This situation appears to explain much urban growth in France before about 1870. Sometimes, on the other hand, an old regional capital might be revivified by the vitality of economic life, and in particular the growth of industry, in the surrounding area. Barcelona may have benefited substantially from the strength of the textile industry in Catalonia. Milan, whose population trebled in 1850–1912, certainly profited from being the centre of one of the few industrial areas in Italy.

Cities grew in number and size, however, mainly for two reasons. On the one hand they were now able, because of the growth of industry, handicraft as well as factory, and the later growth of the service trades and the professions, to offer employment and other opportunities to immigrants from the countryside as never before. The positive inducements which the city could hold out, the jobs, wages, amusements and the new kind of life to be had there, were of the greatest importance. Cities did not grow merely or inevitably because there was surplus population in the countryside. They had to have something to offer, above all in economic terms; and if they did not have it the surplus population would go elsewhere or refuse to move and make the best of things on their inadequate landholdings. This is seen clearly in the case of Italy, where large population growth led not to any great increase in the size of cities (which with one or two exceptions grew quite slowly) but from the 1890s onwards to massive emigration to other European countries, to parts of Latin America and North Africa, and most of all to the United States. Most Italian cities, economically stagnant, simply did not have the capacity to absorb or employ a large increase in their population.

Cities increased spectacularly in size for a second reason. In spite of the stresses and sufferings of urban life, on which a large historical literature now exists, health and conditions of life in general were improving, at least in the second half of the century, for the inhabitants of large towns. Until then these had grown almost entirely through immigration from the countryside; urban mortality had been so high that deaths in the great cities had outnumbered births and growth by natural increase had been impossible. This situation was now changing, though in many parts of Europe with painful slowness. In Paris births had begun to balance deaths by the end of the eighteenth century; and the same position was achieved in London a few years later. Elsewhere its advent was slower. In the major German cities it was reached during the first half of the nineteenth

century, but in Stockholm only after 1860. The Spanish census of 1850–
51 revealed that two-fifths of the population of Madrid had not been
born in the city or even in the province of Madrid: and a study made in
1877 showed that immigration was still the most important source of
growth in the great majority of the major cities of Europe.[65] The effectiveness of improvements in sanitation and public health, and the speed with
which they were introduced and took effect, should not therefore be overestimated. They were a significant element in urban growth, but certainly
less so than the economic inducements which the city offered.

There is no doubt that conditions of life, of housing, health, diet and
education, were for large parts of the urban population atrociously bad
by present-day standards during the nineteenth century. This was especially so during the first half of the century; but down to 1914 and beyond
there remained great areas of misery and deprivation, of slum housing,
unemployment and demoralization, in all the major cities of Europe. This
was partly because of the slowness with which governments, municipal
bodies or any sort of public authority came to feel any active sense of
responsibility in these matters. It was also, however, because for a long
time the administrative mechanisms and technical expertise needed to give
real effect to such a sense of responsibility were lacking. The great cities of
the nineteenth century, partly because of their very size and partly because
of the growing intricacy of so many aspects of life, needed administrations
far more complex, well informed and sensitive to new requirements than
any hitherto known. A great city required officials, detailed regulations,
technical knowledge and information about changing conditions in a way
that a small town or still more a village did not. The administration of
such a city had to supervise and control those it ruled with much greater
care than any central government needed to show for its subjects. It had
to be careful, systematic, businesslike and intelligent; and these were not
qualities for which many municipal administrations were noted during
much of this period.

The most acute suffering, the worst health and housing conditions,
the sharpest cleavage between the poor and the well-to-do, the grossest
examples of the inability or unwillingness of public authorities to meet
this situation, were to be seen in the first half of the nineteenth century,
and notably though by no means entirely in the often explosively growing
industrial towns. In these the resources available to alleviate mass poverty
were often very inadequate; and their administration was often controlled
or strongly influenced by factory-owners (themselves often of working-
class origin) who lacked any tradition of public service or public responsibility. From the 1820s onwards a series of remarkable social investigators
began, first of all in France and a little later in Britain, to reveal the full

implications of this situation. In 1828 Achille Peuot showed that since 1812 the expectation of life in Mulhouse, one of the most rapidly growing industrial cities in France, had been significantly lower at all ages than that for the country in general. Almost simultaneously Louis Villermé found that the Nord *département*, the most industrialized in France, had a far higher proportion of paupers in its population than any other; in Lille, its capital and another rapidly growing French industrial city, nearly a third of the inhabitants were in this position. In 1835 two other investigators showed that in Nantes mortality was higher, and infantile mortality enormously higher, in the poorer areas than in the more well-to-do ones. Another contemporary estimate put the number of Parisians living in poverty and misery at the time of the 1830 revolution at 420,000 in a population of 755,000.[66] In Britain a series of larger and more detailed studies, notably the series of reports issued by the Poor Law Commissioners in 1835–47, culminated in the publication in 1842 of Edwin Chadwick's great *Report on the Sanitary Conditions of the Labouring Population*. Many observers were struck by the physical effects of industrial life, by the fact that young working-class men were markedly smaller in stature than the sons of the middle classes (the system of military conscription in France and the records it generated provided clear evidence of this) and by the lower resistance of the working class to disease. The effects on morals and behaviour seemed even more alarming: it was claimed, for example, that the number of prostitutes in Paris had trebled in 1800–35.[67]

Gross disparities in life-chances of all kinds, most fundamentally in the opportunity of mere physical survival, were of course nothing new; but these enquiries illustrated them in greater and more convincing detail than ever before. They also linked the conditions they described with industrialism, and thus implied that they might not get better as industry and the factory system developed, and might conceivably get worse. The new poverty was not temporary and episodic, the result of a bad harvest or some individual misfortune. Now, concentrated and made clearly visible in the cities, it struck many observers more forcibly than ever before as a permanent condition.

For the respectable and well-to-do this situation seemed full of danger. There had now emerged in the industrial cities, to some extent in all great cities, an industrial working class which was more numerous than in the past, and which was exposed to all the stresses of sudden and severe fluctuations of demand and therefore of employment and wages. This dangerous element in society was largely untouched by the restraints of conventional religion and threatened to escape from the control and guidance of its social superiors which still operated in the countryside. In it immorality of all kinds, crime and disease seemed terrifyingly rife. From it they might spread to infect and weaken all the rest of society. More dangerous still, poverty and ignorance might all too easily make it the prey of radical orators and revolutionary demagogues and turn it in their hands into a weapon for the overthrow of the existing political and even social order. Sir James Kay-Shuttleworth, one of the greatest British reforming officials of the 1830s and 1840s, spoke of 'volcanic elements, by whose explosive violence the structure of society may be destroyed', and another commentator in these years feared 'a social earthquake from fermenting masses of misery'.[68] To some observers the industrial working class seemed scarcely human. 'They live', wrote an English observer in 1850,

precisely like brutes, to gratify . . . the appetites of their uncultivated bodies, and then die, to go they have never thought, cared, or wondered whither. . . . Brought up in the darkness of barbarism, they have no idea that it is possible for them to attain any higher condition; they are not even sentient enough to desire . . . to change their situation . . . they have unclear, indefinite and undefinable ideas of all around them; they eat, drink, breed, work and die; and . . . the richer and more intelligent classes are obliged to guard them with police.[69]

How far and in what ways the industrial city with its poverty and stress encouraged crime and bred criminals, one of the most common accusations during the early stages of industrialization, is a complex question. The answer may well vary considerably as between different countries and even different areas within a single country. In England and Wales, it has been pointed out, the numbers committed for trial for indictable offences increased more than sixfold in the years 1805–48, and the number of convictions grew more than eightfold. This was not merely a result of increased police activity; and crime rates, it is argued, were directly related to economic stress during this period.[70] A more detailed study of English experience, however, concludes that 'there is little ground to think that the immediate pressure of want was a major cause of adult crime, or that cyclical changes in this pressure altered its level'.[71] In France and Germany theft seems to be clearly correlated with economic conditions, rising when times were bad and falling when they improved, at least until the 1870s. It is clear also that in both countries it was more common in cities than in the countryside, and most common of all in great cities; but this may well have been the result not of poverty, which was often greater in the countryside, but of the higher expectations and stronger desire for material possessions generated by city life, and of the greater contact between rich and poor, and hence greater opportunities to steal, in the city. Certainly there seems to be little clear evidence that industrialization and urbanization in themselves encouraged violent crime in either France

or Germany. The policing of cities, however inadequate, was more effective than that of rural areas; and a feeling for order and regularity of
the kind which modern industry generated was in itself a force tending
to reduce violence. It was traditional attitudes and values, not factory
industry or large cities, which generated really serious crime. Corsica, the
most underdeveloped *département* in France, had the country's highest
homicide rate.[72]

It is very understandable that the respectable and the well-to-do should
have been alarmed by the apparent dangers of the new industrial towns.
No European state during the first half of the century had at its disposal
what would now be regarded as an adequate police force, or any effective
instrument except the army for the control of large-scale disorder. In
Britain throughout the formative period of industrialism the cornerstone
of public order was the magistrate, the justice of the peace. But the quality
of these varied enormously. Many found their duties hard to cope with
and in any case their geographical distribution was that of a pre-industrial
age. In the manufacturing areas they were thinly scattered and, since a
very high proportion of them were still landowners or Anglican clergy,
they often did not live in or near the main potential trouble centres in the
new industrial towns. In 1817 it was claimed that a large part of the
Potteries, with a population of 50,000, had no acting magistrates at all of
its own. Two years later it was alleged that in Lancashire the area which
covered the cotton-spinning towns of Oldham, Middleton and Ashton
was quite without magistrates.[73] In any case magistrates without some
effective police force could do little; and until 1829, when the creation of
something like a modern force for London was begun, the country was
policed merely by parish constables occasionally supplemented in a few
areas by paid professional 'thief-takers'. (In Ireland, however, a professional
uniformed police force had been set up, first of all in Dublin, then in the
most disturbed areas and finally in 1822 throughout the island. In that
year it numbered 4,000 and had almost doubled within a decade.)

In continental Europe libertarian resistance to any sort of professional
policing was usually less than in Britain; but in many essentials the position was the same – small, archaic, police forces and a consequent reliance
on the army, in spite of the political odium and complications of using
it, as the only effective protection against serious disorder. The Russian
empire, seen in western Europe as the supreme example of autocracy,
was in fact very lightly policed, a military but hardly a police state. The
hundred million peasants in the Russian countryside in 1900 were still
under the ineffective control of less than ten thousand state policemen,
most of them very badly paid. St Petersburg at the same time, in proportion to its population, had fewer policemen than London or Paris. Rural

Prussia, in which about three-quarters of the population still lived until the 1850s, was policed by a mere 1,500–1,600 *Landgendarmen*; even the Rhine province, where they were relatively numerous, had only one of these for every 11,000 inhabitants. Berlin itself had about 200 police in all – roughly one for every 2,000 inhabitants. The municipal guard, recruited from the respectable and well-to-do, was ineffective in most Prussian cities since the central government distrusted it as a symbol of local initiative and autonomy and service in it was seen as a burden.[74] In France in the years after Waterloo, though there were about 14,000 gendarmes (mainly former army NCOs) scattered throughout the provinces the Paris police amounted to only about 450 men. The government had at its disposal several different police forces; but these were responsible to different ministries, with no central coordination or control. The result was that throughout the century, in France as in other parts of Europe, the army had repeatedly to be called upon to protect society and the state against strikes, threats of insurrection, or any other kind of disorder too large-scale for still inadequate police forces to handle.[75] Even in the parts of Europe where industrialism had first taken root and where it was relatively mature, areas moreover with well-established structures of representative government and relatively modern police forces, the army was always to the end of this period the ultimate guarantor of public order. In Belgium the outburst of spontaneous and virtually unorganized working-class violence in 1886, when there were great strikes and much vandalism and when bands of unemployed workers terrorized much of the Meuse and Hainault regions, was repressed only by the use of the army on a massive scale. During a dock strike in Hull in 1893 gunboats were anchored in the Humber and soldiers were quartered in the town, while in 1911, when a great transport strike paralysed Liverpool, 14,000 soldiers were sent to the city and two warships were stationed in the Mersey.

Nevertheless the second half of the nineteenth century saw all the major European states beginning to develop much larger and more efficient police forces. In Britain the Home Office was given in 1856 power to inspect the police of counties and boroughs. This was an essential step, in the country which more than any other prized local autonomy in all forms of administration, towards coordination between different areas and the imposition of uniform standards. In Prussia the upheaval of 1848–49 had as one of its first results a rapid growth in police strength. The *Landgendarmerie* had grown by 1855 from 1,500 to 2,500, and the Berlin police force had increased from 200 or so to over 1,200. In France under Napoleon III the number of policemen in Paris rose to 4,000 and that of the gendarmerie to about 25,000.[76] The emergence of modern police forces was a major innovation of the nineteenth century, and a very important one. It meant that governments now had at their disposal an instrument for the control of their subjects which was more adaptable, and hence more efficient, than any hitherto seen. Without adequate police forces minor acts of disorder had often gone more or less unpunished, while major ones might be punished, by the use of the army, with disproportionate severity. Now the response could be more flexible, and hence more economical and effective. 'Troops fired; police clubbed.'[77] The transition was an important factor in making much of European society more secure and sure of itself, in giving it a different feel, as the century went on.

The change was greatly assisted by the fact that the nature of the urban working class, so feared and suspected during the first half of the century, was slowly changing. Gradually, through newspapers, through emerging political organization, most effectively of all through mass education, middle-class ideas and values were penetrating, sometimes being forced, downwards to the roots of society. The result was a slow change, difficult to chart in detail but certainly important, in the nature and objectives of popular violence. Until the second half of the nineteenth century this had usually taken a traditional form, that of reaction against some new threat or demand from above which was felt to be oppressive. The breaking of machines seen as threatening employment, riots against high food prices, resistance to a new tax or sometimes to military conscription, were all essentially of this form. Any violence or threats of violence involved were 'reactive' and defensive, even conservative; they were very often meant to preserve or return to some state of affairs regarded as normal and acceptable. By the last years of the century, and still more in the twentieth century, popular demands and popular violence were changing. They were now becoming increasingly a matter of more or less organized groups putting forward more or less thought-out proposals for change and demanding that these be heard and acted on. The large-scale organized strike (a different thing from the localized and spontaneous ones often accompanied by sporadic and casual violence which had been characteristic of the early stages of industrialization) was one symptom of this change. Another was the new weapon of the demonstration, in which a large body of people assembled in a public place and stood or more often marched there, shouting slogans and carrying banners and placards which expressed their demands. This political technique was first seen in action on a large scale in the Chartist agitation in Britain in the later 1830s; and its spread and full development were closely connected with the growth of mass socialist parties in many European states from the 1870s onwards. It was to be one of nineteenth-century Europe's significant political legacies to our own world.

It would be unfair, however, to think that the reaction of the well-to-do to the social stresses of industrialism and the growth of cities was merely a matter of self-interest and self-preservation. Side by side with this impulse went a feeling that to moralize and civilize the industrial worker through education and religion was a praiseworthy act in itself, indeed a moral duty. It is significant that the most intense efforts to achieve this followed, and did not accompany, the period during which the danger of social and political upheaval seemed greatest. The 1850s and 1860s saw the danger of revolutionary change clearly recede in western Europe. In France the revolution of 1830 (when in Paris the most bitter street-fighting had taken place largely in the areas of worst slum housing), the great strikes of silk-workers in Lyons in 1831 and 1834 (both of which had needed large-scale use of the army to suppress them), and the apparently acute danger of social revolution in the capital in 1848, were succeeded by the good decades, the stability and material progress, of the 1850s and 1860s. The Commune of 1871, spectacular as it was, was an expression of nostalgia for the past, an effort to breathe life into a revolutionary tradition now in many ways archaic and even moribund, rather than a pointer to the future. After 1871, under the Third Republic, neither the political régime nor the structure of society was ever threatened in the way seen in 1815–48. The widespread unrest among wine-growers in the south in 1907, perhaps the most serious development of its kind during this period, was a pale reflection of earlier threats and tensions. In Britain in the later decades of the century there were inevitably, as in France and all the rest of developed Europe, some outbreaks of labour unrest serious enough to arouse genuine uneasiness in ruling circles. But these were too transient and too localized to be a real menace of the sort which Chartism had sometimes seemed to present. Nor could such things as the tithe riots in Wales and crofting riots in Scotland in the 1880s be considered any serious challenge to the productive and rapidly developing society which had now taken firm root.

Yet as the threat of really dangerous social disorder receded so the concern with the condition of the poor in the cities grew. In Britain the 1880s saw a marked growth of attention, particularly by the churches, to social questions. This was fed by influential publications such as the anonymous pamphlet *The Bitter Cry of Outcast London* (1883) and William Booth's *Darkest England and the Way Out* (1890). The Salvation Army (1878), the Church Army (1882) and the Christian Social Union (1889), were all outcomes of this sudden increase in sensitivity to social stresses and deprivations, a sensitivity which, influenced by the Christian socialism preached in particular by F. D. Maurice from the 1850s onwards, could take such radical forms as the Church Socialist League (1906).[78] In Germany the 1850s and 1860s had seen the emergence of a Catholic political group in the Prussian *Landtag* with a considerable interest in social problems. This development, in which Bishop Ketteler of Mainz played a leading role, paved the way for the creation after 1870 of the Centre Party with its substantial programme of social reform; while from the Protestant side Adolf Stocker founded in 1878 the Christian Social Workers Party. This, in addition to its marked anti-Jewish attitudes, stood for a deliberate reduction of the gap between rich and poor, for the formation of workers' associations organized on a craft basis and controlling substantial welfare funds for the benefit of the sick and aged, for action to protect the health of workers, and for progressive income and inheritance taxes. In France writers and intellectuals such as the Abbé Lamennais and the Comte de Montalembert had from the 1830s done much to awaken Catholic interest in social questions; and from the 1890s onwards this began to take an increasingly active and sometimes radical form. Both in France and Germany the foundation of separate Catholic and anti-Marxist trade unions was an important result of 'social catholicism' as both an intellectual and an organizational movement.

This type of religion-inspired social consciousness had important limitations. Everywhere it tended to be the work of active and vocal minorities rather than of churches as a whole. Different religious groups sometimes took very different attitudes to the problems of industrialization and urbanization. In Britain the Nonconformist sects and the evangelical wing of the Church of England were much less sympathetic than High Churchmen, while in Germany Lutheranism, now the greatest intellectual prop of the Prussian state and its official ideology, remained solidly conservative. Yet there is no mistaking the sincerity, indeed in many cases the passion, with which a good many churchmen throughout developed Europe were now pressing the claims of the poor. Moreover their protests, couched in terms of moral principle, were now being supplemented by the utilitarian argument that gross poverty, and the disease and ignorance associated with it, dangerously reduced the strength and efficiency of a society and made it more difficult for it to hold its own in a world where inefficiency was doomed to be more and more severely punished. In Britain the 'National Efficiency' movement which developed from the later 1890s onwards argued strongly along these lines and attracted support from a wide variety of differing sources – Fabian socialists as well as imperially minded statesmen and military leaders.[79] In Germany the National Social Association founded by Friedrich Naumann in 1895 showed, in a more aggressive and expansionist form, some of the same preoccupations. By the first years of the twentieth century neo-Darwinian attitudes were becoming in this way a significant spur to social reform and increased provision for education and for the sick and the unemployed.

Unprecedentedly large cities, some of which had grown up very quickly, with unprecedentedly complex economic structures and dependent on unprecedentedly elaborate and rapidly changing technologies, could not be administered by traditional methods. Reform and adaptation of municipal government was one of the most insistent needs of the second half of the nineteenth century, and one which was at least partially met.

In Britain town government remained until the Municipal Reform Act of 1835 a chaotic tangle of traditional authorities, parishes and vestries, archaic in their structure, usually narrow in their outlook and unwilling to spend money on a significant scale (though the existence in many cities of active bodies of improvement commissioners does something to modify this gloomy picture). British experience, however, is a good example of the slow and piecemeal emergence from the middle of the century of a more effective and rational structure of public provision. Legislation of 1848 attempted to set minimum standards of drainage and water supplies; but this was merely permissive and no more than the beginning of a long process. A great Public Health Act of 1875 forbade the building of new houses unless they had running water and internal drainage; it also allowed local authorities to buy or set up gas and water undertakings and to finance hospitals and create parks. In 1909 a Housing and Town Planning Act empowered them to prepare town-planning schemes; and by then small beginnings had also been made in the provision of publicly owned housing for the poor, though as yet this amounted to a mere two per cent of the country's housing stock.

There was no question, however, of British experience in municipal government acting as a model for the rest of Europe to follow, as had happened in the case of factory industry. Every great city had its own problems and found to some extent its own solution for them. Public health, amenities of all sorts, and in particular housing densities and conditions (since in no country was there a national market for housing) showed wide regional variations to the end of this period. Paris differed radically from any British city in that it was strictly controlled by the French government (a legacy of the role in making and breaking régimes which the city had been able to play more than once in the years after 1789). Of all the great European capitals, moreover, it was one of the slowest to provide adequate standards of health and housing for its inhabitants. There were epidemics of cholera there in 1884 and 1892, each of which killed around 1,000 people; and though a law of 1894 provided some government help towards improving working-class housing by means of tax exemptions and low-interest loans this amounted to little in practice.[80] Berlin suffered from its extraordinarily rapid growth, notably during the years 1860–80 when its population doubled. This led, in spite of much new building, to a sharp deterioration in housing conditions. In 1880 male life expectancy there was only thirty years and in 1914 it was still the most densely populated city in Europe. In general, however, the German government after the unification of 1871 was more effective than any other in laying down minimum housing conditions for its people; and German municipal administration became a model which other parts of Europe increasingly admired and tried to imitate. (The British Housing and Town Planning Act of 1909 was inspired in part by German example.) The German municipal bureaucracy was undoubtedly large. Essen, which had employed only 8 full-time officials in 1840, had 377 by 1900 and other German cities had the same experience. It was, however, the most efficient municipal bureaucracy in Europe. More and more it employed, at least in its upper ranks, university graduates who had received formal and specialized training for their work. Increasingly the influence on town government of leading families, church elders, political associations and amateurs of all sorts was in decline. By 1914 the great German cities were run in a more professional and technocratic way than any others in the world.[81]

Through a good deal of nineteenth-century thinking and writing there runs, however, an unmistakable thread of hostility to the city. To many of the most influential intellectuals of the period, particularly literary intellectuals, it seemed that the sacrifices and losses demanded by great towns, because of their size and complexities, far outweighed any advantages they could bring. To abandon the city, reject the machine age and return to an agrarian or small-town society, seemed to writers such as Coleridge and Ruskin in Britain or Dostoevsky and Tolstoy in Russia an alluring prospect. From a rather different standpoint some of the utopian socialists, notably Fourier, came to similar conclusions. By the end of the century, moreover, the city was under attack from another direction – from extreme nationalists and conservatives. To them it housed, on the one hand rootless masses of workers lacking healthy contact with the soil and any pride in their country, and on the other groups of rich people, many of them Jewish, whose business and financial interests bred in them a dangerous cosmopolitanism and made them potentially unreliable, even treacherous, from the national point of view.[82] From one standpoint or another, then, whether as the source of the sufferings of the poor, as the root of dangerous political instability, as the breeding-ground of crime and immorality or as the origin of threats to national unity and strength, the city, and particularly the great industrial city, never lacked for critics.

Yet it was one of the greatest liberating forces of the century, perhaps the greatest of all in that it brought together and concentrated a number of different forces each of which was tending to increase the autonomy and freedom of action of the individual. It played a central role in the great transition now well under way in the advanced parts of Europe from a society based on traditional values and assumptions to one based on rational procedures designed to maximize production and wealth and on an unprecedented degree of individual choice.[83] Obviously industrial and urban society imposed compulsions of its own upon its members. Yet even in the worst days of the early factory age the worker who moved to the industrial city might well be freeing himself from a number of serious restrictions. The city offered, for example, a much greater choice of possible marriage-partners than the village; and if the property of both partners consisted in effect of their own labour-power and nothing more, then the need to preserve an inheritance of land, which did so much to control and restrict marriage in all rural societies, ceased to operate. This meant that the traditional authority of fathers over their children and the traditional advantages of being an eldest son were correspondingly eroded.[84] There was also a marked rise in illegitimate births over much of Europe which was at its height in the decades 1790–1860 and which was clearly connected with the growth of city life, though the nature of the connection is still far from clear. This 'revolution in eroticism' can be seen as another important assertion of individualism, of the new idea of sexuality as a fundamental form of self-fulfilment valuable in itself rather than, as in traditional societies, a means to non-sexual ends such as the working and continuation of a family holding.[85]

If it was easier to marry in the city it was also, as time went on, easier to end a marriage. It was in the great cities that divorce, still very rare in rural areas, began in the later years of this period to become an accepted part of society. By the end of the century divorce was ten times as common in Paris as in the French countryside.[86] In this respect as in others individual choice flourished in the city. The position of the unmarried man or woman, again, was much easier in the city than in the country-side. In peasant society he or she occupied always a secondary and often suspect position: the family was the basic unit of production and the isolated individual simply could not hope to work a holding effectively. In the city lack of a partner or of family support was less of a handicap. The very fact that the populations of large cities were by the standards of the countryside or even the smaller town highly unstable, coming to the city, leaving it, moving within it, again identified it with ideas of change and emphasized the extent to which it was breaking the traditional mould. In Berlin in 1890 nearly 12 per cent of the population arrived in the city during that year and 8.5 per cent left it, while over 56 per cent of the inhabitants moved house (a change of employment was more likely than it is today to mean a change of address because of the undeveloped state of public transport).[87] Mobility on this scale inevitably meant individual choices on a scale unknown in the village. The same growing stress on the individual, it is perhaps not fanciful to claim, can be seen in a quite significant form in the development of new styles of dancing. Until the nineteenth century this had been essentially a group activity, a matter of communal folk dances which quite frequently involved only one sex and which often took place only on special occasions, such as religious festivals, births, marriages and even deaths. It is only in this period that it becomes primarily or largely a matter of one man dancing with one woman, another assertion of individual autonomy and individual choice.[88]

This increasing freedom for the individual had a very important general result which is still with us today. It meant as the century went on an increasing emphasis on rights and a corresponding tendency to play down the duties – to his social superiors and ultimately to God – which had for centuries weighed so heavily on the ordinary man. Charles Booth, in the greatest social survey of late nineteenth-century England, complained that 'The average working man of today thinks more of his rights or of his wrongs than of his duties and his failures to perform them',[89] and to varying extents this was now true of most European countries. A society based on the largely unthinking acceptance of obligations was now being transformed into one which stressed the increasingly forcible assertion of rights.

In other and more material ways the city, at least in the second half of the century, as real wages rose and amenities multiplied, showed its liberating and creative powers. It was simply a much more interesting and stimulating place than the countryside. It has been well said that 'Many people in traditional societies may well have spent most of their leisure time being bored.'[90] In the city boredom was easier to avoid. The fact that its streets were lit at night in itself gave it a glamour and clothed it with an aura of power to which the village could not possibly aspire. Perhaps no other aspect of the city gave contemporary observers so strong and immediate an impression of achievement as this. It offered a wider range of employment than the village, and as the century went on increasingly employment (particularly in the growing range of official posts) which conferred the right to some sort of pension, a thing which agricultural work never did. Unemployment in the city was a harrowing experience; but no more so than the seasonal unemployment of the countryside, which was more difficult to avoid. The large city and the growing industrial town, for all the stresses and sufferings they could involve, were for great masses of Europeans places of hope and at least the possibility of fulfilment compared to the village or the small and traditional town. It is perhaps significant that the most startling revelation of the persistence of widespread primary poverty in England at the end of the nineteenth century[91] was provided by a study of York, ancient and largely untouched by the new economic forces, and not of any new industrial city. In traditional rural society a holiday, which was normally a religious feast, had been enjoyed, indeed could be enjoyed, only in customary ways: it fixed the individual in his environment. In the city, at least in the second half of the century, as parks and museums made their appearance and cheap railway excursions and later the bicycle made travel much easier, it gave scope to the individual to follow his own tastes and enjoy himself in his own way. For the country dweller the city therefore could and often did mean escape from an intensely restricting environment. This was particularly true for women, otherwise doomed in a rural setting to a life of grinding hard work and the most limited of horizons. To go to the town as a servant or a factory worker, as so many of them did, had its own dangers: the armies of prostitutes who could be found in every large city were recruited largely from women who had first encountered city life as servant girls. Three-fifths of the registered prostitutes in Berlin in 1900, for example, were former domestic servants, a fairly typical proportion. But hundreds of thousands of women found these risks worth taking.

THE NEW SOCIETY AND THE OLD

Clearly society in the developed parts of Europe was by 1914 radically different from what it had been a century earlier. The industrialization, the urbanization and the growth in geographical mobility which have been discussed above had combined to bring this about. There were, moreover, a number of secondary but very important changes which also illustrate how far much of the continent had advanced during this period. In the first place Europeans were much better educated at the outbreak of the First World War than they had been at the fall of the Napoleonic empire. The relationship between industrialization, at least in its early stages, and the growth of literacy is not an easy one to disentangle. Factory industry in the first decades of its development may often have reduced literacy rates. Factories usually did not need well-educated workers; and what school system existed in many growing early industrial towns often found it difficult to cope with an explosive rise in their population. Thus in France, in the most industrialized *département*, that of the Nord, the new and developing industrial towns such as Lille, Roubaix and Tourcoing had for a long time relatively low rates of literacy. It was not until the end of the nineteenth century that the two most urban and industrial *arrondissements* of the area, Lille and Douai, began to have the highest literacy rates.[92] Even when school provision was adequate, moreover, the need for children to begin earning a wage as soon as possible meant that the schools might well be underused.

However powerful forces were by the middle of the century pressing for the achievement of widespread, even universal, literacy. As the industrial economy matured the relative importance of clerical and administrative workers, who had by definition to be literate, increased rapidly. As technology became more complex, more a kind of applied science, literacy and some degree of technical training became increasingly essential for anyone who hoped to keep abreast of 'best practice'.[93] On a different level, it was argued that the extension of the right to vote and growing public participation in politics must be accompanied by a wider spread of education. It was dangerous to give any share of political power to a man who could not read and who was therefore incapable of understanding political issues. In France the results of the elections by universal suffrage of 1848 and 1849, both of which produced large conservative majorities,[94] and those of the plebiscites held under Napoleon III, convinced many republicans and radicals of the urgent need for mass education to ensure that never again could the reactionary instincts of the uneducated be used against them.[95] (In 1848 more than half the men who voted in the elections for the Constituent Assembly had been illiterate.)

Simultaneously, however, it was being argued from the conservative side that mass elementary education would act as a very valuable social cement. It would make easier the percolation downwards in society of civilizing influences and would spread, particularly through the influence of the teachers, an understanding of the need to respect the law and established authority. When Guizot introduced in 1833 the legislation which provided for the setting-up of an elementary school in every French parish he explained his action, the first effective effort at mass education in France, by saying, 'We have tried to create in every commune a moral force which the government can use at need.'[96] A British justice of the peace in 1845 put the same essential idea in slightly different terms: 'I have no other conception of any other means of forcing civilization downwards in society except by education.'[97] The result was a marked growth of compulsory mass education in the later decades of the century. In France primary education became universal by a law of 1881. In Britain the Elementary Education Act of 1870 brought the first direct state intervention in the education of the mass of the population; and by 1880 it was compulsory for every child to attend either a publicly supported 'Board School' or one provided by a church or voluntary society. In Russia, in the face of difficulties far greater than in western Europe, a systematic programme was drawn up in 1908 for the achievement of universal and compulsory elementary education by the 1920s. Even without political and quasimoral arguments, necessity by itself would have forced a great extension of schooling. Just as economic progress was by the second half of the century demanding better and more widespread education, so education was contributing to economic progress. As Europe's economic life became more and more market-orientated, as traditional and largely self-contained local economies became merged in much wider national and even international ones, so it became more essential for men to be able to understand price-lists or newspaper reports or instruction manuals. The triumph of the market economy meant an immense increase in the scale of written communication; paper was the commodity whose consumption increased most rapidly during the century as a whole. A literate population was likely to be a market-orientated population and therefore one which was progressing economically. In 1850 Sweden, for example, was already 90 per cent literate; and this was certainly an essential foundation of her extraordinarily rapid economic progress during the rest of this period. Spain by comparison was only about 20 per cent literate at the same date, and even in 1900 only about 40-50 per cent so; these figures more perhaps than any other single factor explain her economic weakness and relative decline during the nineteenth century.[98] It has been argued that a literacy rate of at least 30-40 per cent is needed before a society can make any significant breakthrough at all to the greater wealth and higher real incomes offered by industrialization.[99]

Side by side with the spread of education, and to a considerable extent a result of it, came another social change which is still very much with us today. This was the emergence of the idea of youth as a distinct and identifiable stage in human development, one with its own characteristics and its own rights. As young men (and to a lesser but growing extent young women) began to spend more of their lives than ever before undergoing some sort of educational process it became easier to think in terms of a part of the life-cycle intermediate between childhood proper and the responsibilities of being fully adult. This growth of full-time education to fill a substantial slice of life had still far to go; in the years before 1914 in the more advanced European countries the proportion of school-age children going on to secondary education was still only 2-3 per cent (it seems to have differed surprisingly little between different countries).[100] But the process was clearly under way and generating a momentum of its own; more and more it was becoming difficult for the sons of the middle classes to obtain jobs which produced good incomes and conferred social status without going through a longish period of education. 'The fact is,' a witness told a British Royal Commission in 1868, 'if a boy is not well educated he cannot keep his position in society. Society twenty years ago,

as I recollect it, was a totally different thing to what it is now.'[101] Moreover the progressive limitation of child labour in all developed countries,
and perhaps also military conscription which removed large numbers of
young men at least temporarily from the labour-force, helped to create an
increasingly large youth group of this kind.

Most fundamental of all, the fall in fertility and mortality, as it slowly
seeped downwards in society, was generating attitudes to the young less
severely practical and utilitarian than had hitherto prevailed. More and
more young people were valued for their own sake, not merely as a source
of additional income or their parents' guarantee against destitution in old
age. A complex of interacting forces was fostering the progressive emancipation of the young from the control of their elders. Increasingly rapid
industrial and technological change meant that the skills and patterns
of behaviour which had served the father well enough were now often
useless to the son. The traditional assumption of every age before the
Industrial Revolution that a man could equip himself adequately for life
merely by learning from his elders was now more and more difficult
to maintain. Urbanization and growing geographical mobility, as has
already been pointed out,[102] now made it much easier than in the past for
sons, and to a lesser extent even daughters, to be economically independent of their parents.

On a quite different level it was also possible to see the young, their
energies still unweakened and their purity of feeling still untainted by the
evasions and compromises of adult life, as the force which might regenerate societies which were now, it was alleged, weary, cynical and lacking in
capacity for effort and sacrifice. This view of youth as the hope of the
future, as a distinct category of humanity radically different from its elders
and in some respects inherently superior to them, appealed particularly to
the nationalism which was now the dominant mode of political discourse.
Almost all the new organizations for the young formed during this period
(the Scout movement founded in Britain in 1907 is a good though by
no means extreme case) had nationalist overtones of varying degrees of
stridency.[103] Karl Fischer, the German schoolboy who founded the not
altogether dissimilar *Wandervogel* movement at the turn of the century
wanted explicitly, for example, to interest young people in the need to
preserve German rights and control in the eastern border regions where
they seemed to be threatened by Polish separatism, and also to stimulate
the demand for a German colonial empire. On a more consciously literary
and sophisticated level of nationalist discourse there was an increasing
tendency by the end of the century for writers to make the young, or at
least the educated young, their target. Already in 1888, in one of his early
articles, the French nationalist Maurice Barrès had claimed to be addressing

himself to the 'princes of youth', while a little later in Italy Giovanni Papini, in many ways a forerunner of twentieth-century Fascism, aimed his writings at those 'few hundred young men born in Italy around 1880, that is to say *a part* of that generation that has begun to think and to act with the new century'.[104]

The increasingly industrialized, urbanized, mobile, educated and youth-conscious society was also one which was, at least in some important senses, more 'middle class'. On the political level this statement needs serious qualification. Perhaps France under the Third Republic was the only major European state of which, even in 1914, it can be said that the middle classes (and the vagueness of that term hardly needs to be under-lined) was truly in political control. But one unmistakable feature of the second half of the nineteenth century in the developed parts of Europe was the growth of at least one type of middle class, that constituted by the professional and administrative groups whose size and importance were now increasing rapidly. On the one hand the great traditional professions were becoming better organized and more self-consciously united, and thus better able to act as effective pressure-groups. In Britain the setting-up of the Law Society in 1825 and the British Medical Association in 1856 are examples of this process. More important, side by side with them there was now emerging a wide range of new professional groups, some of them called into existence by the demands of the Industrial Revolution, which were developing much of the same organization and self-consciousness. To take the British example again, civil engineers set up a professional body of their own in 1818, pharmacists in 1841, veterinary surgeons in 1844, architects in 1848, chartered surveyors in 1868 and chartered accountants in 1880. By the last decades of the century there were even signs that 'social work' was beginning to emerge as a quasi-profession which required training and which was based on specific and clearly defined principles and procedures.[105] No developed society could now function without the services of a large and growing body of experts of this kind, men who in most cases were increasingly imbued with pro-fessional *esprit de corps*. In Britain the number of those in professional occupations trebled in 1841-81, while the population as a whole grew by only two-thirds.[106]

Even more striking, however, was the vast growth of clerical and administrative employment, which in its upper reaches at least took on a quasi-professional character. The expansion of education meant a corre-sponding increase in the number of teachers, a group which was already, by the end of the century, beginning in many European states its struggle to be recognized as a true profession. The growth of postal services and railways, again, created large numbers of medium-ranking administrative posts whose holders could claim a middle-class and quasi-professional status. In Britain as early as 1850 there were more men employed in operating railways than in building them. The growing complexity of industry, and in particular the emergence of firms very much larger than those normal in the first stages of industrialization, meant the growth of a new class of professional managers and administrators, men often of great practical ability and experience who had no share, or only a small one, in the ownership of the enterprise which employed them.

Finally, in every country civil services grew sharply in numbers during the century. Every central government directly employed far more people at its end than it had at its beginning. Public health, social services, universal state education, sometimes government-owned industries, generated a multitude of officials and inspectors; and quite apart from this more or less mechanical administrative growth changes in the whole tone and style of society were almost imperceptibly having the same effect. As it became more fluid, more mobile and more individualistic, society ceased to be largely self-regulating as it had been before the industrial and urban revolutions. No longer could traditional institutions, the village community, the guild, the church, provide the conscious and purposeful control which was increasingly demanded. More and more this had now to be provided by central governments working through professional administrators, often of a technical or semi-technical kind. This change was perhaps most marked in Britain, with its long traditions of decentralization and very limited government activity. In 1797 the central government employed only about 1,500 civilian officials of its own: by 1869 it had nearly 17,000 on its payroll.[107] In 1851 the army still accounted for 80 per cent of all state employees; but by 1914 this proportion had fallen to only 55 per cent, though in absolute terms the army was by then much larger. The classical land of *laissez-faire* and local initiative had, inevitably and almost unconsciously, acquired a large civilian bureaucracy of its own. Sometimes this growth of administrative machinery might be slowed by traditional distrust of powerful and pervasive central governments, as in Britain. Sometimes it was limited by the sheer poverty of the society concerned and its inability to pay for an expensive bureaucracy. For this reason there were in Russia by the end of the nineteenth century only about 400,000 civilian government employees, while France, with a population only a third as great, had about a million and Germany about 1.2 million. (These figures include postal workers and those in nationalized industries such as the railways and, in France, the gas industry.) A French author estimated in 1910 that for every 10,000 inhabitants Belgium had 200 government officials, France 176, Germany 126 and Britain 73. Such figures involve difficult problems of comparison and should not be uncritically accepted; but even with this qualification they meant government interference with, and control of, the life of society on a scale never before contemplated. This great growth of government jobs added powerfully to the administrative and managerial component in the expanding middle-class strata of society.

The effects of all this were great. Higher education leading to professional and administrative work acted to some extent as a ladder up which a poor but able man could climb to a higher social status. 'The professions', wrote an English commentator in 1857, 'absorb aspirants from all classes, but return few or none to their source.'[108] Moreover civil servants and officials of all kinds normally enjoyed a very high degree of job security and could look forward to substantial retirement pensions. To a considerable extent the same was true of many members of professional bodies and to some degree even of successful managers in industry. This meant that society now contained a growing element which was largely protected against economic pressures, at least in the short and even the medium term. It had little to fear from the unemployment and destitution in old age which were the scourges of the poor, while at the same time it was shielded against the economic fluctuations which could still ruin so many entrepreneurs. A professional and administrative class had now come into existence which was, to some extent, above the battle, one which did not have to struggle against other social groups, at least in any overt way, for its incomes and its standards of living. Moreover although it was still a small minority even in the most advanced European countries, it was a growing one and, more important, an active and vocal one. If not a ruling class in any strict sense of the term, it was everywhere a class which could exert influence, and one whose position was based on education and intelligence. It was therefore more capable than any other element in society during the generation before 1914 of taking a wide view of political and social problems and of sympathizing with the needs and demands of other elements. Much more than other social groups – the industrial entrepreneur, the farmer, the peasant, the artisan – it could sympathize with the idea of a powerful, centralized and bureaucratic state which used its powers in an enlightened and creative way. Socialism in all its forms therefore owed much to men of this type. The Fabian Society in Britain, founded in 1883–84, was dominated by the outlook of a comfortable professional and administrative middle class. In France Jean Jaurès, the outstanding socialist leader of the pre-war decades, began his career as a professor, while in Russia nearly all the major figures in the early history of socialism – P. B. Struve, M. I. Tugan-Baranovskii, Georgy Plekhanov, for that matter Lenin himself – came from this type of background.

The growing importance and activity of the middle classes, and in particular the emergence of the professional classes in something like their present-day form, was an essential foundation for the rise of feminism. It underlay the increasingly insistent demands for greater equality of status and a wider range of rights and opportunities for women which were being heard by the end of the nineteenth century. Feminist groups were in the main a product of industrializing societies and their leadership normally had a strongly middle-class character. Working-class feminism, where it existed as any kind of organized force, was often quite distinct from the middle-class variety and relations between the two strained or even downright hostile.[109] The victories of the movement, or at least the more clear-cut and obvious ones – admission of women to the professions and, for those who were married, rights of property-ownership – were essentially victories for a limited social stratum of middle-class women. Thus for example in Britain women were given the right to register as doctors in 1876, while a series of concessions in 1870, 1882 and 1893 gave married women the same property rights as unmarried ones and therefore at least the possibility of economic independence of their husbands. In France, again, married women were able to open savings accounts in their own names from 1881 onwards, and in 1903 in Toulouse a woman lawyer pleaded for the first time in a European court. Secondary and even university education was beginning to be available to women: by 1914 both the French and the German universities numbered about 4,000 women among their students. Divorce was made easier in Britain in 1857 and legalized for the first time in France in 1884, while in the 1880s a woman doctor, Aletta Jacobs, was daring enough to set up in Amsterdam the first birth-control clinic. But the immediate practical effects of this opening of higher education and the professions to a limited number of middle-class women should not be exaggerated. Its main result by 1914, though a significant one, was to provide for the first time in one or two countries an adequate supply of well trained female teachers.

The feminist movement over much of Europe was still pathetically weak at the outbreak of the First World War. To flourish it needed not merely an industrialized and urbanized society with some reasonably strong parliamentary tradition but also, it seems clear, an environment strongly tinged with Protestantism and with the individualism to which most forms of Protestantism had always been favourable. Nowhere in Catholic Europe was the movement for women's rights strong. Belgium had a bigger population than Holland and was more industrialized and urbanized. Both countries had strong middle classes and parliamentary forms of government. Yet the movement for women's rights was far weaker in strongly Catholic Belgium than in its neighbour. The same influences explain the fact that in 1906 a petition in favour of women's suffrage presented to the Italian Chamber of Deputies could muster a mere 600 signatures, while simultaneously in tiny Iceland a similar petition was signed by twenty times as many women. It was noted that when in the following year a march through Paris was organized to demand voting rights for women those who took part were mainly British suffragettes living in the French capital – a good index of the essential weakness of the entire women's movement in France.

The demand for the vote, the central objective of radical feminism, had by 1914 achieved very little success. In 1906 Finland and in 1907 Norway gave women the right to vote in parliamentary elections (in the case of Norway with considerable restrictions). Elsewhere, however, the position was very different. Sometimes the achievement of universal suffrage for men meant the end of traditional systems of voting based on property qualifications which had given a limited number of women property-owners some small share of political influence. This happened in Bohemia and the Austrian provinces of the Habsburg empire with the coming of manhood suffrage in 1905–1906; throughout the empire the Social Democrats tended to oppose votes for women as a threat to the extension of voting rights for men. Everywhere in Catholic Europe the demand for women's suffrage was weakened by the fear of socialists and liberals that women, once enfranchised, would use their votes under the influence of the church to oppose any kind of radicalism and maintain the status quo. Even in Britain, though a National Society for Women's Suffrage had been formed in 1867 and a series of bills in favour of voting rights for women passed the House of Commons in 1870, 1884, 1908 and 1914, nothing had been achieved by the outbreak of the First World War. Nor was there any correlation between paid employment and agitation for political rights so far as women were concerned. For several decades before 1914 both France and Italy seem to have had a higher proportion of women working outside their homes than Britain; yet the women's suffrage movement was much weaker in both of these countries.[110]

On a deeper level the position of women was changing. The traditional conception of marriage as essentially a business contract, an arrangement based on mutual practical advantage in terms of property-ownership or the labour-power needed to work a peasant holding, the conception which had been taken for granted in pre-industrial peasant Europe, was now rapidly decaying. The idea of it as the result of free individual choice based on individual tastes and preferences was now seeping from the large city into the countryside and the smaller urban centres. In one small French town, for example, during the two decades after Waterloo, the average age of women at marriage was relatively high (about twenty-five) and about a third of brides were older than their husbands. Quite rapidly, however, the average age of marriage fell to twenty-one; and from about 1865 onwards only one woman in ten was older than the man she married.[111] A basic aspect of human nature, the fact that, given a free choice, men prefer to marry women who are younger than themselves and who are physically attractive, was now increasingly able to assert itself. The economic constraints, the need to use marriage simply as a means to acquire a few acres of land or a hard-working wife, which had been so predominant for most Europeans in previous centuries, were becoming less important. How far this change in fact improved the position of women is perhaps open to debate. In traditional peasant Europe a wife, however overburdened and exploited, had been absolutely necessary to most men. The peasant could ill-treat his wife but he could not work his land without her. To the factory-hand or the clerical or administrative worker, in other words to an increasing proportion of men in the later nineteenth century, a wife no longer had the same indispensable quality: this is reflected in the fact that when she died they no longer remarried almost at once as the peasant had usually tried to do. In this sense, it can be argued, the status of many married women had declined. They were now in danger, particularly among the growing middle-class strata of society, of becoming optional extras rather than the essentials of life they had been in a pre-industrial setting.

Rising standards of living, moreover, tended to add considerably to the amount of routine labour involved in running a house. The carpets which by the end of the century were beginning to be articles of mass consumption had to be swept, the mass-produced furniture which more and more families could now afford had to be polished, the increasingly numerous ornaments and knick-knacks had to be dusted. At the same time some of the more essential aspects of traditional women's work were showing signs of moving outside the home. At least in the more developed parts of Europe and for the better-off part of society, primitive (and at first very expensive) domestic machinery, commercial laundries, more entertaining in restaurants and cafés, processed foods, were all now making the family less of a self-contained productive unit. The peasant wife of pre-industrial Europe had spent much of her time and energy in the fields: her work might be brutally heavy, but it was undeniably important. By the second half of the nineteenth century an increasing proportion of married women were spending their time in work which was physically less demanding but also less essential. Yet in other ways women's status and life chances had indisputably improved. As has already been pointed out, the coming of the factory and the new opportunities for paid employment which it brought, gave opportunities of some degree of personal independence to large numbers of young women and helped to emancipate them from the family and social controls which were so hard to resist in a traditional rural environment.[112]

This argument again must not be pressed too far. The great majority of women, and virtually all married women, remained throughout the century securely under the control of their menfolk; and there is some evidence to suggest that as industrialization developed the proportion of married women working outside their homes and with the degree of independence this might confer usually fell (partly because rising real wages made men more able to support their families single-handed). It has been argued persuasively that this situation explains the greater loyalty of women to organized religion in all its forms, since in the churches, and particularly in the Catholic church, they could liberate themselves from male control in the only way which was socially acceptable. The churches offered an opportunity to organize and share in charities and societies which were exclusively female, and in Catholic countries provided in pilgrimages 'the woman's only socially sanctioned means of escape from home and its daily routine'.[113] It is tempting to believe that forces of this kind account for the tendency for religious vocations in many Catholic countries to be more frequent among women than men during this period; by the 1850s there were more female than male members of religious orders in France, for example, for the first time in the country's history.[114] Over much of Europe the social significance of organized religion was different for men and for women, and much greater in the case of the latter. The struggle between clerical and anticlerical influences in so many Catholic countries during the nineteenth century was in a very real sense a struggle between the sexes – and the fact that the church on the whole was able to maintain its position so well can be seen as evidence of the growing ability of women to hold their own in this. Nor should it be forgotten that over much of the continent the percolation downwards from the middle classes to the population in general of birth-control, and the resulting fall in birth-rates in the later decades of the century, were slowly beginning to free women from the heaviest of their traditional burdens and to widen in the must fundamental way of all the range of opportunities open to them. To strike an accurate balance between all these factors and establish clearly how and how far the status of women changed during this period is not easy; but it is hard to deny that their position in industrialized and urbanized Europe was improving, in spite of class and regional differences which were still very wide.

The most developed and modernized parts of Europe were also slowly becoming, in terms of individual behaviour and personal relations, a gentler and more humane society than ever before. From the later decades of the eighteenth century onwards influences of this kind were percolating downwards from the more comfortable and better educated to the mass of society and very gradually transforming it. This is seen on the most fundamental level in changing attitudes to young children. In some parts of Europe, notably in France which has been most intensively studied in this respect, it was still very common in the later eighteenth century to put newly born children out to nurse, to be fed and looked after by a professional wet-nurse who often sent her own children away in the same manner. In some rural areas, especially those within relatively easy reach of Paris, wet-nursing was an important mainstay of the local economy. It was estimated in 1777 that a sixth of all French children were brought up in this way in the first stages of their life; and even as late as 1913 a tenth of all newborn babies in France still went *en nourrice*.[115] But long before then the practice had begun to decline sharply, with the middle classes clearly leading the way in this development. The Paris municipal wet-nursing board sent out 5,000–6,000 children each year in the first decade of the nineteenth century; by the 1830s this figure had dropped to 1,000. This, it has been argued, indicates a deep-seated change of attitudes on the most basic human level, a spreading throughout the population of mother-love of the kind which is now taken as the European norm.

This change, moreover, and other associated ones – the growth for the first time of a large popular literature on child-rearing and child-hygiene, the slow abandonment of the very ancient practice of swaddling babies in tight wrappings which prevented all movement – were, it is claimed, outcomes of that vast, confused movement of change which the preceding pages have tried to describe. The most provocative writer on the subject has claimed flatly that 'good mothering is an invention of modernization' and has even identified a specific decade, that of the 1860s, as that in which modern-style maternal love finally established itself as a dominant attitude in the French working class.[116] Certainly one very important aspect of modernization, the reduction in both child-mortality and birth-rates which it involved, was important here. As the number of children in a family became smaller, and each tended to live longer and thus be seen by its parents as an identifiable individual in its own right, each also came to represent a greater emotional investment than in the past. In the eighteenth and early nineteenth centuries most Europeans were, by present-day standards, remarkably indifferent to their young children, so prevalent was the expectation that many of them would not survive for long. The great change in the conditions of material life which was clearly under way in developed Europe by the middle of the century was the solvent which weakened and finally swept away these attitudes and cleared the way for those which we now take for granted.

In other ways also and on different and less fundamental levels this growth in gentleness, in the ability to feel for the sufferings of others, can be seen. One of these was the activity and influence of the anti-slavery movement. Another was the growth of pressures for better treatment of animals. Both of these were products of mainly Protestant north-west Europe, of the most economically and socially advanced, the most 'modern', part of the continent. The abolition of the trade in African slaves by Great Britain in 1807 and the Netherlands in 1814 in fact helped in the following decades to provide greater opportunities for Spanish slave-traders; and the trade reached its peak, in terms of the number of Africans taken across the Atlantic, as late as the early 1840s. Nevertheless the religious and humanitarian condemnation of slavery was becoming more and more insistent. It was abolished in the British empire in 1833 and in the French one in 1848. Kindness to animals, even more than the anti-slavery movement, was an urban and middle-class impulse and increasingly, as the century went on, one which was strong in the most industrialized parts of the continent (largely because industrial processes were now more and more independent of animals as a motive power for machines). Here again there is some correlation with the pace of modernization: in Britain the first legislation to protect animals was passed in 1822, but in France, less industrialized and urbanized, not until a generation later in 1850. Moreover a feeling for the sufferings and welfare of animals, like cleanliness and punctuality, had definite class connotations. It was forced by an increasingly self-confident and sometimes self-righteous middle class on a working class and a peasantry which strongly resented interference with traditional amusements often involving gross cruelty to animals, such as cock-fighting, bear-baiting and bull-baiting. In 1838 an inspector of the Royal Society for the Prevention of Cruelty to Animals (founded in 1824) died of wounds received when he tried to make an arrest during a cock-fight. Almost simultaneously bull-baiting in the ancient town of Stamford, where it was a tradition going back for centuries, could be repressed only by the use of troops.[117] Nevertheless here as in so many other aspects of life can be seen the growing influence and final victory of the new values, helped by the way in which rising standards of living and easier travel were opening to almost everyone a wider range of recreations and new possibilities of enjoyment. By the middle of the nineteenth century in the Birmingham area, for example, dog-fights and cock-fights had ceased to figure as working-class amusements and even straightforward drinking had lost ground, whereas cricket matches, rail excursions and visits to museums and theatres were now significant elements in the picture.[118] This change could increasingly be paralleled in other parts of Europe.

On a quite different level a concern to make life less harsh for the weaker members of society, to give them some protection against its uncertainties and the suffering they could inflict, was a motive, though by no means the only or necessarily the most important one, for the introduction in all the major European countries by 1914 of programmes of state-organized social insurance. These varied greatly in scope in different countries. Everywhere, however, they represented a break with the past, an abandonment of the hitherto dominant liberal assumption that it was the responsibility of the individual alone to protect himself against accident, sickness, unemployment and old age. In particular state-provided unemployment insurance, which was likely to involve giving help, even if on a very limited scale, to the 'undeserving' poor, to those who were without work through their own fault, was hard to reconcile with economic individualism. For this reason it was often the last form of state insurance to be introduced. It is interesting, and probably significant, that social insurance schemes seem to have been easiest to establish either in states with relatively authoritarian regimes or in those where democracy was well developed (in the sense of more than half of the male population having the right to vote). In both of these the attitudes and assumptions of middle-class liberal individualism were likely to have only limited influence. Germany, where paternalist attitudes came easily to the groups who ruled, led the way: the Bismarckian legislation covering sickness (1883), industrial accidents (1884) and old age and disability (1889) set a model for much of the rest of Europe to follow.

The impetus behind schemes of this kind continued to grow until the outbreak of the First World War. By 1911, when Switzerland introduced one, every advanced country in Europe had some form of state compensation for industrial accidents. By 1913, when the Netherlands introduced one, all had some kind of state insurance against sickness, though this was often narrowly limited in scope and in some important cases, notably France and Italy, purely voluntary and not compulsory. By 1914 eight European countries provided some form of old-age pension, though only five had taken the final step towards collectively organized welfare by setting up state systems of unemployment insurance. By the standards of the present day all these schemes left much to be desired. Their coverage was limited and the benefits they conferred meagre. Nevertheless they were important, the first steps along a new road. 'Transfer payments' of this kind, coupled with the growth of free public services such as basic education and health care, meant that an individual's economic status no longer depended entirely on his own exertions and his own material assets in income or property. The introduction in Germany of a legal minimum wage in 1891 and the beginning there of the regulation of child labour in 1903–5 were clear indications of the direction events were taking. Individualism and market forces, whose supremacy had never been without challenge even in Britain, the scene of their greatest successes, were now beginning what was to be a long, though slow and hard-fought, retreat. In Germany the Reich Office of the Interior spent only eight million marks in 1890 but 108 million by 1914.

Nineteenth-century society, even in the most advanced parts of Europe, was to present-day eyes riddled with the grossest of injustices. It involved extremes of individual wealth and poverty of a kind intolerable today. The differences in life-chances between different social groups, even in the most basic terms of physical survival and expectation of life at any age, were still great in 1914. Everywhere the system (or lack of system) of education excluded, except at the most basic level, the bulk of the population: in England in 1909 only 1.5 pet cent of the 15–18 age-group was still at school. In some great cities, notably London, the wretchedness of the slums was more striking from the 1870s onwards than it had been earlier in the century. And yet in the parts of the continent which were leading Europe, and later the entire world, to modernity there was working a profound reforming and improving impulse, one which was setting unprecedentedly high standards of what human life should be like, of how men and women ought to behave, of what the minimum tolerable conditions of existence could be. This impulse was far from being entirely a humanitarian one. All sorts of selfish and material calculations also underlay it. Minimum standards of public health could be justified in terms of efficiency as well as humanity; the greatest of all English reformers in this field, Edwin Chadwick, thought essentially along these lines. Public provision for sickness, unemployment and old age could be defended as a means of binding the working class to its rulers and reconciling it to the status quo; Bismarck had seen the German social legislation of the 1880s in these terms. Mass basic education, and the extension of middle-class values to the working class in which it was the greatest instrument, were frequently thought of as the most effective defence, in the long run, of the existing structure of society. Yet whatever the motives the result was the same. Developed Europe, industrialized, urbanized, mobile, literate Europe, was by 1914 a better place to be alive in than ever before, one whose inhabitants enjoyed higher standards and a greater range of opportunities than their ancestors had dreamed of.

THE WEIGHT OF THE PAST: TRADITIONAL EUROPE

The earlier sections of this chapter have been concerned with the forces of change which operated in nineteenth-century Europe. Of course this is not the whole story. Traditional ruling groups remained important, often still dominant, in many European societies and even in some of those most spectacularly affected by economic and technological change. More significant, great areas of the continent in the east and south developed far more slowly, raised their productivity and thus their standards of living less and more painfully, than the western and north-western parts of Europe which were leading the world into a new age. The persistence of forces rooted in the past and their adaptation or lack of it to a new situation, the inability of so much of Europe to share fully in the movement into the new age – these are themes which call for attention.

In much of Europe the landowning nobility remained throughout the century the most important element in the ruling class. Among the major states France was perhaps the only one in which its political power had been, by the middle of the century, decisively and permanently reduced. Its position was being slowly eroded everywhere as new forces – geographical mobility and mass basic education – undermined quasi-feudal loyalties and more or less unquestioning acceptance of noble and landlord leadership. The English economist and political philosopher John Stuart Mill saw this very clearly well before the middle of the century. 'The age which produces railways', he wrote, 'which, for a few shillings, will convey a labourer and his family fifty miles to find work; in which agricultural labourers read newspapers, and make speeches at public meetings called by themselves to discuss low wages – is not an age in which a man can feel loyal and dutiful to another because he has been born on his estate.'[119] This erosion was, however, a slow process. It was quite possible for a landed aristocracy to remain very powerful even in a country where modern industry and everything it implied were growing very rapidly. This was notably the case in Great Britain, whose landed élite was the wealthiest in Europe. The census of landownership taken in 1874–76 showed that 363 very large landowners, with estates of over 10,000 acres, held a quarter of all the land there. Well over half the country was in estates of 1,000 acres or more. This was a concentration of landownership, in the home of the industrial and urban revolutions, which could be paralleled nowhere else. In France estates of over 1,000 acres probably took up only about 20 per cent of the land. In Russia, though there were still some gigantic estates, the share of the land held by nobles was in rapid decline: more was now, after the emancipation of 1861, owned by peasants, and still more by the state. In Prussia there were few large estates of the British type. There holdings of more than 375 acres were regarded as large; and even these, at the end of the 1850s, covered only about two-fifths of the land.[120] By the early 1860s only about 18 per cent of the arable land of Saxony and only 6 per cent of that of Hanover was still in noble hands.

Britain was the pre-eminent country of great estates and very wealthy landowners because there both law and tradition were uniquely favourable to effective entails. Large estates, once formed, were thus much more likely than anywhere else to perpetuate themselves and avoid division between heirs. In the 1850s about half of the land in Britain was entailed. This was ten times as high a proportion as in France, while in Russia entails were hardly possible at all until 1845 and even in 1914 only about one per cent of the land was subject to them. The great landowners of Britain were the richest identifiable social group to be found anywhere in Europe. Until the twentieth century the wealthiest of them were far richer than the most successful British business man and even in the later nineteenth century there may well have been seven or eight landowners worth twice as much as the richest industrialist or banker in the country.[121] The Duke of Westminster, the wealthiest of all, was reputed in the early 1900s to have an income of £1,000 a day, whereas in the century or more from 1800 to 1914 only one Manchester cotton manufacturer left an estate of over a million pounds and only two others more than half a million. It is important to bear such facts in mind when one is asked to think of the century as one dominated by industrialization, the 'rise of the middle class' or the 'triumph of the bourgeoisie'.

Continuing economic importance and social leadership meant for the landowning class in much of Europe also political influence and often political control, at least at the local level. In England the justice of the peace, very often a landowner or a clergyman who was a member of a landowning family, continued to be the most important element in rural local government until the creation of elected county councils in 1888. In Prussia the *Landrat*, who was both the representative of the local landowners and the agent of the central government, remained a powerful figure until 1914: and even as late as that well over half the *landräte* in the eastern provinces were nobles. In Russia, as liberal demands and embryonic national claims gathered strength, the government attempted by creating in 1889 the new office of land captain *(zemskii nachal'nik)* to strengthen the hold of the reliably conservative landowning class on local administration. The one outstanding exception to this generalization is France. There throughout this period the prefect, who was emphatically the agent and representative of the central government, remained completely in control of his *département*; and at least after the 1830 revolution he was hardly ever a noble or a great landowner. There the heritage of the great revolution meant that by the 1870s the leading industrial dynasty, that of Schneider, had an income twice that of the richest landowner.

The picture, however, is not a simple one. Over great areas of eastern and central Europe the landowning class was losing ground rapidly in the face of economic pressures and peasant demands. In Russia the position of the landowners, already declining, was further undermined by the emancipation of the serfs which began in 1861 and whose detailed working-out dragged on through decades of often acrimonious disputes. Losses of land to the peasants as a result of the emancipation; frequently bad management of what remained; the difficulty of making an estate profitable in a country of backward techniques, severe climate and poor communications – all these accelerated the decline of the Russian landowner in the half-century before the First World War. The effort of Alexander III's government to bolster up his position by providing credit through the Nobles Land Bank set up in 1885 had little effect. Throughout these decades sales of noble estates continued on a large scale; the revolution of 1905–7 saw a flood of such sales by terrified landlords. The peasant emancipation in the Habsburg empire which followed the revolutions of 1848, and still more that in Russian Poland after 1864, were even less favourable to the landlord than the much more famous Russian one of 1861. The Habsburg government in Hungary and the Russian one in Poland wished to attract peasant support and weaken the position of a landowning class which they regarded as disloyal and a potential danger. In both cases therefore emancipation was mandatory; and in both the compensation payments to be made by the peasants for the land they acquired were fixed at a low level. In Hungary it was calculated that the lords were paid only about a third of the market price for the land they handed over to their peasants.[122]

Moreover noble and landlord influence at the local level did not necessarily mean corresponding power over central government; and as problems and policies became more complex and governments more active and interventionist it was increasingly at the centre that all important decisions were taken. In Germany the political power of the landed nobility was clearly great at both levels – at the national one probably greater in the generation before 1914 than it had been for a century or more. In 1913 three-quarters of the members of the upper house of the Prussian Landtag (a body comparable in many ways in importance to the imperial Reichstag) were nobles, as well as over a quarter of the members of the lower house. In Britain on the other hand wealth, social status and local importance could not conceal the fact that landlord influence over central government was in steady decline. In Ireland, under political and social pressures not paralleled anywhere else in the United Kingdom, legislation of 1881 and 1903 brought a complete undermining of the landlord's position, transforming him into 'a mere receiver of rents, on terms regulated by the state in favour of the tenant'.[123] In 1894 the landed interest was unable to prevent the introduction throughout the United Kingdom of the death duties which, although their immediate effect was very limited, sounded the death-knell of the great estates. Finally the Parliament Act of 1911, carried into law after an unprecedented political crisis and against bitter opposition from the landlord-dominated House of Lords, asserted the ultimate right of the House of Commons to tax at its own discretion and 'placed the whole of the wealth and income of the population at the disposal of the elected chamber'.[124] Henceforth the wealthiest landowning class in Europe was to be subjected to taxation heavier than correspond-ing groups in any other major state had to bear. This inability of British landowners to determine or often even much to influence government policy is underlined by the fact that Britain was the only major state west of the Russian frontier which made no effort to protect its agriculture against the cheap Russian and American grain which came flooding in from the 1870s onwards.

A final complication in the picture was the fact that the landowning nobility, for so long the ruling class throughout almost the whole of Europe, was changing its character. Almost everywhere it was becoming more and more connected with industrial interests and allied with great entrepreneurs. Such connections were far from new. There was a venerable and widespread tradition of landowners exploiting, often very profitably, mineral deposits under their land. Often also in the past they had organ-ized industrial enterprises based on raw materials produced on their estates. But the second half of the century saw the links between landed interests and industrial ones become closer and more numerous than ever before and sometimes develop into a powerful political alliance. This was most clearly visible in Germany. There the wars of 1866 and 1870–71 rapidly dissipated the resentment and bad feeling which had traditionally reigned between the Prussian middle class and the landowning class, the *Junkers*. Almost overnight the army officer, a member of a group completely dom-inated by *Junker* values and traditions, became a popular hero. Simultan-eously the wealth and power which the industrialists were clearly now creating for Germany began to give them a social status hitherto enjoyed only by landowners, officers and high civil servants. The *Junker* who provided officers and high-ranking bureaucrats to run the new empire, and the industrialist who generated the economic resources needed to sustain its greatness seemed to be the twin pillars on which the Reich now rested. Marriage between members of the two groups became much more frequent than in the past. Sometimes indeed the great landowner and the great industrialist (as more rarely in Great Britain) were the same individual. This was particularly the case in the very important industrial area of Silesia: at the end of the nineteenth century one Silesian aristocrat was the world's greatest producer of zinc, while another employed nine thousand men in his coalmines. Moreover the fact that many industrialists lived outside the great cities (unlike merchants and bankers) and that many *Junkers*, notably in Silesia, had already begun to develop industry on their estates strengthened this movement towards some convergence, even merging, of the two groups. The relations with their workers of many great German industrialists, strongly authoritarian and paternalist, were similar, to an extent never approached in Britain or France, to those of a landowner with his peasants: this was one of the most important ways in which the industrialization of Germany differed from that of her west European neighbours. This situation culminated in the ennoblement of a number of Germany's new industrial leaders – Hoesch, Roechling, Kirdorf, Thyssen. In 1906 the kaiser himself, with the imperial chancellor and a bevy of ministers, generals and admirals, attended the wedding of the daughter and heir of Fritz Krupp, the then head of the firm; and six years later the centenary of its founder, Alfred Krupp, was celebrated in the same way.

Nor was this type of development confined to Germany. In France the nobility during the second half of the nineteenth century became increasingly involved in industry and finance, so that by 1902 30 per cent of the directors of railway companies and nearly a quarter of those of steel companies and banks were noble.[125] The four daughters of Eugène Schneider, the greatest figure in French heavy industry at the end of the nineteenth century, all married noblemen, and one of his grandsons was able to marry into the quasi-royal Orleans family. In Britain by 1914 nearly a third of the members of the House of Lords were company directors, mainly of railways or of insurance or international trading companies. In Austria the most important financial institution, the Credit-Anstalt, had among its founders in 1855 three bankers but also three princes and a count, all from the highest and oldest aristocracy. In Russia too wealthy nobles, and even members of the imperial family, invested in and sat on the boards of industrial enterprises and railway companies.[126]

In 1914 the landed nobility was still in most parts of Europe an important element in the social scene. In Germany, for the last generation or more the most dynamic of all the European states, it was still, in spite of the growing threat from social democracy, in many ways the most potent element in politics. At its highest level, in the greatest noble families, it could claim to constitute one of the most genuinely supranational elements in European life. Such families, at the apex of the social pyramid, could still conduct their lives with little thought for linguistic divisions or national allegiances. Tiny in numbers, they were an international class in a far more genuine sense than the industrial proletariat ever was. Thus the Radziwill family, in territorial terms the greatest of all Polish landowners, had branches in France, Germany and Russia as well as in Poland. Prince

Hohenlohe, German imperial chancellor in 1894–1900, had one brother who was a high official at the Habsburg court in Vienna and another who was a cardinal at the Papal Curia: through his wife (with whom he normally spoke French) he owned estates in Russia far larger than those he possessed in Germany. Count Mensdorff, the Habsburg ambassador in London at the outbreak of war in 1914, was a distant cousin of King George V. Illustrations of this kind could be multiplied almost indefinitely; and the cosmopolitan outlook and influence of this enormously privileged group was one of the significant casualties of the war which began in 1914. Yet it is clear that long before then the European landed class (if this phrase is permissible) was in general losing influence, losing self-confidence, changing its character. As a link with the past, a persisting legacy of pre-industrial, pre-mass-age Europe, it was slowly but steadily declining in significance.

Another great section of traditional society, even more difficult to generalize about, formed a stronger and more durable link with the past. This was the peasantry. It was not, of course, a homogeneous social group; there were for example very wide differences indeed between the peasants of central Russia, accustomed to highly communal methods of organization and action, and those of France, much more individualist and sometimes verging on being commercial farmers. However some valid generalizations can be made about it. Virtually every social commentator in continental Europe during the nineteenth century stressed the profound differences between the peasant and the townsman. In attitudes, values, abilities and interests they seemed to many commentators not merely different but almost diametrically opposed. The French economist Adolphe Blanqui, a very experienced observer, wrote in 1851 of 'two different peoples living on the same land a life so different that they seem foreign to each other, though united [i.e. in France] by the bonds of the most imperious centralization that ever existed. . . . Village and city represent . . . two completely opposite ways of life.'[127] Few of these observers, moreover, had any doubt that the townsman was the intellectual and moral superior of the peasant, that he represented knowledge, progress, the future. The peasant, by contrast, though his very ignorance and conservatism might sometimes make him a stabilizing force in society, was still in many ways essentially uncivilized, the embodiment of the more brutal aspects of the past. Sometimes he seemed hardly human at all. A landowner in central France in 1865 spoke of peasants as '. . . animals with two feet, hardly resembling a man. [The peasant's] clothes are filthy; under his thick skin one cannot see the blood flow. The wild, dull gaze betrays no flicker of thought in the brain of this being, morally and physically atrophied.' It was possible to find evidence to support even judgements as severe as this.

Only five years after these works were written a noble landowner in the Dordogne suspected by the local peasants of Prussian sympathies during the war of 1870 was beaten, dragged around the village, tortured and finally thrown on a pyre to be burned alive.[128]

From at least the 1870s onwards such very sharp distinctions between town and country were beginning to break down. By then urban tastes and values were increasingly being accepted in the countryside, and in this way a society more homogeneous than any seen before was coming into existence. Better roads, railways, later bicycles and even motor vehicles, newspapers and mass education, mass-produced furniture and other household goods, were allowing the peasant to become more and more like the townsman. Increasingly he wore the same clothes, ate the same food and even came to have a similar outlook on many issues. But throughout the century he was normally seen as inferior to the townsman, and resentfully saw himself as such. This inferiority was reflected even in the most basic of all aspects of life; food. It was the peasant who in bad times, and very often in normal ones also, ate inferior substitutes for wheat or even rye bread – chestnuts or acorns in southern Europe, buckwheat, the 'famine breads' containing potatoes, chaff, straw and even worse ingredients which were consumed in Russia after a bad harvest. It was the peasant who ate less meat, tea and sugar and other relatively expensive foods: as late as 1900 the average French peasant consumed only a quarter as much meat as the average townsman and only a fifth as much as the average Parisian.[129] In all sorts of other ways the material inferiority of the peasant was marked. His village street, usually unpaved and therefore dusty in summer and a quagmire after rain, was seldom lit; the visible contrast with the large city glittering with gas or later electric street lighting was therefore sharper than in any earlier age. His own house might well be very inadequately lit: in Provence the *caleu*, a wick burning in a bath of walnut oil, a device unchanged since neolithic times, remained in use until the end of the century.[130]

The distinction between the peasant and the townsman, however, was much more than just a matter of material living standards. It was also frequently one of attitudes and beliefs. The individualism which was the increasingly dominant ideology of the town, at least in western Europe, usually found a much less congenial soil in the countryside, where collective action and decisions were often still deeply rooted in tradition. The greatest example of this, and the one with the biggest practical implications, was the *mir* or *obshchina*, the Russian village community. Over a vast area of European Russia, including all its most fertile parts, it was this peasant commune controlled by its assembly of all heads of families, not individual cultivators, which owned the land and was responsible for the payment of taxes. Since the peasant did not own the land he worked and could not pass it on to his children he had no incentive to invest in it, to use fertilizer, better seeds or more efficient methods, even if he had had the capital and knowledge to make this possible. The result was to make Russian agriculture even less efficient than it would otherwise have been; and the *mir* had therefore become, by the end of the nineteenth century, a major target of agrarian reformers. The last great minister of the imperial regime, P. A. Stolypin, launched a sustained attack on it with legislation of 1906 and 1910–11 which attempted to break it up and introduce into Russia a workable system of agrarian capitalism based on individual land-ownership and rewards for individual initiative and effort. In this he had considerable success; but in the process he generated so much opposition that even if he had not been assassinated in 1911 he would soon have been driven from office. The collectivism and egalitarianism which had under-lain the village commune were still potent forces in much of the Russian countryside, as the great peasant land seizures of 1917 were to show.

Elsewhere peasant communal feeling was not institutionalized on the scale seen in Russia (though the *zadruga* in parts of what later became Yugoslavia had something in common with the *mir*). But it was none the less often a significant force. There was still in many parts of Europe a strong prejudice in favour of seeking a marriage-partner within the village, a feeling which reflected the intense localism and distrust of strangers which had for centuries been engrained in the peasant mind. In many areas the seasonal activities which defined the cultivator's year – harvesting, gleaning after the harvest, the picking of grapes for wine-making – could be begun only when communal authorities decided that it was permissible. In the Vendée in western France, for example, one of the poorer and more backward parts of the country, it was only during the last decades of the century, from the 1870s onwards, that peasant proprietors began to be able to go into their own fields for harvesting without a public proclama-tion allowing them to, or to remove the sheaves after the harvest without waiting for a public announcement of the opening of the paths.[131] Almost everywhere, moreover, until at least the second half of the century, the man who departed from the methods of cultivation or the rotation of crops traditional in his area was regarded with the deepest suspicion and with a hostility which quite often took dangerously physical forms.

In the eyes of the educated townsman the peasant seemed to be stamped as an inferior most of all because of his superstition, his irrationality and his proneness to baseless and exaggerated fears. It is doubtful how far peasants in general anywhere in Europe were religious, in the sense of having any deep feeling for matters of the spirit. What they very often did have, however, was a strong and unthinking attachment to customary rituals and ceremonies and a willingness to resist interference with them, even when that interference was the work of the church itself, of reforming bishops or priests who wished to discourage what they regarded as superstition. Thus in west and south Germany in the early decades of the nineteenth century the strength of popular Catholicism showed itself in an attachment to pilgrimages and religious processions. During these holy pictures were often touched with handkerchiefs or articles of clothing so that the latter could then be used to effect magical cures of the sick. Increasingly both the Catholic church and the secular authorities disliked this sort of religious zeal; yet official efforts to restrict such activities were met by determined resistance.[132] Much popular religious belief, particularly in the countryside, can fairly be described as superstition. Faith in the powers for good of relics or holy pictures easily went hand in hand with faith in the powers for evil of sorcerers and witches. Until the end of the century in many parts of France touching a priest or his garments was thought to have the power to cure the sick, while an English traveller in Quercy, in the remote south-west of the country, was struck in 1894 by seeing bottles of holy water placed on top of chimneys as a protection against lightning.[133] Much of this superstition was generated by fear, the fear which had been for centuries the dominant emotion of peasant life, fear of bad weather, bad harvests, disease, bandits, the exactions of governments and officials, disaster and violence of any kind. In the face of a catastrophe, actual or threatened, collective fears often assumed destructive and self-defeating forms. Thus in May 1816, at a time of approaching famine, thousands of Italian peasants around Bologna laid waste rice fields and deprived themselves of food in the belief that rice cultivation (which had been introduced by the landlords a mere fifteen years earlier) was infecting the air.[134] At the other end of the century, in 1892, during the famine which was then afflicting the Volga basin, a mob in Saratov turned on the doctors supplied by the local authorities in the belief that they were deliberately increasing the sufferings of the victims; they then followed this up by an attack on radical students who liked to think of themselves as the most forthright advocates of peasant rights but who were seen by the peasants as representatives of the feared and resented towns.

In one fundamental respect the situation of the peasant changed for the better over much of central, eastern and south-eastern Europe during the nineteenth century. From the 1860s onwards he was everywhere personally free, after the ending of serfdom as a legal status. This was usually a complex and prolonged process. Very often a decree establishing the principle of peasant freedom would be followed by a long period during which the practical details of that freedom and the price to be paid for it were worked out; frequently it needed some crisis such as the 1848 revolutions to force the process to a conclusion. In Denmark, for example, the original decree came as early as 1788, but all seigneurial privileges and inequalities were not finally removed until 1861. In Prussia the gap extended from 1807 to 1850, in Bavaria from 1808 to 1848; in the Habsburg empire the radical reforming decrees of Joseph II in the 1780s were not worked out to their logical conclusion until the legislation of 1848 and 1853. In Russia the most famous emancipating edict of all, that of 1861, took decades to apply in practice: the complexity of the task can be seen in the fact that a Soviet edition of the edict runs to 466 printed pages. Normally the peasant was required to compensate the lord for the land which he was giving up as part of the emancipation process, either to individual peasant proprietors or, as in much of Russia, to the peasant village community; and though these payments often represented a good deal less than the market value of the land involved[135] they usually led to disputes and long delays in the completion of the emancipation process. Redemption payments in Russia, already greatly in arrears, had finally to be written off during the revolution of 1905–7: in Germany some peasants were still making such payments in the 1920s.[136]

Nevertheless the long-term effects of emancipation were profound. It opened the way (greatly helped by railways, which widened markets for agricultural produce, and by growing literacy, which helped to make the peasant more conscious of market possibilities) for a much deeper penetration of capitalism and a capitalist spirit into the countryside. In Russia in 1861 only 10 per cent of the agricultural output sold was marketed by peasants and 90 per cent by landlords. By 1914 the corresponding figures were 78 and 22.[137] This was an enormous change. But it was one which took time to effect; and in Russia as in most other areas of former serfdom the benefits of the change went to a minority of peasants more active and enterprising than the rest. It was these 'sturdy and strong' peasants on whom Stolypin gambled, in the circumstances not unreasonably, as a future support for the imperial régime. It would be wrong to think of peasants as always and everywhere tending to strengthen the forces of conservatism. Instances can be found of their accepting politically radical leadership, as those of Sicily and southern Italy did that of Garibaldi in 1860. Throughout the nineteenth century, however, the European peasantry as a whole must be regarded as essentially a backward-looking force, a relic of the past, though one whose sheer numbers made it impossible to disregard except in a few of the most highly industrialized and urbanized parts of the continent.

There are other ways in which the influence of the past can be seen still clearly at work in nineteenth-century society. One of these was the persisting, in some ways increasing, importance of personal service as a type of employment and of domestic servants as a category of the employed. In western Europe, it is true, the situation was changing in one important respect. The great aristocratic households of the eighteenth century with their tribes of often grossly underemployed domestics were now relatively much less important. The picture was now dominated by a large number of middle-class families, each employing only a small number. This meant a decline in the proportion of male servants and a growth in that of women ones: fewer footmen, more parlourmaids. But until the last decades of the century personal servants were a growing element in the work-force of even the most developed European countries. In Paris in 1861 they were just over six per cent of the total population: by 1896 almost eight per cent. In 1901 they made up nearly 45 per cent of all working women in the French capital. During the middle decades of the century one woman in every six in England, and one in every five unmarried women, was 'in service'.[138] It was not until the 1880s at the earliest that the great expansion of female clerical and office work (helped by the invention of the typewriter) and the rapid increase in the number of shops (which meant more jobs for shop assistants) began to offer many women in cities significantly wider employment opportunities. Domestic service was in one sense a link with the past. It looked back to an age when industrial employment was limited, when large productive units of any kind were rare, and when the employee could still normally expect at least to see his employer every day. In another way, however, it looked to the future and was an instrument of modernization. It was through working as a servant that many young women were introduced to the city and to modern life generally. Some would eventually return to their native villages with money and new ideas acquired in the town and thus help forward the spread of urban attitudes and values in the countryside. Others, as they gained confidence and opportunities for alternative employment increased, moved into other types of work and settled permanently into the new urban environment. The position of domestic service as a means of making this fundamental transition gave it an importance which was much more than merely economic.

There is one last way in which the past still held nineteenth-century Europe in its grip, one last factor of retardation, the most important of all, which must be mentioned. This was the existence, side by side with the developed Europe of the west and north-west, of a second, 'peripheral' Europe in the east, south-east and south of the continent which lagged far behind, and which entered the new industrial and urban world much more slowly and often with much less success. The Russian empire, the Balkans, Hungary, much of Italy and the Iberian peninsula made up this second Europe; and by all the tests the nineteenth century was learning to apply it compared unfavourably with the north-west of the continent. Its people did not live so long as those of the more favoured regions: in the early twentieth century in eastern Europe on average perhaps ten to twenty years less.[139] They were less well fed, sometimes strikingly so. In two typical villages in the Black Earth area of south Russia investigated at the end of the nineteenth century it was found that the average *annual* per capita consumption of sugar was only 2¹/₂ ounces, and of tea half an ounce.[140] Their food supplies were less secure even at the end of the century: there was a very serious famine in the Volga basin provinces of Russia in 1891–92 and a severe food shortage in Spain in 1898. Agriculture in the 'periphery' was much less productive and efficient than in the more developed parts of the continent. Russia in particular, because of her sheer size, attracted much disparaging comment throughout the century on her backwardness in this respect. 'Over the many thousands of square miles embraced in the grain-growing district', wrote the American consul in Moscow in 1861, 'and amidst the thousands of rich proprietors who claim the title to this remarkable soil [i.e. the Black Earth area of south-central Russia], not one in a hundred possesses a deep-soil plough or improved drill, a patent reaper or a modern threshing-machine.'[141] More than half a century later, at the outbreak of the First World War, the whole of European Russia possessed only 166 tractors against about 14,000 in use in the United States. In 1914 artificial fertilizer was used on only three per cent of the cultivated land of the empire, and the small numbers and poor quality of livestock meant that the supply of natural fertilizers was also inadequate. When the revolution of 1917 broke out half the peasant households in Russia did not own a plough of their own and even after Stolypin's reforms most peasant land was still cultivated using the traditional and wasteful three-field system. The same inadequate equipment and low productivity could be seen in the agriculture of most of the Balkans, of southern Italy and its islands, and of most of Spain (where agrarian 'reform' after 1855 tended to increase the concentration of landownership in the hands of an absentee landlord class and thus impede progress). The contrast with the agriculture of much of Britain, the Netherlands or (the most extreme case of all) Denmark, is very forcible indeed.

The peripheral countries were far less well educated than the developed ones. In southern Europe in the years before 1914 illiteracy rates were about 40–45 per cent and in Russia two-thirds of the population was illiterate (some estimates give a higher proportion though it is also true that by then about three-fifths of Russian children were receiving some sort of education). The periphery was also much less urbanized. In the middle of the century Moscow and St Petersburg together, for example, made up well under two per cent of the population of the Russian empire, though both began to grow fairly rapidly from the 1870s onwards. More serious, what towns there were very often did not play the constructive role of those in the west. St Petersburg, Bucharest, Budapest, Constantinople or Madrid did not provide capital, skills, technical knowledge and enterprise in the way that London and Glasgow did in Britain or Berlin and Hamburg in Germany. Too many of the larger cities of the periphery were centres of administration and conspicuous consumption rather than growth-points for the economies of which they were part.

Peripheral Europe also suffered acutely, by comparison with the more developed areas, from the poorness of its communications. The enormous Russian empire was the outstanding example of this. 'Russia', wrote an experienced observer in 1892, 'is at present suffering from its vastness, and the comparative absence of these great arteries of civilization which alone make more rapid progress possible. She must have more railways.'[142] The railway-building of the years which followed did a great deal to improve this position; but in 1914 the internal communications of the Russian empire were still much poorer than those of any of the great west European states. Even in the later 1870s the inadequacies in this respect of the Habsburg empire made it cheaper to bring cotton yarn from Manchester than from Vienna to the weaving-sheds of Bohemia.[143] Perhaps the most extreme case of the retarding effect of poor communications was Sicily, already for centuries a byword for backwardness and misgovernment. Though there was nowhere in the island more than forty miles from the sea the cost of carrying local produce to a port could be greater than that of growing it or of shipping it from Sicily to Britain, while in 1914 there were still many Sicilians who had never seen a wheeled cart.[144] Poor communications moreover meant a much less mobile population, with all that was coming to mean in terms of adaptability and knowledge of the world. In 1911 a Swiss on average made 31 railway journeys a year, a Briton 29 and a German 25; but in southern Europe the figure was not much more than three and in eastern Europe less than two.[145]

The result of all this was marked industrial backwardness in the periphery in terms both of the quantity and quality of what was produced and of a much lower intensity of industrialization. In 1907 Russian industry used 14.7 horsepower for each thousand inhabitants of the empire – roughly the same as the British figure of the 1830s or the German one of the 1860s.[146] Such time-lags illustrate well the widely differing pace of development in different parts of the continent. In particular the newer 'high-technology' industries which were developing in the generation before 1914 – rubber, aluminium and (with the important exception of northern Italy) motor vehicles – found it very difficult to take root in the periphery. This was partly because, as the century went on, the 'take-off' to industrialization became increasingly expensive. Cotton textiles, the great example of early large-scale industry, made quite modest demands in terms of investment. The capital required for each industrial worker at the beginning of the nineteenth century in Britain, it has been calculated, was of the order of only four to five months' wages. In the mid-century, as French industrialization accelerated, perhaps six to eight months' wages were needed. As techniques developed, however, and machines and other fixed costs became more expensive, this figure rose steadily. By the end of the century, when Hungary began to industrialize significantly, about three and a half *years'* wages were needed to equip each worker employed. The lateness with which the countries of the periphery entered the industrial world, in other words, itself made the entry much more expensive and difficult than it would have been earlier.[147] The high initial investment required largely explains the need for eastern and much of southern Europe to import capital from the west in the early stages of their industrialization. High fixed costs and a relatively unskilled and unproductive labour-force explain another leading characteristic of industrialization in the periphery – the prominence there of very large enterprises which might hope to reap the benefits of large-scale production. This again was most marked in Russia. In 1911 44 per cent of the whole factory labour-force there was to be found in less than 400 giant enterprises, each with over 1,000 workers. In Germany (where large enterprises and consequent economies of scale were much more prominent than in Britain) the corresponding percentage was only 18.5. The cotton-mill at Krönholm, about 50 miles from St Petersburg, founded by the German entrepreneur Ludwig Knoop in 1856, had 12,000 workers and was claimed to be the largest in the world.

There are, almost inevitably, important qualifications to be made to what has been said in the preceding paragraphs. The picture of peripheral backwardness must not be painted too unrelievedly black. The Iberian peninsula in 1914 still showed few signs of a successful transition to modern industrialism. So did nearly all of the Balkans: Romania, for example, though she had been a substantial producer of crude oil for several decades was still importing refined oil products. Elsewhere, however, the picture was more hopeful. Hungary was developing significant industries, in particular the flour-milling in which she now led the world: by 1914 only about half her exports were of agricultural products. Some favoured areas of northern Italy, as has been seen,[148] were industrializing rapidly. At the outbreak of war, in spite of the terrible poverty of the south and the islands, the average Italian per capita Gross National Product was about 80 per cent of the European average.

Most important of all, there had been striking economic change and growth in Russia. Even in the middle decades of the nineteenth century there had been some significant industrial development there: the number of industrial workers increased from 252,000 in 1830 to 565,000 in 1860, mainly as a result of a growing demand for consumer goods which was in turn the result of the slowly growing commercialization of agriculture and increasing ability of some peasants to pay for such things. Much more spectacular growth, however, began from the 1860s and 1870s, in railway-building, in iron and steel production, in the oil industry. Over the whole period 1860–1913 Russian industrial growth averaged about five per cent a year; but the figure conceals wide variations within this half-century. The rate of growth in the 1860s and 1870s was relatively moderate; but in the boom decade of the 1890s it probably reached an average of eight pet cent. It then fell in 1900–6 to less than 1.5 per cent before recovering in 1907–13 to over six per cent. Some aspects of this growth were truly spectacular. In 1870 the Caucasus had produced only two million poods of oil. By 1900, when it produced 631 million poods, Russia had temporarily overtaken the United States as the greatest oil producer in the world and was second only to her in the length of her rail network. At the outbreak of war in 1914 the Russian empire was the world's fourth largest producer of steel and (a significant indicator of qualitative progress), the sixth largest of electrical machinery. These were considerable achievements; and in any case the sheer size of the country and its population meant that, in spite of low average productivity and low standards of living, its aggregate Gross National Product throughout the nineteenth century had been the largest in Europe. In 1914 there were still many millions of cottage producers (*kustars*) in Russia, working in their own homes with hand tools, particularly during the winter when work on the land was impossible. They, and artisans organized in self-regulating groups (*artels*) still produced very large quantities of leather and wooden articles, simple metal goods and other widely consumed commodities. The size of the contribution to Gross National Product made in this way has often been remarkably neglected and undervalued by historians.

Industrialization in Russia differed in at least two fundamental ways from that of western Europe. In the first place it was unique in the extent of its dependence on government help and encouragement. Protective tariffs against imported manufactured goods grew from 1877 onwards after a period of relatively liberal trade policies in the previous twenty years. In 1891 they were markedly strengthened and systematized by a great minister of finance, Sergei Witte, under whom a kind of neo-mercantilism became dominant in Russian commercial and economic policy. (Witte himself was deeply influenced by the work of Friedrich List,[149] on whom he wrote a long pamphlet.) The Russian government insisted, for example, on the use of Russian rails in the building of the Trans-Siberian railway, although better and much cheaper British rails were available. Protection-ism of this kind gave valuable indirect help to developing Russian indus-tries. The return to the gold standard in 1897, perhaps Witte's supreme achievement, was also an important indirect help to industrial growth, since by making the Russian currency more stable and reliable (the rouble had been inconvertible since 1863) it substantially encouraged foreign investment in Russian industry, so that by the end of the century Russia had the largest foreign debt in the world. There was also very extensive direct government support for industry, particularly railway-building. In the 1880s the Russian government began to build railways on its own account; by 1913 it owned 69 per cent of all the empire's mileage. It also gave very extensive guarantees as regards rates of return and security of capital to private investors in railways; in 1914 only eight per cent of the capital invested in Russian railway companies was not covered by guaran-tees of this kind. It seems probable that in the 1890s the government, either by direct investment or through the banking system and the effects of currency stabilization in encouraging foreign investment, made available for industry about three billion roubles.[150] The years just before 1914 saw some change in the pattern of this government assistance. Proportionately less now went to railways and heavy industry and rather more to agricul-ture, for example in an ambitious programme for the building of facilities for grain storage in 1911. By 1913 the Russian empire had for a moment overtaken the United States as the world's greatest exporter of grain. But right until the First World War industry in Russia continued to be dependent on government support to an extent paralleled in no other major European state.

Russian industrialization was also unique in the part played in it by foreign investment. It has been estimated that in 1861 capital from abroad represented less than 13.5 per cent of all industrial investment in Russia, whereas in 1914 it accounted for 35 per cent of a much larger total.[151] In the 1870s and 1880s Germany was the most important source of these capital imports; but France then began to play a leading role, and by the turn of the century British, American and Belgian investment was also very significant. Of the capital of Russian joint-stock companies 26 per cent was foreign-owned in 1890, 45 per cent in 1900 (again the growth during this vital decade is very marked), and still 41 per cent in 1915, when supplies of domestic capital were becoming more plentiful. Foreign investment was not spread evenly across the Russian economy. The great bulk of it was concentrated in mining, iron and steel, oil and heavy engin-eering. In textiles (still one of the most profitable areas) and even in chemicals there was much less. But in the sectors which attracted it its importance was unquestionable. Of the 14 steelworks set up in south

Russia in 1888–1900, for example, all but one depended upon foreign capital, while it was the Nobels and Rothschilds who in the 1870s began the building-up of a substantial oil industry which by 1914 was 55 per cent foreign owned. By the end of the century a high proportion of the greatest names in west European industry – AEG, Siemens and Halske in the electrical industry, Badische Anilin and Bayer in chemicals – had Russian subsidiaries. In 1914 only 15 per cent of the electrical industry was in Russian hands.

Russia by the end of this period therefore presents a series of striking economic and social paradoxes. In terms of gross product she was un-questionably one of the world's great industrial powers, and one of the most rapidly developing. Yet compared to the developed states of western Europe she was as yet a poor country. In 1913 manufacturing and mining still provided no more than a fifth of her national income, while agricul-ture supplied well over twice as much: and a great deal of that manufac-turing and mining was still foreign-controlled. Real income per capita was about a third of that of Germany and little more than a fifth of that of Great Britain. In this respect she had actually lost ground by comparison with some of the west European states: in 1861 her per capita real income had probably been somewhere between a third and a half of that of Britain. The same failure to keep pace can be seen in public health. In 1871 infant mortality in Russia had been about the same as in Germany, Italy and Austria-Hungary a decade earlier. Yet in 1913 it was little changed in Russia while it had fallen substantially in these other countries.[152] The empire was still very markedly what Lenin was to call a 'dual economy', one which combined modern high-technology and high-investment elements (mining, metallurgy, oil, chemicals) with primitive peasant agriculture. Less than a fifth of the population was still urban: it was not until the 1960s that town-dwellers became a genuine majority. Yet Russia's potentialities were almost unlimited: it was already recognized by the more perceptive observers of the pre-war years that she was likely soon to become one of the dominant forces of the world economy. These sharp contrasts, of vast potentialities and still limited achievements, of rich resources and a predominantly poor population, coupled with a dis-credited and vulnerable political structure, were to do much to determine the later course of Russian history.

NOTES

1. J. A. Lesourd and C. Gerard, *Histoire économique, xixe et xxe siècles* (Paris, 1963), i, 225. For slightly different figures see P. Guillaume and J. P. Poussou,

Démographie historique (Paris, 1970), p. 267.

2. R. M. Titmuss, 'The Position of Women: Some Vital Statistics', in M. W. Flinn and T. C. Smout, eds, *Essays in Social History* (Oxford, Clarendon Press, 1974), p. 278.

3. See below, p. 161.

4. S. J. Kunitz, 'Speculations on the European fertility decline', *Economic History Review*, 2nd ser, xxxvi, no. 3 (August 1983), 360.

5. P. Leon, ed., *Histoire économique et sociale du monde*, iv, 3.

6. S. Pollard and C. Holmes, eds, *Documents of European Economic History*, i, *The Process of Industrialization, 1750–1870* (London, Arnold, 1968), 322.

7. M. Levy-Leboyer, *Les Banques européennes et l'industrialisation internationale dans la première moitié du XIX siècle* (Paris, 1964), p. 364.

8. Pollard and Holmes, *Documents*, p. 327.

9. P. Leon, ed., *Histoire économique et sociale du monde*, iv, 3. Europe's gross national product, including agriculture and the service sector as well as industrial production, grew considerably more slowly: see the table in P. Bairoch, 'Europe's Gross National Product: 1800–1975', *Journal of European Economic History*, v, no. 2 (Fall 1976), 276.

10. G. von Tunzelmann, *Steam Power and British Industrialization to 1860* (Oxford University Press, 1978), chs 5–7.

11. R. Samuel, 'The workshop of the world: steam power and hand technology in mid-Victorian Britain', *History Workshop*, iii (Spring 1977).

12. Leon, *Histoire économique*, iv, 335.

13. L. Schofer, *The Formation of a Modern Labour-Force: Upper Silesia, 1865–1914* (University of California Press, 1975), p. 127.

14. S. Pollard, *Peaceful Conquest: the industrialization of Europe, 1760–1970* (Oxford University Press, 1981), p. 141.

15. Bairoch, 'Europe's Gross National Product', pp. 282, 283.

16. R. Cameron, 'Le Développement économique de l'Europe du XIX siècle: le rôle de la France', *Annales*, 1957, no. 2, *passim*.

17. G. Stolper, G. Hauser and K. Borchardt, *Deutsche Wirtschaft seit 1870* (Tübingen, 1964), p. 29.

18. J. A. Lesourd and C. Gerard, *Histoire économique, XIX et XX siècles*, ii, 356.

19. Stolper, Hauser and Bouchardt. *Deutsche Wirtschaft*, p. 34.

20. See pp. 29ff.

21. See pp. 206–9.

22. Pollard, *Peaceful Conquest*, p. 101.

23. Bairoch, 'Europe's Gross National Product', p. 283.

24. I. T. Berend and G. Ranki, *The European Periphery and Industrialization, 1780–1914* (Cambridge University Press, 1982), p. 16.

25. Bairoch, 'Europe's Gross National Product', p. 279.

26. Lesourd and Gerard, *Histoire économique*, ii, 364.

27. See below, pp. 163ff.

28. A. Maddison, *Phases of Capitalist Development* (Oxford University Press, 1982), p. 52.

29. See pp. 156–7.

30. See pp. 87–8.

31. J. Fourastié, *Machinisme et bien-être* (Paris, 1952), p. 52.

32. F. Braudel, *Capitalism and Material Life, 1400–1800* (London, Weidenfeld & Nicolson, 1973), pp. 88–9.

33. E. J. Hobsbawm, *The Age of Capital, 1848–1875* (London, Weidenfeld & Nicholson, 1975), p. 176.

34. W. Hamish Fraser, *The Coming of the Mass Market, 1850–1914* (London, Macmillan, 1981), pp. 156, 161–2.

35. R. E. F. Smith and D. Christian, *Bread and Salt: a social and economic history of food and drink in Russia* (Cambridge University Press, 1984), p. 255.

36. For an interesting discussion of this process of standardization in France see E. Weber, *Peasants into Frenchmen* (Stanford University Press, 1976), pp. 228–31.

37. See p. 155.

38. Marjorie Plant, *The English Book Trade* (3rd edn, London, Allen & Unwin, 1974), p. 405.

39. J. K. Walton, 'The demand for working-class seaside holidays in Victorian England', *Economic History Review*, 2nd ser, xxxiv, no. 2 (May 1981), 253–8.

40. The examples in this paragraph are taken largely from Fraser, *The Coming of the Mass Market, passim*.

41. *The Fontana Economic History of Europe: the emergence of industrial societies*, Pt I (London, Fontana, 1973), p. 146.

42. *Ibid*, p. 122.

43. S. Checkland, *British Public Policy, 1776–1939: an economic, political and social perspective* (Cambridge University Press, 1983), p. 86.

44. Leon, *Histoire économique et sociale*, iv, 295.

45. E. J. Hobsbawm, 'The Labour aristocracy in 19th century Britain', reprinted in *Labouring Men* (London, Weidenfeld & Nicolson, 1964), pp. 296–7.

46. Adeline Daumard, 'L'Évolution des structures sociales en France à l'époque de l'industrialisation (1815–1914),' in P. Leon and others, eds, *L'Industrialisation en Europe au XIX siècle* (Paris, 1972), pp. 326, 320–1.

47. A. H. John, *The Industrial Revolution in South Wales, 1750–1850* (Cardiff, University of Wales Press, 1950), p. 71; D. A. Reid, 'The decline of Saint Monday, 1766–1876', *Past and Present*, no. 71 (May, 1976).

48. S. Pollard, 'Factory discipline in the Industrial Revolution', *Economic History Review*, 2nd ser, xxxiv, no. 2 (May, 1981).

49. A. P. Donajgrodzki, ed, *Social Control in Nineteenth Century Britain* (London, Croom Helm, 1977), pp. 146–7.

50. F. M. L. Thompson, 'Social control in Victorian Britain', *Economic History Review*, 2nd ser, xxxiv, no. 2 (May, 1981).

51. R. Melka, 'Punctuality: an inquiry into the psychology of modern man', *Diogenes*, no. 65 (Spring 1969), 21.

52. On the emergence of this cleavage in Britain, allegedly complete by the 1880s, see P. N. Stearns, *Lives of Labour* (London, Croom Helm, 1975), pp. 241–95.

53. Lesourd and Gerard, *Histoire économique*, i, 262.

54. G. Jones, *The State and the Emergence of the British Oil Industry* (London, Macmillan, 1981), pp. 9, 40.

55. Lesourd and Gerard, *Histoire économique*, pp. 201, 258, 260.

56. Leon, *Histoire économique et sociale*, iv, 262.

57. J. D. Post, *The Last Great Subsistence Crisis in the Western World* (Baltimore–London, John Hopkins University Press, 1977), pp. 39, 71.

58. Berend and Ranki, *The European Periphery and Industrialization*, pp. 95–6.

59. Weber, *Peasants into Frenchmen*, pp. 206, 218.

60. T. J. Nossiter, *Influence, Opinion and Political Idioms in Reformed England: case studies from the north-east, 1832–74* (Hassocks, Harvester Press, 1975), Ch. 11.

61. O. Handlin, 'The Modern City as a Field of Historical Study', in O. Handlin and J. Burchard, eds, *The Historian and the City* (Harvard University Press, 1963), p. 6; Lesourd and Gerard, *Histoire économique*, p. 242; H. Haufe, *Die Bevölkerung Europas: Stadt und Land im 19 und 20 Jahrhundert* (Berlin, 1936), Appendix, Tables 7 and 14, conveniently assembles much statistical information about the growth of towns.

62. F. Bedarida, 'Cities', in A. Briggs, ed., *The Nineteenth Century: the contradictions of progress* (Thames & Hudson, 1970); A. F. Weber, *The Growth of Cities in the Nineteenth Century: a study in statistics* (New York, 1899), p. 105.

63. J. J. Lee, 'Aspects of Urbanization and Economic Development in Germany, 1815–1914', in P. Abrams and E. A. Wrigley, eds, *Towns and Societies* (Cambridge University Press, 1978), p. 283.

64. Weber, *Growth of Cities*, pp. 70, 104.

65. D. R. Ringrose, *Madrid and the Spanish Economy, 1560–1850* (University of California Press, 1983), pp. 34–5; Weber, *Growth of Cities*, pp. 238–9.

66. E. Vedrenne-Villeneuve, 'L'Inégalité sociale devant la mort dans la première moitie du XIX siècle', *Population* (Oct–Dec 1961), 665–98.

67. Leon, *Histoire économique et sociale*, iv, 301–2.

68. Donajgrodzki, *Social Control*, p. 138.

69. *Ibid*, p. 141.

70. H. Perkin, *The Origins of Modern English Society, 1780–1880* (Routledge & Kegan Paul, 1969), pp. 167–8.

71. J. J. Tobias, *Crime and Industrial Society in the Nineteenth Century* (Batsford, 1967), quoted in C. Emsley, ed., *Conflict and Stability in Europe* (Croom Helm, 1979), p. 98.

72. On these questions see in general H. Zehr, *Crime and the Development of Modern Society: patterns of criminality in nineteenth century Germany and France* (Croom Helm, 1976).

73. Donajgrodzki, *Social Control*, pp. 30–1.

74. C. Tilly, Louise Tilly and R. Tilly, *The Rebellious Century, 1830–1930* (Harvard University Press, 1975), p. 218.

75. The role of the French army in this respect is well brought out by J. Vidalenc, 'Armée et police en France, 1814–1914', in *L'Etat et sa police en France* (Geneva–Paris, 1979).

76. Tilly and others, *The Rebellious Century*, p. 221; T. Zeldin, *France 1848–1945*, i, *Ambition, Love and Politics* (Clarendon Press, 1973), pp. 517–18.

77. Tilly and others, *The Rebellious Century*, p. 248.

78. K. S. Inglis, *Churches and the Working Class in Victorian England* (Routledge & Kegan Paul, 1963), *passim*.

79. B. Semmel, *Imperialism and Social Reform: English social-imperial thought, 1895–1914* (Allen & Unwin, 1960). The Fabian socialist Beatrice Webb spoke in a letter of 1904 of 'the ghastly tragedies of the mental and physical decrease of the mass of our race'. (N. Mackenzie, ed., *The Letters of Sidney and Beatrice Webb*, ii (Cambridge University Press, 1978), 204.)

80. Norma Evenson, *Paris: a century of change, 1878–1978* (Yale University Press, 1979), pp. 208, 212.

81. J. J. Sheehan, 'Liberalism and the city in nineteenth-century Germany', *Past and Present*, no. 51 (May 1971), *passim*.

82. C. E. Schorske, 'The Idea of the City in European Thought: Voltaire to Spengler', in Handlin and Burchard, *The Historian and the City*, p. 108.

83. For a discussion of this transition from the standpoint of a sociologist see B. R. Wilson, 'Sociological methods in the study of history', *Transactions of the Royal Historical Society*, 5th ser, xxi (1971), 101–18.

84. J. R. Gillis, *Youth and History: tradition and change in European age relations, 1770–present* (New York–San Francisco–London, Academic Press, 1974), p. 47. See also Martine Segalen, *Amours et marriages de l'ancienne France* (Paris, 1981), p. 68.

85. Michael Phayer, *Sexual Liberation and Religion in Nineteenth Century Europe* (Croom Helm, 1977), pp. 82–6.

86. Weber, *Peasants into Frenchmen*, p. 235.

87. *Ibid.*, pp. 368–9.

88. J. Michael Phayer, *Sexual Liberation and Religion in Nineteenth Century Europe* (Croom Helm, 1977), pp. 82–6.

89. *The Life and Labour of the People of London*, (Macmillan, 1892–97) vii, 427.

90. Weber, *Peasants into Frenchmen*, p. 235.

91. B. Seebohm Rowntree, *Poverty: a study of town life* (London, 1901).

92. F. Furet and J. Ozouf, *Reading and Writing: literacy in France from Calvin to Jules Ferry* (Cambridge University Press, 1982), pp. 201–3, 211–17.

93. R. Cameron, 'Pourquoi l'industrialisation européenne fut-elle si inégale?', in P. Leon and others, *L'Industrialisation en Europe*, p. 529.

94. See p. 92.

95. Furet and Ozouf, *Reading and Writing*, p. 125.

96. T. Zeldin, *France, 1848–1945*, ii, *Intellect, Taste and Anxiety* (Clarendon Press, Oxford, 1977), p. 150.

97. R. Johnson, 'Educational policy and social control in early Victorian England', *Past and Present*, no. 49 (Nov. 1970), 97.

98. Cameron, 'Pourquoi l'industrialisation . . .', pp. 530–1.

99. M. J. Bowman and C. A. Anderson, 'Concerning the Role of Education in Development', in C. Geertz, ed., *Old Societies and New States* (New York, Free Press of Glencoe, 1963), pp. 247–79.

100. P. Flora and A. J. Heidenheimer, eds, *The Development of Welfare States in Europe and America* (New Brunswick–London, Transaction Books, 1981), p. 245.

101. Gillis, *Youth and History*, pp. 100–1.

102. See p. 176.

103. This point is developed, and perhaps overstressed, so far as Britain is concerned, in J. Springhall, *Youth, Empire and Society: British youth movements, 1883–1940* (Croom Helm, 1977).

104. R. Wohl, *The Generation of 1914* (Harvard University Press, 1980), pp. 40, 160.

105. Judith Fido, 'The Charity Organization Society and Social Casework in London, 1869–1900', in Donajgrodzki, ed., *Social Control in Nineteenth Century Britain*, pp. 207–30.

106. Perkin, *Origins of Modern English Society*, p. 429.

107. *Ibid*, p. 123.

108. Gillis, *Youth and History*, p. 69.

109. R. J. Evans, *The Feminists: women's emancipation movements in Europe, America and Australasia, 1840–1920* (Croom Helm, 1977), pp. 31–2, 144–53.

110. Joan W. Scott and Louise A. Tilly, 'Women's work and the family in nineteenth century Europe', *Comparative Studies in History and Society*, xvii, no. 1 (Jan. 1975), 37.

111. Evelyn Ackerman, *Village on the Seine: Tradition and Change in Bonnières, 1815–1914* (Ithaca, Cornell University Press, 1978), pp. 62–3.

112. See above, p. 176.

113. Weber, *Peasants into Frenchmen*, pp. 351–2; Zeldin, *France, 1848–1945*, ii, 992–3.

114. Phayer, *Sexual Liberation and Religion*, pp. 94–7.

115. On wet-nursing in general see G. D. Sussmann 'The wet-nursing business in nineteenth-century France', *French Historical Studies*, ix, no. 2 (1975), 304–28.

116. E. Shorter, *The Making of the Modern Family* (Collins, 1976), pp. 168, 195. Shorter's provocative ideas on the history of family relationships are summarized in his 'Différences de classe et de sentiment depuis 1750; L'exemple de la France', *Annales*, 29 année, no. 4 (July–August 1974).

117. The attack on brutal traditional amusements is discussed in B. Harrison, 'Religion and recreation in nineteenth-century England', *Past and Present*, no. 38 (Dec. 1967), 98–125.

118. Reid, 'The decline of Saint Monday', pp. 82–4.

119. *Edinburgh Review*, lxxxi (1845), 513.

120. These figures are taken from D. Spring, ed., *European Landed Elites in the Nineteenth Century* (Baltimore, Johns Hopkins University Press, 1977), pp. 2–6.

121. W. D. Rubinstein, 'Wealth, elites and the class structure of modern Britain', *Past and Present*, no. 76 (August 1977), 103–4.

122. On these aspects of peasant emancipation see J. Blum, *The End of the Old Order in Rural Europe* (Princeton University Press, 1978), pp. 388–93, 398–9.

123. Checkland, *British Public Policy*, p. 192.

124. *Ibid*, p. 181.

125. Zeldin, *France, 1848–1945*, i, 405.

126. Blum, *The End of the Old Order*, p. 423.

127. Quoted in Weber, *Peasants into Frenchmen*, p. 9.

128. Weber, *Peasants into Frenchmen*, pp. 4, 251.

129. *Ibid*, p. 142.

130. *Ibid*, p. 413.

131. Zeldin, *France, 1848–1945*, i, 139.

132. Phayer, *Sexual Liberation and Religion*, p. 68.

133. Weber, *Peasants into Frenchmen*, p. 27.

134. Post, *The Last Great Subsistence Crisis*, p. 72.

135. See above, p. 195.

136. On redemption mechanisms and problems generally see Blum, *The End of the Old Order*, pp. 388–93.

137. Olga Crisp, 'The Pattern of Russia's Industrialisation up to 1914', in P. Leon and others, eds, *L'Industrialisation en Europe au XIX siècle* (Paris, 1972), p. 469.

138. Theresa M. McBride, *The Domestic Revolution: the modernisation of household service in England and France, 1820–1920* (Croom Helm, 1976), pp. 13–14, 34.

139. Berend and Ranki, *The European Periphery and Industrialization*, p. 52.

140. W. H. Bruford, *Chekhov and his Russia: a sociological study* (Kegan Paul, 1948), p. 47.

141. Pollard and Holmes, *Documents of European Economic History*, i, 10–11.

142. W. Barnes Steveni, *Through Famine-Stricken Russia* (London, 1892), p. 91.

143. Pollard, *Peaceful Conquest*, pp. 247–8.

144. D. Mack Smith, 'The latifundia in modern Sicilian history', *Proceedings of the British Academy*, ii (1965), 115.

145. Berend and Ranki, *The European Periphery and Industrialization*, p. 100.

146. Pollard, *Peaceful Conquest*, p. 238.

147. Pollard, *Peaceful Conquest*, p. 221.

148. See above, pp. 143–4.

149. See below, p 244.

150. Olga Crisp, 'The Pattern of Russia's Industrialisation', p. 451.

151. D. C. M. Platt, *Foreign Finance in Continental Europe and the United States, 1815–1870* (Allen & Unwin, 1984), p. 40.

152. P. R. Gregory, *Russian National Income, 1885–1913* (Cambridge University Press, 1982), pp. 5, 159.

4

States and nations

THE TRIUMPH OF NATIONALISM

The most important political fact of the nineteenth century in Europe was the growth of nationalism. During this period the belief that the nation was the natural and inevitable form of large-scale political organization, and the only one which was morally valid, became increasingly widespread and sometimes fanatical. By the middle of the century the approaching triumph of the nation-state was clearly visible to every intelligent observer. 'Today,' wrote an Austrian diplomat in 1848, 'the magic word which moves the masses, not the whole body of peoples but those who form the world of the intelligent, is called *nationality*.' 'With the national idea', wrote the Italian nationalist leader, Baron Ricasoli, a year or two later, 'there can be no compromise. Face to face with this the other liberties must yield place.'[1] This was merely an unusually forthright statement of what by then was becoming a dominant point of view. Over much of central and eastern Europe nationalism in the second half of the century carried out a great work of political destruction and creation. It undermined the multinational states inherited from the past, the Ottoman, Habsburg, and to a lesser extent the Russian empires. In their place it set up or attempted to set up new national states. Everywhere it involved a rejection, often violent and contemptuous, of political structures which attempted to unite a number of different nationalities. In 1851, for example, the Italian writer Pasquale Mancini (quoting his great German predecessor, J. G. von Herder) could claim that a multinational state 'is not a body politic but a monster incapable of life';[2] and two generations later, as nationalism began to dominate the Near East, its greatest Turkish proponent, Zia Gökalp, could write that 'today all of us realize that the idea of a state or homeland supposedly common to diverse nationalities is nothing but a mere concept, devoid of all zeal, enthusiasm and devotion'.[3] By the end of the nineteenth century there were even clear signs that the power of nationalism was no longer confined to Europe and the areas of permanent European settlement overseas. By then it was becoming an almost universal phenomenon, the greatest force in the political world which we still inhabit today. The claim of Marx and Engels in the *Communist Manifesto* that 'national differences and antagonisms between peoples are daily more and more vanishing' reflects the essential optimism and cosmopolitanism which distinguishes all the Communist classics; but it bore little relation to the facts even in 1848 when these words were written and still less in the generations which followed.

It is impossible to provide a truly satisfactory definition of nationalism, one which fits all the facts and to which there are no exceptions. But however we define it, the French Revolution marks the beginning of its emergence as the dynamic force it was to become in the following century. Patriotism, and the dislike of foreigners which easily develops from it, can be seen centuries before this, at least in western Europe. It seems likely, for example, that as early as the twelfth century the canonization of a number of monarchs (Charlemagne in France, Edward the Confessor and Canute in England) did something to implant in the peoples concerned an embryonic consciousness of some distinct collective personality.[4] The Hundred Years War clearly gave a considerable impetus to feelings of this kind in both England and France. The long struggle for independence of England had the same effect on the Lowland Scots; while in Castile the *Reconquista*, the expulsion of Moorish power from Spain, had even more far-reaching results. More peaceful forces also helped to create embryonic nations. The increasing use of the vernacular languages in administration, and more importantly in literature, was binding together more closely the inhabitants of each great linguistic area in western Europe and differentiating it from its neighbours where different tongues were spoken. Increasingly unified legal systems and codes of law had, in a less fundamental way, the same effect. The increasing subordination of church to state, the main result of the Reformation over much of Europe, strengthened embryonic national feeling in many areas. The growing numbers and importance of middle-class groups, which acted to some extent as a cement uniting society and bridging the gulf between rulers and ruled, nobles and peasants, helped to lay the foundations of national consciousness. In the nineteenth century nationalist ideas and writing were to be overwhelmingly middle-class products. Above all the emergence of relatively powerful monarchies – France, Spain, England, Russia and Sweden – created a good deal of the political and territorial framework within which nineteenth-century nationalism was to function.

By the 1760s and 1770s, moreover, Rousseau was expressing theories and emotions which were to recur repeatedly in the thinking of the next 150 years. His deep dislike of the cosmopolitanism of much eighteenth-century thought; his assertion that 'the greatest miracles of virtue have been produced by patriotism'; his advocacy in the *Social Contract* (1762) of the teaching to children of a civil religion which would replace Christianity; his insistence in the projected constitutions which he drew up for Corsica and Poland on the preservation of national peculiarities merely because they were national – all these were to find an increasingly responsive audience in the nineteenth and still more the twentieth centuries.[5] Far more than any other writer, Rousseau begins the close association of nationalism with democracy which was often important in the nineteenth century; and the very frequent use of the word *nation* (as opposed to *royaume, état, empire* or *pays*) in the *cahiers* of 1789 can be taken as showing that by then a feeling of national unity of something like a modern kind existed in France.[6]

This feeling was one of the most important forces underlying the revolution. It was given practical expression in the great reform of local government in France in 1791, which centralized administration more than ever before in Paris. It can also be seen in the first real efforts by any European government (though half-hearted and short-lived) to stamp out minority languages, in this case Breton, Provençal, and the German dialects spoken in Alsace. There was even a suggestion that no male citizen be allowed to marry unless he could read, write and speak French.

In political and constitutional theory the new emphasis on national unity is visible above all in the clause of the Declaration of the Rights of Man of 1789 which proclaimed that 'the principle of all sovereignty resides essentially in the nation. No body or individual may exercise any authority which does not proceed directly from the nation.' On the level of mass psychology the same feeling is seen best in the federation movement which reached its climax in the demonstrations in Paris and the provinces during the summer of 1790. On 14 July 1790 perhaps fifteen million people throughout France and perhaps 300,000 in Paris attended ceremonies which marked the first anniversary of the fall of the Bastille. This was the first national holiday in history and a true landmark in the development of the modern world. These demonstrations were above all an assertion of the will of the participants to intensify and safeguard the unity of the French nation and the integrity of its territory. This will was soon to find practical expression in the annexation of the papal enclave of Avignon and in the nullification of the undoubted legal rights in Alsace of various German princes. The years 1789–91 thus saw a quite unprecedented assertion of belief in the nation as an ultimate value before which others must give way. Modern nationalism, intolerant, demanding, dynamic and creative, the nationalism of the masses, had been born.

The victories of the French Revolution and the Napoleonic empire did much to stimulate national feeling in Europe. Positively, they displayed the military and political power which a great nation could wield if it were effectively united and well led. Negatively, they were effective through the hostile reaction which French conquest and exploitation aroused in some areas, notably in much of Germany. Some of the rulers of Europe grasped dimly the significance of these developments. For example Alexander I of Russia, in the ideas for the political reconstruction of the continent which he drew up in the autumn of 1804, argued that as far as possible its states should in future be composed of 'peuples homogènes', each in harmony with its government.[7] But the immediate importance of all this should not be exaggerated. Neither in Germany nor in Italy, at the end of the Napoleonic wars, did more than a small educated segment of the population dream of creating a centralized state. In the former some of the intellectual foundations of such a state had indeed been laid. Pietist religious emotion, the most living aspect of German Protestantism in the eighteenth century, helped to produce a mental climate favourable to national consciousness through its stress on the communal feeling of believers and on the importance of will and emotion in spiritual life as against the intellectualism of the Enlightenment. Immanuel Kant, the greatest philosopher of the later eighteenth century, was himself far from being a nationalist. But his stress on the autonomy of the individual will, and on moral effort and self-control as the only real source of morality, helped to create an intellectual atmosphere in which a nationalism emphasizing will, effort and sacrifice could take root.[8]

But intellectual forces of this kind were slow-acting and confined in their immediate effects to a small educated minority. By far the most effective popular movement of the period against French dominance of the German-speaking world was that in the Tyrol in 1809. Yet the Tyroleans were quite unaware of belonging to a German nation. They fought in defence of the ancient customs and traditions of their province, now threatened by French-inspired reforms, and from loyalty to the Emperor Francis II, their hereditary ruler. The volunteer units which in 1813 played some role (though one later greatly exaggerated by many nationalist writers) in driving Napoleon's armies out of Germany were overwhelmingly middle-class. In a still predominantly peasant country they included few peasants and from east of the Elbe virtually none. Joseph von Görres, the greatest German publicist of the early nineteenth century, was fully justified in complaining in 1814 that 'a great part of the people have not yet been touched by the new life [i.e. by nationalism] . . . another part has been merely persuaded by talk . . . only the smallest group has really understood, and it is on this group that the hope for the future rests'.[9] Very few Germans at the end of the Napoleonic wars envisaged or wanted any more drastic political change than the restoration, perhaps with a considerably strengthened central government and with a federal army, judicial system and tariff structure, of the Holy Roman Empire which had been swept away in 1804. Moreover nationalism in Germany at the end of the Napoleonic period still retained a large element of eighteenth-century cosmopolitanism. The national idea there was for a generation to come to reflect some of the universalism and rationalism of the Enlightenment. Thus the first eleven articles of the constitution of the German Confederation were incorporated in the Final Act of the Congress of Vienna, giving them an international character and, arguably, some right of intervention to uphold them to the European powers in general. Moreover even such radical nationalists as Freiherr vom Stein and the great historian Niebuhr continued to see a unified Germany as part of a greater unity formed by the Christian states of Europe and not merely as an end in itself.

In Italy the desire for political unity was even more limited in scope and effectiveness. Already during the eighteenth century several writers of importance – Muratori, Genovesi, Algarotti, Baretti – had stressed the need to develop Italian as a true national language and to purge it of the French words which had been added to it in considerable numbers. Already the poet Alfieri had proclaimed that a united Italy would help to bring freedom to other nations without states of their own, thus anticipating one of the dreams of Mazzini. Already Vincenzo Cuoco, a writer who had in 1806–15 served the governments of Joseph Bonaparte and Joachim Murat in Naples, had preached the necessity of educating the mass of the people in ideas of unity and independence. But all this agitation was still confined to small groups of intellectuals. The ordinary Italian was almost as far as he had ever been from envisaging or desiring national unity. Neapolitans, for example, still spoke of travellers coming from the north as having 'arrived from Italy'.[10] Indeed particularism was considerably stronger in Italy than in Germany; an Austrian official in Lombardy spoke of her as 'this land where mutual envy and jealousy are taken in with the mother's milk'.[11] For several years after the Congress of Vienna Metternich played with the idea of establishing a defensive federation of the Italian states under Austrian leadership; but his hostility to national unity, in Italy as in Germany, was complete. He even tried to encourage particularist feeling in Lombardy and Venetia, the Italian provinces now placed under Habsburg rule, since this would act as a barrier against the success of any genuine Italian nationalist movement.

It is true that in two important European states, Russia and Spain, Napoleon I had encountered bitter and successful national resistance to his attempts at conquest. But in neither of these had the emotions visible during the early nineteenth century much in common with modern nationalism. In both they were inextricably bound up with religious feeling. In Spain the Peninsular War of 1808–14 was provoked largely by the attempts of the French régime in Madrid, in 1808–9, to attack the power and wealth of the Catholic church and to suppress the Inquisition and many of the religious orders. In essence it was a religious war against the ideas of the eighteenth-century Enlightenment, of which the French invaders were the representatives. In Russia also resistance to France was associated with religious emotion more than with modern secular nationalism. When Alexander I declared war on France in 1805, the Holy Synod ordered that there should be read in the churches on every Sunday and feast-day a proclamation which denounced Napoleon, not merely as the enemy of Russia and the tsar, but still more as the foe of the Orthodox church. The charges which it brought against him were religious, not political, ones. Both in Russia and in Spain, therefore, nationalism of a kind undoubtedly existed in 1815; but in both it was defensive, religious, and highly conservative. It had little in common with the forces which were to redraw the frontiers of all central and south-eastern Europe during the following century. The national feeling of Poland was even more limited. It was one of the ruling class only and had as yet made no impact on the peasantry, the vast majority of the population. The Polish nation, like that of Hungary, was still one merely of the nobility and landowners, while in some of the most developed parts of Europe, Belgium and the Swiss cantons, there was no national tradition and hardly anything that could be called national consciousness.

Nationalism in 1815, therefore, was weak. Over most of Europe it was still embryonic or backward-looking. Yet it was also a force, and a growing one, in European affairs. The statesmen at Vienna, however much most of them disliked it, were not completely without an understanding of its potentialities. Already in 1809 Napoleon, during the brief but violent struggle with Austria of that year, had envisaged an appeal to the national feeling of the Hungarian squires as a weapon for possible use against the Habsburgs. Three years later he had threatened Alexander I with the raising of an army of 200,000 Poles for use against Russia, and with the resulting loss of the Polish territories gained in the partitions of the later eighteenth century. Most significant of all, perhaps, was the fact that from 1805 onwards the Austrian government had attempted, with some success, to create by propaganda a substitute for the national unity which was impossible in a multinational empire. This substitute was *Kaisertreue*, personal loyalty to the emperor and the Habsburg family, a force which more than anything else held the empire together until 1918.

The first political newspapers in the Habsburg hereditary lands were founded for this purpose in 1808–9; and even the theatre was used as a means of strengthening the fidelity of the masses to the ruler.[12]

Throughout the century which followed the settlement of 1814–15 nationalism strengthened its hold on the minds of even the most pacific of men, so that by 1860 John Stuart Mill could declare in his *Represensative Government*, one of the sacred books of nineteenth-century liberalism, that it was 'in general a necessary condition of free institutions that the boundaries of government should coincide in the main with those of nationalities'. Meanwhile its character and the ideas which underlay it were developing in complicated and unforeseen ways.

The nationalist mysticism which had already been seen in embryo during the French Revolution, the idea of the nation as a divine creation, the supreme focus of men's loyalties and even the source of morality, became much more pronounced and widespread as the nineteenth century progressed. This was particularly marked in Germany where, at least during the first half of the century, the output of nationalist theorizing was more extensive, more varied, and of higher intellectual quality than anywhere else in Europe. Thus Wilhelm von Humboldt, one of the outstanding German liberals of the early decades of the century, came at last to believe that 'there are only two realities, God and the nation'.[13] It became increasingly common to think of the nation as the creation, not of the objective facts of linguistics or geography, but of the workings of a mystical entity, the national spirit. 'Our fatherland is with us, in us,' wrote the historian Leopold von Ranke in 1836. 'Germany lives in us. We enact it, whether we choose to do so or not, in every country we enter, in every zone. We stand upon it from the very beginning and cannot escape it. The mysterious something that informs the lowest among us precedes any form of government and animates and permeates all its forms.'[14] Well before the end of the eighteenth century Burke in England and Herder in Germany had begun to argue along these lines; and although in Burke's hands the idea of national spirit was a highly conservative one it could also be easily made to serve revolutionary ends. Moreover if each nation had its own distinctive spirit, its own particular genius and aptitudes, it was easy to go a step further and think of each as having a distinctive mission of its own and as playing its own indispensable role in the divine scheme of things. The decline of conventional forms of religious belief almost certainly aided the growth of this pseudo-religious approach to national dreams and ambitions. In Germany such ideas fell on fertile ground. They were central to Herder's thought; and in the early decades of the nineteenth century a galaxy of important writers – Fichte, Hegel and Schleiermacher – took them up in differing ways. The last of these, for example, proclaimed that 'God has pointed out to every people its particular mission on earth and has breathed into it its particular spirit, in order that in this way He may be glorified by each one through its particular mode'.[15]

It was in the writings of the greatest Italian nationalist prophet, Giuseppe Mazzini, that some of these cloudy and unhistorical concepts assumed their politically most important form. To him nationality was truly a religion; national unity must be based upon religious belief and be itself a form of religious belief. The fundamental truths he thought of as known intuitively, leaving to reason only a subordinate function. The duties of men were more important than their rights; for individuals existed to fulfil a mission in the service of humanity, and liberty was no more than the ability to choose between different ways of doing this. Nations could be constituted only by the will of the individuals composing them, by those individuals recognizing a common duty and its consequences and affirming a common purpose. Each had its own specific moral mission to perform. 'Every nation has a mission, a special office in the collective work, a special aptitude with which to fulfil it: this is its sign, its baptism, its legitimacy.'[16] A world of sovereign nation-states, each fulfilling its God-given task, would therefore be one of peace and happiness. Mazzini was much more than a selfish or parochial nationalist. His ideas were always essentially universalist. To him the idea that the nations of Europe as soon as they had gained their freedom would spontaneously unite in some form of association was fundamental; and his last significant work, the *Politica Internazionale* (1871) was a vision of a Europe of free peoples thus voluntarily associated. The national state was to him the norm towards which all political life and action should tend, not merely a panacea for specific grievances. 'The nation', he wrote, 'is the God-appointed instrument for the welfare of the human race.'

In practice, however, it was inevitable that the idea of national mission should normally be put forward in support of the demands and grievances of some specific national group. Mazzini himself was preoccupied above all by the struggle for Italian independence and unity, although his knowledge of the country, and in particular of the vast non-political majority of its population, was very slight. He had a mystic reverence for Rome and the imperial traditions for which it stood, and expected the achievement of Italian freedom to begin the transformation of Europe to which he looked forward. In France also the idea of a mission providentially reserved for the French people can be seen running from the liberal Michelet and the positivist Comte in the middle years of the century, through the conservative Barrès in its last decades to the Catholic poet Péguy, whose influence was considerable in the years before 1914. Michelet, though a distinguished historian, could speak without embarrassment of nationalism as a 'religion' and of 'our two redemptions' by Joan of Arc and by the revolution of 1792, while Comte hoped for the union and regeneration of all humanity under the leadership of France. Perhaps the most extreme form of the idea that each nation has its own mission to perform, its own distinctive moral obligation to fulfil, can be seen in the assertion by the poet Mickiewicz in his *Books of the Polish Nation and of the Polish Pilgrims* (1832) that for Poland had been reserved the messianic destiny of becoming a martyr in the cause of human freedom, the 'Christ among the nations', a claim which was soon to be echoed by other Polish poets, Krasinski and Slowacki. Nothing perhaps brings out more clearly than these claims the essential irrationality of this belief in national mission or the covert arrogance which often underlay it.

The first half of the nineteenth century saw another and often more constructive development in nationalist theorizing. This was the increasing tendency to turn to history to support national claims and buttress dreams of national greatness. Allied with this very often went efforts to record and study the folklore, folk customs, folk art and folk music which were thought to express the distinctive character of each nation; for by preserving these the national character could be protected against the onslaught of the increasingly influential natural sciences, which were by their nature cosmopolitan and international. In the eighteenth century history had been either a branch of literature or a source of precepts useful to the politician or the moralist, 'philosophy teaching by example' in Bolingbroke's well-known phrase. Nearly all the greatest historians of the period had been cosmopolitan in outlook and often international in their choice of subjects; Gibbon and Robertson are the outstanding British examples of this. What national histories had been produced had usually been written in purely political and dynastic terms. The generation which followed the French Revolution saw a rapid change in this position, a change reflected in Friedrich von Schlegel's remark that 'history is the self-consciousness of a nation'.[17] Historical writing was now conceived more and more in terms of separate peoples and states, of nations and nation-states. Ranke, the greatest historian of the century, wrote largely though by no means entirely of nation-states, and particularly of the conflicts between them. This meant that he was far more concerned with questions of foreign policy than any previous writer of comparable stature; and this concentration on the history of diplomacy and war was one of the greatest of his legacies to his successors. The first half of the nineteenth century saw the educated classes of Europe become increasingly historically minded,[18] and the history they read was more and more written in terms of nations. In a different way this growing nationalist influence in historical studies can be seen in the publication from the 1820s onwards of a number of great national collections of printed documents which are still indispensable to the historian today – the *Monumenta Germaniae Historica* from 1824, the *Documents inédits sur l'histoire de France* from 1833, and in England the 'Rolls Series' from 1836. In Russia the first real attempt at a national history, that by Nikolai Karamzin published in 1826–29, both reflected and stimulated an upsurge of national feeling; while the Slavophil Konstantin Aksakov can be found in the middle of the century suggesting that in order to teach the peasants the history of their country and imbue them with a proper pride in it every village library should contain a collection of Russian medieval chronicles.[19]

The fact that history was now being written so much in a national form had important results. It meant, particularly perhaps in central and eastern Europe, that it tended to become largely the story of national rivalries. Thus the first great history of Bohemia, that by Palacky published in 1836–67, depicted the country's past in terms of a long struggle for mastery between Germans and Czechs. In a similar but less dangerous way the creation of the first chair of Finnish history, at the university of Helsinki in 1856, and the publication of the first important history of Finland, by Koskinen, from 1869 onwards, did much to strengthen Finnish resistance to both Swedish and Russian influences. Much nineteenth-century historical writing, therefore, reflected and intensified existing national antagonisms; and as it influenced, at least in the long run, the history taught in schools, it played an important part in creating a truly mass national feeling, with all its attendant dangers.[20] Increasing historical-mindedness also meant that in parts of Europe which had been subjected to long periods of foreign rule there was a tendency for renascent national pride and national claims to hark back to political units which had existed in the more or less remote past, even though these had not in any sense been national states. Thus Serb national feeling drew encouragement from memories of the Serb-dominated empire of Stephen Dushan, which in the fourteenth century had covered most of the Balkan peninsula. Similarly Greeks were inspired to hopes of future greatness by memories of the Byzantine empire. Later even Bulgars could look back to an age of greatness when Tsar Simeon, early in the tenth century, had made Bulgaria the leading power in south-eastern Europe. Often the historical inspirations and models most useful to nationalists were those taken from a past so remote and little-known that they were largely immune from effective scrutiny by historians. In England Boadicea; in France Vercingetorix, the Gaulish leader who had resisted Julius Caesar; and notably in Germany Arminius, who had destroyed an invading Roman army (and to whom a great monument was erected in 1841–75 with money raised largely by popular subscription) were all pressed into service in this way.

Hand in hand with this interest in national history went one in folklore and folk culture, notably in those parts of Europe where sovereign national states were unknown or struggling into life. A people which was not politically independent could at least exist as a 'folk nation' and by so doing perhaps lay the foundations of eventual sovereignty. By the beginning of the nineteenth century the idea that each national literature was the reflection of a distinctive national spirit was becoming more and more generally accepted. Herder, the originator of so many trends in cultural nationalism, had already done much to spread the idea that a people's folklore, and particularly its folk poetry, was the supreme expression of its essential character and the greatest of all national possessions. Himself one of the first great collectors of folk-songs, he helped to stimulate in Germany a new wave of interest in this aspect of the national heritage; of this the great collection of folk-tales by the brothers Grimm published in 1812–15 was the outstanding literary result. Elsewhere in Europe a similar interest and similar efforts can be seen. In Russia, the poet L. A. L'vov published as early as 1790, with Ivan Prach, the first serious collection of the country's folk-songs. In Finland H. G. Porthan had produced even earlier, in 1766–68, his *Dissertatio de Poesi Fennica*, the first attempt at a real study of Finnish folklore; while in 1835 Elias Lönnrot published for the first time the national folk epic, the *Kalevala*.[21] In Wales the Royal National Eisteddfod began to be held annually from 1858: and by 1914 such festivals of traditional poetry and music had become almost a national mania of the Welsh.

Parallel with this interest in national history and folklore, and even more important, went in many parts of Europe an intense and possessive interest in the national language. Nineteenth-century nationalism, in so far as it can be defined in objective terms, was above all linguistic nationalism. More and more, as the century progressed, language came to be regarded as the ultimate criterion of nationality and as the proof of a nation's existence and right to exist. One of the earliest of the societies set up from the 1830s onwards to fight for Flemish culture and rights in the new kingdom of Belgium called itself *De Taal is Gansch het Volk* (The Language is the Whole People), a title which sums up this attitude. The idea of language as the ultimate badge of nationality, like that of national mission, was of mainly German origin. It too was first given currency by Herder and then spread by other German writers, notably Fichte. Like the belief in national mission, it deepened the divisions between different national groups; for it could be argued that since language expressed the innermost being, the soul, of the nation, it should be kept free from contamination by foreign words. If these were allowed to invade it they would inevitably bring with them foreign ideas to pollute the mind and spirit of the nation. A pure language derived from a single source, an *Ursprache*, was therefore inherently superior to a composite one built up of different elements (an idea which had been taking shape in Germany over the last three centuries). Thus Fichte, in his *Reden an die Deutsche Nation* (1807–8) could argue that the Germans alone were fitted to regenerate the world, since they alone had preserved their original language uncontaminated. The French and English, on the other hand, though mainly of Germanic stock, had allowed their languages to degenerate into mixed and partly or largely non-Germanic ones, which he thought of as dead.

Relatively few, even among scholars, were willing to push the argument as far as this; but throughout this period the emphasis on language as the decisive factor in national allegiance tended to increase. This had very important practical implications. It meant that nationalist movements, particularly in the less developed parts of Europe, were very often associated with the revival of national languages which had sometimes survived merely as peasant dialects. Quite often these languages were more or less deliberate and almost artificial creations, the work of nationally-minded scholars. In the early and middle decades of the century a whole series of Slav languages was rediscovered in this way and equipped by devoted scholars with grammars, orthographies and even the beginnings of a literature. Dobrovsky and Jungmann among the Czechs; Šafarik and Kollar among the Slovaks (one of the best examples of a national group whose renaissance was made possible by the resurrection of its language); Gaj among the Slavs of the Illyrian coast; Kopitar among the Slovenes and Karadjitch among the Serbs, were all active in this way. In Norway Ivar Aasen published a dictionary (1846) and a grammar (1848) which produced a national language from a welter of local dialects. The most extreme case of all is the creation in the Basque provinces of Spain at the end of the century of a new hybrid literary language from a group of over twenty dialects some of which were mutually unintelligible. In Finland the Aurora Society had been founded in 1770 to develop the national language; and during the nineteenth century fears of russification helped Finnish to expand at the expense of Swedish. The first chair of Finnish was set up at Helsinki in 1851. In Greece, after independence had been achieved in the early 1830s, every effort was made to purify the language of foreign words and make it resemble as closely as possible that of classical times. The restoration of the ancient tongue, it was believed, would restore the genius of classical Greece in the modern nation. The Greek constitution of 1911 therefore strictly prohibited any corruption of the national language – a remarkable if naive illustration of the idea that the latter enshrines the very soul of the people. Even in Lithuania the first scientific grammar of the language was published in the 1840s. The *reductio ad absurdum* of the idea that a real nation could not exist without a distinctive language was reached in the early twentieth century in Scotland. There the programme for a proposed 'Scottish Party' issued in January 1907 called for a compulsory qualification in Gaelic for every holder of state office in the country, though the language had not for almost a millennium been spoken by a majority of Scots.

There were two media in particular through which linguistic nationalism could be fostered. These were the schools and the press, above all the newspaper press. Both of these powerfully encouraged the growth of cultures which were not local and traditional, not based on subgroupings of a relatively small and even intimate kind such as village or regional communities, but increasingly homogeneous over large areas, areas defined by state frontiers. These new national cultures were based on mass access to the printed word and the ideas it conveyed. They were increasingly hostile to traditions and allegiances of any kind, social, economic or religious, which intervened between the individual and the more and more demanding national community to which he owed a primary and overriding loyalty. The hostility of German nationalists after 1871 to both Social Democracy and the Catholic church is a good example of the sort of 'integral' nationalism which the schoolmaster and the newspaper were now making possible. The growth of universal, or at least widespread, primary education went during the century in step with the growth of popular nationalism: the second could hardly have existed without the first. During the early years of the century Fichte had hoped for the national regeneration of Germany through a system of education based on the principles of the Swiss theorist Pestalozzi; and F. L. Jahn, the most xenophobic of the German nationalists of the period, had drawn up a detailed programme of national education which stressed patriotic history, compulsory manual work, gymnastics and military sports. Their hopes were not realized; but in Prussia a department of public instruction was established in 1807 (an important legacy of the military collapse of the previous year) and the abolition of fees in state schools was begun in 1833. In the same year France began to create a system of national elementary schools. Holland began the creation of a national system of education in 1806, Greece in 1823, Belgium in 1842, Portugal in 1844, Romania in 1859, Hungary in 1868, and even Bulgaria, still not formally an independent state, in 1881. The adoption of a uniform national curriculum in German schools in 1872 was one of the most important efforts to consolidate the political unification of 1866-71. In the more backward parts of Europe the growth of primary education was sometimes striking, at least on paper. In 1800, for example, the Pashalik of Belgrade had possessed only two elementary schools, in both of which the teaching was in Greek. By 1870 the principality of

Serbia, which covered roughly the same area, had 441.[22] It is true that some of these systems of popular education, especially in poor and badly governed states, promised much more than they performed; as late as the 1880s only about 9 per cent of the population of Serbia was even barely literate. Everywhere, however, education was falling more and more under the control of governments. In Catholic Europe it was increasingly being taken from the hands of the church, the one supranational organization which still possessed real vitality. Everywhere greater numbers of ordinary men were acquiring, with literacy, some access to political ideas; and this very often meant nationalist ideas.

The emergence of a small and weak nationality depended in its early stages even more upon the development of some national literature, and notably of newspapers in the national language, than upon the growth of an educational system. The importance of these factors can be seen repeatedly in eastern, central and south-eastern Europe, and in the Near East, during this period. One of the best illustrations is the Armenian nationalist movement which began to attract some attention in Europe at the time of the Congress of Berlin and the growth of which stimulated great massacres of Armenians by Turks in the 1890s. Its rise was in large part the result of the rapid development from the 1840s onwards, particularly in the Armenian areas under Russian rule, of a literature written in the vernacular. The first Armenian newspaper to be published on Armenian soil appeared in 1855, the first Armenian novel in 1860; it was not until the 1870s and 1880s, on the other hand, that schools began to be widespread in the Armenian-speaking areas of Asia Minor. There are many other instances of the way in which vernacular literature and newspapers could generate national feeling and all too often sharpen national antagonisms. Thus the foundation in Prague of the first important Czech political paper, in 1846, marks an important stage in the evolution of Czech national consciousness; while the establishment in Hungary five years earlier of *Pesti Hirlap*, the journal which helped to make Kossuth a national figure, is an even better illustration of the point. In Russia embryonic nationalism among the Jewish community was fostered by the revival of Hebrew studies and the growth of a modern Hebrew literature. Abraham Mapu of Kovno (1808–68) was the first novelist to write in Hebrew; and in 1869 a Russian Jew, Peter Smolenskin, founded a monthly magazine printed in the language and designed to counteract the growing tendency for Jews to become assimilated to their Gentile environment. The appearance of the first popular Flemish newspaper, the *Volksblad*, at Ghent in 1870, was both a sign of the growing strength of Flemish nationalism and a factor tending to strengthen it still further. The same was true of the first daily newspaper in Catalan, which began publication in 1879. In Latvia the first newspaper of any significance began to appear in 1862; by 1914 the biggest Latvian paper had a circulation of 100,000 – considerably more than some important Russian ones. In Germany the first great political daily, Cotta's *Allgemeine Zeitung*, was founded in 1798. By the 1840s the growth of the popular press had helped to produce there for the first time something like a genuine national public opinion. It is significant that the rapid growth of tension between Germans and Danes in the duchy of Schleswig during the 1830s was accompanied and accelerated by the foundation of a politically minded newspaper by each of the antagonists – the *Kieler Korrespondenz-Blatt* by the Germans in 1830 and the *Dannewirke* by the Danes in 1838.

Linguistic and folk nationalism was clearly, in many ways, a creative element in the life of nineteenth-century Europe. It resurrected and refurbished languages which had sunk to the status of peasant dialects. It rediscovered forgotten literatures, some of them of real value. It gave a powerful impetus to the study of national history and folklore. It encouraged the production of a number of great dictionaries, for example those of Grimm and Adelung for German, Linde for Polish and Jungmann for Czech. In a few cases, notably in Bohemia from the end of the 1860s, it stimulated the growth of important national theatres. It was the largest single element in that general cultural nationalism which can also be seen clearly, to the great enrichment of music, in the 'national' composers of the later decades of the century – Smetana and Dvořák in Bohemia, Mussorgsky in Russia, Grieg in Norway – or in collections of folk tunes such as those published in Spain by Felipe Pedrell. It meant that the distinction, important throughout eighteenth-century Europe, between a high culture which was cosmopolitan (though essentially French in origin) and a popular one with local and vernacular roots was increasingly bridged, at least in western Europe. Sometimes folk-nationalism of this kind could be carried to ridiculous lengths, as in proposals for the creation or revival of 'national' costumes. The Babeuf conspirators in 1796[23] had planned to adopt a national uniform which would distinguish the French from all other nations and thus keep them free, as the people destined to change the world by their example, from foreign contaminations. A few years later Jahn in Germany adopted a 'national' dress of unbleached cloth worn with flowing hair and beard, while in Russia the extreme nationalist Admiral Shishkov advocated a return to the costumes of the seventeenth century, those worn before Peter I contaminated Russian life with his borrowings from the west. But in general the rediscovery of national pride and traditions associated with the revival of national languages had undoubtedly constructive effects.

Linguistic nationalism could have much less beneficial results. It often meant that a ruling nation deliberately impeded the development of the language of a subject one. Such a ruling group was likely to resist strongly demands for the teaching in schools of 'inferior' languages or for higher status or equality for them in the administration and the judicial system. The outstanding example of this type of linguistic oppression is the policy pursued by the Hungarians, or at least by their ruling class, throughout the second half of the century. It was only as late as 1843–44 that the use of Magyar was made compulsory in official business and education in Hungary proper. But after the *Ausgleich* of 1867 the Hungarians, in spite of the passage of a relatively liberal Law of Nationalities in 1868, increasingly discriminated against the languages of the Serbs, Slovenes, Romanians and other groups which found themselves under Magyar rule in the eastern half of the Habsburg empire. By impeding or forbidding the teaching of these languages in schools the subject-nationalities which spoke them could be 'decapitated', since their natural leaders would be forced to attend schools in which Magyar was the medium of instruction. The fact that the civil service, which used Magyar as the language of administration, was the main source of employment for educated men in these backward areas, also constituted a standing temptation to able and ambitious Slovaks or Serbs to abandon their own nationality and attach themselves to the dominant Magyar one (the teaching of Magyar in schools was made compulsory in 1879). This system of linguistic discrimination and oppression, the most sustained of the nineteenth century, was made possible only by the fact that after 1867 the membership of the Hungarian parliament was grossly biased against the subject-nationalities. Thus the Slovaks, if they had been represented in it in proportion to their numbers, would have had 45 deputies; in fact they had only three. The Romanians, who suffered more than any other group from Magyar domination, were entitled on a population basis to 68 members but had only five to speak for them.[24]

A similar effort by a ruling nation to impose its language on weaker peoples under its control can be seen in the Russian empire. The Polish revolt of 1863 led to severe repressive measures which included efforts to weaken the Polish language and Polish schools; while for forty years after 1864 the printing of books in Latin characters in Lithuania was forbidden. In 1876 the printing and import of books in Ukranian, with a few exceptions, was also forbidden: permission to print a Ukranian grammar was refused on the ground that 'the printing of the grammar of a language which is condemned to non-existence cannot be permitted'.[25] The 1880s saw strenuous efforts to russify the Baltic provinces, efforts inevitably directed largely against the German schools there. In Finland also there were attempts from the end of the century to propagate Russian more or less forcibly; it was quite unjustifiably made the language of official business in 1900 and of the Finnish senate in 1912. In a similar way and with similar objectives the teaching of Polish was forbidden in 1887 by the German government in the schools of Prussian Poland, while a nationalist society, the *Ostmarkverein*, made strenuous though not very successful efforts to spread the use of German there.

The nationalism of the nineteenth century, and especially of its second half, was also new in the extent to which it was tinged with racial feeling. The idea that humanity could be divided into more or less clearly defined racial groups and that these groups had differing hereditary characteristics and could be arranged in some kind of hierarchy was already old when the century began. Early in the eighteenth century, for example, the Comte de Boulainvilliers had argued that all tendencies towards political or intellectual freedom in France came from the Germanic element in the French people; while in 1775 the German J. F. Blumenbach, in his *De Generis Humani Varietate Nativa*, a book which founded the modern science of physical anthropology, seemed to place the belief in separate races on a more secure intellectual footing than ever before. In 1810 Jahn urged in his *Volkstum* that the Germans must keep themselves racially pure and undefiled since it was their task to civilize the world by force.

It was only in the middle decades of the nineteenth century, however, that racial beliefs became a well-established part of the nationalist creed. There were several reasons for their growing popularity. The great vogue of phrenology in the first decades of the century, the widely accepted belief that the shape of a man's skull decided his character and abilities, gave them considerable impetus. It strengthened the idea, already well established in the eighteenth century, of a systematic correspondence between mind and body, of mind as a purely biological function. As there were clear physical distinctions between different broad groups of humanity it became easy to believe that these must imply corresponding differences of character and intellect.[26] During the second half of the century the measurement of skulls and the calculation of cranial indices (the ratio of the maximum breadth of the skull to its maximum length) for different national or regional groups became a favourite pastime of anthropologists. Such calculations also served as foundations for many theories about the racial make-up, and therefore the moral and intellectual value, of the different European nations.[27] The growth of anthropology and sociology as pseudo-sciences (the first International Congress of Anthropologists met in 1865 and its successors annually from 1867 onwards) helped to give racial beliefs academic respectability and to make them an accepted part of the thinking of the great majority of Europeans. Already in 1853–55 Alfred de Gobineau had published his *Essai sur l'inégalité des races humaines*, the most important of all statements of the idea that civilizations decay because of the weakening and bastardization of superior races by mixture with inferior ones. He also put forward more clearly and forcibly than any previous writer the assertion that the 'Aryan' race was the creator of European civilization, the source of its vitality and therefore the element in it whose purity must be guarded most jealously. History, he affirmed, 'shows us that all civilizations derive from the white race, that none can exist without its help, and that a society is great and brilliant only in so far as it preserves the blood of the noble group that created it, provided that this group itself belongs to the most illustrious branch of our species'.[28] By the beginning of the twentieth century ideas of this kind had been abandoned by serious scholars. By then the greatest students of societies and their structure – Pareto, Durkheim, Weber – had discarded such naive beliefs. But at a more popular level they remained widespread and almost unchallenged.

Racial mythology was also spread by the mental attitudes fostered by Darwinian biology. Just as certain chance variations of an animal or plant species were better fitted than others to their environment at any given moment, and therefore more likely to survive and propagate themselves, so certain human groups were 'superior' to others. This 'social Darwinism' could be both 'internal' and 'external'. It could be used to provide a pseudo-scientific explanation for the superior status enjoyed by certain groups within a given society, a defence of the ruling classes' right to rule. It could also be turned outwards and used to support the alleged superiority of one national group to another, or to all others. It underlay the very interesting association often seen between national movements and ideas of the necessary physical strengthening of the individual through sports and exercises, often of a traditional kind. The revival in the later nineteenth century of hurling (Gaelic hockey) in Ireland and horse-racing in Hungary, the emphasis of Jahn and his followers in Germany on gymnastics, the Sokol gymnastic movement in Bohemia in the second half of the century, are all examples of this. In fact the analogy between humanity and the world of animals and plants was a very bad one. Social Darwinists stressed the need to protect the 'superior' groups from the competition of the 'inferior' ones which continually threatened to overwhelm them, while in the animal or vegetable world the superior variations, those best adjusted to their environment, would, on the contrary, inevitably and automatically flourish at the expense of all others. Social Darwinism, however, was far from being merely a conservative force. Darwin's ideas were enormously influential and eagerly welcomed by a great many intellectuals and writers because they gave very impressive backing to a current of ideas which was already flowing strongly in nineteenth-century Europe, that of belief in progressive, deterministic change.[29] Social Darwinism had great appeal because it provided a simple law, that of an endless and unavoidable struggle for survival and growth, which seemed to explain a great range of social phenomena. Better still, it justified them; and in the most influential of all terms, those of science or pseudo-science. It is not a coincidence that it was most popular in the United States, where struggle and competition, especially in economic life, were more uncontrolled than anywhere else in the world. All the important critics of an unthinking application of Darwinian ideas to social problems came from western Europe, where tradition and religious forces still did much to limit social and economic competitiveness.

Racial beliefs and assumptions, confused and unscholarly as they were, had important practical results. They made it possible to think of international rivalries in racial terms. This tended to increase the bitterness of these antagonisms and to make them appear, in so far as they were based on the alleged physical realities of race, natural and insoluble. Thus the Russian Slavophil writer M. P. Pogodin could speak of the Germans as 'hostile to the Slavs because of some physiological quality'.[30] The acute antagonism between French and Germans after 1871, in particular, included on both sides a considerable element of racial mythology; and the feeling of inferiority to the Germans and British which is clearly visible in much French writing during the later nineteenth century was based largely on a reluctant and resentful belief in the superior strength and virtues of the more 'Nordic' peoples. The defeat of 1870–71 led at least two of the greatest French intellectuals of the day, Ernest Renan and Hippolyte Taine, to explicit admissions of German racial superiority to the French. It was also more and more widely believed that a state, to be strong, should have a population which was racially as well as linguistically homogeneous. The still largely cosmopolitan liberalism of the first half of the century, reflected in the historian Lord Acton's remark that 'a state which is incompetent to satisfy different races condemns itself', was now in full retreat.

The main victims of this growing insistence on racial uniformity were inevitably the Jews. It is not a coincidence that it was a minor German nationalist writer, F. C. R. Ruhs, who in 1815 published the first scholarly, or pseudo-scholarly, anti-Semitic book, *Über die Ansprache der Juden an das deutsche Burgerrecht*. In this he demanded that Jews be excluded from all political rights in Germany as well as from trade guilds, public offices and the army: they should also be forced to wear a yellow patch on their clothing to make them instantly recognizable. Even in France, which had led Europe in the grant of equal rights to Jews, a good deal of hostility to them, mainly of radical and left-wing origin, is visible by the middle decades of the century. The socialist P.-J. Proudhon, for example, believed in an international Jewish conspiracy which he identified with the power of the great banking family of Rothschild. The catastrophe of 1870–71 encouraged a tendency to use the Jews as a scapegoat for national humiliation and to see in their presence in France an element of national weakness. In 1886 Edouard Drumont published his *La France Juive*, the most famous anti-semitic work of the period: by the end of the decade it had gone through over 100 editions. The 'integral nationalism' of such writers as Maurice Barrès and Charles Maurras, with its emphasis on the continuity of French traditions and its bitter hostility to all shades of liberalism, was directed against the Jews even more than against the Protestants, naturalized foreigners and other elements which it alleged to be outside the French nation and hostile to its unity and greatness. For several years after 1896 the case of Captain Dreyfus, a Jewish officer wrongly condemned in 1894 for selling military secrets to Germany, raised anti-Semitic passions in France to new heights and even led to demands for discriminatory laws against Jews. The eventually successful demands of his supporters for a revision of his case, and the resistance to them, cut across many class and party dividing-lines and brought the Third Republic near to collapse.

In Germany the legal emancipation of the Jews had been completed in 1867–70. There, and still more in Austria-Hungary, they were heavily concentrated in the universities, in the arts and professions, and in the capital cities of Berlin, Vienna and Budapest. (About a quarter of the population of the Hungarian capital was Jewish by 1914, and of the twenty-one daily papers published in Berlin in the 1870s thirteen were owned by Jews.) This made it easy to exaggerate their very real economic and intellectual influence, and to arouse against them the resentment of craftsmen, peasants and shopkeepers whose existence seemed threatened in an age of increasingly large economic units, of stock exchanges and great banks. In 1881 a quarter of a million Germans signed a mass petition calling for the prohibition of Jewish immigration, the removal of Jews from public office and teaching posts in schools, and a reduction of their numbers in universities. It is significant that Karl Lueger, the anti-Jewish mayor of Vienna from 1897 onwards, depended for support entirely on the poorer parts of the city; in the wealthier areas he could never shake the hold of the liberals. The very powers of survival of the Jews, their ability to hold out against long periods of sustained discrimination and even persecution, and their alleged tendency to increase in numbers, made them seem dangerous in the eyes of many observers.

Anti-Semitism also helped to focus, in central Europe as to a lesser extent in France, the emotions of romantic conservative nationalists who hoped for a revival of guilds, a strengthening of peasant agriculture and the introduction of high protective tariffs, and who were hostile to liberalism and often to representative government of any kind. In its more extreme forms this sort of anti-Semitic feeling degenerated in central Europe into 'nostalgic primitivism, noble savagery – a rejection of the elaborate, sophisticated, intellectual and legalistic urban concepts which we associate with nineteenth-century civilization'.[31] Meanwhile in Russia, where Alexander III was himself strongly anti-Semitic, Jews were in 1882 barred from settling in rural districts, even within the Pale of Settlement in the western provinces to which they were still in the main confined, while the device of the *numerus clausus* limited their access to secondary or university education.

The immediate importance of this anti-Jewish feeling can be exaggerated. In Italy it was always relatively weak in spite of the violence of much nationalist feeling there from the 1870s onwards. In Great Britain, though distinct traces of it can be found in the literature of the early twentieth century (notably in the works of Kipling and of the Catholics Belloc and Chesterton) it had little practical significance. In France the Dreyfusards were victorious: Dreyfus was vindicated and reinstated and rose to the rank of general. In Germany the two decades before 1914 saw a decline of extreme and active anti-Semitism in national politics, though this was achieved at the cost of a growing tacit acceptance of milder anti-Jewish prejudice by the parties generally. Even in Russia the sensational Beilis case of 1911–13, when a Jew in Kiev was accused of the ritual murder of a Christian child, ended in his acquittal in spite of the efforts of nationalist anti-Semites, backed by Nicholas II himself, to have him condemned. The fear aroused by the spectre of Jewish power in many parts of later nineteenth-century Europe becomes more ridiculous the more it is studied. The importance of Jews in international and state finance had declined considerably from the greatest days of the Rothschilds in the early decades of the century. Moreover many Jews everywhere were now almost pathetically anxious to identify themselves with their Christian environment. Sigmund Freud, as a student in Vienna in the later 1870s, was for five years a member of an ultranationalist pan-German society. So were Victor Adler, the founder of the Austrian Socialist Party, and probably even Theodor Herzl, the creator of the organized Zionist movement.[32] Yet clearly the intolerant and racially minded nationalism of the later nineteenth and early twentieth centuries was paving the way for the unprecedented crimes and catastrophes which accompanied the Second World War. It was also generating by reaction an important Jewish nationalist movement. In 1882 Leo Pinsker provided, in his *Autoemanzipation*, the first important statement of the Zionist position, asserting the need for the Jews to have a territory and state of their own. Fourteen years later Herzl's *Judenstaat* repeated this demand and added the argument that the existence of a Jewish state would make easier the complete assimilation of those

Jews who chose to remain outside it. The first Zionist congress met in Basle in 1897.

CHALLENGES TO NATIONALISM

The implications for the European state system of the growth of nationalism were enormous, though its significance in this respect varied greatly in different parts of the continent. In Britain, France and most of northern Europe, where relatively large unified and centralized states had existed before the evolution of modern nations, its most usual associations were with liberalism and later even with social democracy. There it tended on the whole to be a force making for consolidation rather than drastic change in the international status quo.[33] In Germany and Italy, on the other hand, it gave birth to great new states, though in each the work of unification was in the main controlled by men who were not nationalists. In both, by contrast with western Europe, it was the nation, increasingly conscious of its existence, which created, or at least helped to create, the state. In east-central and south-eastern Europe nationalism was in the main a politically divisive force. It helped to reduce the Ottoman empire in Europe by 1914 to a mere fragment of what it had been a century earlier. In the Habsburg empire and perhaps even in Russia it seemed to threaten the disruption of the two other great multinational states.

There were limits to its power. The united Germany formed by 1871 was not a 'Great Germany'. Outside its frontiers, in the Russian Baltic provinces, in Transylvania, in Switzerland, above all in Austria and Bohemia, lived millions of Germans who were not its subjects. In Austria a pan-German movement led by Georg von Schönerer, which wished to merge the German parts of the Habsburg empire with Germany, emerged during the 1880s. But it had no practical result and merely added one more to the difficulties and tensions with which Francis Joseph and his ministers had to cope. Again the Italian nationalism which had triumphed so rapidly in the decade 1860–70, with powerful outside aid and against relatively weak resistance, soon showed its practical limitations. It proved quite unable to obtain for Italy the south Tyrol and the Trentino, the *Italia Irredenta* about which many Italian patriots (though much less often Italian governments) felt deeply. Ireland, after decades of struggle against British rule, seemed by the beginning of the twentieth century as far as ever from independence; and the forms taken by Irish nationalism were by then becoming milder. The Home Rule movement from the 1880s onwards had little in common with the desperate nationalist rebellion of 1798 or the Fenian violence of the 1860s. Often the effective size of a national movement bore no relation to the amount of noise it made. A good judge estimated, for example, that even in 1918 the number of 'educated and nationally conscious Slovaks' was only 750-1,000.[34] Also it was still possible, in spite of nationalist dogmatizing, for durable states to be created even though they lacked any unity of language or history. In Switzerland, populated by three major linguistic groups and with a history largely formed by the particularist feelings of the individual cantons, some approach to national feeling can be seen emerging by the middle of the century, after the brief *Sonderbund* war between Protestant and Catholic cantons in 1847. Moreover many expert observers in the years before 1914 believed that the internal problems of the Habsburg monarchy could and would be solved. Almost until it was on its deathbed in 1918 most of the nationalities under its rule continued to seek satisfaction for their grievances within the empire rather than outside it. After 1867 only the Czechs and Italians were offering consistent opposition to the status quo. Supported by the army and bureaucracy and by the still powerful feeling of loyalty to the dynasty, greatly aided by the complete lack of unity between the subject-nationalities, which sometimes disliked each other more than they did their German or Hungarian rulers, the Habsburg régime showed surprising vitality. It successfully surmounted the crises of the later 1890s, the greatest internal threat it ever had to face; and in the decade before the First World War it seemed if anything to be gaining strength. What doomed it was not the power of national feeling in its territories but its foreign policy, its inability and unwillingness to adopt the strict neutrality in international affairs which alone might have saved it. The way to its collapse was opened by the determination of the emperor and his ministers to maintain the fiction that it was a great power. It was this which led inevitably to its fatal involvement in the conflicts of the true great powers and thus to the catastrophe of 1914. It was destroyed, in the last analysis, by nothing more sophisticated than military defeat. The same is true of Russia, where it was only the terrible losses suffered by the inefficient army in Poland in 1915, and the collapse of 1917, which made possible a precarious and often short-lived independence for the Finns, the Poles, the Ukrainians and the Baltic and Caucasian peoples.

Nationalism during this period was therefore by no means an irresistible force. Like every other in political and social life it triumphed where, and only where, conditions favoured it. Yet its achievements, though many of them were negative and destructive, were vast. It was able, in the second half of the nineteenth century, to involve whole peoples in international conflicts in a way hitherto unknown except in a few states of western Europe. Attempts to unite the nations of Europe in some supranational way, on a regional basis or on one of alleged racial and linguistic affinity, might sometimes supplement national feeling; but they were quite unable to offer an acceptable alternative to it. All of them were intellectually vaguer than nationalism (itself not notable for intellectual precision). They tended to stress, in their more mystical forms, the links between kindred peoples constituted by community of blood or, still vaguer, community of soul. They were therefore less concerned than most nationalist movements with territorial details, and less identified with existing states and governments. In their more extreme forms they could come to express an almost tribal attitude. But such vague and grandiose concepts could never compete effectively for the allegiance of the common man with a straightforward nationalism focused on relatively clear-cut objectives and grievances.

Thus the Scandinavianism, the feeling that Denmark and Norway-Sweden were so closely akin that they should cooperate politically and if necessary militarily, which was widespread in these countries during the middle decades of the century, amounted to little in practice. In 1848, when Denmark seemed threatened by the Prussian army, 5,000 Swedes helped to defend the island of Fünen; but in the much more serious struggle of 1863–64 with Prussia the Danes received significantly little aid from their Scandinavian kinsmen. In the same way the idea of a Balkan federation, a union of the peoples of the peninsula once they had been freed from Ottoman rule, proved quite unable to withstand the divisive effects of national rivalries, though it continued to be put forward at intervals throughout the century.

More important, the Slavophil and Panslav movements which from the 1820s onwards stressed the essential unity of the Slav peoples, their linguistic affinities and spiritual communion in the Orthodox church and the need for them to stand together against their traditional enemies, the Turks and the Germans, were always essentially movements of intellectuals. Moreover Panslavism, though the original impetus behind it came largely from the Slavs of the Habsburg empire, was in practice dominated by Russians and largely an instrument and extension of Russian nationalism. The schemes for a great Slav federation, perhaps with Constantinople as its capital, which were put forward by Panslav writers, all envisaged this as something to be achieved under Russian leadership and control. Pogodin, the author of the earliest of them, boasted in 1838 that 'Tsar Nicholas is nearer to Charles V's and Napoleon's dream of the World State than those two ever got'. Later N. Y. Danilevsky, in his *Rossiya i Evropa* (1869), a verbose and mystical statement of the extreme Panslav position, demanded that such a federation, dominated by Russia, must include the non-Slav Magyars, Romanians and Greeks 'whom historic fate, for better or for worse, has irrevocably linked up with us, having squeezed them, so to speak, into the Slavonic body'.[35] Also Panslavism made little appeal to some of the most important of the Slav peoples. Among the Czechs, and later the Serbs and the Bulgarians, it aroused some response. But in Panslav eyes the Poles, a Catholic or Uniat people who regarded themselves as the cultural superiors of the Russians, had betrayed Slavdom by voluntarily going over to the west and submitting to the rule of a westernized nobility. There was considerable controversy over the admission of Polish representatives to the Slav Congress which met at Prague in 1848; and Polish demands before and during the revolt of 1863 for the return of the areas of western Russia formerly under Polish rule – Kiev, Chernigov and Minsk – did much to strengthen Panslav hostility to them. Also the close association of the more conservative Panslavs with Orthodox Christianity made it difficult for the Croats, also a major group of Catholic Slavs, to feel much sympathy with them. Until 1848 or even 1867 the Croats remained one of the most loyal to the dynasty of all the peoples under Habsburg rule. The Bulgars were reliably Orthodox and their language was closer than any other Slav tongue to Russian. Moreover they owed their autonomy after 1878 entirely to the expenditure of Russian blood and money. Yet even they did not hesitate in the 1880s to flout the wishes of their great Slav kinsman when these conflicted with their own national interests and national pride.

Panslavism, therefore, was never in practice what it claimed to be – a force capable of endowing the Slav peoples with a unity which would transcend their separate nationalisms. It was much more a vehicle for Russian national feeling and expansionism. It was also a force which was never much liked by the rulers of Russia. The tsarist régime at least until late in the century was largely indifferent to national questions and national intolerances,[36] while the radicalism of many Panslavs on such questions as the abolition of serfdom, freedom of the press and the internal administration of the country in general made them objects of suspicion rather than of admiration in official circles.

There were in nineteenth-century Europe a number of important currents of internationalist theorizing, pacifist, free-trading and socialist; but none of these was ever able to compete effectively with nationalism for the allegiance of the ordinary man. The earliest Peace Society was formed in the United States in 1815. The British Peace Society, founded in the following year, presented its first petition to Parliament in 1842 (in protest against the wars then being fought in China and Afghanistan) and a series of International Peace Congresses was held in 1848–53. In the 1840s several Utopian socialists, notably the Frenchmen Constantin Pecqueur and Victor Considérant, published books envisaging the possibility of permanent international peace. In 1867 another Frenchman, Frédéric Passy, the most important figure in the history of pacifism during the later nineteenth century, founded in Paris the *Lique de la Paix*; and in the same year a peace congress at Geneva, with Garibaldi somewhat incongruously as chairman, decided that Europe must be reorganized as a federation of free and democratically governed peoples. From 1889 onwards there were annual Universal Peace Congresses and in 1892 an International Peace Bureau was set up at Berne. The Nobel Peace Prize was founded in 1897 and first awarded in 1901, while the Carnegie Endowment for International Peace was established in 1910. Pacifist agitation and ideas of European federation encouraged the movement which became visible in the 1870s for the codification of international law and even played some part in the setting up in 1899 of the permanent Court of Arbitration at The Hague (though this, in spite of its title, was no more than a panel of jurists). The result of this was that the decade before 1914 probably saw a more widespread belief in the possibility of international cooperation and a more general optimism as to the possibility of achieving permanent peace between the great powers than had ever been known before.

But all this was no more than a fringe movement. Pacifism was weakened by many factors – by disunity between extremists who refused to accept war under any conditions and moderates who were willing to recognize a defensive war as legitimate; by divisions between the various schools of thought, Christian, socialist, Mazzinian, free-trading liberal, which hoped for some kind of European union;[37] by the tendency of many pacifists to think of states as mere aggregations of individuals, not as organisms;[38] and most of all by the sheer inability of pacifist ideas to attract the ordinary man. It was all very well for Henry Richard, the leading British pacifist of the period, to denounce nationalism in 1864 as 'a poor, low, selfish, unchristian idea, at variance with the very principle of an advanced civilization'. It none the less had a dynamism, a vulgar power, which pacifism never acquired. Gladstone, one of the supreme liberals of the century, had no doubt in 1893, towards the end of his life, that the loss of national spirit was 'the heaviest and most deplorable and the most degrading loss that any country can undergo'.

The same lack of dynamism and popular appeal doomed the current of internationalist ideas based on free trade and associated above all with the British statesman and publicist, Richard Cobden. Cobden defined his basic idea as 'as little intercourse as possible betwixt the *Governments*, as much connection as possible between the *nations* of the world'. These unofficial and non-governmental contacts, above all commercial ones fostered by free trade, by complete liberty in the international movement of people, goods, capital and ideas, would inevitably draw the nations together in a way that statecraft, treaties and diplomacy had conspicuously failed to do. From this basic assumption and from the deep hostility to governments and traditional foreign policies which underlay it, flowed a number of conclusions. Cobden and his followers rejected totally the concept of the balance of power, the search for which one of them described as 'like hunting for the philosopher's stone, or perpetual motion'. Though they were not pacifists (Cobden made it clear that he accepted the right and need of a state to defend itself against attack) they were bitterly hostile to large and expensive armed forces, and to colonial empires. Above all they were totally opposed to intervention by one state or people in the affairs of another: non-intervention they justified not merely in terms of expediency and material advantage but also as the most Christian attitude to international affairs. They realized that this sometimes meant tolerating flagrant injustice, such as the existence of slavery in the United States; but this argument was met by the contention, unproved and unprovable, that injustice inevitably weakens those who commit it and thus in the long run cures itself. Finally from this stress on non-intervention and distrust of statesmen and diplomats there stemmed a rejection of any move towards world government or even the creation of international institutions. Thus though Cobden was a convinced supporter of the use of arbitration to settle disputes between states he wished this to take place on a purely *ad hoc* basis by agreement of the governments concerned: he always opposed the creation of any kind of international court of arbitration.

This current of ideas had an ancestry of some distinction. The assumption that unofficial, and above all economic, contacts between peoples are fundamental and constructive while official diplomacy is at best superficial and more often pernicious, that the best foreign policy is to have no foreign policy at all, derives from the French Enlightenment of the later eighteenth century. By the end of that century such assumptions had won widespread acceptance in the United States, a country which Cobden deeply admired and to some extent feared as the greatest world power of the future. In the mid-nineteenth century Cobdenism's open hostility to so many forms of traditional authority – armed forces, diplomatic services, aristocratic rule in general – recommended it strongly to radicals of many types. Thus at the sitting of the Frankfurt Parliament on 22 June 1848, when the foreign policy of the new German national state was debated, the young left-wing Hegelian, Arnold Ruge, proposed, with a specific mention of Cobden and his followers, the calling of a congress of peoples to prepare the way for general disarmament and establish peace and unity in Italy and Poland. He also pointed to the United States and Switzerland as examplars of the new form of international relations.[39] His proposals were quite ineffective; but for a number of years Cobdenism had appreciable influence at least in Britain. This does something to explain the isolationism, sometimes verging on timidity, of British foreign policy during the 1860s and early 1870s. One aspect in particular of his ideas, the hope that in the future economic forces, not nationalism, would dominate international life, aroused a considerable response among European intellectuals. The French socialist Proudhon for example argued, totally unrealistically, in 1851 that 'there is no longer any nationality or father-land in the political sense of the term. . . . Political economy is the queen and mistress of the age.'

Nevertheless Cobdenism was powerless to combat the growth of nationalism. Cautious, cold-blooded, self-regarding, it made no easy appeal to the feelings and had none of the crude dynamism of nationalist emotions. In spite of its democratic top-dressing it was always the creed of an élite, never a mass movement. Its complete lack of widespread support even in Britain was dramatically illustrated by the violence of the popular Russophobia of 1853–54, which shocked and disillusioned Cobden himself. The ideas which he stood for had some lasting significance, at least in the Anglo-Saxon world. Some of them provided part of the intellectual background of British radical writers such as Angell and Brailsford before the war of 1914 and of President Wilson during and after it. But in the development of international relations Cobdenism, if not exactly a blind alley, was never to become a main thoroughfare.

The sheer amount of international organization, governmental and non-governmental, increased enormously from the 1860s onwards. Nearly 3,000 international gatherings of different kinds were held in the period 1840–1914 and in the century which followed the Vienna peace settlement 466 private and non-governmental international organizations were set up, together with 37 governmental ones.[40] Many of these, for example the International Union of Esperantist Vegetarians, were trivial. Others, such as the Telegraphic Union set up in 1865 or the International Postal Union established in 1874, were of very great practical value. They provided clear evidence of a greater need, and probably a greater willingness, than ever before to cooperate internationally for practical purposes. Yet they did very little to weaken national feeling in Europe. Virtually all these international unions and associations were based simply on calculations of practical advantage. They had little or no emotional appeal for the ordinary man, even when he was aware of their existence.

Moreover the later decades of the nineteenth century, when international organizations were being created in large numbers, were also paradoxically a period of increasing economic nationalism, of rising tariff barriers and frequent tariff wars. From the French Revolution onwards it had been clear that self-consciously national states were likely to pursue nationalist economic policies. The revolutionaries revoked the unpopular commercial treaty of 1786 with Great Britain, which had opened the

French market much more widely than ever before to many British products; and the great Jacobin government of 1793–94 adopted a strongly protective tariff policy. Almost simultaneously a neo-mercantilist element in German nationalism can be seen in embryo with the publication in 1800 of Fichte's *Geschlossene Handelstaat* (though Fichte had been an economic liberal in his younger days and never completely reconciled his later ideas with his earlier ones). It is also visible in some of the writings of Hegel. It was not until 1841, however, that Friedrich List provided the most important theoretical foundation of late nineteenth-century economic nationalism by publishing his *Das nationale System der politischen Ökonomie*. Inspired by the example of the United States, where he had lived for seven years, consumed with envy and admiration for the wealth and power of Great Britain, he wished to unify Germany through internal free trade and a national system of posts and railways.[41] This unified Germany was to be equipped, through the workings of a system of protective tariffs, with flourishing industries, colonies and a large overseas trade. She must diversify her economy, which must cease to be based mainly on agriculture. She must increase her productive power, since in this way alone could she win real military security. Britain had achieved a position of unparalleled strength through industrial development originally fostered by protective tariffs. A policy of free trade now suited her interests and could be safely followed by her; but Germany, unless she adopted a protectionist policy, would never be able to build up her industries and trade in the face of British rivalry and would condemn herself to permanent inferiority. Once she no longer needed to fear foreign competition she too might revert to free trade, though care must be taken to see that this did not cause any decline in her economic life. The government of the new Germany must guard jealously the country's economic well-being. Legislation might well be needed to maintain a healthy balance between agriculture and industry and between employers and workers; special subsidies might be necessary to maintain the national mercantile marine.

The immediate effects in Germany or elsewhere of List's book were not great. From the 1840s to the 1860s free-trading attitudes were clearly gaining ground over most of Europe. In this movement Britain led the way. The Corn Laws of 1815, which had imposed very severe restrictions on the import of foreign grain, were abruptly swept away in 1846 and the remnants of the Navigation Acts, which since the mid-seventeenth century had restricted the country's trade in various ways, met the same fate in 1849. Two famous Gladstonian budgets of 1853 and 1860 completed the triumph of free trade in Britain. In Prussia tariffs had been low ever since 1818; and in 1850 the hitherto protectionist Habsburg empire moved towards freer trade (largely in the hope of easing its entry into the

Zollverein). There were significant movements towards reducing tariffs in the Swiss Confederation in 1850–51 and in Belgium in 1849–53. In 1860 a great Anglo-French commercial treaty, the most important international trading agreement of the century and negotiated on the British side by Cobden himself, gave this movement further impetus: the 1860s saw trade between the European states less impeded by tariff barriers than at any other time during the century. By the 1870s, however, the position was once more changing. By then there had emerged a 'historical school' of German economists, some of them (notably their leader, Gustav Schmoller) of very high ability. These increasingly challenged the idea, fundamental to all the classical economists, that economic life, like the natural sciences, was governed by laws which were universally valid. More and more they stressed the need to adapt the economic policies of a state to fit its own interests, problems, traditions and resources – in other words to adopt an essentially nationalist attitude to economic affairs. They also stressed increasingly the obligation of the state to safeguard the well-being of its subjects by positive action and not to leave them, as classical economics demanded, at the mercy of free competition and the uncontrolled workings of market forces. In 1872 the leading members of the 'historical school' met at Eisenach a number of leading German lawyers and civil servants sympathetic to their ideas and issued a manifesto condemning economic liberalism. They demanded that the state should foster every aspect of German economic life; they also set up the Union for Social Politics, which worked in the following years for a protective tariff policy combined with state insurance of workers against illness, accident and old age. In 1876, moreover, a powerful protectionist influence began to play upon the German government from a different direction. In that year the conservative leader von Kardorff founded the Central Alliance of German Industrialists for the Promotion and Preservation of National Labour to work for a protectionist tariff policy. This demand for high tariffs was soon successful. In 1879 Bismarck broke with the National Liberals, hitherto his main supporters in the Reichstag, and imposed duties on imported iron, steel and grain. Policies of this kind found eager imitators. In Italy the move towards a protective system had begun in 1878. In France, where the free-trade tendencies of Napoleon III had always been unpopular, tariffs rose from 1881 onwards: the Méline tariff of 1892 made her a highly protectionist country. In Russia duties on imported industrial products and raw materials crept steadily upwards during the 1880s and were raised steeply in 1890 and 1891. Of the major industrial states of Europe only Britain and Belgium still clung to free trade.

Even in Britain a National Fair Trade League was formed in 1881 by manufacturing interests which were likely to benefit from protection; and as foreign, above all German, competition with British industry increased, so the advantages of abandoning free trade seemed to grow. In 1903 a leading Conservative, Joseph Chamberlain, placed himself at the head of the movement for tariff reform (in other words protection) and in so doing split his party. Much of the theory behind the movement was derived from German sources – the stress on employment rather than profitability, on industry rather than finance, on production rather than exchange, on the national economy and not on the cosmopolitan international one posited by classical economics. Several of the British academic advocates of protection, notably W. J. Ashley and Sir Halford Mackinder, were certainly influenced by the work of List. Moreover the tariff reform movement shared the emphasis on social welfare which was so prominent in the writings of many German protectionists: Chamberlain had been, in the 1890s, the first British statesman to show serious interest in the possibility of a system of old-age pensions and workmen's compensation for industrial accidents. The movement failed. Free trade was still too deeply entrenched in Britain and still promised too many genuine advantages, particularly cheap food, to be overthrown. But Chamberlain more than his opponents, represented the forces which were to influence powerfully Britain's future.

The move towards higher tariffs which developed from the 1870s onwards gained momentum from the industrial slump which struck Europe in 1873 and whose results were prolonged, in the form of the so-called 'Great Depression', until 1895. But it was much more than a mere response to a temporary worsening of economic conditions. Many historians have thrown doubt on the severity of the 'Great Depression', or even on its existence; and protective tariffs had gained substantial intellectual support and an intellectually respectable ideology well before the difficulties of the middle and later 1870s entered the picture. Growing protectionism was a rejection of the liberal idea of an increasingly unified international economy. It extended to economic life the assumption that the world was, and ought to be, composed of sovereign national states, each concerned only with its own interests and inevitably the rival of its neighbours. It meant that economic development in Europe had to be thought of in terms of political units with firm and unchanging frontiers rather than, as always hitherto, in those of natural economic regions which often transcended political or linguistic boundaries. The logical culmination of this process was the 'tariff war' in which each of two competing states attempted, by damaging the trade of the other, to extract political or economic concessions from it. The history of Europe in the last decades of the nineteenth century was studded with such struggles, some of which had considerable political importance – between France and Italy in 1887–98; between

Russia and Germany in 1893; between France and Switzerland in 1893–95. Increasingly nationalists preached the need to make the state as far as possible self-sufficient, at least in essentials, even at heavy economic cost.[42] Thus Italy, to take the most striking example, though she had no coal of her own and only very limited resources of iron ore, painfully built up, in the early twentieth century, a highly inefficient steel industry.

The decades which saw international organization achieve unprecedented scope and complexity therefore also saw economic nationalism reach heights hitherto unknown; and of the two tendencies the second undoubtedly reflected more faithfully the feelings and prejudices of the ordinary man.

Nor was Marxism, the political doctrine whose importance was increasing most rapidly during the later nineteenth century, in practice an effective obstacle to the spread of nationalism. Marx's thinking was thoroughly internationalist, though problems of international organization play a very small part in his writings. His account in *Das Kapital* of the workings of the capitalist system is based on *laissez-faire* assumptions as undiluted as those of Cobden, while the *Communist Manifesto* takes it for granted that the movement towards free trade is irresistible. To him the nation and the nation-state were transitory phenomena sustained for the most part by the bourgeoisie. The historically determined and inevitable function of the proletariat was to overthrow them by revolution. Both he and Engels wished on occasion to use national feelings for their own purposes. In particular they called for the restoration of Poland within its 1772 frontiers as a barrier against Russian influence in Europe, though they realized that this meant putting millions of Ruthenians and White Russians under Polish rule. But neither had the slightest sympathy with the aspirations of small peasant nations, which they saw merely as obstacles to the inevitable progress of mankind towards a more advanced economic system. Their internationalism was centred on a small number of large, well-defined historical nations, most of which were also great industrial powers and thus capable of developing a truly revolutionary psychology among the mass of their population. The small Slav and largely peasant peoples of central and east-central Europe – Czechs, Slovaks, Serbs, Croats – they thoroughly disliked. Nor had they any active sympathy with the 'colonial' peoples now falling under European control. As good progressives of their own day they supported the annexation of California by the United States, stressed the constructive aspects of British rule in India and opposed the rebels of 1857, thought the forcible opening of China to European influences necessary and welcomed the defeat of native resistance under Abd-el-Kader by the French in Algeria.

However Marxist practice was often very different from Marxist-theory; and the achievements of Marxism in later nineteenth-century Europe were those of Marxist parties working within the framework of the national state rather than those of an effective international movement. After the foundation of the Second International in 1889 the idea that the workers should struggle against the state in the cause of revolution was more and more replaced in practice by the belief that they might accept existing states and their governments while they waited more or less passively for revolution to break out. 'The revolution was treated as an inevitable event which no amount of effort could accelerate or postpone, and which could be pushed into a vague future where it ceased to have any importance for practical politics; in the meantime concrete benefits were to be gained by cooperation with the state.'[43] The degree to which this attitude was accepted by Marxists differed from one country to another; and Rosa Luxemburg, perhaps the most interesting Marxist theorist of the years before 1914, continued to insist passionately on the irrelevance of national questions and antagonisms in an age increasingly dominated by aggressive world empires.[44] But in general the already inadequate resistance which Marxism was able to make to the growing power of the nation state became weaker from the 1890s onwards. The Stuttgart congress of the International in 1907 showed the unwillingness of the German Social Democrats to commit themselves to a general strike in the event of war, as their more radical French counterparts were urging; and the 1910 congress at Copenhagen was marked by a good deal of nationalist tension between the British and the German delegates. After this meeting the Czech Social Democrats formed their own party: this was a significant defeat for the idea of a single multi-national grouping which would embrace all the socialists of the Habsburg empire.

The impotence of socialism as an antidote to the effects of national rivalry was now becoming clearly visible to some observers. It was pointed out, for example, that some of the repercussions of the increased international mobility of labour showed the hollowness of the pretence that working-class solidarity transcended national boundaries. Everywhere the appearance of low-cost immigrant labour aroused working-class resentment, sometimes to the point of riots, strikes and even murder. (The vicious hostility to Italian immigrants in France, particularly in Lyons, is a good example.) Yet other equally intelligent contemporaries continued to deceive themselves. In the years before 1914 it was easier than ever before to mobilize left-wing feeling on an international scale in protest against any spectacular act of oppression or injustice. The anti-Jewish pogroms in Russia in 1905 and the judicial murder of the Spanish anarchist Francisco Ferrer in 1909 both aroused reactions of this kind, and by so doing gave fresh currency to the myth that an effective international socialist movement existed. It was possible, therefore, for an English radical to argue, only a few months before the catastrophe of 1914, that socialism 'is even now perhaps the most formidable factor in the preservation of the peace of Europe'.[45] This bubble was mercilessly pricked by events. The outbreak of war in 1914 aroused hardly a flicker of effective resistance from European socialism. 'All our fine talk,' wrote another English radical, though of a very different stamp, 'all our glowing shibboleths, are proved to be mere surface froth.'[46]

NATIONALISM IN THE NON-EUROPEAN WORLD AND THE CHALLENGE TO EUROPE

By the end of the nineteenth century there were signs, faint as yet but unmistakable, that the nationalism which had developed in Europe would soon be worldwide. It was now becoming the most dynamic and explosive element in Europe's relations with much of the rest of the world. By 1914 it had spread to much of Asia and the Near East, an inevitable result of the conquest or domination by Europeans of great areas there with distinctive civilizations of their own.

That conquest inevitably carried some flavour of humiliation for the peoples concerned. European rule or influence, however beneficial its results, was bound to appear to at least some extent as a threat to indigenous values and traditions, notably religious ones. Inherent in the situation, therefore, were forces which could generate a reaction against the conquerors; and more or less incoherent popular resentment of European influence was slowly growing in the later decades of the century over much of Asia and the Near East. In 1860 the British, then at war with China, had had no difficulty in employing as many coolies as they wanted; in 1884 the French, when they declared war on China over the situation in Annam, found that no Chinese in Hong Kong would do any work on French ships entering the port.[47] Popular feeling of this kind owed nothing to European intellectual influences or to a conscious adoption of nationalist ideas. It was rather an instinctive defensive reaction to outside pressure and western arrogance, one which stressed traditional loyalties and pieties and was perhaps particularly marked in parts of Asia which fell under direct European political and military control. Most of all in the Muslim world, where religion was still a more fundamental unifying force than political allegiance, 'race', or even language, traditionalism remained strong. In North Africa, for example, religious institutions were the main centres of resistance to western influences. The Azhar mosque in Cairo, the Zaytuna mosque in Tunis, the Qarawiyyin mosque in Fez, all acted in this way, as did the religious order of the Sanusiyya in Tripoli. In a rather similar manner the marked development of Christian missionary work in India from the end of the 1850s produced efforts by Syed Ahmed and Syed Amir Ali to revivify Islam as a bulwark against this increased western challenge.

This defensive religious reaction to the growth of infidel power over Muslim lands is seen most clearly in the growth of Pan-Islamism, which began to develop in the 1870s and which the Ottoman Sultan Abdul Hamid attempted for the next generation to use as a prop for his own power and a means of increasing his influence. The Pan-Islamists wished to accept from Europe only material techniques – railways, telegraphs, industrial and military methods – and then to use these against the European empires for the restoration of Islamic unity and greatness. Support for this came at first in the main from India and central Asia – areas where many millions of the faithful were now under British or Russian rule.[48] The greatest of Pan-Islamic theorists, however, Djamal-al-din al-Afghani (1838–97), was born in Meshed, in a country (Persia) still largely untouched by western ideas. Though he later lived under British rule in Egypt and for a short time in India, his outlook remained little affected by non-Islamic thought. His low opinion of the Turks, to whom he considered the Arabs much superior, and the general radicalism of much of his thought, estranged him from the Ottoman régime; but his influence throughout the Islamic world was considerable during the last decades of the nineteenth century. His desire to reform Islam, to make it a religion of struggle, effort and heroism, and thus an effective weapon against the encroachments of Europe, was doomed to failure. His wish to transform the Ottoman empire into a federation of autonomous khedivates which might be joined by Persia and Afghanistan and supported by the Muslims of India, was totally unrealistic.[49] Yet he undoubtedly expressed a kind of nationalism, and one which owed little to European thinking or example.

In rather a similar way B. G. Tilak, the most dynamic and extreme of the major Indian nationalist leaders from the 1890s until his death in 1920, was little affected by European ideas, though much of his education was along British lines. He was intensely conservative in his attitude to social questions, a bitter opponent of measures to limit child-marriage, develop education for women or introduce compulsory vaccination against plague. He supported cow-protection societies and was a student, though an unscholarly one, of the Hindu scriptures. Freedom from foreign rule was to him above all a means of restoring in India the unchallenged predominance of Hindu orthodoxy. Even his nationalism, for most of his life, was more a kind of regionalism confined to his native Maharashtra.

In 1901 he wrote that it was 'wrong to conclude ... that the Marathas, Punjabis, Bengalis, etc., all these different peoples have one nationality'. Only from about 1905 did he begin to think in terms of an Indian state. In all this he contrasts strongly with his great political opponent, G. K. Gokhale, a moderate who was deeply influenced by European, above all British, political ideas, and who believed passionately in the value of western education.[50]

Side by side with these traditionalist anti-western reactions, and to some extent a product of them, something that can reasonably be described as national feeling was also slowly emerging in parts of Asia and the Near East. This was in the main the outcome of western education and political ideas, the latter spread by the western invention of the newspaper. To say, as one writer has done, that 'nationalism outside Europe is a sustained exercise in unreality, for there is no nation to start with',[51] is to put the case too strongly. But the remark drives home the essential point that the nations of the extra-European world are usually the creations, though unplanned and often undesired ones, of Europe. It was precisely this European character of so many national movements in the colonial world which by the end of this period was winning them the support of many liberals in Europe: imitation, after all, is the sincerest form of flattery. The creation of Indian, Chinese, Egyptian, Arab, Persian and eventually Turkish nationalism was very largely the work of Europeans (or in a good many cases Americans) who, by developing modern systems of education, made it possible for organized and self-conscious national movements to exist. Everywhere European conquest or influence meant some growth of European education. Sometimes this was considerable; as in India, where in 1885–1900 the number of students in colleges and universities more than doubled (from 11,000 to 23,000) and the number of children in secondary schools rose from 429,000 to 633,000. Sometimes it was much less; as in Russian Turkestan, where as late as 1911 there were only eighty-nine modern schools accessible to the natives of the area. Sometimes it was the work of missionaries rather than of governments; as in much of the Ottoman empire, where American missionary schools helped to lay the foundations of Armenian nationalism and American Protestant and French Catholic ones were influential in parts of the Arab world. Often western intellectual influences were exerted effectively by training in Europe or the United States students from Asia or the Near East. Foreign-educated leaders of this kind were of great importance in the transformation of Japan into a modern state from the 1860s onwards, and the two greatest Asian nationalists of the twentieth century, Sun Yat-sen in China and Gandhi in India, both received a western professional training outside their own country (Gandhi in London, Sun Yat-sen in Hong Kong). The foundation in 1911 of *Sarikat Islam,* the first significant nationalist organization in the Dutch East Indies, probably owed something to the fact that the number of Indonesians educated in Holland, hitherto extremely small, increased markedly in the early years of the twentieth century.

With western education came often a new and partly westernized middle class which was henceforth to lead the national movement in many areas. This development was very noticeable in India, the part of Asia in which western education was first implanted and most rapidly developed. An Indian writer is fully justified in claiming that 'in spite of the attempts of conservative administrators and Indian extremists to belittle the importance of the middle class, it must be admitted by any impartial historian that the main credit for the regeneration of India belongs to this class, primarily a product of the system of education introduced in the nineteenth century'.[52] Inevitably also with western-type schools and universities came western political thought and translations of western books. The ideas of European liberals and nationalists could be used to attack the moral basis of European dominance and to justify Asian or Near Eastern movements against it. Sun Yat-sen was powerfully influenced by the works of Mazzini, as were many Indian nationalists and two of the most important Egyptian ones, Mustapha Kamil and Zaghlul Pasha.[53] Western political ideas could also be appealed to as evidence that the Europeans were betraying their own best traditions in their efforts to rule other peoples, and even western law could sometimes be used as a weapon against Europe. As early as the 1860s, for example, the Chinese government commissioned several translations of European works on international law in the hope that this would help it to resist the claims of foreign governments and their representatives in China.[54]

For the most part, therefore, the anti-European nationalism which was emerging at the end of the nineteenth century was a compound of two elements. On the one hand there was suppressed and sometimes almost unconscious resentment of foreign influence or conquest, and of the arrogance Europeans so often displayed in their dealings with those they regarded as inferiors. This increasingly widespread feeling could be sparked into violent but spasmodic activity by economic difficulties, by religious fanaticism, or by some striking instance of European disregard of native susceptibilities. Its most spectacular manifestations were the successful popular resistance in Persia, organized by Muslim religious leaders, to the grant by the shah in 1890 to an Englishman, Talbot, of a concession for the sale of tobacco; and the better-known anti-foreign Boxer movement in China in 1900. Side by side with this unsophisticated protonationalism, and exploiting it, existed in many areas growing nationalist movements of an intellectual and organized (and therefore urban and usually 'middle-class') kind. These were the direct products of western influences and usually aimed at the creation of national states with liberal and democratic constitutions. This self-conscious nationalism in Asia and the Near East found practical expression in the foundation of political parties and even more in the setting-up of newspapers.

The rapid development of the newspaper press was central to the growth of national feeling outside Europe, even more so perhaps than it had earlier been within that continent. Its importance is seen clearly in the Near East, particularly in the Arab parts of it. The first newspaper printed in Arabic was published in Cairo in 1828; but the real growth of the press in Egypt began only half a century later. In the 1890s it became very rapid. The forty periodicals which appeared in 1892 had more than quadrupled in number by 1899; and in 1900 Mustapha Kamil, the real founder of organized Egyptian nationalism, began to publish his *al-Liwa* (*The Standard*). In 1861 an official newspaper began to be published in Tunis by the government of the bey, though the first unofficial Arabic paper did not begin to appear there until 1888. In 1883 the large but dispersed Muslim minority in the Russian empire gained a mouthpiece for the first time with the appearance at Bakhchiserai in the Crimea of *Terguman* (*The Interpreter*). In the Ottoman empire proper political journalism was slower to take root. The official *Moniteur Ottomane* began to appear in 1831, though only in French; and in 1860 Butrus Bustani set up in Beirut the *Nafir Suriya* (*Clarion of Syria*), the first political journal in the history of the province. By 1876 thirteen periodicals of different kinds were being published in Turkish. However the régime of the Sultan Abdul Hamid from 1876 onwards saw the end for a generation of any semblance of freedom for the Ottoman political press; and its real growth came only in the years immediately before 1914. But when it did come it was explosive. By mid-1908, immediately after the Young Turk revolution, 474 periodicals, including a large number in Arabic, Armenian and Greek, were appearing. In India also the growth of the newspaper press was an indispensable part of the whole nationalist movement. The years 1883–88, when modern nationalism began to emerge, saw a quadrupling of the circulation of vernacular newspapers in Bengal, the most politically conscious part of the subcontinent; while in the decade after 1878 the circulation of Indian-owned newspapers in Bombay grew from less than 12,000 to almost 60,000. Tilak's influence depended largely on his paper *Kesari* (*The Lion*) which he began to publish in 1881; and the British administration showed its grasp of the situation by efforts to control the press by legislation in 1878 and 1910.

It is true that many of these newspapers and periodicals were ephemeral and in themselves unimportant. Most of them had small circulations.

Often they were written in a style which only a small educated minority could understand. Nor was their political outlook always necessarily nationalist, at least in a direct sense. Thus the remarkable Tatar intellectual Ismail Bey Gaspirali (Gasprinsky), the publisher of *Terguman*, though he hoped for the spiritual and eventually political unity of the Muslim world, aimed like the Indian moderates at cooperation with the west (he had received part of his education in France) and the modernization of his people by educational reforms. Yet newspapers did more than anything else to spread nationalist ideas to great numbers of people hitherto politically inert and to transform nationalism over much of the non-European world from an intellectual cult to a mass movement.

The first decade of the twentieth century saw a great acceleration in the growth of this nationalism, which now began, for the first time, to show its potentialities. In India the National Congress had been founded in 1885; but it was at first a very moderate group and its main creator was a British official, A. O. Hume. By the 1890s, however, Tilak was building up a violent Hindu movement directed against the Indian Muslims as well as the British. In 1897 the murder of a British officer marked the first use of terrorism as a weapon to enforce nationalist demands. In 1906 the division of the province of Bengal for administrative purposes provoked bitter and widespread popular resistance fomented by the more extreme nationalists. In the following year Congress, meeting at Surat, was hopelessly split by the growing feud between moderates and extremists; and for nearly a decade it virtually ceased to exist. But terrorism and the repression to which it led were now growing rapidly. In 1908 Tilak was arrested by the British authorities: the strike of Bombay textile workers which followed can be considered the effective beginning of mass nationalism in India. In 1911 the partition of Bengal (clearly justified as an administrative measure) was revoked. The events of the last fifteen years had been a turning-point in the history of India. A nationalist movement with a partly westernized leadership and at least potential mass support had emerged.

In China conditions were much less favourable to the growth of organized nationalism. Society was controlled, as it had been for more than two millennia, by a class of scholar-officials whose ultimate allegiance was to a way of life and thought, not to a nation, a territory or a dynasty. This class, moreover, was traditionally and profoundly hostile to any forces in Chinese life which it did not control. The Manchu Ch'ing dynasty, tottering under the impact of foreign pressures and internal disorder, wished above all to maintain its own position. The Dowager Empress Tzu Hsi, who controlled the government for more than a generation before her death in 1908, relied on manoeuvre and adroit concessions to control both the foreigner and internal opposition: it was inconceivable that she should put herself at the head of a popular nationalist movement. Moreover China was still a linguistically and ethnically divided country. The highest ranks of the imperial government were dominated, until its collapse in 1911, by Manchus, not by the Han Chinese who made up the overwhelming majority of the population. Resentment of this fact was becoming more and more open and widespread. In 1907 an imperial proclamation declared for the first time the formal equality of the two groups and approved intermarriage between them; but Chinese hatred of Manchu rule was not assuaged. It has been said, perhaps with some exaggeration, that 'revolutionary enthusiasm between 1900 and 1911 was in fact very little more than racial antagonism to the Manchus'.[55] Nevertheless from the beginning of the century onwards railway-building, the growth of newspapers, translations of foreign books[56] and the education of increasing numbers of Chinese outside their own country – in the United States, Hong Kong, Europe and most of all Japan – were slowly generating genuine nationalism. This nationalism was of a clearly western, European, type. As it developed it therefore tended more and more to blur the hitherto very sharp and jealously guarded distinction between Chinese and foreign ideas. More and more, western methods and standards were penetrating Chinese thought and society and taking root there. Thus in 1905 the centuries-old system of competitive literary examinations for government posts, which had done more than anything else to inhibit the intellectual development of China, was abolished. It was replaced, at least on paper, by a system of universal education borrowed from Japan (which in turn had borrowed it from Europe). In 1908 the government even announced the principles on which it proposed, at some unspecified future date, to draw up a constitution.

This modernization was much too slow to satisfy the nationalist groups which were now arousing feeling against the dynasty and the old system. These groups combined western political objectives with methods of organization modelled on the secret societies which had for centuries been the traditional outlet for political discontent in China. In 1894 Sun Yat-sen founded the China Revival Society among exiles and emigrants in Hawaii; in 1905 he set up the Alliance Society in Tokyo. In China itself the Recovery Society, the Dragonflower Society and the Society of Justice were established in 1903–4. By then the forces which were to produce the revolution of 1911 and the collapse of central government which followed were clearly in existence. Westernization and nationalism had been slow to take root in China; but when they did their effect was explosive.

In Persia also the process of nationalist revolution, once it got under way, was rapid. Here too its immediate result was to destroy a tottering traditional form of government without putting anything workable in its place. Until the end of the nineteenth century Persia was not part of the contemporary world. An English scholar wrote of a visit to it in 1887–88 that

> ... the atmosphere was mediaeval; politics and progress were scarcely mentioned, and the talk turned mostly on mysticism, metaphysics and religion; the most burning political questions were those connected with the successors of the Prophet Muhammed in the seventh century of our era; only the most languid interest in external affairs was aroused by the occasional appearance of the official journals.[57]

This other-worldly calm was already deceptive. Communication with the outside world was becoming more frequent. As a result agriculture and such industries as carpet-weaving were becoming more commercialized and the peasant more exploited by the landlord. European political ideas were beginning to enter the country, both directly from western Europe and indirectly through Russian Transcaucasia, which played an important role in the early history of Persian nationalism. Newspapers hostile to the shah's régime had begun to appear as early as the 1870s, though they were all published abroad, usually in Cairo, Calcutta or Constantinople. Yet Persia remained very backward, both politically and economically. This backwardness, combined with the power and ambitions of her great northern neighbour, the Russian empire, doomed the attempted revolution of 1905–9 to humiliating failure. In 1906 the shah was forced to agree to the issue of a constitution and the meeting of a parliament (*Majliss*). But a western liberal régime in this disunited and misgoverned country was a mere dream of intellectuals. In April 1909, after a long period of confusion and disorder, Tabriz, the main centre of constitutionalist strength, was captured by Russian forces. This virtually ended the constitutional experiment: the *Majliss* was dispersed, with the help of Bakhtiari tribesmen, in December 1911. Nevertheless the revolution was a turning-point in Persian history. It created nothing permanent; but it gave the death-blow to the old régime. 'The Persians', wrote a somewhat idealistic American observer in 1912, 'were anxious to adopt wholesale the political, ethical and business codes of the most modern and progressive nations. They burned with that same spirit of Asiatic unrest which pervades India, which produced the "Young Turk" movement, and which has more recently manifested itself in the establishment of the Chinese republic. The East has awakened.'[58]

When these words were written the awakening had already become unmistakable in the Ottoman empire and Egypt (still in theory a part of that empire but in fact under British control since 1882). As early as the 1860s resentment of European bullying of the Turkish government had combined with imported European ideas of political liberty and nationality (again derived largely from Mazzini) to produce the Young Ottoman movement. But this proved transitory and superficial. The failure of the constitutional experiment of 1876, and the decades of repression which followed under Abdul Hamid, meant that political activity of all kinds was very effectively driven underground wherever the sultan's writ ran. Nevertheless the 1880s and 1890s saw the publication abroad by political exiles, mainly in Paris, of a number of anti-Hamidian newspapers; and two ineffective congresses of Ottoman liberals met in the French capital in 1902 and 1907. By then it was being increasingly felt, above all in military circles, that the safety of the empire in the face of European pressure demanded the end of the sultan's nervous and inefficient autocracy. In 1906 a young captain, Mustapha Kemal, founded in Damascus the political secret society *Vatan* (Fatherland): this soon merged with the more important Society of Union and Progress which had its main centre in Salonika. An army mutiny which broke out in Macedonia in July 1908 spread rapidly to the rest of European Turkey; and by the end of the month the sultan had surrendered to it. In April of the following year the 'Young Turk' revolution was completed by his deposition and exile.

It was not a nationalist revolution in the normal sense of the term. The Young Turks preached not nationalism but 'Ottomanism' – loyalty to the empire of all its subjects whatever their race, religion or language. A Law of Associations of August 1909 forbade all political organizations based on ethnic or national groups, while Zia Gökalp, later to be the greatest ideologue of Turkish nationalism, spoke of the empire as 'the free and progressive empire of the East', where races and nationalities would eventually fuse as they were doing in the United States. 'Ottomanism', however, was now a dream: events had far outstripped it. In Armenia, in Albania, in the Arab parts of the empire, national feeling was growing. In 1905 the émigré *Ligue de la Patrie Arabe*, meeting in Paris, had demanded an independent Arab state extending from Mesopotamia to Suez and from the Mediterranean to Oman, with a liberal and constitutional government. This was an extremist claim; the great majority of the Arabs under Turkish rule still asked for no more than autonomy under a highly decentralized form of government. Nevertheless an Arab nationalist movement was now rapidly emerging. It was created largely by Syrian Christians and strengthened by a remarkable growth of the newspaper press (in 1908–14 about sixty new papers appeared in Beirut and about forty in Baghdad, though most of them were very ephemeral). Even the hitherto unknown idea of a Turkish nation was slowly beginning to take shape. Fed by

European studies of the early history of the Turks, and by the influence of Turkish-speaking Tatar exiles from the Russian empire, there was even a growth of pan-Turkish or 'Turanian' dreams in the years before 1914. These visions of a political union of all the Turkish-speaking peoples of Russia, Afghanistan, Persia and even China with those in the Ottoman empire were utterly impracticable. They never had real influence outside a small circle of intellectuals and officials. But this growth of nationalism which, it must be emphasized, followed rather than caused the revolution of 1908–9, sealed the fate of the empire as a multinational state. The conception of it as such was now being discarded not merely by its subject peoples but also more and more by its rulers. Turkish nationalism was still strongly opposed by the deep-rooted conception of the unity in Islam of all true believers, a unity which must not be undermined by their division into national groups. Thus in 1913 one influential writer could claim that nationalism was 'a foreign innovation as deadly to the body of Islam as cancer is to man', while another argued that 'our Turkishness is nothing but a symbolism. We are all assimilated in Islam, and we are only Muslims.'[59] But these were voices from the past, though still influential ones. The last years of the Ottoman empire saw this abandonment of multinationalism expressed in efforts to enforce the exclusive use of the Turkish language in the schools and administration. These provide a Near Eastern parallel to the earlier linguistic intolerance of the Magyars in Transylvania and Slovenia, of the Germans in Posnania, and of the Russians in Poland, the Ukraine and the Baltic provinces.

In Egypt the British-dominated administration from 1882 onwards was much less repressive than those of Abdul Hamid in Constantinople or Nasr-ed-Din Shah in Tehran. The result was that Egyptian nationalism was able to develop more freely than that of the Turks or the Persians. Here as elsewhere direct rule by Europeans was more conducive to the growth of national feeling than that of ineffective traditional autocracies.[60] The two greatest sources of national consciousness, education and the newspaper press, both developed rapidly in Egypt during the later nineteenth century. The founding of large numbers of schools (by private initiative rather than government action) produced an educated or semi-educated class proportionately larger than in any other part of the Arab world. In 1875 there were 7,450 pupils in western-type schools in Egypt; by 1914 there were over 48,000.[61] Politically minded newspapers had begun to be a significant force even in the 1870s, before the British occupation. The journalist Abdullah al-Nadim, the main spokesman for the resistance to the British conquest of 1882, 'can be regarded as the first of the popular Egyptian nationalists'.[62] By the 1890s relations between educated Egyptians and the British officials who in effect governed the country were deteriorating sharply, in part at least because of the attitude of Lord Cromer, who as consul-general in Cairo, dominated the administration for almost a quarter of a century.[63]

In 1907 the first important organized political groups in Egypt, the People's Party, the Constitutional Reform Party and the National Party, took shape. Economic strains, the result of rapid population growth and the dangers inherent in dependence on cotton as an export crop, helped to give them some popular backing. In 1910 came the first important example of nationalist terrorism, with the murder of the prime minister, Butrus Ghali. National feeling, however, was still very far from being united except in hostility to the British régime. On the one hand stood those who, under the influence of pan-Islamic ideas and encouraged by the Young Turk revolution of 1908–9, wished to restore the effective authority of the sultan in Egypt. Facing them were the more radical nationalist groups which hoped to create an independent and sovereign Egyptian state. The latter were the first effective representatives in the Arab world of true exclusive national feeling; for the idea of an Egyptian nation 'involved not only the denial of a single Islamic community, but also the assertion that there could be a virtuous community based on something other than a common religion and a revealed law'.[64] To the great majority of Arabs, and of Muslims everywhere, this was still a strange and radical idea in 1914.

There was thus a sudden and very striking rise in the activity of nationalist movements all over Asia and the Near East in the years 1905–9. In each of the areas concerned, Egypt, the Ottoman empire, Persia, India and China, local forces and conditions played a part in this. But underlying the whole process and giving it a certain unity was the effect of the Russo-Japanese war and of the defeat of Russia, astonishing to almost all observers in Europe, with which it ended. Even before 1904–5 it was not altogether unknown for brown or yellow armies successfully to resist white ones. It has been argued that in the Franco-Chinese war of 1884–85 in Tongking 'for the first time soldiers of a yellow race had fought hand to hand with Europeans and not been disgraced'.[65] More spectacularly, in 1896 the Ethiopians had largely destroyed at Adowa an invading Italian army (or at least one officered by Italians: its rank and file was mainly African). But neither of these struggles had been on a scale comparable to that between Russia and Japan or had been reported to the world in the same detail. Neither, therefore, had anything like the same results. Victory was by no means easy for Japan. By the end of the war she was economically exhausted and Russia's military position was improving: Japan could not have fought it to a conclusion without financial help from Britain and the United States. (Of the 1,000 million American dollars which it cost her about half came from loans floated in London and New

York, with Germany contributing a little.) But it was a real and conclusive victory. For the first time a great European empire had been defeated by an Asian national state. Everywhere that anti-European nationalism had taken root it was given fresh life and energy. In Egypt Mustapha Kamil was inspired to write a book, *al Shams al-mashriqa* (*The Rising Sun*), which acclaimed Japan for 'demonstrating to the people of the East that it is possible for them to rise again, if the requisite effort is made'; while the poet Hafiz Ibrahim prophesied that the war 'would summon the men of the East to triumph'.[66]

In India, where there had been considerable admiration for Japan even before the war, Gokhale urged his followers to study her development since the Meiji restoration of 1867–68 in order to prepare themselves for the self-sacrifice which their country demanded. In the Russian empire itself the abortive revolution which followed defeat made possible the meeting of an All-Russian Muslim Congress in August 1905 and the formation of the Russian General Muslim Party. On a wider canvas it had considerable influence in strengthening the forces of revolt, national and social, in many parts of Asia.[67] In Persia the first European-style novel, *Siyahatnama-ye Ibrahim Beg*, held up Japan as a model to be copied. Even in Afghanistan the publication in 1916–17 of a translation into Pashto of a five-volume Turkish history of the Russo-Japanese war was one of the first literary results of rising national consciousness.[68]

The Russo-Japanese conflict thus marks a real dividing-line in the history of Europe's relations with Asia and even with the Near East. In world history it is more important than the struggles, parochial by comparison, which in 1854–71 remodelled the European state-system. Paul Cambon, the French ambassador in London, was correct in prophesying that it would 'weigh upon the whole century'.

NATIONALISM AND PROGRESS

Recent writers on the rise of nationalism, especially European ones contemplating the devastation caused by two world wars fought mainly in their own continent, have tended to stress its negative and destructive side. The effects of national feeling in separating peoples from one another, in increasing tensions between states, in making racial and linguistic intolerance more widespread and dangerous, have been repeatedly underlined. Certainly the texture of national feeling in Europe coarsened as the nineteenth century progressed. Whereas the writers of its earlier decades had usually stressed the virtues and constructive potentialities, real or imaginary, of the national group to which they belonged, by its end it was increasingly national military and political power, actual or potential, which was glorified. Thus in France for nearly two generations after 1815 nationalist dreams of territorial expansion and the achievement of the Rhine frontier could still be combined with the idea that the country had a great role to play in the liberation of the Poles or Italians from foreign rule. This generous and outward-looking attitude was quite absent from the thinking of Maurras and his followers in the two decades before 1914. In the first half of the nineteenth century it had been possible to see nationalism as the expression of a truth about the nature of men and societies which was itself general and supranational; whereas in 1899, at the height of the Dreyfus affair, the French nationalist writer Maurice Barrès could say that 'German and English truths are not French truth, and can poison us'.[69] Nevertheless the positive aspects of nationalism were enormously important throughout this period. It was the greatest of all forces for evil, but also for good.

It presupposed in theory, and its supporters sometimes sought to realize in practice, a certain fundamental equality between different members of the nation. The essence of a nation, the condition of and justification for its existence, was unity against the outside world; and there could be no real unity between masters and slaves. The national state was therefore implicitly hostile to the type of society which had been normal in Europe during the eighteenth century and was still normal in Asia at the beginning of the twentieth – one based on a complex of social orders, each with different rights and obligations, and a structure of local and regional privileges and peculiarities. 'A country', wrote Mazzini in his *Duties of Man*, 'is an association; there is no true country where the uniformity of that right is violated by the existence of caste, privilege, and inequality.'[70] He therefore quite logically advocated important social reforms in Italy as the necessary foundations of national unity. The same assumptions inspired a poster issued by a French nationalist group during the election of 1900. 'They call themselves Socialists', it complained of its opponents, 'and in twenty years they have not achieved a more equal sharing of the burdens of taxation, or old age pensions. For Nationalism means care for the interests of all the members of the community. Patriotism involves a spirit of solidarity, mutual aid, and fraternal charity.'[71] Built into nationalism therefore, at least in Europe, was an inherent tendency towards some degree of social equality. Moreover this aspect of it was being continually reinforced in practice during the nineteenth century by the growth of communications, which meant that all citizens, at least in the more advanced states of Europe, tended increasingly to dress, behave and even think in the same way.

The egalitarian tendencies of nationalism, like so many other aspects of it, can be seen clearly for the first time during the French Revolution. Not only did the revolution make all Frenchmen equal before the law. It also produced the most far-reaching suggestions hitherto put forward in any European state for the establishment of a system of social security. The constitution of 1791 proclaimed the duty of the government to aid education, relieve the poor and infirm and provide work for those unable to find it. The more radical Jacobin constitution of 1793 asserted that public assistance was a sacred debt owed by society to the unfortunate. Bertrand Barrère, one of the leading members of the Convention, proposed in May 1794 that aged and infirm workers and peasants and impoverished mothers, wives and widows should receive state pensions, and that there should also be state medical provision for the sick. He urged that 'the distressing word "poverty" be eradicated from the vocabulary of republicans'.[72] It is worth noting that the man who put forward these humanitarian proposals was noted for the virulence of his hostility to Great Britain, against which he preached war to the knife. The combination of public spirit and egalitarianism at home with violent nationalism and xenophobia abroad is already visible. The more advanced areas of western Europe offer plenty of other examples during the following decades of social radicalism united with national feeling. Thus Fichte proposed in his *Geschlossene Handelstaat* (1800) that when a citizen died all his property should revert to the state, carrying nationalist egalitarianism to a length which no writer of the century was to surpass.

Even the anti-Semitism with which extreme nationalism tended to become associated in the last decades of the nineteenth century often contained, especially in Germany and the Habsburg empire, a distinct element of social and economic radicalism. The programme of Adolf Stocker's Christian Social Workers' Party was in some respects as complete a rejection of the status quo as that of the Social Democrats. In the same way the equally nationalist and anti-Semitic *Soziale Reichspartei*, founded in 1881, demanded the introduction of a ten-hour working day and the abolition of all direct taxes levied on the poor. During most of the nineteenth century anti-Semitism came as much from the left as from the right in European politics. It was propagated by radicals as much as by conservatives and Catholics. The most important task of nationalism from the 1870s onwards all over western Europe was to win the industrial worker away from ideas of class war and the international solidarity of the proletariat, as preached by the Marxists, and convert him to belief in the paramountcy of national interests for all elements in the community. In this, aided by high tariffs, education and sometimes social legislation, it had by the outbreak of the First World War been triumphantly successful. 'Although socialism in Europe is constantly gaining strength', wrote Gökalp in 1913, 'we see clearly that it gives way to the national ideal in time of war. Not only during political wars but even in economic competition, class ideals are subordinated to national ideals.'[73] Socialism and liberalism have both at different times been the objects of widespread popular hostility, at least in some parts of Europe. This has never been the case with nationalism. In the nation and perhaps in it alone the common man, irrespective of class, can fulfil himself.

This unifying element in nationalism, the tendency to see all members of the national group as in some sense equals in the struggle against foreign competitors and domestic foes such as the Jews, was not universal. It was in the main confined to western Europe, where social distinctions were already less extreme than in most other parts of the civilized world. In much of central and eastern Europe, in Hungary, Croatia and Poland, the nationalist leaders were drawn in the main from the landowning gentry and the peasantry was not regarded as part of the nation in any effective sense at all. This was shown dramatically when, in 1906, the Emperor Francis Joseph was able to end a bitter controversy with the Hungarian ruling class over the language of command in the Hungarian army (at its height orders had been given though never carried out for an invasion and military occupation of Hungary) merely by threatening to introduce universal suffrage in the eastern half of his empire. Elections on this basis would have shown at once that the Hungarian gentry-nationalists represented hardly anyone but themselves – not even the Hungarian peasant who also spoke Magyar but who was almost as badly oppressed as the Slovaks or Romanians. In so far as there was any peasant support for nationalism in most of central and eastern Europe before 1914 it was usually based on the hope that it would pave the way to redistribution of land and an increase in peasant holdings. But none of the national movements of this overwhelmingly peasant area originated from the peasantry; and those which contained a large peasant element – for example that of the Slovaks – tended to be weak. In many parts of Asia and the Near East also the nationalist leaders tended to have little interest in social and economic reform. This was partly because many of them, particularly in the Near East, were local notables or members of well-to-do families. More important, it was widely assumed that national independence could be achieved without real change of this kind. Economic and social improvement could wait until the purely political objectives of the national movements had been gained; after that it would follow almost automatically. Some socially constructive aspects of non-European nationalism can indeed be seen, notably perhaps in the first real effort in some parts of the world to improve the status of women.[74] They were as yet superficial, however, their impact limited to a small, urban and usually well-to-do segment of the population. They had therefore little reality before 1914 compared to those in western Europe. But though so limited they were still genuine.

Nationalism has shown itself during the last century or more as the only force capable of involving the ordinary man deeply and personally with the state of which he is a member. A state merely dynastic and monarchical, as most of those of eighteenth-century Europe were, could never hold the active allegiance and gain the passionate loyalty of its subjects as a national one can. A state based on conquest, tradition or dynastic rights could exist and even flourish though the great mass of its inhabitants cared little for it and took no interest in its doings except when it affected their daily lives by taxing or conscripting them. One based on national feeling, on the other hand, has its whole *raison d'être* in the loyalty of its subjects, in the unity they feel with one another and in the pride they feel in that unity and in the state which symbolizes and guarantees it. The national state is the supreme practical embodiment of the idea of the popular will; it exists because its subjects, or the dominant part of them, demand that it shall. National feeling alone can generate the active popular assent which is now considered necessary to justify the existence of any political unit. In the modern world the nation is the community which legitimizes the state, and the only one which can do so. To the nation many things are now permitted which would be forbidden to any other grouping of humanity. A rebellion against foreign rule by a nation, or some group which claims to be one, can be accepted and even acclaimed by great numbers of people who would indignantly refuse to countenance a similar movement based on class or religion. This position of privilege the nation had already achieved over most of Europe by 1914. Since then events have somewhat weakened its emotional attraction in the continent which gave it birth. But it remains today to the majority of humanity, however mistakenly, the medium through which progress is best assured and advanced. In this sense it is the greatest political legacy of the nineteenth century.

NOTES

1. W. K. Hancock, *Ricasoli and the Risorgimento in Tuscany* (London, 1926), p. 163.
2. T. Schieder, 'Typologie und Erscheinungsformen des Nationalstaats in Europa', *Historische Zeitschrift*, ccii (1960), 60.
3. N. Berkes, ed., *Turkish Nationalism and Western Civilization: selected essays of Zia Gökalp* (London, Allen & Unwin, 1959), p. 81.
4. B. Guenée, 'État et nation en France au Moyen Age', *Revue Historique*, ccxxxii (1967), 22.

5. To some extent, such ideas aroused a response even in Rousseau's lifetime. There are, for example, signs of an increasing stress in French art-criticism from the 1760s onwards on the desirability of choosing national and patriotic themes as the subjects of paintings (J. A. Leith, *The Idea of Art as Propaganda in France, 1750–1799* (Toronto University Press, 1965), pp. 81–6: and Louis XVI and his ministers commissioned a number of strongly patriotic paintings and statues for the annual Luxembourg exhibitions in Paris.

6. A. Aulard, *Le Patriotisme français de la Renaissance à la Révolution* (Paris, 1921), p. 89.

7. See his instructions to Novosiltsev, the envoy he was about to send to London, of 23 September 1804, in *Vneshnaya politika Rossii XIX i nachala XX veka. Seriya pervaya* (Moscow, 1960–72), ii, 142.

8. See E. Kedourie, *Nationalism* (London, Hutchinson University Library, 1960), Ch ii, *passim*.

9. Hannah A. Straus, *The Attitude of the Congress of Vienna towards Nationalism in Germany, Italy and Poland* (New York, Columbia University Press, 1949), pp. 19–20.

10. H. Wienstock, *Rossini: a biography* (Oxford University Press, 1968), p. 46.

11. A. G. Haas, *Metternich, Reorganization and Nationality, 1813–1818* (Wiesbaden, 1963), p. 160.

12. W. C. Langsam, *The Napoleonic Wars and German Nationalism in Austria* (Columbia University Press, 1930), Chs ii and iii; and A. Robert, *L'idee nationale autrichienne et les guerres de Napoléon* (Paris, 1933), *passim*.

13. G. L. Mosse, *The Culture of Western Europe: the nineteenth and twentieth centuries, an introduction* (London, Murray, 1963) p. 44.

14. F. Meinecke, *Cosmopolitanism and the National State* (Princeton University Press, 1970), p. 205.

15. C. J. H. Hayes, *Nationalism: a Religion* (New York, Macmillan, 1960), p. 47.

16. G. Salvemini, *Mazzini* (London, Cape, 1956), p. 51. This idea could have negative as well as positive implications. Mazzini denied the Irish the right to national independence, since to him they had no specific national mission to perform and represented no moral idea.

17. Mosse, *The Culture of Western Europe*, p. 42.

18. See p. 354.

19. S. Lukashevich, *Ivan Aksakov, 1823–1886* (Harvard University Press, 1965), p. 32.

20. By the 1890s, for example, the teaching of history in the elementary schools of Prussia was intensely nationalistic, more so indeed than the official regulations required (W. C. Langsam, 'Nationalism and History in the Prussian Elementary Schools under William II', in E. M. Earle, ed., *Nationalism and Internationalism* (Columbia University Press, 1950)).

21. It was in fact compiled by Lönnrot from a large number of dispersed fragments, and to some extent written by him; but its doubtful status as a work of folk literature did not prevent its playing an important role in the growth of national consciousness among the Finns.

22. T. Stoianovich, 'The pattern of Serbian intellectual evolution, 1830–1880', *Comparative Studies in Society and History*, i (1958–59), 248–9.

23. See p. 360.

24. The nearest approach in western Europe to a linguistically 'decapitated' nationality were the Flemings, whose national movement was very largely one of the lower classes of the Flemish provinces of Belgium against the dominant French-speaking middle class. The Irish were also to a large extent a 'decapitated' people; but here the decisive factor was the persecution of catholicism in Ireland from the sixteenth to the early nineteenth century, not a primarily linguistic oppression.

25. A. Fischel, *Der Panslavismus bis zum Weltkrieg* (Stuttgart–Berlin, 1919), p. 379.

26. The first clear statement of the idea that skull shape is the principal criterion of race was made by W. F. Edwards in his *Des Caractères physiologiques des races humaines considérées dans leur rapport avec l'histoire* (Paris, 1829). It is significant of the tenacity of the belief in phrenology that so great if opinionated a scientist as A. R. Wallace, who had worked out independently a theory of evolution by natural selection very similar to that of Darwin, could write in 1898 that 'In the coming century Phrenology will assuredly attain general acceptance. It will prove itself to be the true science of mind' (*The Wonderful Century* (London, 1898), p. 193).

27. The crudity of much of this type of argument is well illustrated by the contention of one author that, on the assumption that Mongols averaged 83 cubic inches of brain capacity and Aryans 92 cubic inches, then 400 million of the latter would in the aggregate possess 3,600 million cubic inches more of brain than the former. This he went on, must through the superior 'intellectual force' which it gave the Aryans have a great effect on 'historical development' (G. G. Zerffi, 'On the possibility of a strictly scientific treatment of universal history', *Transactions of the Royal Historical Society*, n.s., ii (1874), 391).

28. M. D. Biddiss, ed., *Gobineau: selected political writings* (London, Cape, 1970) pp. 140–1.

29. An idea of which Marxism was a different and equally important expression. It is significant that Marx wished to dedicate the first part of *Das Kapital* to Darwin (who refused the compliment). There is also some obvious underlying similarity between Darwinism and the belief of the classical economists that unlimited competition will lead to the victory of the best and cheapest of a number of competing products.

30. N. V. Riasanovsky, *Nicholas I and Official Nationality in Russia, 1825–1855* (University of California Press, 1959), p. 148.

31. P. G. J. Pulzer, *The Rise of Political Anti-Semitism in Germany and Austria* (New York, Wiley, 1964), p. 65.

32. W. J. McGrath, 'Student radicalism in Vienna', *Journal of Contemporary History*, ii, no. 3 (1967), 184.

33. This point should not be pushed too far. The peaceful emergence of an independent Norway in 1905 and of an independent Iceland in 1918, and the persisting strength of Irish nationalism, show that even in western Europe nationalism could easily become a force disruptive of existing political units.

34. P. Vysany, *Neo-Slavism and the Czechs, 1898–1914* (Cambridge University Press, 1977), p. 6.

35. F. Fadner, *Seventy Years of Pan-Slavism in Russia: Karazin to Danilevsky, 1800–1870* (Georgetown University Press, 1962), pp. 201, 328.

36. Thus in 1849 Nicholas I told the Slavophil Samarin, with reference to the position in the Baltic provinces, that 'You want to make Russians out of Germans by force, but we really should not do it that way, since we are Christians' (S. Monas, *The Third Section: police and society in Russia under Nicholas I* (Harvard University Press, 1961), p. 264).

37. See P. Renouvin, *L'idée de fédération européenne dans la pensée politique du XIX siècle* (Zaharoff Lecture for 1949: Oxford, 1949), *passim*.

38. Cobden, for example, argued in 1849 that 'the intercourse between countries is nothing but the intercourse between individuals in the aggregate' (A. C. F. Beales, *The History of Peace* (London, Bell, 1931), p. 90).

39. H. Gollwitzer, *Europabild und Europagedanke* (Munich, 1964), pp. 259–60.

40. See the table given in F. S. L. Lyons, *Internationalism in Europe, 1815–1914* (Leyden, 1963), p. 14; and on a specialized aspect of the subject Brigitte Schroder, 'Caracteristiques des relations scientifiques internationales, 1870–1914', *Journal of World History*, x (1966–67), 161–77. Sixty-nine international congresses of different kinds are said to have met in Paris in 1889 alone (L. L. Lorwin, *Labour and Internationalism* (London, Allen & Unwin, 1929), p. 69).

41. The Germany he envisaged was to be a *Grossdeutschland* including Denmark, Holland, Belgium, Switzerland and south-eastern Europe.

42. This meant that international division of labour, which had been a prominent feature of the economic life of Europe in the third quarter of the nineteenth century, was strikingly reduced. Measured as the ratio of world trade to world production at constant prices, it fell from an index figure of 129 in 1876–80 to one of 89 in 1896–1900 (though it then recovered somewhat to 102 in 1911–13) (A. Maizels, *Industrial Growth and World Trade* (Cambridge University Press, 1963), p. 80).

43. Royal Institute of International Affairs, *Nationalism* (London, 1939), p. 312.

44. For a brief discussion see J. A. Petrus, 'The theory and practice of internationalism; Rosa Luxemburg's solution to the national question', *East European Quarterly*, iv (1970–71), 442–56.

45. H. N. Brailsford, *The War of Steel and Gold* (London, 1914), p. 195.

46. Margaret Cole, ed., *Beatrice Webb's Diaries, 1912–1924* (London, Longmans, 1952), p. 34.

47. E. V. G. Kiernan, *British Diplomacy in China, 1880 to 1885* (Cambridge University Press, 1939), p. 185.

48. D. E. Lee, 'The origins of Pan-Islamism', *American Historical Review*, xviii (1942), 283. A good though late statement of much of the Pan-Islamic point of view was given by an Uzbek leader in 1914: 'If you study contemporary science you will be in a position to construct telegraphs, build railroads, transport hundreds of thousands of troops from one end of the earth to the other in twenty days ... to comprehend the secret meaning of the Koran, to prepare rifles and cannon for the

defence of Islam, to liberate our fatherland from the hands of the foreigners . . . to free our nation from the yoke of the infidel and to restore Islam to its earlier heights' (H. S. Dinnerstein, 'The Sovietization of Uzbekistan', *Harvard Slavonic Studies*, iv (1957), 503).

49. There is a useful short discussion of his political ideas in M. Colombe, 'Islam et nationalisme arabe à la veille de la première guerre mondiale', *Revue Historique*, ccxxiii (1960), 88–92; see also in particular E. Kedourie, *Afghani and Abduh* (London, Cass, 1966). The exact nature of some of Afghani's ideas is still far from clear, since for tactical reasons, or even those of personal safety, he often over-stressed in his expression of them their Islamic elements. See the discussion in Nikki R. Keddie, 'Religion and irreligion in early Iranian nationalism', *Comparative Studies in Society and History*, ix (1961–62), 279–84.

50. The contrast between the two is discussed in detail in S. A. Wolpert, *Tilak and Gokhale: revolution and reform in the making of modern India* (University of California Press, 1962).

51. K. Minogue, *Nationalism* (London, Batsford, 1967), p. 88.

52. S. P. Sen, 'Effects on India of British law and administration in the 19th century', *Journal of World History*, iv (1957–58), 879.

53. In India Mazzini's works were translated into Bengali and his autobiography into Marathi, while the extremist leader Lajpat Rai wrote his biography (S. Ghose, *The Renaissance to Militant Nationalism in India* (Bombay, 1969), pp. 218–19).

54. I. C. Y. Hsu, *China's Entrance into the Family of Nations: the diplomatic phase, 1858–1880* (Harvard University Press, 1960), pp. 125ff, 132ff.

55. J. Ch'en, *Yuan Shih-k'ai* (London, Allen & Unwin, 1961), p. 102. The first cabinet in Chinese history, which was formed in April 1911 only a few months before the collapse of the dynasty, included nine Manchus (five of them members of the imperial clan) and only five Han Chinese.

56. In 1850–99 Chinese translations of European or American books on the sciences (particularly the applied sciences) outnumbered those on the social sciences and humanities by four to one. In 1902–4, however, the corresponding ratio was one to two: the flow into China of western political and social ideas had enormously accelerated (J. K. Fairbank, 'China's response to the West: problems and suggestions', *Journal of World History* iii (1956–57), 405, n. 11).

57. Quoted in T. C. Young, ed., *Near Eastern Culture and Society* (Princeton University Press, 1959), pp. 136–7.

58. W. Morgan Schuster, *The Strangling of Persia* (New York, 1920), pp. 245–6.

59. N. Berkes, *The Development of Secularism in Turkey* (Montreal, McGill University Press, 1964), pp. 374–5.

60. In the same way in the autocratically governed Emirate of Bukhara, which was merely a Russian protectorate, new ideas of any kind were sternly discouraged whereas in the areas of Turkestan governed directly by the Russians they were allowed to circulate a good deal more freely (R. A. Pierce, ed., *Mission to Turkestan: being the memoirs of Count K. K. Pahlen, 1908–1909* (Oxford University Press, 1964), p. 74).

61. G. Baer, 'Social Change in Egypt, 1800–1914', in P. M. Holt, ed., *Political and Social Change in Modern Egypt* (Oxford University Press, 1968), p. 159.

62. A. Hourani, *Arabic Thought in the Liberal Age, 1798–1939* (Oxford University Press for RIIA, 1962), p. 197.

63. His earlier experience in India led him to stress good financial administration, low taxation and the safeguarding of the position of the smaller farmers and cultivators, to the virtual exclusion of purely political considerations (R. Owen, 'The influence of Lord Cromer's Indian experience on British policy in Egypt, 1883–1907', *St Anthony's Papers: Middle Eastern Affairs*, no. 4 (Oxford University Press, 1965), 109–39).

64. Hourani, *Arabic Thought in the Liberal Age*, p. 193.

65. Kiernan, *British Diplomacy in China*, p. 185.

66. D. Hopwood, *The Russian Presence in Syria and Palestine, 1843–1914* (Oxford University Press, 1969), pp. 127–8.

67. For a short Soviet account see G. F. Kim and F. I. Shabshina, *Proletarskii internatsionalizm i revolyutsii v stranakh vostoka* (Moscow, 1967), pp. 33–57.

68. V. Gregorian, *The Emergence of Modern Afghanistan: politics of reform and modernization, 1880–1946* (Stanford University Press, 1969), Ch. viii.

69. J. Lestocquoy, *Histoire du patriotisme en France* (Paris, 1968), p. 168.

70. Royal Institute of International Affairs, *Nationalism*, p. 89.

71. D. R. Watson, 'The nationalist movement in Paris, 1900–1906', in *The Right in France, 1890–1919* (St Anthony's Papers, no. 13: Chatto and Windus, 1962), p. 63.

72. C. J. H. Hayes, *The Historical Evolution of Modern Nationalism* (new edn, New York, Macmillan 1948), pp. 76–7.

73. Berkes, *Turkish Nationalism*, p. 82.

74. On the beginnings of this process in Turkey see Berkes, *The Development of Secularism in Turkey*, pp. 386–7. In particular a new Law of Family Rights recognized for the first time in 1917 the right of women to bring legal proceedings for divorce and tried to discourage polygamy. Mahmud Tarzi, the leading figure in the early history of Afghan nationalism, was a strong advocate of women's rights (Gregorian, *Emergence of Modern Afghanistan*, p. 172).

5

Europe and the world

For long after 1815, indeed until the 1870s or even the 1880s, colonial issues counted for little in international relations within Europe and attracted little active public attention in the European states. These two generations saw a steady growth of the economic, technological and military superiority of Europe to the rest of the world, and therefore an increasing possibility of European dominance on a scale and of a completeness hitherto unknown; yet the interests of both governments and peoples in empire-building in other continents remained in general at an obstinately low ebb.

For this there were a number of reasons. No European state during the generation after 1815 depended economically on its colonies to the extent that several had done in the eighteenth century. The remnants of the Spanish empire after its final collapse in the mid-1820s were, with the exception of Cuba, almost valueless. The declining importance of imports of cane sugar and the abolition, at least in theory, of the slave trade, had greatly reduced the value of what was left of the French colonial empire. Even in Britain trade with the colonies (including India) had ceased by the early 1790s to be the largest element, as it had been during most of the eighteenth century, in the country's total overseas trade; and the adoption of free-trade policies, which reached its climax in the 1850s and 1860s, seemed to reduce still further the commercial value of the empire. In any case a rapidly growing population and domestic market, and heavy demands for investment at home, particularly to mechanize the textile industries and build railways, meant that Britain's interest in exporting either goods or capital was significantly less than it later became. Even for cotton textiles, the manufactured product which had led the way towards modern industrialism, the home market was growing faster than the export one during the first three or four decades of the nineteenth century, while as late as 1840 Britain still exported less than a twentieth of her rapidly increasing production of coal. Moreover apart from raw cotton,

of which the United States was overwhelmingly the greatest supplier, there
were few essential raw materials which she as yet needed to import in very
large quantities from outside Europe. Her industrial development and her
investment were both still directed primarily to home markets and
depended primarily on home resources. In these circumstances there was
little incentive to expand her overseas empire, either formal or informal.
Governments and peoples still welcomed, or at least did not oppose, territorial gains which seemed likely to be economic assets; the vast expansion
of British power in India which marked the four decades after Waterloo
was accepted largely because it was thought to be, at least in the long run,
profitable. Indian possessions, after all, paid their own defence costs, which
no other British colony did, and also gave employment, as soldiers and
officials, to many Englishmen and Scots. It was also widely assumed that
British trade with India depended on British political control there. But
there were few parts of the world, and in particular few large overseas
territories, which it now seemed worth while for a European state to
conquer and administer. The only one of significance, apart from India,
was the Dutch East Indies, which in 1831–77 contributed over 832 million florins to the treasury of Holland.[1] Trading stations and naval bases
might still be a good investment. Extensive overseas empires in general
were not. Moreover the extraordinary naval and industrial predominance of Britain for almost half a century after 1815, a period during
which she was the only truly great industrial and naval power in the
world, meant that there was little of the sharp competition on more or
less equal terms for colonial territories and overseas markets which had
been seen during much of the eighteenth century. The absence of this
competitive spur in itself does much to explain the general lack of desire
to expand outside Europe during this period. This state of affairs of course
suited Britain well. 'We have possession', wrote Wellington in 1829, 'of
nearly every valuable port and colony in the world, and I confess that
I am anxious to avoid exciting the attention and jealousy of other powers
by extending our possessions, and setting the example of gratification of a
desire to seize more territories.'[2]

History also seemed to show that large colonies of settlement overseas
were a very doubtful asset. The four decades before Waterloo had seen the
disruption of the two greatest colonial empires in the world, those of Britain
and Spain, a disruption which was the result of revolts by discontented
colonists against the rule of the mother country. This easily produced in
western Europe the belief that any large body of Europeans settled overseas would inevitably, as their strength and self-confidence grew, seek
independence. Like ripe fruit falling from a tree, they would separate
from their begetter in Europe. No European statesman during this period

believed that colonial independence was desirable for its own sake; but many felt it to be inevitable in the long run. 'The normal course of colonial history' wrote an observer as late as 1869, 'is the perpetual assertion of the right to self-government.'[3]

This pessimism about the prospects of maintaining permanently any substantial overseas empire of settlement partly explains the fact that for over forty years, between the Canada Act of 1791 and that which abolished slavery in the British empire in 1833, the British Parliament passed no legislation of any significance bearing on the internal government of the colonies. It is true that in Britain, the one European power which still retained a large colonial empire, defeatism of this kind slowly weakened. From the later 1820s onwards interest in settlement in the colonies, for long at a very low ebb, revived considerably, in part as a result of the writings of Edward Gibbon Wakefield and the theories of colonization which he preached.[4] In 1826–27 a Select Committee of the House of Commons reported in favour of some state-aided emigration. In 1839 the Durham Report on the position in Canada, though many of its recommendations were not applied in practice, paved the way for the growth of representative government there in the 1840s and struck a note of confidence in the future of the British empire which had been little heard for half a century or more. The colonial secretaries of the 1830s and 1840s, unlike their predecessors for over a generation, were all in varying degrees reformers and innovators; and the creation in 1833 of the Judicial Committee of the Privy Council as a kind of supreme court of the empire again shows the growth of a more positive attitude to the colonies. The leading writers on political and economic problems of the later eighteenth century – Tucker, Bentham, Adam Smith himself – had been hostile to large colonial empires, as had David Ricardo, the greatest economist of the years immediately after Waterloo. Yet from the 1830s onwards economists at least were becoming more favourable to the idea of empire.[5]

Nevertheless the belief that overseas possessions, or at least those which needed to be administered and defended on a considerable scale, contributed nothing of value to Britain and might be actively harmful to her, was very slow to die. Even at the end of the 1850s Cobden, a convinced free trader and a bitter opponent of colonies as sources of wars, of waste of resources and of administrative nepotism, could write that it would 'be a happy day when England has not an acre of territory in Continental Asia'.[6] Above all the cost of colonial garrisons was a standing grievance to the radicals and to many of the Whigs; and in particular the obligation to defend Canada aroused great uneasiness at times when relations with the United States were strained.

Finally there were, at least in Britain, quite powerful moral objections to any further growth of empire. It was easy for missionary and evangelical groups, whose influence was at its height in the 1830s and 1840s, to identify colonies, particularly tropical and subtropical ones, with conquest, slavery, exploitation and the sacrifice of helpless natives to European greed, rather than with civilization and progress. Feelings of this kind underlay the abolition of slavery in the empire in 1833 and the appointment two years later of an important parliamentary committee of enquiry into the treatment of aborigines in British colonies. Humanitarian and missionary pressure-groups were by no means always united on the policies they wished the government to pursue. There were at times, for example, considerable differences in this respect between the Wesleyan Missionary Society and the London Missionary Society.[7] In India, moreover, where really great interests were at stake, missionary influence had never much political importance. Elsewhere however, particularly in Africa, the missionaries and their allies were at times able to exert great influence on official policy, and usually in a way hostile to territorial expansion. In 1835–36, Lord Glenelg, the colonial secretary, refused under pressure of this kind to accept the annexation of part of the territory of the Xhosa people which had been carried out by Sir Benjamin D'Urban, the governor of Cape Colony. Again the clauses protecting Maori interests which were inserted in the treaty of Waitangi (1840), by which British power was established in New Zealand, were the result of missionary pressures.

The period 1815–70 was thus one during which there was little direct economic incentive for even the most rapidly developing of the European powers to acquire new colonies. It was also one in which the climate of opinion, both popular and official, was normally tepid and sometimes hostile where overseas expansion was concerned. It nevertheless saw a striking territorial growth of three European colonial empires, those of France, Russia and most of all Britain.

Apart from the acquisition of very important naval bases and trading stations – Singapore in 1819, Aden in 1839, Hong Kong in 1842 – there was a rapid expansion of British power in India. The remaining strength of the Maratha princes was finally broken by 1819. Some Burmese territory was gained in 1825; Sind annexed in 1843; the Punjab conquered by 1849; more Burmese territory annexed in 1852 and the kingdom of Oudh in 1856. In 1877 Baluchistan fell under British control. In spite of serious setbacks – a difficult, unnecessary and unsuccessful war in Afghanistan in 1839–42, and the great sepoy mutiny of 1857 – British rule in India presented a picture of rapid and almost irresistible growth. Elsewhere New Zealand had been annexed in 1840 and Natal proclaimed a British colony in 1843.

By comparison the expansion of the French empire was slower and less spectacular. In 1830 the conquest of Algeria, which was to occupy the next two decades or more, got under way. France thus began, for the first time for almost seventy years, to possess a real colony of settlement. By the middle of the century there were over 100,000 Frenchmen established there, though a high proportion of these were military colonists. Tahiti became a French protectorate in 1843 (though it was not annexed until 1888) and in 1861–67 there was a piecemeal growth of French control in Cochin China and Cambodia. From 1854 onwards Louis Faidherbe, one of the most remarkable colonial governors of the period, began a considerable expansion of French power in Senegal.

The growth of the Russian empire in Asia was comparable to that of the British one. Difficulties of communication, the barrenness of the country and the severity of the climate made the conquest of central Asia very difficult; in 1839–40 an effort to capture the city of Khiva, a centre of the slave trade and a base for raids into Russian territory, was a disastrous failure. But the decrepit and badly ruled states of the area were helpless to resist the systematic Russian advance which began in the early 1860s. In 1865 Tashkent fell; and in July of the next year the governor-generalship of Turkestan was formed. In 1868 Bukhara accepted a Russian protectorate. In 1873 Khiva was taken and also became a protectorate. Meanwhile in 1858 Count N. N. Muraviev, governor-general of eastern Siberia since 1847 and one of the great empire-builders of the century, had forced the Chinese government to cede to Russia the territory it had formerly held on the left bank of the river Amur. Two years later the cession was confirmed, together with that of the large though almost uninhabited area between the river Ussuri and the Pacific Ocean, including the site of the future port of Vladivostok. In 1851 the slowly growing trade between Russia and China was encouraged by a treaty which opened two new trading centres in Chinese Turkestan to the Russians.

The other great European empire of this period, that of the Dutch in the East Indies, expanded territorially hardly at all. But its economic value and its hold on Java, incomparably its most important territory, were intensified by the development from the early 1830s onwards of the 'culture system' by which the native population, instead of paying taxes in money, delivered specified quantities of produce to the government.

Side by side with this growth of European territorial empires went, notably in the case of Britain, that of 'unofficial empire', of spheres of influence or control based on trade, investment, or agreements with native rulers. Indeed until at least the 1870s this quite as much as the annexation of territory was the means by which Europe's political and economic influence radiated to the rest of the world. Thus the Persian Gulf was completely controlled by Britain. Her influence was dominant in the little Gulf state of Musquat from the beginning of the century. The appointment of a British political agent there in 1800 was followed in 1839 by a commercial agreement, in 1846 by a customs agreement and in 1864 by an agreement for the use of Musquat as the terminus of a British submarine cable. Bahrain placed itself under British protection in 1861. In so great a state as China influence so open and complete as this was impossible for any one European power to achieve. But even there the leading position of Britain in the empire's seaborne trade encouraged at times in London hopes of some political predominance. In August 1842, by the treaty of Nanking, Britain had begun the imposition on China of a 'treaty tariff' which was not to be altered without the consent of the powers, and of a system of extraterritorial rights for foreigners which was to last far into the twentieth century. This opened the way for the treaties which France and the United States negotiated relatively easily with the Chinese government in 1843–44. In March 1856 the foreign secretary, Lord Clarendon, in instructions to Sir John Bowring, the British representative in China, even spoke of the possible establishment of some form of British protectorate over the decaying Manchu empire to prevent its domination by Russia. Two years later, when he negotiated the treaty of Tientsin with the Chinese, Lord Elgin, the British plenipotentiary, insisted on the establishment of a permanent British diplomatic representative in Peking (an innovation bitterly resisted by the Chinese government) partly in the hope that this might help to revive the empire under some kind of British diplomatic protectorate.[8]

In Egypt the influence of Europe, with France in the lead, was becoming irresistible from the reign of the Khedive Said (1854–63) onwards. By the later 1850s foreigners were settling in the country at a rate of about 30,000 a year. In 1865, attracted by the boom in cotton production which accompanied the American Civil War, 80,000 arrived. There was a rapid multiplication of economic concessions and privileges of all kinds granted to foreigners; and from 1858 onwards a growth in the indebtedness of the government to west European creditors. Under the Khedive Ismail (1863 79) this indebtedness, very rapidly increased by loans raised often on ruinously unfavourable terms,[9] became crushing. By the 1870s a collapse was clearly approaching. The way had been cleared for the international control of Egyptian finances established in 1876, and for the British occupation of 1882. In a rather similar manner, though the interests involved were much less important, an international commission was set up in 1868 to supervise the chaotic finances of the bey of Tunis.

In the Ottoman empire proper foreign borrowing on a considerable scale began with the raising of loans in London in 1854 and 1855. From

1865 onwards the proceeds of new loans were used almost entirely to pay off the interest on existing ones, while European investment in banks, port facilities and railways slowly grew. By October 1875 the Turkish government had been forced into default on the interest payments on its foreign borrowing; while the Russo-Turkish war of 1877–78 was followed by the stationing of British 'military consuls' in eastern Anatolia and a general disposition on the part of the powers, notably Britain, to scrutinize with jealous care any action which the Sultan Abdul Hamid and his ministers took or proposed to take. In 1879 Lord Derby, a former foreign secretary, complained that 'the daily surveillance of which Turkey is the object in her domestic affairs has reduced her sovereign authority to practically zero'. Finally in 1881 the Ottoman empire, like Egypt five years earlier, had to submit to foreign control of a considerable part of its finances when in December of that year the Decree of Mouharrem established an International Council of the Ottoman Debt. Although the working of the decree in practice was by no means unfavourable to the Turks (the total amount of the foreign debt was drastically written down and very few of the employees of the Council were Europeans), it illustrated strikingly the growth of Europe's unofficial or semi-official control in the Near East.[10] By 1914 the debt administration employed more officials than the Turkish ministry of finance.

In a less obtrusive way a kind of British 'unofficial empire' can be seen in large parts of Latin America for much of the nineteenth century. Thus in Brazil, where she predominated in foreign trade and had enormous importance in banking and railway-building, Britain had secured great commercial concessions by a treaty of 1827. Though the Brazilian government refused to renew this when it expired in 1844, it was not until 1887 that the country could finally nullify the consular privileges and extraterritorial rights granted to the British earlier in the century. In Argentina also large-scale British investment, at least from the early 1860s onwards, tended to create what some Argentines at least, with much exaggeration, considered a kind of indirect British financial control. It is important to remember, moreover, how little Britain's unofficial and even her official empire in these decades depended, at least directly, on her army and navy. Little of her own limited military strength was committed on a regular basis to Asia or Africa and none to Latin America. It was at least as much the support of local élites and forces – Indian princes, sepoy troops, Brazilian or Argentinian landowners – which made possible this imperial growth.

All this expansion, open or covert, official or unofficial, amounted to a very formidable growth of European territorial and economic power, above all in Asia and the Near East. Whereas in 1835 seventy British naval vessels were serving on non-European stations, twice as many, with a third of the total establishment of seamen and marines, were doing so a generation later.[11] Certain moments saw displays of British world power of a completeness scarcely possible before. Such were the few days in December 1840 which saw the almost simultaneous arrival in London of news of the capture of the Chinese island of Chusan, of a victory in Afghanistan and of the conclusion in Alexandria of the agreement by which Mehemet Ali acknowledged the defeat of his ambitions in Syria and Asia Minor; or the few months in 1857 when Britain crushed a great military revolt in India, sent an expedition to the Persian Gulf and thus forced Persia to renounce her territorial ambitions in Afghanistan, and captured Canton from the Chinese.

Yet in no case was imperial expansion before the 1870s the result of a consistent and wholehearted demand for it in the European state concerned. Sometimes it was the outcome of an incoherent striving for national status. This was particularly so in France, where the role of the colonies acquired during this period was essentially one of prestige, to 'dispute with England the mastery of the seas, to affirm before the world the presence, the grandeur, the expansion of France'.[12] Often territorial expansion was the work of some enterprising official or soldier on the spot rather than of ministers or public opinion in a European capital. The slowness and difficulty of communications before the coming of the telegraph made it relatively easy for a commander or governor-general in India or Turkestan to act on his own initiative and present his government in London or St Petersburg with a *fait accompli* which it was in practice impossible to undo. Thus the annexation of Sind in 1843 was the work of Sir Charles Napier, the military commander involved, and Lord Ellenborough, the governor-general of India. The directors of the East India Company (still until 1858 formally the ruling body in British India) disliked it and recalled Ellenborough; but they could not undo his work.

Whether the expansion of Russia in Asia in the middle decades of the century was really unwelcome to the country's rulers and forced on them by aggressive soldiers and officials, as has often been argued, is open to dispute. Nicholas I consistently backed Muraviev in the Far East; and Alexander II gave some of the original impetus to expansion in central Asia in the 1860s, an expansion which was strongly supported by his great war minister, D. A. Milyutin. General M. G. Chernaiev, after his capture of Tashkent in 1865, was recalled, ostensibly in disgrace, for disobedience to orders not to attack the city; but he received decorations and honours for what he had done in Turkestan and his career suffered no damage. On the other hand the ministry for foreign affairs, its attention focused on Europe and the Near East to the virtual exclusion of all else, was consistently hostile to ventures in Asia. Its attitude is well expressed in a letter (written in opposition to a proposal to annex Samarkand) of Stremoukhov, the head of its Asiatic section, to General Heiden, the chief of the general staff, in July 1867.

We are constantly told [he wrote], that for the maintenance of Russia's glory and prestige it is essential to take some fortresses or beat Asian hordes in the field. Fortresses are taken one after the other, hordes are completely beaten, good frontiers are achieved; and then it appears that another conclusive victory is essential, that the really good frontier lies further on, that our prestige has not been raised high enough by previous successes. Your Honour must agree that such a method of proceeding must at last be ended, for it is suited neither to the dignity nor the real interests of the government.[13]

Neither Count K. R. Nesselrode, chancellor until 1854, nor his successor, Prince A. M. Gorchakov, liked Asian ventures. Finance ministers such as Count Kankrin and Baron Reutern, alarmed by the military and other expenditures involved in a programme of imperial expansion, were equally hostile to them.

During the period from 1815 to the 1870s, then, the Europeanization of the world was proceeding apace; but it was accompanied by little justificatory theorizing and few really serious international frictions. Such imperial impulses as were felt in the capitals of Europe during this period were muted, intermittent and half-hearted compared to what they were soon to become.

By the 1870s there were signs that this position was changing. During this decade, for the first time during the nineteenth century, the growth of empires began to attract widespread popular attention in the great states of western Europe. It soon stimulated discussion and debate on a scale unequalled for nearly three generations. In Britain the Royal Colonial Institute was founded in June 1868 for the study of the problems raised by overseas expansion. The speech made at the Crystal Palace by Disraeli, the leader of the Conservative party, in June 1872, in which he challenged the view that the British colonies of settlement must eventually become independent and regretted that there was no common imperial tariff or system of defence which would make Britain 'a great country, an imperial country', has been taken as symbolizing the growth of a new and more positive attitude to the overseas empire. (Though when he was in power in 1874–80 Disraeli showed little personal interest in colonial problems.) By the 1880s the idea that the empire might be more effectively united by some form of federal constitution was becoming influential. An Imperial Federation League was founded in November 1884; and colonial conferences at which the great colonies of settlement were represented were held in London at intervals from 1887 onwards, though their practical achievements were not great. In France the catastrophe of 1870–71 helped to encourage ideas of expansion outside Europe as a substitute for the recovery of Alsace-Lorraine which German power made, for the time being at least, impossible. This changing attitude to overseas empire can be seen in a remarkable growth of interest in exploration and geographical discovery, notably in Africa,[14] and in the publication in 1874 of perhaps the most famous book of the century on colonial questions, A. Leroy-Beaulieu's *De la colonisation chez les peuples modernes*.

In Germany ideas of expansion overseas had begun to develop, though as yet on a small scale, even before the war with France. In 1867 Lothar Bücher, an important foreign ministry official, had suggested the acquisition of German bases in Timor and the Philippines; and in 1871 a group of merchants in Hamburg urged the annexation of the French possessions in Cochin China, Miquelon, St Pierre and Martinique. The 1870s and early 1880s saw a considerable output of writing in Germany on colonial questions, all of it, at least by implication, anti-British. But the country had no colonial tradition comparable to that of France and still more Britain. European problems were to most Germans, and certainly to Bismarck himself, incomparably more important than doubtful colonial opportunities in Africa or the Pacific. Even the formation of an active pressure-group, the *Kolonialverein*, in 1882, and the publication by it from 1884 onwards of a newspaper, the *Kolonialzeitung*, had little immediate effect on this position. Nevertheless the idea of expansion outside Europe had now entered the arena of serious political discussion in Germany for the first time. In Belgium, again, the Crown Prince Leopold had urged the creation of a colonial empire in a pamphlet written as early as 1863, and had considered projects of expansion in such diverse areas as China, Egypt, Borneo, the Philippines and the Transvaal. In 1876 a geographical congress meeting under his auspices in Brussels (he had become King Leopold II in 1865) decided to organize on an international basis the exploration of the vast and still unknown area of Africa between the Zambezi and the Sudan. The *Association Internationale Africaine* which it set up at once aroused a good deal of uneasiness in London and Paris. Even in Russia there were signs that conquest and expansion in Asia were beginning to attract some popular interest and support, partly at least because of their anti-British implications. Thus two Russian nationalist newspapers in the 1870s hailed the projected railway from the eastern shores of the Caspian to Bukhara, through newly conquered Turkestan, as 'a very worthy answer to the opening of the Suez Canal'.[15]

The decade 1870–80 did not see, by comparison with the 1880s or 1890s, any very rapid growth of European territories overseas. But during it were laid many of the psychological foundations for the swift, at times almost chaotic, expansion which was to follow and to mean that in the four decades before 1914 about a quarter of the land surface of the world changed hands. More and more emphasis was now being laid on the importance of colonies as contributors to the power and prestige of the mother country. More and more it tended to be argued that, as a Frenchman put it, 'there has never been a great power without extensive colonies. The apogee of the grandeur of empires always coincides with the maximum of their colonial expansion, their decadence with the loss of their colonies.'[16] The complex of traditions and snobberies which regarded events in Europe as more important than any in other parts of the world, and state service as carrying greater prestige if performed in Europe than overseas, was still very powerful even in the greatest imperial powers. Within the Russian foreign ministry the Asiatic department continued until the end of the tsarist régime to be regarded as at least socially inferior to that which handled relations with the states of Europe. Officers in British regiments maintained the now well-established tradition of looking down on those who served merely in an Indian one. But attitudes of this sort were now increasingly out of step both with public feeling and with the facts.

The new attitude to overseas possessions was seen first of all in Africa, in a great burst of European expansion there in the early and middle 1880s. In 1882 Britain, without any conscious planning on the part of her leaders, established a military occupation of Egypt which was to last for four decades. By the early 1890s Lord Salisbury and his cabinet had decided that no other European power should be allowed to control the Nile valley; and in 1896 the conquest of the Sudan, ruled since 1884 by a native religious leader, the Mahdi, and his successor, the Khalifa, was begun. Two years later it was essentially complete, with the destruction of a Sudanese army at Omdurman and the defeat, in the Fashoda crisis, of French ambitions in the area. Finally the Boer war of 1899–1902 gave Britain, after many difficulties and even humiliations, possession of by far the most immediately valuable territory to be found anywhere in Africa and branded her in the eyes of many observers as incurably avaricious and expansionist. France, her protectorate over Tunis established in 1881, conquered from 1887 onwards a huge though largely barren and thinly populated area covering the middle Niger, the northern Ivory Coast and the western Sudan. By 1905–6 the foundations were being laid of the protectorate over Morocco which she proclaimed seven years later. German agents were at work signing treaties with native rulers in south west Africa in 1883 and with those of Tanganyika in the following year. By the end of 1884 those areas, and Togoland in west Africa, were in German hands, while the Berlin African Conference of 1884–85, which attempted to lay down internationally agreed rules for the partition of Africa, was a clear sign of Germany's sudden emergence as a significant influence in the territorial expansion of Europe overseas.

In Asia the imperial prizes to be scrambled for were far more alluring than almost anything to be found in Africa. A French protectorate over Annam, established in 1884–85 after a difficult war with China, hitherto the suzerain power, was supplemented in 1893 by another over Laos. By the end of the century the Chinese empire seemed about to collapse and thus provide the powers of Europe with territories and markets of the sort hitherto achieved only by the British in India. The collapse of China in 1894–95 during the short and disastrous war of these years with Japan was followed by the series of demands on her for bases, for trading and railway-building concessions, even for the recognition of exclusive spheres of influence in different parts of her empire, which rose to a crescendo in 1898. By then Russia was establishing a virtual protectorate over Manchuria. Her merchants, her missionaries, most of all the armed guards stationed in the Manchurian provinces for the protection of the Chinese Eastern Railway begun in 1896, made her effectively master of the area.[17] The anti-foreign Boxer revolt which affected much of northern China in 1900 was made in St Petersburg the pretext for large-scale military action: by April 1901 there were about 100,000 Russian soldiers in Manchuria. The transformation of it and perhaps of all the north Chinese provinces into a Russian colony, so much feared in Britain, was prevented by Japan; and after the war of 1904–5 the rivalries of the great western powers in the Far East lost a good deal of their intensity and immediacy. Nevertheless China remained incomparably the greatest of all colonial prizes, though one by its very size difficult for any power, or even group of powers, to grasp. In no part of Asia was European economic activity increasing more rapidly: quite apart from a good deal of railway-building and investment in government loans the value of China's foreign trade almost trebled in the years 1895–1914 and the foreign population of Shanghai, by far the greatest centre of European trade, rose from less than 4,000 in 1890 to over 10,000 twenty years later.

In the Near East the rivalries of the powers, though less spectacular and perhaps less acute than in China, were more prolonged and almost equally important. A rapid increase in German activity in the Ottoman empire, seen notably in the proposed railway from Konia to Baghdad and eventually to the Persian Gulf, for which the first concession was granted in 1899, aroused fears in both Britain and Russia. Though the 'Baghdad Railway' was hardly the threat to the status quo which it at first appeared, and though the antagonisms it generated were largely assuaged by Russo-German and

Anglo-German agreements of 1911 and 1914, it illustrates well, particularly in the exaggerated hopes it aroused in some quarters in Germany, the way in which the spirit of international competition for imperial advantage was becoming more intense in this as in other parts of the non-European world. In Persia also the same factors can be seen giving birth to greatly increased Anglo-Russian tension. The grant by the Persian government in 1872 to a British subject, Baron Reuter, of rights giving him a dominant position in many aspects of the country's economic life was from the beginning a dead letter. Nevertheless through the alarm it gave rise to in Russia it began a process of rivalry between British and Russian influences in the increasingly decrepit Persian state, in which Russia by the 1890s was clearly gaining the upper hand. Her defeat by Japan and the fear and dislike of Germany which was now increasingly strong in both London and St Petersburg explain the conclusion in 1907 of an Anglo-Russian convention whose Persian clauses were its most important part: a large Russian sphere of influence was carved out in the northern half of the country and a much smaller British one set up in the south-east. Nevertheless this agreement, though attacked by some Russian soldiers and diplomats as too favourable to Britain, did little to halt the growth of Russia's dominance. From 1909 onwards large parts of northern Persia were under her military rule. By 1912, when Shah Mohammed Ali offered to accept a Russian protectorate over the entire country, there were 14,000 Russian soldiers there. By 1914 negotiations were under way for a new Anglo-Russian agreement which would divide all of Persia between Russian and British spheres of influence; and even the very threadbare fiction of her sovereignty could hardly have survived but for the outbreak of war in Europe.

Thus during the four decades before 1914 European influences, political, military, economic, cultural, were imposed on an unprecedented scale on every part of the non-European world. In 1880 most Africans could still expect to live out their lives without direct experience of European rule or direct contact with European ideas. In China, perhaps even in the Ottoman empire, both already smarting from the experience of western material superiority, it was still possible to hope that a little judicious borrowing of western techniques might enable society and government to survive in their traditional form. In the international backwater of Persia even the idea of a serious European threat to custom and tradition had hardly begun to be formulated. By 1914 these comfortable assumptions had disintegrated under the brute force of events. Now even the Afghan mountaineer, the Mongolian herdsman or the tribesman in the African rain-forest could scarcely hope to escape for long the devastating and fruitful influence of Europe.

THE ROOTS OF EXPANSION

It was for long fashionable to attribute the great growth of European empires from the 1870s or 1880s onwards mainly or even exclusively to the working of economic forces. The search for markets in Africa or Asia which the European states could monopolize, the quest for valuable raw materials, the desire to invest surplus capital profitably in the newly acquired colonies – these have long been widely accepted as the mainspring of this spectacular eruption of European world-mastery. Some of the leading figures in the imperialism of the later nineteenth century themselves subscribed to beliefs of this kind and sometimes stated them very forcibly in their efforts to rally support for their policies. Thus in France from the later 1870s onwards many writers and speakers stressed the economic strength which the country must acquire, at least in the long run, from the possession of a great colonial empire. Jules Ferry, the leading advocate among French politicians of colonial expansion, is a good example of this. Across the Channel Cecil Rhodes stated the case rather differently and with almost hysterical violence in a well-known letter of 1895.

In order to save the forty million inhabitants of the United Kingdom from a bloody civil war [he wrote], our colonial statesmen must acquire new lands for settling the surplus population of this country, to provide new markets for the goods produced in the factories and mines. The Empire, as I have always said, is a bread and butter question. If you want to avoid civil war, you must become imperialists.

With greater moderation, Leopold II of Belgium had proclaimed a decade earlier in defence of his African schemes that

Our cities are gorged with the products of the most diverse industries; nowhere will they find so great a market to absorb them. The most intelligent of our youth demands wider horizons on which to expand their abounding energy. Our working population will desire from the virgin regions of Africa new sources of prosperity and render more in exchange.[18]

At a rather different level of analysis the English liberal J. A. Hobson, in his very influential *Imperialism* (1902), argued that the forcible imposition of European rule upon so much of the non-European world was the result, not so much of capitalism itself, as of imperfections in the form which it had assumed by the later nineteenth century in the advanced states of western Europe. In particular, he thought, the growth of industry and development of financial mechanisms had meant the piling up of a disproportionate share of the national wealth in the hands of relatively few people and gross inequality in its distribution. The poverty of the mass of the population meant it was unable to consume enough of the product of modern industry to make its continued expansion profitable. In Britain, France and Germany (though Hobson's argument was essentially concerned with Britain) there was therefore an inescapable tendency for the rate of profit on domestic investment to decline. The result was that in all the great industrialized states of western Europe there was a vast amount of surplus capital seeking profitable outlets; since these could not be found at home its owners tended to invest in mines, plantations or other enterprises in Africa and Asia, and then to call on their governments to protect these investments by conquering and administering the territories concerned.

This type of argument was not new. The classical economists of the first half of the nineteenth century had believed in a natural tendency of profits to fall; and as early as 1839–41 the English writer Herman Merivale had put forward in very general terms, in a series of lectures given at Oxford, ideas somewhat similar to those of Hobson. Wakefield, in his *Art of Colonization* (1849), had argued that Britain's economic difficulties in the 1830s stemmed largely from a glut of capital seeking investment at home. By 1850 David Livingstone, the greatest of the missionary-explorers who did so much to make south-central Africa known to Europe, had decided that capital exports were likely to play a great role in the future growth of the British empire. Moreover Hobson (who was always interested much more in Britain's domestic social and economic problems than in overseas expansion for its own sake) considerably modified many of his contentions in later writings. Nevertheless echoes of his book have been audible down to our own day; and many of its arguments lent force to the Marxist analysis of the growth of empires which was now attracting attention in continental Europe.

Marx himself always regarded colonial expansion as an essentially pre-capitalist phenomenon and showed little interest in it. His whole outlook was dominated by Europe and European conditions and many of his comments on non-European societies, for example the concept of a distinctive 'Asiatic mode of production' put forward in the preface to his *Contribution to the Critique of Political Economy* (1859), do not fit easily into his thought in general. Certainly his contempt for Indian society, 'undignified, stagnatory and vegetative', and for that of China, 'that living fossil', made him willing to see the growth of European empires as often a movement of the greatest progressive significance.[19] A developed Marxist theory of imperialism began to emerge only in the early years of the twentieth century in the works of the Austrian writers Bauer and Hilferding, while in particular the argument that imperial expansion was inevitable, an inescapable result of the workings of capitalism, was given its most dogmatic form in the *Akkumulation des Kapitals* of the German Marxist

Rosa Luxemburg. None of these owed much to Hobson: but Lenin's *Imperialism, the Highest Stage of Capitalism* (1916), which is still by far the most widely read statement of the Marxist standpoint, was deeply indebted to him.[20]

There is no doubt that some parts of the Hobson–Lenin thesis have a shadowy relationship to the truth. British expansion during the later nineteenth and early twentieth centuries was certainly accompanied by a great growth in capital exports. In the period 1875–1914 total British domestic capital increased by about 80 per cent (from roughly £5,000 million to over £9,000 million) while British investment abroad grew during the same years at well over three times this rate.[21] Clearly investment overseas did in some ways stimulate prosperity in Britain during this period, particularly since much of the money it earned was spent on British goods (notably railway equipment) and on freight charges paid to British shipowners.[22]

Yet it is doubtful whether any writer other than a convinced Marxist would today uphold a theory of late nineteenth-century colonial expansion which explained it solely or even mainly in terms of economic factors. The insuperable weakness of the Hobson thesis, or of any which makes economic forces the mainspring of the movement, is simply that it does not fit the facts. No European government during this period, not even that of Britain, was the tool of a class of financiers and merchants as economic explanations of the growth of empires imply. The ease with which Hobson assumed, completely without evidence, the primacy of financial interests in the making of government policies is very striking.

'Does anyone seriously suppose', he wrote, 'that a great war could be undertaken by any European State, or a great State loan subscribed, if the house of Rothschild and its connections were to set their face against it?'[23] Twelve years later events gave a conclusive answer to this question, for in the final crisis of 1914 the London Rothschilds at least struggled vainly to avert an Anglo-German conflict.[24] When forced to choose, governments much more often than not subordinated possible economic advantage to political and diplomatic necessities. An excellent specific example, chosen almost at random from many others, is the systematic discouragement from the 1870s onwards by the British colonial office, for political reasons, of the grant of far-reaching monopoly concessions by the sultan of Johore to British capitalists.[25] Another and more important one is the way in which in 1889 Bismarck, in the interests of improving relations with Britain, disavowed the efforts of the German adventurer Karl Peters to extend German territory in east Africa and create a 'German India' there; indeed for that matter the chancellor had disliked Peters' first expedition to the area in 1884.

Business was the servant of diplomacy (the great French loans to Russia in 1906–14 are an obvious case in point) rather than its master. Moreover the enormous amounts of capital which Britain invested abroad during the later nineteenth century went overwhelmingly, not to the newly acquired African colonies, or even to the sphere of influence which she was acquiring in China, but to the great temperate raw-material and food-producing areas of the world – to the United States, Canada, the Argentine, South Africa and Australasia. By 1911, according to the best contemporary calculation, there was about £688 million of British money invested in the United States and £587 million in Latin America, while Canada, Australasia, India and Ceylon, and South Africa each accounted for between £350 and £400 million. By comparison only £29 million was invested in the British colonies in West Africa, only £22 million in the Straits Settlements and the Malay States, and only about £33 million in all the other overseas colonies of Britain combined.[26] It must be remembered, also, that in the Americas or in the colonies with extensive white settlement European investors could not force themselves on unwilling borrowers. On the contrary Americans, Australians, Argentinians and Canadians needed to borrow more than Europeans needed to lend to them, and therefore tended often to seek out and attract foreign capitalists. The initiative in the investment process, in other words, came very frequently from outside Europe, from the borrower rather than the lender. These facts are not easy to square with the current of thought, or rather the set of assumptions, which Hobson and Lenin represent.

Also some at least of the acquisitions made by Britain from the 1870s onwards – British New Guinea is the extreme example – were economically worthless. They offered few immediate opportunities for British investment and only very scanty ones in any foreseeable future. This does not in itself destroy Hobson's argument, for quite a small investment in some unimportant tropical area could conceivably, if the investors had political influence and the ear of the government, generate military and political action to protect it. Moreover it is notoriously difficult to estimate at all accurately the value of any colony to the metropolitan power concerned; one completely unprofitable in itself may be well worth holding as part of a complex of imperial possessions which is lucrative as a whole.[27] But it is clear that none of the enormous areas which Britain acquired in Africa and elsewhere during the later nineteenth century were economically necessary to her in any normal sense of that phrase. None of them, with the partial exception of the Boer republics of the Transvaal and the Orange Free State, annexed in 1902 at the end of the Boer war, could compete with the United States or Britain's old colonies of settlement as sources of food and raw materials, or as markets. None of them, again with the notable exception of the gold-producing South African republics, could provide important opportunities for profitable investment. The British East Africa Company collapsed in 1895, the Royal Niger Company in 1899. The British South Africa Company, the most important of Cecil Rhodes' creations, paid not a single dividend during the whole period of its responsibility for the administration of Rhodesia. To argue that capitalism in Britain needed for its functioning political and military control of Nigeria, or Uganda, or Rhodesia, or Upper Burma, or even the Transvaal, is nonsense. In 1890 the *Economist* dismissed the scramble for African territory as 'a quarrel of tenth-rate magnitude over interests of scarcely any national importance'. There is no real evidence that British (or for that matter French) merchants and traders were in favour of a great growth of European political control in Africa or even in many parts of Asia; and it should be remembered that the *Kolonialverein* found its supporters mainly in south and west Germany and aroused little response in the great trading cities of Hamburg and Bremen.[28] Moreover the sequence of events postulated by Hobson was often reversed in practice. Far from investment leading to annexation it was often annexation and the beginnings of development which followed, particularly in railway-building, which made it for the first time sensible to sink money in the area concerned. Thus really large-scale investment in what is now Zambia began to be possible only with the exploitation of the great copper deposits there in 1926; but this was the result (in this case a surprisingly tardy one) of the establishment at considerable expense to the British government of railway links with the outside world.

All this certainly does not mean that there were no economic forces behind British imperial expansion. The country's need for raw materials which only non-European sources could supply grew very rapidly in the generation before 1914. By the outbreak of war it was importing minerals such as tin, copper and even iron ore in a way which had not been necessary until late in the nineteenth century. More striking and potentially threatening still was its complete dependence on the world outside Europe for supplies of essential new primary products such as rubber and above all petroleum (of which it already imported 484 million gallons in 1913). Moreover the very limited value of the new colonial markets, especially in Africa, which seems so obvious now, was much less obvious in the 1880s or 1890s, when accurate information about their potentialities was hard to come by. The slowing of British economic growth in the 1870s and 1880s began to arouse for the first time fears that Britain might in the foreseeable future be overtaken not merely by the United States but by Germany; this did something to stimulate a search for new economic opportunities overseas. More important, the increasing protectionism of the great European powers, and of the United States, raised the spectre of Britain's progressive exclusion from many of her most valuable existing markets and again stressed the apparent need to develop new ones. 'Everywhere', lamented Lord Salisbury in 1895, 'we see the advance of commerce checked by the enormous growth which the doctrines of Protection are obtaining. We see it with our three great commercial rivals France, Germany and America. The doctrines of protection are stronger and stronger and operate to the exclusion of British commerce wherever their power extends.'[29] Moreover Britain had for long depended far more than any continental European country on trade with the world outside Europe and with North America. As early as 1860 49 per cent of her exports went there, and by 1913 53 per cent. Any threat to this trade from the imperial activities of the other great powers was therefore certain to arouse alarm in London. From the mid-1880s onwards successive British governments therefore became more willing than in the past to apply political pressure in the Ottoman empire, Persia, the Far East or Latin America to safeguard British financial and trading interests there when they seemed threatened by the 'unfair' competition of foreigners supported by their governments.[30] But these activities were essentially defensive, like British foreign policy in general. They aimed not at expanding British territory but at safeguarding Britain's existing world position and protecting her merchants, bankers and to a lesser extent industrialists in an international environment increasingly hostile to them.

There is also no simple economic explanation of the growth of the French and German empires. French foreign investment from the 1870s onwards was very considerable indeed. But it went mainly to the Near East and later to Russia (where just over a quarter of it was concentrated by 1914), with considerable amounts to Latin America. The amount of French money sunk in Africa, the greatest area of European territorial expansion from the 1870s onwards, was always small by comparison; and it is notable that much of it went to parts of the continent which were not politically under French control. In 1906 the colonial ministry estimated that about 1,500 million francs were invested in the French colonies. At the same time, however, there were about 3,000 million francs invested by Frenchmen in parts of Africa controlled by other powers (particularly in Egypt, where up until 1914 French investment continued to be considerably larger than British, and indeed slightly larger than that of all the other European states combined). Here again it is difficult to see any obvious correlation between the investment of money and a subsequent march of empire. What raw materials her colonies produced were not essential to France, for they could all be obtained without the expense and responsibility of political and military control; while as markets the profitability of her colonies was limited, since her industry simply was not developed enough to meet all their needs. Though the share of her overseas possessions in France's external trade rose from 5.7 per cent in 1882–86 to 10.2 per cent in 1909–13, in the early twentieth century they consistently traded more with foreign states than with the mother country.[31] In the French empire, as in the British, trade and investment followed the flag rather than vice versa. Even in Tunis, a much more developed, accessible and potentially profitable area than most of tropical Africa, it was not until several years after the proclamation of the French protectorate that French capital began to be invested on a significant scale. Moreover right up until to 1914 the French colonies were exploited in a purely traditional way, essentially as they had been for generations past. Old-style trading companies, not banks or new-style financial monopolies, were the agents of exploitation. There were financial interests involved in the growth of the French empire: but they were not 'finance capital' of a Leninist kind.[32]

The German empire fits little better into the framework of any theory which makes economic pressures or necessities the mainspring of imperial growth. It has been argued that the acquisition of colonies was to Bismarck largely a means of providing a safety-valve for the social discontents generated in Germany by a period of very rapid and rather uneven economic growth.[33] In his eyes, the argument runs, enlarged markets overseas might help to promote social stability and preserve the traditional social hierarchy at home, as well as assuaging the political tensions within Germany which had been merely papered over in 1871. But it should be noted that even if the argument is correct, it hardly squares with the Hobson–Lenin thesis, for it elevates the policies of one man to the controlling position with which that thesis endows impersonal economic forces. Certainly the German colonial empire, in so far as any rational economic calculation underlay it, was much more a guarantee for the future than a response to any immediate needs. Much of it was acquired in a few months in 1884–85, at a time when the industrial and financial development of Germany, though going ahead very rapidly, was far from having reached its peak.

Though German industry was always much more controlled than that of Britain by banks and financial institutions, the formation of the great cartels which restricted or eliminated competition in some of its most important branches, a development to which Lenin attached great significance as a sign of the dominance of 'finance capital', reached its height only after 1900. The colonies were acquired, in other words, at a time when there were still plenty of opportunities to invest money profitably in Germany herself and no need to search for much more doubtful ones in Africa or New Guinea. Indeed it proved almost impossible to persuade Germans to put money into their new possessions on any substantial scale. All the chartered companies through which Bismarck and his successors tried for a good many years to administer most of the empire had great difficulty in raising capital. That which ruled German east Africa paid no dividends whatever until after it had abandoned its sovereign rights in 1891 and begun to receive an annual government subsidy. By 1895 the New Guinea Company was so deeply in difficulties that it too had to appeal to the government for help. Nor had ordinary commercial undertakings much better luck. The South West Africa Company, formed in 1892 to exploit the minerals of Damaraland, raised its capital of 20 million marks in Britain; and several other companies active in south west Africa were under foreign influence. The South Cameroons Company, which attempted to develop a trade in rubber, was dominated by Belgian capital, while a very large share of the trade of all the German colonies remained in the hands of British firms.[34] As late as 1914 there were only about 416 million marks of German capital invested in the empire, as against seven or eight times as much in Latin America; and the colonies accounted for only 0.5 per cent of the total value of German foreign trade. That any significant proportion of German industrialists or bankers ever desired to possess so valueless a collection of territories for rational economic reasons is hard to believe.

Two final arguments can be brought against simple monocausal economic explanations of 'imperialism'. If it is regarded as the result of economic maturity, of a high degree of industrialization and the existence of a surplus of capital seeking profitable employment, how can the growth of the Russian and Italian empires (and to a lesser extent that of Portugal) be fitted into this framework? Both Russia and Italy were during the later nineteenth century backward countries by the standards of western Europe. In spite of the remarkable development of industry in Russia from the 1890s onwards neither was highly industrialized, as Britain and Germany were, even in 1914. Neither could export capital on a significant scale; on the contrary both imported it in large quantities. In Russia particularly the industrial boom of the 1890s was financed largely by imported capital and some industries, notably oil, were dominated by foreign money. Yet none of this prevented both Russia and Italy having imperial ambitions of essentially the same kind as those of Britain, France and Germany, ambitions which, in Russia's case, were of world importance. The most successful and lasting territorial expansion achieved by her during the second half of the nineteenth century, that in central Asia, was the result of a complex of motives. Of these one, and an important one, the desire to develop Turkestan as a producer of cotton for the Russian textile industry, was economic. But the others – the desire for a secure frontier and an end to the slave-raiding and other provocations offered by Khiva and Bukhara;

fear of a growth of British influence in the area and hopes of threatening British power in India by possession of it; the desire of officers and officials on the spot for action and personal prestige – clearly were not. Certainly central Asia was not regarded as an essential or even very important field for Russian investment. Nor was Asia in general, indeed, ever seen as very important in the overall picture of Russian trade: in 1913 Persia, her most important Asiatic market, accounted for only three per cent of the Russian empire's exports. Nor did her inability to export capital prevent Portugal playing an important role in the partition of Africa; while Italian adventures there from 1884 onwards were undertaken by the statesmen mainly concerned, Depretis and Crispi, largely to distract attention from difficulties within Italy and a generally depressing domestic position. No simple, schematic, material explanation will account for the fact that more or less simultaneously a number of states with widely differing social and economic structures quite suddenly developed remarkably similar expansionist tendencies.

It has also been powerfully argued that capitalism, even a capitalism marked by protective tariffs and cartels as much of that of Europe was by the early years of the twentieth century, is fundamentally a form of economic organization which strengthens international peace and co-operation. The warlike and conquering impulses which played a large part in the construction of great overseas empires are therefore, it is contended, essentially foreign to it. 'A purely capitalist world', according to the greatest proponent of this line of thought, 'can offer no fertile field to imperialist impulses.'[35] Imperial expansion is therefore not the result of the needs and pressures of capitalists. It springs rather from the surviving influence of pre-capitalist social groups and political forces – military men, hereditary aristocracies and autocratic governments – and from the irrational and anti-capitalist prejudices and emotions associated with them. 'Imperialism . . . is atavistic in character . . . In other words, it is an element that stems from the living conditions, not of the present, but of the past.'[36] This is an incomplete view of the problems involved, and one based too exclusively on the experience of Germany, where the army and to a lesser extent the ruler retained great prestige throughout this period. But it is a highly suggestive and original view and one which opens wide and important perspectives on this enormously complex set of phenomena.

It is valuable above all because it emphasizes the great truth that deeply rooted psychological and emotional factors are at least as important as any material ones in explaining the great burst of European expansion which began in the 1870s. The crucial weakness of Hobson and his fellow-radicals such as H. N. Brailsford, as well as of the Marxists, was their belief that men and governments were dominated by rational (by which they meant material) considerations. To them imperial expansion must serve, or at least be thought to serve, the rational, material interest at least of ruling groups if not of nations as a whole. With even greater naïveté, they assumed that men can make accurate calculations and forecasts of what will serve their selfish interests. Patriotism, national or racial pride, occupy a relatively small part of the picture they draw.[37] This view was quite unrealistic. Even before the 1870s national rivalries had played a direct role in European imperial expansion and there had been cases of territory being seized to keep it out of the hands of a rival power and not for any intrinsic value of its own. Muraviev's activities in the Far East in the 1850s, for example, had been inspired in large part by fear of British control of the coastline of north-east Asia and its possible consequences for Russia.

From the 1870s onwards factors of this kind became more important. Intensified national feeling was now breeding more bitter rivalries, more active envy, more acute fears, between nations. The relative stability of the position in Europe and the difficulty of altering the status quo there meant that more and more during the generation after 1870 antagonisms and ambitions unable to find free expression on the continent were deflected outside it. Expansion in Indo-China, in Senegal, or across the Sahara can be seen as a substitute for the recovery of Alsace-Lorraine which the structure of international relations and her own relative weakness denied France, at least for the time being. The ambitions which Italy could not realize in the Trentino or along the Dalmatian coast could find some expression, though this was very much a second-best, in Eritrea, Ethiopia or Tripoli; and the partial thwarting of Russian hopes in the Near East in 1878 may have given impetus to the growth of her power in central Asia and the Far East. From the early or middle 1880s 'imperialism may be seen as the extension into the periphery of the political struggle in Europe'.[38] Once the process of colonial expansion had clearly begun, particularly in Africa with the British occupation of Egypt in 1882, it became increasingly easy for each government to fear that its rivals might steal a march on it and obtain more than their share of territory and future economic opportunities. And this fear was little less even if the territory in question were largely valueless and the opportunities it offered hardly worth having. There was thus a strong temptation to forestall any possible action by a rival power, to seize in the hope that they might some day and in some way be valuable colonies which were only too clearly a burden in the present. 'Obsessed by their own rivalries, none of the European powers was prepared to stand aside while others extended their territories, or to withdraw and leave a void into which a potential enemy might move.'[39] A striking and little-known example of these feelings is the unsuccessful efforts of the Habsburg government in 1913-14 to lay the foundations of a colony which might have incorporated much of the southern coast of Anatolia. This curious ambition was inspired entirely by considerations of prestige; it was an emotional reaction against a situation in which the Habsburg empire was the only major European power with no colonial possessions of its own, not a serious attempt to gain any material advantage.[40] In such a climate of feeling the argument that a new acquisition would not pay in an economic sense went unheeded. Justified or not, it was beside the point. Moreover the national pride which demanded the acquisition of new colonies forbade *a fortiori* the loss of old ones. The best evidence of this is the sense of national humiliation and crisis aroused in Spain by the surrender in 1898, after defeat by the United States, of Cuba and the Philippines, neither of which was of great economic value.

This competitive impulse was not confined to governments and ruling groups. For short periods at least it could affect large parts of the population in all the great states of western Europe. Successful military commanders in colonial campaigns could become national heroes, as Generals Chernaiev and Skobelev did to the Panslavs of Russia in the 1870s and 1880s because of their share in the conquest of central Asia, or as Roberts and Kitchener did in Britain. One cynical Russian minister, reacting to the popular enthusiasm inspired by the capture of Tashkent in 1865, remarked that there was 'something erotic in everything that happens on the distant frontiers of the empire'. The enthusiasm with which the ordinary man almost everywhere rushed to the colours in 1914 showed unmistakably how deeply nationalism was now engrained in him; and a popular 'social imperialism' was one of the major offshoots of this from the 1880s onwards. Even Hobson did not demand the abandonment by the European powers of their colonies; he urged merely that in their administration the interests of the natives should be given absolute priority. Jaurès, the greatest French socialist of the period, admitted that France had a civilizing and pacifying mission in Morocco which justified her presence there. The Amsterdam congress of the Second International in 1904 envisaged the emancipation of European colonies, but only as a long-term, not an immediate, objective. That in Stuttgart three years later, which condemned all colonial expansion, did so only by a narrow majority which was made possible by the votes of delegates from small states without colonies.

But the attachment of the ordinary man to the idea of overseas empire was always essentially shallow. He was seldom willing to make great personal sacrifices for it as he was for the defence of his homeland. Imperial expansion was always the work of a political, economic and often intellectual élite, never a true mass movement. In Britain active popular support for the growth of empire was probably greater than anywhere else in Europe. Lord Curzon, one of the supreme embodiments of the idea of imperial power, could claim with some justification in 1898, when feeling of this kind was at its peak, that imperial expansion 'is becoming every day less and less the creed of a party and more and more the faith of a nation'.[41] Two years later a former high official of the government of India pointed out that 'the main difference is that whereas formerly we did [sic] our Imperialism quietly, so that people hardly knew what they were about, we now proclaim it upon the house-tops'.[42] Distorted echoes of Darwinian ideas; popular literature which stressed imperial themes and responsibilities; a growing realization of Britain's economic vulnerability as her industrial leadership was eroded by German and American progress; all contributed to a widespread belief in the empire as a pledge of continuing greatness and a vast contribution to the progress of mankind.

Yet it is very questionable whether imperial pride really dominated the thinking of more than a minority, even in Britain, except for a few years from the middle 1890s onwards. Except in this short period expansion overseas was gratifying to national self-esteem, very acceptable so long as it did not cost much money or involve serious international difficulties, but essentially a luxury, a 'political arabesque'. This attitude can be seen in the readiness of the government, on a number of occasions, to sacrifice Britain's colonial ambitions to the needs of the white dominions which were so much more important to her than anything she could hope to gain in tropical Africa or the islands of the Pacific. Thus in 1899 it agreed, under pressure from Australia, to the fortification of Pago-Pago in Samoa by the United States; and in 1904 Britain abandoned territorial demands in west Africa in order to ease the position of Newfoundland in the Anglo-French negotiations of that year. Even where the great colonies of settlement, Canada, Australia, South Africa and New Zealand were concerned, imperial pride was often tempered by resentment of their selfishness and their excessive demands on the mother country over such things as defence costs. So stout a patriot as Sir John Fisher, First Sea Lord, complained that 'the colonies one and all grab all they possibly can out of us and give nothing back. They are all alike.'

Elsewhere in Europe imperial expansion never achieved even the temporary control of public opinion which it gained in Britain. Feeling in France in favour of a great overseas empire was often vocal. It can be seen in the formation of a series of pressure-groups which sometimes made serious studies of the problems involved in colonial expansion – the *Comité de l'Afrique française* which was formed in protest against the Anglo-French agreement of 1890 on west Africa; the *Union coloniale française* set up in 1893; the *Comité de l'Asie française* formed in 1901 to ensure that France took advantage of the apparently imminent partition of the Chinese empire; on a different level the *Ligue coloniale de la jeunesse* which came into existence in 1894. But there was never a colonial party, in any strict and organized sense, in France. Almost fifty colonial societies functioned, some very briefly, in the quarter-century before the First World War. But in 1914 those of them still in existence had a total membership of probably less than 5,000. The Fashoda crisis of 1898 aroused real passions in France; but this was because of national rivalry with Britain, not because many Frenchmen really wanted a huge and valueless colony in the Sudan. The Moroccan crises of 1905–6 and 1911 aroused almost equally strong feelings; but it was the conflict with Germany, not the acquisition of Morocco as such, which focused French emotions.[43] No conceivable colonial gain could compete in appeal to public or governmental opinion with the recovery of Alsace-Lorraine; and during the Boer war Theophile Delcassé, perhaps the greatest foreign minister of the Third Republic, played with the idea of offering Germany all the French possessions in Indo-China in exchange for the lost provinces.

In Belgium the resources of the huge *Domaine de la Couronne*, which had been created by Leopold II and covered perhaps a sixth of the whole area of the Congo Free State, were used in part for the building of parks, monuments and bathing-places. The country thus benefited from the colonial adventures of its ruler in a more visible and immediate way than most other parts of western Europe did from their possessions overseas. Yet in spite of this there was no real public interest in the Congo or in Leopold's very real though brutal achievements there: in 1908 it was only with reluctance that the government allowed the Free State to become a Belgian colony.

In Germany fairly widespread popular ambitions, which gave an undoubtedly colonialist tinge to public opinion, helped to make possible the acquisition of an empire in 1884–85 and perhaps to some extent forced Bismarck to acquire one. 'The immediate cause of the colonialist movement was not profit, or population, or living standards. It was the acquisition of Germany's place in the sun through the efforts of a German people united by a dynamic principle.'[44] Yet here also it was impossible to sustain public feeling permanently at a high level; and the gross misgovernment to which most of the German colonies were subjected for more than two decades after their annexation did a good deal to discredit the idea of colonial expansion with considerable sections of German opinion.

Nevertheless, even when all these reservations have been made, it remains true that the generation or more before 1914 witnessed an unprecedented growth of public attention in western Europe to imperial issues and the rise of empires. It might be difficult or impossible to persuade the ordinary man to take a sustained interest in colonial questions or to invest in distant and doubtfully remunerative territories. It was relatively easy to make him believe that national greatness depended on the possession of a colonial empire, and to rouse in him powerful emotions when that empire or its expansion seemed to be threatened by a rival.

The growth of empires was also nourished by another and higher current of feeling. This was the belief that the advance of European power meant progress, self-realization, in the long run at least the possibility of freedom, for the peoples subjected to European rule. This faith in the right and duty of the white man to civilize the world, and if necessary to override in doing so the resistance of peoples too barbaric and societies too stagnant to understand the greatness of the benefits they were being offered, was a progressive force and one with noble aspects. It allowed the idea of empire to rise even to the level of 'an unformulated philosophy of life and politics'.[45] Underlying it were a deep sense of responsibility and a very real humanitarianism. Where Europe penetrated, she brought, in spite of frequent mistakes and not a few serious crimes, essential progress. The ending of slavery as a legal status; a tendency, however slight, for the position of women to improve; efforts to suppress at least the more dangerous forms of witchcraft – all these are obvious illustrations of this. Nationalism was the greatest driving force behind expansion overseas. But humanitarianism, a sense of responsibility and a willingness to embark on great constructive tasks in the more backward parts of the world, were also important. It is certainly significant that many of the greatest empire-builders were also supporters of reform and improvement, at least of a paternalist kind, at home. Thus Muraviev worked for the emancipation of the serfs in Russia and Lord Milner, one of the authors of the Boer war and the creator of the Union of South Africa, had as a young man helped to found Toynbee Hall, the Oxford University settlement in London's East End. Similarly Hubert Lyautey, the chief creator of French rule in Morocco, had as a young man made a remarkable statement of social idealism in his *Du rôle social de l'officier* (1891), while in Germany Friedrich Naumann, founder in 1896 of the *Nationalsozial Verein*, did much to link the ideas of social reform and imperial expansion and went so far as to argue that 'by raising the physical, mental and moral standards of the German worker, the democratic movement is making a direct contribution to the German policy of expansion'.[46]

Of the soldiers and officials who created and expanded European empires during this period few seriously doubted the moral justification of what they were doing. Their consciences were clear, their moral earnestness sincere, their self-confidence unbounded and their successes correspondingly great. Since they clearly thought well of themselves, those they ruled often thought well of them also. Though their sense of superiority to their subjects rested, in the last analysis, on the superior material strength of Europe as compared with the rest of the world, it was not, at least consciously, entirely a matter of material power. Underlying it was also a profound feeling of moral superiority, based ultimately perhaps on the still widespread belief in the truth of the Christian revelation and the falsity of all other religions; and the truth or otherwise of this belief made no difference to its practical importance. It is almost certainly not a coincidence that the greatest British empire-builders in tropical Africa, Sir Harry Johnston and Frederick Lugard (later Lord Lugard) both came from devoutly Christian homes: Lugard's mother had been a missionary and his father was an army chaplain in India. One very genuine side of empire-building is revealed in Johnston's declaration to the Basoga tribe in Uganda in 1900: 'We were like you long years ago, going about naked, with our war paint on, but when we learnt Christianity from the Romans, we changed and became great. We want you to learn Christianity and follow in our steps and you too will be great.'[47]

To the best imperial administrators the position in Africa and most of Asia seemed essentially simple. Their peoples desperately needed just and efficient rule. This Europeans alone could provide; and it was their duty to provide it. Justice and efficiency, tempered with mercy, were the ideals which they at least intermittently served. They had not yet been persuaded to believe that democracy had any place in a political structure sustained in the last analysis by power. It could even be argued that the possession of an empire and the fulfilment of the obligations this implied was a moral benefit to a European people, safeguarding it against deterioration by forcing on it efforts, sacrifices and decisions which it would not otherwise have had to make. 'As for the priceless asset of national character,' said Lord Curzon, a supreme example of this attitude, in 1907, 'without a world to conquer or a duty to perform, it would rot to atrophy and inanition. . . . In Empire we have found not merely the key to glory and wealth but the call to duty and the means of service to mankind. Let us no more forswear Empire than we would abjure our own souls.' And he went on, significantly, to warn that 'commercialism and materialism are dangers against which the Imperialist requires to be specially upon his guard'.[48] Some years earlier, soon after his arrival in India as viceroy, he had made the point even more forcibly in a private letter.

No one is an Englishman who has not been to India. It is a vast mystery, a prodigious experiment, a genuine glory. But I do not honestly think that the romance is what appeals to me most. It is all duty. I hate to see a British official not slaving his heart out: a department slack or careless: society frivolous or rotten: Tommy Atkins coarse and contemptuous: the British ideal shattered or impaired.[49]

This is undoubtedly an ideal of service. It is also an ideal of power; and it was the achievement of power which generated the ideal of using that power for constructive and morally right purposes. The best of all French examples of this stress on the moral improvement to be derived from the heroism and self-sacrifice needed in the creation of a colonial empire is the account of duty and fulfilment in north Africa to be found in Ernest Psichari's *Terres de soleil et de sommeil* (1908); and Psichari's conversion to catholicism in 1913, after a long and agonizing personal crisis, illustrates once more the religious impulses which underlay the finest aspects of Europe's expansion in this period. The romanticism, often little changed from its early nineteenth-century form, which is one element in such writing, is also unmistakable.

Finally the personal factors which underlay the accelerated growth of European power in the world from the 1870s onwards should be emphasized. It was a process which owed much to a relatively small number of outstanding individuals. In Africa particularly, where communications remained primitive until far into the twentieth century, the 'man on the spot' for long retained much of the importance which he was now tending to lose in Asia. In the new African empires adventurers such as Rhodes, Lüderitz and Peters, administrators such as Johnston, Lugard and Lyautey, were able to exert deep and lasting influence. No explanation of the events of this period can be complete unless it allows for what one writer has called 'the individual, the maladjusted European individual who, biding his time and place, made his mark on the partition of Africa'. Not all the Europeans who played leading roles in the conquest and partition of Africa were maladjusted; but few of them, had they stayed at home, could have made for themselves careers at all comparable in scope and importance with those they forged overseas. To small but very important groups of energetic individuals, imperial expansion offered an opportunity, a freedom to exercise initiative, to shoulder great responsibilities and win great rewards (in prestige and individual distinction rather than in material terms) which would have been otherwise unattainable. Enterprising young officers and administrators often found in the colonies a refreshing freedom from the conformity and promotion by seniority of Europe, an opportunity to break with routine and lead a freer and more satisfying existence.[50] A colony which added nothing to the strength of the country which owned it might thus provide very attractive opportunities and deep satisfactions for its creators. This fact is certainly more relevant to the history of European expansion than the conventional wisdom on the subject allows.

By the early years of the twentieth century the explosion of energy which had carried European dominance across the jungles and savannahs of Africa, into the steppe of central Asia and to the decaying states of

Persia, China and the Ottoman empire, had begun to exhaust itself. Slowly Europe was losing her world leadership, at least in its military and economic forms. After 1905, the affairs of one of the great areas of international tension, the Far East, were largely controlled by two non-European powers – Japan and the United States. Russia, though still deeply interested in Manchuria and Mongolia, had stabilized the position there by an agreement with Japan in 1907. This, coupled with the convention with Britain signed in the same year, meant that she had in effect abandoned for the time being overt expansion in Asia in order to free her hands for action in Europe.[51] Already, moreover, Great Britain had been forced to conciliate her new potential rivals in the Pacific: the United States by the Hay–Pauncefote treaty of 1901 and Japan by an alliance made in 1902. By 1909 it was already beginning to be realized that Britain's Far Eastern possessions were safe only so long as this alliance lasted.[52]

The shift in the world balance of power (or more accurately the emergence for the first time of something like a true world balance of power) can be seen in a different way in the growing independence of the British dominions. Canada sent a minister of her own to Tokyo in 1907, the first time one of them had ever done such a thing, and began to create her own navy in 1909. Australia set up her own Department of External Affairs in 1901 (though it was said ten years later to be incapable of translating an ordinary letter from French into English). The efforts of the Round Table movement from 1909–10 onwards to promote some form of closer and more institutionalized unity between Britain and her dominions would have been powerless to halt this development even had they not been cut short by the war of 1914. Indeed after the Imperial Conference of 1907 the word 'commonwealth' began to replace 'empire' in British usage, a significant sign of the growing emphasis on dominion independence. On the economic level, the threat to Europe's leadership was a good deal more obvious than on the political one. Even the beginnings of a threat to her position as the world's banker can be discerned. In 1899 an important foreign loan (in this case to Mexico) was floated for the first time in the United States; and by 1914 American investment in European industry, though still very small by comparison with the enormous outflow of capital from Europe to the Americas, was noticeably increasing. The growing nationalism which was now showing itself in so much of Asia[53] was in most cases still very undeveloped; and in black Africa hardly anything that could be called national feeling was visible in 1914. Nevertheless it was already clear to many observers that in the realm of ideology also the dominance of Europe would henceforth be under increasingly heavy fire.

Above all the European powers themselves were more and more preoccupied from the early years of the twentieth century onwards with purely or mainly European problems. The development of new groupings as a result of the Anglo-French and Anglo-Russian agreements of 1904 and 1907; the competitive growth of armaments and the very real danger of war in 1908–9; the collapse of the Ottoman empire in the Balkans in 1912 and its results – these far more than affairs in Africa, Persia or the Far East preoccupied the statesmen of Europe in the decade before 1914. The few imperial problems of these years which did assume real importance in European politics, those of Morocco and the Baghdad railway, had their origins in areas close to Europe and were in many ways integral parts of the political rivalries of the continent rather than true colonial issues. The sudden burst of expansionism seen during the later nineteenth century was thus, considering its enormous geographical scope, remarkably concentrated in time. Taking shape by the 1870s, well developed by the middle 1880s and at its height by the middle 1890s, it was dying away after about 1905.

THE RESULTS OF EXPANSION

Yet the significance for the world of this expansionism is difficult to exaggerate, especially when it is remembered that it followed the growth of the British, Russian and to a lesser extent French empires which took place during the early and middle decades of the nineteenth century. These two processes combined meant that the world was becoming more European, increasingly an outgrowth of Europe. More and more it was becoming a unity, politically, economically, intellectually; and its unity stemmed from Europe. Great areas of it had been settled by Europeans. However much the United States and to a lesser extent the British dominions might stress their distinctiveness and their peculiar excellences, nothing could conceal the fact that they were all, in essence, outgrowths of north-western Europe. More and more the world was bound together physically, by railways and telegraphs built by Europeans, by cables laid down by Europeans, by steamships designed and commanded by Europeans. The capital which made possible so much economic development in the rest of the world came largely from Europe; banks, stock exchanges and modern industry were European inventions. Moreover a quite moderate amount of European investment could, by the encouragement it gave to economic and social change and its generally innovating effect, revolutionize the whole life of great parts of the world. African tribes, Muslim obscurantists in central Asia, headhunters in Borneo, the Stone Age aborigines of New Guinea, were all to varying extents now exposed to at least some aspects of modern civilization. Though native traditions and peculiarities were almost ineradicable in the countryside, towns throughout the world were slowly tending more and more to resemble each other, to approximate to a norm which was European in origin. Thus the novelist Thackeray, as early as 1844, found Alexandria 'scarcely Eastern at all'; while one of the visitors to Port Said in 1869 for the opening of the Suez canal thought the newly founded city 'like a San Francisco in miniature', and a traveller in Siberia in 1902 found Irkutsk 'like a restless, bustling, Western American town near the region of gold diggings'.[54] Everywhere Europeans spread the idea, or rather the faith, upon which, more than on any other, modern life is founded – the belief that change for the better through man's mastery of his physical environment is always possible. 'Europe today', wrote a commentator in 1919, 'is no more than a portion of the "European world". The earth, almost in its entirety, is European in outlook, spirit and accomplishment.'[55] The extent to which the world had been Europeanized and thus unified by 1914 can certainly be exaggerated. A system of true world politics was then still only in embryo. There was still only one power, Great Britain, with important interests in every continent; and the war which broke out in that year and which is dignified by the title of the First World War was for most of its duration merely a great European struggle. But during the previous half-century the economic and intellectual unification of the world had gone ahead at an unprecedented rate, even if the political results of this process were rather slow to show themselves.

The expansion of Europe during the nineteenth and early twentieth centuries is difficult to analyse and explain convincingly, and even to describe concisely and accurately, chiefly because it was unplanned and chaotic. The attitudes to their colonies of the great powers, and the policies they pursued there, differed widely because of the differences in their own histories, traditions and systems of values. Thus France, though with some doubts, pursued a policy of assimilating her overseas possessions politically and culturally to the mother country, of turning Arabs, Berbers, Senegalese or Annamites as far as possible into Frenchmen. This attitude can be seen at least as early as the constitution of 1795, which declared the colonies to be 'integral parts of the Republic' and divided them into départements. By contrast Britain relaxed, after the Mutiny of 1857, the considerable efforts which had been made during the previous generation to impose on her Indian possessions the social, economic and administrative values current in London; while in her African colonies she tended increasingly, as the nineteenth century drew to a close, to work through chiefs and other native authorities whose power she consolidated and used for her own purposes. Germany, since her empire was very largely the outcome merely of rivalry with Britain, had until 1907, when the first state secretary for the colonies was appointed, hardly any positive ideas about the way in which her new territories should be administered.[56]

On a different level, the great development of modern education in British India, and the wide dissemination there of the English language which resulted, contrasts strikingly with the position in the Dutch East Indies. There at the end of the nineteenth century there were only a few thousand who could read and write out of a total population of perhaps 30 million, while there was considerable official resistance to the idea of allowing the natives to learn Dutch. Again there is an important difference between the willingness of many able officers and administrators to serve in the British colonies and the difficulty which other powers, without any colonial tradition, encountered in persuading men of real calibre to make careers in their newly acquired possessions. Thus Russian Turkestan was notorious for long after its conquest for the corruption of its administration; the history of the German colonial empire was punctuated by scandals and atrocities; and the lurid early history of the Congo Free State was partly the outcome of the great difficulty which Leopold II found in recruiting honest and able men to govern it. Even the quality of French colonial administrators left much to be desired. The fact that the European powers had differing resources and outlooks meant inevitably that the impact they made on the outside world also differed, in nature and scope.

Moreover that outside world comprised a vast range of societies at almost every level of size and sophistication. Its reaction to European influences was correspondingly varied. In much of east and central Africa, for example, where a number of different factors (particularly the devastating effects of the Arab slave trade) had conspired to keep the inhabitants at a very low level of social and economic development, European conquest did not mean the same as in many western parts of the continent, where society and economic life were a good deal more advanced. In Asia the differences, social, cultural, religious, historical, between India, the Ottoman empire, China and Persia were enormous. The one thing they had in common was that the traditional structure of authority had in all of them been weakened and shaken before European pressures became really intense.

Most of all Japan differed spectacularly from the rest of the non-European world. Alone in that world she had developed before the European impact two supremely valuable assets – some genuine sense of patriotism and national unity, and a relatively effective system of education. (In the 1850s perhaps 40 or 50 per cent of her male population was literate, a higher rate than in most of Europe.) The result was that in spite of her smallness, her limited resources and the fact that she imported relatively little capital from abroad, she showed a unique ability to adopt

European ideas and methods, either directly or at second hand through the United States, and to use them to transform with astounding speed many aspects of her life.[57] By developing a modern (in other words European-type) army and navy she safeguarded herself against the sort of bullying by Europeans from which China suffered so much. By developing modern industries she avoided the de-industrialization which the competition of cheap European factory-produced goods with the products of handicraft industries meant for much of nineteenth-century Asia. Even as early as 1862 she had been represented at the Great Exhibition of that year in London. By the end of this period she had made herself, at least in embryo, a world power. The effect upon the extra-European world of the expansion of Europe was thus the aggregate result of a large number of complicated interactions, each of which was unique. The outcome of each was in turn determined by a host of factors which are difficult to evaluate and sometimes even to identify.

There is, finally, one aspect of this European world leadership which must strike any impartial observer: the general ease with which it was achieved. In a few areas – Algeria is perhaps the outstanding example – there was prolonged resistance to European conquest. In some others, such as Afghanistan and Ethiopia, geography gave a high degree of protection against invasion by European armies. China, the greatest of all non-European societies, offered until near the end of the nineteenth century a sullen though increasingly ineffective resistance to western influences of almost every kind. But in general it is the inability, and still more the frequent unwillingness, of Africa and Asia to protect themselves against European dominance which is impressive. Nothing is more striking than the ease with which small, sometimes very small, numbers of Europeans were able to transform large parts of the world. Apart from the Maratha and Sikh states few Indian principalities offered sustained resistance to the spread of British rule. When the nineteenth century ended the whole of the subcontinent, with a population already approaching 300 million, was controlled by an army which included only 70,000 white soldiers and of which a large part was stationed permanently on the Afghan frontier. The acquisition of the huge colony of Turkestan, extending over a generation, cost the Russians in all probability less than 1,000 men killed in battle. Even in Egypt, where nationalism was rapidly gaining strength, a population which by 1900 approached 10 million was controlled by a British army of occupation which sometimes numbered less than 5,000. Numerically most striking of all, in 1896 about 3 million people in southern Uganda were ruled by perhaps 25 British officials.

Whatever the forms it assumed and the methods by which it operated, European rule was in general accepted by its new subjects, at least in its early stages, with remarkable docility. To some extent this was a result of the irresistible military superiority usually given the Europeans by their weapons and organization. Victories of such brutal completeness as those of the Russians over the Turkoman tribes at Geok Tepe in 1881, or of the British over the Sudanese at Omdurman in 1898, left the defeated no alternative but immediate submission; and the difficulty of military resistance was illustrated in dozens of smaller engagements and less well-known episodes.[58] The colonial wars of the nineteenth and early twentieth centuries often cost the European armies which fought them heavy losses: but these were the result of disease, not of the strength of native resistance. European dominance was also acceptable, however, because it could often 'gather to itself a legitimacy which was traditional'.[59] It did this by presenting itself as the successor of recognized native authorities or by basing itself on the simple right of conquest, which was generally and unquestioningly recognized as a source of legitimate power. It is important to remember that before nationalism had begun its work the idea that a people had an inherent and natural right to independence was almost unknown in Africa, and felt rather than formulated even in the most advanced parts of Asia. Rule by Europeans was also often welcomed by certain social groups, notably merchants and traders, for the new economic opportunities and the higher status and prospects of advancement which it brought them. Most of all, however, it was generally acquiesced in, sometimes positively welcomed, because usually it brought peace and physical security, giving to the areas in which it was established at least the concept of economic development and later of social change. Only a minority of the peoples conquered by Europeans during this period felt that their independence was worth defending very energetically or that the change of rulers was harmful to them. 'Colonization', it has been said, 'could never have existed at all had there not existed a willingness on both sides that it should.'[60] This is an exaggeration, but it exaggerates an important truth.

In a world dominated by nationalism, both the most creative and the most destructive of all European ideas, former colonial peoples do not remember European rule with gratitude. To do so would involve facing too many unpleasant facts. In some cases they are justified in recalling it with active resentment, for example in that of the Javanese subjected for so long to the oppressive and mean-spirited rule of the Dutch. Yet hardly any of them would now wish to turn back the clock to pre-colonial days and undo the effects of European conquest. It is doubtful whether any present-day African state really envies Ethiopia, which preserved its independence when the rest of the continent was being partitioned between the European empires. The freedom which the Negus Menelik ensured for his country when he defeated the Italians at Adowa in 1896 was the freedom to remain a backward and inefficient despotism, without serious economic development, without modern education, and with a society which for decades continued to regard slavery as normal. It is equally doubtful whether Siam (Thailand) really benefited from the largely fortuitous events which prevented her being annexed or dominated, as more than once seemed likely, by either Britain or France. In Afghanistan as in Ethiopia, freedom from European rule meant in practice freedom from the greater knowledge, wealth and efficiency which conquest by Europeans produced elsewhere.

Worse still was the fate of areas such as the Middle East, which had the benefits neither of genuine and creative independence like Japan nor of relatively efficient and honest foreign rule like India. They reaped few of the material advantages which either could bring in terms of communications and industry. In 1913 India had 56,000 kilometres of railways and the entire Ottoman empire only 3,500. The whole area from Constantinople to Afghanistan was at the outbreak of the First World War in commercial terms merely a source of primary products (mainly foodstuffs, with a very little oil from Persia and Iraq and some minerals from Turkey). India and Japan, on the other hand, were already substantial exporters of textiles; and Japan was rapidly developing exports of more sophisticated manufactured goods. Moreover although the Ottoman empire imported in proportion to its population vast amounts of European capital this was used not, as in India or Japan, to lay railway-lines, build factories or dig irrigation canals, but to meet debt charges, military expenses or war indemnities. The loan of 1870 for railway-building in the European provinces of the empire was the only one raised by the Ottoman government for economic development as opposed to military and other unproductive uses and by the early 1870s, with bankruptcy clearly imminent, 60 per cent of all Ottoman government revenue was being used to service the foreign debt. By 1914 India and Japan had each an appreciable number of universities with respectable standards: the only Middle Eastern area which began to compare with them in this respect was the tiny Lebanon. Yet the social disruption and demoralization generated by the European impact was probably greater in the Middle East than in India, and certainly greater than in Japan.[61] Most clearly of all the modern history of China provides 'shattering evidence of what could happen to a great country which was wrenched out of its isolation but was not colonized, whose old order disintegrated in contact with the West but for whom nobody assumed responsibility'.[62] To argue about whether the creation of great European empires was morally right is futile. Judged by their results they have been justified, in spite of the crimes, follies and stupidities with which their former subjects can justly reproach them. It is impossible to defend every act and omission of every imperial power during the wonderful century which ended in 1914. It is almost equally difficult, however, for a European not to feel pride in the sheer energy and confidence which underlay the increasing Europeanization of the world during this period, or in the faith and idealism which at least in part inspired it.

NOTES

1. J. S. Furnivall, *Netherlands India: a study of plural economy* (Cambridge University Press, 1939), p. 211. The money was used to reduce government debt and taxation, and to build railways and fortifications in the Netherlands.
2. *Despatches of Arthur Wellesley, First Duke of Wellington* (London, 1837–39), vi, 48–9.
3. A. G. L. Shaw, 'A revision of the meaning of imperialism', *Australian Journal of Politics and History*, viii (1961), 206.
4. *A Letter from Sydney*, his most important work, was published in 1829.
5. D. O. Wagner, 'British economists and the Empire', *Political Science Quarterly*, xlvi (1934), 248–76.
6. O. MacDonagh, 'The anti-imperialism of free trade', *Economic History Review*, 2nd ser, xiv (1961–62), 496.
7. J. S. Galbraith, 'Myths of the "Little England" era', *American Historical Review*, lxvii (1961–62), 43–8.
8. I. C. Y. Hsu, *China's Entrance into the Family of Nations: the diplomatic phase, 1858–1880* (Harvard University Press, 1960), Ch. iii.
9. In 1863–76 the Egyptian foreign debt rose from £3.3 million to £91 million.
10. It is perhaps worth while to point out that in 1897 a somewhat similar international financial commission of control was set up in Greece, whose financial position was also by that time desperate, with the right to collect certain taxes and use the proceeds to service past foreign loans. Tutelage of this kind was not reserved exclusively for non-European states.
11. C. J. Bartlett, 'The mid-Victorian Reappraisal of Naval Policy', in K. Bourne and D. C. Watt, eds, *Studies in International History: essays presented to W. Norton Medlicott* (London, Longmans, 1967), p. 191.
12. H. Brunschwig, *Mythes et réalités de l'impérialisme colonial français, 1871–1914* (Paris, 1960), p. 16.
13. A. L. Popov, 'Iz istorii zavoevaniya Srednei Azii', *Istoricheskie Zapiski*, ix (1940), 217.
14. *The Société de Géographie de France*, which was founded in 1821, had never more than 300 members until the 1860s. By 1873 it had 780 and by 1881 2,000. Eleven provincial geographical societies were founded in France during the decade 1871–81; and by the latter year of the 30,000 members of such societies throughout the world nearly a third were to be found in France alone (Brunschwig, *Mythes et réalités*, p. 23).

15. Popov, 'Iz istorii', pp. 225–6.

16. The Abbé Raboisson, in his *Études sur les colonies et la colonisation au regard de la France* (1877) quoted in Brunschwig, *Mythes et réalités*, p. 27.

17. Before 1895 there was not a single Russian merchant or missionary anywhere in Manchuria. By 1902 there were 30,000–40,000 railway guards there; and the Russian population of the town of Harbin alone amounted to over 12,000. See Rosemary K. I. Quested, 'The Russian sphere of influence in China, 1895–1917' (London M. A. thesis, 1957), Ch. i, *passim*.

18. Quoted in W. Woodruff, *Impact of Western Man* (London, Macmillan, 1966), p. 5. See the similar claims by Rhodes and Joseph Chamberlain quoted in B. Porter, *Critics of Empire: British radical attitudes to colonialism in Africa, 1895–1914* (London, Macmillan, 1968), pp. 45–7.

19. S. Avineri, ed., *Karl Marx on Colonialism and Modernization* (New York, Doubleday, 1968), *passim*.

20. There is a good account of the evolution of Lenin's ideas on this subject in W. H. B. Court, 'The Communist Doctrines of Empire', in W. K. Hancock, ed., *Survey of British Commonwealth Affairs*, Pt I (Oxford University Press, 1940), 293–305.

21. The difficulties of compiling reliable figures for British foreign investment in the nineteenth and early twentieth centuries are well brought out in A. H. Imlah, *Economic Elements in the Pax Britannica* (Harvard University Press, 1958), Ch. iii.

22. See W. W. Rostow, *British Economy of the 19th Century* (Oxford University Press, 1948), Chs. iii and vii; A. K. Cairncross, *Home and Foreign Investment* (Cambridge University Press, 1953), Chs. vi and vii.

23. *Imperialism*, 1902 edn, p. 64.

24. See p. 55.

25. K. Sinclair, 'Hobson and Lenin in Johore: Colonial Office policy towards British concessionnaires and investors, 1878–1907', *Modern Asian Studies*, i (1967), 335–52.

26. Sir G. Paish, 'Great Britain's capital investments in individual colonial and foreign countries', *Journal of the Royal Statistical Society*, lxxiv (1911), 167–87.

27. See the discussion in E. M. Winslow, *The Pattern of Imperialism: a study in the theories of power* (Columbia University Press, 1948), pp. 55–60. The most complete collection of figures relating to the profitability of European colonial empires is still Grover Clark, *The Balance Sheets of Imperialism* (Columbia University Press, 1936).

28. M. Walker, *Germany and the Emigration, 1816–1885* (Harvard University Press, 1964), p. 216.

29. D. C. M. Platt, *Finance, Trade and Politics in British Foreign Policy, 1815–1914* (Oxford University Press, 1968), p. 364.

30. The earliest clear example of this appears to be the action of Salisbury in 1885 in empowering the British minister in Tokyo to support British commercial interests in Japan, which were then being threatened by the unprecedented backing given by the German minister to his compatriots. (Platt, *Finance, Trade and Politics*, pp. 272–4.)

31. See the table in Brunschwig, *Mythes et Réalités*, p. 99.

32. J. Bouvier and R. Girault, *L'Imperialisme français d'avant 1914* (Paris – The Hague, 1976), pp. 326–7.

33. H.-U. Wehler, 'Bismarck's imperialism, 1862–1890', *Past and Present*, no. 48 (August 1970), 119–55. This summarizes the analytical parts of his very voluminous *Bismarck und der Imperialismus* (Cologne, 1969).

34. W. O. Henderson, 'British economic activity in the German colonies, 1884–1914', *Economic History Review*, xv (1945), 55–65.

35. J. S. Schumpeter, *Imperialism and Social Classes* (Oxford, Blackwell, 1951), p. 90. The two essays which make up this book were first published in German in 1919 and 1927.

36. *Ibid*, p. 84.

37. Though it should be said that Lenin in his book – which he significantly subtitled *A Popular Outline* – admitted that beside the economic one there were numerous 'old' motives for imperial expansion, though he did not discuss these.

38. D. K. Fieldhouse, 'Imperialism; an historiographical revision', *Economic History Review*, 2nd ser, xiv (1961–62), 205.

39. G. Barraclough, *An Introduction to Contemporary History* (London, Watts, 1964), p. 161.

40. F. R. Bridge, 'The Habsburg Monarchy and the Ottoman Empire, 1900–1918', in Marian Kent, ed., *The Great Powers and the End of the Ottoman Empire* (London, Allen & Unwin, 1984), pp. 44–5.

41. H. Nicholson, *Curzon, the Last Phase* (London, Constable, 1934), p. 13. He claimed in the same year that 'Parliament will have to know Asia almost as well as it knows Europe; and the time will come when Asiatic sympathies and knowledge will be, not the hobby of a few individuals, but the interest of the entire nation' (*Ibid*, p. 38).

42. Sir M. Durand, *Life of the Rt Hon Sir A. C. Lyall* (London, 1913), p. 381.

43. C. Andrew and A. S. Kanya-Forstner, *The Climax of French Imperial Expansion, 1914–1924* (Stanford University Press, 1981), pp. 24, 30.

44. Walker, *Germany and the Emigration*, p. 221.

45. E. Stokes, *The Political Ideas of English Imperialism* (Oxford University Press, 1960), p. 10.

46. Quoted in H. Gollwitzer, *Europe in the Age of Imperialism, 1880–1914* (London, Thames & Hudson, 1969), p. 140.

47. R. Oliver, *Sir Larry Johnston and the Scramble for Africa* (London, Chatto & Windus, 1957), pp. 258–9.

48. 'The true imperialism', *The Nineteenth Century and After*, lxiii (1908), 157–8.

49. O. Lyttelton, *From Peace to War: a study in contrast, 1857–1918* (London, Bodley Head, 1968), p. 63.

50. Some interesting details of French soldiers and officials for whom service in the colonies opened opportunities unknown at home can be found in Brunschwig, *Mythes et réalités*, pp. 164–5. For Britain R. Meinertzhagen, *Kenya Diary, 1902–1906* (London, Oliver & Boyd, 1957) illustrates some of the same feelings.

51. See the comments of Izvolskii, the Russian foreign minister, made at the final ministerial conference on the agreement with Britain, in *Krasnyi Arkhiv*, nos 69–70 (1935), p. 36.

52. A. J. Marder, *From Dreadnought to Scapa Flow* (Oxford University Press, 4 vols, 1961–70), i, 236–7.

53. See pp. 249ff.

54. W. M. Thackeray, *Notes of a Journey from Cornhill to Grand Cairo*, 1888 edn. p. 118; J. Marlowe, *The Making of the Suez Canal* (London, Cresset Press, 1964), p. 265; J. Foster Fraser, *The Real Siberia* (London, 1912), p. 83.

55. W. R. Shepherd, 'The expansion of Europe', *Political Science Quarterley*, xxxiv (1919), 44.

56. It is typical of her backwardness in this respect that one of the first actions of Dernburg, the newly appointed minister, was to visit London to study the working of the Colonial Office.

57. Colonel Teruda, who commanded the 1st regiment of the Japanese army at the siege of Port Arthur in 1904–5, the greatest single operation of the Russo-Japanese War, had himself as a young man fought in the internal struggles of the mid-century in Japan wearing armour and carrying a battleaxe (E. Ashmead-Bartlett, *Port Arthur: the siege and capitulation* (Edinburgh–London, 1906), p. 265).

58. Thus, for example, the British and French armies which defeated the Chinese at Palikao and opened the way to Peking in 1860 lost only 51 killed and wounded in doing so, while the Chinese left at least 1,000 men on the field. In the battle of Mahram in 1875 well over 1,000 Kokandis were killed by the Russians, who lost 6 dead and 8 wounded. In the British invasion of Tibet in 1904, 2,700 Tibetans were killed while the invaders lost fewer than 40. At Geok Tepe, the supreme illustration of these military inequalities, 6,500 bodies were found in the captured fortress and another 8,000 people were killed in the flight of the garrison and inhabitants: the Russians lost 59 men. Even at Adowa in 1896 the Ethiopians lost about twice as many men as the humiliatingly defeated Italian army.

59. D. A. Low, 'Lion Rampant', *Journal of Commonwealth Political Studies*, ii, (1964), 241–2.

60. A. P. Thornton, *Doctrines of Imperialism* (New York, Wiley, 1965), p. 194.

61. These comparisons are based on C. Issawi, 'Middle East Economic Development, 1815–1914: The general and the specific', in M. A Cook, ed., *Studies in the Economic History of the Middle East* (Oxford University Press, 1970).

62. H. Luthy, 'Colonization and the making of mankind', *Journal of Economic History*, xxi (1961), 494.

6

Armed forces and war

For nearly four decades after 1815 armed conflict between the great powers of Europe was unknown. This was by no means a period of unbroken peace. It saw, apart from the barbarities of the Greek War of Independence, a considerable though short-lived struggle between Russia and the Ottoman empire in 1828–29. It also saw the frequent use of armies on a large scale for the maintenance of order and of the political and social status quo within many of the states of Europe. The role of the Austrian army in suppressing the liberal revolts which broke out in Naples and Piedmont in 1820–21, the sending of a considerable French expeditionary force to Spain in 1823, the events of June 1848 in Paris and the crushing of the Hungarian nationalists by Austrian and Russian armies in 1849, are all obvious examples of this. But the complete absence during these decades of anything resembling the tides of war and conquest which had washed over Europe in the years 1792–1815 is very striking indeed. At no time in modern history until our own day has the continent enjoyed so long a period of peace between its great states.

The lack of armed conflict on a large scale meant inevitably that military factors, though still very important, no longer bulked quite so large in the affairs of Europe as in the days of the French Revolution and Napoleon. After the strains and sacrifices of that quarter-century, most powers were content, indeed eager, to reduce the size of their armies and navies. Mass armies, apart from their cost, had now unpleasant associations with political radicalism, even violent revolution. Governments also tended to avoid for as long as possible the introduction into the organization and armament of their forces of expensive novelties which might have unpredictable results. In France in particular, which had in the past two decades imposed new dimensions of military effort upon the other powers, there was a marked reaction after Waterloo against the army and the idea of military glory. The harsh conscription of the last years of Napoleon I and the severe measures taken against those who attempted to evade it (the levying on villages of heavy collective fines, the billeting of soldiers on the families of delinquents, the use of flying columns to round up deserters and evaders) had had a profound effect on popular feeling. Moreover the army played no political role in France between Waterloo and the middle of the century: it identified itself with no particular régime. It did nothing to bring about the fall of Charles X in 1830 and as little to prevent that of Louis-Philippe (which was widely regretted in military circles) in 1848. Even in 1851, when exceptional conditions forced it to take an active part in politics, it was difficult to find many high-ranking officers willing to support the Bonapartist *coup d'état*. In this respect again the contrast with the revolutionary epoch, or at least with the years 1795–99, is striking; and this lack of military ardour and influence in politics can also be seen in several of the other major European states during the generation after Waterloo.

Nevertheless the armies of the great powers were slowly evolving into forces very different from those of the eighteenth century. Except in Britain all of them, in varying ways, were based at least in part on some form of conscription; though the element of compulsion was softened, or disappeared altogether, where the educated and better-off classes were concerned. In Prussia, the most militarized European state, a law of 1814 limited the service demanded of conscripts in the field army to the relatively short period of five years (reduced to four in 1831): this meant that exemptions in favour of the middle classes were less necessary than in states such as France and Russia, where the term was much longer. But even in Prussia by the 1850s less than a quarter of the young men who became available each year for service were in fact called up; and those of them who had attained a reasonably high standard of education served for a shorter period than their fellows and under better conditions. It has been argued, perhaps with some exaggeration, that 'in part the middle-class German became educated in order to avoid the burdens laid upon him by militarism'.[1] In France conscription had been forbidden by Article xii of the Constitutional Charter of 1814; but it was reintroduced in fact, though the hated word was not explicitly used, in 1818. The law of that year, inspired by Gouvion St Cyr, one of Napoleon's marshals, provided for the conscription annually of 40,000 men, who were to be chosen by lot from the 300,000 or so who became eligible each year for service and were to serve for six years. This system, coupled with the fact that the well-to-do young man who drew a 'bad number' could buy a substitute, meant that the whole burden of service in the ranks fell on the poorer classes, especially on the peasantry. In spite of this and other defects, however, it remained unaltered in essentials though frequently modified in detail (notably in 1832) until the later 1860s. In Austria the position was similar; there too only a small part of each year's contingent actually served and those who could afford it could purchase substitutes. Moreover the Landwehr, the militia created during the Napoleonic Wars, was never popular with the Habsburg government. It was weakened by stages and finally abolished in 1831. In Russia, until the passage of the universal service law of 1874, the obligation of military service rested not upon individuals, as elsewhere in Europe, but upon communities. Villages and sections of towns were forced to supply men for the army when called upon, usually in the proportion of about one in every twenty-six liable. As in France and Austria, substitutes could be bought; and any possibility of universal service was ruled out not merely by the unmanageable administrative problems this would have created, but also by the fact that a serf recruit ceased to be a serf when he entered the army. A 'nation in arms' was therefore impossible in Russia except at the cost of a great social revolution; and the abolition of serfdom in the 1860s was the logical preliminary to the extension of the obligation to military service.

Conscription was by no means new. In primitive forms it had existed in Russia since the beginning of the eighteenth century, and in Prussia since the 1730s. But by 1815, as a result of the great military upheavals and efforts of the previous quarter of a century, it was more widespread, more generally accepted (so long as it did not call for real sacrifice by the ruling groups in society) and less inefficient than ever before. It was still limited in its scope: Prussia was the only state which possessed really substantial reserves of trained military manpower for use in a long war. Neither the French nor the Austrian forces, by contrast, had adequate quantities of second-line troops with which to support their field armies in case of need; while the Russian army, though very large, was so short of reserves that in 1849 its intervention in Hungary, which involved little fighting, was made possible only by a special draft of 134,000 men for the purpose. Almost everywhere, in the decades after 1815, the great bulk of the crop of potential recruits escaped service altogether and formed a reserve of manpower which, however large, was totally untrained. But if they differed widely in their methods of recruitment from the armed masses of the twentieth century, the armies of the first half of the nineteenth differed almost as much from those of the Maréchal de Saxe or Frederick the Great.

They were also more modern than the armies of the *ancien régime* in that they were increasingly officered by professionals who regarded military service as a permanent career. In some types of unit, notably guards and cavalry regiments, aristocratic and dilettante influences often remained strong; but elsewhere, and particularly in artillery and engineer formations, the emphasis on professional competence was increasingly heavy. A movement towards greater professionalism had already been seen in the eighteenth century in the creation of a number of important schools for officers in most of the greater European states. This development, however, was comparatively limited in scope: not until well into the following century was the victory of the professional complete. In France the idea of the career officer was, after the revolution, more fully developed than anywhere else. No longer, as under the old monarchy, could officers spend most of their time on their estates during long periods of leave, or in winter quarters far from the men under their command; while the proportion of officers, even in the highest ranks, who were not of noble origin increased sharply. Elsewhere the idea that the officer corps should not be dominated by the nobility was in 1815 less generally accepted. In Prussia a royal order of August 1808, issued when the state was still reeling under overwhelming defeat by France, had declared that henceforth social discrimination in this respect should end. Yet there aristocratic influences in the selection and promotion of officers remained stronger than anywhere else in Europe. The struggle between liberal and conservative forces in the higher command of the army and the government generally, which culminated in 1819 in the dismissal of the liberal war minister, Boyen,[2] reinforced the position of the officer corps as an aristocratic and highly conservative caste. Such military conservatism left a deep imprint on both the domestic and the foreign policies of Prussia. It meant that in 1848 the army was the most effective and reliable support of the monarchy and the old régime, and that for the next decade its leaders regarded it as essentially a kind of glorified police force dedicated to the suppression of political and social radicalism. They therefore disliked any foreign adventure which might distract them from this fundamental task and tended to approve even of the surrender to Austria at Olmütz in 1850.

In the Habsburg empire regimental officers were for the most part of relatively humble social origins; but the higher reaches of the officer corps remained throughout the century strongly aristocratic. They were also, at least until its middle years, marked by the cosmopolitanism and variety of national origins which had since the early seventeenth century distinguished the officers in Habsburg service. Officers not merely of German and Magyar but also of Italian, French and even English, Scottish or Irish descent were to be found in the Austrian army.[3] In Russia a few officers were promoted from the ranks and a certain number, drawn mainly from the wealthier landowners, were trained in the Cadet Corps schools, of which there were twenty-three in 1855. But the great majority were recruited from *Junker* volunteers, members of minor landed families, many of them very poor, who began their service as sergeants in line regiments. Only in the guards regiments was the officer corps aristocratic in any genuine sense.

The same slowly growing professionalism can be seen in the central organization of the great European armies. Though the Cossacks continued to make up an important part of the Russian forces and Arnauts and Bashi-Bazouks to figure among those of the Ottoman empire, the irregular and semi-regular formations which had hitherto played an important role in some other European armies were now generally in decline. Thus the Grenzers, the inhabitants of the military frontier set up by the Habsburgs during the sixteenth century in Croatia and Syria for defence against the Turks, rapidly lost the very real importance they had for long enjoyed in the structure of Austrian military power. As recently as 1809 the military border had put over 100,000 men in the field during the great struggle of that year against Napoleon; but this was its last significant appearance on the international stage. Its importance was now rapidly declining; and though the border regiments were mobilized as late as 1866 for the war with Prussia they played no significant part in it and had ceased to exist by 1873.[4] In the Ottoman empire also Mahmud II, though greatly handicapped by lack of good officers, had by the later 1830s built up an army of almost 40,000 men trained and organized along more or less European lines. This supplemented and increasingly replaced the chaotic and undisciplined forces, often raised by provincial governors, on which the government had for generations been forced largely to rely. However irregular forces of Kurds, Arabs and Circassians remained for a long time of some real significance in the Ottoman military picture – about 50,000 of them were raised during the Crimean War – and religious prejudice ensured that non-Muslims were not effectively recruited to the Turkish army until after the revolution of 1908. This growth of central control and centralized efficiency is visible also in a slow improvement in the organization of the war offices of several great European states. Thus in Russia Nicholas I, who had a real though narrow concern for the well-being of his army, reorganized the war ministry in 1832 and again in 1836. He had already introduced in 1831 a new Recruit Code governing every aspect of the treatment of recruits, while the 1830s saw a marked improvement of the appallingly bad commissariat system from which the Russian army had always suffered: in 1850 almost nine times as many soldiers were receiving a ration of meat as in 1826.[5]

In Prussia the growth of central planning and control was to be seen above all in the evolution of what was to become the most admired and perhaps the most admirable military institution in Europe – the great general staff. Organizations of this kind can be traced back, in an embryonic form, to the 1760s; and developments in communication (which made it possible for armies to operate in widely separated divisions) and in cartography were making them, by the early nineteenth century, steadily

more essential in war. None, however, achieved the efficiency or importance of that of Prussia. Established in its nineteenth-century form as part
of the reorganization of the Prussian war ministry by Scharnhorst after the
catastrophe of 1806–7, it became separate from, though still subordinate
to, the ministry in 1821. Henceforth its chief became the main adviser of
the king in operational matters, while the war ministry was confined to
the political and administrative control of the army. During the first half
of the century the great days of the Prussian general staff were still in the
future. It became of first-class importance only from the war with Denmark
in 1864. Already, however, it was a planning organism, a concentration
of directing intelligence, such as no other army possessed. In Russia the
general distrust of intellectual effort under Nicholas I, and the ludicrously
disproportionate emphasis laid on drill and parade-ground manoeuvres,
meant that the rudimentary general staff in existence there had little
importance. In France the tradition of Napoleon, who had planned and
controlled his campaigns with relatively little staff work to assist him,
meant that the army had little staff tradition or organization. In the
Habsburg empire also the general staff was little regarded and of poor
quality, as the wars of 1859 and 1866 were to show; and intellectual
analysis of military problems was despised and suspect. Field Marshal
Radetzky, until his death in 1857 the greatest and most representative
figure in the Austrian army, proclaimed that 'war is obviously an art and
no science'.[6] By 1815, therefore, the germ of a profound difference in this
respect between the Prussian army and those of other great European states
was already visible; but only time was to show its real importance.

The strength of the forces making for change in the military life of Europe
during the generation after Waterloo should not be exaggerated. Everywhere they were opposed by powerful conservative traditions, by a multitude of inheritances and vested interests from the past. In the Austrian
army, for example, there persisted until after the middle of the century the
old custom of appointing *Inhaber*, or proprietors of regiments. These
controlled the appointment and promotion of cadet officers in their regiments and even the transfer to them from other units of officers under a
certain rank. They thus benefited from the sale of commissions which
continued to be a feature of the Habsburg army until 1848. Each regiment
continued, as in the past, to be known by the name of its proprietor and
not by a number, as was now normal in other European armies; and it was
not until 1868 that the last of these proprietorial rights were abolished.

The idea of war as something which must absorb the whole energies
of a people was still, in spite of the unprecedented size and intensity of
the Napoleonic struggles, far from being completely accepted, as the very
limited and half-hearted forms of conscription in force clearly showed. It

was still very common in times of peace, moreover, as it had been through-out the eighteenth century, for a considerable proportion of many armies to be sent on leave as an economy measure or employed on civilian work of some kind. In the Habsburg empire, where shortage of resources was a perpetual problem, a well-informed observer wrote in 1840: 'In peaceful times it is usual for a third or even a greater part of the men to be on leave, and to keep only those who are indispensable for duty.' In some years in the 1820s, indeed, almost half the men in the Habsburg army were on leave at any given moment, while in France even as late as the 1870s regimental commanders sent many of their men home during the winter because they could not afford to feed them. The assumption, easily made in the twentieth century, that in time of war civilian interests must be sacrificed to military necessities, was still strange and repulsive. Thus in 1832 the French army commanded by Marshal Gérard, which was besieging the fortress of Antwerp then held by a Dutch garrison, agreed, in order to avoid damage to the town, to attack only that side of the citadel which faced open country.[7] The traditional view of war as a kind of gentlemanly though lethal game was still alive: as late as 1855 Marshal Canrobert, the French commander during the siege of Sebastopol, com-plained of the Russians using hooks and ropes to take prisoners during sorties from the fortress on the grounds that 'these are not arms for gen-tlemen'.[8] The military theorizing of the decades after Waterloo, like their military practice, looked backwards as well as forward. Certainly General Karl von Clausewitz, by far the most influential writer on military subjects whom they produced, argued in his *On War* (*Vom Kriege*) published in 1832, that it was absurd to introduce into war, which was 'an act of violence pushed to its utmost bounds', ideas of moderation. Yet he also realized quite well that limited wars were possible and would continue to occur, and that it was wrong to assume that future struggles must be total ones with the very survival of the contestants at stake.[9] Moreover Baron Jomini, the other great military theorist of the period though one now less well remembered, continued to think in largely eighteenth-century terms. To him, as to all theorists of the old régime, the acquisition of territory by skilful manoeuvre was at least as important as the destruction of the enemy's army. He did not emphasize, perhaps over-emphasize, the import-ance of moral and psychological factors in warfare as Clausewitz did. In his voluminous writings, particularly his *Art of War* (1836), 'he carried down into the age of Bismarck a habit of mind and feeling formed in the very last days of Frederick the Great and Voltaire'.[10]

But no nostalgia for the past, no inherited tradition, could in the long run have any effect against the vast and accelerating changes which were now taking place in military and naval technology. Like every other aspect of life, at least in western Europe, armies and navies were now being revolutionized by the development of new tools, new machines and new methods.

The old smooth-bore musket of the Napoleonic period, little altered in essentials for generations and hardly superior as a weapon to the longbow of the later Middle Ages, was now being changed out of all recognition. Percussion caps (developed in Britain though not adopted by the British army until 1840) could now prime its charge even in wet weather, thus considerably reducing the vulnerability of well-trained infantry to cavalry attack. Better gunpowder reduced the inevitable fouling of the barrel when it was fired. Breech-loading as opposed to muzzle-loading weapons allowed a much higher rate of fire to be achieved. Above all the introduction of rifled barrels made possible far greater range and accuracy than ever before. By the early 1840s the Prussian army had adopted on a large scale the Dreyse rifle (the 'needlegun'), the first successful breech-loading infantry rifle; and in 1847 the Minié bullet, excellently adapted for use in rifled weapons, was evolved in France. The effect of these changes was startling. With an old smooth-bore musket under good conditions a man, standing and fully exposed, might be hit by 40 per cent of the shots fired at him at 100 yards. By comparison the Dreyse rifle was accurate up to 400 yards; the Minié one was accurate up to about 650 and had some effect at twice that distance.[11] The tactical implications of this – in making frontal attacks on well-defended positions almost impossibly costly, in allowing large areas of ground to be swept by the fire of a relatively small number of men, in increasing the importance of field fortifications, which alone could offer shelter from this appallingly increased fire-power – were far from clear to contemporaries. But it was realized that the nature of war and of armies was changing spectacularly. 'The armies which have just taken the field', wrote a competent observer in 1870 at the beginning of the Franco-Prussian War, 'differ from the armies commanded by the first Napoleon or the Duke of Wellington almost as much as the latter differed from Roman Legions.'[12]

Moreover by the middle of the century these unprecedentedly powerful and destructive armies were beginning to be given unprecedented mobility by the use of the railway. The first definite proposals for the use of railways for strategic purposes (in this case for the defence of western Germany against French attack) were put forward as early as 1833 by a Westphalian industrialist, F. W. Harkort. Two years later a special commission was set up to consider their possible military uses. Helmuth von Moltke, later chief of the Prussian general staff and the most significant military figure of the century, was keenly alive to their possibilities from the later 1830s onwards. The first large-scale transport of soldiers by rail took place in 1846, when over 12,000 men of the Prussian army were moved, with horses and equipment, to destroy the independence of the free city of Cracow. In 1850, during the Austro-Prussian crisis which ended in the Olmütz agreement, the Austrians were able to move 75,000 men by rail over a distance of 150 miles to the Silesian frontier, though it took them nearly a month to do it.[13] These were not in themselves revolutionary achievements. Few parts of Europe by the middle of the century possessed railway networks dense enough to allow the rapid movement of really large forces over considerable distances. Few armies had the organizing power and the experience to make full use of the railways at their disposal. But they were achievements which pointed towards greater ones in the future.

It must not be thought, however, that the great improvement in the firepower and mobility of armies seen during these decades was matched by a corresponding one in all the material aspects of military life. In particular disease continued to take a very heavy toll, especially in the armies of the more backward states such as Russia. In the Polish campaign of 1831, for example, only about 7,000 Russians were killed in action or died as the result of wounds; but 85,000 died of disease. The French ambassador in St Petersburg reported in the early 1820s that in the Imperial Guard 6,000 men out of a total of 60,000 died each year; and during the generation before the Crimean War the annual death-rate in the Russian army averaged 37.4 per thousand – about three times as high as in the corresponding civilian age-groups in Russia.[14] It is not surprising that a traveller at the end of the 1830s found that 'its ranks are considered by every Russian, high or low, as the Ultima Thule of misery and hardship'.[15] Other European armies, with death-rates averaging about 20 per thousand, were much better off; but even in them the soldier was considerably more exposed to disease than was his civilian counterpart.

The technical changes which were having such an effect on the potentialities of armies were seen in an even more pronounced form in the development of navies during these decades. The first steam-propelled warship, the *Demologos*, was built by the American Robert Fulton in 1814, though she never took part in any naval action. Almost simultaneously the British Admiralty began to experiment with small steamers, which were used for towing men-of-war out of harbour in the face of contrary winds, and to some extent as packet-boats. The Russian navy laid down a steam warship, the *Skoryi*, in 1817 and in 1824 the *Diana*, a steamer belonging to the East India Company, saw service in the first Burmese War. Steam power, however, was adopted by the navies of Europe only slowly and with some reluctance. There was a substantial technical argument against its use on a large scale in that early steamers, with their highly inefficient engines, consumed enormous quantities of coal. They thus completely lacked the greatest advantage of the sailing warship – its almost unlimited endurance. If they were to be used to control the oceans they must be supported either by a worldwide system of bases and supply depots at which they could refuel, or by a large and vulnerable train of colliers. Britain, the greatest naval power and the one true world power during much of the nineteenth century, felt these defects much more than other states which used their fleets on a smaller scale and over shorter distances.[16] It is not surprising, therefore, that she was slow to adopt the steamship for more than limited and specialized functions. The first French and Dutch war steamers crossed the Atlantic in 1824 and 1827 respectively, the first British one only in 1833. Nevertheless the Admiralty appointed a chief engineer and inspector of machinery in 1835; and by the end of 1841 about a fifth of all the British warships in commission were steamers.

In spite of its considerable disadvantages and the dislike with which conservative naval officers almost unanimously regarded it, the steam-driven warship was now launched on a course of rapid and accelerating progress. By the middle of the century the screw propeller, more efficient and less vulnerable than the paddle-wheel, was beginning to be used for propulsion: the American navy laid down a screw warship, the *Princeton*, in 1842, while the British one had over forty screw-propelled ships, nearly all small, by 1847. In 1848 for the first time a British ship of the line, the *Blenheim*, was fitted with an auxiliary screw, in spite of fears that the installation of machinery in such ships would spoil their sailing qualities. The French replied with the *Napoléon*, similarly equipped, in 1850.

By then the use of iron for naval shipbuilding was slowly beginning to make headway. Like steam power, it was opposed in part for reasons of mere instinctive conservatism and in part for apparently good technical ones – the danger from flying splinters if an iron ship were struck by a projectile; the greater difficulty of plugging leaks in an iron ship as compared with a wooden one; the difficulty as yet of producing large quantities of iron plate of uniform quality. Though experiments with iron merchant-steamers had begun by 1815 it was not until 1839 that the British navy acquired its first iron steamers. Other states, which lacked Britain's metallurgical resources, were even slower to use the new material; and in the later 1840s and during most of the 1850s there was even a movement away from iron construction because of its undoubted disadvantages. But the increasing weight of engines and guns, coupled with the facts that iron greatly reduced the appalling fire risks from which wooden ships had always suffered and that iron vessels were cheap to build and maintain, meant that the future lay with it.

The steam-driven, screw-propelled, iron-built warship which was beginning to take shape by the middle of the century was increasingly armed with guns which fired explosive shells instead of solid shot; this meant that its fire-power was far greater than ever before. From early in the century General H. J. Paixhans had been arguing in France that the warships of the future would be shell-firing and that the day of the cannon-ball was over. In 1822, in his *Nouvelle force maritime,* he provided the first systematic study of the possibility of a navy of steam-driven, iron-built ships of this kind. Though for long his ideas were neglected in his own country the French government decided in 1837 that in future shell-firing guns should be mounted in ships of the line and frigates. The British Admiralty was forced to follow suit in the following year, though armament of this kind continued for some time to be associated in Britain with steamers rather than with sailing men-of-war. The full implications of the change, and in particular the need it created for warships to be given protective armour, were hardly visible to most contemporaries. Once more, however, a great step forward in the evolution of modern armed forces had, almost unconsciously, been taken.

Every innovation of this period in naval technology met with instinctive hostility in Britain because it seemed to threaten the naval supremacy which she had established by 1815. That had been built on the wooden sailing warship armed with smooth-bore guns firing solid shot or grape. The development of a totally new type of fighting ship would nullify Britain's existing advantages, it was felt, allow rivals to compete with her on more even terms than in the past, and even expose her to invasion. Well before the victory of the new iron steamers had become complete fears for the future of British naval power were being loudly voiced. The end of the Napoleonic Wars had been followed by a drastic reduction in the size of the navy. In 1815 Britain had 214 ships of the line in commission, though many of these were in poor condition. By 1822 she had only sixty-eight ready for sea, and by 1835 only fifty-eight. The next four years saw a large increase in her naval strength (the manpower of the navy rose by about a third in 1835–39) stimulated mainly by fears of the apparent growth of Russian power at sea. In 1844, however, at a moment when Anglo-French relations were very strained, the publication by the Prince de Joinville, a son of Louis-Philippe and commander-in-chief of the French navy, of his *Notes sur l'état des forces navales de la France* aroused acute alarm in Britain over the possibility of invasion by steamer-borne forces from across the Channel. Wellington himself was deeply worried by the new state of affairs, and perhaps not without reason; for although the British fleet was still much larger than the French one the inspector-general of fortifications estimated in 1846 that if the country were invaded there would be only about 10,000 regular troops available to defend it. Another burst of agitation over possible invasion from France during the winter of 1851–52 (largely stimulated by the Bonapartist *coup d'état* of 2 December 1851 in Paris) led to the passage of an ineffective Militia Bill in the summer of 1852 in an effort to improve the country's defences.

These flurries of alarm can be explained partly by the unsettling effects of rapid technical change and partly by the possibility (always greatly exaggerated in Britain) that two or more of the country's naval rivals might unite against her. In the 1820s and 1830s there was in particular a widespread belief in the likelihood of a Franco-American combination of this kind. All these fears, however, were empty; and many of them could be seen to be empty by any intelligent contemporary even without the advantages of hindsight. A country such as Britain, rich in coal and iron and with the most advanced metallurgical and engineering industries in the world, could only benefit from the coming of the new warship. Hitherto the import of timber and masts for shipbuilding from the Baltic and North America had been an important adverse element in her balance of payments. Now she could begin to dispense with such imports and increasingly to export machinery, coal and even complete warships to other countries. From 1850 onwards the Russian navy bought a number of iron gunboats in Britain, while an official enquiry of 1849–51 in France brought out how heavily the French navy now depended on British engines, engineers and coal.

WARFARE TRANSFORMED, 1854–1871

The long period of almost unbroken international peace which Europe had enjoyed since the defeat of Napoleon was ended by the outbreak in 1853–54 of the Crimean War. Itself in many ways inconclusive and even unimportant, this began a series of struggles between the great powers, the only one of the century after Waterloo. When the provisional government of France signed with Prussia the armistice of 28 January 1871 it ended a period of less than two decades during which a sequence of wars, short and not very bloody but supremely important, remodelled completely the political geography of Europe. The exposure of the weaknesses of Russia; the decline of the Habsburg empire; the beginnings of Italian unity; the spectacular overthrow of France; above all the emergence of the new Germany as a great power threatening to dominate Europe – all these had by 1871 been achieved by military struggle. The exhaustion, the desire for peace and stability even at heavy cost, which had made military adventure so unpopular for long after 1815, had now receded into the past. War as a means of altering the status quo, of serving the cause of liberalism or national unity, was now acceptable to a wider range of opinion than ever before. The pacifist movement, active and vociferous by the middle of the century,[17] had clearly little influence even in the English-speaking countries from which it originated. The Crimean War was greeted in Britain by a violent though short-lived burst of enthusiasm, while in 1859 French soldiers leaving for Italy were wildly cheered by the radical republican working-class suburbs of Paris. By the later 1860s, it is true, signs of an antimilitarist reaction were becoming visible in radical circles in France (Léon Gambetta, the symbol of national resistance in 1870-71, had urged as a young republican candidate in Paris in 1867 the abolition of all standing armies); but this was of little practical importance.

The wars of this, the most dynamic period in the history of nineteenth-century Europe, made it possible for the first time to see the accumulated effect of the technological development of the previous four decades; and this stimulated still more violent changes. The annihilation of a squadron of wooden Turkish men-of-war by one of shell-firing Russian warships at Sinope on the northern coast of Asia Minor in November 1853 showed that armour was essential in naval warfare now that the age of the explosive shell had begun. The fighting in the Crimea therefore saw the first use of ironclad warships, when in October 1855 three French floating batteries protected by iron plating bombarded the Russian fortifications at Kinburn. Within the next decade, or little more, the modern warship emerged. In 1859 the launching of the French *Gloire*, an armoured, screw-driven vessel of nearly 6,000 tons, marked an immense advance on anything hitherto known. In the next year Britain replied with the *Warrior*; and the rapid development of both guns and armour in the 1860s culminated in the *Devastation*, laid down in 1869 and completed in 1873, which marked a new epoch in naval architecture. The Crimean War had thus helped to produce a type of vessel which was to rule the seas for the next three generations. It also saw the construction of the first military railway, the narrow-gauge line built (very slowly and inefficiently) by a private contractor with navvies sent out from England and running from the port of Balaclava to the Anglo-French lines around Sebastopol. It saw the production of 'the first truly modern weapon'[18] in the form of the 'built-up' breech-loading Armstrong gun of 1855. It saw the first serious use of floating mines, in the defence of the Russian Baltic naval base of Kronstadt, and the resulting development by the British and French of primitive minesweeping devices. Most of all it made clear the now inescapable and rapidly increasing interdependence of military and industrial strength, a lesson which was to be driven home a few years later by the American Civil War. Henceforth no state could hope to be a truly great military power without first becoming an important industrial one. Russia was not defeated merely because of the poorness of her military leadership (which was hardly worse than that of the British and French armies) or the threatening neutrality and eventual unconcealed hostility of Austria (which led the Russian commander in Poland, Marshal Paskievich, to insist on keeping large forces there in case of Austrian attack). In addition to these factors her technical inferiority to her enemies was a marked and serious handicap. An army which possessed, as hers did in 1853, only 6,500 rifles in all, was at a crippling disadvantage in the field against forces equipped with modern firearms. Most of all her economic weakness, her lack of developed industry, of an even remotely adequate railway network, of the financial resources needed to sustain the burden of a long war, made victory impossible.

On the technological level, therefore, the Crimean War must be regarded as a turning-point in the history of warfare in modern times. But in another respect it was a very misleading guide to the form which international conflict was to take from the 1870s onwards. It was not a mass war. It was fought by armies mainly, and in the case of Britain entirely, composed of long-service professional soldiers. The damage it did to civilian interests and the disruption it caused to normal civilian life was generally small.[19] Even the most clearsighted contemporary could hardly have seen in it the embryo of the gigantic struggles of the twentieth century. The same is true of the short-lived Franco-Austrian conflict of 1859. Here again on both sides the armies were essentially professional forces. On both sides the numbers on the battlefield were small by the standards which were to become generally accepted after 1870: the Austrians had at first only 75,000 men available, a figure which was later doubled by the arrival of reinforcements, while the French had about 130,000 and their Piedmontese allies about 64,000. As in the Crimea the interest of the struggle, in which the leadership on both sides was unimaginative and second-rate, was essentially technical. In it the French army used rifled field artillery for the first time, benefiting from the greater range and accuracy of fire which rifling made possible. Most significant of all, this war saw the first large-scale use of railways for military purposes. In 1859 the French were able, by using them, to transport across the Alps in less than three months 205,000 men and 130,000 horses, with large amounts of equipment and supplies. By the standards of the later nineteenth century this was no spectacular achievement; but it was one hitherto unprecedented; and the inferiority of the Austrian railway system, and of the use made of it by the Austrian commanders, was an important reason for the victory of Napoleon III.

The classical demonstration of the military potentialities of railways, however, one which placed for ever beyond question their importance in this respect, was that given by the Prussian army in 1866.[20] Von Moltke, who had become chief of the general staff in 1857, had equipped it in 1864 with a railway section. His enormous and deserved reputation as a military organizer rests in the last analysis on his efficient exploitation of the Prussian railway system for military purposes. In 1866 he was able to transport the Prussian armies to the Bohemian frontier much more rapidly than the Austrian ones could move. He thus more than counterbalanced the advantage Austria drew from the fact that she had begun to mobilize five days earlier than her rival. (Though it has to be remembered that as soon as they left the railheads the Prussian forces, like the German ones in France in 1870–71, had to move and supply themselves by methods which had not changed since the days of Napoleon I.) Von Moltke was also able, by telegraph from his office in Berlin, to move the different army corps under his control along widely separated lines of communication and to concentrate them just before the decisive battle of Sadowa, a strategy which might have led to serious difficulties had he been faced by a more active and aggressive opponent. He himself arrived at the front only just before the battle was fought. Sadowa was a victory for the Prussian needle-gun, which had a high rate of fire and could be loaded by a soldier lying flat on the ground, over the Austrian Lorenz rifle, in spite of the superior range and accuracy of the latter. It also showed clearly the better training and greater intellectual energy of the Prussian commanders as compared with their Austrian opposite numbers. The officers in control of the staff work of the Austrian Northern Army, Generals Henikstein and Krismanić, were both relieved of their commands just before the battle. Benedek, the commander-in-chief, had always been hostile to book-learning and to any study of the intellectual and theoretical aspects of war, as had the emperor himself. [21] In the last stages of the struggle at Sadowa he plunged into the fighting, seeking to rally his troops in person rather than to retain any control of the movements of his army as a whole. But the campaign of 1866, as distinct from the battle which was its culmination, was won mainly by the more efficient use of communications, above all of railways, by the Prussians. It is significant that in this year the Prussian army created the first specialized units of railway troops, intended to repair lines destroyed by the enemy and destroy those of the enemy, ever seen in Europe.

The political importance of the war of 1866, in making Prussia supreme in Germany, in paving the way for the collapse of the constitutional opposition which had seemed to William I and his ministers so threatening during the previous five or six years, in altering the European balance of power and arousing French fears and suspicions, has already been discussed.[22] On the purely military level also its repercussions were great.

To Napoleon III the war revealed the power of the new rival to France which had emerged so suddenly across the Rhine. It also brought forcibly home to him the crucial weakness of the entire French military system – its lack of trained reserves. Already in 1859 he had made peace with Austria partly because the limited reserves of trained military manpower at his disposal (a mere 74,000 men) made it highly dangerous to risk facing Prussia on the Rhine as well as the Habsburgs in northern Italy. After Sadowa Prussia was calling up about 100,000 men each year for military service against the mere 56,000 who were being drafted in France. Clearly this disparity could become disastrous if it were allowed to continue. In October 1866, therefore, Napoleon proposed that the annual intake of men to the French army be increased to 160,000 a year. But such a measure was certain to be bitterly unpopular, above all with the middle classes who saw their hitherto privileged position, at least de facto, with regard to military service threatened with complete destruction. Two months later the war minister, Marshal Niel, put forward a milder proposal for the creation of a large militia force, the Garde Nationale Mobile, on the lines of the National Guard which had existed during the revolution and under Louis-Philippe. Even this encountered violent opposition; and the law which was eventually passed in January 1868 did little to strengthen France's shaky military position. Under it the new militia was to receive so little training that it would be almost useless in time of war. In fact before 1870 none of its units received any at all except in Paris; and the first enrolments provoked violent demonstrations in a number of French towns. An effort to create by the same law a large pool of trained men by providing that henceforth soldiers, after four years with the colours, should spend five in an army reserve, was also a failure, mainly because the new reserves were given no training in the use of the new and very effective *chassepot* rifle which the French army adopted in 1867. The selfishness of the middle classes; the personal weakness and illness of the emperor; the considerable opposition within the army to any dilution of its professional and long-service character; the belief of liberals and republicans that to strengthen the army was to strengthen the imperial régime; most of all the refusal of most Frenchmen to believe that the country was in real danger or needed to train more of its citizens as soldiers – all these meant that France entered the war of 1870 very unprepared for a long struggle or one which involved heavy losses. [23] The standing army numbered about 380,000; but it had in effect no reserves of manpower, and this was a fatal weakness. Even the warnings of Prussia's dangerous military strength provided by Colonel Stoffel, the able French military attaché in Berlin, were disregarded by the government and finally withheld from it by General Leboeuf, the war minister.

Nor were other efforts to strengthen France much more successful. Niel set up in 1869 a commission to study the existing regulations for the use of the French railways in wartime and to draw up new and more effective ones; but his death soon afterwards meant that nothing effective was done before war broke out. In 1870 there were still only three lines running from Paris to the eastern frontier, and of these only one was double-tracked throughout. Moreover France had few lateral railway lines useful for military purposes; in particular the important one from Metz to Verdun had not yet been completed at the beginning of the struggle with Prussia. The greater density of the German railway network put the French army at a fundamental disadvantage from the moment the first shot was fired. Again the *mitrailleuse*, one of the first practicable machine-guns, which had been developed in France in 1867 and might, properly used, have been a war-winning weapon, was never exploited to the full. It was produced on a relatively small scale, so that in 1870 the French army had only about 200 in all, and kept so secret that the men who were to use the new weapon in the field were not properly trained in its use. Moreover its tactical possibilities were not really grasped. In 1870 it was used almost entirely at long ranges, where it could be easily destroyed by the superior Prussian artillery. Indeed the French army ever since 1815 had suffered from its officers' lack of intellectual activity and interests. In it understanding and desire for understanding of new methods and techniques were generally at a low ebb by comparison with the position in Prussia.

The factors sketched in the last two paragraphs go far towards explaining the catastrophe of 1870. Greater reserves, and swifter mobilization and movement through more effective use of a bigger railway network, meant that the German states had from the beginning a heavy numerical superiority on the field of battle. When the war broke out, on the eastern frontier of France 243,000 French soldiers confronted 400,000 Germans; while the German states then had in all 866,000 men under arms against only 430,000 in France, of whom 66,000 were in Algeria or Rome and 60,000 new recruits. The Prussian army, which had needed five weeks for mobilization and deployment in 1866, now required only eighteen days, though a much larger force was involved. By contrast the French railways, inferior in number and capacity, were very inefficiently used; in all 16,000 French trucks were captured by the invading forces because it was impossible to withdraw them over lines already blocked with other traffic.

The numerical preponderance of the German armies, coupled with the marked superiority of their artillery and the confusion and ineffectiveness of most of the French leadership, ensured victory for Prussia and her allies. The superiority of the *chassepot* rifle to that used by the Germans; the undoubted though limited effect produced by the *mitrailleuse*; the ingenuity shown in the defence of Paris (in the use of armoured trains, and of balloons as a means of communicating with the outside world) could not offset the crushing superiority of the enemy in numbers and organization. Nor could the new forces improvised from September 1870 onwards by Gambetta and Freycinet or the pathetic faith of many extreme republicans and radicals, inspired by the example and myths of 1793, in the invincibility of a people in arms even if it had not been trained to their use. When the war ended there were in France over a million German soldiers, to whom the republican government improvised after the fall of the Second Empire could oppose only 200,000 French ones. The importance of rapid mobilization, of staff work, of the numbers which only a system of widespread compulsory service could produce; these lessons had been driven home with a speed and completeness which deeply impressed every European government.

War was assuming a new dimension. The battle losses of 1870–71 were not heavy. The Germans had won a crushing victory which altered the whole face of European politics at a cost of only 28,000 dead. But both sides had raised unprecedented forces and France had fought to the last gasp before surrendering – the first time in history that any great European state had done so. By 1871 'total war' of the twentieth-century type was beginning to be a physical and psychological possibility. The effects of new weapons and the growing complexity and expense of war were to be seen in the crudest and most material form simply in an unprecedented expenditure of ammunition. Well-informed contemporaries had found it remarkable that a few of the Prussian soldiers at Sadowa had managed to fire as many as ninety rounds during the battle.[24] Yet in the fighting around Metz in 1870 a single French army corps fired 2 million cartridges in two days – more than the entire Prussian army had used in 1866.[25] And this unheard-of consumption of ammunition, as of resources of all kinds, was to increase rapidly in the decades that followed. A British war correspondent estimated that in the defence of Plevna in 1877 the Turkish garrison fired 60,000 rounds for each casualty it inflicted on the besieging Russians.[26] In 1870–71 the changes which had affected European armies since 1815, in their weapons, their transport, their organization and the planning of their operations, their sheer size, were for the first time given full scope and their results shown with dramatic effect. Napoleon I, though at the height of his power he had at least 44 million people under his direct control, never had as many as a million men under arms simultaneously: the largest force he ever tried to manoeuvre as in some sense an entity numbered about 450,000. By 1914 great states could envisage the mobilization if necessary of a tenth of their population and the engagement of armies of two million men. During the intervening century warfare had been transformed; and if this process can be said to have a decisive turning-point it is in 1870–71.

TECHNOLOGY AND MASS ARMIES, 1871–1914

The Franco-Prussian war set off a round of military reforms which affected almost every major state in Europe. This was seen most strikingly in France, where a law of 1872 drastically overhauled the system of recruiting which had so spectacularly failed the country two years earlier. Henceforth every Frenchman, on reaching the age of eighteen, was to be subject to military service in one form or another for a period of twenty years. The period of active service with the colours was fixed at five years (in 1877 it was reduced in effect to four) and the system of substitutes, with the numerous abuses it had fostered, was abolished. This was still far from being a system of truly universal military service, for exemptions on family or educational grounds remained numerous. Thiers, as Chief of the Executive Power the leading figure in French politics in 1871–73, was strongly opposed to the idea of a short period of service for all Frenchmen capable of bearing arms and secured its rejection by the National Assembly. But France had now moved closer to universal service than at any time since the last days of Napoleon I. Simultaneously an effort was made to improve military administration and planning by the creation of the Conseil Supérieur de la Guerre, though this did not in fact begin to function effectively for another fifteen years. The establishment in 1872 of a commission to study the use of the French railways in time of war and the creation three years later of the first French railway troops showed that a systematic effort was now being made to rectify one of the great weaknesses of 1870; while the French general staff was reformed on the Prussian model in 1874 and the Ecole Supérieure de la Guerre set up four years later as a kind of staff college. A new willingness to learn from foreign example can perhaps also be seen in the addition during the 1870s of eight military attachés to the five France had already maintained in foreign capitals before the war: by 1914 she had twenty-four.[27] Accompanying all this there was a very sharp rise in spending on military equipment. More than ten times as much was spent in this way in the decade 1875–84 as in that of 1855–64.[28]

At the same time there was a profound change in the attitude to the army of the ordinary Frenchman. The collapse of 1870 and the political uncertainty of the next decade or more made it a symbol, the only one now available in France, of national unity and resurgence. To great numbers of people it seemed that the resurrection of French power and self-confidence which the squabbling and selfish politicians were failing to achieve could be attained only through the discipline, and the spirit of patriotism and sacrifice, which the army typified. At no time during the century was the social prestige of the army officer so high in France as during the two decades after 1870; and this had the result of raising the intellectual level of the officer corps and attracting to it recruits from the better-educated and aristocratic elements of French society. The prestige of the army is seen in the fact that the government had in practice remarkably little real control over it during the later nineteenth century. In particular there was until 1899 no government control over promotions, which were decided by *commissions de classement* composed entirely of officers; while the war minister, nearly always a serving general, was essentially an ambassador accredited by the army to his civilian colleagues. The increasing conservatism of the higher command which resulted from this position paved the way for the Dreyfus case,[29] and this destroyed conclusively the belief, so widespread in the previous twenty years, that the army could unify all Frenchmen. In 1906 a decree gave civil officials precedence over military men of corresponding rank so that, for example, a prefect now took precedence of a general commanding an army corps. This reversal of a ceremonial hierarchy established in France since the days of the Consulate can be taken as symbolizing the collapse of the remarkable autonomy which the army there had enjoyed for over a generation, an autonomy which was an unexpected and unplanned result of the defeat of 1870.

In Germany as in France, among the victors as among the vanquished, the war had important military repercussions. The German army, like that of France, gained in status and influence from the conflict. The events of 1870–71 had revealed more than once acute tension between Bismarck, dominated by political considerations, and the army commanders, indifferent to all but military advantages and necessities. After 1874, when the practice was introduced of the Reichstag voting money for military expenses for a period (at first seven years) in advance, any real parliamentary control of the army vanished. An ordinance of 1878 gave field marshals precedence not merely over ministers but over the Reichschancellor himself. Moreover a growing tendency developed, especially after the resignation in 1883 of the relatively liberal war minister, General von Kameke, to remove from the control of the war ministry, and hence from possible discussion in the Reichstag, many aspects of army life. The military cabinet of the kings of Prussia, which had been established in 1858, was now becoming more powerful; and though Bismarck was able, as long as he remained in office, to balance it against the civilian one which he controlled, there was a continual threat that military influences upon German policy might become dangerously great. In 1869 the military attachés of Prussia in foreign capitals had been allowed to correspond directly with the war minister and the general staff. Henceforth their reports did not have to be transmitted through the heads of the missions to which they were attached; and Count Waldersee, who succeeded Moltke in 1888 as chief of the general staff, encouraged them to report to him not merely on military affairs but also to an unprecedented degree on political ones in the capitals where they were stationed. In particular the military attaché in St Petersburg achieved during the later decades of the century a position of great importance as a direct and personal channel of communication between the kaiser and the tsar. In 1883, moreover, the general staff attained greater independent power than ever before when its head was given the right of direct access to the kaiser and no longer had to approach him through the war minister. The effort of a number of military leaders, led by Waldersee, to organize in 1887 a preventive war against Russia was the most striking example in the Bismarckian period of this growing readiness of soldiers to interfere in high politics. The 1870s and 1880s, though they saw no fundamental changes in the recruitment or organization of the German army, were thus a period in which its autonomy, self-confidence and political pretensions grew. This growth owed a good deal to the prestige given the Prussian war machine by the victory of 1870-71 and to the increased preoccupation with military security which was everywhere in Europe one of the main results of that victory.

The repercussions of the Franco-Prussian war on the quality and organization of armies were widespread. In Russia it helped to stimulate a far-reaching overhaul of the army in 1874, the work of a great war minister, Dmitri Milyutin. This not merely abolished corporal punishment but, more important, radically reformed the system of recruiting. The period of service was reduced to fifteen years (six with the colours and nine with the reserve) though this was drastically shortened for recruits with educational qualifications or for those serving in remote parts of the empire. Each year's levy of recruits was to be chosen by lot, since the army could not hope to train all those liable for service. With all its defects this was a fairer and, for those chosen, less onerous form of recruiting and service than Russia had ever hitherto known. Moreover the Russian army was now entrusted for the first time with the task of providing illiterate recruits with some primary education; and in 1874-91 about 1.5 million men learned to read and write, at least after a fashion, in this way.[30] For a short time in 1901-2 a former war minister, General Vannovsky, was minister of education, a metamorphosis perhaps unique in modern history. From the 1870s therefore we can see in Russia a position not unfamiliar today in the less developed parts of the world – that of the army as, in some ways at least, an engine of progress. The deficiencies of the Russian army in terms of the general educational level and technical knowledge of the ordinary soldier were severe, however, even in 1914. During the war of 1904–5 with Japan it was still possible for Russian soldiers, not understanding the significance of telephone wires, to cut them down and use them to make shoelaces and belts. Nor could Milyutin or any other minister do much to remedy one of the most serious of all the army's weaknesses – the often poor quality of its officers and in particular the high average age of the senior ones (because pensions were so poor that many simply could not afford to retire). In 1902 the average age of Russian generals was seventy, and there was still one ninety-two-year-old on allegedly active service. Nevertheless the Milyutin innovations were the most ambitious programme of military strengthening and renewal attempted by any European power during the nineteenth century.

Even in Britain, of all the great powers the most unmilitary and the worst organized for war on anything more than a colonial scale, there were stirrings of reform. In 1871 Edward Cardwell, as secretary of state for war in the great Gladstone cabinet of 1868–74, was able to abolish the sale of commissions and thus, at least in theory, give greater scope to poor men of ability in the British officer corps. In the same year the first annual army manoeuvres were held in Britain, an innovation largely inspired by German example, while in 1873 an intelligence section was formed to advise the commander-in-chief, the Duke of Cambridge. The practical significance of all this can easily be exaggerated. The abolition of purchase had little effect on the standards applied in practice in the appointment and promotion of officers. Parliament's refusal to spend money on an adequate scale meant that there were no manoeuvres at all in 1873–97; and financial starvation ensured that the army was chronically under strength throughout the last decades of the century. Nothing was done to create a general staff or a chief of staff on the Prussian model, even after a parliamentary commission had recommended this in 1890, until the establishment of the Committee of Imperial Defence in 1902.[31] That the current of army reform which was sweeping over much of Europe in the early 1870s could make some headway even in this hostile environment is a considerable tribute to its inherent strength. In August 1914, at the outbreak of war, Britain had 733,000 men, an unprecedented number, serving in the regular and reserve forces and in the new territorial army created from 1908 onwards. In Italy also, poor and completely lacking in any tradition of unified military organization or effort, there was considerable army reform, especially of the system of conscription, in 1870–76; while in Spain a selective form of conscription was introduced in 1874 as a product of the short-lived republic established in the previous year.

A major result of the spectacular remodelling of the European state system achieved in 1859–71 was a competitive increase not merely in the quality of armies but in their size, an increase which accelerated in the years before 1914. The growth was not so much a matter of standing armies as of the building up of enormous reserves of trained manpower, reserves formed by giving compulsory military training to an increasingly high proportion of all eligible males. During the last generation of the nineteenth century the total strength of the forces which the European powers could put in the field in case of war may have increased for this reason by as much as 10 million men. A tendency for standing armies to grow can also be seen, however, notably in France. There hatred of the new Germany and desire for revenge for the disaster of 1870 inspired heroic military efforts, at least by any hitherto accepted standard, in the 1870s and 1880s. The result was that by 1880 France was, in some ways at least, militarily superior to Germany. She had by then a standing army of 435,000 men to set against the 403,000 at which the German one had been fixed in 1874 by the Reichstag, and 367 field batteries against a mere 300 (with rather inferior guns) on the German side.[32] By 1887, when the German standing army was increased to 461,000, it had regained a slight numerical superiority to that of France; and this it henceforth retained and increased as the size of both forces grew. But it is important to re-member that the leading role played in Europe by Germany in the age of Bismarck depended on diplomacy, on the Bismarckian system of alliances and the isolation of France, as much as on armed strength. The fact that there was no imperial direct taxation (Bulow fell from office in 1909 over an unsuccessful attempt to introduce an inheritance tax) was a particular obstacle to large increases in German military spending.

If a war had broken out during these years it is far from certain that the German army could have decisively defeated the reconstituted French one, even if France had fought without allies. The position, in fact, was the exact opposite of that which existed in 1905–14. Then the blunders of her statesmen and diplomats meant that many Germans felt their country isolated and endangered.[33] Yet after the defeat of Russia by Japan and her weakening by revolution Germany really was, for the first time, militarily dominant on the continent. By 1911 her standing army numbered 645,000 against only 524,000 in France; and there was little effective Franco-Russian military cooperation before 1914. In 1912 Germany's military expenditure per head of population exceeded that of France for the first time. Moreover the introduction of genuinely universal military service by France in 1905, with a two-year period of active service for all physically fit males, and even the raising of the period of service to three years in 1913, could not offset the effect from the 1870s onwards of the rapid rise in the population of Germany and the stagnation of that of France. Nor could rather desperate expedients such as the extension of conscription to Algeria in 1911.

The leaders of the German army envisaged it as an élite force unswervingly loyal to the emperor and its commanders, and therefore one from which civilian influences of an undesirable – that is liberal and still more socialist – sort were to be completely excluded. Above all any contamination of the officer corps in this way must be uncompromisingly resisted. Yet it was clear that in German society influences of the kind which the German military leaders so detested were in many ways becoming stronger. If there were true universal service the army must become more representative of that society, and therefore tainted with disloyalty. If the term of service were shortened in order to give training to a higher proportion of the population it would become difficult to indoctrinate recruits effectively with the true Prussian spirit of loyalty and obedience to superiors. The supreme catastrophe would be the tainting of the officer corps, which was in any case becoming markedly less aristocratic in the later years of the century, by liberal bourgeois. Such developments would mean that the army ceased to be a reliable pillar of the political and social status quo in the new and essentially unstable Germany.[34] Whether these forebodings were justified is extremely doubtful. It seems much more likely that conscription, at least in Germany, helped to indoctrinate young men, especially those from the countryside, with the values and assumption of the new industrial society and to turn them into more reliable and docile workers than they would otherwise have been. It fostered collaboration between classes rather than struggle.[35] Nevertheless fears of this kind were widespread and influential at the highest level in German military circles right down to the catastrophe of 1914. Few leading German military figures after 1871 were seriously interested in expansion, territorial or economic. What preoccupied them was principally the maintenance of the sort of Germany which had now come into existence, the protection of the traditional Prussian virtues and pieties, the product of an agrarian society, against the inroads of the modern industrialized world – and as an aspect of this the safeguarding of their own position. This led, for example, to a tendency to prefer recruits from rural areas to those from towns and from the highly industrialized parts of the country. The great and vociferous expansionist forces which undoubtedly existed in Wilhelmine Germany owed little to military backing. Prince Philipp zu Eulenburg, German ambassador in Vienna and much the most influential adviser of William II in the early years of his reign, wrote in 1896 that 'Imperialism is unthinkable in Prussia, if only because its prerequisite would be the republicanization of the officer corps'[36] and even in the great imperialist decade of the 1890s this view would have been echoed by most conservatives. After 1871 Bismarck had imposed on Germany, for his own and Prussia's purposes, a narrow and essentially political definition of its nationality. More and more this was now being challenged by a wider and much more aggressive ethnic definition, one which stressed the need to include within the nation so far as practicable all Germans in Europe, whether or not they lived within the 1871 frontiers of the Reich. This attitude was considerably strengthened by the increasingly bitter conflicts in Bohemia between Germans and Czechs and the emotions they aroused in Germany. Bismarck's first priority had been the establishment within a geographically limited German state of a structure of government which would be permanently controlled by Prussia. To the expansionist forces which were showing themselves by the 1890s it seemed increasingly that governments and even states were unimportant by comparison with the nation, the *Volk*, the unique source of permanent values. This *völkisch* nationalism was by implication bitterly hostile to the narrow aristocratic and military influences which counted for so much in the empire of William II. The Pan-German League, the most extreme of all the expansionist pressure-groups of the years before 1914, drew its support not from officers or landowners but from humbler people, professional men and particularly teachers. It was precisely its populist character which made it radical. It is significant that its military members were often of non-noble origin and ill at ease in an army still so much led by nobles, and that it was always on bad terms with the Agrarian League which, although also strongly nationalist, was dominated by the great landowners of eastern Germany and altogether a much more socially conservative body.[37]

The result of this situation was that throughout the forty years which followed the triumph of 1870-71 there were within the German military establishment very powerful forces which opposed further growth of the army. When in 1889-90 the war minister, General Verdy du Vernois, proposed the shortening of the period of military service from three to two years and the calling up of a correspondingly greater number of recruits this was successfully opposed as tending to weaken the professional core of the army and strengthen the reserve formations at its expense. In the same tradition General von Einem, war minister in 1903-9, strongly disliked any rapid expansion of the army, arguing that 'any healthy sort of organization will simply disappear if every increase in the troops of our possible enemies immediately produces a similar expansion of our own'.[38] In January 1913 his successor rejected a suggestion by the general staff (which was in general less attached than the war ministry to the social exclusiveness of the officer caste) that three new army corps be formed, since this 'would expose the officer corps to democratization', while a high-ranking war ministry official claimed that any large increase in the size of the army would, by destroying the predominance of noble officers, produce a revolution within a few years. This military conservatism, reinforced by the unwillingness of the Reichstag to vote very large sums for military expenditure, was able to ensure that Germany's military strength was less than that of France in proportion to her population and resources. In the 1870s her recruiting effort, on a population basis, was about 25 per cent inferior to that of her defeated rival, and in the 1880s and 1890s it fell short by as much as 30 per cent. In 1910 the German standing army was equivalent to only 0.79 per cent of the total population of the country, as against 1.53 per cent in France. Germany was now caught in a dilemma. Social stability seemed to demand an army which, though by no means small, was limited in size. Yet the international situation demanded a very large army. The powerful military influences which resisted any dilution of the aristocratic character of the officer corps thus did much to limit the country's military strength. Moreover the narrowmindedness of the German military establishment, and its determination to uphold its position at almost any cost, meant that in the higher command of the army there was virtually no understanding of the new potentialities of economic warfare (though in this respect Germany was by no means unique) and little interest in many of the new weapons and techniques which were now becoming available. The military potentialities of aircraft were now beginning to be discernible.[39] In Britain, for example, the Aerial League of the British Empire was formed in 1909 'to secure and maintain for the Empire the same supremacy in the air as it now enjoys on the sea'. Yet in 1912 the German army possessed only 100 of the new machines while the French one had almost four times as many. (The Russian army did quite well in this comparison with 263: the Habsburg one very badly with only 42.) Nevertheless Germany could not but be influenced by the growing military rivalries of this period, as the steady growth of her army bears witness; and this influence was becoming increasingly marked during the series of crises which punctuated the decade before 1914. Even had there been no war her standing army would have grown in that year to a total of 830,000 men (an increase of 30 per cent in two years) and her recruiting effort would have begun for the first time to approach that of France in intensity. The Reichstag passed an unprecedentedly large arms bill in June 1913. In the same year French expenditure on military and naval equipment alone accounted for over 5.5 per cent of all government spending. With the exception of one other year (1899) this was the highest such proportion ever attained in France.

A growing emphasis on military strength and preparedness can be seen during the period 1871–1914 not merely in France and Germany but in all the major capitals of Europe. During these decades the military expenditure of Russia trebled, while the growth of her railway network made it easier for her to use effectively her great but unwieldy strength. By 1914 she was spending on her armed forces almost as much in absolute terms as Germany, while her standing army was the largest in the world: plans had been made before the outbreak of war for its growth from 1.28 to 1.7 million. Even in Austria-Hungary the amount spent on the army almost doubled during these decades; but it was now clear that she could not match Germany or Russia in this respect and was ceasing to be a truly great military power. In 1913 the military expenditure of the almost completely landlocked territories of Francis Joseph was no more than that of Britain, which had no land frontiers whatever to defend in Europe. His subjects still spent on beer, wine and tobacco more than three times as much as on the empire's armed forces. In the years before the outbreak of the First World War the Dual Monarchy called up for military service a smaller proportion of its population than any other major continental state: Hungarian opposition prevented until 1912 any increase in the annual intake of recruits. In 1914 it had still in use heavy artillery produced as long ago as 1880 and was outgunned even by the Serbian army, which had fifty-four artillery pieces to each of its divisions against the Habsburg thirty-eight. Conrad von Hötzendorf, the fire-eating Austrian chief of staff, opposed the monarchy's participation in the Hague disarmament conference of 1907 on the grounds that 'the present condition of our army has already an appearance of permanent limitation of armament'.[40] This weakness was not entirely the result of lack of money, for funds could always be found for the maintenance of the large and expensive bureaucracy. It was caused much more by the nationalities problem of the monarchy, and in particular by the unwillingness of the Hungarians to contribute adequately to the upkeep of forces which might be used in a crisis to assert against them the power of the emperor. It meant that even before 1914 the Dual Monarchy had ceased to be able to fight a war with real hope of success except against a second-rate opponent such as Serbia or Italy. Any more exacting struggle must emphasize and make explicit its position as a military client of Germany. Indeed distrust of Austrian military capacity had played a considerable part, as early as the 1890s, in inducing Count Schlieffen, the German chief of staff, to base his plans for a future war on the idea of an all-out attack on France in which the Habsburg armies would take no part.

The enlarged armies of the European powers were made increasingly effective fighting forces during the later nineteenth and early twentieth centuries by the accelerating progress of military technology and the swift development of weapons. New explosives meant that both artillery and small arms became effective at greater ranges, while it was now possible to use rifles of smaller calibres than ever before, thus lessening their weight and that of the ammunition for them without any loss of killing-power. Moreover the rate of fire attainable was growing enormously, partly because of the adoption in the 1880s of the repeating rifle and still more because of the development of the machine-gun, a weapon for long underestimated by every European army. The effect of a long process of innovation can be seen most clearly if the position in 1914 is compared with that of a century earlier. Under Napoleon I a field-gun could fire 150 rounds a day and might be effective up to about 1,200 metres. By 1914 it could fire 300–400 rounds at an average effective range of 6,000–7,000 metres. The muskets used by Napoleon's soldiers could fire, at the very most, five times a minute. By 1914 a repeating rifle could easily fire twelve times a minute, accurate up to 800 yards and lethal at several times that range, while a machine-gun could fire at anything from 250 to 400 rounds a minute.[41] Fire-power had multiplied many times in intensity, range and accuracy.

This had repercussions on tactics and fortifications of the kind already seen, in a modified form, in the middle decades of the century. It meant that fortresses of the type which had existed in Europe since the sixteenth century had been made totally obsolete by the growth in the range and power of artillery. They were now being replaced by fortified areas whose defences were of steel and concrete and were placed as far as possible underground. The importance of field fortifications behind which an army could protect itself, made clear by the American Civil War, was underlined still further as the rifle and machine-gun developed. By the end of the nineteenth century the infantryman in every European army normally carried an entrenching tool as an essential part of his equipment. Greater fire-power also made it possible, as had already been shown in the 1850s and 1860s, for a defensive position to be successfully held by relatively few men. Under Napoleon I a concentration in battle of around 12,000 men for each kilometre of front had been normal (this was the density of Wellington's army at Waterloo). Yet during the war of 1899–1902 in South Africa the Boers successfully repulsed British attacks with defensive concentrations of as little as 400–600 men per kilometre; and under very different conditions in the great battle of Mukden in 1905 the Russian concentration against the Japanese was never anywhere more than 5,000 men to the kilometre.[42]

There was no rapid and spectacular alteration in the naval balance of power in Europe during this period as there had been in the military one in 1870–71. The British fleet remained, as it had done for almost two centuries, the greatest in the world. Nevertheless at sea technological change was even more rapid than on land; and at sea as on land it bred increased feelings of insecurity and growing national rivalries.

Throughout the last decades of the nineteenth century both the armour which protected ships of war and the guns with which they were armed improved rapidly. Indeed the history of naval architecture during this period can be seen in terms of a race between guns and armour in which the former always set the pace. Every improvement in the size and power of naval guns forced designers to armour ships more heavily, at least in their vulnerable parts, and to develop more effective armour-plate. The result was a very rapid growth of the ability of battleships both to give and to take punishment. Thus the *Warrior*, launched in 1861, had armour $4^1/_2$ inches thick and guns each of which weighed $4^1/_4$ tons; the *Inflexible*, launched exactly twenty years later, had armour 24 inches thick and guns which weighed 81 tons. Of the total weight of the French *Gloire* (1858) the armour represented 18 per cent and the armament 8 per cent; in a typical battleship of 1914 the percentages were 34 and 18.[43] On the one hand the development of slow-burning explosives in the 1880s made possible much higher muzzle velocities than hitherto with elongated projectiles. This, combined with rifling, greatly increased the effective range of all artillery, while from about 1890 smokeless powder, better sights and rangefinders and better fire control were all helping to increase the striking power of the naval gun. On the other hand the invention of the open-hearth process greatly cheapened steel plates and made them, from about 1885 onwards, a practicable alternative to the iron ones hitherto used to protect warships. Once established, steel plate was rapidly improved, with the development of 'harveyed' steel in Britain in the early 1890s and of the still better nickel steel by Krupp a year or two later. This rapid growth in the size of guns and the thickness and weight of armour meant inevitably a rapid growth in the size and cost of warships. In France for example the *Gloire* had a displacement of 5,600 tones, the *Richelieu* (1873) one of 8,500 and the *Patrie* (1901) of 14,900, while by 1914 there were French battleships of 25,500 tons under construction.

When in 1906 the British admiralty launched the *Dreadnought*, the first 'all big gun' warship with her main armament of ten 12-inch guns, and also began to develop systematically a new type, the battle-cruiser, more lightly armoured than the battleship but faster and as heavily armed, half a century of development in design had reached its logical culmination. Though future capital ships were to be larger, faster and more heavily armed than those built in 1906–14, they were not, until the aircraft and the submarine made all capital ships obsolete, to be essentially different in type. Moreover these unprecedentedly powerful ships in existence by 1914 were able to attain higher speeds with more efficient use of fuel, first by

the adoption of the turbine from the 1890s onwards and then by the first
serious use of oil fuel in the years just before the outbreak of the First
World War. Rapid technical changes meant rapid, sometimes alarmingly
rapid, obsolescence.

The best ship existing in 1867 [wrote a leading authority] would have been more
than a match for the entire British Fleet existing in 1857, and, again, the best ship
existing in 1877 would have been almost if not quite equal to fighting and beating
the entire Fleet of only ten years earlier. By 1890, the best ships of 1877 had
become well-nigh obsolete and by 1900 the best ships, even of 1890, were hardly
worthy of a place in the crack Fleets of the country.[44]

At least as important during this period as the improvement of existing
types of warship was the development of new ones – the torpedo-boat
and the submarine. The automotive torpedo, invented in 1860, had been
adopted by every major navy by the early 1870s. This soon led to the
building, notably by France, of large numbers of small and very fast craft
designed entirely to attack with the new weapon the larger and slower
ships of an enemy. To these torpedo-boats an answer was found partly in
the development from the 1880s onwards of the quick-firing gun and
partly in the building, above all in Britain, of 'torpedo-boat destroyers',
ships powerful enough to pursue and catch them. A practicable submarine
(made possible by the development of the electric accumulator battery)
was also first seen in France, which was building these startling new
vessels in considerable numbers by the end of the 1890s. The British
admiralty ordered its first submarines in 1900; the German one did the
same only in 1906. By 1914 every large navy in the world had submarines; but their potentialities, and particularly the fact that they might
be used as an efficient weapon of blockade, were still not adequately
grasped. Germany, where the invention of the diesel engine had added
greatly to their efficiency, possessed only nineteen submarines fit for sea
in August 1914. At the height of the First World War she was to have
354.

Even in the last years of this period navies were only beginning to think
of using the innovation which was to do most of all to revolutionize war
at sea – the aeroplane. Yet in 1911 an aircraft was launched from a ship
for the first time, when one flew from a specially constructed flightdeck on
the British battleship *Africa*. Five years later another landmark was reached
when a Russian battleship in the Gulf of Riga was hit by a bomb dropped
from a German aircraft – the first time that a ship had been damaged in
this way.

It seemed to many observers on both sides of the English Channel that
these spectacular technical developments might mark the end of British

predominance at sea; and from the early 1890s onwards international rivalries began to express themselves in the competitive growth of navies as they were already doing in that of armies. Until the middle or later 1880s, in spite of the enormous changes of the previous generation or more in shipbuilding and armament, the naval expenditure of the major European states did not increase. There was even a sharp fall in French naval expenditure during the decade after 1867. Individual ships rapidly became more complex and expensive; but fewer were built, especially of the large and costly battleships. Technical change, though it sometimes, as in the past, created a sense of insecurity in Britain (for example in 1884, when accelerated French building once more aroused uneasiness) did not in general force her to spend more on her navy. The naval estimates laid before Parliament in 1861 were not equalled until 1885. After about 1890 this position rapidly changed. National rivalries meant that naval estimates rose rapidly everywhere during the next two decades.

Until the end of the century it was from France and Russia that the threat to Britain's seapower and security appeared to come. In 1882 the Russian government drew up for the first time a systematic plan for a great increase in the country's naval strength. Fifteen battleships and ten cruisers were to be built; and these numbers were later increased. Another big building programme was drawn up in 1898, the date from which the Russian empire began to maintain a powerful fleet in the Far East. In France also the rate of building increased during the 1880s and 1890s, notably after the adoption of the ambitious Gervais programme of 1891; and in particular the new torpedo-boat seemed there to offer a cheap and effective riposte to the far superior British strength in battleships. A group of naval theorists, the *Jeune École*, of whom Admiral Aube was the most influential, stressed the possibility of inflicting crippling losses on Britain in any future war by the use of torpedo-boats and later submarines against her fleet, and of commerce raiders against her merchant shipping. The idea of commerce-raiding by fast cruisers, which drew support from the success of Confederate efforts of this kind during the American Civil War, also played an important role in Russian theories of naval warfare during this period.

There was a large element of exaggeration and wishful thinking in these theories, as the experience of 1914–18 was to show; and in the construction of large warships Britain, with her highly developed metallurgical and shipbuilding industries, was still in a position of decisive superiority. Armour-plate was not easy to produce, and in particular the backwardness of Russia's steel industry added very considerably to her difficulties in building a large navy.[45] Moreover one result of uneasiness about French and Russian intentions was a considerable improvement in the efficiency of British dockyards from the 1880s onwards. In 1885 it had been noted that no British ironclad had ever been put into service within five years of the keel being laid, and that some had taken up to nine years to build. By contrast in the period 1889–1905 it took on average a little over three years to complete a British battleship (the *Dreadnought* was built and fitted out, by a special effort, in just over a year), whereas it needed five years to build a French one and even longer to build a Russian one. Nevertheless it seemed to many people in Britain by the end of the 1880s that either France or Russia singly might now, armed with new weapons, be a serious adversary at sea, and that together they could place the country in imminent danger. A few years later the emergence of the north African port of Bizerta as an important French naval base and the growth of Russian naval power in the Far East seemed to add substance to these fears. The result was the passage in 1889 of the Naval Defence Act, which led to a large increase in British building, and the development during the next decade of a naval rivalry with France and Russia which was sometimes acute. From 1889 onwards it was officially held desirable that the strength of the British navy, at least in battleships, should be equal to that of the two next strongest navies in the world combined. Henceforth the 'two-power standard' was to be accepted in Britain as the most obvious measuring-rod of the adequacy of the fleet.[46] The Navy League was formed in 1895 to help mobilize public opinion in the cause of strengthening the fleet, while in that year, for the first time during the nineteenth century, the navy estimates were larger than the army ones (by 1914 they were to be nearly 60 per cent higher). A year earlier Gladstone had been forced to resign the premiership and end his political career by the desire of the rest of his cabinet for an increase in the rate of naval building.

There is no mistaking the intensity and genuineness of the fears provoked in Britain in the 1890s by the bogey of French and Russian competition at sea. From 1894 onwards there were strategists who advocated the complete withdrawal of the British fleet from the Mediterranean in time of war, while it was increasingly agreed that it would be impossible to keep the Suez Canal open in face of French and Russian hostility. Yet by far the most serious threat to British security was to come later, with the rise of the German navy in the early years of the twentieth century. The idea of a large German navy was not new. In 1849 Prince Adalbert of Prussia had drawn up plans for one; and in 1873 von Stosch, the head of the imperial admiralty (significantly, an army officer with no naval experience) had put forward proposals for the building of a considerable fleet. Only after 1890, however, did such ideas begin to have practical importance. William II deeply envied and admired the position of Britain as a world power, a position which clearly depended above all on her strength at sea. The achievement of the great colonial empire and the world power status which he felt were Germany's right, and which the misfortunes of her history had hitherto denied her, clearly involved the building of a large navy, if necessary in opposition to that of Britain. The growing influence over the kaiser of Admiral von Senden-Bibran, the head of his naval cabinet, did much to strengthen these ideas. William was also deeply impressed by the American Admiral Mahan's famous book, *The Influence of Sea Power upon History* (1890), the most influential work ever written on naval strategy, of which he ordered a translation to be placed on board every ship in the German navy. Its insistence on the supreme importance of a 'fleet in being' strong enough to control the seas and deny freedom of movement to any opposing force, its low view of the effectiveness of commerce-raiding as a means of warfare, lent weight to the growing pressure in Germany for the building of a powerful force of large warships. In 1892 William gave Captain Alfred von Tirpitz, the leading advocate of such a fleet, the right of direct personal access to him. In 1897 Tirpitz became minister of marine; and some German industrial interests were now beginning to be aware that a programme of large-scale naval construction might be very profitable to them.

But the drive for a large German navy was much more than a matter of a day-dreaming ruler, ambitious officers and greedy businessmen. It was a movement which aroused genuine and widespread popular support in Germany. There by the end of the century was clearly visible a powerful current of anti-British feeling fed from several disparate sources. Conservative agrarians disliked Britain as the outstanding example of the democracy and parliamentary government which they loathed: liberals saw in her Germany's greatest industrial and colonial rival. 'In domestic politics, socially, economically, they were deadly enemies; but in foreign policy they were united in hostility to England.'[47] In Britain moreover the competition of German industry was painfully felt in the 1890s – more so than after the turn of the century, when it began to appear less of a threat. On both sides there were publicists ready to proclaim that conflict was inevitable. For example the biologist Peter Chalmers-Mitchell wrote in the *Saturday Review* in February 1898: 'Here is the first great racial struggle of the future; here are two great nations pressing against each other, man to man, all over the world. One or the other has to go; one or the other will go.'[48] More and more it could be plausibly argued in Germany that future expansion demanded that Britain be either defeated or forced to come to terms with a threat to her naval power and hence her security. 'Without a strong fleet', wrote the greatest German shipping magnate, Albert Ballin, in February 1909, 'Germany will be very much reduced as a power for friend and foe alike in a future war: with a strong fleet the German empire will hold the balance in its hand for a long time perhaps. . . . In the brutal struggle of nations for light and air, strength alone counts in the final analysis.'[49] The formation in 1898 of the Navy League, a pressure-group under imperial patronage dedicated to the cause of a great German fleet, and the extensive propaganda it carried on,[50] helped to focus these increasingly widespread anti-British feelings. Also the navy was one of the few truly national institutions Germany possessed. Unlike the army, it was not permeated by aristocratic influences; and it was associated with the most modern aspects of German life – efficient heavy industry and the approach to parliamentary government represented by the Reichstag. These facts very considerably increased its popularity: it is noteworthy that its claims always aroused in the Reichstag more sympathy than those of the army.

All these forces combined to produce in 1898, in spite of the reluctance of many members of the Reichstag to spend much money on the fleet, a new Navy Law which considerably increased the rate of building. The more important Second Navy Law of 1900, whose introduction was accelerated by William II to take advantage of the bitter anti-British feeling aroused in Germany by the Boer war, provided for the laying down by 1917 of no fewer than thirty-four battleships (Germany had possessed only six in 1898, and small ones at that) as well as eleven heavy and thirty-four light cruisers. This legislation involved a definite decision, accepted by the politically conscious part of the German people, to challenge British leadership at sea. Henceforth the building of a big navy was for the kaiser and many Germans a matter of prestige at least as much as of any rational calculation of profit and loss. As Bethmann-Hollweg, the imperial chancellor, said in 1912 to a member of the British embassy in Berlin, Germany desired a navy not merely to protect her coasts and commerce but for 'the general purposes of her greatness'; and the very vagueness of this desire added to its dangers. From about 1905 onwards fear of German power at sea was to be the greatest of all factors influencing British public opinion against Germany; while there were real fears in Berlin, especially in 1904–5, that Britain might attempt to destroy the still incomplete German navy by a surprise attack like that made on Copenhagen and the Danish fleet in 1807. Yet national honour made it impossible for the German government to give way to British demands that the rate of naval building be slackened, unless very large political concessions, above all a promise of British neutrality in a continental war, could be obtained in return. The result was that a series of efforts by Britain to reach some agreement on the naval question all failed. The most serious of these, the mission to Berlin in February 1912 of Lord Haldane, the secretary of state for war, produced no result partly because the negotiations were not very competently conducted (Haldane was by no means an expert on naval affairs) but mainly because of the repeated refusal of the British government to give an unconditional promise of neutrality in any future war in which Germany might be engaged.[51] Indeed Haldane's visit was followed by the publication of new legislation, the so-called *Novelle*, which envisaged a further considerable strengthening of the German fleet. Yet the objective of making that fleet so strong that war with Germany would constitute for Britain an unacceptable risk was not achieved. German naval strategic planning throughout the Tirpitz era remained remarkably erratic and confused.[52] The most detailed quantitative study of the relative strengths of the two fleets concludes that there was only one year, 1911, in which the German threat to British naval power was 'large'.[53] The strength of the British fleet, and above all of its largest ships, was now concentrated in home waters, leaving only a small force in the Mediterranean. The development of Rosyth, on the east coast of Scotland, as a new naval base which could be of use only in a war with Germany, had been under way for some time; and in 1912 the admiralty began to prepare special charts of the German coasts intended for operational use. The fact that Tirpitz seems not to have foreseen at all such a concentration of British naval strength in the North Sea is a telling indictment of the narrowness and dogmatism of his ideas. Above all Britain could and did outbuild Germany. At no time did expenditure on the fleet amount to more than a third of all German spending on the armed forces. In 1913, in spite of the *Novelle*, it fell to as little as 22 per cent. The greater size of the British shipbuilding industry, and the strong public feeling which forced Parliament to vote increasing sums for naval building, allowed Britain to maintain, though at a cost which deeply pained many of the more radical and pacifist liberals, a decisive margin of superiority.

The armed forces of Europe in 1914, the product of two generations or more of unprecedentedly rapid development in weapons and organization, were still in some ways surprisingly backward-looking and enslaved by the past. Much of their thinking on military tactics failed to take account of the enormous difficulties which the development of modern weapons had now placed in the way of mass attacks of the traditional kind, or even of the movement of large bodies of men in the open. In France particularly, where the country's inferiority to Germany in numbers and material resources was now impossible to ignore, official orthodoxy in the last years of peace stressed the alleged ability of a really determined and well-led attack, culminating in a bayonet charge, to carry even a strong position defended by entrenchments and men armed with up-to-date weapons. The victories of the Japanese in Manchuria in 1904–5, which were achieved by mass frontal attacks and aided by the defensive attitude and general inertia of the Russian armies, gave considerable support to this belief (in spite of the heavy losses – 84,000 Japanese dead and 143,000 wounded – which they involved). Only the catastrophic failure of the French offensive in Lorraine in 1914 could destroy it, though the destruction was then rapid and total. The importance which every army continued to attach to cavalry is understandable, since the horseman was still of some value, in an age when motor transport was in its infancy, for scouting and reconnaissance. But the belief, in an age of modern artillery, machine-guns and barbed wire, that the cavalry charge had still a place on the field of battle, and the reluctance with which this belief was abandoned even after 1914, shows how deep-rooted the conservatism of many military leaders still was. As late as 1909, again, it was envisaged that in time of war French field-guns would fire on an average only four rounds a day; and it was not until 1915 that the French soldier ceased to wear the traditional red trousers, which made him so visible to enemy riflemen, and was given a more rational dress. Perhaps equally remarkable is the fact that it was not until 1905, fifty years after the evolution of the modern battleship had begun, that boarding stations and cutlass drill ceased to be part of the regular training given to ratings in the British navy.

No writer or theorist before 1914 realized at all adequately what a war of the future, fought between great industrialized states able to raise mass armies and maintain them for years on end, would be like. For such a realization not merely technical knowledge but still more analytical imagination of the highest kind was needed; and this was not a quality with which the military and naval leaders of Europe were richly endowed. With very few exceptions they continued to think in terms of clear-cut and relatively rapid victory, to be achieved by essentially traditional means. This was largely because they assumed that a long war was an economic impossibility. The great Moltke had stressed as early as 1869 in his orders to German commanders that economic necessity demanded that a future war be ended quickly. Four decades later Tirpitz and Schlieffen were accepting unquestioningly the same assumption. In the two decades before the outbreak of war civilian writers such as H. G. Wells and Arthur Conan Doyle in Britain, or Albert Robida in France, showed a deeper imaginative grasp of the new possibilities than any professional soldier.[54]

Not even they, however, could foresee all the implications of a war of the future. In particular the potentialities of economic warfare, the extent to which in time of war governments could and would take control of the entire economic life of the nation through rationing, price controls and forms of industrial conscription, was not at all understood. Thus Ivan Bloch, in his *La Guerre* (Paris, 1898–1900), the most detailed and convincing effort to understand the new nature of armed conflict, took it for granted that in time of war prices would be left at the mercy of ordinary market forces. This, he argued, meant that food prices in Britain would be greatly increased if even a single enemy cruiser were left at liberty to prey on her trade routes, and that Russia and the Dual Monarchy, the only great European states with a surplus of home-grown food, were those best fitted to stand the strain of a long war. In a rather similar way Sir Norman Angell, in his very widely read *The Great Illusion* (London, 1910), which undertook to prove that war under modern conditions could not possibly pay the victors, assumed that an essentially liberal and individualistic economic system would continue to function, within each belligerent country and internationally, if a conflict broke out. More important, he assumed that the behaviour of states was essentially rational and would remain so even in time of war. He failed utterly to grasp the intensity of the group hatreds, the vindictiveness and gratuitous destructiveness, which a great international conflict must now release. If highly educated civilians and men of affairs such as Bloch and Angell failed to understand the economic, social and above all psychological implications of a great war, it was not likely that soldiers and sailors would do so.

In every great European state, therefore, armed forces in 1914 were larger, more expensive, more national, more eager for conflict and endowed with enormously more destructive power than in the year of Waterloo. Everywhere, as the cost of armies and navies grew and simultaneously demands for better education and more lavish social services were voiced, conflicts within governments over the allocation of resources between these competing uses grew sharper. Everywhere it became increasingly difficult for poor and industrially undeveloped states, however large, to attain the military strength which could now be based only on wealth and advanced technology. Everywhere generals and admirals claimed, with complete sincerity, to be the guardians of national security and prestige; so that in 1914 their influence on the formulation of policy in many parts of Europe was at least as great as at any moment in history. Many national leaders all over Europe foresaw that war was likely in the not too distant future: some of them, notably in Germany, wished and hoped for it. No one, however, envisaged or desired a struggle such as the one which broke out in July and August of that year, a war which was the culmination not merely of military and naval developments but of the vast economic growth and the triumph of nationalism which had so deeply marked the history of nineteenth-century Europe.

NOTES

1. A. Vagts, *A History of Militarism* (London, Allen & Unwin, 1938), p. 189.
2. See above, pp. 8–9.
3. Readers of Anthony Trollope's *Autobiography* will remember that in 1834, when the family had been forced by his father's debts to take refuge in Belgium, he was offered a commission in an Austrian cavalry regiment, in spite of his being shortsighted and having no military experience or background whatsoever (Fontana edn, 1962, p. 41).
4. The decline of the military border can be followed in G. E. Rothenberg, *The Military Border in Croatia, 1740–1881* (University of Chicago Press, 1966), Chs. vii–x.
5. J. S. Curtiss, *The Russian Army under Nicholas I, 1825–1855* (Duke University Press, 1965), p. 231.
6. O. Regele, *Feldmarshall Radetzky: Leben, Leistung, Erbe* (Vienna–Munich, 1957), p. 431.
7. It is true that this well-known episode took place in somewhat unusual and ambiguous circumstances. France was not at war with Holland, though she was cooperating with Britain in the expulsion of Dutch forces from the southern Netherlands and the creation of an independent Belgian kingdom. But it is probably a fair illustration of the point made in the text.
8. Curtiss, *The Russian Army under Nicholas I*, p. 340.
9. E. M. Earle, ed., *Makers of Modern Strategy* (Princeton University Press, 1944), pp. 108–9. There is a good account of Clausewitz's ideas in G. Ritter, *The Sword and the Scepter: the problem of militarism in Germany* (Coral Gables, Florida, University of Miami Press, 1969–70), i, 48–70.
10. Earle, *Makers of Modern Strategy*, p. 91.
11. These figures are given by H. Nickerson, 'Nineteenth-century military techniques', *Journal of World History*, iv (1957–58), 348–58.
12. Lt Col F.-R. Chesney and H. Reeve, *The Military Resources of Prussia and France and Recent Changes in the Art of War* (London, 1870), preface, p. vi.
13. These details are taken from E. A. Pratt, *The Rise of Rail-Power in War and Conquest* (London, 1915), Ch. i.
14. General Andolenko, *Histoire de l'armée russe* (Paris, 1967), p. 216; Curtiss, *The Russian Army under Nicholas I*, pp. 248 50.
15. Captain Jesse, *Notes of a Half-Pay in Search of Health: Russia, Circassia and the Crimea in 1839–40* (London, 1841), ii, 142.
16. The repercussions on naval tactics and strategy of the coming of steam power are well discussed in B. Brodie, *Sea Power in the Machine Age* (Princeton University Press, 1941), Chs vi–vii.
17. See pp. 240–3.
18. *New Cambridge Modern History*, ix (Cambridge, 1962), 284.
19. British efforts to blockade Russia encountered many political and other difficulties and were not very effective (see Olive Anderson, 'Economic warfare in the Crimean War', *Economic History Review*, 2nd ser, xiv (1961–62), 34–47).

20. There had already been spectacular illustrations of what railways could achieve during the American Civil War. Thus late in 1863 a Confederate force of 10,000 men was moved by rail over a distance of nearly 1,000 miles in less than eight days. Almost simultaneously a Federal army of 20,000 was moved 1,200 miles at an average speed of 200 miles a day (H. Nickerson, *The Armed Horde, 1793–1939* (New York, Putnam, 1940), p. 169). But the significance of these achievements was hardly at all grasped in Europe at the time.

21. Francis Joseph, no doubt largely under the influence of 1848, felt strongly that the strength of his army lay in 'loyal and knightly' rather than in learned officers (J. C. Allmeyer-Beck, 'Das Heerwesen', in F. Engel-Janosi and H. Rumpler, eds, *Probleme der Franzisko-Josephinischen Zeit, 1848–1916* (Munich, 1967), p. 69).

22. See p. 23.

23. A more detailed discussion of these issues can be found in A. F. Kovacs, 'French military institutions before the Franco-Prussian war', *American Historical Review*, li (1945–46), 217–35; and Gordon Wright, 'Public opinion and conscription in France, 1866–70', *Journal of Modern History*, xiv (1942), 26–45.

24. Chesney and Reeve, *Military Resources of Prussia and France*, p. 116. The Prussian army as a whole fired only about 200,000 rounds – slightly more than one for each rifle available (G. A. Craig, *The Battle of Königgrätz* (London, Weidenfeld & Nicholson, 1965), p. 184).

25. Nickerson, *The Armed Horde*, p. 194.

26. *Ibid.*, p. 205.

27. A. Vagts, *The Military Attaché* (Princeton University Press, 1967), p. 31n.

28. F. Crouzet, 'Recherches sur la production d'armements en France, 1815–1913', *Revue Historique*, ccli (1974), 56.

29. See p. 235.

30. P. L. Alston, *Education and the State in Tsarist Russia* (Stanford University Press, 1969), p. 94.

31. For a discussion of the problems of the British army in the later nineteenth century see A. V. Tucker, 'Army and society in England, 1870–1900: a reassessment of the Cardwell reforms', *Journal of British Studies*, ii (1962–63) no. 2, 110–41.

32. H. Contamine, *La Revanche, 1871–1914* (Paris, 1957), pp. 39–40.

33. See above, pp. 52–3.

34. Friedrich Engels, starting from a totally different set of political assumptions, reached the same conclusion. 'Contrary to appearance', he wrote in 1891, 'compulsory military service surpasses general franchise as a democratic agency. The real strength of the German social democracy does not rest in the number of its voters but in its soldiers. . . . By 1900 the army, once the most Prussian, the most reactionary element in the country, will be socialist in its majority as inescapably as fate.' (Earle, *Makers of Modern Strategy*, p. 169.)

35. V. G. Kiernan, 'Conscription and Society in Europe before the War of 1914–1918', in M. R. D. Foot, ed., *War and Society: historical essays in honour and memory of J. R. Western* (London, Paul Elek, 1973), pp. 144–91.

36. J. C. G. Röhl, *Germany without Bismarck: the crisis of government in the Second Reich* (London, Batsford, 1967), p. 191.

37. R. Chickering, *We Men Who Feel Most German: a cultural study of the Pan-German League, 1886–1914* (London, Allen & Unwin, 1984), pp. 103–4, 114–15, 127–8.

38. J. Steinberg, 'The Kaiser's navy and German society', *Past and Present*, no. 28 (July 1964), 108–9.

39. The first bombing from a powered aircraft took place on 1 November 1911, when during the Italo-Turkish war the Italian Lieutenant Gavotti dropped four small bombs on a Turkish army camp in Libya.

40. N. Stone, 'Army and society in the Habsburg Monarchy, 1900–1914', *Past and Present*, no. 33 (April 1966), 107.

41. J. Perré, *Les Mutations de la guerre moderne* (Paris, 1962), p. 120.

42. *Ibid.*, pp. 121–2.

43. L. Nicholas and A. Reussner, *La Puissance navale dans l'histoire* (Paris, Editions Maritimes et Coloniales, 1958–1963), ii, 152. A discussion of the development of guns and armour during this period, with much technical information, can be found in Brodie, *Sea Power in the Machine Age*, pp. 213ff.

44. Sir W. L. Clowes, *The Royal Navy: a history* (London, 1897–1903), vii, 68.

45. Italy and Japan were hampered in the same way; and even the United States could not produce armour-plate until an Act of 1886 made it mandatory to use only domestic products in the building of the new American fleet which was then projected.

46. Though in the 1890s some supporters of an overwhelmingly strong British fleet would have liked to achieve a superiority of five to three over France and Russia combined, in order to allow for the fact that in wartime a considerable proportion of Britain's strength at sea would be absorbed by commerce protection and other duties.

47. E. Kehr, 'Englandhass und Weltpolitik', in his *Primat der Innenpolitik* (Berlin, 1965), p. 170.

48. Quoted in A. J. Marder, *The Anatomy of British Sea Power* (Frank Cass, 1964), p. 300.

49. L. Cecil, *Albert Ballin: business and politics in imperial Germany, 1888–1918* (Princeton University Press, 1967), p. 155.

50. During the Reichstag elections of 1907, it distributed 15 million pamphlets. By then it had about a million members, as compared with the 15,000 of its British namesake.

51. The best account of the Haldane mission, based largely on archive materials, is in Cecil, *Albert Ballin*, pp. 181ff.

52. P. M. Kennedy, 'The development of German naval operations plans against England, 1896–1914', *English Historical Review*, lxxxix (Jan. 1974), 56–60.

53. J. H. McRandle and J. P. Quirk, 'An interpretation of the German Risk Fleet Concept, 1899–1914', *Purdue Faculty Papers in Economic History, 1956–66* (Homewood, 1967), pp. 500–1.

54. On discussions during this period of the nature of wars of the future see I. F. Clarke, *Voices Prophesying War, 1763–1984* (Oxford University Press, 1966), Chs iii–iv.

7

Romanticism, evolution, consciousness: the movement of ideas

In every aspect of intellectual and cultural life – in the physical sciences, in music and the arts, in thinking about politics and society – the nineteenth and early twentieth centuries were a more complex age, more dynamic, more varied, more rapidly and incessantly changing, than any preceding one. To summarize it is therefore to falsify, perhaps even seriously to falsify. Yet if a summary is to be attempted much of its life can be grouped under one or another of the great tides of thought and feeling mentioned in the title of this chapter. In the first half of the nineteenth century the triumph of romanticism was never complete. Yet that period gave freer play than ever before to fundamental emotional drives and appetites which the eighteenth-century Enlightenment had tended to neglect and which have remained a great force in European life ever since. In the later decades of the century evolutionary ideas, in the widest sense of the term, revolutionized thinking about the nature and purpose of human life and seemed to open to it a whole new vista of possibilities. From the 1890s onwards the most original thinkers tended to concentrate their efforts more and more on the mysteries and irrationalities of man's nature and to see the problems of man in society in a new light, in terms of consciousness rather than in those of mechanism or even ideas. Throughout these wonderfully productive generations change, by the standards of the past sometimes almost apocalyptic in its violence and suddenness, was building up a mental climate very different from that of the eighteenth century. Political hopes and fears, artistic dogmas, pessimism about the way the world was going and messianic hopes of a future unlike anything hitherto known – all were now more intense and more widespread than ever in the past. The marvellous intellectual and artistic fecundity of the period was both the measure and the outcome of its tensions and dilemmas.

Romanticism is one of the vaguest of the many vague terms in the vocabulary of the historian. It is scarcely possible to find any characteristic shared by all the romantics of the first half of the nineteenth century, or to draw up any confession of faith to which they would all have subscribed. Nevertheless the word is not meaningless: it is possible to make a number of general statements about romanticism which are as well grounded as most generalizations. It meant most fundamentally of all a stressing of the individual, of his potentialities, of his autonomy as against society or any group within society, of the value of his feelings, spontaneous and unforced, as the yardstick against which the world must be measured. This meant that it erected against the ideals of moderation and elegance which had dominated much of the eighteenth century the new one of the exceptional spirit leading, and entitled to lead, the mediocrities by whom he inevitably found himself surrounded. Such a spirit, as an English painter convinced of his own genius put it, was 'sent into the world not to obey laws but to give them'.[1] This ideal was a deeply anti-egalitarian one. Allied with the Rousseauist belief that the emotions, especially those of love and grief, were felt more intensely and with greater purity by a minority of *beaux esprits* than by ordinary mortals, it contributed considerably to the essentially aristocratic atmosphere which marked much of the romantic movement during its greatest decades. It is notable how many of the literary leaders of that movement, at least until the 1830s – de Vigny, de Musset and Chateaubriand in France, Leopardi and Manzoni in Italy, Byron in England, Novalis and Arnim in Germany – were aristocrats by birth as well as in feeling. Though there were lesser examples of the ideal of genius (for example the composer Beethoven, who even during his lifetime was hero-worshipped by a limited circle of admirers) the supreme one was that of Napoleon I. More than any other figure in history he impressed on his own generation, and still more on succeeding ones, a new view of what the individual could be and accomplish. The enormity of his demands, even the speed and completeness of his downfall, seemed merely to add to his stature. During his reign, wrote Alfred de Musset in 1836,

The life of Europe was concentrated in one man; all were trying to fill their lungs with the air which he had breathed. Every year France presented that man with three hundred thousand of her youth; it was the tax paid to Caesar, and, without that troop behind him, he could not follow his fortune. It was the escort he needed that he might traverse the world, and then perish in a little valley in a deserted island under the weeping willow.[2]

Above all he seemed great because his achievements were so completely the product of his own individuality, because he was the most overwhelming of all examples of the self-made man. His greatness, wrote Chateaubriand after his fall, lay supremely in the fact that 'he owed everything to himself, and without any other authority than that of his own genius made thirty-six million subjects obey him in an age when no illusions surrounded a throne'. That Napoleon should have aroused this romantic enthusiasm is one of the paradoxes of history; for he was himself very much a child of the Enlightenment. He thought in terms of reason and common sense and had a utilitarian view of men as essentially rational and essentially the same everywhere. Nevertheless he aroused an enthusiasm without precedent. Only after him had it been shown to the full what 'genius' might accomplish.

Genius is, more than anything else, originality. The cult of originality and spontaneity, indeed of the subjective in general, is therefore another aspect of the romantic emphasis on the individual. In this sense the romantics rejected uncompromisingly the classicism dominant in European artistic life during the seventeenth and early eighteenth centuries. This had suspected, indeed actively discouraged, originality. The core of classicism in the arts was the belief that all worthwhile achievement depended on finding a sound model, looking up to it and imitating it. Voltaire, in many respects a profoundly conventional man, had been a whole-hearted adherent of this doctrine. Rousseau by contrast asserted that the highest achievement came from a refusal to be bound by precedents or to imitate approved models: in this belief (which he did not originate) he appealed profoundly to the romantics. Thus Beethoven, for example, disliked hearing the music of other composers since this, he felt, might threaten the originality of his own writing. This attitude could easily acquire overtones of conceit and intellectual snobbery; and the history of romanticism offers plenty of examples of more or less conscious poseurs using the alleged originality of their ideas and intensity of their emotions as props for their own egos – Rousseau himself, Chateaubriand, Byron.[3] On a still lower level even the occasional extravagance in dress in which some romantics indulged[4] can be seen as a trivial example of this stress on the individual and the original. Nevertheless it is difficult to deny that the romantic insistence on the rights of originality and of the free individual spirit had enormous constructive importance. It permitted many excesses and follies. Carried to extremes it could come close to an assertion that truth was not objective and independent of the seeker but rather something created by the very search for it. This subjectivity in turn could carry the dangerous implication that the motives behind an action were more important than its consequences, that the value of a cause or an idea lay in the emotions it could inspire rather than in its own intrinsic merits. Nevertheless the emphasis on the claims and rights of originality imparted a new tone, more open, more experimental, more questioning and dynamic, to many aspects of European life. Allied with this high valuation of originality, moreover, and indeed an offshoot of it, was the idea of youth as more original and more creative than age, and hence superior to it – an idea completely strange to the eighteenth century. It is from the triumph of the romantic attitude that one of the most potent myths of the modern world, that of the injustice to youth of selfish and envious age, takes its origin.

The individual was a natural being and one unique in himself. Side by side with a stress on the individual, therefore, went a stress on nature, and in particular on the concrete and specific in nature. This had clearly several different roots. One may have been the new confidence generated by the scientific progress of the eighteenth century, which meant that nature was ceasing to be seen as something normally hostile. Whereas hitherto she had been regarded with fear or at least with awe it was now possible to look on her with wonder, a considerably more comfortable emotion. Another may have been the growing political power and social importance in western Europe of a middle class more vulnerable than aristocracies had traditionally been to the expansive emotions which natural scenery tended to arouse, and to their free expression. Another lay in the assertion, stemming principally from Rousseau, that man was a part of nature rather than of a corrupt society, and that peace and harmony could thus be achieved only by a kind of surrender of the self to nature and by close communion with her. Moreover the nature which the romantics admired was not that of seventeenth and eighteenth-century classicism, smoothed, generalized and kept at arm's length. It was one made up of specific and individual entities, one in which each river, mountain, forest, had its own characteristics and individuality, just as in the human world each society and culture was unique. 'To Generalize is to be an Idiot', wrote the poet and artist William Blake. 'To Particularize is the Alone Distinction of Merit. General Knowledges are those Knowledges that Idiots possess. . . . Minute Discrimination is not Accidental. All Sublimity is founded on Minute Discrimination.'[5]

Like the emphasis on the worth of the individual, that on the virtue and curative power of nature could be dangerous. In intellectual and artistic life it meant that mere sincerity could be exalted above skill, and ignorance excused on the grounds of truly felt emotion. In politics it created, above all in France from 1793 onwards, a radical mythology of the superior virtue of 'the people' (which could be regarded as a kind of natural force) and of the purifying violence of the uneducated. This, at least until the failure of the radical revolutionary movement of 1848, could be used to justify many sorts of arbitrary authority and in particular a very rough-and-ready popular justice.[6] None the less the romantic view of nature, like the romantic view of the individual, was a force tending to liberate thought and feeling. A certain amount of emotional excess, of silly effusiveness, even perhaps of arbitrariness, was a price worth paying for this liberation.

Romanticism was thus a great innovating force. Yet one of its most important innovations was to give immense importance to history and the historical. Its vision of the world as the outcome of an age-long process of development and growth, its interest in origins, was the most truly revolutionary of all its characteristics. 'Our century', wrote a commentator in 1818, 'is singular in that it apprehends by memories, as it makes politics by memories.'[7] Nearly forty years later the greatest French novelist of the century, Gustave Flaubert, declared flatly that 'we are above all in a historically minded century'.[8] Every new political and social ideology to emerge during the nineteenth century was to one extent or another a vision of history. By the 1820s or 1830s Europe presented the hitherto unknown spectacle of a civilization beginning to be truly conscious, in an imaginative as well as an intellectual way, of its history, of one increasingly attuned to historical habits of thought. This change of intellectual climate, one of the most profound any society has ever undergone, almost certainly owed something to the political cataclysms unleashed by 1789. The upheavals of the revolutionary and Napoleonic periods had forced the ordinary man, more than ever before, into history, had begun for the first time to make him conscious of it as a process of change, and expressly of man-made change. History had become a mass experience.[9] The sudden growth in the size of armies which forced millions of conscripts into some kind of personal contact with historical events played a part in this; and some of these half-comprehending pawns may even have been stimulated to the beginnings of a new awareness by the sight of Napoleon himself, history incarnate, riding by.

The new outlook can be seen ramifying through European thought and feeling. It was deeply important for scholarship, for it underlay the work of the great German historian Leopold von Ranke and his followers, and hence the beginning of truly modern historical writing. But it was much more than an academic movement. The emotional appeal of history, notably in the enormously popular and influential novels of Sir Walter Scott, was very wide. The view of it which the ordinary man absorbed from these novels was to a hitherto unknown degree one which stressed peoples and the lives and characteristics of ordinary individuals rather than monarchs, churches or aristocracies. It was therefore one able to achieve unprecedented popularity and arouse unprecedented interest. Through the work of Scott and his imitators the educated minority of European society came to put a quite new value on history, to see how the past influenced the present and, inevitably, often to read the present back into the past.[10] Fragmentary, biased and unscholarly though this popular view of history was, it meant the addition of a new and very pervasive element to the stream of Europe's intellectual life. More and more universal principles, as explanations of events, were abandoned in favour of modes of thinking which were historical and in some sense evolutionary. For the first time an interest in origins came to play a great, indeed a dominant, role in European thought.

The purely practical implications of this historicism were considerable. By its stress on the differing pasts of particular human groups, and on the persisting legacy of these differences to the present it helped to stimulate the growth of nationalism.[11] For the same reason it tended to devalue the idea, so popular in the eighteenth century, of a simple code of rules governing human behaviour which was universally, or at least very widely, valid. So far as law was concerned this naïve faith in codification came under fire principally from the great German jurist F. K. von Savigny, the founder of the 'historical school' of jurisprudence, and his followers.[12] In a more superficial way the historicism of the romantics, and particularly the strong interest of many of them in the Middle Ages, led, notably in Germany, to a hankering after a revivified traditional society based on guilds and corporate bodies. This dream was made possible only by the fact that most of Europe had still been barely touched by the Industrial Revolution and that the immensity of the economic and social changes soon to overtake much of the continent was still hardly dreamed of by most contemporaries. It seemed none the less to offer a system of political and social organization which avoided the different evils of autocracy, liberal parliamentarism and socialism, and was therefore to retain some of its appeal throughout the century.

This type of traditionalism had strong religious, and particularly Catholic, overtones: another aspect of the romantic era was a marked revival of religious feeling and of a widespread desire to believe among the educated classes of Europe. To this statement, as to every other about romanticism, there are obvious and important individual exceptions. The composer Berlioz, for example, in some ways the archetypal 'romantic' personality, managed to combine the writing of a considerable amount of religious music including at least one masterpiece (his *Childhood of Christ*, 1854) with a personal attitude to religion close to that of the eighteenth-century Enlightenment. Moreover a good deal of the religious feeling of the first half of the nineteenth century was a matter of religiosity, of 'stained-glass Christianity', rather than of genuine or profound faith. Often it was the external appearances of religion – liturgy, vestments, buildings – rather than its essence, which appealed to artists and intellectuals, while the centuries-old justification of it as a mere engine of social control was still repeatedly put forward. Both attitudes, notably the former, find expression in the most popular and successful pseudo-religious work of the age, Chateaubriand's *Génie du christianisme* (1802). Much of this religious revival was little more than a feeble emotionalism, a luxuriance in nostalgia for a medieval Christian past which was largely a figment of the imagination, and an indulgence in vaguely elevating feelings. Some of it sprang from a dislike and distrust of scientific explanations of nature, since these seemed to rob her of her mystery and therefore of some of her power. The German writer Novalis (Friedrich von Hardenberg), as romanticism was rising to its apogee in the last years of the eighteenth century, had spoken of 'the dignity of the unknown' – an idea which would have been incomprehensible to the age of Newton. Similarly Keats in his *Lamia* (1819) complained that

Philosophy will clip an angel's wings,
Conquer all mysteries by rule and line,
Empty the haunted air and gnomed mine –
Unweave a rainbow . . .

and a somewhat similar stress on the essential mystery of the natural world appears in one of the supreme expressions of romanticism in music, the great passage in which Faust, in Berlioz's *Damnation of Faust* (1846) invokes nature as 'Nature immense, impénétrable et fière'. To speak without qualification of a romantic cult of the irrational and inexplicable would be an exaggeration. But some leading romantic writers – Wordsworth is an example – showed the dawning of an intuition that there are areas of the mind which are beyond the reach of reason or even conscious thought; and for the first time there was a fairly widespread interest in madness, in which it was thought the essential characteristics of the individual could be seen exposed and defenceless, as a subject for writers and painters.[13]

After these tentative and very incomplete efforts at a definition of romanticism one is driven to admit the impossibility of the task, even if definition takes merely the crude form of description. The phenomena are simply too numerous, and too rich in their variety and contradictions, to be bound by any formulae. From one point of view, to be a romantic was to stress the individual and the unique, genius, originality, spontaneity. Yet at the same time the romantic sense of history emphasized the impossibility of escaping completely from the past and asserted that the development of human institutions was continuous, not something that proceeded by jumps. Moreover the populism which some of the more politically radical romantics affected, like the organic conception of the state and the emphasis on corporate bodies and peasant communities which appealed to others, did not square easily with assertive individualism. It is possible to speak without too gross inaccuracy of a typical or at least widespread romantic mood, that of nostalgia, nostalgia for an irrecoverable personal or collective past,[14] for a future as yet unattained, or merely for something, it was hardly known or perhaps cared what, different from the here and now. Allied with this went a cult of the emotions and a condemnation of anything which impeded their free expression, so that the young Mikhail Bakunin, for example, was able in 1838 to excuse his disobedience to his father by claiming that 'duty excludes love; and everything that excludes love is wicked and mean'.[15] All this has been described by a hostile observer as 'the indulgence of infinite indeterminate desires ... an endless and aimless vagabondage of the emotions with the imagination as their free accomplice'.[16] It cannot be denied that there is truth in the indictment. Yet the romantic age was not one of dreamy inertia or elegiac futility. It did not reject responsibility and effort. It throbbed with activity and was rich in achievement. A more friendly commentator has spoken, with equal or greater truth, of 'the most salient feature of romantic *practical* life – its energy and the harnessing of its energy to the production of large-scale works'.[17] Again, moreover, one is faced by the contradictions within individual personalities which make dogmatic generalization so vulnerable. Thus Novalis, the most extreme of German early romantic writers, was by training an expert mining engineer; while Turner, so unrestrainedly romantic in much of his painting, was also a hardheaded business man with a highly unromantic sexual life.

Moreover romanticism is not a phenomenon which can be defined strictly, or perhaps at all, in chronological terms. The Abbé Prévost's *Manon Lescaut* (1731) is undoubtedly a romantic novel, while even earlier in the eighteenth century Joseph Addison in the *Spectator* had praised geniuses who had something 'nobly wild and extravagant' about them and were not dominated by mere imitation of approved models. The essentially romantic contrast between nature and convention, the glorification of the former and condemnation of the latter, was fundamental to the thought of Rousseau before the romantic age proper had begun. For that matter an idealization of the emotions, a kind of romantic subjectivism, can be seen as early as the twelfth century, in legends such as that of Tristan and Isolde and in the work of the troubadours. Romanticism, which in its most general sense is an irreducible aspect of the human, or at least the modern European, personality, has thus no clearly defined origin in time; nor has it any end. Overlaid, sometimes distorted, by newer habits of thought and conventions of feeling, it remains one of the foundations, perhaps the most deeply rooted of all, of the modern European's consciousness of himself and of the world.

In spite of its psychological dynamism and its power of emotional attraction the triumph of romanticism was never complete even in the era, roughly

1790–1840, when its power was at its height. There were always important areas of thought which escaped it.

Economics, the one social science which had already taken secure root
in European intellectual life, continued to be based on a purely Enlightenment tradition of rational analysis. It continued to assume that human
conduct was subject to clear and discoverable rules. Writers such as Ricardo
or McCulloch remained bastions of an eighteenth-century mode of thought,
and the analytical and quantitative approach to the subject which was
now universal was sharpened by the appearance of the first efforts at a
strictly mathematical treatment of it.[18] More important, the most pervasive
current in the political thought of the age, that of liberal individualism,
was deeply rooted in anti-romantic assumptions. Every great liberal thinker
– Locke, Adam Smith, Bentham, Mill – assumed that man was fundamentally a hedonist, that he would always seek pleasure and avoid pain.
There was no place here for the assumption of the more extreme romantics that a great man must suffer greatly and will even seek such suffering,
that in de Musset's words 'nothing makes us so great as suffering greatly'.
Moreover it was generally assumed (Mill is the main exception here)
that there was no means of distinguishing qualitatively between different
pleasures. When they conflicted the quantitatively greater must triumph,
since the end of all action was the achievement of the greatest possible
quantity of pleasure. To both the achievement of pleasure and the avoidance of pain, security of property, which guaranteed to the individual the
fruits of his efforts, was fundamental; hence its basic significance to liberal
ideologies of every shade as compared with its relative unimportance in
what romantic political theory there was.

All liberals took for granted the basic rationality of man; for unless he
were rational he could not measure pleasure and pain and balance the one
against the other in any given situation. All, because of this assumption,
were to varying extents believers in education as a cure for political and
social evils. All thought of societies as essentially aggregations of individuals, knowable once the characteristics of these individuals were
known. To them there was no essential difference, as there was to a
romantic, between man in society or in history and man as an isolated
and unrestricted individual. Most, to varying extents, were unhistorical
in their habits of thought and reluctant to admit that the past could be
useful, or even interesting, to the present. All (with Mill again as a partial
exception) thought of the obstacles to good government merely in terms
of prejudice arising from ignorance or from corruption inspired by vested
interests, not in those of something inherent in human nature or in the
historical situation of a particular society. It is significant that Bentham,
the most radical of utilitarians and individualists, strongly disliked the

work of Savigny and his followers. The whole drift of classical liberalism, at its best the noblest and most truly aristocratic of political creeds, was towards the enlargement of liberty (which to a liberal meant nothing if not the liberty of the individual) and towards the rational conduct and direction of human life. But in its march towards these objectives it largely turned its back on the emotions, on the imagination and to a large extent on history, and hence on much of the essence of romanticism.[19]

The conflict between these two great forces can be overemphasized. In practice many important liberals, like many romantics, were sympathetic to the claims of nationalities, or at least of 'historic' nationalities such as the Poles, Greeks and Italians. More fundamentally, liberalism and romanticism shared common ground in that both centred on the individual. But the individual of whom liberals spoke was rational and a calculator; he was autonomous, an atom in the aggregation of atoms which was society. To the romantic on the other hand he was a sentient being, interesting in direct proportion to his capacity for feeling: he was also part of a society which, even if unjust and offensive, was usually thought of as having some organic characteristics.

In practical terms during the period 1815–48 liberalism meant above all political and constitutional reform, reform designed to subject rulers and governments to a law embodying fundamental truths and values and thus to make authority impersonal and objective. By being restricted in this way rulers and governments would be forced to respect the rights of individuals, a sphere into which they should never penetrate and for the safeguarding of which all states existed. This did not mean democracy in anything resembling its twentieth-century form. It did not necessarily mean even genuinely representative government. In France, in many ways a bastion of advanced ideas, most liberals remained deeply distrustful of democracy. In 1839 one of their leaders, Montalembert, could class it with monarchy as a force aiming at despotism and ten years later Guizot, prime minister and in his own way a genuine liberal, could denounce 'the idolatry of democracy . . . this idea which must be extirpated'.[20]

Liberalism and romanticism, then, so dissimilar in many ways in their assumptions and their 'feel', could often cooperate up to a point in practice. But though the romantic current was wide enough and vague enough to embrace, in some of its forms, a good deal of liberalism, it was more fundamental, more all-embracing and more lasting in its effects. This is because romanticism, defying definition, pervaded the arts and the whole culture and mental climate of the age in a way in which the more defined and intellectualized liberal creed did not and could not. Scott or Beethoven, Turner or Manzoni, still speak to us directly and contribute directly to our consciousness of the world and humanity. Modern achievement in the arts and the modern European mind spring from the sometimes anarchic-ally violent attitudes generated by romanticism. The liberal political con-stitutions of this period, by comparison, are now of purely historical interest; and even many of the works of the great liberal ideologues may share the same fate in an age in which political thought, in the traditional sense of the term, appears to have come to an end.

The confused and largely embryonic socialism of the first half of the nineteenth century, like liberalism, inherited most of its characteristics from the eighteenth century. Here again there are problems of defini-tion, for socialism was still a heterogeneous assembly of creeds, prophe-cies, fantasies and dreams which, like romanticism, resists clear definition. Two main schools of thought can be distinguished within it. On the one hand was that which traced from the Jacobin régime of 1793–94 in France and which was uncompromisingly activist and power-orientated. Represented from the 1830s onwards most clearly by the fanatical pro-fessional revolutionary Auguste Blanqui, it believed that the new age could be ushered in, in any existing society, only by a violent *coup d'état* which must be the work of an enlightened minority, the agents of an inexorable historical process. Once established in power, this minority would establish a régime based on complete social and political equality, the end towards which history was inescapably moving. After some unavoidable coercion the majority, their eyes opened by education, would embrace the new régime with enthusiasm. It would then become permanent and unalterable, since no man, as a rational being, could wish to change it. Aspirations of this kind were first given practical expres-sion in the Babeuf conspiracy of 1796 in Paris. Through the *Conspira-tion pour l'égalité* of Buonarotti, a history of that conspiracy published in 1828 which became 'the manual of the communist movement in the 1830s and 1840s and the chief source of its ideology',[21] they were to remain part of the European, later the world, revolutionary vision until our own day.

Side by side with this harsh and uncompromising scheme there developed another current of thought, represented in Great Britain by Robert Owen and in France by Charles Fourier and to a lesser extent Louis Blanc and that most idiosyncratic of thinkers, Pierre-Joseph Proudhon. These writers, dominated less by ideas of historical inevitability than by a desire for justice and for the lessening of human suffering, disliked the totalitari-anism, the violence, the centralization of power which were essential to the Jacobin–Babouvist–Blanquist outlook. They dreamed rather of a new society, achieved peacefully or with a minimum of violence, in which patterns and initiatives would emerge from below. Owen and Fourier, the most extreme representatives of this attitude, envisaged the dissolution of central authority and its transfer to small self-contained communities based on a perfect division of labour.

All these groups and prophets, however, violent and authoritarian or peaceful and decentralizing, shared a belief in the rational nature of man and the possibilities of his improvement. Almost all believed that a new ordering of human society which would be completely virtuous, and therefore eternal and unchanging, could be both conceived of and achieved in practice. In these beliefs they were the heirs of the Enlightenment. The eighteenth-century concept of man's character and ideas as something created by society, the product of environment and therefore to be moulded and ennobled by purposeful change in that environment, finds its most extreme expression in the works of Owen:

Every day will make it more and more evident that the character of man is, without a single exception, always formed for him; that it may be, and is, chiefly, created by his predecessors: that they give him, or may give him, his ideas and habits, which are the powers that govern and direct his conduct. Man, therefore, never did, nor is it possible he ever can, form his own character.[22]

There follows from this a belief in human perfectibility, a belief without which perhaps no thoroughgoing form of socialism is conceivable; but the individual is envisaged as being perfected entirely from outside, without effort, far less suffering, on his own part. The contrast with the romantic vision of man as active, autonomous, a creature endowed with genius and energy expressed largely in a capacity for suffering, is very striking.

A lack of emotional sympathy for many aspects of the romantic vision is also visible in the work of the most original socialist thinker of the early nineteenth century, the Comte Claude Henri de Saint-Simon. It is significant that to him Napoleon I seemed admirable above all as a successful administrator and scientific legislator, not as a heroic symbol of individual genius and energy. He saw the future society as dominated by 'industrialists' (by which he meant all productive workers – farmers, scholars, artists, labourers), as a hierarchy based on capacity and function, essentially administrative and pacific. This was a much more original and farsighted view than that of any other writer of the period. It fits neatly into no conventional intellectual pigeon-hole; but least of all into the romantic one. Moreover the vaguely defined 'universal association' at which the Saint-Simonians aimed, and which came to be typified for them above all by the building of great international railways, ignored the national allegiances which romanticism indirectly did so much to stimulate. Saint-Simon believed that his ideal society would give the individual the highest degree of freedom; but this freedom could be produced only by the widest possible 'association' of men. It is true that this idea of 'true' freedom as possible only through the willing incorporation of the individual in a wider whole plays a prominent part in much of Rousseau's thought. It is also true that Saint-Simon did not share the distrust of the emotions shown by eighteenth-century writers with a philosophy of history, such as Condorcet. On the contrary he stressed their role as a link between men, and their growth in scope and importance throughout history; while after his death his ideas provided the basis for a highly emotional quasi-religious cult among his followers. Nevertheless, fundamentally the Saint-Simonian doctrine was irreconcilable with many of the basic romantic attitudes.

It is possible to speak of a romantic political conservatism based on traditional loyalties to throne and altar or on a hankering after a corporative society of a would-be medieval kind. Nevertheless most of the politically important conservatives of the first half of the century, in so far as they gave any systematic expression to their attitudes, did so in terms of the Enlightenment rather than in romantic ones. Metternich, the most significant of them in practice, shows many of the less convincing characteristics of eighteenth-century thought. These are visible in his dogmatism, in his liking for large and superficial generalizations and in his much too ready belief in the existence of general laws governing the actions of states (something closely akin to the 'maxims of state' of Louis XIV or to the 'geometrical methods' in diplomacy of which Prince Kaunitz had boasted in the later eighteenth century). From a different standpoint his pragmatism, his belief that 'the whole secret is to survive, and he who achieves it takes his place in history', or that 'to govern is to keep on one's feet and go forward', is an equally unromantic attitude. The most famous and extreme conservative writer of the Restoration era, the Piedmontese Xavier de Maistre, shows traits which mirror aspects of romanticism. Like the romantics he stressed national peculiarities. Like them he was reluctant to admit the existence of a human nature independent of time and place. 'The philosopher who wants to show us by *a priori* reasoning what man must be', he wrote, 'does not deserve an audience.'[23] Like many romantics he emphasized heavily the irrational forces of custom and loyalty which hold society together. But his pessimistic insistence on the wickedness of natural man, whom society must compel to be virtuous, and above all his deep distrust of spontaneous feeling and of the autonomy of the individual, both so likely to lead to disobedience and rebellion against sanctified authority, make him a leading anti-romantic.

Romanticism then was not a system of ideas, political, social, economic or even artistic. It was something more pervasive – a loose assembly of sometimes contradictory assumptions, above all a way of feeling. The distinguishing feature of a romantic was not that his conclusions were revolutionary or reactionary, progressive or conservative, but that he reached them by an essentially non-rational and subjective route. Romanticism was a mould in which any idea might be shaped, a palette from which it might be coloured. It did not depend on any specific idea or even any specific emotion but was rather something which pervaded life itself, something which could always be recognized though never defined. No political or social ideology escaped the romantic influence. Intangible and many-sided, it suffused the mental climate of Europe during the first half of the nineteenth century, above all through its influence on the arts. It strengthened and spread a new idea which had begun to take shape before the French Revolution – that of the artist as necessarily in some sense detached from society, a free, critical and creative intelligence responsible only to himself. In its more extreme forms it thought of him as superior to ordinary humanity and a potential saviour of society, of art as an adjunct to, perhaps even a substitute for, religion. This cult of the artist is seen clearly, for example, in the great burst of admiration for Shakespeare, who had been criticized or ignored in continental Europe during much of the eighteenth century.[24] It also generated a new emphasis, particularly in music, on the sacredness of the artist's creation and the inadmissibility of adapting or 'improving' it. The wholesale cutting and altering of the scores of operas by conductors, theatre-managers and others, so normal in the first half of the century, was increasingly frowned on by the 1850s or 1860s. A similar attitude is also perhaps visible in the unprecedentedly close connections now established between the different arts, for since the musician or painter was no longer regarded primarily as a technician or a craftsman he was influenced by literature, and to some extent influenced it, more than ever before. In the eighteenth century it had still been normal to think of a hierarchy of the arts, and in particular of a hierarchy of different forms and genres within each art, so that for example poetry was assumed to be inherently superior to prose and 'history painting' to portraits or landscapes. Now all artistic effort, in print, in sound, in paint, and all practitioners of the arts, were for the first time being merged in the vague and sanctified categories of 'art' and 'the artist'.

Side by side with these grandiose claims went, from artists increasingly compelled to find an audience among the middle classes, increasing complaints of the philistinism and insensitivity of their new patrons. More and more the artist felt that he worked in the last analysis for his own satisfaction and that this took precedence over the comprehensibility of his work to the general public – the attitude summed up in Turner's comment in 1842 on one of his later pictures that 'I did not paint it to be understood'.[25] In particular the fact that until the middle of the century the majority of the greatest writers belonged, or at least aspired to belong, to the upper ranks of society, almost certainly sharpened the contempt which some of them were coming to feel for the general reading public. The estrangement between art, at least if it pretended to depth or novelty, and the life of the ordinary man, a major characteristic of the modern world, was now clearly developing.

The subjectivism of the great romantics and their admiration of strong emotions also helps to explain the marked rise during the early nineteenth century in the relative importance of music, which became the pre-eminent romantic art. It achieved this position in part because of the immediacy with which it acted on the hearer. 'It is in sound', argued the French writer E. P. de Senancour, 'that nature has placed the most forcible expression of the romantic character. . . . We admire what we see, but we feel what we hear.'[26] In the same way the German writer E. T. A. Hoffmann (himself also a composer) claimed that music was 'the most Romantic of all the arts – one might even say that it alone is purely Romantic'. Music was also valued, however, because it was the most intangible, indeed irrational, of the arts. 'The musician', wrote Schopenhauer, 'reveals to us the inner essence of the world and becomes the interpreter of the most profound wisdom, while speaking a language which reason does not understand.'[27] On a more superficial level, the prestige of music may have been raised indirectly by purely technical and organizational changes – the development and perfection of instruments such as the clarinet and French horn; the adoption of modern orchestral notation (usually said to have been first used by Cherubini in 1803); the growth in size of orchestras and the emergence of the first great composer/conductors, Mendelssohn and Berlioz, in the 1830s, followed a generation later by the first great virtuoso conductor, Hans von Bülow. These innovations, by making music more complex, dictated slower and more deeply pondered methods of composition. No longer could a composer end one opera on Christmas Eve and begin another on Boxing Day, as Handel had done. This in turn strengthened the ideal of the composer as a dedicated artist rather than a technician producing a relatively simple article in response to a commercial demand. No longer could he boast, as Vivaldi had done a century earlier, that he could write a concerto faster than the copyist could make out the parts for the different instruments. The idea of the composer as a craftsman plying a skilled trade (and a largely hereditary one, as the examples of Bach, Mozart or Beethoven show) was now being replaced by that of him as an artist driven by an irresistible inner compulsion to pursue his art against every discouragement which an uncomprehending world could offer. This was the picture drawn, with great skill, by Berlioz and Wagner in their autobiographies; and it is symptomatic of the new artistic self-consciousness created by romanticism that only from the mid-nineteenth century do such personal confessions begin to appear. It is interesting and perhaps significant, moreover, that this idealized view of music and musicians (and to a large extent of the arts in general) should have become so influential in an age when capitalism, in the eyes of its detractors the most selfish and materialist of all social and economic systems, was so rapidly gaining ground almost everywhere.

THE EVOLUTIONARY CREDOS

From the middle of the century the intellectual atmosphere changes dramatically. Neither the romanticism nor the liberalism of its earlier decades could resist erosion by events. On the political level the liberal ideologies and programmes which seemed on the point of complete triumph almost everywhere west of the Russian frontier in the spring of 1848 were by the 1850s in retreat over much of Europe. The very speed and ease of the short-lived victory of 1848 may have contributed to this. In France and much of Germany stiffer resistance by the old régime, a more genuine struggle for power, might have made the revolutions more radical and thoroughgoing, the policies of the revolutionaries more realistic and their success more permanent. As it was, the upshot was the emergence of a new generation of conservative leaders – Bach, Schwarzenberg, Bismarck, in some ways Napoleon III – who were tougher, more realistic and more self-confident than Metternich and his contemporaries. The extent of the immediate setback for liberalism can certainly be exaggerated. Even in Germany, the part of Europe for which 1848 was most obviously a turning-point in this respect, the conservative reaction after 1849 was not total. Almost everywhere written constitutions were a more important aspect of monarchical rule than ever before. Yet something had been lost. The liberalism of the first half of the century, whose emphasis on individual rights had been one of the noblest aspects of the culture of that era, had had a good deal of the bloom rubbed off it by events. Not merely the political defeats of 1848–49 but still more fundamentally the fact that for the first time the Industrial Revolution was beginning to affect the daily lives of many millions of people in continental Europe, creating new problems and new tensions, meant that the old élitist liberalism was in the long run doomed.

The temper of the times was now increasingly hostile to sweeping abstract ideas, to wide-ranging generalizations based on deduction from a few simple intuitive premises. 'I find', wrote Charles Darwin in 1874, 'that my mind is so fixed by the inductive method, that I cannot appreciate deductive reasoning. I must begin with a good body of facts, and not from principle (in which I always suspect some fallacy) and then as much deduction as you please.'[28] The attitude which he described had already been gathering strength for at least a generation before these words were written. The future now seemed to lie with specific and relatively exact disciplines, with history and above all with the physical sciences. More and more emphasis was coming to be laid on the idea that truth could be arrived at only through the analysis of data, the collection and collation of observable facts, not through intuitions or metaphysics. Much was thus to be gained in rigour and professionalism. But something also was to be lost in buoyancy and generosity of outlook. Nor was the new dispensation more favourable to the warmth and vagueness of romanticism. Romantic feeling could never cease to be important, for it responded to the inescapable emotional needs of the majority of Europeans. Indeed the German writer Friedrich Nietzsche, who did not die until 1900, can be regarded as one of the supreme European romantics. His insistence on the importance of will, on the greatness of the heroic individual faced by a mean and philistine society which he despises, his contempt for the physical sciences, even his final collapse into madness, are all typical of extreme romanticism. Nevertheless just as the predominance of liberalism and individualism in discussion of political and social problems was slowly declining, so was that of romanticism in the arts and in modes of feeling.

The new tone, scholarly as much as intellectual, powerfully influenced by the prestige of the physical sciences and of inductive reasoning, is seen most significantly in the predominance of evolutionary modes of thought during the second half of the nineteenth century. These ideas, in their broader aspects, were far from new. In thinking about the physical universe they were already well established many years before Darwin published his *Origin of Species* in 1859. The idea that species in the organic world were not fixed, but somehow subject to change, had already been put forward by the great French naturalist Buffon in the later eighteenth century. In 1827 the geologist Charles Lyell had arrived at the belief that new animal species originated from existing ones, though he was unable to explain the mechanism by which this happened. Three years later his great *Principles of Geology* pictured the earth as changing gradually over a very long time-span, becoming what it is as the result of a slow process of gradual change which could be explained in terms of provable physical laws. This was a milestone in the undermining and eventual discarding of the orthodox Christian catastrophist doctrine of a sudden once-for-all creation. A little later the astronomer J. P. Nichol, in a series of books written from 1839 onwards, also sketched an evolving universe and used the word 'evolution' apparently for the first time.[29]

Thinking about human society and institutions was also being affected by similar influences. More and more theories of society were becoming theories of social development. The historicism of the first half of the century and its concern with origins laid some of the foundations for an evolutionary attitude to such questions; and by the 1830s Auguste Comte was raising in his 'positivist' doctrines an impressive structure of evolutionary social speculation. Comte's system assumed that history was an inexorable process which could be understood but could not be diverted from its predetermined course. Man had an innate desire to understand the world and control it; in different ages his modes of thought, his very consciousness, were different, so that in the future even newborn children would be unlike those of the past. From a 'theological' mode of thinking man had evolved to a 'metaphysical' one. He would now move on to a scientific or 'positive' one marked by the growth of a new science of society whose practitioners would become a kind of priesthood. Some of these ideas, in a less developed form, are to be found in the work of French thinkers of the previous century, notably Turgot and still more Condorcet. Indeed one writer has called Comte 'the heir of Condorcet'.[30] However Comte linked man with society not, as the Enlightenment had done, through reason, but through emotion. The society he envisaged was, like that of Saint-Simon whose secretary he had been, an organic one given life by a generalized love of humanity felt by all its members. Moreover Comte did not accept the enlightened and liberal belief that men could change society through their own efforts. They were subject, like the rest of the universe, to laws of nature which could be discovered and described but not altered. Comte's doctrines were completely independent of the idea of biological evolution, which plays no part in his thought. They were, however, the most important example of the way in which theories of society were acquiring an evolutionary aspect even before the middle of the nineteenth century. (Comte published his six-volume *Cours de philosophie positive* in 1830–46, long before Darwin had become a figure of any significance.)

There were several reasons why this should have been so. An evolutionary theory of society, by appearing to anchor social development firmly to recorded or at least recordable facts, above all the facts of history, rather than to the arbitrary wills of men, could foster a sense of security. This, in the disturbed decades of the middle of the century, was to many people very welcome. If society evolved in accordance with discoverable laws along a predetermined course then the efforts of idealists and revolutionaries to disrupt or radically alter it were doomed to failure. In this way social evolution could come to seem almost a conservative force. From a different point of view evolutionary theories of society appealed to some observers since they implied the essential unity of mankind, in the sense that all societies, however dissimilar in the exterior, were following the same path and appeared different merely because they had progressed varying distances along it. In extreme cases the idea of an evolutionary law of development binding together all mankind and the entire universe could become a kind of substitute religion. Thus the English blue-stocking Harriet Martineau, who had already lost her faith in orthodox Christianity, was inspired by reading Comte to write that 'We find ourselves suddenly living and moving in the midst of the universe – as a part of it and not as its aim and object. We find outselves living, not under capricious and arbitrary constitutions, unconnected with the constitution and movements of the whole, but under great, general, invariable laws, which operate on us as part of the whole.'[31] Finally the influence of the Industrial Revolution, altering every aspect of life with unprecedented speed, accustomed Europe as never before to rapid change and made it easier than ever before to envisage society as something in the process of continuous development. One consequence of this was an increasing tendency among Europeans to look down on the non-European peoples, particularly those of Asia, because of the obvious failure of the latter to develop their societies and intellectual life at anything approaching the European rate. During the eighteenth century the stability of the Chinese empire, for example, had been admired; now its stagnation seemed the clearest of all badges of inferiority.

In the field of political ideas (though 'political' is here much too restricted a term) Marxism is the supreme example of an evolutionary doctrine. It also seems clear, however, that the strictly revolutionary element, with its strong determinist overtones, became considerably more pronounced in Marx's work from about 1850 onwards. The young Marx of the 1830s and 1840s drew his ideas from a wide range of sources. One, deriving from the Enlightenment and again in particular from Condorcet, was the belief in man as naturally virtuous and rational and thus able to realize his full potentialities for good as soon as he had been freed from the crippling restrictions and superstitions of the past. From this stemmed a considerable element of utopianism. From Fourier Marx absorbed the idea that in the society of the future man would no longer be subjected to the division of labour with its stultifying effects on his interests and capacities, and from Owen the belief that in particular the distinction between industry and agriculture could in such a society be reduced or even abolished. A second strain in his thinking, imbibed from French historians such as Thierry, was the concept of history as a series of struggles between different social classes. These struggles were to be seen above all in the events of the great French Revolution of 1789; it was the study of these which particularly occupied Marx during the summer of 1843, the period in which most of his fundamental ideas took shape. From acceptance of class struggle as the motive force in history it was not a very long step to acceptance of the Babouvist–Buonarottist–Blanquist vision of revolution as the product of a successful conspiracy, of a *coup d'état* by a revolutionary élite and a temporary dictatorship resulting from it.[32] Underlying all these beliefs and aspirations was the faith which inspired every radical thinker of the generation after 1815 – the belief that history had some objective meaning and that it was inexorably marching towards the fulfilment of that meaning, each step in the process inevitably leading on to the next. In the case of Marx this faith stemmed in the first place from the philosopher Hegel, the predominant intellectual influence in the Germany in which he grew up. Certain aspects of Hegel's thought, notably his vision of history as progressing not smoothly but by revolutionary jumps, influenced Marx throughout his life. Nevertheless by the mid-1840s he had begun to find orthodox Hegelianism unsatisfactory. In particular Hegel's vision of the laws of thought as ultimately identical with the laws of events, each with a pattern of growth discoverable by the use of reason, meant that in the end mind must be reconciled to the world as it is, whereas Marx wished to turn thought 'into an instrument for transforming the world in accordance with the principles of philosophy'.[33] However from Hegel he derived the basic idea of societies and civilizations as evolving in terms of a pattern of development, and of the ultimate interdependence of political, economic and social institutions.

The young Marx of the 1840s was still very much a humanist. To him the freeing of the individual from 'alienation', the liberation and enrichment of the individual consciousness, was supremely important. He was a good deal of a utopian, and even something of a romantic in the way in which he envisaged revolution in terms of 1793, in those of neo-Jacobin heroism. It was, indeed, the certainty which he shared with all other European radicals that history was about to repeat itself which explains his confidence in the victory of the revolution in 1848. The *Communist Manifesto* of that year, the work of Marx and of his lifelong friend and associate, Friedrich Engels, 'spells out the implications of a world-view which owed more to reminiscences of 1789–94 than its authors would have been willing to admit'.[34]

By 1850 Marx could no longer deny the failure, at least for the time being, of the hopes which had run so high in 1848; and this frustration probably does a good deal to explain the bitterness which tinged his writings for the rest of his life. Disappointed hopes enforced a revision of attitudes and priorities. When in September 1850 he and Engels withdrew from the now moribund Communist League they began an abandonment of the kind of revolutionary voluntarism typified by Blanqui, with its romantic overtones of individual and élitist heroism. Henceforth they were to become more and more sceptical of attempts to 'pre-empt the revolutionary process'. More and more they were to fall back on the idea of revolution as something scientifically inevitable, the unavoidable result of a process of social and economic evolution. The 'forces of production' would steadily grow as technology developed and the organization of labour became more sophisticated; but the social 'relations of production' would not alter correspondingly. As the economies of the great capitalist states developed, so ownership of capital and of the means of production would become concentrated in fewer and fewer hands. Though the capitalist system would be able to produce more and more, poverty would be the lot of an increasing majority. The worker, who could live only by selling his labour-power to the capitalist, would suffer increasing impoverishment, relative if not absolute.[35] The middle classes, small traders and manufacturers, farmers and artisans, would be gradually crushed by the forces of capital concentration. They would thus come to form part of an impoverished and increasingly frustrated majority, numerically overwhelming, which, goaded beyond endurance, would be driven to revolution. Since capitalism had enormously expanded international contacts, such a revolution would spread rapidly from its point of origin to engulf all the advanced countries and would be worldwide in its effects. Capitalism, like the 'tribal' and 'feudal' forms of organization which had preceded it, would thus inevitably collapse and be transformed once it had made its contribution to the growth of the productive forces of humanity.

This vision of the future, of which only the crudest summary is given here, was elaborated at great length, with a mass of statistical and historical detail, in the first volume of Marx's largest work, *Das Kapital*, which appeared in 1867. It meant a fundamental change of emphasis in his thinking. The fulfilment and true freedom of the individual still remained the objective of revolution and the end of the historical process. As far as the making of revolutions was concerned, however, his 'alienation' and his revolutionary consciousness, so important in the early works of the 1840s and still important in those of the 1850s, were now threatened with submersion in a vast and impersonal process of social evolution governed by laws analogous to those of the physical world and quite impossible to divert or restrain.

Marx himself never surrendered by any means completely to pseudo-scientific determinism. He never provided a systematic discussion of the materialist philosophy on which it was based (this was attempted rather by Engels) or himself used the terms 'historical materialism' or 'dialectical materialism', which were later to become the small change of discussion among Marxists. In 1871 the outbreak of the Commune in Paris (though only one of its leaders was in any real sense a Marxist) seemed to revive for a moment[36] some of the belief in revolutionary voluntarism which had run strongly in Marx until 1849–50. (This was not unreasonable, since the Commune was dominated by obscure local clubs and committees and was largely the work of local militants acting spontaneously and without central direction.) Neither he nor Engels ever ceased to be influenced by the traditions and mythology of 1789 and 1793. They continued to believe that in a moment of great external danger (attack by Russia, or by Russia and France in alliance) their followers in Germany, where there was from the mid-1870s onwards an increasingly large Social Democratic Party inspired by Marxist doctrines, might be called upon to lead the nation as the Jacobins had led France in 1793. On the other hand Marx at times also played with the idea that extension of the franchise might, at least in a few advanced countries, produce the new society without a revolutionary upheaval; since he found it inconceivable that the workers, once given the vote, would not at once use it to overthrow the existing social system and replace it by socialism. In particular in a speech in Amsterdam in September 1872 he envisaged that the conquest of power by the proletariat, essential and inevitable everywhere, might be achieved in Britain, the United States and Holland by peaceful means.

Until his death in 1883, therefore, Marx managed to retain a considerable degree of intellectual elbow-room and to avoid becoming the prisoner of set dogmas. As a mass creed, it may be argued, the appeal of Marxism has always lain less in its claims to be 'scientific' than in the fact that it offers to the believer a kind of moral drama played out in history, with a hero (the working class), a villain (capitalism with its contradictions and its dehumanizing effects), and the promise of a happy ending to the struggle between them with the triumph of virtue. Nevertheless the effect of Marx's writing from the 1860s onwards was, on balance, to strengthen the element of inevitability and predictability in his doctrines. After his death Engels, with the German Social Democrats August Bebel and even more Karl Kautsky, developed this 'scientific' aspect of Marxism to the virtual exclusion of its other sides.[37] In their hands it became 'merely a subspecies of evolutionary positivism';[38] and indirectly they introduced into it an element of fatalism and quietism which was to have disastrous results. Marxism came to have, for its adherents, some of the characteristics of a religion.[39] But since it alone among religions was 'scientific', based on irreducible and unshakable facts, it alone could truly promise believers inevitable and indeed imminent triumph. Bebel, at the national congress of the German Social Democrats in 1891, when the party for the first time adopted a purely Marxist programme, claimed that the victory of socialism in Germany was so near that few of his audience would not live to see it. Engels in the following year prophesied victory for the German Social Democrats within a decade. Moreover this triumph, it was increasingly felt, would come more or less peacefully through the use of the franchise and the parliamentary system. From these assumptions it followed that little positive effort or revolutionary dynamism would be needed to produce the collapse of the existing economic and social structure. More and more Marxist theoreticians (usually themselves of middle-class origin) substituted elaborate pseudo-scientific theories for observation of the facts of everyday life. More and more Marxism became an 'opium of the intellectuals'. The effect was to drain the German socialist movement, and consequently the Second International founded in 1889 in which it was the leading element, of much of their real vitality even before the coming of war in 1914 dramatically exposed their true inner weakness.

Though by the end of the century Marxism had become overwhelmingly the most important form of socialism in continental Europe, it was still in the 1860s and 1870s only one of a number of forms of socialist belief. The first Socialist International, set up in September 1864, was an extremely loose organization with a fluctuating membership. In it many different schools of thought and shades of feeling, often not socialist at all in any genuine sense, were represented. The Italian members of its General Council, for example, were completely dominated by Mazzini, an explicit opponent of socialism in any form; while rationalist societies, free thinkers, mutualist credit movements, ex-Carbonari, former Chartists, radicals of every stripe, all found a place in it. A strain of romantic voluntarist thinking remained active among its adherents and retained considerable appeal, in spite of the repeated setbacks it encountered in practice, for those unwilling to wait until the forces of economic and social evolution had produced their 'inevitable' results.

This attitude in an extreme form, with its impatience of intellectual analysis, its urge to action at almost any price, its incurable optimism, is seen in the chaotic career of the Russian anarchist Mikhail Bakunin. Bakunin had no ideas, in the strict sense, worth discussion. It was not until 1866, only a decade before his death and more than twenty years after he had become a revolutionary, that he produced, in his *Revolutionary Catechism*, a reasonably clear statement of his aims, none of which was original. The state was to be swept away, nations to be organized as federations of autonomous communes, complete economic and social equality to be introduced and marriage and the right of inheritance abolished. What is significant in him is not the intellectual content of these vague declamations but his tone and psychology. In his incarnation of the spirit of revolt for its own sake, his constant dream of revolutionary action even in circumstances in which it had not the slightest chance of success, his unshaken belief until almost the end of his life that violent revolutionary passions were everywhere latent in the masses and awaiting only the call to action, his contempt for 'learned doctors and self-appointed tutors of humanity' such as Marx, his endless self-dramatization and lack of practical ability and elementary common sense, he typifies many of the worst characteristics of an exaggerated and flawed romanticism. 'Whenever man has tried to reduce his animal character to an abstraction', he wrote in 1869, 'he has become its plaything, its slave and most often its hypocritical servant.'[40] The description of him as 'one of the obscure ancestors of one aspect of Fascism',[41] is fully justified. With the methodical and orderly Marx, in his personal life in general a believer in the middle-class virtues, this undisciplined member of the Russian gentry had nothing in common but the vein of authoritarianism which both shared. The vicious personal rivalry between them which disrupted the First International was almost inevitable.

Not all revolutionary activists after the middle of the century were as self-indulgent and unrealistic as Bakunin. But many shared some at least of his tastes and attitudes. In particular his passion for ineffective secret societies, which owed a good deal to the example of the Carbonari, with their elaborate and childish rituals, and to that of the societies founded by Buonarotti from the first years of the century onwards, struck a note to which many would-be revolutionaries still easily responded. In Russia the *Zemlya i Volya* organization, formed in the early 1860s, was strikingly reminiscent of Buonarotti's creations, and the *Narodnaya Rasprava* founded a few years later by the revolutionaries Nechaev and Tkachev was also very similar to them. This proliferation of extremist societies explains in large part the exaggerated fear of revolution which continued to be felt by the ruling classes over much of Europe until at least the 1870s. Right down to 1914 secret societies using blood-and-thunder rituals continued to flourish in the more backward parts of Europe;[42] and it is one of the major merits of Marx and Engels that they saw clearly the impotence of most such bodies when it came to carrying out any revolution worthy of the name.

Bakunin's morbid passion for violence also found some response among his contemporaries. It began the association of anarchism with acts of individual terrorism, an association first seen in his contacts with the young Russian anarchist Nechaev in Geneva in 1869–70. This fatal link, especially after the spectacular anarchist outrages of the 1890s in France associated with the names of Vaillant, Ravachol and Gallo, finally destroyed any faint chance there may have been of widespread acceptance of what is, in essence, the most idealistic of all forms of political and social belief. The extreme romantic individualism which was the mainspring of Bakunin's career is also echoed in the survival until at least the 1870s of the type of international revolutionary who, often unencumbered by much in the way of ideological baggage, found his way from one unsuccessful revolt or attempted coup to another. Such were, for example, the Italian anarchist Amilcare Cipriani, who fought in Garibaldi's army against that of the pope at Aspromonte in 1862, then in Crete against the Turks and finally in the Commune of 1871 in Paris; or the Russian Sergei Kravchinsky (Stepniak), who took part in the Bosnian rising of 1876 against Turkish rule, then in the attempted anarchist revolt in Benevento province, near Naples, in 1877, and then achieved fame by the assassination of the chief of the Russian secret police in St Petersburg in 1878. A still more striking example is that of the French professional soldier General Cluseret who, after service in the Crimea and Algeria, fought under Garibaldi in Italy and in the Union army in the American Civil War, joined the Fenian movement for Irish independence and was condemned to death *in absentia* in England, attempted with Bakunin to carry out an anarchist coup in Lyons and Marseilles in 1870, served for a short time as war minister of the Commune and then took part in an Albanian rising against the Turks.

Of the non-Marxist socialists of the 1850s and 1860s the most interesting and important, however, was not Bakunin but the Frenchman Pierre-Joseph Proudhon. The confusion and inconsistency of his voluminous writings make him a difficult thinker to discuss briefly and fairly; but all his ideas were based ultimately on an intense individualism, an insistence on the autonomy of the individual and the respect owed him. This led him, until his last years, to a rejection not only of government and every form of social inequality but even of law and many conventional ideas of justice. Proudhon desired above all else the complete liberation of man, his subjection only to standards and norms which he himself created and not to any imposed upon him by society. This is a romantic attitude and marks out Proudhon as in a very real sense a romantic thinker. His ideal society, though he never defined its workings in any detail, was a 'mutualist' one in which individuals and groups bargained directly with one another for the exchange of goods and services, a society regulated and given internal cohesion not by coercion but by public opinion. This vision, coupled with his dislike of large-scale industry and cosmopolitanism and with his in many ways intense traditionalism (notably in his attitude to women) had almost nothing in common with Marxism. Moreover he consistently stressed that his aims could be achieved only by peaceful methods: for a time in the 1850s he even hoped that Napoleon III might be converted to his ideas. In particular he attached overwhelming importance for the

realization of his vision to the creation of free credit through the establishment of a *banque du peuple*. This, he claimed, would be 'the solvent of all
authority' which would 'change the basis of society, shift the axis of
civilization';[43] and in 1849 he attempted unsuccessfully to set up such an
institution. In his last years (he died in 1865) his ideas became in some
ways less extreme. He was driven to accept the need for some minimum
of government in even the freest of societies, though he insisted that this
government must be a federal one, with the component units given as
much independence as possible and the right to secede from the federation
if they wished. He also began, for the first time, to envisage the urban
working class as a potentially effective revolutionary force; the elections
of 1863 to the Chamber of Deputies in France, when Paris returned five
anti-government deputies, seem to have been for him a turning-point in
this respect.

No political theorist of the nineteenth century, not even Saint-Simon
himself, is more idiosyncratic than Proudhon. Yet neither this nor the
defeat and partial oblivion to which his ideas were doomed should be
allowed to obscure his importance in his own lifetime. To Marx he seemed
a formidable opponent. In the early years of the First International it was
the followers of Proudhon much more than those of Bakunin whom the
Marxists saw as a threat. In particular Proudhon's ideas of producer
cooperatives and free credit facilities found considerable support in a France
where most workers were still artisans or craftsmen; and the fact that
until at least about 1880 France remained indisputably the main centre of
European socialism meant that any ideologue with influence there became
automatically a figure of European importance. In Spain also Proudhon's
influence was for a time significant. Francisco Pi y Margall, one of the
four short-lived presidents of the chaotic Spanish republic of 1873–74,
had absorbed his ideas as an exile in Paris in 1866–69, was influenced
both by his credit schemes and by his federalism, and translated into
Spanish his last book, *Du principe fédératif*.

In political and social thought, then, the third quarter of the nineteenth
century sees a distinct weakening of individualist liberalism with its rationalist and Enlightenment background. It also sees an ebbing of romanticism. That of the right, of the monarchist-clerical-corporative type, had
never been of great intellectual importance and was now being replaced
by a tougher, more flexible and more realistic conservatism of which
Bismarck was the supreme practical exponent. That of the left, volitionist
and implicitly élitist, was now increasingly overshadowed by Marxism.
There had been, as old faiths and certainties faded, a widespread movement towards inductive thinking, towards 'science', and therefore towards
mental attitudes which were in some sense evolutionist.

The most clearly formulated, most spectacularly successful and most durable of all evolutionary ideas were, of course, those of biological evolution through natural selection put forward by Charles Darwin. But to thinking about society and its problems he contributed only indirectly. Rather he gave unique and irresistible prestige to a mode of thought which had already in large part triumphed over its competitors. He did not create an evolutionary sociology or anthropology; they already existed or were coming into existence before *The Origin of Species* was published in 1859. Even the voluminous English writer Herbert Spencer, the most influential of evolutionary sociologists, was not a Darwinist in any strict sense. His theories of society as evolving, in accordance with a natural process, from a 'homogeneous' to an increasingly 'heterogeneous' state, which would culminate in the complete adaptation of man to his social environment and hence his complete freedom, had been formulated in essentials before 1859. Indeed it may be argued that Darwin made, or at least should have made, an evolutionary theory of society more difficult to sustain than it had been before he wrote; for Darwinian evolution, like every truly great scientific discovery, raised new questions while answering existing ones. In particular the sheer complexity of the biological world which Darwin helped to reveal struck a blow at the assumption that the laws of nature (and therefore the laws of society as an aspect of them) were necessarily few and simple; though this fact was successfully concealed by his numerous popularizers and followers.

There was a further and more fundamental difficulty, however, inherent in the application to society of pseudo-Darwinian ideas. Was an advanced society, one relatively far along the path which all human societies were fated to travel, somehow ethically or spiritually superior to a less advanced one? Believers in evolutionary theories of society were anxious to believe that it was; but there was nothing in Darwin's work to indicate that this was logically so. What he had done was to develop a theory of evolution by natural selection from among the random variations in any species which were constantly occurring in the course of nature. Evolutionary change in organisms was thus accounted for in a completely mechanical and material way. Purpose did not enter into the picture. Moreover if man were subject to the same laws of development as other organisms and distinguished from them merely by his superior intellectual powers, why should he ever obey any ethical rule or moral law? Evolutionary materialism seemed to lead inevitably to ethical nihilism, to a denial of objective meaning either in the universe or in history. It could describe and account for what existed, but it could not say what ought to exist: indeed it made it meaningless even to ask what ought to exist. Nature seemed to have become a force which worked blindly and without purpose.

Darwin in his later work tried to escape from this quandary by arguing that as man had evolved he had developed a moral sense which made him sympathize with races and societies other than his own, and with the sick, the old and the weak. But if conventional morality were readmitted by the servants' entrance in this way, what became of the uninhibited struggle for survival which was thought to be the mainspring of all social change and progress? This difficulty might be evaded by arguing that among mankind, as distinguished from the lower animals, this struggle was between groups, not individuals, and that therefore morality had survival value since it fostered group cohesion. Thus Karl Pearson, one of the ablest of Darwin's scientific followers and the founder of the science of biometry, argued in a lecture given in 1900 that 'the safety of a gregarious animal – and man is essentially such – depends upon the intensity with which the social instinct has been developed. The stability of a race depends entirely upon the extent to which the social feelings have got a real hold on it.'[44] But even this dubious line of argument did not dispose of the difficulty. If the criterion of progress were merely the capacity to survive and expand, did not the military strength and success of a group, its ability to crush rival groups, become the most convincing index of its progressiveness? This conclusion particularly worried Spencer who, as a good Victorian radical, strongly disliked the growing militarism which was becoming apparent among the great powers by the 1870s or 1880s.

Nevertheless these difficulties seemed until the end of the century less important than the optimistic lessons to be drawn from Darwin's work. In the intellectual history of the nineteenth century he was the only figure to attain the kind of universally admitted greatness which Newton had achieved in the world of the old régime. As early as 1863 the English churchman and novelist Charles Kingsley had to admit that 'Darwin is conquering everywhere and rushing like a flood by the mere force of truth and fact'. In Protestant Europe, which had produced no Voltaire, he offered the first really great challenge, so far as the ordinary man was concerned, to traditional religious assumptions, and a far more thoroughgoing and searching one than Voltaire had ever undertaken. Nor did his ideas lead, as logically they should have done, to callousness towards the unfortunate and the incompetent. On the contrary, it is one of the paradoxes of intellectual history that the age of Darwinism was also one of unprecedented effort, over much of Europe, in social reform and organized (finally state-organized) charity. The dynamism, the high valuation of effort and responsibility, which marked the age, were too strong to be paralysed even by the most seductive form of scientific determinism. So was its optimism. The belief in pain as natural and inevitable, and even in orthodox Christian terms good, was by the end of the century clearly being abandoned all over western Europe. Yet no side of intellectual or artistic life escaped the influence of evolutionary ideas. In every aspect of that life there was now an unprecedentedly widespread tendency to accept as given the superiority of the present to the past and the need to move forward from the position which the present had reached.[45]

One very important caveat is, however, necessary. The preceding pages have been concerned with systems of ideas all of which, with varying degrees of justification, claimed to be innovative and in some sense scientific. All of them were the work of men who could claim, again more or less accurately, to be intellectuals. But these were a small minority of society, the mass of which remained deeply attached to beliefs which were highly traditional and instinctively opposed to fundamental change of any kind. The 1850s and 1860s, decades which saw the birth of Marxist socialism and Darwinian evolution, held out the promise, to a minority prepared to think in truly radical terms, of a unified explanation of all human existence which would be completely materialist, an attack at least by implication on traditional religious belief which would be unprecedentedly far-reaching. Side by side with this, moreover, went another and equally threatening assault, that from searching and questioning biblical criticism which, from the 1830s onwards, threw doubt on some of the foundations of Christianity, even on the divinity of Christ himself. Of this the *Leben Jesu* (*Life of Christ*) of the German theologian D. F. Strauss (1834–35) was perhaps the most important single example.

Yet the nineteenth century was also a great age of religion, in some ways very arguably the greatest of all. The French Revolution had made religious belief and the churches which embodied and fostered it appear as perhaps never before as the essential pillars of social and political stability; and in some parts of Europe the events of 1848 strengthened this impression. Moreover this was more than a merely negative emotion, a matter of mere self-defence by ruling groups against the power of change which had first shown themselves with such disruptive force in the 1790s. A revival of active and often popular faith showed itself in a number of ways, and was often most marked in some of the most progressive parts of western Europe.

One of the most visible of these was the building of new churches, often in an effort to Christianize and thus civilize the new, explosively growing industrial cities where churches, it seemed to many observers, were shamefully few. Thus the Church of England in three or four decades (1840–76) restored over 7,000 churches in need of repair and built over 1,700 new ones. Much the greater part of the cost of this, the enormous sum of over £25 million, was met by voluntary contributions. No other achievement of Victorian England – economic growth, political reform, imperial expansion

– attracted as much disinterested enthusiasm as this. In Scotland the newly established Free Church, after it broke away from the parent Church of Scotland in 1843, built 654 new churches in four years, a truly remarkable achievement for a country so small and still in some ways so poor. The same powerful religious impetus can be seen in a tendency in some countries for the number of ministers of religion to increase. France had more priests (almost 57,000) by 1870 than at any other time in the nineteenth century. In Ireland, a very striking case, which in 1850 had 5,000 priests to serve a population of about five million, half a century later there were 14,000 for a population which had now fallen by about a third. Missionary work outside Europe, in Asia, Africa and the Pacific islands, showed the same growth, the same faith-generated energy. By 1900 there were, including native priests and ministers, 41,000 Catholic and 18,000 Protestant missionaries at work in the non-European world. All this growth and activity, moreover, was underlain and made possible by a corresponding strengthening of popular faith perhaps most clearly seen in some Catholic parts of the continent. New popular pilgrimages were developed and some of these, aided by the new railways, attracted unprecedented numbers of the faithful. In 1844 a million people are said to have made the pilgrimage to Trier in the Prussian Rhineland to see part of a coat allegedly worn by Christ on the cross; and by the 1890s the relatively new centre at Lourdes, which dated only from 1858, was regularly attracting half a million pilgrims each year. Mystical and emotional forms of Catholicism, such as the cult of the Virgin and the Sacred Heart, grew in strength in many parts of Europe and in others, such as the Catholic areas of Germany in the middle decades of the century, there was a tendency for the age of young people at confirmation to fall.

All this powerful religious feeling inevitably had political implications. It could sometimes be seen as challenging the claims of secular governments and lead to conflict with them. The most striking example of this came in the new Bismarckian Reich. The suspicion and dislike of the Catholic church which was deeply rooted in Prussian ruling circles had already led to bitter disputes in the 1830s during which the Archbishop of Cologne was himself imprisoned in 1837; and in the 1870s Bismarck, who knew that many Catholics in south and west Germany looked to Vienna rather than Berlin for leadership, made a determined effort to reduce drastically the power of the church in the new Reich. The May Laws of 1873, and in particular the effort they made to bring the training and appointment of priests under state control, aroused bitter opposition. By 1876 every Catholic bishop in Prussia was either in exile or in gaol and many parishes had no priest. This *Kulturkampf* (Struggle of Cultures) became less intense after 1878–79 with the accession of a more conciliatory pope, Leo XIII, and the alliance between the new Germany and the Habsburg empire; but it was not formally ended until 1887. It was not a complete defeat for Bismarck. Some aspects of the legislation of the 1870s, notably civil marriage and state inspection of Catholic schools, were retained. But the strength and popular support shown by the new Catholic Centre Party during the struggle meant that political Catholicism had been consolidated in Germany as never before. The Centre Party won more than four-fifths of the Catholic votes cast in the Reichstag elections of the 1870s.

In France again from the 1870s the traditional antagonism between republican anticlericalism and widespread Catholic conservatism and monarchism showed how deep its roots were. There also the continuing influence of Catholicism in politics, the strength of the challenge it could still offer to the more and more secular state, was seen in a long and often bitter struggle, largely over education. A law of 1882 established the principle that state schools should be entirely secular and free from all religious influences, and four years later members of religious orders were forbidden to teach in them. From 1892 onwards Leo XIII made a considerable effort, the *Ralliement*, to improve relations between church and republic. But the more vocal forms of republicanism were too anticlerical, and the more intense forms of Catholicism too hostile to the republic and often too mystical and anti-Jewish in their outlook, for this to have real success. More legislation in 1904 attempted to expel even more completely religious influences from education; and in the following year this process culminated in the abrogation of the Napoleonic concordat of 1802 with the papacy and the formal separation of church and state in France.

The nineteenth century, then, was a great age of religion both in belief and action, one in which churches could still be a serious obstacle in the way of the increasingly demanding, interventionist and secularized state. During his long pontificate Pope Pius IX (1846–78) seemed more and more to exemplify this cleavage with uncompromising explicitness. His enunciation of the doctrine of the Immaculate Conception of the Virgin as an article of faith in 1854 was a response to conservative Catholic pressures. The Syllabus of Errors which he issued ten years later ended with a sweeping declaration that the pope ought not to come to terms with progress, liberalism or modern civilization in general. The Declaration of Papal Infallibility of 1870, the fruit of long debate in a church council meeting in Rome, seemed the supreme rejection of the whole tenor of Europe's developing intellectual life and was greeted with dismay by many liberals within as well as outside the church. But the long reign of this extremist pope was merely the most striking illustration of an intellectual cleavage which was now more clear and pervasive than ever before – that between an élite, though a growing one, which tried to understand the world in rational, analytical and at least quasi-scientific terms, and a majority whose outlook was traditional and still largely rooted in religion. The political and social importance of the intellectual contribution made by some of the outstanding figures of the mid-century – Darwin, Marx, de Tocqueville, perhaps Mazzini, Cobden and List – is clear. But it must not be forgotten that they represented, as genuine intellectual novelty must in any age, only a relatively small segment of society in general.

THE EXPLORATION OF CONSCIOUSNESS AND THE GROWTH OF SELF-DOUBT

The generation between the 1840s and the 1870s thus enriched and complicated the stock of ideas and beliefs available to the educated European. By 1914 he had at his disposal an even wider, indeed an unprecedented, variety of political, social and artistic creeds among which to choose.

In Marxism, particularly in Germany and central Europe, the dominant strain remained the 'scientific' and determinist one which Engels had done so much to foster. But its dominance was never unquestioned. Even in Germany it was challenged during the 1890s by the 'revisionists' led by Eduard Bernstein, who pointed out that Marx's prophecies of an increasing relative impoverishment of the working class and a growing concentration of the means of production in fewer hands were clearly not being fulfilled. Trade cycles were becoming less pronounced, order and prosperity were growing, social tensions were being appeased: in a word, some of the objectives of socialism were already being achieved in Germany without a revolution and without even the establishment of popular government. The Social Democrats, Bernstein and his followers argued, should therefore abandon the increasingly threadbare pretence of being a revolutionary party and work for gradual and progressive social change, for democracy and international conciliation, by peaceful means. These attitudes were widely supported by the Social Democrats of south Germany, where the party was much more integrated with society generally than in the rest of the country, and also by many party members, for example trade union leaders or practising professional men, whose daily work forced them into contact with the wider non-socialist world. But the party ideologues such as Kautsky for whom the party as it stood was an enclosed and self-sufficient society, in some ways almost a mirror-image of the German imperial society in which it was embedded, would have nothing to do with Bernstein's ideas. In the Hanover and Dresden congresses of the German Social Democratic party in 1899 and 1903 these heretical arguments were decisively rejected; and the party leadership was tactically justified in its conservatism. A church is always in danger if it modifies essential doctrines; and to abandon the myth of inevitable and more or less imminent proletarian revolution would have undermined seriously the faith and morale of many ordinary party members. Moreover the Social Democrats had never any chance of exercising real power in Germany. Its wellsprings in the court, the army, the bureaucracy and heavy industry, were always far beyond their reach. Bernstein, as events were to show, was wrong in believing that Germany could achieve effective political democracy unless by revolution or military defeat. Nevertheless the revisionists, in spite of their failure, had thrown into relief the unreality, at least in the more advanced countries of Europe, of much of the now dominant strain in Marxism. They had exposed its shallow optimism about the inevitability of revolution, and the lack of real predictive power, which vitiated its claim to be scientific.

From a different standpoint the increasingly quietist Marxism of Germany came under fire during the later nineteenth century from France, where the romantic and élitist element in socialism, the concept of it as a creed of struggle involving the forcible conquest of power by a consciously revolutionary minority, showed much greater vitality. In France socialist political groups in the 1880s and 1890s were small, quarrelsome and usually militant. Moreover many of the most able and prominent French socialists – Jaurès, Viviani, Millerand, Briand – entered public life in the 1890s as independents with no fixed allegiance. Not until 1905, after many vicissitudes, was a united party, the *Section Française de l'Internationale Ouvrière*, formed by the fusion of the two main surviving French socialist groups. Even this was a much smaller and less disciplined body than the German Social Democratic party; indeed it was in large part the very fewness and lack of rigid organization of the French socialists which allowed them to retain a revolutionary dynamism which the wealthy and centralized German party was increasingly losing.

While one wing of the French socialist movement was more militant than the German one, another was more moderate, or at least more realistic. In France there was in the 1880s and 1890s a considerable 'Possibilist' tendency, typified by Paul Brousse and his followers, which was willing to contemplate gradual and piecemeal reform and to cooperate to some extent in the working and defence of existing institutions: the foundation of the Second International in 1889 was accompanied by a good deal of friction between the Broussists and the German Social Democrats. Moreover the greatest French socialist of this period, Jean Jaurès, was of a very different stamp from the leaders of the German party. A man of wide culture and humanity, he accepted materialism, but not as the sole and self-sufficient motive force in history. In his most important theoretical work, published in 1895, he argued that 'it is . . . not necessary to oppose the materialist and the idealist conceptions of history to one another' and that 'history, at the same time that it is a phenomenon unfolding in accordance with a mechanical law, is also an aspiration realizing itself according to an ideal law'.[46]

French socialism in general, unlike that of Germany or Austria, was always interested in history rather than in economics: this largely explains its more flexible and less dogmatic character. Most important of all, in France, a country with a genuine if often chaotic system of representative government, socialism could have practical influence in a way impossible in Germany or the Habsburg empire. In 1899 Millerand became a minister in the cabinet headed by the radical Waldeck-Rousseau. This stimulated bitter controversy as to whether a socialist should ever cooperate in this way with the government of a capitalist state (especially as the same cabinet included as minister for war the Marquis de Gallifet, notorious for his role in the suppression of the Commune in 1871). The congress of the International which met in Paris in 1900, after long discussion, grudgingly legitimized action such as that of Millerand; but only in exceptional cases and if it received the consent of the party of which the individual concerned was a member. The contrast between the flexibility and indeed confusion of the position in France, and on the other hand the great and almost monolithic German party consistently excluded from power, is the best of all indices of the very different political, social and indeed intellectual structures of the two countries.

The Marxism which was now spreading throughout Europe[47] was thus never a completely unified movement. Nor was it ever free from challenge by forces and ideas which were, at least in theory, more radical. In particular anarchism remained a competitor of some importance and one which, in spite of the excesses of its extremists, the bomb-throwings and assassinations which outraged opinion throughout Europe,[48] embodied the most fundamental of all criticisms of existing society. However anarchism never became a coherent movement either in theory or in practice: it was contrary to its essential nature to attempt to become one. Some of its adherents were gentle pacifists like the Russian Prince Kropotkin, others pathologically violent social misfits.[49] Some stressed the need for cooperation in the society of the future, others adhered to the most extreme and subjective type of romantic individualism. Some looked to a genuine social revolution, others were interested merely in rejecting the conventions of personal morality. Some were important figures in intellectual and artistic life – for example the geographer Elisée Reclus and the painter Camille Pissaro – others were poorly educated workmen. A movement simultaneously so incoherent and so radical could attract gifted individuals: it is impossible to deny the beauty of the anarchist vision at its best. But it had never any chance of practical success. In Italy, drawing on the tradition of conspiracy and armed revolt left behind by the Risorgimento, it had considerable influence until the 1890s. In the Jura area of Switzerland, the only part of Europe in which Bakunin had been able to attract genuinely widespread support, an anarchist tradition lingered on. In Spain, uniquely, the influence of anarchism increased, after its introduction to the country at the end of the 1860s, right up until 1914. The *Alliance Internationale Ouvrière*, a loose association of anarchist groups, was formed in 1880: it was not until 1896, after bitter controversy, that the Second International excluded anarchist parties from membership. But except in Italy and Spain, backward areas with long histories of defeat, frustration and conspiracy, the effective appeal of anarchism was very limited.

Indirectly, through ideas associated with it, it had a wider influence. From the 1880s in France there was a remarkable rise, among the growing trade unions and their sympathizers, of syndicalism, of the vision of existing society overthrown and replaced through purely industrial action, without reliance on any political party. This attitude, deeply hostile to politics in the normal sense of the term, was based in part on a working-class distrust of middle-class intellectuals, whatever their ideas. Traces of this distrust are clearly visible in the Commune of 1871 and even as early as 1848. It found practical expression in France in the creation, from 1887 onwards, of militant labour organizations, the *Bourses du Travail*, and their union in a federation in 1892. Fernand Pelloutier, its remarkable young first secretary-general, was deeply influenced by anarchist ideas and wished to make the *Bourses* educational centres which might equip the workers to become members of the new society of the future. Syndicalist attitudes, and in particular a deep distrust of all political parties, remained very important in the French labour movement, and hence in French politics, until 1914. In Spain they were even more significant. There the trade unions of Catalonia, the only industrialized area of the country, were strongly syndicalist by 1907, when they united in the *Solidaridad Obrera*. The general strike which this called in 1909, and the savage fighting and repression in Barcelona which followed (the *Semana Tragica* – Tragic Week) strengthened this tendency still further. The *Confederación General del Trabajo*, formed in 1911, was to remain for a generation the most important syndicalist organization in the world. Even in Britain, though their practical importance was not very great, syndicalist ideas had considerable influence on a number of trade union leaders and contributed to the growth of the interesting though short-lived Guild Socialist movement from 1906 onwards.

All this appeared, to some observers, to face Marxism with a formidable competitor. 'Syndicalism has taken the place of the old-fashioned Marxism', wrote one in 1912. 'The angry youth, with bad complexion, frowning brow and weedy figure is nowadays a syndicalist; the glib young workman whose tongue runs away with him today mouths the phrases of French syndicalism instead of those of German social democracy.'[50] In fact the threat to Marxism was less than it seemed. Syndicalism, like the anarchism to which it was related, was by its very nature unfitted to evolve an effective programme or a systematic international organization. It can best be seen as an expression of the discontent, widespread in Europe during the generation before 1914, of men trapped in a society in which conditions, though generally improving, were doing so too slowly to satisfy them, and of their passionate readiness to see in merely industrial action a swift and effective solution to their problems.

The highest and most extreme form of this industrial action was the general strike. Though the German Social Democrats always disliked the idea of this, it was possible to argue that its efficacy as a means of extorting concessions from the ruling classes had now been proved in practice. In Belgium there was a series of successful large-scale strikes in 1886, 1887, 1891 and 1893 in support of demands for extension of the franchise. In 1902 a successful general strike was called in Sweden for the same purpose. More spectacularly, the mass strikes which were a feature of the upheaval of 1905 in Russia strengthened considerably the syndicalist idea of the general strike as the supreme revolutionary weapon. Side by side with more or less rational arguments, however, went a mystique of the general strike, a belief in it as a symbolic action which, irrespective of the objective facts of the situation, could arouse and sharpen, with unique effect, the feelings, memories and aspirations of the workers. The supreme statement of this attitude is Georges Sorel's *Réflexions sur la violence*, published in 1908, in which the author speaks of the general strike as 'the myth in which Socialism is wholly comprised, i.e. a body of images capable of evoking instinctively all the sentiments which correspond to the different manifestations of the war undertaken by Socialism against modern society', and as providing 'that intuition of Socialism which language cannot give us with perfect clearness'.[51] This view sees humanity as impelled to action not by reason or the clear enunciation of ideas but by vaguely apprehended feelings aroused by myths which are themselves endowed with numinous power. Of all the political visions of this period it is perhaps the one furthest removed from the liberal tradition, and indeed from Marxism also. Yet none has better withstood the test provided by the events of the twentieth century. Even before Sorel's book was written Gustave Le Bon had gone some distance towards providing, in his

Psychologie des foules (1895) a scientific basis for belief in the effect of myth and emotion in moving the masses. The very vagueness and non-rationality of myths of the Sorelian type makes them almost indestructible, since they can, more easily than any other view of society and social action, change and refine themselves to fit changing practical experience.

The decline of liberalism, its loss of self-confidence and vitality which had begun to be visible by the middle of the nineteenth century, continued until 1914. Classical liberalism had, fundamentally, depended on a belief in the existence of transcendental truths and in the absolute value of the individual. By the 1890s these assumptions were becoming more difficult than ever to sustain. They had already been undermined by the advance of positivism and quantitative thinking, which made law seem the product merely of a particular time and place rather than something transcendental, applying to all men. Right and wrong, good and bad, justice and injustice thus became merely matters of utility or expediency. Positive law (which was ultimately the product of will and coercion) was now increasingly regarded as the only law. There was no longer, as there had so notably been to so many thinkers of the Enlightenment, an ideal law with which it could be compared. Rights were no longer those of man in general. They were merely those of the citizens of a particular state and subject to alteration or even nullification by that state.[52] The growing dominance of positivist modes of thought from the 1840s to the 1880s was thus progressively taming liberalism, robbing it of the intellectual vitality it had possessed in the days of Adam Smith or Humboldt or even Mill.

In the externals of politics, in terms of constitutional guarantees, voting rights, political phraseology, this change showed itself only slowly over much of the continent. Until 1914 a great deal of party-political debate in many countries continued to be conducted in terms of the slogans and catchwords of constitutional liberalism. The realities, however, had changed – most rapidly and importantly in Germany. There the victories of Prussia and Bismarck in 1862–71 ended any possibility of liberal idealism playing a dominant or even a leading political role. The surrender of 1866 is a watershed in this respect. After this the majority of Germany's liberals, represented from 1867 by the new National Liberal party, were in effect supporters of an efficient and militarist conservative régime. Before very long German liberal jurists were arguing that the individual 'is for the State nothing but an object serving the State's ends', and that 'only as a member of the State . . . is man the bearer of rights'.[53] The role the liberals had formerly played as defenders of the individual against the state machinery was now increasingly to be played by new forces, those of political catholicism and social democracy. The Progressives (later the National People's party) who had not gone over to support of the régime after 1867 now found themselves increasingly powerless. Narrow in outlook and distinguished largely by a dogmatic opposition to protective tariffs, they were able in the years before 1914 to play some role in German politics only through intermittent alliances with the Catholic Centre party and the Social Democrats.

Even in Britain, where the liberal tradition was longer and more deeprooted than anywhere else in Europe, liberal attitudes were becoming more difficult to sustain. From the 1850s and certainly from the 1870s onwards the demand for greater efficiency in every aspect of the national life was being uttered more and more insistently. It is visible in the remodelling of the civil service and audible in repeated proposals for drastic improvement and broadening of the educational system. A heavy emphasis on efficiency of any kind agreed more easily with a positive or scientific than with a traditional liberal mode of thought; and the achievements of British rule in India seemed a striking example of what could be done by a government freed from liberal restraints and dedicated to practical progress. The most acute British conservative of the nineteenth century, James Fitzjames Stephen, wrote in the later 1870s that India was 'the best corrective in existence to the fundamental fallacies of Liberalism', and 'the only government under English control still worth caring about'.[54]

There was in Britain nothing approaching the loss of nerve and self-confidence suffered by liberalism in Germany after 1866. Nevertheless there was a certain narrowing of sympathies and erosion of idealism as the century drew to a close. Some of the certainties of its middle decades, both about the truth of liberal assumptions and about the readiness of the world to accept them, began to decline. To some extent this can be illustrated in terms of political events. Thus the adoption by Gladstone and the Liberal party in 1885 of a policy of Home Rule for Ireland produced a strong hostile reaction, justified in the main by arguments based on power and efficiency, among English intellectuals. Whereas in 1876 an agitation against Turkish massacres of Bulgarians had been spectacularly successful, a similar one in 1895–97 against Turkish massacres of Armenians was a complete failure, in spite of the fact that ten times as many Armenians as Bulgarians were slaughtered and that the two agitations were led to a considerable extent by the same individuals. Fundamental liberal attitudes – individualism, belief in the essential rationality of man, belief that the validity of law depended upon its content and not merely upon its source, and a consequent refusal to glorify the state – were still deeply rooted in Britain. But even there liberalism had lost some of its moral and more of its intellectual vitality.

Its decline continued unbroken almost everywhere in Europe until the First World War. From the 1890s onwards, however, its most insidious intellectual adversary was not positivism or even Marxism but the new views of the nature of man, both as an individual and as a part of society, which were being put forward by a number of profoundly original thinkers. These thinkers – Vilfredo Pareto and Gaetano Mosca in Italy, Sorel in France, on a different level Sigmund Freud in Vienna – were all, in different ways and to different degrees, preoccupied with the irrational or non-rational aspects of human psychology. All agreed in rejecting the classical liberal view of man as autonomous, rational and capable by the exercise of his reason of achieving true liberty. To them he was the master of his fate only in the most superficial and limited way, only in so far as instincts and passions, driving forces of whose very existence he was often unconscious, would allow him to be. It was in this uncompromising rejection of the idea that society and its problems could be understood by mere knowledge of objective facts, that human nature could be explained in terms of the natural sciences and their methods, that their originality lay. Sorel's theory of the 'myth' and his vision of spontaneous, non-rationalized, revolutionary activity; Pareto's theory of 'residues', the unchanging or very slowly changing elements in human conduct which were beyond the reach of rational thought; Freud's discovery of the unconscious mind and development of a theory of unconscious motivation from his *Interpretation of Dreams* (1900) onwards, are all examples of this. The strangeness of many of these ideas, and the size and difficulty of the books in which some of them were presented, limited their impact upon even the educated classes of Europe before 1914. In both the Slavonic and the English-speaking worlds they were still in that year almost unknown. But they offered the most fundamental of all challenges to liberalism and to the belief in progress which it helped to generate. Their devaluation of the importance of rational thought in social and political life did something to pave the way for the aggressively antirational cults of the 1920s and 1930s. In particular in the writings of Pareto, Mosca and the German Robert Michels politics were made to centre, as never since Machiavelli, around a brutally clear distinction between rulers and ruled and the manipulation by the rulers of the emotions and irrational urges of their subjects.

The chaotic variety and kaleidoscopic changes of the political and social ideas of the two generations before 1914 are mirrored in the confusedly luxuriant growth of their art, music and literature. This gigantic subject, which would require a whole assembly of specialists to do it justice, can only be touched on here. Certain rough equivalences between intellectual life in general and that of the arts can none the less be suggested. Richard Wagner, in his prolific writings, in his aesthetic theorizing, in his dream of the *Gesamtkunstwerk*, the work which would unite harmoniously within itself music, literature and the visual arts, can be classed with Marx and Darwin as one of the great system-makers who overshadowed so much of the life of the third quarter of the nineteenth century. The year 1859, which gave birth not merely to the *Origin of Species* but also to Marx's *Critique of Political Economy* and Wagner's *Tristan und Isolde*, can be seen as the beginning of a new era in intellectual life. Certainly in the Wagnerian movement which influenced so much of European music from the 1880s onwards, notably in France, it was Wagner's ideas and theories as much as his music itself which appealed to intellectuals; and a similar dream of uniting all the arts in a vast symposium which would engage simultaneously all the senses inspired several later composers, for example the Russian Alexander Skryabin.

In a more specific way the dominant positivism, materialism and individualism, and the still widespread belief in political democracy, of the third quarter of the century can be equated with the realist movement in art and literature, of which the painter Gustave Courbet and the novelist Émile Zola, both French, were the most popular representatives. Courbet said that 'through my affirmation of the negation of the ideal and all that springs from the ideal, I have arrived at the emancipation of the individual and finally at democracy. Realism is essentially a democratic art.'[55] Zola's largest work, the Rougon-Macquart series of novels, of which he published twenty volumes in 1871–93, betrays the same faith in the material and the scientific in its significant subtitle, *A natural and social history of a family under the Second Empire*; and his interest in social mechanisms and indifference to psychological subtleties and the deeper aspects of individual personality is typical of this whole literary and artistic current.

In a rather similar way the growing disintegration of old certainties – in the essential rationality of man, in the reality of progress – is reflected by the end of the century in a growing rejection of fixed standards, in an attraction towards the ambiguous, towards the suggestive rather than the precise and explicit, in a willingness to experiment with a bewilderingly wide variety of new modes of expression. In music this tendency can be seen most strikingly in the work of Claude Debussy, the greatest composer of the generation before 1914. The shimmering vagueness of so much that he wrote during the later 1880s and 1890s, and above all of his *La Mer* (1905) and *Images* (1909–12), has much in common with the work of the Impressionist school of painters which dominated forward-looking French and therefore to a large extent European art in the 1870s and early 1880s. In 1882 Renoir, one of the greatest of them, spoke to Wagner of 'the Impressionists in music' – probably the first time the term had been applied to the sister-art.[56] The new uncertainty and experimentalism can also be seen, in a more extreme form, in the progressive abandonment of the idea of fixed tonality, which had been since the end of the sixteenth century one of the assumptions on which European music was based. This abandonment had indeed been foreshadowed considerably earlier in the nineteenth century. In parts of his *Euryanthe* (1823) Weber had already gone some distance towards it. Liszt, the most prophetic of all great nineteenth-century composers, had in his later works gone further. One of the last piano pieces written by him before his death in 1886 (though published only seventy years later) had been a *Bagatelle sans tonalité*. It was only a few years before 1914, however, that this movement, with its increasing reliance on complex chromatic harmonies, culminated in the work of the young Austrian, Arnold Schönberg, in music which was clearly and systematically atonal. The two decades before the First World War were, in literature and the arts, a period of wonderful richness and achievement in Europe, a last superb flowering of energy and sensibility before the cataclysm of 1914. But it is impossible to ignore an increasing stridency, an increasing extremism and radicalism pursued for its own sake, which can be seen, without an illegitimate use of hindsight, as an indication of underlying tensions and uncertainties. In painting the reaction against realism took not merely the form of Impressionism, which could be seen as a different and truer view of reality, but the much more radical one of the Cubism created by Picasso, Braque, Gris and Derain (on foundations laid earlier by Cézanne) in Paris in the years after 1907. Some of their contemporaries in the German and central European world – Munch or Kandinsky, for example – can be seen in their sometimes anguished efforts to probe their own innermost feelings and to expose on canvas the depths of their consciousness as expressing in art the psychic drives postulated by Freud. By the eve of 1914 another school of radical innovators in Russia, the Constructivists of whom Malevich and Tatlin were the outstanding representatives, were launching from a different direction an equally violent assault on traditional standards and certainties. The most 'scientific' of the radicals of European art, they rejected the personal and subjective and used for the first time materials such as steel to make large impersonal constructions in space. From a number of widely differing standpoints, therefore, most of the greatest artists of the age were attacking and even ridiculing the whole traditional concept of the Fine Arts. Moreover the coming of the great international art exhibition (the first ones were held in Munich in 1886 and 1888) and the increasing ease with which pictures could now be more or less accurately reproduced in quantity, meant that the artist now had access in an unprecedented way to the works of other ages and other civilizations. One result was that the art of the non-European world now influenced European painters and sculptors as never before. In particular that of Africa, hitherto ignored, now attracted admiration precisely because it was so clearly and completely remote from European models and values, so un-European, so apparently unsophisticated. It thus appealed to a Europe increasingly unsure of the inevitable rightness of its own traditional standards. In music the same movement away from the old certainties and the same desire for the exciting, the pseudo-primitive, even the brutal, culminated in a roughly similar fashion with the publication by the Italian Futurist, Luigi Russolo, in Milan in 1913 of his manifesto *The Art of Noise*. A decade earlier the Gramophone Company, from its headquarters in London, had set on foot the first large-scale and systematic effort to record the native music of India, China and Japan: Europe's musical life, like its artistic one, was now being enriched and confused by the revelation of non-European achievements and possibilities. In literature new discoveries such as those of Freud, coupled with growing lack of confidence in the standards of the past, were beginning to breed a hitherto unheard-of scepticism about the ability of mere words to express every possible shade of human feeling and experience; this was another and a very fundamental aspect of the flight from rationalism.

A good deal of this extremism in the arts had only a limited influence on the future. Some of it by its self-consciously *outré* character has perhaps attracted more attention than it really merits. It must be remembered also how limited the response of the general public was to most of it. Nearly all Frenchmen preferred highly skilled and conventional painters such as Bouguereau and Meissonier to any of the Impressionists or Post-Impressionists, not to speak of the Cubists; while in 1914 few Viennese would have considered Schönberg in his recent work a composer at all in the sense that Brahms had been. Nevertheless this growing extremism injected a note of unease into the cultural life of this great pre-war generation. The range of cultural possibilities, the apparently vertiginous rate of cultural change, made for a sense of uncertainty and impermanence. 'The nature of our epoch', wrote the Austrian poet and playwright Hugo von Hofmannsthal in 1905, 'is multiplicity and indeterminacy. It can rest only on *das Gleitende* (the moving, the slipping, the sliding), and is aware that what other generations believed to be firm is in fact *das Gleitende*.'[57] These words were written by a subject of the great power most clearly menaced by internal dissolution and collapse. They were also written by a citizen of Vienna, a capital in which, more than anywhere else in Europe, a highly cultured *haute bourgeoisie*, effectively excluded from political power by the defeat of liberalism, had developed a deep interest in the arts and especially in their individual and subjective aspects. But Hofmannsthal's statement is only one expression of a feeling increasingly widespread among the small minority upon whom the high culture of Europe depended. It can easily be paralleled by others: for example by the manifesto issued in February 1909 by the Futurist movement in Italy which proclaimed that 'everything moves, everything runs, everything is being rapidly transformed'.

The life of the mind thus presents in the Europe of 1914 a picture of confusion. On the one hand there was still plenty of hope and apparently much reason for hope. It was undeniable that the last century and especially the last generation had seen in most parts of the continent a vast improvement in the conditions of physical life, in terms of health, longevity, nutrition and comfort. To the ordinary man as distinct from the intellectual belief in progress still seemed natural. A naïve positivism, a belief in progressive advance through the accumulation of knowledge and in the rationality of man, still dominated the thinking of ordinary people, even of most educated people. It was still possible, for some extreme political radicals, essentially in the tradition of the eighteenth-century Enlightenment, to believe that in the future science might regulate the whole life of a regenerated humanity to the exclusion of emotions and traditions which were a crippling inheritance from the past.[58] On the other hand the new tributaries which were beginning to flow into the great river of European thought and feeling were distrustful of, even destructive of, such hopes and certainties. Crude ideas of social evolution had now been discredited in the eyes of the intellectually creative minority; in part by the increasing difficulty its members now found in believing in the reality of progress, in part by the fact that field research by anthropologists had now exploded the earlier assumption that all societies must pass through the same sequence of stages as they developed. Most fundamental of all, belief in the rationality of man and therefore in the possibility of his achieving complete freedom by taking thought and acting on his thoughts, the noble and beneficial liberal illusion to which the nineteenth century owed so much, seemed to the intellectual avant-garde increasingly untenable. In their eyes 'the people', virtuous and incorruptible, in which the idealists of 1848 had placed such hopes, was now being replaced by 'the masses', irrational, violent and emotional, a source of suspicion and menace rather than of confidence. Everywhere in the marvellous luxuriance of music, literature and the arts, can be felt this slow erosion of assumptions and certainties still widely and unthinkingly held. A new intellectual atmosphere was forming, one in some ways as brilliant and productive as its predecessor, but one less robust, less self-confident and masculine, more uneasy and tentative. Politically the nineteenth century ended in 1914. In the world of ideas and the arts the beginning of the end for nineteenth-century Europe had come two decades earlier.

NOTES

1. E. George, *The Life and Death of Benjamin Robert Haydon* (2nd edn., Oxford University Press, 1967), p. 34.

2. *Confession d'un enfant du siècle*, quoted in J. B. Halsted, ed., *Romanticism* (London, Macmillan, 1969), pp. 338–9.

3. Stendhal, who met Byron in Milan in 1816, acutely noted that 'Lord Byron greatly resembled Rousseau in the sense that he was constantly occupied with himself and with the effect he produced on others' (H. G. Schenk, *The Mind of the European Romantics* (London, Constable, 1966), p. 140).

4. For example, Rousseau's partiality at times for 'Armenian' dress, the ostentatious scarlet waistcoat worn by the poet Théophile Gautier at the first night in 1830 of Victor Hugo's play *Hernani* (a symbolic victory for romanticism in the French theatre over the classical tradition) and perhaps the whole phenomenon of 'dandyism' in French literary circles in the middle decades of the nineteenth century.

5. An annotation to Sir Joshua Reynolds' *Discourses*, quoted in Halsted, *Romanticism*, p. 354.

6. The best, though a late, statement of this populist romanticism is to be found in the works of the French historian Jules Michelet. See particularly his *Le peuple* (Paris, 1846) and the preface to his *Histoire de la révolution française* (Paris, 1847–53).

7. Quoted in S. Mellon, *The Political Uses of History: a study of historians in the French Restoration* (Stanford University Press, 1958), p. 2.

8. G. Conard, ed., *Correspondence de Gustave Flaubert* (Paris, 1926–33), iv, 61.

9. For a discussion of this idea see G. Lukács, *The Historical Novel* (London, Merlin Press, 1962), Ch. i, *passim*.

10. A good example of this is the persistent effort of liberal writers in France after 1815 to relate the revolution to the whole of the country's past and to stress the element of political struggle which had existed under the monarchy and prepared the way for 1789. Both this attitude and the conservative one which saw the revolution as a catastrophic break with the past involved 'reading history backwards' (see Mellon, *The Political Uses of History*, Chs ii–iv *passim*).

11. See p. 225.

12. For Savigny's condemnation of the optimism and universalism of the eighteenth century see the extract from his *Of the Vocation of our Age for Legislation and Jurisprudence* (1814) in Halsted, *Romanticism*, p. 202; and on his work in general W. Kantorowicz, 'Savigny and the historical school of law', *Law Quarterly Review*, liii (1937).

13. This is visible, for example, in the attention given to it by Théodore Géricault, the greatest French painter of the early nineteenth century.

14. An outstanding illustration of this is Berlioz's account of his return in 1848 and again in 1864 to the scene of his first adolescent love affair in 1815 (D. Cairns, ed., *The Memoirs of Hector Berlioz* (London, Gollancz, 1969), pp. 455–6, 499–501).

15. E. H. Carr, *Michael Bakunin* (London, Macmillan, 1937), p. 29.

16. I. Babbitt, *Rousseau and Romanticism* (New York, Houghton Mifflin, 1919), p. 79.

17. J. Barzun, *Classic, Romantic and Modern* (London, Secker & Warburg, 1962), p. 87.

18. The earliest important work of the kind is A. A. Cournot, *Recherches sur les principles mathématiques de la théorie des richesses* (Paris, 1838); for a discussion of previous and more incomplete efforts in this direction see R. D. Theocaris, *Early Developments in Mathematical Economics* (London, Macmillan, 1961), *passim*.

19. This very bare summary of the main ideas of liberal individualism rests largely upon H. K. Girvetz, *From Wealth to Welfare: the evolution of liberalism* (Stanford University Press, 1951), Chs i–ii.

20. T. Zeldin, 'English ideals in French politics during the nineteenth century', *Historical Journal*, ii (1959), 47–8.

21. K. D. Tönnesson, 'The Babouvists: from utopian to practical Socialism', *Past and Present*, no. 22 (July 1962), 71.

22. *A New View of Society* (1813), quoted in M. Salvadori, ed., *Modern Socialism* (New York, Harper & Row, 1968), pp. 73–4.

23. J. S. McClelland, ed., *The French Right (from de Maistre to Maurras)* (London, Cape, 1970), p. 40.

24. During the early nineteenth century in Germany A. W. von Schlegel and in Russia V. A. Zhukovsky translated him, while in England Hazlitt wrote perhaps the most famous of all assessments of his work. Later in France Hugo pronounced him the greatest of all modern writers. He had enormous influence on Berlioz, while Beethoven envisaged an opera based on *Macbeth*.

25. G. Reynolds, *Turner* (London, Thames & Hudson, 1969), p. 190.

26. F. Baldensperger, *Sensibilité musicale et romantisme* (Paris, 1925), p. 34.

27. *Ibid*, p. 100.

28. F. Darwin, *The Life and Letters of Charles Darwin* (London, 1887), iii, 193–4.

29. Darwin himself did not make use of it until the fifth (1869) edition of the *Origin of Species*.

30. J. W. Burrow, *Evolution and Society: a study in Victorian social theory* (Cambridge University Press, 1966), p. 15.

31. *Ibid*, p. 106.

32. Marx read Buonarotti's book in 1844 and hoped to arrange for a German translation of it to be made by the radical Moses Hess.

33. G. Lichtheim, *Marxism: an historical and critical study* (London, Routledge, 1961), p. 37.

34. *Ibid*, p. 62.

35. In the *Communist Manifesto* Marx and Engels had insisted that there would in the future be an absolute fall in the living standards of the workers; but by the later 1860s they were talking merely in terms of their relative poverty, since it was difficult to deny that their position had by then improved markedly over much of Europe in absolute terms. Marx in the first volume of *Das Kapital* specifically admitted at least the possibility of a rise in real wages.

36. In his *The Civil War in France* (London, 1871). On Marx's ambiguous attitude to the Commune see S. Avineri, *The Social and Political Thought of Karl Marx* (Cambridge University Press, 1968), pp. 239–49.

37. Engels' attitude is summed up in his famous claim at Marx's grave that 'as Darwin discovered the law of evolution in organic nature, Marx discovered the law of evolution in human history'.

38. Burrow, *Evolution and Society*, p. 101n.

39. M. Drachkovitch, *De Karl Marx a Leon Blum. La crise de la Sociale-Democratie* (Geneva, 1954), pp. 17–20, where a selection of quotations illustrating this point is given.

40. B. T. Tchou, ed., *Ni dieu ni maitre. Les anarchistes* (n.p., 1969), p. 177.

41. E. H. Carr, *Michael Bakunin* (London, Macmillan, 1975: First published 1937), p. 439.

42. For example the South Slav nationalist *Ujedinenje ili Smrt* society, responsible for the murder of the Archduke Franz Ferdinand in June 1914. Its initiation ceremony for new members took place in a darkened room lit only by a candle and before a small table on which on a black cloth lay a crucifix, a dagger and a revolver. The society's seal bore a skull and crossbones, a dagger, a bomb and a bottle of poison together with the inscription *Ujedinenje ili Smrt* (Union or Death). The whole apparatus is strongly reminiscent of that used by the Carbonari in Italy a century earlier. (See R. J. Rath, 'The Carbonari: their origins, initiation rites and aims', *American Historical Review*, lxix (1963–64), 356–65.) The Irish Republican Brotherhood, founded in the 1850s and revived after about 1907, is another good example of the continuing strength of the conspiratorial tradition.

43. A. Ritter, *The Political Thought of Pierre-Joseph Proudhon* (Princeton University Press, 1969), p. 171.

44. W. Warren Wagar, ed., *The Idea of Progress since the Renaissance* (New York, Wiley, 1969), p. 109.

45. For a good example of this attitude in music see the comments of Emmanuel Chabrier, one of the most fanatical of Wagner's French admirers, on the great German composer's place in a kind of evolutionary development of opera (R. Myers, *Emmanuel Chabrier and his Circle* (London, Dent, 1969), p. 115).

46. A. Fried and R. Sanders, eds, *Socialist Thought: a documentary history* (Edinburgh University Press, 1964), p. 414.

47. The Belgian Workers Party was formed in 1885, and Austria and Switzerland acquired Social Democratic parties in 1888. In Britain small Marxist organizations, the Social Democratic Federation and the Socialist League, were founded in 1883 and 1884, and an Italian Socialist Party, which was vaguely Marxist, in 1892. The Group for the Liberation of Labour, the first Russian Marxist Party, was created by exiles in Switzerland in 1883. The Social Democratic Party of Hungary was founded in 1890 and the Polish Socialist Party in 1892.

48. The most important were those of President Carnot of France in 1894, of the Spanish prime minister, Cànovas del Castillo, in 1896, and of King Umberto of Italy in 1900.

49. It is noteworthy how many of the anarchist extremists of the later nineteenth century had had deeply unfortunate early lives since they were illegitimate or abandoned by one or both of their parents (J. Joll, *The Anarchists* (London, Eyre & Spottiswoode, 1964), pp. 131, 134, 139; J. C. Longoni, *Four Patients of Dr Deibler: a study in anarchy* (London, Lawrence & Wishart, 1970), pp. 18, 22, 85, 133–5).

50. *Beatrice Webb's Diaries, 1912–1924*, ed. M. Cole (Longman, 1952), p. 7.

51. M. Salvadori, ed., *Modern Socialism* (New York, Harper and Row, 1968), p. 155.

52. There is a good discussion of this erosion of the intellectual foundations of liberalism in J. H. Hallowell, *The Decline of Liberalism as an Ideology, with particular reference to German politico-legal thought* (London, Kegan Paul, 1946), esp. Ch. i.

53. Hallowell, *The Decline of Liberalism as an Ideology*, pp. 82, 100.

54. J. Roach, 'Liberalism and the Victorian intelligentsia', *Cambridge Historical Journal*, xiii (1957), 64. The indifference to India of W. E. Gladstone, the greatest Liberal statesman of the second half of the century, makes a significant contrast.

55. Quoted in Joll, *The Anarchists*, p. 166.

56. E. Lockspeiser, *Debussy: His Life and Mind* (London, Cassell, 2 vols, 1962–65), ii, 19. It should be noted, however, that the works of Debussy's last years before his death in 1918, smaller-scale studies and sonatas, were 'pure' music without the strong visual overtones of the better-known and larger-scale earlier compositions.

57. C. E. Schorske, 'Politics and the psyche in *fin de siècle* Vienna: Schnitzler and Hofmannsthal', *American Historical Review*, lxvi (1960–61), 943–4.

58. See the picture of extreme left-wing, and especially anarchist, circles in Paris immediately before 1914 drawn in Victor Serge, *Memoirs of a Revolutionary, 1901–1941* (London, Oxford University Press, 1963), Ch. i, esp. p. 23.

Conclusion

This was an age of change and growing power in Europe – change often slow in the first half of the nineteenth century, then accelerating in a quite spectacular way; and material power nourished by constructive change. By 1914 most of the Europe of Napoleon and Metternich had altered almost beyond recognition; it was now in many ways as remote and irrecoverable as the Round Table of King Arthur. On the eve of the First World War an inhabitant of north-west Europe (especially if he were male and middle class) could justifiably feel that he, and his father and grandfather, had helped to change the world, to direct and quicken the movement of humanity, as no three generations ever before. In political life the decisive stage in this process of change came, for much of the continent, in 1848–49 and during the next two decades. In military life the state funeral in Vienna in 1858 of Field Marshal Radetzky, 'Vater Radetzky' to the rank and file who fought under him, symbolized the end of the old Europe, the outdating of the brave, loyal, drunken, illiterate peasant armies of the past which was to be made brutally clear by the Prussian successes of 1866 and 1870. In intellectual life it is impossible to draw dividing-lines of even this superficial kind; but even here the publication of Darwin's *Origin of Species* in 1859 and the most important works of Marx between 1848 and 1867 again help to mark this wonderful third quarter of the century as a watershed. It was in this unprecedented fertility, not merely in new techniques and ideas but in new mental attitudes, that Europe's power and her leadership of an outside world by contrast static and unchanging was rooted. By 1914, in so far as there were any worldwide norms of political, economic or intellectual life they were based on a European experience which was now being more and more completely imposed on other continents.

The picture, from a European point of view, is thus one of brilliant success. But two qualifications should be made, even at the end of a survey so inevitably incomplete as that provided in this book. In the first place there were several different Europes. This is true in more than the obvious sense of sharp contrasts between different geographical areas, between the parliamentarism of England and the autocracy of Russia, or between the brilliant achievements of Germany and the stagnation and defeat of Spain and to a lesser extent of Italy. These contrasts, if the continent is looked at as a whole, were indeed striking. Side by side with progressive and innovating Europe, the Europe which was changing the world, there remained peripheral Europe, poor, unindustrialized, economically and socially stagnant, the 'African' Europe of Andalucia, Sardinia and Sicily, the bitterly divided Balkans, the peasant Europe of the east struggling to modernize. In Sicily, for example, the yield of wheat on the great estates at the time of Italian unification was probably about the same as it had been under the Roman empire. In its most extreme form the old pre-modern and pre-industrial Europe can be found in the completely tribal society of Montenegro, where the blood-feud remained the most important of all social institutions and where throughout the nineteenth century the cutting-off and public display of the head or nose of a murdered enemy was still a highly desirable accomplishment. It would be ridiculous to pretend that Montenegro was anything more than completely exceptional, a kind of ethnographic museum-piece, and an unimportant one at that (though there were still significant areas in the Balkans and Mediterranean Europe where the blood-feud flourished). But even a passing reference to it helps to make the point that Europe was still enormously varied, that there were very many people in it throughout this period who lived in a quite different mental and moral as well as physical world from that of the liberal industrial capitalism, the technological progress, the 'scientific' socialism, in terms of which this book has for the most part been written. Even in states which were in some formal sense political unities the contrasts could be enormous. In Italy in 1913 eleven per cent of the population of Piedmont was illiterate; but in Calabria the rate was seventy per cent. In the Habsburg empire a few years earlier six per cent of the German population and only three per cent of the Czechs were illiterate; but seventy-seven per cent of the Ukrainians and Ruthenians were. Even progressive Europe, moreover, was far from any complete unity of outlook and feeling. There were profound intellectual and even spiritual cleavages within the most advanced and rapidly developing parts of the continent. In particular there was clearly, by the middle of the nineteenth century, a growing division in the life of much of western Europe between an outlook which was rational, pacific, individualist, 'middle class', often inspired by English experience and often more or less openly selfish, and another which was radical, populist, often idealist, at least potentially violent and in its implications revolutionary.

The first was well typified in political terms by the French statesman Adolphe Thiers and in intellectual life by another Frenchman, the historian

Hippolyte Taine. It can be seen victorious, in somewhat differing forms, in the régime of Louis-Philippe, in the Third Republic in France, and in many aspects of the history of Great Britain during this period. The second is represented in its clearest form by Mazzini in Italy and, in a more coarse-grained manner, by Jahn a generation earlier in Germany. It, more than anything else, gave some cutting edge to the outbreaks of 1848 and, far more than any form of socialism, inspired the greatest political and social tragedy of the century, the Commune of 1871 in Paris. Both outlooks drew sustenance from aspects of the great liberal current which was the most pervasive force in the world of political ideas throughout this period. But they took from it very different things and used them for very different purposes. The cleavage between them, one of temperaments at least as much as of ideas, was in many ways fruitful: it was also pregnant with danger for the future. The revolutionary populism of the nineteenth century was to breed many of the forces which devastated Europe for a generation after 1914.

This successful and creative Europe inevitably lacked complete unity in another way. Inescapably society, even in the more developed and progressive parts of the continent, contained large elements of ignorance, of resistance to change, of deep-rooted traditionalism inherited from the past. Progress in the nineteenth century has to be described largely in terms of an unprecedented victory of market forces in economic life and ideas of contract in much of life in general. But this victory was won by an active, self-confident and self-conscious minority which could impose itself on a majority still very much aware of the importance of tradition and inherited status. Nearly all history is written in terms of educated and articulate minorities, sometimes small ones – and often rightly so, since in many contexts, particularly those of change, these minorities are what matter. This is as true of the nineteenth century as of most other periods; for even the rise of organized public opinion in the European states which was one of its important features was the work of minorities and even individuals rather than a spontaneous growth. It must never be forgotten how many of the great events of the century unrolled against a backcloth formed by the incomprehension, apathy and even hostility of the ordinary man. The lack of positive mass support for political unification in Italy and its limitations even in Germany,[1] the failure of millions of Frenchmen to sympathize with the strivings of 1848 and 1871 in Paris, the general indifference of the British worker, in the country which had created the first industrial society, to any form of systematic socialist doctrine, all underline the fact that the great movements of change, powerful and pervasive as they were, had clear limitations. Though the machinery of government was everywhere becoming more active, in 1914 it still impinged remarkably little on day-to-day life. The role of the state in economic life in particular was smaller than it had been in the eighteenth century as well as much smaller than it was to become in the twentieth. Moreover on a less political, and deeper, level a surprisingly large inheritance of traditional fears and pieties survived.

It is remarkable, for example, that in Britain, the home of parliamentary government, the millennia-old belief in the magical powers of rulers should have lingered on, at least in some remote areas, throughout much of this period. Faith in the curative properties of the royal touch was not yet completely dead there, though the abandonment from the early eighteenth century of the hallowed practice of 'touching for the king's evil' had now forced it to assume new forms. Coins bearing the head of Charles I were handed down from father to son in the Shetland islands, for use as a remedy against skin diseases, until at least the later 1830s. Much later, crofters in parts of northern Scotland still regarded sovereigns as cure-alls simply because they bore the queen's head; the fact that the ruler in question was the profoundly unromantic Victoria did nothing to shake this belief. Later still, in 1901, a handkerchief allegedly stained with the blood of Cardinal York, the last legitimate descendant of the Stuart line who had died in 1807, was in use as a magical remedy against scrofula.[2] More significant, perhaps, is the fact that in Halle, in one of the most highly educated parts of Europe, the building of a new bridge across the Elbe in 1843 inspired widespread fears that its safety was to be guaranteed by walling-up a child within its foundations to appease the hostile forces of nature – fears through which there reverberate folk-memories reaching back to pre-Christian times.[3] These examples of the pervasiveness of irrationalism and tradition could very easily be multiplied many times over.

This aspect of the nineteenth and early twentieth centuries has been relatively little studied. Such neglect is at least partly justifiable; for beliefs and attitudes of this kind had a merely negative significance. They could slow change and impede innovation; but they could create nothing. Nevertheless it is important, in the last lines of a book concerned essentially with change, to stress, however briefly, that every progressive force and institution of this period – reforming bureaucracies, modernizing armies, innovating technologies, increasingly productive industries – worked in an environment of which popular apathy and incomprehension, often popular hostility, made up a large part. These feelings and most of those who held them were doomed to be pushed into the background and to become merely part of 'the sludge of history'. But if the history of Europe during this period can ever be adequately written from the standpoint of the ordinary half-comprehending, backward-looking man (which is perhaps open to doubt), they will bulk much larger in such a work than they have done in this book.

It is legitimate to stress the human importance of these conservative, backward-looking factors in nineteenth-century Europe, the continuing significance of the ordinary man's instinctive attachment to the past. Modern history is essentially the history of change; and this means that to many historians the elements of continuity in Europe's evolution, the extent to which any situation was inevitably rooted in and influenced by what had gone before, are easy to underestimate. Nevertheless it would be very misleadingly one-sided to end on a predominantly conservative note. Fundamental processes of change had been visible, at least in parts of western Europe, for at least two generations before 1815. They increased their impetus, though over large parts of the continent quite slowly, for half a century after that date. But by the 1880s the speed with which the continent was being transformed was unprecedentedly great. Over considerable parts of it an agrarian society which was centuries old was giving way to one in which most people lived in towns, even in great cities, and in which urban standards and values could be imposed on an often resentful rural minority. This, coupled with the influx of agricultural products from the Americas and Australasia and the resulting fall in agricultural prices from the 1870s, usually meant a fall in the incomes, and soon in the importance, of the landowners who were still almost everywhere the traditional ruling class. Intensified by the extension of voting rights, these processes often meant a marked decline in aristocratic political power. In Great Britain, the most striking case in point, the legislation of 1884-5, which gave the right to vote to agricultural labourers, meant that the landed nobility and squirearchy, already struggling to cope with falling rent-rolls and land values, rapidly lost a control of county administration and even of the representation of the counties in Parliament which had been unchallenged for centuries.

Of course this tendency for aristocratic and landowning power to decline was by no means uniform. The French nobility had never recovered the position lost after 1789; and the Russian landowning class saw its position more and more undermined by economic change. Yet in Hungary, by contrast, the prominence of a number of great patrician families remained almost as marked as in earlier generations. Yet in these years 1880–1914 we can clearly see a whole series of interlocking factors – mass literacy, mass circulation newspapers, mass political parties – which were bringing a new age into existence. Almost if not quite as fundamental in its effects was the unprecedented speed of economic change – new industries, revolutionary technological innovations, frighteningly great cities – and its tendency, in some parts of the continent at least, to generate government intervention to soften its impact on the ordinary man and his life-chances.

Europe in 1914, therefore, for all the large inheritance from the past which it inevitably contained, was in rapid change, a change more often than not for the better so far as the majority of its people were concerned. When he made a telephone call, when he switched on the electric light, when he rode in a motor-car or even on a bicycle, when, greatly daring, he might even in a handful of cases fly in one of the new aeroplanes, an ordinary man could not fail to recognize that he lived in an age when change was inescapable and progress, in many respects at least, a reality. Intellectuals and aesthetes might have forebodings about the future. But the majority of Europeans still looked forward with a consciousness of having achieved much in the past and with confidence in what was to come.

NOTES

1. See pp. 23-4.
2. These illustrations come from M. Bloch, *Les rois thaumaturges* (Paris, 1924), p. 396.
3. Iona and P. Opie, *The Oxford Dictionary of Nursery Rhymes* (Oxford University Press, 1951), p. 275.

Select Bibliography

The lists which follow are summary and therefore somewhat arbitrary. This means that many books of importance are omitted from them. In their compilation books have been preferred to articles. A conscious effort has been made to concentrate on books in English at the expense of those in other languages.

GENERAL

There are at least three multi-volume series which deserve mention here. The largest is the *New Cambridge Modern History*, each volume of which contains chapters by different authors. These volumes therefore lack the unity and structure which a single author can give; but they none the less contain a great amount of detailed and reliable information. The relevant ones are: vol. ix, *War and Peace in an Age of Upheaval, 1793–1830*, ed. C. W. Crawley (Cambridge University Press, 1965); vol. x, *The Zenith of European Power, 1830–70*, ed. J. P. T. Bury (Cambridge University Press, 1960); vol. xi, *Material Progress and World-Wide Problems, 1870–1898*, ed. F. H. Hinsley (Cambridge University Press, 1962); and vol, xii, 2nd edn, *The Shifting Balance of World Forces, 1898–1945*, ed. C. L. Mowat (Cambridge University Press, 1968). The period is also covered in three volumes of the Longmans *General History of Europe* series. These are F. L. Ford, *Europe, 1780–1830* (London, Longman, 1970); H. Hearder, *Europe in the Nineteenth Century, 1830–1880* (London, Longman, 1966); and J. Roberts, *Europe, 1880–1945* (London, Longman, revised edn 1986). These are less detailed than the *New Cambridge Modern History* volumes, but unlike them have the substantial advantage of including bibliographies and maps. In the Fontana *History of Europe* series there are again three relevant volumes: J. Droz, *Europe between Revolutions, 1815–1848* (London, Collins, 1967); J. A. S. Grenville, *Europe Reshaped, 1848–1878* (London, Fontana/Collins, 1976); and N. Stone, *Europe Transformed, 1878–1919* (London, Fontana, 1983). The third is particularly provocative and stimulating: all include useful bibliographies. *The Nineteenth Century: Europe 1789–1914*, ed. T. C. W. Blanning (Oxford University Press, 2000) is a series of short and up-to-date chapters of high quality, while R. Gildea, *Barricades and Borders: Europe 1800–1914* (2nd edn, Oxford University Press, 1996) contains much detailed information. The most stimulating coverage of this period by a single author is to be found in the three volumes by E. J. Hobsbawm, *The Age of Revolution: Europe 1789–1848* (London, Weidenfeld & Nicolson, 1962), *The Age of Capital, 1848–1875* (London, Weidenfeld & Nicolson, 1975) and *The Age of Empire, 1875–1914* (London, Weidenfeld & Nicolson, 1987). Two older and more conventional books which are still useful are D. Thomson, *Europe since Napoleon* (revised edn, Harmondsworth, Penguin, 1966) and J. B. Joll, *Europe since 1870: an international history* (London, Weidenfeld & Nicolson, 1973).

There are many good books on individual countries: here again a large element of arbitrariness inevitably enters into the choice. On Germany, whose remarkable development contributed so much to the history of nineteenth-century Europe, three standard large-scale works are G. A. Craig, *Germany 1866–1914* (Oxford, Clarendon Press, 1978) J. J. Sheehan, *German History, 1770–1866* (Oxford, Clarendon Press, 1987) and D. Blackbourn, *The Fontana History of Germany: 1780–1918: the long nineteenth century* (London, Fontana, 1987). On France there is the remarkable work of T. Zeldin, *France, 1848–1945*, vol. i, *Ambition, Love and Politics*; vol. ii, *Intellect, Taste and Anxiety* (Oxford, Clarendon Press, 1973–77). Sometimes the detail in this enormous book of over 2,000 pages becomes excessive; but it is crammed with fascinating information. R. Magraw, *France, 1815–1914: the bourgeois century* (London, Fontana, 1983) is written from a political standpoint with which not everyone will agree but includes a good up-to-date bibliography. C. Charle, *Social History of France in the Nineteenth Century* (Oxford–Providence, Berg, 1994) is useful; but the most comprehensive recent book is R. Tombs, *France, 1814–1914* (London, Longman, 1996). R. Price, *A Social History of Nineteenth-Century France* (London, Hutchinson, 1987) is also a good book. Russia is covered in the very solid and informative H. Seton-Watson, *The Russian Empire 1801–1917* (Oxford, Clarendon Press, 1967) while H. Rogger, *Russia in the Age of Modernization and Revolution, 1881–1917* (London, Longmans, 1983) is more recent and thematically arranged. On the Habsburg monarchy and its problems R. A. Kann, *The Multinational Empire: nationalism and national reform in the Habsburg monarchy, 1848–1919* (New York, Columbia University Press, 1950) and A. J. May, *The Habsburg Monarchy, 1867–1914* (Cambridge, Mass., Harvard University Press, 1951) have not been superseded. C. A. Macartney, *The*

Habsburg Empire, 1790–1918 (revised edn, London, Weidenfeld & Nicolson, 1971) is a very substantial work. A. Sked, *The Decline and Fall of the Habsburg Empire, 1815–1918* (London, Longman, 1989) is short, clear and balanced.

So far as Italy is concerned there is much of interest in S. J. Woolf, *A History of Italy, 1700–1860: the social constraints of political change* (London, Methuen, 1979), while D. Mack Smith, *Italy: a modern history* (Ann Arbor, University of Michigan Press, 1959) and for the later part of the period C. Seton-Watson, *Italy from Liberalism to Fascism, 1870–1925* (London, Methuen, 1967) are now standard works. Of the many books on the lesser European states perhaps the only ones worth mentioning here are Barbara Jelavichi, *History of the Balkans* (Cambridge University Press, 1983), the two volumes of which include much information on the Slav and Magyar peoples of the Habsburg monarchy as well as on the Balkans proper, and S. K. Pavlowitch, *A History of the Balkans, 1804–1945* (London, Longman, 1999). Finally on Great Britain, among a number of excellent works, may be mentioned N. Gash, *Aristocracy and People: Britain 1815–1865* (London, Edward Arnold, 1979); R. T. Shannon, *The Crisis of Imperialism, 1865–1915* (London, Hart-Davis MacGibbon, 1974); and two volumes in the Longmans *History of England* series, edited by W. N. Medlicott: A. Briggs, *The Age of Improvement, 1783–1867* (London, Longman, 1959) and D. Read, *England, 1868–1914* (London, Longman, 1979). C. Matthew, ed., *The Nineteenth Century: The British Isles, 1815–1901* (Oxford University Press, 2000) is a series of good thematic chapters by different authors.

CHAPTER 1. THE POLITICAL AND ECONOMIC BALANCE OF POWER

F. H. Hinsley, *Power and the Pursuit of Peace* (Cambridge University Press, 1963) is a well-known general study of the European state-system and ideas about international organization, mainly from the end of the eighteenth century onwards. On the international events of the period the literature, essentially in the form of conventional diplomatic history, is enormous. Useful general works are: R. Albrecht-Carrié, *A Diplomatic History of Europe since the Congress of Vienna* (revised edn, New York, Harper, 1973); A. J. P. Taylor, *The Struggle for Mastery in Europe, 1848–1918* (Oxford, Clarendon Press, 1954); and M. S. Anderson, *The Eastern Question, 1774–1923: a study in international relations* (London, Macmillan, 1966). R. Bullen and F. R. Bridge, *The Great Powers and the European States System, 1815–1914* (London, Longman, 1980) is a concise and clear summary. C. J. Bartlett, *Peace, War and the European Powers, 1814–1914* (London, Macmillan, 1996) is even more brief. For the first decades of this period the magisterial work of P. Schroeder, *The Transformation of European Politics, 1763–1848* (Oxford, Clarendon Press, 1994) supersedes all other books, while the most important international issue of its middle years is thoroughly treated in W. E. Mosse, *The European Powers and the German Question, 1848–1871* (Cambridge University Press, 1958). The last three decades of the nineteenth century are covered in great detail in two books by W. L. Langer which, though published many years ago, have still not been superseded: *European Alliances and Alignments, 1871–1890* (2nd edn, New York, Knopf, 1962) and *The Diplomacy of Imperialism, 1890–1902* (2nd edn, New York, Knopf, 1956).

The years before 1914 and the approach to the First World War have given rise to an enormous historical literature. A number of volumes in the Macmillan *Making of the Twentieth Century* series deserve mention even in so brief and arbitrary a list as this, as they often extend their chronological coverage back into the later years of the nineteenth century and link the domestic politics and problems of the powers with their international behaviour: J. F. V. Keiger, *France and the Origins of the First World War* (London, Macmillan, 1984); D. C. B. Lieven, *Russia and the Origins of the First World War* (London, Macmillan, 1983); V. R. Berghahn, *Germany and the Approach of War in 1914* (London, Macmillan, 2nd edn, 1993); S. R. Williamson, *Austria-Hungary and the Origins of the First World War* (Basingstoke, Macmillan, 1991) and Zara S. Steiner, *Britain and the Origins of the First World War* (London, Macmillan, 1977). G. Barraclough, *From Agadir to Armageddon: anatomy of a crisis* (New York, Holmes & Meier, 1984) is brief and highly provocative. D. Stevenson, *Armaments and the Coming of War, 1904–1914* (Oxford, Clarendon Press, 1996) is a scholarly and important study, and D. G. Herrmann, *The Arming of Europe and the Making of the First World War* (Princeton University Press, 1996) is good on the same subject. British leadership in Europe, in some respects at least, during the nineteenth century, and the growing German challenge to it can be followed in the essays in C. J. Bartlett, ed., *Britain Pre-eminent: studies of British World Influence in the Nineteenth Century* (London, Macmillan, 1969) and in the thorough study by P. M. Kennedy, *The Rise of the Anglo-German Antagonism, 1860–1914* (London, Allen & Unwin, 1980). There are useful brief surveys in Muriel Chamberlain, *'Pax Britannica'? British Foreign Policy 1789–1914* (London, Longman, 1988) and C. J. Bartlett, *Defence and Diplomacy: Britain and the Great Powers, 1815–1914* (Manchester University Press, 1993). F. R. Bridge, *The Habsburg Monarchy* among the Powers, 1815–1914 (New York–Oxford, Berg, 1990) brings out well the essential weakness of Austria-Hungary's position.

CHAPTER 2. THE MECHANICS OF GOVERNMENT: FREEDOM AND AUTHORITY

E. N. and P. R. Anderson, *Political Institutions and Social Change in Continental Europe in the Nineteenth Century* (Berkeley, University of California Press, 1967) is an ambitious effort at a synoptic view of this very large subject, while for the decades after 1815 J. L. Talmon, *Political Messianism, The Romantic Phase* (London, Secker & Warburg, 1960) throws much light on the relationship between practical politics and their intellectual background. D. Pinkney, *The French Revolution of 1830* (Princeton University Press, 1972) is the best book on its subject and is based on very extensive archive materials. Pamela M. Pilbeam, *The 1830 Revolution in France* (London, Macmillan, 1991) is short and useful. On the revolutions of 1848 the literature is very large. The essays in F. Fejto, ed., *The Opening of an Era: 1848* (New York, Fertig, 1966: first published in English, 1948) are still worth reading. On events in France the best single book is probably G. Duveau, *1848: the making of a revolution* (London, Routledge & Kegan Paul, 1967), while J. R. Rath, *The Viennese Revolution of 1848* (Austin, University of Texas Press, 1957) is the only substantial treatment in English of this aspect of the events of the year of revolutions. On Germany there is F. Eyck, *The Frankfurt Parliament, 1848–1849* (London, Macmillan, 1968). Sir L. B. Namier, *1848: the revolution of the intellectuals* (Oxford University Press, 1971: first published, 1946), which deals mainly with Germany, is a short and now classic analysis.

On France after the mid-century upheavals T. Zeldin, *The Political System of Napoleon III* (London, Macmillan, 1958) is short and stimulating; T. A. B. Corley, *Democratic Despot: a life of Napoleon III* (London, Barrie & Rockliffe, 1961) is more general and conventional and J. F. McMillan, *Napoleon III* (London, Longman, 1991) is a short chronological treatment. D. Mack Smith, *Mazzini* (Yale University Press, 1994) is an important biography. For Germany T. S. Hamerow, *The Social Foundations of German Unification, 1858–1871* (Princeton University Press, 1969) is very good on changes in German society during this period and their political implications, while there are very large-scale treatments of Bismarck's career in L. Gall, *Bismarck: the White Revolutionary* (2 vols, London, Allen and Unwin, 1986) and O. Pflanze, *Bismarck and the Development of Germany* (3 vols, Princeton University Press, 1990). There are a number of good books on the Third Republic in France; but the most suggestive and penetrating treatment in English is that to be found in vol. i, Part III of T. Zeldin, *France, 1848–1945*, details of which are given in the first section of this bibliography. The development of the Second Reich after Bismarck's fall can be followed in the excellent book by J. C. G. Röhl, *Germany without Bismarck: the crisis of government in the Second Reich* (London, Batsford, 1967) and in the same author's *The Kaiser and his Court: Wilhelm II and the government of Germany* (Cambridge University Press, 1994). Russia, whose political and social problems dwarfed those of any other European state, is also well catered for in writing in English. Two important articles are: M. Szeftel, 'The Form of Government of the Russian Empire prior to the Constitutional Reforms of 1905–06', in J. S. Curtiss, ed., *Essays in Russian and Soviet History in Honour of Geroid Tanquary Robinson* (Leiden, 1963); and M. Raeff, 'The Russian autocracy and its officials', *Harvard Slavic Studies*, iv (1957). D. T. Orlovsky, *The Limits of Reform: the Ministry of Internal Affairs in Imperial Russia, 1802–1881* (Cambridge, Mass., Harvard University Press, 1981) is solid and informative as is F. W. Wcislo, *Reforming Rural Russia: State, Local Society and National Politics, 1855–1914* (Princeton University Press, 1990). D. C. M. Lieven, *Nicolas II, Emperor of all the Russias* (London, John Murray, 1993) is a balanced and well-written biography. On a more general theme there is much information in R. J. Goldstein, *Political Repression in Nineteenth-Century Europe* (London, Croom Helm, 1983).

On the growth of newspapers and a public opinion formed by them, one of the most significant developments of the period, there is information in C. Bellanger and others, eds., *Histoire générale de la presse française*, vol. ii (Paris, 1969), in Irene Collins, *The Government and the Newspaper Press in France, 1814–1881* (Oxford University Press, 1959) and in the massive and fascinating volumes of *The History of the Times, 1785–1948* (4 vols in 5, London, *The Times*, 1935–52). The very important subject of the development of statistics and their use for governmental and administrative purposes is covered for the country which in general led the way in this respect in M. J. Cullen, *The Statistical Movement in Early Victorian Britain* (Hassocks, Harvester Press, 1975).

CHAPTER 3. ECONOMY AND SOCIETY: THE NEW AND THE OLD

The growth of Europe's population, a highly technical subject with a large literature of its own, has received only very summary treatment in this book. General discussions can be found in P. Guillaume and J. P.

Poussou, *Démographie historique* (Paris, 1970) and T. McKeown, *The Modern Rise of Population* (London, Arnold, 1976). The emphasis placed by the latter on improved nutrition and hygiene as the most important causes of population growth is criticized in two articles in the *Journal of Interdisciplinary History*, xiv (1983): Susan C. Watkins and E. van de Walle, 'Nutrition, mortality and population size: Malthus's court on last resort', and Ann Carmichael, 'Infection, hidden hunger and history'.

There are several important general economic histories of Europe to be mentioned. The largest-scale one in English is the *Cambridge Economic History of Europe*, of which the two parts of vol. vi, edited by H. J. Habbakuk and M. Postan, *The Industrial Revolutions and After: Incomes, Population and Technological Change* (Cambridge University Press, 1966) are full of relevant information. The last three chapters of vol. vii, Part 2, edited by P. Mathias and M. Postan, *The United States, Japan and Russia* (Cambridge University Press, 1978) provide a substantial account of Russian economic growth. Two of the volumes in C. Cipolla, ed., *The Fontana Economic History of Europe* (London, Collins–Fontana, 1972–76) are relevant and useful. They are: vol. iii, *The Industrial Revolution*, and vol. iv, *The Emergence of Industrial Societies*. In French P. Leon, ed., *Histoire économique et sociale du monde*, vol. iv, *La domination du capitalisme, 1840–1914*, ed. G. Garrier (Paris, 1978) is very comprehensive and useful, perhaps the best one-volume treatment in any language of its period, while the first of the two volumes of J. A. Lesourd and C. Gérard, *Histoire économique, XIXᵉ et XXᵉ siècles* (Paris, 1963), though more summary, is also of use. D. S. Landes, *The Unbound Prometheus: technological change and industrial development in Western Europe from 1750 to the present* (Cambridge University Press, 1969) is a famous book which is unusually well written. A more recent discussion is C. Trebilcock, *The Industrialization of the Continental Powers, 1780–1914* (London, Longman, 1981), which is more concerned with models of growth and which includes a useful statistical chapter. C. Morazé, *The Triumph of the Middle Classes: a study of European values in the nineteenth century* (London, Weidenfeld & Nicolson, 1966), a translation of a French work, is less strictly economic and less analytical. A. Maddison, *Phases of Capitalist Development* (Oxford University Press, 1982) is a short and stimulating account, essentially an essay, from the standpoint of a professional economist, while W. Ashworth, *A Short History of the International Economy since 1850* (3rd edn, London, Longman, 1975) is brief but useful. P. Leon and others, eds, *L'Industrialisation en Europe au XIXe siècle* (Paris, 1972) is a collection of essays (some of them in English) many of which are worth attention. S. Pollard, *Peaceful Conquest: the industrialization of Europe, 1760–1970* (Oxford University Press, 1981) is balanced, and clearly written, while

I. T. Behrend and G. Rankl, *The European Periphery and Industrialisation 1780–1914* (Cambridge University Press, 1982) discusses the areas which lagged behind in the great wave of nineteenth-century growth. Two articles of general scope which deserve mention among many such are S. Pollard, 'Industrialization and the European economy', *Economic History Review*, 2nd ser., xxvi, no. 4 (Nov. 1973), and P. Bairoch, 'Europe's Gross National Product: 1800–1975', *Journal of European Economic History*, v, no. 2 (Fall 1976). I. Inkster, *Science and Technology in History* (Basingstoke, Macmillan, 1991) contains much information though it is not always easy reading.

There are many useful books on individual countries, of which it is possible to mention only one or two here. For Great Britain S. Checkland, *British Public Policy, 1776–1939: an economic, social and political perspective* (Cambridge University Press, 1983) is very good on the interrelationship between government policies, political ideas and economic life, while H. Perkin, The *Origins of Modern English Society, 1780–1880* (London, Routledge & Kegan Paul, 1969) is now a standard work. Two books translated from French: F. Crouzet, *The Victorian Economy* (London, Methuen, 1982) and the early chapters of F. Bedarida, *A Social History of England, 1851–1975* (London, Methuen, 1979) are also very useful. A short comparative study is P. O'Brien and C. Keyder, *Economic Growth in Britain and France, 1780–1914: two paths to the twentieth century* (London, Allen & Unwin, 1978), which concludes that the comparison is more favourable to France than has usually been thought. C. P. Kindelberger, *Economic Growth in France and Britain, 1851–1950* (Cambridge, Mass., Harvard University Press, 1964) is more detailed and analytical and R. Price, *An Economic History of Modern France, 1730–1914* (London, Macmillan, 1981) is a short descriptive account with a heavy emphasis on the importance of communications. Two useful collections of essays are: J. Komlos, ed., *Economic Development in the Habsburg Monarchy in the Nineteenth Century: essays* (New York, Columbia University Press, 1983) and Olga Crisp, *Studies in the Russian Economy before 1914* (London, Macmillan, 1976). P. Gatrell, *The Tsarist Economy, 1850–1917* (London, Batsford, 1986) is also clear and concise.

The most general discussion of problems of 'social control' is C. Tilly, Louise Tilly and R. Tilly, *The Rebellious Century, 1830–1930* (Cambridge, Mass., Harvard University Press, 1975). On urban growth the classic work of A. F. Weber, *The Growth of Cities in the Nineteenth Century: a study in statistics* (New York, 1899: reprinted Ithaca, Cornell University Press, 1963) is still very important, as is A. R. Sutcliffe, *Towards the Planned City: Germany, Britain, the United States and France, 1780–1914* (Oxford, Basil Blackwell, 1981). An outstanding story of urban growth is well covered in Patricia Herlihy, *Odessa, a History, 1794–1914* (Harvard University Press, 1986). There is an excellent account of the end of serfdom in J. Blum, *The End of the Old Order in Rural Europe* (Princeton University Press, 1978); but the best study of modernization in any European country is E. Weber, *Peasants into Frenchmen: the modernization of rural France, 1870–1914* (Stanford University Press, 1976) which is very well written and full of interesting information. Pamela M. Pilbeam, *The Middle Classes in Europe, 1789–1914: France, Germany, Italy and Russia* (Basingstoke, Macmillan, 1990) is informative but a little dull; and D. Lieven, *The Aristocracy in Europe, 1815–1914* (London, Macmillan, 1992) is excellent though confined to Great Britain, Germany and Russia. D. Cannadine, *The Decline and Fall of the British Aristocracy* (Yale University Press, 1990) is a very detailed study and A. J. Mayer, *The Persistence of the Old Regime: Europe to the Great War* (London, Croom Helm, 1981) is stimulating though it overstates its case. An important aspect of social relationships is discussed in J. R. Gillis, *Youth and History: tradition and change in European age relations, 1770–present* (New York–San Francisco–London, Academic Press, 1974). R. J. Evans, *The Feminists: women's emancipation movements in Europe, America and Australasia, 1840–1920* (London, Croom Helm, 1977) brings together much information in a small compass, while on a different level E. Shorter, *The Making of the Modern Family* (London, Collins, 1976) is a stimulating though controversial discussion. Joan W. Scott, and Louise Tilly, 'Women's work and the family in nineteenth-century Europe', *Comparative Studies in History and Society*, xvii, no. 1 (Jan. 1975) is an article of importance.

CHAPTER 4. STATES AND NATIONS

There is a considerable literature on the development of nationalism before the nineteenth century. Detailed studies which may be mentioned are: K. F. Werner, 'Les nations et le sentiment national dans l'Europe mediévale', *Revue Historique*, ccxliv (1970); B. Guenée, 'État et nation en France au Moyen Age', *Revue Historique*, ccxxxvii (1967); J. Godechot, 'Nation, patrie, nationalisme et patriotisme en France au XVIIIe siècle', *Annales Historiques de la Révolution Francaise*, xliii (1971); and H. Rogger, *National Consciousness in Eighteenth-Century Russia* (Cambridge, Mass., Harvard University Press, 1960). Short and stimulating general discussions from differing points of view can be found in: E. Kedourie, *Nationalism* (2nd edn, London, Hutchinson, 1960); E. Gellner, *Nations and Nationalism* (Oxford, Basil Blackwell, 1983); and E. Hobsbawm, *Nations and Nationalism since 1780* (Cambridge University Press, 1990).

More extended treatments of a generally historical kind can be found in Royal Institute of International Affairs, *Nationalism* (London, Oxford University Press, 1939); F. Hertz, *Nationality in History and Politics* (London, Kegan Paul, 1944); L. L. Snyder, *The Meaning of Nationalism* (New Brunswick, N. J., Rutgers University Press, 1954); and B. C. Shafer, *Nationalism, Myth and Reality* (London, Gollancz, 1955).

There are many books which deal with the growth of national feeling and the achievement of national unity in individual countries. G. L. Mosse, *The Nationalization of the Masses: political symbolism and mass movements in Germany from the Napoleonic Wars through the Third Reich* (New York, Fertig, 1975) is interesting on the development of national monuments and symbols of all kinds, an area of the subject which has particularly attracted historians in recent years. H. Schulze, *The Course of German Nationalism from Frederick the Great to Bismarck, 1763-1867* (Cambridge University Press, 1991) is brief but to the point. F. Meinecke, *Cosmopolitanism and the National State* (Princeton University Press, 1970), a translation of a famous German book which first appeared as long ago as 1907, deals with Germany in spite of the generality of its title. On France there is a useful collection of documents edited by R. Girardet, *Le Nationalisme français, 1871-1914* (Paris, 1966) and a brief but interesting account in J. Lestocquoy, *Histoire du patriotisme en France* (Paris, 1968). On Italy M. Vaussard, *De Petrarque à Mussolini. Evolution du sentiment nationaliste italien* (Paris, 1961) is concerned predominantly with the nineteenth century. On Catalonia a fundamental work is the very detailed study by P. Vilar, *La Catalogne dans l'Espagne moderne: Recherches sur les fondements économiques des structures nationales* (Paris, 1962; 3 vols), while the other regional nationalism which has complicated the history of modern Spain is discussed in S. Payne, *Basque Nationalism* (Reno, University of Nevada Press, 1975). Rosalind Mitchison, ed., *The Roots of Nationalism: studies in northern Europe* (Edinburgh, John Donald, 1980), is a collection of short essays on national feeling in the Nordic countries, Ireland, Wales and Scotland. Panslavism is well covered in M. B. Petrovich, *The Emergence of Russian Panslavism, 1856-1870* (New York, Columbia University Press, 1956) and F. Fadner, *Seventy Years of Panslavism in Russia: Karazin to Danilevskii, 1800-1870* (Washington, Georgetown University Press, 1962).

On the spread of European nationalist ideas to the societies of Asia and the Arab world which was developing by the end of the nineteenth century it is possible to mention only one or two titles. A. Seal, *The Emergence of Indian Nationalism: competition and collaboration in the later nineteenth century* (Cambridge University Press, 1968) remains the best general study of its subject. On Arab nationalism, which has been much written about in the last two or three decades, there are: F. Gabrieli, *The Arab Revival* (London, Thames & Hudson, 1961); A. Hourani, *Arabic Thought in the Liberal Age, 1798–1939* (London, Oxford University Press, 1962); and H. Sharabi, *Arab Intellectuals and the West: the formative years, 1875–1914* (Baltimore, John Hopkins University Press, 1970). J. Westwood, *Russia against Japan, 1904–05: A New Look at the Russo-Japanese War* (Basingstoke, Macmillan, 1986) is probably the best short account of its subject.

CHAPTER 5. EUROPE AND THE WORLD

D. K. Fieldhouse, *The Colonial Empires: a comparative survey from the eighteenth century* (2nd edn, London, Macmillan, 1982) is a solid narrative and descriptive account which provides much of the essential factual information, as does the same author's *Economics and Empire, 1830–1914* (London, Weidenfeld & Nicolson, 1973). His *Colonialism, 1870–1945* (London, Weidenfeld & Nicolson, 1981) is much more summary and more of an interpretative essay. H. Gollwitzer, *Europe in the Age of Imperialism, 1880–1914* (London, Weidenfeld & Nicolson, 1969) is an interesting short account of the intellectual background to European expansionism in its period and A. P. Thornton, *Doctrines of Imperialism* (London, Wiley, 1965) is a stimulating discussion though one which sometimes pushes its arguments too far. W. Baumgart, *Imperialism: the idea and reality of British and French colonial expansion, 1880–1914* (Oxford University Press, 1982) is a short study which combines information and analysis very satisfactorily. Of a great many articles dealing with the more general aspects of the imperial phenomenon the following at least are worthy of mention: D. S. Landes, 'The nature of economic imperialism', and H. Lüthy, 'Colonization and the making of mankind', both in *Journal of Economic History*, xxi (1961); D. K. Fieldhouse, ' "Imperialism": an historiographical revision', *Economic History Review*, 2nd ser., xiv (1961–62); and W. J. Mommsen, *Theories of Imperialism* (London, Weidenfeld & Nicolson, 1981), a good short discussion.

A good general discussion of German imperial ambitions is W. Baumgart, *Deutschland im Zeitalter des Imperialismus (1890–1914)* (3rd edn, Frankfurt am Main, 1979), while there is also a good account in H. Brunschwig, *L'Expansion allemande d'outre-mer du XV siècle à nos jours* (Paris, 1957). R. Chickering, *We Men Who Feel Most German. A Cultural Study of the Pan-German League, 1886–1914* (London, George Allen & Unwin, 1984) throws much light on the social background to expansionism in Germany. On France the best general account is still H. Brunschwig, *French*

Colonialism, 1871–1914 (London, Pall Mall Press, 1966). Two more recent works, J. Thobie, *La France impériale, 1880–1914* (Paris, 1982) and J. Bouvier and R. Girault, eds, *L'Impérialisme français d'avant 1914* (Paris–The Hague, 1976) are concerned mainly with French foreign investment and capital exports, which they assume rather too uncritically to have been the main driving force behind French expansionist ambitions. So far as Britain is concerned the most important general studies are P. J. Cain and A. G. Hopkins, *British Imperialism* (2 vols, London, Longman, 1993) and A. Porter, ed., *The Oxford History of the British Empire*, vol. iii, *The Nineteenth Century* (Oxford University Press, 1991). Still worth reading is D. C. M. Platt, *Finance, Trade and Politics in British Foreign Policy, 1815–1914* (Oxford University Press, 1968). The same author's 'Economic factors in British policy during the "New Imperialism"', *Past and Present*, no. 39 (1968) and 'The national economy and British imperial expansion before 1914', *Journal of Imperial and Commonwealth History*, ii, no. 1 (1973) are useful, and R. Hyam, *Britain's Imperial Century, 1815–1914* (London, Batsford, 1976) is both informative and readable. L. E. Davis and R. A. Huttenback, *Mammon and the Pursuit of Empire: The Political Economy of British Imperialism, 1860–1912* (Cambridge University Press, 1986) is a very good book. A useful assembly of up-to-date articles on European ambitions in one particular area of potential expansion can be found in Marian Kent, ed., *The Great Powers and the End of the Ottoman Empire* (London, Allen & Unwin, 1984), while D. R. Headrick, *The Tools of Empire: technology and European imperialism in the nineteenth century* (New York, Oxford University Press, 1981) is a useful reminder of the extent, often forgotten, to which European expansion in this period depended on the continent's technological superiority to the rest of the world. D. Geyer, *Russian Imperialism: The Interaction of Domestic and Foreign Policy, 1860–1914* (Leamington Spa, Berg, 1987) concentrates on economic explanations of Russian expansionism, while D. Gillard, *The Struggle for Asia, 1828–1914* (London, Methuen, 1977) deals well with Anglo-Russian imperial competition.

CHAPTER 6. ARMED FORCES AND WAR

There is a good general introduction in T. Ropp, *War in the Modern World* (Cambridge University Press, 1962), which includes a large bibliography. J. Gooch, *Armies of Europe* (London, Routledge & Kegan Paul, 1980) is very brief but good on the social and political background to armies and warfare and also has a useful bibliography. The second volume of M. Kranzberg and C. W. Pursell, eds., *Technology in Western*

Civilization (2 vols, Oxford University Press, 1968) contains a good chapter by E. Katzenbach on the mechanization of warfare in the period 1880–1919. On naval developments the best general treatment is perhaps still B. Brodie, *Sea Power in the Machine Age* (Princeton University Press, 1941). A. Gat, *The Development of Military Thought: The Nineteenth Century* (Oxford, Clarendon Press, 1992) ranges more widely than its title suggests.

The history of the French army during much of this period is covered in two books by D. Porch, *Army and Revolution: France, 1815–1848* (London, Routledge & Kegan Paul, 1974) and *The March to the Marne: the French army, 1871–1914* (Cambridge University Press, 1981). R. Girardet, *La Société militaire dans la France contemporaine, 1815–1939* (Paris, 1953) is an important general study with much on the social and intellectual background to French military developments. H. Contamine, *La Revanche, 1871–1914* (Paris, 1957) is more narrowly military in scope but full of information. Two articles in English worth mentioning are: R. Holroyd, 'The Bourbon army, 1815–1830', *Historical Journal*, xiv, no. 3 (1971), and A. F. Kovacs, 'French military institutions before the Franco-Prussian War', *American Historical Review*, li (1946). On the German (or more accurately the Prussian) army there are several well-known books in English: G. Craig, *The Politics of the Prussian Army, 1640–1945* (Oxford University Press, 1955); G. Ritter, *The Sword and the Scepter: the problem of militarism in Germany*, of which the first two volumes (Coral Gables, Florida, University of Miami Press, 1969–70) are relevant; and M. Kitchen, *A Military History of Germany from the Eighteenth Century to the Present Day* (London, Weidenfeld & Nicolson, 1975). In German the best general treatment is probably C. H. Herrmann, *Deutsche Militärgeschichte: eine Einführung* (Frankfurt, 1966). On more restricted subjects D. Showalter, *Railroads and Rifles: soldiers, technology and the unification of Germany* (Hamden, Conn., Shoe String Press, 1975) is the most up-to-date study of its kind and M. Kitchen, *The German Officer Corps, 1890–1914* (Oxford University Press, 1968) is detailed and thorough. D. E. Showalter, 'Army and society in imperial Germany: the pains of modernization', *Journal of Contemporary History*, xviii, no. 4 (Oct. 1983) is a useful article. On the Russian army J. S. Curtiss, *The Russian Army under Nicholas I, 1825–1855* (Durham, N.C., Duke University Press, 1965) is a thorough study and J. H. L. Keep, *Soldiers of the Tsar: Army and Society in Russia, 1462–1874* (Oxford, Clarendon Press, 1985) is a very good book. J. Bushnell, 'The tsarist officer corps, 1881–1914: customs, duties, inefficiency', *American Historical Review*, lxxxvi, no. 4 (Oct. 1981) is highly critical of its subject, though probably not unjustifiably so. On the Habsburg army there are in English G. Rothenburg, 'The Austrian army in the age of Metternich', *Journal of Modern History*, xl (1968), and the same author's *The Army of Francis Joseph* (West Lafayette, Indiana, Purdue University Press, 1976). The wider significance of the relatively weak and inefficient British army is treated in E. N. Spiers, *The Army and Society, 1815–1914* (London, Longman, 1980) and in A. V. Tucker, 'Army and society in England, 1870–1900: a reassessment of the Cardwell reforms', *Journal of British Studies*, ii (1962–63). On the Italian army there is J. Whittam, *The Politics of the Italian Army, 1861–1918* (London, Croom Helm, 1977). A very interesting general work on a subject markedly neglected by historians is M. Van Creveld, *Supplying War: logistics from Wallenstein to Patton* (Cambridge University Press, 1977).

On naval developments in general there may be mentioned, in addition to the book by Brodie, the second volume of L. Nicolas and A. Reussner, *La Puissance navale dans l'histoire* (2 vols, Paris, 1958–63). Large aspects of the history of the British navy are covered in C. J. Bartlett, *Great Britain and Sea Power, 1815–1853* (Oxford University Press, 1963), A. J. Marder, *The Anatomy of British Sea Power: a history of British naval policy in the pre-Dreadnought era, 1880–1905* (repr., London, Frank Cass, 1964) and P. Kennedy, *The Rise and Fall of British Naval Mastery* (London, Lane, 1976). There is by now a large and in general very good literature on the naval ambitions of the Wilhelmine Reich: important examples are W. Hubatsch, *Die Aera Tirpitz. Studien zur deutschen Marinepolitik* (Göttingen, 1955); V. R. Berghahn, *Der Tirpitz-Plan: Genesis and Verfall einer innenpolitischen Krisenstrategie unter Wilhelm II* (Dusseldorf, 1971) and H. H. Herwig, *'Luxury' Fleet: The Imperial German Navy, 1888–1918* (London, Allen and Unwin, 1980). A useful short article in English is J. Steinberg, 'The Kaiser's navy and German society', *Past and Present*, no. 28 (July 1964). A very thorough and interesting specialized study is P. G. Halpern, *The Mediterranean Naval Situation, 1908–1914* (Cambridge, Mass., Harvard University Press, 1971).

CHAPTER 7. ROMANTICISM, EVOLUTION, CONSCIOUSNESS: THE MOVEMENT OF IDEAS

The extremely varied and wide-ranging nature of the subject means that any list of suggested reading here must be even more arbitrary than for the earlier chapters. J. W. Burrow, *The Crisis of Reason: European Thought 1848–1914* (New Haven–London, Yale University Press, 2000) is wide-ranging with a good bibliography but not an easy read. Useful synoptic views will be found in G. L. Mosse, *The Culture of Western Europe: the nineteenth and twentieth centuries* (London, John Murray, 1961); and for shorter periods in M. D. Biddiss, *The Age of the Masses: ideas and society* in Europe since 1870 (Harmondsworth, Pelican, 1977) H. Stuart Hughes, *Consciousness and Society: the reorientation of European social thought, 1890–1930* (London, McGibbon & Kee, 1959) and Chapters 3–6 of J. B. Joll, *Europe since 1870*, which is mentioned above. On romanticism J. L. Talmon, *Romanticism and Revolt: Europe, 1815–1848* (London, Thames & Hudson, 1967) is short and stimulating, with good illustrations. H. G. Schenk, *The Mind of the European Romantics* (Oxford University Press, 1979) is also important, while three collections of extracts from primary materials and the comments of historians which may be useful are: A. K. Thorlby, ed., *The Romantic Movement* (London, Longmans, 1966); J. B. Halsted, ed., *Romanticism* (London, Macmillan, 1969); and E. K. Bramsted and K. H. Melhuish, eds., *Western Liberalism. A History in Documents from Locke to Croce* (London, Longman, 1978). Some works on particular currents of political and social ideas are: F. Manuel, *The New World of Henri Saint-Simon* (Cambridge, Mass., Harvard University Press, 1956); J. Beecher, *Charles Fourier: The Visionary and his World* (Berkeley–Los Angeles-London, University of California Press, 1986); W. M. Simon, *European Positivism in the Nineteenth Century* (Ithaca, Cornell University Press, 1963); A. Ritter, *The Political Thought of Pierre-Joseph Proudhon* (Princeton University Press, 1969); Gertrude Himmelfarb, *Darwin and the Darwinian Revolution* (London, Chatto & Windus, 1959); M. Ruse, *The Darwinian Revolution* (University of Chicago Press, 1979); and R. Hinton Thomas, *Nietzsche in German Politics and Society* (Manchester University Press, 1983).

The literature on Marx and Marxism is enormous. Among the more important general works are: D. McLellan, *Karl Marx: his life and thought* (London, Macmillan, 1973); S. Avineri, *The Social and Political Thought of Karl Marx* (Cambridge University Press, 1968); and G. Lichtheim, *Marxism: an historical and critical study* (London, Routledge & Kegan Paul, 1961). Aileen Kelly, *Mikhail Bakunin: A Study in the Psychology and Politics of Utopianism* (Oxford, Clarendon Press, 1982) is the best book on its subject. The growth of racist ideas has also attracted much scholarly attention during the last generation or so. Important works in English are: M. D. Biddiss, *The Father of Racist Ideology: the social and political thought of Count Gobineau* (London, Weidenfeld & Nicolson, 1970); P. J. Pulzer, *The Rise of Political Antisemitism in Germany and Austria* (London, Wiley, 1963); and L. Poliakov, *The Aryan Myth: a history of racist and nationalist ideas in Europe* (London, University of Sussex Columbus Centre, 1974). A very different thread in the pattern of European thought is discussed briefly and effectively in J. B. Joll, *The Anarchists* (London, Eyre & Spottiswoode, 1964). Another aspect of the subject is covered in O. Chadwick, *The Secularization of the European*

Mind in the Nineteenth Century (Cambridge University Press, 1975), though the more recent F. J. Coppa, *The Modern Papacy since 1789* (London, Longman, 1998) is disappointing. R. Wohl, *The Generation of 1914* (London, Weidenfeld & Nicolson, 1980), is illuminating on many of the strains and uncertainties which were beginning to show themselves at the end of this period in European social and intellectual life.

Index

Aasen, Ivan, Norwegian philologist, 227

Abdul Hamid II, Sultan of Turkey, 236, 240, 243, 253, 258

Abyssinia, see Ethiopia

Academic Legion, in Vienna (1848), 94

Acton, John Emerich, baron, British historian, on nationalism, 234

Adalbert, Prince, of Prussia, 341

Addison, Joseph, English writer, 357

Adelung, Johann Christoph, German scholar, 230

Aden, 273

Adler, Victor, Austrian Social Democrat, 236

Adowa, battle of (1896), 259, 304

Adrianople, treaty of (1829), 12

AEG, German electrical company, 209

Aehrenthal, Alois von, count, Austrian statesman, 121

Aerial League of the British Empire (1909), 335

Afghani, Djamal-al-Din al, Pan-Islamic theorist, 250

Afghanistan, 40, 51, 277
  and Russo-Japanese war, 260
  British war with (1839–42), 273

Africa, British battleship, 339

Africa
  colonial expansion in, 280–1
  artistic influence of, 391

Agadir, crisis (1911), 52–3

Agrarian League, in Germany, composition of, 334

Agriculture, 151

Aircraft
  military use of, 335
  naval use of, 339

Aix-la-Chapelle, congress at (1818), 4

Aksakov, Konstantin, Russian Slavophil, 225

Albert I, King of the Belgians, 60

Albert, Prince Consort in Great Britain, 86

Albert (pseud. of Martin, Alexandre), French socialist, 90, 98

Alexander I, Tsar of Russia
  and treaty of general guarantee, 22
  and Holy Alliance, 22
  and revolt in Greece, 35
  and reform in Russia, 6
  ministries created by, 68, 72
  and nationalism, 219

Alexander II, Tsar of Russia, 19, 121
  supports colonial expansion, 277

Alexander III, Tsar of Russia, 122

Alfieri, Vittorio, count, Italian poet, 220

Algarotti, Francesco, count, Italian writer, 220

Algeciras, conference at (1906), 51

Allgemeine Zeitung, German newspaper, 230

Alliance Internationale Ouvrière, 27, 160, 384